The Journals of Alfred Doten

THE *Journals* OF ALFRED DOTEN

1849-1903

EDITED BY WALTER VAN TILBURG CLARK

VOLUME THREE

UNIVERSITY OF NEVADA PRESS

Reno, Nevada   1973

University of Nevada Press, Reno, Nevada   89507
© University of Nevada Press 1973. All rights reserved
Library of Congress Catalog Card Number 72–76826
Printed in the United States of America
Designed by Adrian Wilson and John Beyer
ISBN 0–87417–032–X

Contents

The Long Decline

Books 59–74
March 23, 1885 – Dec 31, 1898

In Carson, Alf's spirits rise at once, and the upward turn continues as he once more becomes local on the Enterprise *in his beloved, if fading Virginia, and he and Mary can visit one another for quite happy weekends. But the* Enterprise *is fading, too. Alf bitterly sees himself passed over each time the managing editor position is open, is reduced to a half-time job and half-fare railroad pass, both just charity, and is then "left out" altogether. He attaches inordinate importance to the nearly-defunct Pioneer Society and its presidency, and to his perennial last hope, the Centennial Mining Company, meeting its assessments by ignoring long-standing bills. He tries other things, from selling insurance down to sending eulogistic obituary notices to relatives in hopes of a gratuity, but whiskey takes up the small returns and he has to take slights and insults as well as handouts. Finally he must retreat to Reno as a kind of prisoner of his family, pledged to give up drinking. Old-time newspaper friends do what they can, but the whole state is down, journalistic times and tastes are passing him by, and clearly no one has much faith in him anymore. The clippings he increasingly pastes into the journals are less and less his own work. After a brief stand against the whiskey, he is "down town" as regularly as ever and, long barred from the conjugal bed, discovers an increasing amount of "decayed veneration," especially from son Alf.*

BOOK NO. *59*

Virginia City and Reno
March 23, 1885 – Dec 31, 1885

March 23 . . . Rose at 8:30 oclock A.M. having slept only 3 hours . . . Got a shave & breakfast and then went to Enterprise office and entered upon my duties . . . Got along very smoothly – Through at midnight – Went up to Piper's new Opera House and saw the closing of the Knights of Pythias ball . . . Was with Piper for 2 or 3 hours afterward, talking over matters & things & the past, etc – Bed at 4 in my room, No 7, Douglas' building . . . Room $8 a month rent –

March 24 . . . Worked as usual . . . Took a box at Postoffice today, No 584, at $1 per quarter –

March 27 . . . Mining report day today – Weekly – I got mine up in good style but had to rustle to do so, having been out of practice, & having many an old end to pick up . . .

March 28 . . . Telegraphed wife that I would see her tomorrow evening – Worked late tonight – Bed 3 –

Sunday, March 29 – Cloudy but pleasant – Rose at 6 – down town – shave – breakfast & at 8 left for Reno – local passenger & freight train – slow – Reno at 12 M – All right at home – PM took walk with wife & our two boys down by RR depot – Found my freight from Austin had arrived this morning – $40.50 – Evening at home – Played banjo for 1st time for months, & Sam, Alf and Bessie sang with me – Bed at 8½ – At 4:30 PM today, the special train of Adelina Patti, the famous singer came dashing into Reno and stopped about 20 minutes at the depot – 6 cars – She had all her troupe, hotel and cooking arrangements along – Whole town rushed to depot – Worse than a Gold Hill dog fight for attraction – Wife & I went, too, & both saw Patti, and after train left, everybody dispersed like going home from circus –

March 30 – Cloudy but pleasant – After breakfast took morning train, at 7:10 – Wife went with me to depot – Va at 10 – About town picking up items – Worked very hard tonight – Bed at 2:30 –

March 31 . . . Morning, freight train brought my desk & trunk – got them taken to my room and I fixed desk in running order . . .

April 1 . . . April Fool Day – Very little observed about town – Fire early this morning on the Divide, back of the Ashland House, burned two unoccupied wooden buildings . . .

April 2 . . . Senator J P Jones came in on special train from Reno . . . last evening . . . He was around among the mines some today, & at 5:25 he left on train for San F. – Told me he was going for his wife, & would bring her home to Gold Hill next Monday – Saw him off – Worked late in office & read at home some – Bed at 5 . . .

April 3 . . . Rained and snowed more or less all the AM – Very sloppy – Had to wear my rubbers – Was up to Savage office & got items on Hale & Norcross & Chollar from Supt Keating – PM wrote mining report as usual – Evening worked in office – Bed at 2:30 . . .

April 4 . . . My old editorial chair, bequeathed to me by old man Lynch who had the News before I did, arrived from Reno this morning, & I had the pleasure of sitting in it at the Enterprise office today . . .

Sunday, April 5 . . . Evening about town some – Great attendance at the churches, it being Easter Sunday – Home & overhauled the drawers, etc of my desk – Badly demoralized as to contents, through bad handling – Bed at 5 –

April 7 . . . Grant for several days has been telegraphically reported to be dying slowly but surely, from cancer at root of his tongue and throat . . . and tonight telegrams said he was thought to be dying of hemorrhage therefrom – but at 10:30 was resting comfortably . . .

April 10 . . . Mining report day – Got along finely –

April 11 . . . John Mackay arrived on Comstock for 1st time in several months – from San F – Other mining men came also . . .

Sunday, April 12 . . . Evening about town – Wrote letter to Eunice – Bed 2 –

April 13 . . . This evening I called on S D Baker, Secy Centennial, & paid my present assessment, $18.50 . . .

April 14 – Cloudy, with some nice showers in the morning – The Hale & Norcross stock & mine excitement which has grown since I have been here, broke today – quite a backset from recent good prices – Big masquerade ball tonight at Piper's Opera House by Hall & Zimmer's band – I was there in time to see the grand tableau and entree – About 70 couples – Galleries crowded with spectators at 50 cents each – After got through at office I went back to see the fun – found so many to talk with, etc, including John Piper, that I did not get to bed until 4 – S D Baker was prostrated about 9 oclock this evening, at his home, by a severe stroke of paralysis, affecting entire right side – Fearful blow to him –

April 15 . . . Col F F Osbiston from Idaho Springs, Colorado, and George Senf, "Graphy," from Sacramento, arrived this morning to see the prospects . . .

April 16 – Sky variable – High SW wind – Big bonanza thought to be developed in Hale & Norcross, as big improvement made in ore in west crosscut No 4 on 2900 & No 2 on 3,000 levels – Mackay and Osbiston both down in mine this PM – H & N stock up big today – Mackay and Graphy both left for California this evening – 5:25 train – I was down to depot and saw them off – I wrote letter to Yerington begging pass for self & wife over the V&T RR and sent it by that train – Called on S D Baker this PM short time – confined to bed – Bed at 2 – very cold – Ice formed tonight, ¼ of an inch thick –

April 17 – Cloudy, cold & blustering, with frequent snow squalls . . . Mining report day – Was out to Savage office twice to get report on Hale & Norcross . . . Grand bal masque by Prof Gosse tonight at Opera House . . . Biggest crowd I ever saw on any such occasion in this city – Staid till 3 oclock when it broke up . . . Colder than last night – Guess it played havoc with fruit crop, etc –

Sunday, April 19 . . . Snow stormy . . . at 8 left on train for Reno – Bought round trip ticket $3 – At Carson Yerington called me into his office in the depot, & after some little persuasion gave me pass for wife & self . . . Till Dec 31st . . . Found all right at home except all children had the whooping cough . . .

April 20 . . . Wife saw me off . . . Lawyer Bonnifield on board, also Henry Nofsinger, the capturer of Clarence Gray, the murderer of R H Scott at Paradise last December – He was on his way to Carson to secure the State reward of $500. If he gets it he will also get $500 offered by

Scott's partner, and $150 by citizens of Paradise – Bonnifield is his law-
yer – Goes before the State Board of Examiners this PM at Carson – I
took down all the items from Bonnifield, for *Enterprise*, and he presented
me with $5 . . .

April 21 . . . Today at Carson, Nofsinger was awarded the $500 . . .

April 22 – Clear & pleasant – Got a $20 postal order today and mailed
it in letter to wife – US Senator Jas G Fair arrived at Carson this morning from Washington – Came up here this PM in a buggy, arriving at
about 5 PM – At 8 he had a grand serenade by Cara's band – Big crowd
on C st in front of International – I was up to his reception in parlor, &
had shake hands & glass of wine with him & others – Quite a crowd in
parlor – Then all went out on front balcony, where he made short speech
to crowd – M N Stone, D E McCarty & Bob Keating also spoke, and
each wound up by inviting the crowd up to refreshments – It came like
the locusts in Egypt & in 10 minutes not a drink or a cigar left – Through
in office at 2 – Bed 2:30 –

April 24 – The same – Senator Fair was about town & the mining works
considerably today, seeing lots of friends & the people generally – An old
crank named Knapp was around him this PM for short time & followed
him up, having words with him in relation to a lot sold by Knapp to the
Gould & Curry for dump ground some time ago – Knapp threatened to
shoot Senator but was arrested and jailed by Sheriff – Fair was at office
this PM & saw Col Shaw & gave him a $50 greenback, & left another with
him to give me . . . in appreciative acknowledgment of courtesies in
the paper – Very nice – He left on evening train for San F – I was down
to depot & saw him off . . .

Sunday, April 26 . . . At 8 went to old Pioneer Hall to meeting of the
old stiffs – Only about 8 present – About town awhile . . .

April 28 . . . Evening reported monthly meeting of Board of School
Trustees . . . I got a postal order today of $6 to send to Summerfield to
pay Mike Finigan and other expenses attendant upon packing and sending my things from Austin –

April 29 . . . Wrote a letter to wife this PM, & sent it on evening train –
I enclosed our new pass over the V&T RR, inviting her to come up on a
visit next Saturday or Sunday – Evening, Col Shaw was on one of his
gambling and drinking spells & was only in the office working half an
hour during the entire run of the work – I stood in on his part of the work

and fixed up all the telegraph etc – in fact got up about the whole paper myself . . .

May 1 . . . Got letter from wife telling that she was coming up this evening – I worked lively at my mining report & got it over half up before 7 when I went to train & met wife & took her to supper at Fitzmier & Armbrust's – Then took her to Doc Kirby's, & left her to pass evening with Lucy – Finished mining report and read proof of it – Then took wife up to my room – and went back to office at 11 – Through at 2 & to bed with wife –

May 2 . . . Wife & I took breakfast and then a walk to Gold Hill – where she was to meet Mrs Dwight, Gov Adams' mother . . . Got there just a little too late . . . found that Mrs D had gone down to Stevenson's in his buggy – Gov gone up to Va – buggy returned & took wife & Mrs R down there also . . . Wife & the others staid at Stevensons all day – I was about town 3 or 4 hours visiting the business places, saloons, etc – Rode up on Dazet & Chataine's liquor delivery wagon – Work as usual – Wife came up in office about 8 – Piper came in, & got us to go up to Opera House & see his new drop curtain, just put up – Very fine – Scene in Venice – Took wife to room & went to office & worked till 1 – Home – Bed 1½ . . .

Sunday, May 3 – Clear & pleasant – Rose at 10 – Took breakfast at Heffron's at 12 M – Home again – At 1 PM walked to Gold Hill – Stopped in awhile at Mrs Robinson's – Also was at Mrs Fraser's a short time, next door to the *News* property – And I, as well as Mary, took good look at what used to belong to us, the trees I planted, etc – Somewhat dilapidated but still in fine order – Then we walked down to Chubbuck's . . . to dinner – Had roast turkey, etc – Also very pleasant social chat with Chubbuck & wife – At 5:30 were at Gold Hill depot . . . and wife left for Reno – I was at Charley Tobener's saloon for a while with others, & at 7 PM took evening train for Va – Was about town awhile & with John Piper at Opera House – went with him to Heffron's & had *pan roast* of oysters – Home at 12 – Bed at 1 – lonely –

May 4 . . . Evening, dedication of Piper's New Opera House – I was there & saw the whole performance – Very fine indeed – About 250 people there – Rather of a poor house considering the occasion – After show, a dance till 12 oclock . . . Paid my room rent this PM to Joe Douglass . . . Also paid . . . my Exempt dues to May 1st $6 –

May 5 . . . R M Clarke Jr, son of the well known Carson attorney . . . shot himself in the head with a Smith & Wesson 38 caliber revolver, at his room over W F & Cos Express office – died in 2 hours – cause, gambling & dissipation & probably using money that did not belong to him – He was messenger & delivery clerk for W F & Co – Body sent to Carson tonight . . . Evening I attended coroners inquest & got all the testimony . . .

May 6 . . . Got a letter from Sardis Summerfield . . . returning the $6 postal order I sent him at Austin – He has resigned as teacher there and come to Reno . . . Evening, 1st appearance of "Peck's Bad Boy" Company at the Opera House – This is the 1st company Piper has had in his new theater – I was in and saw a little of it – Very amusing – thats all – Unnatural, and not good – Influence bad . . . The Combination pump broke Sunday night & once or twice since & the Hale & Norcross has been flooded in lower levels . . .

May 7 . . . Letter from wife, returning our pass –

May 9 . . . Evening the Col went to Carson & left Jim Townsend to fix up the telegraph for him, etc . . .

Sunday, May 10 . . . Took train at 8 – lovely ride to Reno – green trees, green grass and all that sort of thing . . . All right at home . . .

May 11 . . . Took train at 8 . . . This PM I wrote notice of a pretty little steam pressure indicator . . . George C Phillips of Silver City is the maker . . . made it for his own use, as an improvement in two or three points over the previous styles – He gave me $5 to make the item . . . Got off at 2½ – Was at Simon Fraser's saloon afterward awhile – Bed at 4 –

May 12 . . . W W Hobart in town – met him & we had good old chat together – leaves for Carson tomorrow, & back to San Francisco, where he is Secy of Spring Valley Water Co – T R McGurn was attached for $300 this PM, and being afraid of other bouncings he sold everything to W J Hester. 3 grocery stores and a wood yard, personal property etc – Evening McGurn sent for me & I went up to his rooms in the Marye Building – He told me the whole story, so I could write it up correctly – Went to ball of Red men awhile, at Opera House . . .

May 13 . . . Mike Farrell & wife from Austin on a visit to Gold Hill –

May 14 . . . Got letter from wife – death notice in it, clipped from SF

Chronicle of death of Mrs Hiller, at Butte Montana, May 6 – aged 67 years – remains brought to Oakland for burial . . .

May 15 . . . The cold snap of the last 2 or 3 nights has killed all the fruit in this county . . .

May 16 . . . Wife arrived on train at 10 – Breakfast at Chaumond's – Bought some clothes for our boys – then she went to Gold Hill . . . came up on the evening train – I met her & she & Mrs Chubbuck et al went to skating rink – I to office . . .

Sunday, May 17 . . . At 11 went to breakfast at Chaumond's – Good – Then we went out on the Geiger Grade for a walk – nearly to Hall's Laundry . . . Home at 2 to my room – made fire & we read and enjoyed each others society lovingly till nearly 5 – then dined at Chaumond's and went to train . . .

May 18 . . . Big fire about 10:40 oclock – Original Keystone Mining Company's works – Worth awhile ago $30,000 – Supposed incendiary fire – Col Shaw rode out there in a buggy & took the items – He wrote it up . . .

May 19 . . . Got letter from Sam Crescenzo, Austin, asking about stocks . . . wrote letter to Harry Clauson, Ogden, enclosing one of my CP tickets for him to sell – Also letter to C C Powning of Reno *Journal*, telling him not to forget my passes, which he thinks he can sell for me . . .

May 21 . . . Got my hair trimmed today by Brodek, 1st time since I was in Austin last – March 17 . . .

May 22 . . . Ice froze an ⅛ of an inch thick . . . Around lively today, & got up good mining report . . .

May 23 . . . The Colonel's wife & children came up from Carson this morning, so he was with them most of the day – Evening he went to Carson with them – Jim Townsend did the telegraphic . . .

Sunday, May 24 . . . At 8 AM left on train for Reno – Took along dirty clothes, etc, and a 2 quart candy jar which I got filled with olives yesterday at Hatch Bros – Finest kind of Queen olives – Spanish imported . . . Found all right at Reno except Goodie – She had worms, or a cold, or something similar – very feverish dull & sleepy – The young ones as well as the old ones pitched into the olives lively, for we are all very fond of them . . . At the RR depot when trains came from Va and the East –

Met Powning – gave him my Ogden ticket to sell – Had long chat with him . . .

May 25 . . . My little Goodie better – Left on 7:10 train . . .

May 27 . . . Met Lew Stevenson on C street this noon, arrived from Leadville where he has been for the last 3 or 4 yrs, mining, etc – I think he is glad to get back, and feels like the Prodigal Son of his father C C Stevenson . . .

May 28 . . . At 1 PM an open buggy & 2 horses awaited me at the Enterprise office, and my old friend & pard, Dan B Sohl was the driver, to take me to Gold Hill to inspect a new refrigerator room at C J Waider's meat market, & report thereon in shape of advertisement – Dan is in from Montana, where he has been prospecting around for the last year, & is glad to get back . . . The refrigerator room . . . is "Stevens' patent cooling room," a very nice invention for cooling and keeping meats in hot weather – ice on top, etc . . .

May 29 . . . Evening the Col was on a drunk & didnt stand in – He came in about 10 & cut out some editorial, and in ½ an hour left for the Sawdust Corner gambling tables – He won at the game and felt hilarious – Duffy, one of the printers had to be detailed to run the eastern telegraph – Bed at 3 . . .

May 30 – Clear & warm – 83 deg – Memorial Day – Regular celebration as usual – military & civic procession & exercises at Opera House – I attended Opera House, but didnt go out to cemetery – Telegram from wife said she & Alfie were coming up on evening train – I met them & took them to dinner & then up to room & left them – Col Shaw went to Carson, leaving Jim Townsend to run his telegraph – I got through at 2 – home to bed at once – √

Sunday, May 31 . . . Wife & Alfie & I took walk this PM over beyond Gould & Curry dump etc – They left on 5:25 PM train . . .

June 1 . . . Col Shaw off at Carson or Reno and Jim Townsend did his telegraph for him . . .

June 2 . . . PM reported County Commissioners – Col Shaw returned . . . & worked all night . . .

June 3 . . . Met L W Getchell of Austin this PM – Came in Sunday to attend meeting of Board of Regents of the State University at Reno . . .

Evening attended Fourth of July adjourned meeting at Exempt Firemen's Hall . . .

Sunday, June 7 . . . Went down to Reno by morning train – Found everybody all right, Goodie also – After dinner I took my children all out to walk through NE part of town – Then I went down to depot at 8 to see trains come in, & see Powning, et al . . .

June 8 . . . Home to Va at 10 – Work as usual – Col & Getchell at Reno, both being Regents of the State University, to select a new site at Reno for that institution, which is to be removed from Elko – Col didnt return tonight – Jim Townsend did his telegraph . . .

June 9 . . . Evening Col Shaw not got back from Reno, and old Jim Townsend filled in for him . . .

June 10 . . . Three or four light snow squalls . . . Col Shaw got back this evening & went to work as usual – Sent a letter to James B Egan, Austin, relative to a fine English Gordon Setter pup . . . that Jack Bradley ships him tonight . . . This PM Ed Swift of Gold Hill met me on C street, and in consideration of having stood in with him in getting started on his street sprinkling contract he presented me with $5 . . .

June 11 . . . PM sent letter to wife enclosing pass, so she can come up if she likes – Water broke into the 3,000 level of the Hale & Norcross near face of main north lateral drift & about 150 feet from Savage south line – 5 or 6 inches of it – The stock tumbled a dollar from $8½ . . .

June 12 . . . Received an express letter from Harry A Clawson of the Union Depot Hotel, Ogden, Utah, telling me he had succeeded in selling my railroad ticket for $25, which he enclosed to me in greenbacks . . .

June 13 . . . AM got telegram from wife that she & Sammy would come up on evening train – Met them & took them to supper & to my room . . . McGurn sent me four bottles of "J H Cutter OK Old Bourbon" whisky and a box of 25 "Clean Sweep" cigars – to my room – This was in appreciation of my services in fixing up his ad and local the other night . . .

Sunday, June 14 . . . We breakfasted at Chaumond's . . . took walk way up along Summit st & other upper streets, from Mill st south & down Taylor street home . . . Saw wife & Sammy off at 5:35 . . . after dining at Lowery & Morrill's . . .

June 16 . . . Col Shaw off his nut . . . On a gambling drunk, etc – I filled in all right . . .

June 17 through 20 [AD pays a Centennial assessment of $27.63 and notes that Jim Townsend has stood in for Shaw twice.]

Sunday, June 21 . . . Left for Reno on 5:25 PM train . . . Stopped about depot in Reno awhile . . . walked up town – met Matt. M Gillespie & had quite a chat – He is in from Bodie, prospecting around . . . Home at 9 – The great Barrett circus was on the road up to Va as I came down . . . 30 cars in all . . .

June 22 – Clear, warm & pleasant – Matt Gillespie was on the train with me this morning for Va – As we got up onto C street, it looked like the flushest of times – No less than 5 different crowds at intervals along street around as many chance games, bogus jewelry auctions, patent medicine vendors, etc – Lots of people in from Gold Hill, Silver, Dayton and all adjacent localities – All come up to circus this PM & evening – At 11 AM the grand circus procession came down C street from toward Divide – Fine Band of music in chariot, long string of caged wild beasts in dens very artistically painted with scenes of wild beast etc – lots of Ladies & gents in pretty rig followed – Finest horses I ever saw & finest street pageant – Office awhile – When I was paid off my regular $30 at 1 PM it was $4 short, from Cohen the bookkeeper having paid it to the collector for Poll tax – I walked down to the circus ground away down below Alexanders milk ranch – Nearly half mile below C st – Hot – Bully circus & pretty good menagerie – More circus than I ever saw before anywhere – I staid to the concert afterward which wasn't much – side shows ditto – I made Matt Gillespie take dinner with me at Chaumond's today . . . at noon – Evening at office awhile, had item about little boy getting right hand badly torn by foolishly poking into the aperture beneath the bars of the cage this morning – The largest of the Coal Black tigers nailed the hand as a cat would a mouse – Hurt so that little Alonzo Curran couldnt go to the circus – Evening I walked down to circus . . . Had talk with general manager about the tiger & boy trouble – Then with W T Blaser the press agent, who being a musician was filling in as player in the band . . . We came up town together, and he will pass my family into the circus at Reno, Wednesday – Through in office at 2 – Bed 4 –

June 23 . . . Wrote letter to wife, telling about Blaser and how to get into the show . . .

June 26 . . . Got letter from Bessie & wife telling about the good time they all had at the circus, and how Blaser gave them 7 tickets . . .

June 27 . . . Through in office at 2 – got out in saloon across the way, McGrath's, & struck a lot of printers and had to stay with them till daylight – Went home perfectly sober but cussing myself for being a dam fool – jolly enough but not profitable, though only cost me 4 bits . . .

Sunday, June 28 . . . Wrote letter to wife, enclosing pass & telling her I couldnt come down . . . Attended monthly meeting of Pioneers – only President Storer, Bob Patterson, Dr Delevan, myself, S D Baker, Eli M Skaggs and C M Brown the undertaker – Knocked about town awhile afterward . . .

June 29 . . . Got telegram to meet wife at evening train – Did so – We dined together at Lowery's – Then took her to room and went back to office . . .

June 30 . . . Wife & I rose at 10 – Went shopping awhile along C st – Breakfast at Chaumond's – At 2 PM she took 'bus for Gold Hill to visit old Jane Noble, Mrs Chubbuck et al and take the train there . . .

July 1 – AM clear & warm – 80 deg – Paid my Odd Fellows dues $3.75 and my Postoffice box rent $1 . . . Met Capt Harry Johns on C street about noon – One of my old chums in Austin – Cornishman, about 40 yrs old and I think a mighty good man – Said left Austin awhile ago & went to Bernice to work, as he is a thorough miner in Austin for years – Got through at Bernice & thought would try it here – Said would like a job in the mines – Just then I saw Sam Jones, Supt of Crown Point, Belcher & Con Va, etc, passing on sidewalk – & stopped him & spoke to him about Capt Harry – Said tell him to meet me somewhere shortly, and speak to me & I'll set him to work – So I told Harry & we parted – Thus he got a job in 15 minutes after we met – The Col gambling badly today & this evening & night – Jim Townsend in his place – Through at 2 – Home – read etc – Bed 4 –

July 3 . . . Busy on the mining report – Got letter from wife enclosing pass – Lots of flags up today and evening, for the 4th – Lots of saloons open all night, with plenty of customers . . .

July 4 . . . We have to run a paper tomorrow . . . 2 holidays together wont do – I telegraphed to Melville Curtis, Reno for full list of names of his company and band from Austin – Replied "full list in *Reveille* of

Thursday" – Found it and printed it tonight – Wrote letter to wife enclosing pass & telling her to come up on morning train – telegraphed her also –
Was about town all day taking items – About 9 oclock I had occasion to
go to my room – in the entry or hallway I tumbled over a drunken man
and knocked my right shoulder out – I got it back directly . . . pained
me bad, but I worked with it . . .

Sunday, July 5 – Clear & warm – 86 deg – At 10 AM was at train
arrival – Big crowd to see the Austin folks – The band came, in uniform,
accompanied by about 28 of the company, in citizens dress – They played
in front of the International. I took them all in for a drink with Bob Patterson – Then they marched up C street, playing, to National Guard Hall
where they were entertained by the Nationals, with beer, lemonade, punch
etc, & a collation – Made it their headquarters – Some of them were taken
in carriages out to the big Combination shaft – They cruised about the
city considerably taking a look at things – PM I was with them awhile at
Hall, as I knew most all of them, but most of day I spent at home with my
wife – the day was hot, and my room comparatively cool and my shoulder pained & troubled me considerably – We breakfasted at Chaumond's
and dined at Lowery – At 5:25 PM we left on train for Reno, with all the
Austinites on board – At Carson we found a terrible fire raging – 2 large
blocks in heart of town almost – On arrival at Reno wife went home, & I
staid about depot, etc, awhile chatting with the Austinites – Home at 10 –
All well, Alfie & Goodie sound asleep in bed – My flags were up on the
house – Mary having attended to that – Bed at 11 – Painful nights sleep –

July 6 – The same – 87 deg – Sam & Alf went nearly to the depot with
me in morning – Met lots of the Austinites – They go home tomorrow –
Chamberlain & others will take the band out to the Insane Asylum today
to show them the concern and give the patients some music – On the train
were the four famous athletes Duncan C Ross, Jim Cannon, Dempsey and
Cleary – Mike Smith, formerly of the Vesey House, Gold Hill was with
them as agent and manager – I was made acquainted with them all –
They are on the way over from California, having showed last at Nevada
City, and will show at Pipers Opera House tonight – I worked as usual
today, but with very lame shoulder – Col Shaw was at Carson when fire
occurred, so he staid and got all the particulars and wrote them up tonight
. . . with a big diagram which he drew – I was at Opera House and
reported the performance of the athletes – Had chair behind one of the
wings & good view of the whole – wrestling and sparring – stripped nearly

naked – violent exercise – they sweat profusely – Office at 10 – Wrote up all and through at 1 – Home at 2 – Bed at 3 – Slept better, as arm is getting better –

July 7 . . . Capt Harry Johns told me this PM that he is going to work in Crown Point tomorrow . . . much pleased . . . Barry & Fay Comedy Co at Opera House, in "Irish Aristocracy" . . .

July 9 . . . Went out to Savage office – Called in to see Mercedes Navarro, my old landlady who lives on South C street at that point with her daughter Emma . . . Col Shaw on the gamble tonight – had Jim Townsend in his place . . .

July 10 . . . On mining report – Got letter from wife & one from Sam Crescenzo, Austin, asking about best investment in stocks . . . Also received Journal of the Assembly 1885 from Secy of State John M Dormer –

Sunday, July 12 . . . Evening at 9 left office – heard of a dead man found in bed in Lentz' lodging house near corner of B st & Sutton Avenue – Name Anton Anderson, a tailor by trade, stranger in this city – Very well dressed and several dollars in his pocket – Shot right through brain & died at once – Been dead over 24 hours before discovered – stunk badly – Pistol in hand – clear case of suicide – sent press dispatch of it to San F in name of Cohen, agent or reporter here . . .

July 15 . . . This evening Dan B Sohl of Gold Hill called in office to see me – got married this evening to Miss Julia M Ford of Silver City – Sent keg of lager to office – I gave him good send off – Old folks objected, & she ran away with him – Being 27 yrs old she concluded she was at age of discretion . . .

July 16 . . . Wife & Bessie came up on morning train, & I met them & took them to breakfast at Lowrey's . . . Took them to dinner at Allen & Chaumond's . . . Got work well ahead – At 8 went to room & took them to Opera House – good audience – Mestayer-Vaughn Comedy Co in queer play of "We Us & Co" – Very funny – We had all the laughing we wanted . . . A telegram this evening said Johnny Skae died this PM in San Francisco –

July 17 . . . They went to Gold Hill this PM – walked & came back on evening train . . . Wife & I wrote letter to Eunice today –

July 18 . . . About 1 PM, Old Aunt Jane, our old nurse, came up from

Gold Hill in 'bus & spent the PM with us – Dined with us at Chaumond's – Had bully dinner . . . Col Shaw has been all right and worked regularly & well all the week –

Sunday, July 19 . . . We rose early enough for wife & Bessie to get off for Reno on morning train at 7:20 – I saw them off – Was about town awhile . . .

July 21 . . . My 56th birthday – Nothing unusual happened to signalize the occasion – Work as usual . . .

July 22 – Clear, warm & very pleasant – PM was at assay office of the Con Cal & Virginia Mining Co – & Frank Fielding, assayer, showed me through . . . About 6:30 PM a fight between Lowrey and Morrill, Proprietors of the Grand Central restaurant, in which Mrs Morrill took a hand – created quite excitement on street – Settled by both parties selling out to Crosby & Co, who took possession at once – I got through at 12 – but our eastern telegrams told that Grant was just about to die, even saying death rattles in throat, so we kept the paper open & I staid with telegraph office till 4 – Nothing further, & I got to bed at 5 –

July 23 . . . Flags all at ½ mast all over town, as Grant died about 8 o'clock this morning . . .

July 24 . . . Was up to ball of class of '84 – Pretty good crowd & time . . . Sent wife a gold note of $20 in letter this evening –

July 25 . . . Telegram from wife says will come up in morning – PM engaged with County Commissioners meeting . . .

Sunday, July 26 . . . Wife & Goodie came on morning train . . . We went to breakfast at Morrill's Grand Central Restaurant . . . Dined at 5:30 at Chaumond's French Rotisserie – Evening attended meeting of Pioneers . . .

July 27 . . . At 4 PM took them to dinner at Chaumond's – then to the train . . . attended & reported meeting of citizens at Court house, to arrange for a Grant memorial . . .

July 31 . . . Went up to Opera House to report Father Upchurch's reception – He is founder of the A.O.U.W. [Ancient Order of United Workmen] and arrived from San Francisco this morning – Theater densely crowded – Fully 1500 people present – Biggest crowd I ever saw in a

Comstock hall – Addresses, music, singing, a silver brick presented by the AOUW & ball wind-up – Fine affair . . .

Sunday, Aug 2 . . . Took train at 7:20 for Reno – At Steamboat the thermometer scored 97 in the shade . . . PM staid at home – Sat on front porch with wife & mother & the children – coolest place we could find – Our thermometer stood at just even 100 – Terrible on a fat fellow like me – wilted collars badly – After sunset much cooler – Wife & children & I walked out together . . .

Aug 3 . . . About as hot this PM as yesterday – Rose at 6 – Packed my journal books and some more books, etc into my old valise – Got a drayman to take it to the train for me – Wife went to depot with me – Met Powning there – Says he sold my ticket from here to Ogden for $25 & will "hand the money to Mrs Doten" . . . PM mostly in office [at Virginia City] . . . Evening hard at work in office – Col off on another drunk and gamble . . . Bed at 4 . . .

Aug 6 . . . Caledonian Picnic today at Treadway's Park, Carson – 9 cars – good crowd – I gave Capt Hinds my ticket to go with & he reported the racket . . . telegrams today told of sudden death of Judge B C Whitman of Apoplexy last evening – Was taken . . . in Union Club room at 6 PM & only lived a few hours – Old Comstocker . . .

Aug 8 . . . Grant Memorial services and obsequies today – Services & exercises at Opera House – Big crowd – I reported . . .

Sunday, Aug 9 . . . Was at train & met wife this morning – PM she visited the Stevensons, at Gold Hill . . . Took a walk out on some of the northern streets after dinner . . .

Aug 10 . . . Wife & I visited together most of day – at our room . . . At 4:30 took wife to dinner, Chaumond's, then to the cars . . . James W Marshall the discoverer of gold in California, died at Kelsey, Cal, this morning –

Aug 12 . . . Evening found in Alta of yesterday news of Bob Lowery's death in San Francisco – Wrote nice notice of him . . .

Aug 13 . . . Evening was at meeting of Pioneers in Bob Pattersons International saloon – private room – Only 5 present – quorum – adopted my "Memorial of Condolence" to be sent to the Grant family – Went to office – Fixed her up & inserted it all right for morning paper . . .

Aug 14 . . . 92° – Bed 2 – Received from Secy of State a copy of the Senate Journal for 1885 –

Sunday, Aug 16 . . . At 5:25 PM took train for Reno . . . Met wife with Sam & Alf on sidewalk by Postoffice & went home with them . . .

Aug 17 . . . Wife & Bessie & the boys went to depot with me – Through in due time – Brought from home my "Mary & little lamb" coal oil lamp – Went to Fredericks after I arrived & got chimneys fitted to it – Only 2, unbreakable chimneys for 4 bits . . . Fixed up a form for Lee McGown, the Secretary of the Pioneers to engross that Memorial of Condolence . . . Overhauled my journals, & made transcript of record as to time 1st V&T RR got through to GH & Va – Did it for Yerington's son Ed . . .

Aug 18 – Cloudy & sultry – About 12:30 big rain set in for about ½ an hour – rained like the Devil, in regular old cloudburst style – Everybody out to see it rain – Streets sheets of water, and gutters all running full – Sewers well flushed – big torrents down the cross streets – Not much damage done down the canyons – Whole city & mountain got good wholesome washing off . . . Got my lamp filled and trimmed . . . and had it burning . . .

Aug 20 . . . At noon I got T B Storer, President of the Pioneers, to go with me to Lee McGown Secy and sign that Memorial of Condolence . . . put in envelope directed to Col Fred Grant, New York City . . . I mailed it myself . . .

Aug 22 through 24 [Mary & Goodie visiting – As usual.]

Aug 25 . . . Morning I saw Mary and Goodie off on the train . . . Daggett & wife came up on evening train – from California – He has been Minister to the Sandwich Islands for last 3 years & now, being superseded by G W Merrill gets back to Nevada for 1st time . . . was about town & in saloons like a dam fool till 2:30 . . .

Aug 28 – Clear & very pleasant – 85° – Mining day – Work as usual – At 11 John Cavanaugh killed in Hale & Norcross mine – Winze station for 3100 level – Putting in a blast – Archie Pollock holding drill, and Cavanaugh striking – About a carload of rock fell from roof of station, striking him in left side of head & breast, killing him almost instantly – Pollock escaped unhurt – Deceased about 40 yrs old, native of Ireland & leaves wife & 2 children at north end of city – I got all items, telegraphed below to press, then went to office and wrote it up for paper – Then went up to Charley Brown's undertakers shop & waited till body was brought in – saw it – Fine physique – large man – 6 ft – 200 lbs – Bed at 3:20 –

Aug 29 – The same – PM reported coroner's inquest on John E Kavanaugh's death – Evening attended & reported regular meeting of school trustees at 4th Ward Schoolhouse – then, at 9, reported big wrestling match at Opera House, between Adam Butler of San Francisco and Alf Williams of Gold Hill – Fair house – Williams won – $100 and net receipts was stakes – Through in office at 1:30 – Bed at 3:30 –

Sunday, Aug 30 – Clear & hotter – Took train for Reno at 7:20 AM – At Franktown got detained by a telegram from Carson – the yardmaster there had forgotten to hitch on an extra coach for the excursion this PM from Reno to Steamboat – Our conductor went back to Carson and got it in 55 minutes – so we were just that later reaching Reno – Quite a crowd at the Steamboat Springs as we passed, brass band etc – Mary & Alfie came to meet me as I passed up street – Had dinner together, all of us – All well – Very Hot – 95 deg – PM rested – Evening we had banjo & songs on the front porch, and flute in parlor afterward – Sammy said it was the happiest evening he had seen for a long time – Bed at 9 –

Aug 31 – Clear & hot – Back to Va at 10 AM – Alarm of fire as I reached office – Ran to it – Small storehouse of 200 barrels of coal oil, near the Ophir works – on E st between Carson & North sts – building destroyed and some of the oil – Loss about $2,000 – At 4 PM Jonah Williams shot in International saloon by Con Collins in a quarrel over $2 at the gambling table – faro – Ball struck left side & passed around back, & can be felt on opposite side, & will be taken out tomorrow morning – Drs Kirby and Webber attend him – Bed at 2 –

Sept 2 . . . Bed at 4:30 – Ran with Steve Gillis awhile in saloons, after got through in office – Like a damfool – But no hard drinking – mostly talking –

Sept 3 – Same – This evening I commenced telegraphing for the Cal Associated Press, from here, for pay – $10 per month – getting my dispatch off at 12 oclock – 2 items, 47 and 25 words respectively – About Brophy being nearly killed by an accident in the Douglass mill, Dayton yesterday, and a fire in McGurn's North C st store this AM – PM attended examination of Con Collins for shooting Jonah Williams – Bed at 4 –

Sunday, Sept 6 – Morning cloudy & cool, with a light shower at 4:30 – I rose at little before 6 – fixed up & went down to depot – Big Miners

Union Picnic excursion to Treadway's Park, Carson – Left at 7:45 AM –
6 flats & 4 coaches – I rode in local passenger coach on my pass, as I had
given Jim Townsend my complimentary ticket – At Gold [Hill] 2 more
flats & a coach joined us . . . 2 hours to Carson stopping all along to
take on more passengers – Crowds also came in carriages – Weather
cleared off fine & pleasant & not too hot – Lots of fun at grounds – 4
teams target shooting – The Nevada Rifle Association team got 1st prize –
Gold Hill boys, Junior Hose, won Firemens race – Lots of games & sports –
music & dancing – Train got back to Va at 7:30 – When evening train
for Reno came along I got aboard – Through to Reno on time – All
right at home – Bed at 10 –

Sept 10 . . . Sent my second dispatch tonight to the Ass. Press or
Chronicle, S.F., telling about H K Alexander, carpenter in Eureka Mill,
Carson river, falling this morning through a hole in the floor 12 ft to
floor below, breaking collar bone & nearly killing him . . .

Sept 11 . . . Got letter from wife, also one from Mrs R H Lindsay . . .
enclosing a very long winded account of her recent trip over in the upper
mining belt in the old gold regions of California . . . Big time I guess –
Also got printed list of the tax payers of Lander County . . .

Sept 12 – Clear & pleasant – Excursion to Reno of Masons & others to
attend ceremony of laying corner stone of new State University this PM –
under auspices of Masonic fraternity – Col Shaw went, he being one of
the Regents of the University – Over 150 went from here – Left at 9:30,
special train, & came back at 9:30 – Wife came along – I was up to Opera
House to see the glass ball shooting of Miss Lilian Smith, the greatest
rifle shot in the world – truly wonderful shooting – Took wife to room &
left her – Through at office at 12:30 Home at 1 Bed at 1:30 √

Sept 13 through 16 [AD to Reno with Mary, back, "as usual" & notes
coming on of his annual catarrh or hay fever.]

Sept 17 – Clear & pretty warm – Wrote & mailed letter to Sam Clemens,
"Mark Twain," Hartford Conn, & one to James W Paige No 13 Haynes
St Hartford Conn – With them I mailed a package to Paige of minerals –
Comstock ore from Hale & Norcross mine, Ruby silver from Austin, Aluminum ore & piece of the metal Stephanite from Austin – Tourmaline and
a piece of the bogus "tin ore" from Antelope Valley, Mono County California – Postage 19 cts – Bed at 2 –

Sept 19 – Same – Got ahead with my work so as to go to Reno in the morning – Through in office at 1, & started for home – Heard pistol shot down by International – Ran down there – Sam, a China washman on B st had shot at a dog belonging to George Roth, a shoemaker on B st – Dog was muzzled, but made a rush at Chinaman & he had a big navy revolver on and shot at dog but missed – nearly hit owner of dog, who told him there was no danger, & was trying to catch the dog – officers took Chinaman to jail – Went to office & wrote up the item – Home – Bed at 3:30 –

Sunday, Sept 20 – Clear & hot – Morning train to Reno – Gov Adams on board – I sat and chatted with him all way to Carson – Found Sam, Alfie and Goodie down with scarlet fever or something like it . . . over 90 deg – I sat around & sweated . . .

Sept 21 . . . Home at 10 – Had to get off cars at old Va depot, as a cave at north end of E st tunnel prevented our going through . . . caused by some sewers rotting the timbers . . . Paid Centennial assessment today $27.63 . . .

Sept 22 . . . Wrote letters to wife and A L Bancroft – Got draft from ALB this morning for $25.70 – Gold Hill News account balance – I sent it back *protested* – & sent letter to them tonight . . .

Sept 23 . . . Letter from wife recd, enclosing letter that should have been sent to Bancroft & Co, San F . . .

Sept 24 – Cloudy – Cold – Very sudden change – 1st rain of Fall season about noon today in light showers, with light dash of snow – I went back to room & put on thicker undershirt & stockings & coat – At Frederick's auction store today I bought at private sale a nice little coal oil hand stove for $2.50 – also gave me lot of books, & an oil can – I get in telegrams to the San Francisco papers . . . now almost daily . . . Worked late in office tonight – fixing up for tomorrow – Fixed up concluding portion of cousin Annie's account of her & Bob, et als, camping trip out in the mountains, over in Plumas & Sierra Counties a few days ago – Through at 3 – Soon as I struck the street I caught suicide of James Brock, a Mason Valley man, 40 yrs old, out on South C street – overdose of morphine – cause, family troubles and gambling – Went to International saloon & got full item from Dr Webber – Went to telegraph office & telegraphed it to SF Chronicle – Bed at 4:30 – Cloudy & cold – Thermometer at Gillig's front went down to 45 this PM – Wrote short note to Bancroft & Co enclosing their letter from me which I sent by mistake to my wife –

Sept 26 . . . Wife & Alfie came on evening train . . .

Sunday, Sept 27 . . . Breakfast at Morrills, dinner at Chaumond's & saw them off on 5:25 PM train – Wrote resolutions on death of Robert E Lowery and went to regular monthly meeting of the Pacific Coast Pioneers . . . & they were adopted . . .

Sept 28 through 30 [AD reports that his catarrh is getting better, thanks to his using castor oil in his nostrils, does a little carpentering in his room & buys a gallon coffee pot to heat water in.]

Oct 1 . . . Met Johnny McMartin at dinner at Morrill's . . . locomotive engineer on Southern Pacific RR . . . pleasant chat over old times – Used to be in Gold Hill . . . PM I reported County Commissioners . . . Evening, Daggett gave free lecture at Opera House on "The Past and Present of the Hawaiian Kingdom" – Crowded house – Read his lecture – took 2¾ hours – Rather prosy – I heard 15 minutes of it – Wrote it up – Bed at 3:30 – Rapid delivery PO system went into effect today in the U.S.

[AD pastes here a clip from the *Evening Chronicle* of Virginia City:] "Squirting with injective force into the very heart of the conflagration" and "funeral obsequies" may be very fine specimens of "high-toned aesthetic fanciful tropes of speech," in the estimation of the "veteran journalist" employed in editing the local department of the morning paper. The general opinion of the reading public, however, is that the coiner of such sentences is either an ignoramus or a damphool.

Oct 2 . . . Lively day – On my way out to the Chollar and Savage offices at noon, I found a fire ahead, near the junction of B & C sts – In a Tailor shop – Friedlander's . . . Burned off part of roof . . . Then when to the Chollar and Savage offices – then down town – At 4 PM another fire alarm – Stovepipe in cabin back of Gould & Curry works on D st – No harm done but big excitement – I telegraphed . . .

Oct 3 . . . Evening train took Daggett & wife off for Washington . . . J S Kaneen & wife & family leave for Los Angeles tomorrow evening to make future home – He having always been prominent man here, Mayor, County Commissioner etc, his friends got him up a nice Farewell testimonial in shape of grand ball at National Guard Hall – Over 100 couples present – Music, dancing and a parting address by Hon J A Stephens, responded to by Kaneen, also by D O Adkison, the Postmaster – Dance kept up till after midnight – $1 admission – for lemonade, cigars for occasion . . .

Sunday, Oct 4 . . . At 5:25 took train for Reno – At 8 oclock, when 6 miles from Reno, going at 45 miles an hour, we ran into a band of cattle, killed 7 & got ditched or derailed – Whole train off – Carriage from Reno brought us in at 10:30 to Lake House . . .

Oct 5 . . . Train got on track at 8, ran in to Reno at 8:30, & at 9:30 I took passage on train for Va . . . Watty Hall died this morning –

[Clip, *Enterprise:*] The train for Reno, consisting of the mail car, express car and two passenger coaches, drawn by the locomotive Reno, which left this city at 5:25 P.M. on Sunday, met with one of the queerest accidents which has happened on the Virginia and Truckee Railroad for years. The train bowled along at its usual excellent rate of speed, on time, and was going about forty-five miles an hour, when, at 8 o'clock, about six miles south of Reno, it suddenly ran into a small band of twenty-five or thirty head of cattle. They had broken the fence and got out of Wright's field for the purpose of luxuriating in the good feed to be found on both sides of the track. They were on the east side in the tall wild rye grass, and were probably lying down, but even if they were standing up they could not readily be seen. The rush of the train and the glare of the headlight evidently startled them, for they rushed directly upon the track ahead of the locomotive. Tom Clarke, the well-known engineer, one of the most experienced and careful on the road, immediately jerked the airbrake into full action, but before there was much slowing down, beef was flying in the air on all sides. One fated beast went directly under the cowcatcher and threw the locomotive off the track. The entire train passed over the carcass, and all followed the locomotive, every car being derailed in a few seconds. The air-brakes acted well, but the strongest and most effective brake of all consisted in the wheels cutting through the ties into the soft ground peculiar to that locality. The train came to a dead standstill in a little more than its own length from the time the locomotive left the track.

A LIVELY SHAKING UP

Was experienced by the messengers in the mail and express cars and by the passengers, especially in the smoking car, as they went bouncing among the ties. Those in the rear car, including ladies and children, felt comparatively less of the shock. None were thrown from their seats, and not a person on the train was hurt or even badly frightened. As soon as possible the men all jumped out to see what had happened, and with lanterns and candles viewed

THE WRECK.

The locomotive and all the cars stood well upon the roadbed, or rather into it, and the smoking car was the only one showing a leaning toward going over. But the ties were not only cut up into stove-wood but were scraped up in piles against the brakes and trucks, thus contributing still further toward the sudden stoppage of the train. The rails, of course, were turned over and shoved out of place. There was a culvert four or five feet deep, and the cars must have passed over it on the rails turned on their sides, for the front wheels of the rear car were found thus supported on the side groove of the rail, directly over the culvert. The railroad beneath the cars was certainly demolished, and it looked as though the brake beams and trucks were badly broken and injured.

SLAUGHTERED CATTLE.

One dead cow lay across the cow-catcher, or pilot, and just at the rear of the last car lay the animal which the train had passed over and caused its complete derailing. Further back were five others, dead, dying or hopelessly crippled. Four were doubtless killed outright, and the other three had their legs broken or were so badly injured that they had to be killed. A broken fence showed where they got out of their pasture, near by. The survivors went voluntarily back through the break, with little or no persuasion, and were glad to stay there, and parties from the neighborhood passed along and quietly put the wounded ones out of their misery.

RELIEF FROM RENO.

The place where this accident happened was opposite the Lake schoolhouse and the Eads ranch, and about 150 yards from Dry Creek. Just as soon as Conductor Bray ascertained the extent of the calamity, he went into a pasture near by, captured the first horse he could find, borrowed a saddle and struck out for Reno at a lively rate through the dust and darkness. He found the west-bound Central Pacific train waiting, but when the cause of the detention was learned, that train passed on, having lost only half an hour in waiting. Bray at once telegraphed the particulars and nature of the disaster to Carson, and procuring a big basketfull of lunch for his passengers rode back, carrying the basket on his arm. Meanwhile, James Dealy, of the Lake House, Reno, and two or three other passengers had started out for Reno on foot, and the result was that the omnibus and two carriages from the Lake House stables promptly came out to the wreck and took all the passengers, except half a dozen men who preferred to stay in the cars, including one condemned prisoner from Inyo county, California, in charge of an officer, who was taking him to San Quentin. The passengers were all safely landed at the Lake House at just 10:30 o'clock, free of charge for their accommodating ride. The passengers all agreed that it was a pretty good thing to have Jimmy Dealy for a fellow-passenger sometimes. The hospitable lessee of the stable also offered to take any of them to whatever part of the town they wished to go, but most of them preferred to stop at the Lake House and the rest footed it to their own destination.

THE WRECKING TRAIN,

Consisting of a locomotive and a car well loaded with ties, rails, jackscrews, etc., and plenty of men who understood the business, arrived at midnight from Carson and immediately went to work. Commencing with the rear car they raised it up with their screws and other appliances, built the railroad under it and ran it back out of the way. They did the same with the rest, one after the other, and finally got the locomotive on. Strange to say, the brakes nor any portion of the running gear had not sustained any injury whatever. A beam of the forward truck of the mail car was a little checked, and that was all. The train was on the track and started for Reno at 8 o'clock A.M., and after about an hour's stop for passengers and for the train hands to get breakfast, it pulled out for Virginia at 9:35 A.M. Owing to sand having got in, or something of the sort, the locomotive Reno had to stop a couple of times on the road on account of a "hot box," and was left at Carson. The locomotive Genoa took the train up to Virginia, arriving at 12:30.

ALL RIGHT.

Although some of the passengers were disappointed in not being able to connect with the west-bound train at Reno, none complained, for they could plainly see that no one could possibly be blamed in the matter. Nobody had been hurt, and little damage was done, except to the cattle, and all admired the diligent promptness with which the temporary difficulty had been obviated. Indeed, this novel wrecking experience was rather interesting than otherwise.

Oct 6 . . . Attended Watty Hall's funeral this PM – Myself and John Brady marched at head of procession, escorted remains from Exempt Firemens' Hall . . . to the depot – shipped on evening train for Lone Mountain –

Oct 8 . . . Baldwin Theatre Co playing at Opera House tonight & 2 nights more – Big house – I was there few minutes – Good – play was "The Wages of Sin" – Col Shaw got his wife up today from Carson & they have taken house on north C street . . .

Oct 9 . . . The Baldwin theatre Co played "Called Back" this evening – Got letter from Jas W Paige, Hartford, Conn . . . thanking me for the specimens I sent him . . . He is the one Mark Twain wrote me about –

Oct 10 . . . Wife came up on morning train – ate together at Chaumond's and walked with her out to the 4th Ward Schoolhouse & she went on to Gold Hill to see Jane etc – She returned on 'bus at 7 PM . . . took her to theater & left her to see play of "The Veteran" . . . Col Shaw was at Carson today attending Bd of Regents . . . Returned on 7 PM train & stood in some during evening, with old Jim Townsend to assist him – Then he went off gambling again – Received season ticket to State Fair yesterday, but as it was complimentary only to *myself* & not family, I sent it back to them this evening, for *correction* or *retention* –

Sunday, Oct 11 . . . Home all day – Wife had headache . . . At 9 I

went to theater – The Baldwin Theater Co playing one more night . . . .
"Wages of Sin" . . . Very good house & excellent play . . .

Oct 12 . . . Up at 6:30 with wife . . . & at 8 she left for Reno . . .
PM J W Whitcher Atty at law notified me that he had recd my four notes
of 5 yrs ago from Bancroft & Co for collection . . . They amount to a
little over $100 – Bed at 2:30 –

Oct 13 . . . Wrote letter to A L Bancroft & Co . . .

Oct 14 . . . John Mackay passed Reno this evening at 8 oclock on
regular train – bound for San F – Morris Aveplich of the Hale & Norcross went down with buggy to bring him up, but he went through –

Oct 16 . . . Got letter from Bancroft & Co – very peaceable & quiet in
tone . . . Got letter from wife, enclosing a Reno Fair correspondence
for the paper . . . I ran in a part of it under head of "Reno Notes" –
Bed at 3:30 –

> [From the *Enterprise:*] UNGRATEFUL.—The Austin *Reveille* editor [J W
> Maddrill], after systematically and faithfully copying the sanguine effu-
> sions of the Virginia *Chronicle* on the bonanza developments of the Com-
> stock for several months past, generally taking them bodily without credit
> and passing them off as his own, suddenly sours on the proposition and
> has the cheek to accuse the *Chronicle* of "systematically lying about
> stocks," and "booming the stock market in view of the most discouraging
> quotations." Next thing he will be accusing the *Chronicle* of lying about
> the mines, and sour on his own scissors.

Sunday, Oct 18 . . . Took 5:25 train for Reno . . .

Oct 19 . . . Took morning train & was at Va at 10 AM – Went to
Judge J W Whitcher's office – signed 4 notes to A L Bancroft & Co . . .
aggregating $167.68 – Took up my old notes . . . $101.70 – The additional . . . is the interest on them – Then I got a $20 greenback and
mailed it to my wife – PM a meeting of the Nevada Silver Association at
Pipers Opera House, and in evening Hon Wm M Stewart, formerly US
Senator from this State made an address at the same place on the Silver
question – Good house – Col Shaw reported – I worked in Office . . .
On train coming up this morning was Ex Gov Kinkead of Nevada and
Alaska. I being old chum of his, chatted with him most of the way up
from Carson where he got aboard . . .

> [From the *Enterprise:*] AT THE FRONT.—John H. Dennis, in his Tuscarora
> [Nevada] *Times-Review*, plaintively remarks: "Hairless dogs are all the

rage in New York. Isn't it about time that hairless men also came to the front?" Yes, that shiny pate of the venerable Dennis has been a conspicuous feature among the baldheaded brigade in the front rank at the ballet and melodeons of the Pacific Coast for the past thirty-five years.

Oct 23 . . . Evening the great Haverly Minstrel combination at Opera House – crowded full – $750 house . . . 40 of them – 35 on parade through the streets about 1 PM – 16 pieces of music – all hands wore plug hats . . .

Oct 24 . . . Got lots of copy ahead so I could go to theater evening – Secured pass and 3 seats – Wife & Sammy came up on train – took them to room, then to theater – Best performance of kind I ever saw – The Cragg family with them, wonderful acrobats – Office till 1:30 – Home – Bed 2 –

> [Clip, *Times-Review* of Tuscarora, Oct 24:] Old man Doten, of the Virginia Enterprise has never forgiven the writer for unintentionally disturbing the course of a love affair of the former, with an Indian maiden of some fifty summers, named Olympia, at Fort John, California, in the halcyon days of previous. Hence his sarcastic allusion to our tressless caput.
> [Clip, *Daily Reveille* of Austin, Oct 26:] The old stiff who slobbers over the local columns of the Enterprise must have had a sober moment and while in that unusual condition tried to be funny about the REVEILLE. Stick to your free whisky, old man.

Oct 28 – Cloudy – Bed 2:30 –

Oct 29 . . . I elected a Trustee of Centennial at meeting this PM –

Oct 30 – Clear & pleasant – Got letter from Sam Crescenzo, Austin, about stocks, one from Wells Drury, Carson, about a lecture by H C Dane at Carson, enclosing comps – and one from A Richardson, Agt Cal Ass'd Press San Francisco, dispensing with my services as agent here – John Mackay arrived from SF today for a brief visit – I met & shook hands with him at Con Va office – Mining day – busy as usual – Home at 3 – wrote long letter to A Richardson . . . Bed at 6 –

Oct 31 . . . Madame Janauschek & dramatic co at Opera House 3d night tonight – Thursday evening she played "My Life," on Friday night "Mary Stuart," matinee this PM "Countess of Mansfield" (I took wife there & left her after the 1st act) and this evening "Macbeth" – I saw the 4th & 5th acts – This ends the Janauschek engagement – Wrote & sent a letter to Sam Crescenzo, Austin today –

Nov 4 . . . 1st snow and 1st freeze of the season – The latest telegram from San Francisco tonight was to the effect that Sharon, who has been sick from malarial fever the last two or three weeks, was lying very ill at the Palace Hotel tonight, and that his life was despaired of –

Nov 5 . . . Uncle Billy Sharon still alive but arranging his worldly affairs, calculating to die very shortly –

Nov 7 . . . Saw two last acts of "East Lynne," as played by Miss Jeffreys Lewis and good dramatic company – It was done very well . . .

Sunday, Nov 8 . . . At 5:25 PM left on train for Reno . . .

Nov 9 . . . Left wife [erasure] . . . Evening at show of "Rag Baby" theatrical company at Opera House – Very funny – Bed at 3 –

Nov 10 . . . Stole a big dry goods box as I came home . . .

Nov 11 . . . The big dry goods box I stole last evening, or this morning, I chopped up this AM, & have now a pretty good amount of fuel . . .

Nov 12 . . . Sent letter to . . . R R Parkinson of the Carson *Tribune* . . . He found advertisement of Brown's Iron Bitters in local columns, speaking of *blood "corpuscles"* – These local ads of B I Bitters come in sheets, ready printed, for insertion each day for the year round – This one, Old Parkinson of the *Tribune* thought I wrote, same as all the rest, and shoots off this in his paper of yesterday:

> [Clip:] The idea of old Alf Doten attempting to describe corpuscles is too funny for notice. Stick to the main brace and azimuth, old shipmate, and don't get out of soundings.

Col Shaw went to Reno this morning, leaving old Jim Townsend to do the *Enterprise* for him . . .

Nov 13 . . . Sharon died at 3:32 this PM in his Palace Hotel, San Francisco – Flags at ½ mast in Carson and here –

Nov 14 . . . Evening at 8 I walked out to the Fulton Foundry, on the Divide, and saw a model quartz mill made to send to the New Orleans and London expositions – It is ¼ the size of the regular quartz mills connected with Comstock ore reduction – Made by a Comstock boy, 23 yrs old, named E J Squier – Was put in practical operation 1st time this PM – A really wonderful piece of work, considering that the boy did it all himself, engine, boiler, & all – Col Shaw drunk & gambling tonight – Didnt stand in at all . . .

Nov 16 . . . Flags ½ mast in Carson, on the mills along the river, lots of others in Gold Hill & away down the canyon – and only a half dozen in Virginia – All in mourning token of funeral of Sharon this PM in San Francisco – Most of the principal stores in Va closed from 1 PM & till funeral was over . . .

Nov 17 . . . Home from office at 2 – snow 9 inches deep and still snowing . . .

Nov 18 . . . Lots of cutters out – Gold Hill 'bus on runners . . . Wires down today till 3 PM when 2 wires worked to San F & the East . . .

Nov 20 . . . 6 PM John B Fegan of Gold Hill, one of the old Comstockers, died – apoplectic fit – Fell down in his back yard while feeding his chickens . . . No hard drinker & he wasnt drunk . . .

Nov 21 . . . Wife came on morning train at 10 – Breakfast at Chaumond's – took walk out on South C street – Left her in room at 3 PM & went to my regular work – Home again at 7, & took a home lunch with her – can oysters, grapes, crackers, a boiled quince, etc . . .

Sunday, Nov 22 – Moderate snowstorm all day – About an inch accumulated, making the side and cross walking very slushy and greasy, so to speak – We rose at 9, after a second mutual and complete communication – which hasn't happened or been effected since the first time or year, and all in 6 hours – Ate lunch, breakfast at home – cooking coffee on stove – can of oysters, crackers etc, & fruit – Dined at Chaumonds & she took train at 5:25 for Reno – I didn't go down to train with her as it was too slippery for *me* – Went home to room & wrote a memorial of condolence on Sharon for the Pioneers, as he was a life member of the Society – Got it done at 7:30 & hurried down to regular monthly meeting of the Pioneer Society at their Hall on B street – I was made chairman of committee on Sharon, with Dr James Delavan and Lee McGown – We reported my memorial directly and it was unanimously adopted – Home – Slept awhile – Rose, and wrote out the copy of memorial, & full report of meeting, and another item or so for the *Enterprise* – Finally bed 7 –

Nov 24 . . . Chester Hatch, who has just returned from a ducking hunt to Sink of Carson, presented me with a pair of ducks today – fat & nice . . .

Nov 25 . . . Paid my present Centennial assessment – $46.10 – 5 cents per share . . . Through in office at 1:30 – Bed at 5 – going to Reno tomorrow – Was weighed today in Hatch's store – *199 pounds* –

[Clip, *Enterprise,* Nov 25:] William Martin Gillespie arrived in this city Sunday morning from Honolulu. He was in the last stages of consumption and was taken to the County Hospital, where he died yesterday morning. . . . He was Secretary of the Constitutional Convention in 1864, which framed the first Constitution of this State, and henceforward always took an active part in political matters in connection with the legislative and State organization. During several sessions he was legislative reporter of the ENTERPRISE, and as a practical reporter he had few equals, yet as a journalistic writer he did not amount to much, and in fact had little pretentions, although he was contemporaneous with Mark Twain, Dan De Quille and other local journalistic lights of the time.

He left the Comstock and Nevada eight or ten years ago, and was more or less connected with the San Francisco journals for a short time and went to the Sandwich Islands. In Honolulu he was somewhat journalistically connected, but his health failed, and finally consumption marked him for a victim. . . . The old Nevada pioneer finds home and rest at last.

Nov 26 – Clear & very pleasant – rose at 7 – took train at 8 for Reno – took along my dirty clothes, pair of ducks, and a gallon demijohn of sweet cider – All right at home – Ruel Waggoner, and Katie & Louise Hammond of Austin, now attending the Bishop's school were present at dinner at 4, 2 turkeys, cranberry sauce, pie, cake, etc – 11 of us in all – After dinner I strung up old banjo & we had a little concert – Millie and Miss Chrissie Andrews went with a young fellow to a grand masquerade ball – Bed at 9 –

Nov 27 . . . [Back in Virginia City] Through in office at 2 – Bed at 4 – Got letters today from Will W Booth, in a store at Belleville, Nev, and J B Marshall, Bodie, Cal – Col Shaw gambling tonight & not on paper – old Jim Townsend stood in for him –

Nov 28 . . . In accordance with telegram received from H M Yerington, at Keeler on the C&C RR, I took morning train to Mound House and inspected a lot of marble from Inyo county, Cal – Just arrived – 2 carloads – going through to San Francisco & Sacramento today – 1st shipment – Quarries 5 miles this side of Owens' lake – Fine marble – Takes fine polish . . . When I returned from Mound House this AM another telegram from D A Bender at Hawthorne telling me to send telegram to the Associated Press, San F, about the marble – I did so . . . Got Fillebrown to wake me at 7 this morning –

Sunday, Nov 29 – Cloudy & thawy – Slept till noon – about 9 hours –

Shaved etc & went on street at 2 PM – Knocked about town – Took T H Fillebrown to dinner with me this PM, in return for his favor in waking me yesterday – We dined at the Grand Central and had turkey dinner – Was at Pipers short time and secured ticket & seat for Emma Nevada concert Thursday evening – Home at 10 – Bed 11 – Very dark & cloudy & threatening –

Nov 30 . . . I went to lumber yard on north C st and got 2 14 ft boards, 14 inches wide, dressed on one side, also a 12 ft length of flooring, 6 inch wide . . . going to put up shelving . . . Col Shaw still on the gamble and did not put in appearance at all again tonight – Old Jim Townsend worked in place –

Dec 1 – Clear & pleasant – Rose at 11 AM – Work as usual – Sent letter to wife, enclosing pass – Evening big saloon opening of Louis Hirschberg, in front and under my room, in Douglass building – next south of Mallon's store – Saloon named the "Crystal" – Finest saloon in the city – Immense crowd till way past midnight – big free lunch of roast pig, etc – Big run of custom to compensate – Liveliest "opening" I ever saw here – Bed at 3 – Col Shaw stood in as editor again tonight –

Dec 3 – Same – Emma Nevada arrived by morning train – I saw her pass along C street in carriage on return from Gold Hill – I got in my work early and went to Opera House to my reserved seat at 7:30 because of the immense rush – Very fine concert – commenced at 8:15 – Cohen reported it – as he is the self constituted theatrical critique of the Enterprise . . .

Dec 5 . . . Evening I got in early work & went to see the "Mikado" at Opera House – Big house – Very funny – Enjoyed it much – of the "Pinafore" order – musical burlesque – Home at 2 – wrote letter to M H de Young of SF *Chronicle* . . .

Dec 7 . . . Had my big blanket overcoat which my folks got dyed last week in Reno for $4 to a nice dark brown . . . commenced carpentering my new clothes closet . . . Col Shaw went to San F this evening on a private detective arrangement in connection with libel suit of G J Reek of Eureka vs the Enterprise . . . Old Jim Townsend in his place . . . Play of "Under the Gaslight" at Opera House this evening by Virginia Dramatic Company – They had a good house – The company all young fellows & girls – Did very well for amateurs – Bed at 3:30 –

Dec 9 – Cloudy & cold – Capt G J Hinds died at 7 AM – PM I met Charley Legate, & he & I paid a visit to Miss Harriet Hinds at the Wm

Tell House – She is niece to the Captain, & arrived from Boston yesterday morning on purpose to see to him – She will take the corpse home to the scenes of his childhood starting on Friday – Hinds was local on the *Enterprise* in January and February, after Dan was discharged and until I took hold – He died at the Hospital of dropsy of the abdomen – Been tapped twice in last 3 weeks – 3 gallons each time – Taken with bleeding at stomach about 2 months or 6 weeks ago, superinduced by heavy, constant drinking and no eating – Would rather drink than eat – took to his bed and dropsy followed – I work as usual – Bed at 3:30 – snowing furiously – Wrote a good obituary sendoff for Hinds tonight for mornings paper –

Dec 10 – Cloudy & cool – The snowstorm this morning did not amount to much – Dan Delaney, a miner in the Combination shaft was shot by officer Linehan about 5:30 oclock this morning on C street near the Delta saloon – Delaney was making himself troublesome and resisted arrest – Linehan shot four shots – One entered his groin, another his right breast, & the third made flesh wound on outside of his thigh – The other ball missed him – Badly wounded but may live – Bed at 3:30 – Today I bought from a traveling agent with one arm, David Wilson, one printed right to use "Rex Magnus," or Professor D M Marks' recipe for preserving fruits, vegetables, meats, fish, etc in a natural state for 30 months or more – full directions for making the liquid – His price is $5 but I became very well acquainted with him, & being a newspaper man he sold the right to me for a dollar, cash –

Dec 12 – Clear & pleasant – Wife came on morning train – Went to breakfast together at Chaumond's – Then I went with her down almost to Osbiston shaft & left her to visit Mrs Tony Fox – Home – She came in an hour afterward – She visited at Kirby's awhile – I went to work as usual at 4 – Col Shaw badly demoralized at drinking & gambling – Jim worked in his place & was himself pretty tight – The editorial end of the paper was decidedly demoralized – Fire up on Stewart street, bet Sutton & Bonanza Avenues – 2 story house of Wm Kane – About all burned up – I was to it – Through in office at 1 – Bed 1:30 √ – Wife & I dined at room this evening, fresh raw can of Eastern oysters, crackers, etc – Nice –

Sunday, Dec 13 – Same – We rose at 10 – I went up to Jake Becker's bakery & got 10 cts worth of fresh rolls, also got 3 boxes sardines for 4 bits at Ford's – opened one & we had boiled sweet potatoes, coffee, sardines, rolls and fresh Honey Lake apples for breakfast – PM at home with wife – We had turkey & chicken dinner at Grand Central restaurant – Saw her off on evening train at 5:25 – Home to room – Started writing *"Nevada"* for M H De Young of *SF Chronicle* – sketch of the resources, mineral & agricultural, including the last year principally, with a view at the future of the State – Laid down & slept about 3 hours on bed –

Dec 14 – Rose at daylight – Finished my de Young article on "Nevada" at 4:30 PM . . . 957 words . . . Col Shaw drinking & gambling & [did] not put in appearance till nearly 10 oclock . . .

Dec 15 . . . Through at 2 . . . Left Col Shaw in office when I came away, very intent on reading up the New York exchanges – Unusually busy for him – Evidently trying to do penance for his bad behavior and neglect of his position of late – Perhaps will read himself to death before morning –

Dec 16 . . . At noon held meeting of Centennial Trustees at Odd Fellows Building . . . Overhauled lot of bills sent over by Supt Wheeler – Mine shut down about a week ago – for season – Had just reached bedrock at 250 feet & found gold bearing gravel . . . Received 1st volume of Personal Memoirs of U S Grant, just arrived – $5 – Paid agent C A Mather for it . . .

Dec 18 . . . Home at 2 – wrote letter to A Richardson, Ag't Cal. Associated Press, San Francisco, enclosing bill $20 for press telegrams furnished by me during the months of September & October last . . .

Dec 19 . . . Dan Delaney, shot by officer Linehan a week ago last Thursday morning died at 3 PM – leaves a wife & 5 children . . .

Sunday, Dec 20 . . . Took morning train at 8 for Reno . . . The Hammond girls, Katie and Louise, are now stopping with us for their vacation at Bishop Whitaker's school . . .

Dec 21 . . . [Back to Va] PM attended & reported Coroner's inquest in Dan Delaney killing . . .

Dec 22 . . . PM I was at the same Coroner's inquest . . . got rest of it in evening from Coroner Stoddard, also verdict of jury . . . I sent a letter this evening . . . with $3 greenbacks enclosed for one dozen *No 4*, flexible, best English catheters . . . Forefathers Day today – No note of it except a few lines by me in the *Enterprise* this morning –

Dec 23 . . . PM reported the examination of Patrick Linehan before

Justice Kehoe for the killing of Dan Delaney – Bob Lindsay was there as counsel for the prosecution, with Dist Atty Stephens, Deal and Mack for defense . . .

Dec 24 . . . Went to Justice Kehoe's court & reported continued examination of Linehan – Concluded at 12 M – Then attended meeting of trustees of Centennial . . . Voted to pay all bills – Then went out to Chollar and Hale & Norcross and got mining items – Went to Con Va office for same purpose – met John Mackay there . . . At 7 PM went with Bob Patterson to his residence corner of Taylor & F streets to see Christmas tree of his little daughter "Elva" . . . About 20 of his old stiff friends there, and we all had some egg-nog & I went back to office . . . lots of drinking and folks ranging the streets having a good time –

[Articles in the *Enterprise* clarify the Linehan-Delaney business – Linehan pleaded self-defense in drawing and, his pistol being a self-cocker, that Delaney had "shot himself" in the struggle – His actions seemed dubious enough, though, to bind him over to the grand jury, on $5,000 bond.]

Dec 25 – Cloudy & threatening – Rained about 4 AM, then froze, making it quite icy – Rose at 6:45 – Left on the 8 AM train for Reno – Had along a demijohn of sweet cider . . . also 4 bits worth of shrimps – Found all right at home & greatly excited over the lots of presents from our folks in the East . . . A perfect bonanza, as good or better than any Christmas yet – Eunice also sent a big box of presents – The Hammond girls . . . also received a big box full of presents from their folks in Austin – PM Alfie managed to drop his new red morocco purse . . . containing 3 bits, a lot of beech nuts, some string, 2 buttons and other treasures, down a privy hole – I had to tear up the seat and fish some time for it, but I got it – cleaned it up etc – Among the few small presents I had was a little box from Lizzie at Plymouth – it contained a handful of "Wintergreen" or "Boxberry" plums, something I haven't seen since '49 . . .

Dec 26 . . . Home to Va on morning train – Knocked around as usual – Bed at 5 –

Sunday, Dec 27 . . . Bed till 12 – shaved & was about town, in office etc – After dinner I went home & slept couple of hours till 7:30 – Then went & attended regular monthly meeting of the Pioneers . . .

Dec 28 – Clear & very fine day – Rose at 9 – Was down at the train at 10 & met wife – Ate at room – Had fried, fresh canned Eastern oysters for breakfast – and fricasseed chicken for dinner – She left on evening train – Evening I attended the annual election of the Va Exempt Firemen's Association . . . I had been put on the ticket as one of the board of 5 trustees, but got only 16 votes out of 35 and was beaten by one vote – Col Shaw did not put in his appearance at all this evening – until about 2 o'clock, when I was about quitting – He had been out gambling and drinking all the time . . .

Dec 30 [AD gets more lumber & saws it up to make "shelf, table, window cupboard etc" & presides over a short Centennial meeting] – In compliance with letters from Gallatin & Folsom, Reno, I signed . . . a note to them for $345.93 for hardware . . . furnished in building my house in Gold Hill, when they were there too . . . they simply wanted a renewal which I granted, they throwing off all the *interest* to date – And I am generous enough to respond by throwing off the principal, thus making the thing square . . . Col Shaw gambling bad – He didn't put in his appearance at all – Sent Jim Townsend to fix up telegraph for him about 1 oclock . . . Alice Harrison and pretty good stock company from the East played "In Hot Water" at Pipers Opera House . . .

Dec 31 . . . Paid my rent, $8, Odd Fellows dues to Jan 1, $3.75, and Exempt Society dues to Jan 1, $5 – Mining day today, as no paper tomorrow – Very busy – Col Shaw still on the gamble – Jim Townsend worked in his place tonight, and the Col staid with faro in the International saloon game . . . At 12 oclock tonight there was much gun & pistol shooting, fire crackers and general hilarity in honor of the advent of the New Year –

BOOK NO. *60*

Virginia City and Reno
Jan 1, 1886 – Sept 30, 1886

Jan 1, 1886 . . . Wrote letters to H M Yerington enclosing railroad pass for renewal – to Gallatin & Folsom, Reno, about my new note . . . to I J Lewis & Co Austin, enclosing 50 cents for split curtain rings or to take a drink with . . .

Sunday, Jan 3 . . . Met Capt Harry Johns – went with him to his room on A st & he gave me a $20 piece as a New Years present – Also was with Fred Say formerly of Say's station on the Idaho road . . . wrote letter to M H de Young of SF Chronicle enclosing bill $20 for writing that descriptive sketch of Nevada, which appeared in the New Years edition . . . Also wrote letter to wife and one to A J Graham, the famous phonographer, 744 Broadway, N.Y. for some of his phonographic works, enclosing 25 cents – all in greenbacks – 22 deg tonight –

Jan 4 . . . Got letter from wife – Also envelope from V&T RR Co enclosing pass for self & wife . . .

Jan 6 . . . This PM I met W A (Pap) Abbott & he told me he was going to get married to Miss Emma Winterbauer tomorrow PM & I must give him a nice marriage notice, & I went with him to Sutherland of the Enterprise job office & he paid $18 for 200 wedding cards with envelopes etc – and he gave me $7.00 in coin to treat with . . . Old Pap Abbott is about 60 yrs old, Emma is 23 – May and December –

Jan 7 . . . Evening I was at train at 5:25 & saw Pap Abbott & his fair young bride take their departure for California, they having got married at the rectory of St Paul's Episcopal Church at 4:30 PM . . . I wrote old Pap & his wedding up properly . . . At about 10 attended banquet of the Red Men at Dunlop's restaurant – after joint installation of Pocahontas Tribe of this city and Piute of Gold Hill . . . Got a watch for present to wife today from Fredrick the jeweler . . . Nickel silver – $7.50 . . .

Jan 8 . . . At 11 AM attended & presided at meeting of the Centennial stockholders – agreed to declare a stock dividend of 40,000 shares of the stock in the treasury, pro rata among all hands, leaving 16,500 shares . . . in pool for the Trustees to sell at not less than 25 cts for working or debt paying purposes . . . assessment of 2 cts per share levied – Got letter from SF Chronicle enclosing PO Order for $10 in payment for my descriptive sketch of Nevada, saying that was enough for the work . . .

Jan 9 . . . At 9 in the evening attended the banquet at conclusion of joint installation of officers of the five Odd Fellows lodges . . . responded to toast to "The Press" in a few words – 105 seated at tables . . .

Sunday, Jan 10 . . . Voted at new election for President of Exempts . . . J P Smith, 25, C C Bowman 11 . . . Evening about town . . . Wrote . . . to M H de Young . . . protesting against only paying me $10 . . .

Jan 11 . . . Evening at Opera House awhile – Leavitts European Special Company all in specialties – Very good – Went then to joint 3 lodges installation of the Knights of Pythias at old Pioneer Hall, which now belongs to them . . . In letter to wife today I sent a $20 greenback –

Jan 12 . . . I went to lumber yard and got a couple more boards . . . Also got from the Gould & Curry works a big block . . . for chopping . . . to set up at end of wood box in my room . . .

Jan 16 . . . Train arrived at 10 – wife also . . . We cooked our breakfast on my little stove – Had 4 little rock cods and a crab . . . Old Jane Noble came up . . . & spent afternoon – Wife took her to dinner at Chaumonds & then saw her off . . . I worked in office – Went home to wife & we had a can of fresh Booth Eastern oysters, 75 cts – Also had that bottle of champagne John Piper gave me when his daughter Louise married Ernst Zimmer a few weeks ago – office again . . . L W Getchell of Austin arrived in town Tuesday morning, direct from a visit to his folks in Maine . . .

Sunday, Jan 17 . . . At 8 AM left for Reno . . . All right at home – The children all came running to meet us – Spent jolly time – Snowed quite lively all the PM . . . Gave wife $20 to help along . . . Received letter from A Richardson . . . enclosing check . . . for the $20 owing me for telegraphing . . .

Jan 19 – [Back in Va] Heaviest snowstorm of the season . . . Drifted badly . . . V&T train an hour late . . . Telegraph troubled considerably . . .

Jan 20 . . . Snowed at intervals & blew fiercely most of the day – fearful in the evening – Worked at making my window cupboard . . . I did all my eating at home this day, cooked a can of "Our Taste" oysters costing 2 bits which I had in my larder, had also crackers, butter, etc, also what brandy I wanted for sustenance, consequently I made it a very particular . . . point not to spend one single cent in the city of Virginia, at saloons or anywhere else – And I *didnt*. Never succeeded before –

Jan 21 – Still storming . . . Lots of sleighs out, especially in evening, when it was clear & fine & moonlight . . . Telegraph cut off all day to SF, so no stock report . . . I ate at home again today, and had big tuckout on fresh herring, fried . . . Also bought three pickerel at McGurn's fresh from the East, frozen – They called them "pike," but I 'spect they are pickerel – Anyhow they look, as near as I can remember, like the pickerel I used to catch on the ponds back of Plymouth, fishing through the ice in Winter with "pickerel traps" . . . Bought me a new pair of rubbers today & wore them . . . Sidewalks very slippery . . . Bed 3:30 – Snowing & blowing furiously . . . 2nd edition of the storm –

Jan 22 . . . Evening at 10 went with Col Shaw to Joe Mallon's rooms to farewell party given to Mr & Mrs Bigelow – B has been cashier of the Nevada Bank in this city for several years past, goes to San Francisco tomorrow evening to take position in the parent bank & reside there hereafter – Very nice party – All the elite of the city were there – I only staid ½ an hour, & back to office . . .

Jan 23 . . . Al. J Mills got married this evening to Miss Nellie Paul – Al. is one of the *Chronicle* printers & he sent in some cake & wine into the office . . .

Sunday, Jan 24 . . . Went to bed at 5:30 this morning, & had only just got asleep when my stovepipe came down with terrific crash – I bounced out – good fire in stove . . . hot – leg of stove got out & it tumbled over – H-ll of a time barelegged – Got step ladder out in the entry & made out to get stovepipe fixed all right again – Went down to Depot at 7:30 – found train of last evening only got to Washoe City on account of washouts on road and the Vivian was caved in, so I couldn't even get to Carson, so I went back home – Bed . . . Met Judge Flanningham, Secy of the Centennial, and went to the office & he gave me my stock dividend certificate . . . makes 2,015¼ shares in all . . .

[Clip, *Enterprise:*] One cold night not long ago, Spykens, who rooms in a big brick building on C street, made a nice coal fire in his little stove and warmed his feet before going to bed. He also made a nice pot of tea, drank a cup or two and left the pot on the stove. Then he rolled comfortably into bed. He had just commenced to snore regularly when he was suddenly awakened by a terrible crash. Out he bounced, landing with his bare feet on the long hot stovepipe which lay on the floor, inducing some vigorous words about sheol-fire and His Satanic Majesty. The room was filling with smoke and gas so he jerked down the upper sash of his window, lighted a lamp, grabbed a couple of towels to protect his hands and tried to get that twelve foot stovepipe up where it belonged. But it was crippled by its fall and inclined to part in the middle.

By cautious manipulation he had almost got the elbow into the hole up near the ceiling, when one front leg of the stove dropped out, and over came the stove, dumping the red-hot coals onto the floor, together with the pot of hot tea. Spykens dropped the pipe, yelped out a religious remark, danced a short war dance, then grabbed a pail of water and dashed it over the coals, shouting, "First water for Fours, yi, yi!"—He used to belong to the old Volunteer Fire Department. Then he threw the contents of his washbowl into the stove, and stood victorious amid a cloud of steam, smoke and white ashes. He felt like a whole fire department, and wanted to be on a long ladder, rescuing women and children from the upper windows. He imagined he heard groans of somebody dying amid the ruins, but it was only the next roomer snoring. *"Sleeping!* is he?" exclaimed the exasperated Spykens. "Confound him, let him burn up." But the fire was out.

Then he rushed through the dimly-lighted hall after a stepladder, and in turning a corner his old nightshirt caught onto something which tore it nearly all off except the upper part and the sleeves. Just beyond, at the head of the front stairs, he met a printer coming up to bed. That terrified compositor turned and fled, firmly assured that he had seen a ghost or old Jimmy Squarefoot himself. It took several drinks at a down-town saloon to brace up his shattered nerves, and he got roaring drunk, and staid so the next day, and the foreman had to put on a "sub" at his case.

Spykens found the ladder, placed it in position, and was carefully raising that stovepipe on end when it broke in two amidships, and the upper portion banged down across his head and shook about a peck of soot all over him. Then he wished the spirit of his old father, who used to be a sea captain, could only be there a few minutes to suggest some appropriate remarks. He looked in the glass and didn't know himself from a charcoal peddler or a Digger Indian in mourning costume.

But that stovepipe, had to go up anyhow, and it went up in two pieces, fished or splinted in the middle with a bootjack, a walking-stick, the fire poker and some string. It took him the rest of the night to clean up, and the first tinner he could find in the morning was given a contract for a new stovepipe, which is braced and wired up so elaborately that nothing short of an earthquake can tumble it down.

Jan 25 . . . New snow this morning, about 3 inches . . . Evening at 8:30 went up to the Scottish festival, at Pythian Hall, on B street, to banquet & jollification of Caledonia Club in honor of birthday of Robert Burns . . . 2 tables in hall – lots of women & children besides the club – speeches, music, singing etc . . .

Jan 26 through Feb 5 [AD works long hours, getting to bed from 3 to 5 AM, gets a haircut, buys a new stove pipe & gets a "tinner" to put it up, pays Jane Noble $25 of $100 she "voluntarily loaned us when Mary & family left Austin" and "Spiro Vucovich $20 which I borrowed of him 7 yrs ago" and his rent, receives more letters inquiring about stocks, makes a trip to Reno, which is delayed by derailed ore cars, & fixes up a warming plate extension on his stove & a plank shelf to break coal on in his coal box.]

Feb 6 – Clear & pleasant – Through in office at 2 – Home – shaved & pooped around – got nice breakfast of pure old Java coffee with an egg into it by way of milk – 3 slices nice pickled pork, fried, with four fried eggs, crackers etc – The first boss breakfast of my little restaurant – Enjoyed it hugely – And this day I ate at home – having the tail end of that oyster stew for dinner – Am swindling the restaurants – Got all ready to go to Reno and at 6 oclock laid down on top of the bed to be called at 7 by the janitor, Billy –

Sunday, Feb 7 – Same – Billy called me at 7 – Took train at 8 – Reno at 12 – Found all right at home – PM after dinner, wife, Sammy, Alf & Bessie took a walk over to near the new State University at north part of town – Called at residence of Curtis, the architect of University, & delivered a message from Col Shaw . . .

Feb 8 – US Senator Jas G Fair . . . rode beside me on same seat all the way to Carson – Had a good talk with him . . . Paid my new Centennial assessment today, $40.30 . . .

Feb 9 . . . Fair and his companion, E J Coleman, took a ride around among the various mining works today – and left on the 5:25 train for Reno and Washington – [four-line erasure]

Feb 12 – Strong SW winds this last day or two – blow up a storm – Mining day & busy as usual – Capt Harry Johns got caved on in 1700 level of Crown Point this morning at 8 – Was putting in a cap timber on 2nd floor above the level when cave came from roof – smashed plank he stood on and he fell 8 feet – Cut & torn all over – Both collar bones broken & probably lungs hurt – Back badly contused & strained – PM I went down to see him and found him at the Capitol lodging house – Had quite a chat with him – Was about town awhile, & rode home on the 'bus – Stood in as usual – Was at St Valentine Domino party at Odd Fellows Hall for about an hour *"spectating"* – Office at 11:30 and just saved my distance – Met old Doc Spalding – Volney E Spalding who used to keep a high toned 2 bit saloon on South C st in the early times – He is here on a recuperative visit, or as he says to "get his breath" – About 72 yrs old – Came yesterday & will stay short time – I sent following telegram this evening (night rate) . . . Thomas C Johns, Austin, Nev. "Harry both collar bones broken and back badly strained. Cave – Crown Point. Well cared for – Have seen him – Will write" – Bed at 4 –

Feb 13 through 19 [Weather pleasant – AD exchanges wires with Thomas Johns & writes him a letter, goes to Reno, taking with him "a fine shad & a big flounder" he has kept on ice in the Crystal Saloon, & has some beer & a talk with Thomas Johns when he arrives – Notes that Harry Johns is doing all right.]

Feb 20 . . . At 10 was at train & wife came . . . At noon Jane came . . . Wife went with Jane to GH on evening train . . . & returned on 7 o'clock train – I . . . shaved & put on clean shirt, & at 6 PM took bus for GH. Cara's brass band, 6 pieces on board – We went together to the Kentuck works and marched with the crowd of miners, about 90 down to Stevensons, a mile, to celebrate his 60th birthday (today) good time – Rode back at 10 with Lew Stevenson on buckboard – Office & wrote up . . .

Sunday, Feb 21 . . . Rose at 11 AM – Wife violent headache – made fire & cup of coffee for her – At 11:30 Lew Stevenson from Gold Hill came with carriage for us to go down there to dinner . . . Enjoyed a very pleasant PM . . . At 5:35 train came along, & wife left for Reno, & I for Va on foot – read, scribbled, slept, etc. Bed 2 –

Feb 22 . . . Washingtons Birthday . . . flags up everywhere, & fluttering from the balconies – National & Emmet Guards paraded finely with full ranks & National Guard Band – Lots of people in town enjoying holiday . . . Hugh Lamb, foreman of all the bonanza mines for several years died at 6:10 this evening of "acute bronchitis" after 4 wks in bed – 51 yrs old . . .

Feb 23 . . . Rode with Supt Lyman down to the Osbiston shaft & took look at the works . . .

Feb 24 . . . Hugh Lamb's funeral today – 74 carriages – Escorted by over 400 miners . . .

Feb 25 . . . Through in office at 2 & on my way home heard through Gold Hill carrier boys that Frank Currier, the Railroad station agt in GH had just died of pneumonia – Bed at 3 –

Feb 26 – AM cool & blustering – cloudy – PM more so – very dusty – toward evening lively, cold snowstorm set in & continued – Morning I was down to train at 10 & saw the Mexican Typical Orchestra arrive – Quite a crowd there to see them – 34 in all – Evening, being busy on mining report, I could not attend until performance nearly out – Very fine – good house – Sweetest music I have heard for many a day – Telegraphed wife this PM about pass, & she says she will come tomorrow – Through in office at 2 – Home – still snowing – fully 5 inches on the ground – Cold – Made good fire – wrote letter to M H de Young on Chronicle, S.F. offering to be special agent for local telegraphic reports at $20 per month – Bed at 5 –

Feb 27 . . . Freezing all day in the shade – Snow 6 or 7 inches deep – Wife came up on morning train – We went to breakfast at Chaumond's but dined at home . . . Evening took wife to Theater – Mexican Orchestra – Slim house, & cold, but good performance . . .

Sunday, Feb 28 . . . We got light breakfast, & left on the 8 oclock train for Reno – The Mexican troupe on board – They got off at Carson . . . PM sharpened all the small knives and scissors in the house – for all hands – Gave Sammy a small handle full of small tools, awls etc – Evening amused children very much, drawing "Niner pictures" . . .

March 1 . . . About 3 inches of snow in Reno, and still snowing – Found about 8 inches in Va . . . Evening Col Shaw gone to Reno – Frank Duffy, one of the printers, did telegraph for him – I got to bed at 4 – still snowing . . .

March 2 through 6 [Snowstorms continue – AD as usual.]

Sunday, March 7 – Rose at 11 – Down town – Met Billy Woods – Used to be a lawyer here – Whitman & Woods was the firm – Col W S Woods they call him now – He is over here from San Francisco where he has been living for the last 7 or 8 yrs in the law business – as atty for the Sharon estate, looking out for some legal matters connected therewith – Had a long chat with him – He finds lots of old timers to shake hands with – Will go back tomorrow – Evening at home – Wrote letter to Fair in Washington asking him to *copper* my old friend W P Pratt on the Va Postmastership, as there is liable to be a change before long [Pratt fired AD from the *News* in December, 1881] – Bed at 3 – Jimmy Durant, the old Enterprise carrier, died in Reno Insane Asylum, brought up here last evening – Buried this PM by Odd Fellows and Knights of Honor – Good sized funeral – Wife died in Reno 6 months ago – Leaves 2 children –

March 8 – Partially clear, warm & pleasant – Rose at 11 AM – about town – PM met Parsons the newspaper carrier – He got very bad cold – taking rum & gum *copiously* for it – He got so drunk that myself & T H Fille of the railroad [illegible scribbles] – Oh dear! I got so sleepy right there that it looks like *I* was drunk as well as Parsons – Met him near the International & saw he was under the influence of liquor – Never saw him so before and N B Parsons has been a carrier here for about 20 years – or more – Used to carry the Gold Hill News while I owned it – He rooms at the Chapin House out on South C st – I tried to get him home & he went with me but reeled so that T H Fillebrown, whom we met, consented to accompany us – he on one side & I on the other – Parsons bigger than both of us – Had a very rough time – He fell half a dozen times, and last of all I got 3 or 4 men to pick him up and carry him bodily to his room & bed – saw that his money $47 in his pocket, and his papers, documents, account books in pockets were all right in hands of his landlady, Mrs Cavanagh – and left Fillebrown to attend to him – I sent my Anti-Pratt letter by mail this evening to Senator Jas G Fair, Washington, DC. – Through in office at 2 – Bed at 4 – Clear most of yesterday & till midnight, when commenced snowing again –

March 9 . . . Evening I was at theater – The Lew Morrison Comedy company in "The Galley Slave" – Big house – Fine play . . .

March 10 through 14 [Two more storms – AD as usual and to Reno – "banjo & songs with my children."]

March 15 – Cloudy & threatening – Evening & night strong winds &

sprays of snow and rain occasionally betokened a storm that didnt come to any responsible extent – Rose at 6, as usual & went to depot – wife also – The train from California 5 hours late – went back home & cut Sams & Alfie's hair – Loafed around the Depot till train came at 11:20 – Big train of 13 cars & 2 locomotives – Big lots of passengers now, owing to railroad war, & worst cut rates ever known – Cause of delay was freight train off track & wrecked considerably, 20 miles west of the Sierra Nevada summit, near or at Blue Canyon – We left Reno at 11:40 & got through at 2 to Va – Heard news Miles Goodman appointed Postmaster here – Sent telegram to wife: "Miles Goodman nominated Senate today Postmaster. Somebody gets salt pork." Put in good lively work & got through in office at 2 – Home – made good fire, wrote long letter to Mary, telling her principally about an interview old W P Pratt had with me in *Enterprise* office this PM – relative to the "Nevada Potatoes" article which found a controversy between *Enterprise* and Va Chronicle – Those in *Chronicle* were signed "P" & he was afraid I would think *he* was the man – It was "old Put" of the Enterprise compositors – Bed at 7 – Long 4 page letter –

March 16 . . . Tom Johns came in to see me & we had long chat together also a drink or two at saloons – Harry is getting along very well, and able to be out on the street . . .

March 17 . . . St Patrick's day . . . no observance of the day beyond a few green neckties etc – Big ball in evening by the Emmet Guard – their anniversary as well as St Patrick's – proceeds to go to the Irish Parliamentary Fund to assist Parnell, et al, in securing Home Rule for old Ireland. One of the biggest balls ever given in this city – Big success in every respect . . .

March 18 – Morning, heavy snowstorm – About a foot fell – Fine sleighing – At 12 M took my first sleigh-ride of the season on the bus to Gold Hill – Stopped at the Capitol boarding house to see Harry Johns & Tom – Took dinner or breakfast with Harry – He is getting along finely – Went to the Crown Point works with Tom to get him a job – Couldn't see the foreman – About town a little – Rode home with J B Dazet on his liquor delivery wagon – Bed 4 – Clear – 24 degrees above zero – Evening train cut off by a derailed ore train this side of Mound House –

March 19 . . . Wrote letter to G W McHardy, Austin, returning him a long article he wrote on the Silver Question for *Enterprise* – Too d—long & verbose – Bed at 5 –

Sunday, March 21 . . . Found all right at home – PM, Bessie, Sam, Alf & 2 other little boys went with me to see big base ball game on old circus ground west of public school house, between the "Dude" nine and the "Prints" nine – They were all in uniform – big crowd of spectators including ladies and gents in 7 or 8 carriages – quite interesting – some like a circus – Score – Dudes, 11; Prints, 33. . . . This is the first regular base ball game I ever saw –

March 22 . . . [Back in Va] work as usual – I have $100 ahead today in my little treasury of earnings outside of regular salary since have been on the *Enterprise* – one year tomorrow – and it under the *upper little drawer* – Bed at 3 – Col Shaw getting off again *bad* – drinking and gambling . . .

March 25 . . . The Buffalo Bill Combination arrived on morning train . . . Several hundred people on hand . . . Lots of people from outside, like a circus day – Evening I was at their performance at Opera House – Crowded house – Pretty good – worth the money – $1, and 50 cts . . .

March 26 . . . Senator Jones arrived at Gold Hill yesterday morning . . . left in evening for SF to join the other Senators & Congressmen who came with him with remains of Senator Mather of Cal – They go back to Washington by the Southern route –

March 27 and 28 [Mary to Virginia City, and then AD goes back to Reno with her – AD sees Virginia City baseball team beat the Dudes.]

March 29 . . . R M Daggett & wife on board – just over from California – They went through to Va & will stop anyhow till after election . . . Seid Ali, commonly known as Billy "Side Alley," an East Indiaman, was killed about 6 oclock this evening in lower part of the city . . . by an old Italian scavenger, St Jacobo, who goes around with cart etc clearing up the streets etc – There was a woman concerned in the scrape – [erasure] – Jealousy caused Billy to get after St Jacobo with a big knife 14 inches long . . .

March 30 through April 5 [AD notes that March is going out like a lion, sends a pail packed with sugar, halibut & candy to Mary, works as usual, visits family & friends in Reno, gets a letter from Senator Fair & another from "Silver Question" McHardy, of Austin, receives a copy of the *New York Tribune Almanac* & a sample of the new LePage's liquid glue for which he has sent. On March 31 he pastes another clip into the journal, this one from the Plymouth, Massachusetts, *Old Colony Memorial:*]

It is thirty-seven years today (March 18th) since the Bark Yeoman sailed from Plymouth, bearing the Pilgrim Mining Company, about fifty in number, to the Land of Gold. Of the entire party we believe but one, Alfred Doten, brother of the editor of this paper, still remains on the Pacific coast. At various times the members of the company have found their way back, or passed beyond the boundary of this existence, but Alf has never set his face homeward in all this time, and is now the sole representative of Plymouth's original "forty-niners" on the Western slope of the continent.

April 6 – Cloudy, blustering, & disagreeable – Judge J W Whitcher came on the paper today in place of Col Shaw who was discharged yesterday by the Board of trustees – Mr Yerington included & present – Col Shaw has been drinking, gambling and trifling with his position and neglecting his duty too much, especially the last week, & this is the effect and the result – Col went to Carson today to see Yerington & have the decision reversed, but didnt succeed – I helped Whitcher all I could to fix up the telegraph & gave him all the points possible in the business, he being a novice – Evening sent letter to wife, with pass – Through at 2 – Bed 4 –

April 9 . . . Prof Gosse's annual grand bal masque at Opera House – Looked in short time – Splendid affair – fine costumes – Nearly 100 couples on the floor . . . Immense crowd of spectators filling every inch of galleries and stage . . .

April 10 . . . Morning train an hour late on account of heavy delayed trains from California – RR travel immense yet, although the recently vastly cut rates have raised a little – About 500 passengers pass daily . . . over the Central Pacific . . . Signor Bosco with his slight of hand performance, illusionist etc and gift distribution performance opened at Opera House tonight for 3 nights – Had big house . . .

April 14 – Comstock April weather – Springlike, but a little cloudy occasionally, with a few flakes of snow floating down through the air – Cohen, business manager of the *Enterprise* received $20 from McHardy, Austin this morning, so his communication on the Silver Question goes in on the outside tomorrow morning – 1st page – Takes 2 columns – I revised & corrected it, put a proper head on it and drew attention to it in the local – William Thomas, formerly of Gold Hill, a miner who married daughter of old Capt Harry George, was arrested night before last, when he came off shift at 11 oclock at Combination shaft, on charge of incestuous connection with his own daughter, Rosa, 11 years of age, for about a year past – Put in jail & will have examination tomorrow before Justice Kehoe –

I bought a selection of groceries etc this PM at McGurn's store, amounting to $7.45 – Had all packed in one box and shipped by freight to wife in Reno – Work as usual – Bed at 3 –

April 15 through 18 [AD as usual & home to see family – late through a mixup about the V&T pass.]

April 19 . . . Arrived Va at 11:20 – P.M. reported preliminary examination of Wm Thomas . . . closed doors – nasty evidence & very bad for def't . . .

April 20 . . . PM the Thomas incest case concluded [Thomas was held to answer before a grand jury in the amount of $2,500] – Bed 4:30 – Received this morning a gallon of fine "Thistledew" whisky from J B Dazet from his store on South C st – complimentary & useful . . . Am reading Dana's "Two Years Before the Mast" a few chapters at a time when I get the chance – Rec'd revised Statutes of Nev from Dormer today –

April 21 . . . Was at Justice Kehoe's court attending a rape case – John Lepava & little 9 yr old girl – "Assault with intent to commit rape" was language of the complaint – Postponed till Friday – Wrote & sent letter to wife, with $20 greenback and the pass in it . . .

April 22 through 24 [Weather clear, AD as usual and repudiates first of the due notes from Bancroft Co, saying he can't pay, catches a bad cold, breaks a tooth & is visited by wife & Alfie.]

Sunday, April 25 . . . Wrote "Memorial of Respect" for memory of Dr Volney E Spalding a member of Society of Pioneers – Took same to regular monthly meeting . . . Only 3 members present, Old President T B Storer, Charley Rawson & myself . . . Old "Stiffs" pretty near played out . . . Read awhile on "Two Years Before the Mast" . . .

April 26 . . . Evening attended 67th anniversary of Odd Fellowship at National Guard Hall . . . Ladies of Rebekah etc, and a full house – Speeches, singing, etc – succeeded with clearing hall & good square dancing – kept up till past 2 . . .

April 28 . . . Stocks are very much down the last 2 or 3 days . . . Everybody feeling blue . . . Read "Two Years Before the Mast" till 3:30, when, as it was just showing the least gray of dawn . . . I walked nearly up to the Corporation house above B st to see the new comet said to be appearing in the northeast – Didnt see it – Home & read till 5, when

I finished reading it through – Most interesting book I ever read being an Argonaut myself of '49 only a few years behind Dana – Bed at 5:30 feeling queerly happy from the reading of that realistic work –

April 29 . . . Evan Williams, just returned from Centennial mine, was in town today – He is Pres't of the Co – Secretary Flanningham up from Gold Hill – We three held a sort of informal meeting . . . Put notice in Enterprise – I paid my present assessment . . . $60.50 – Biggest ass't we have yet levied, yet it does not quite put the Co out of debt from last year – The Celia Alsberg–Lew Morrison–W E Sheridan Dramatic Co played "Measure for Measure" tonight – good house –

April 30 . . . Met Tom Johns today – Going to have his family with him next Wednesday, he thinks . . . Going to reside on A street – "Cymbeline" was played tonight to a good house . . .

May 1 – Clear & pleasant – Chief of Police Bob Morrison has absconded – Last seen walking on the Geiger Grade beyond the Sierra Nevada works yesterday afternoon about 3 o'clock – Being ex officio city license collector he is found to be about $1,680 short, and a defalcator to that amount so far as known – Has been losing heavily at faro for some weeks past – The Board of County Commissioners this PM at their regular monthly meeting elected Harrold Farnum to fill his vacancy as Chief of Police – Measures have been taken, telegraphically and otherwise, to arrest him – Through in office at 1:30 – Home – Bed at 3 – I paid Postmaster, Judge D O Adkison $20 today which I borrowed of him to help get out to Austin with my family some years ago.

Sunday, May 2 – Same – Rose at 7 & took train for Reno at 8 – Had along a lot of apples and oranges, dirty clothes etc in my shawl strap . . . PM took all four of my little ones out to walk – along the river, & over to Bob Lindsay's – Millie working at Bobs – working in kitchen, etc, at $3 per week – Evening at home – got out my old fiddle, tuned it up & played it more than I have at any time for 20 yrs – Bed at 10 – √

May 3 . . . [Back in Va] PM annual meeting of Centennial M Co . . . 72,000 shares represented – New Board of Trustees elected – Evan Williams, M Kinzle, Alf Doten, Wm S James, H C Gorham – Williams re-elected President, J P Flanningham, Secy., and Bullion & Exchange Bank, Carson, treasurer . . .

May 5 . . . Went up to Friedman's, pawnbroker, and bought an elegant little banjo for Bessie – 11 inch hoop – 18 inch finger board – 10 brackets – nickel plated rim for $5 – Tom Johns wife & 2 children arrived from Austin today . . . I spent considerable time tuning & fixing up that new banjo, and when I came home tonight at 2 oclock, I had to sit down and enjoy it as well as I could & not disturb my neighbor – Bed 4 –

May 6 . . . Met Tom Johns. Had an armfull of grub packages, taking up to his family – I went up with him – 4 room house on Howard st bet Union st & Sutton Avenue – Introduced to wife & 2 little boys . . .

May 7 . . . Air full of clouds of dust . . . Noon I went out to Chollar, Norcross etc & got reports – terrible dose of dust . . .

May 8 . . . Evening at 9 I went up to Opera House – Had to get in back way on account of big crowded audience – Alf Chartz was my reporting partner & we had also to get in upon the stage by rear entrance from A st – It was a hard glove fight for $250 a side – 6 rounds fought, & Slattery declared winner as Rodda refused to come to time for the 7th round, he claiming "foul" striking . . .

Sunday, May 9 . . . Off at 8 for Reno . . . Had quite a job fixing up the clothes line, as we will do our washing at home in preference to sending it to the new steam laundry, just started to drive out the Chinese – We have had our washing done by a Chinaman heretofore – Evening banjo & songs . . .

May 10 . . . Ice thick as window glass on water in washtubs – Afraid all the fruit is killed . . . [Back in Va] Evening was at Opera House short time & saw last act of "Mixed Pickles," being played by J B Polk and dramatic Co, Exceedingly funny piece . . . Ed Swift of Gold Hill was awarded the contract for sprinkling the streets in this city & GH . . . He commenced yesterday & the dust is laid pretty well – Got photo of Bro Sam . . . *Dont know him.*

May 11 . . . Wrote letter to Hon Jas G Fair . . . asking him to send me a copy or so of the *Congressional Directory* for 1886 – Also . . . to Sherman, Clay & Co., musical merchandise men enclosing $1, asking them to send me a "Rothwell" nightingale flageolet, and a catalogue . . .

May 12 – Same – pleasant, cool day. Work as usual – Wrote 7 page letter to Z A Willard, Murphy's, Calaveras County California . . . He knew me through my sister Lizzie in Boston – is anxious to know about concentration. I copied my letter after writing it, as some of it may be handy to use sometime . . . Evening was short time at ball of Pocahontas and

Apache Tribes, Va & GH Red Men, at Opera House – Full and good & lively – They had a "war dance" on the stage with camp scenery etc – Had my little dog "Kyzer" guarding the tent – Also had big stuffed deer, & a Cal lioness, with Kyzer, from Pioneer Hall – Bed at 2:30 –

May 13 . . . Evening was at theater awhile and saw Harrison & Gourlay in "Skipped by the Light of the Moon" . . .

May 14 . . . The Sparks Co in "A Bunch of Keys" or "The Hotel" at Opera House . . . Very good house . . .

May 15 . . . Went down to train & met wife . . . took wife to theater . . . Second night of Sparks Company and "A Bunch of Keys" – Very poor house . . . About 40 people present, and about ½ *deadheads* . . . Two nights of same play wont do in Va . . .

May 16 through 19 [AD to Reno & back, as usual, receives second volume of Grant's memoirs, the flageolet, which he returns because it is an octave too high, & various other objects he's written for, and undergoes a three-day bout of diarrhea.]

May 20 . . . Got note from Bob Lindsay telling me to send copy of indictment in the Thomas incest case – Went to Court Clerk's office & made copy myself and sent it . . . At 1 PM attended 1st meeting of the campaign of State Central Committee – Held at Exempt Firemen's Hall – Well attended from all parts of the State – I made a pretty full report . . .

May 21 through 29 [Weather clear & hot – AD "as usual" in all matters (except that he gets drunk one PM when Mary doesn't arrive), visits in Reno, sees M B Curtis in *Samuel of Posen,* reports the graduation exercises of the class of '86 and offers to sell his Austin property to an inquirer for $200 cash.]

Sunday, May 30 – Showers – Rose at 7 – no breakfast – left on 8 oclock train for Reno – Through at 12 – Found all right – Took breakfast – Children & wife went with me to same train and at 1:50 PM wife & I & Alfie left on it & the other children went home feeling very sad because my visit was so short . . . The morning was pleasant, but sky clouded toward noon, and in PM as we came up across Washoe valley, rain began to sprinkle – stopped an hour & 15 minutes in Carson – Walked about town, passing up street south of Mint to next street and along it, & down the street past Cap Avery's Hole in the Wall saloon to front gate of Capitol square – It was beginning to rain so hard that she & I & Alfie had to hurry to depot – got in the car, and ate some of the best cherries I ever saw, 2 bits worth, which I bought at a fruit stand – Left on time, with 6 carloads of wood – raining lively – On up grade after leaving bed of Carson river the wet, slippery track & heavy load made us go slow & even quite stop at times, & got to Mound House a few minutes behind time – The regular express mail & passenger train which leaves Va at 5:25 here met us, also the incoming C&C train – Transfer of passengers etc took place between the three trains, Wife & Alfie getting aboard & leaving on return to Reno – Stopped about 15 minutes – still raining – our train had hard pulling & slipping all way to Va, stopping 10 minutes at Gold Hill – Through to Va at 7:45 or 45 minutes behind time – A lively & pleasant days trip for me, and wife & Alfie enjoyed their part of it much – Rained hard from Mound House to Va, & we found it had been raining very hard at Va since 4 PM – Big streams flowed down cross streets & everywhere & water stood in big puddles . . . Went to room – Took a little lunch there – Was about town short time . . . This is 1st rain since middle of April . . .

May 31 . . . Fine day for Memorial Day services . . . Flags all at full-mast – Procession of military, G.A.R. & Mex Vets & citizens in carriages – Had a spat or two with drunken fellows, the mines laying off today – Attended & reported services at Opera House . . .

June 4 . . . Rec'd copy of Congressional Directory – 49th Cong from Senator Fair . . . neat bound copy, with my name, Alf Doten, stamped in gilt letters on the cover . . .

June 5 . . . Public Schools picnic from here to Treadways Park, Carson – 15 cars, including 10 flats, left here at 8 AM, took on 1 coach & 2 flats at Gold Hill – Big lot of women & children – No accident nor trouble . . .

Sunday, June 6 – Clear & hot – Took 8 AM local train for Reno – At Carson Seymour Pixley had been found dead, lying on the floor of his carpenter shop about 100 yds north of the RR depot – about 9 AM – I went & took a look at him – He had not been home to his family since the noon previously, and inquiry and search being made this morning resulted in finding him – He lay on the floor on his back, feet toward & near door – Autopsy resulted in finding he died of aneurism of the heart – I arrived Reno on time at 12 M – Going up street met Andrew Nicholls of Austin & had pleasant chat – Found folks all well . . . Thermometer said 92 deg – Evening cooler – Wife & I & children sat on front porch before dark, & had banjo & songs – Bessie got up a little surprise party for us – Had porch trimmed with a few locust limbs & sprinkled with water – Then she & Goodie, with little paper crowns on their heads, that Bessie had made, represented Maids of Honor to their Majesties the King and Queen, myself and wife, & Sam & Alf were Pages – Bessie treated us to a glass of lemonade all round, with a strawberry in each glass – Very agreeable little family episode and a *genuine* surprise to wife & I. About train time 8 PM, I went down to the depot – Met Nicholls and also C W Hinchcliffe there – They are in as Representatives from Austin to the meetings of Grand Chapter RAM, and Grand Lodge, F&AM, tomorrow and next day – Sat & talked with them an hour or so in barroom of Depot Hotel – Bed at 10 – OKF

June 7 . . . Va on time . . . Found letter from Dr F Hiller, my old friend and coadjutor years ago in this city – Now in S.F. wife dead & daughters all married – wants to know about some mines here – PM met Billy Birch down town, was introduced & had long & pleasant chat – Very agreeable gentleman – Like him – Also met Ben Cotton – Stood in lively on office work and at 8 went to Opera House – Birch & Cotton's San Francisco Minstrels – About 20 of them – They paraded B & C streets with brass band this PM – Evening big house – $624.50 receipts . . . A right jolly good minstrel show . . .

June 8 . . . The brass band of the Minstrels played on C street this PM in front of the 2 newspaper offices – Joe Marshall delivered me my Statistician for 1886 . . . Evening I saw the closing portion of the Minstrels . . .

June 9 . . . Tony Fox got killed about 10:30 this evening by accidental fall into pit of big fly wheel at the Combination shaft works, of which he was temporarily a night watchman – Waited & saw his corpse brought to Charley Brown's at 1:30 or later – All broke up . . .

June 10 . . . Tony Fox will be buried Saturday – He joined the Order of Chosen Friends in this city about a year ago, and his insurance policy in the Order gives his family $3,000 cash –

June 12 . . . This PM at 3 oclock I marched in funeral procession of Tony Fox from Odd Fellows building down C street to Mill st, walked with Lee McGown – Dr Delavan and Vincent Elliot were the only other Pioneers with us . . .

June 13 through 17 [AD to Reno & back, as usual, mixes 2½ gallons of the "Rex Magnus" preserving formula & "pickles" ten pounds of cherries, two baskets of Reno strawberries and four pounds of California blackberries purchased at McGurn's store.]

June 18 . . . Evening Independence celebration meeting . . . I so busy on Mining report I could not attend either that or the play at Opera House – the Harry Lacy company in "The Planter's Wife" – Fine play, good company and good house . . . In addition to my mining I had to write long account of J C Currie's suicide – At 9 oclock this morning J C Currie, old timer, ex Mayor of City – in auction & commission business here for many years – well known by everybody – shot himself in right temple with English bulldog 45 calibre revolver – died instantly – Laid himself on bed in room at rear of his store and deliberately let himself out – Cause – business troubles, poverty, old age and general delapitude and discouragement – Leaves a widow here . . .

June 19 through 21 [AD sees last two acts of Lacy Company's *East Lynne,* visits family & returns & writes several letters, including one ordering four copies of the *Sweet Singer of Michigan,* and one to Wakelee & Co, San Francisco, ordering a dozen more catheters.]

June 22 . . . PM I bought another banjo of Friedman for seven dollars . . . 11 inch drum & 18 inch finger board with inlaid frets – It has 16 brackets . . . I worked at tuning it up . . .

June 23 . . . Mrs Henry Dods took strychnine this evening & died shortly – Dods engineer at Ophir works – She 28 yrs old – They have little boy 3 yrs old – Dont know cause . . .

June 24 – Clear & warm – Inquest on Mrs Dods this PM – He testified that she had chastized their little boy more severely than he liked, and they had a little spat over it – He went out to work in the garden – Came in to supper & found it cold on the table – He put on his hat & coat & went down town, & soon after heard she had poisoned herself – ran home & found her *dead* – Jury verdict in accordance . . . Evening was up to Opera House awhile to Juvenile Mikado Masquerade, given by Prof Harry J Gosse – They performed 1st act of "The Mikado" on the stage, giving all the original dialogue, music, etc – Big audience – Then they had grand march, and more maskers joined in, and finally spectators helped to fill floor – Big ball till late – Bed at 3:30 –

Sunday, June 27 – Same – Rose at 6 & took 7:20 train for Reno – Found all right there – After dinner I took all my children out to walk – Went out as far as the town reservoir, over half a mile beyond the Bishops school, north – fully a mile & ½ from home – Long walk for all of us – Evening Ruel Waggoner and Millie came . . . he is her beau – Almost engaged to be married – Wife & I had a long and square talk with Ruel on the question in Millie's presence – She has been running with him every evening and too much, so that it should be put a stop to for fear of scandal – He promised not to run her quite so hard – Then he saw her home to Lindsay's – Bed at 11 – √

June 28 . . . [Back in Va] Paid my quarterly dues today to Secy Mt Davidson Lodge I.O.O.F. $3.75 – Also paid my room rent – $8 –

June 29 . . . Settled my banjo business with Friedman, I returning the two extra banjos I have had on trial . . . Have now got 2 really good banjos. Both 18 inch neck and 11 inch head – Wooden lined hoop, "Te dooden doo" . . .

June 30 . . . I went down to GH today to see the Foreman in the C Point, Jimmy Livingston, about getting the Johns boys work – Tom goes on tomorrow – Harry will after a while – Got three big gallon glass jars to put up fruit in on the Rex Magnus proposition . . .

July 3 . . . Grand celebration in Carson of Independence Day today, as the 4th comes on Sunday – The Artillery and Nationals went down, also quite a number of citizens – Probably 250 or 300 . . . Here in this city getting ready to celebrate – flags & decorations going up – Big celebration at Steamboat Springs tomorrow . . . Wrote letter to L P McCarty . . . relating to eating arrangements of the Pacific Coast Press Association at the hotels or restaurants on the 24th, when they will come . . .

Sunday, July 4 . . . Left at 7:30 for Reno – Hitched on behind the big excursion to Steamboat . . . The excursion & the picnic were fine & all satisfactory to all who liked & cared for it – I didn't and came through on the "local" train to Reno, being in Steamboat about ½ an hour – Nothing there except some good shade, a nice little stream of water, the baths etc, and plenty of chance to spend money for whisky . . .

July 5 . . . Wife & I left on the 7:10 AM train for Va . . . Reno Guard on board – Also big crowd of citizens . . . At Carson big lot more got aboard, also the Carson Juvenile military Co of little boys with dummy muskets – Got through to Va at 10:30 . . . The military met us & escorted the Reno Guard & the Carson youths up – Wife & I went to my room, & at 11 AM saw the procession pass down C street . . . was reviewed by the Governor & dispersed – Exercises in National Guard Hall followed – & I had to desert wife & be there . . . & at 5:25 had to see her off . . . Evening & night passed off with but very few rows . . .

July 6 . . . Cooked & eat at home today . . . Made a nice stew of pork, beef, green peppers, tomatoes etc – Was at Opera House short time seeing Reed's Minstrels . . .

July 7 . . . Evening attended annual meeting of the Society of Pacific Coast Pioneers – Was elected as one of the Vice Presidents . . .

July 8 . . . John W Mackay and W S Hobart arrived this morning – Received 2 banjo instruction books today . . .

July 9 . . . John Mackay & Hobart left for Cal this evening – Bed at 3 – I bought a box of apricots, about 12 lbs, for $1, also 4 lbs gooseberries 50 cents – Pickled down one of the Chub jars full . . . also pickled & packed the best of the gooseberries . . .

July 10 – Same – Hotter – 86 deg – Paid present assessment of 2 cts per share on Centennial today to Secy Flanningham, amounting to $40.30 – Met Charley C Thomas, Supt of Sutro Tunnel & he gave me $5 to give to the Pacific Coast Pioneers as a donation . . . I worked at fixing up Bessie's banjo in 1st class style, new pegs etc – Also wrote in her banjo book, on the fly leaf "Bessie Tahoe Doten (With a Banjo) From her father, Alf Doten, On her Twelfth Birthday, July 13, 1886, Reno Nevada" – Wrote letter to W D C Gibson, Indian Agent, Pyramid Reservation, bespeaking for Millie the place heretofore occupied by Amanda Ayer, as assistant matron, in case is vacancy through Amanda's marriage which takes place on the 21st – Through in office at 2 – Home – wrote the Gibson letter etc, shaved, & got things ready to go to Reno – Didnt go to bed at all –

Sunday, July 11 – Clear & infernal hot – Left on 7:20 AM train for Reno – Had heavy bundle in shawl strap – box of apricots, papers, dirty clothes – Bessie's banjo etc weighing in all 23 pounds – Made me sweat profusely carrying from depot to home – Found all right and made Bessie the happiest little girl in the world – Kept quiet as possible at home all the PM for thermometer stood at 100 in the shade – breezed up at sunset & wife & I & the young ones took short walk along street to Mrs Egar's house where they lived when I got back from Austin – It took fire & burned down at 3 oclock on Thursday morning – unoccupied except by

Mrs Egar who slept in a back bedroom formerly occupied by my mother-in-law – Insured for $800, all it was worth – Evening we had Bessie's banjo & songs on front porch, I playing it – Open air concert – After that Bessie, with Sam for confederate gave us a regular parlor show – magician, slight of hand performance – Did several tricks very neatly, winding up with filling a big empty pitcher with nice lemonade in a very mysterious way and treated us all to a full glass of lemonade each – Bed at 10 – sweltering hot all night √ – Difficult to sleep –

July 12 . . . Took 7:10 passenger train for Va . . . Brought my old banjo up – Took it apart, cleaned it nicely – took neck to Fredericks & got him to varnish it – Clouded up at noon & in PM had a pretty good rain, enough to lay dust and cool the air finely . . .

July 13 . . . PM a few thunder clouds . . . I fixed up a lot of tin whistle flageolets – 4 A's and 3 high D's – concaved the mouth pieces, rasped off their roughness and sand papered and polished them all off smooth & bright . . .

July 14 . . . PM clouded up & gave good thunder showers for couple of hours – flushing out sewers & purifying the air . . . Made up another fresh lot of "Rex Magnus" – 9 quarts . . . Had to throw away today all the cherries and blackberries I put up . . . as they had soured & spoiled – My other fruits hold good yet . . .

July 15 . . . PM good thunder showers . . . Big cloudburst in mountains back of Carson, obstructed railroad 2 or 3 miles from town with logs, bark, brush etc this PM . . .

July 17 – AM clear, hot & sultry – PM showers, and at 4 PM a grand cloudburst, the heaviest ever here – rained fearfully & did much damage to houses & furniture throughout Va & Gold Hill, through flooding & mud – Washout on railroad near Julia mining works . . . No big rain beyond Am Flat & not much north of this City – special to the Comstock. Bed 3 –

Sunday, July 18 . . . Went to Reno – Met John W Mackay at Carson on way to Va . . . After dinner went over to Lindsay's with my 4 children – The L's gone [to] Lake Tahoe – Millie there sick with nervous rheumatism, & mother attending her – Been sick nearly a week – Evening gave Bessie & Sam lessons on the banjo – Bed at 9 –

July 20 . . . [Back in Va] Made a new calico necktie – Bed at 3 –

July 21 . . . My 57th birthday . . . It passed off without any extra event worth mentioning – Bed at 3 – When I was at Reno, Sunday, got copy of Memorial and Rock, Charley's paper . . . in which was quarter item of death of my old boyhood's friend, George F Cobb – Died at his house in Baltimore June 29th – disease of the kidneys, from which he had long suffered . . . Good Bye George – Thus another tie is broken that has bound me to old home . . .

July 22 – I strung up my big old banjo today & put it in tune . . .

July 24 . . . 7:20 was on hand & left for Mound House – Got off & waited there for up train from Reno . . . got aboard – The Pacific Coast Press Association on board – 47 in all – including 22 ladies – wives, daughters etc . . . Affiliated with W H Barnes, Prest & L P McCarty, Secy & Treasurer of the Excursion – They left SF Monday morning last & have done Lake Tahoe & Carson . . . Very lively crowd – They went down Combination & C & C shafts into the mines – As many women went as there did of the men & they stood it better . . . They ate according as I had arranged . . . left on 5:25 . . . for Reno . . .

Sunday, July 25 . . . At 7:20 left for Reno . . . Millie still sick at Lindsay's, and mother over there taking care of her . . . On the train . . . met "Gov Nye" an old mining friend in Austin – He has made a raise of a few thousand dollars, in the "Neiad Queen" mine and is going east to Cape Cod, where he was born, on a visit – Bruce, another Austin miner was with him . . . we met O'Neil, another Austinite & we all had a drink together – At 8 in the Evening wife, Bessie & I went down to the RR depot to see "Rozzie" Gray, who told by letter to wife that she was to pass through from visit East, to her home in San Leandro . . . We found her & had a nice sisterly & brotherly chat with her . . . while the train stopped for dinner . . .

July 26 . . . Back to Va . . . Bought me a new felt hat today for 6 bits – Long *felt* want supplied –

July 28 . . . After I got through in office at 2 I was across street in Mike Flynn's saloon, after a drink – Met George Skelding, Special advance agent and arranger for the great Sells Brothers Circus & menagerie . . . We had long & interesting conversation – He is an old timer in this section as well as all over the world, and always in the circus & show business – He is the original of Jules Verne's story of "Around the World in Eighty Days" – Bed at 6 –

July 31 – Clear & warm – wife arrived at 10 in company with Col Parker & other educational folks from the Teach Institute been held in Reno during week – About 20 of them – They visited mines & left again tonight – Phil Kearney Post GAR of this city left also – Big crowd saw them off – Wife & I dined at room – big crab etc – Work as usual – Bed 2 – Wife helped me on paper this evening by writing letter from Reno about Institute –

Sunday, Aug 1 – Clear & hot – 84 deg in Va – Bed till 9 √ – Breakfast at home, can oysters, eggs, fresh buns, fruit, tea, etc – PM down town awhile – We dined at French Rotisserie & took train at 5:25 for Reno – At Carson the Col Parker crowd were to have got aboard but they were just too late . . . They saw the tail end of the train in the distance . . . Lots of passengers aboard for S.F. taking advantage of cheap rate to go to the Grand Army Reunion . . . Since yesterday morning, nine trains of 15 coaches each, thoroughly well filled have passed through Reno . . . Many trains also have gone the Southern route via Los Angeles – We found all right at home – Millie recovered sufficiently to be out at Andrews' ranch 2 or 3 miles from town on a visit . . . At 11:30 the train with General Logan on board arrived, & put up for the night – Big time – firing of anvils, brass band, speech from Logan, etc – Big crowd to see him – 15 cars – 500 people on board . . . Three 15 car trains full of the Grand Army passed through tonight – Made big thundering noise, reminding some of the war – [General John A Logan was an unsuccessful Republican candidate for vice-president in 1884.]

Aug 4 . . . [Virginia City] A G Koch, a German tinner & plumber whom I have known ever since I have been here, shot & killed himself this morning at his place of business on C street short distance north of Enterprise office – Financial embarrassments the cause – leaves wife & 3 children – 49 yrs old . . .

Aug 5 – Same – Sells Bros great Circus and Menagerie came this morning from Reno where they showed yesterday PM & last evening – PM I got 2 tickets at Enterprise office – and took Harry Johns with me to circus – Big street parade – Heard the Calliope for the 1st time – Dreadful music – scary to all decent animals – Pretty good show – Evening had biggest house – About 6,000 people – Tent as big as Barrett's last year, & all the seats jam full – About 12:30 George Skelding came up in office to see me, & we went across to Mike Flynn's & had a drink together – He came up from Reno this evening, & left with the circus tonight for Carson where it shows tomorrow – Bed at 4 –

Sunday, Aug 8 . . . Went to Reno on morning train . . . PM at home – Bessie had a trapeze show in the woodshed with a dummy acrobat, the other kids and myself as audience – This comes of their going to Sells big circus . . . Evening she gave a small, rude but neat magic lantern show in parlor – Bed 10 –

Aug 9 . . . Our train [to Va] was filled, every seat, with returns from SF & Grand Army . . . Had to throw away my tomatoes . . . as they were soft & *"working"* . . . Afraid gooseberries are fermenting . . . Meeting of prominent citizens held this evening at Odd Fellows Hall to make preparations for receiving General John A Logan . . .

Aug 10 . . . Evening attended adjourned citizens Committee on Logan reception . . .

Aug 11 . . . Democratic primaries . . . Liveliest I ever saw, without any fighting of any consequence – Gov Jewett W Adams won his delegates by big majority in the whole county, Theodore Winters beaten . . .

Aug 13 – Clear & warm – Logan & party arrived at 1 PM in special car from Carson – They got to Carson at 8 last evening from the lake, so had to sleep late this morning – Flags all over city – like 4th of July – 13 in Logan party, with several Carsonites of note – Taken in carriage through principal streets to International, B street entrance – Music – Logan & Gov Alger of Michigan spoke from C street balcony to big crowd – Stood in hotel office & everybody passed through & shook hands with him – In evening, after dinner, they were serenaded by band, & he & Alger spoke again from C street balcony – Bed 3:30 – 85° today –

Aug 14 . . . The Logan party rode to Sutro, came through the tunnel, and to the 1600 level of the Combination shaft – Logan and Alger and 3 ladies were lowered to the 3200 & saw some of the drifts, etc, & all they need to see of a mine – Logan, Alger & 3 or 4 more of the party left for Carson at 4 PM to go to the state prison & see the prehistoric tracks in the quarry yard . . .

Sunday, Aug 15 . . . Found all right at Reno – I took with me to Reno in my shawl & strap, three packages of "Crushed Indian" and two big crabs that I bought on Friday and have had in Louis Hirschberg's ice closet ever since . . . We all had lots of crab & they were good – Thermometer showed 97 deg this PM in shade . . . Millie came home from Andrews' ranch this evening – She is feeling much better . . . Evening me & mine sat on front porch & had flageolets, banjo & songs – also mosquitoes . . .

Aug 16 . . . Reached Va at 10:50 . . . Evening was at Opera House short time & saw about half the play of the "Golden Giant," by McKee Rankin & Cal Theater Co – Very good – $232 house, though . . .

Aug 17 through 21 [Hot – As usual – Centennial levies another two-cent assessment – Mary to Virginia City.]

Sunday, Aug 22 . . . Wife & I took light breakfast at room & morning train at 7:20 – Got off at Empire & in a few minutes up train took us back to M.H. There we got aboard C&C train for Dayton where I was engaged to witness working model of Whittier Dredge in river, for raising quicksilver, amalgam etc – Dr J H Rae, the owner & Prest of the Co took us in tow as his guests – Paid all traveling expenses – took us to his house, where his wife is, & I left Mary there, & we went over & saw the dredge work in the river, about 100 yds from the RR depot – dined with Dr & wife & son et al at Union Hotel – Other parties came from Va to see dredge, Sol & Louis Frankel, brothers, F E Fielding and Matt. Rider of the Con Va assay office, & others – PM very windy & dusty – fearfully so – Hadn't been in Dayton for 12 years . . . Left on return at 5 PM . . . At Mound House wife took train for Reno, & I for Va . . .

Aug 23 . . . Got my sleep well up – Got in my dredge visit for paper in morning – makes over a column . . .

Aug 24 – Clear & pleasant – As usual – Evening I was at Opera House awhile & heard most of concert of the Wizard Oil company – Half a dozen of them, including Mrs Harry Christie, a strong, clear soprano, who did the piano. Fine quartette – Sang all sorts of songs, sentimental, comic and otherwise – Irish, Dutch, Jubilee songs, etc – Had big house at 4 bits admission – although they have been singing free concerts every evening for a week from their wagon on the street – Bed at 3:30 –

Aug 25 through 31 [Hot – As usual – Buys "½ doz new collars – $1," is visited by Mary, covers a fire on the Divide, goes to Reno and notes that Millie is "recovering from rheumatic fever – Worn to a skeleton" – Takes a look at the Chollar croppings with his friend Lawson of American Flat.]

Sept 1 – Clear & pleasant – 72 deg – Put up 2 half gallon Woodbury patent fruit jars, costing 2 bits each . . . Catauba grapes in one – and Muscat grapes in other – Whole cost $1.10 – Evening grand reception of the Carson lodge of AOUW by the lodges of this city and Gold Hill – Procession with music through streets from RR depot, they coming through in a special car – Select Knights, 30, led off in full uniform – Held exercises at Odd Fellows Hall – literary, musical etc – Bed at 3 – Senator J P Jones arrived from Reno on special car at 11 tonight at Gold Hill – Direct from Washington –

Sept 2 – Same – John W Mackay arrived this morning from San F – Stewart, Woodburn, Gov Adams & other big magnates, mining & political also came – Big crowds of wire pullers, [illegible] etc, all talking politics – Bed at 3:30 – I registered my name today as a voter in Storey county once more at Justice Kehoe's office – I was No 1029 on the list –

Sept 4 . . . Grand picnic excursion of the Miners Union of Storey & Lyon Counties at Treadway's Park . . . 12 carloads . . . Plenty went in carriages, etc – Big time . . .

Sunday, Sept 5 . . . Wife arrived on morning train . . . We had a splendid breakfast at room – Nice steak cooked with green peppers & onions – tomatoes, cucumbers, grapes, fresh rolls, cakes, nice coffee, etc – Really luxurious, & best breakfast I ever ate in this city – We staid at home all day, enjoying each others company – She left on the 5:25 . . .

Sept 6 . . . Cohen took $10 out of my pay today to pay for announcement ad of Judge Adkison, which he got me to go security for as he is candidate for Justice of the Peace . . . I found Bob Patterson, & he & I went to J C Hampton & got him to send for a new flag for the Pioneers . . . 20 ft flag – stars & stripes . . .

Sept 8 . . . Put up patent jar of crabapples & Muscat grapes mixed . . . Eyes very sore . . .

Sept 9 . . . "Admission Day" – Anniversary of admission [of] California into the Union – Flag up on Pioneer Hall – No other observance here except no stock board, the Gov of California having declared it legal holiday – State Democratic Convention at Elko today – Only got as far as preliminary organization . . . Second concert of the Wizard Oil Company . . . $200 house – They had $165 house at other performance . . . Yet they have been giving free open air concerts for the last three or four weeks on the street, selling "Wizard Oil" from their wagon – Really wonderful crowd – Had to wear glasses this morning 1st time in my life on the street – Clouded glasses . . .

Sept 10 . . . The convention at Elko got through today – Jewett W Adams nominated for Governor by acclamation – Salute fired in his honor this evening in lower part of city . . .

Sept 11 . . . Republican primaries for delegates to State Convention . . . only one ticket in the field – all unpledged . . .

Sept 15 [AD still suffering from annual hay fever – Has to dump all his preserved grapes & crabapples down the privy – Makes three bottles of preserving syrup and gives recipe] – About 11, just as I had got things straightened up in my room, somebody knocked at door – Opened it and there was my old friend and . . . ranch neighbor in the Berryessa district . . . away back in 1860 or thereabouts, J C Morrill – Looked just as natural as life . . . knew him at a glance & we affiliated at once – Had long chat . . . Went to International Hotel together & found his new wife in parlor & had chat – Morrill has sold out his old ranch for $2.25 per acre – $26,000 in all – Is taking a cruise, looking around, with a view to a home in his old days – Left on evening train for Carson – Will go over to Lake Tahoe tomorrow for couple of days, & back to San Jose . . . Was up to ball of Miners Union at Opera House awhile . . .

Sept 16 through 20 [AD writes letters ordering a "London Flute – two Richter 10 hole harmonicas," a lemon drill & a pair of cuff holders – His catarrh so bad he must continue to wear dark glasses – Notes that politicians are gathering & that Sammy is doing better than Bessie on the banjo & can already play "My Bonnie Lies Over the Ocean."]

Sept 21 . . . Got Tom Rickey to . . . pay for new flag for the Pioneer Society today . . . 20 ft long, cost, made to order, $26 – Rickey is candidate for Governor, & I advised him to *make a point* in this way . . .

Sept 22 . . . Rep primaries for County Convention – quiet – K of P fraternal visit to Carson tonight . . .

Sept 24 . . . Left on 7:20 train for Carson – Big crowd of delegates etc – Republican State Convention – Met at 1 PM – Got as far as permanent organization at 4 PM & adj till 9 AM tomorrow – Bed 2 –

Sept 25 . . . Called by policeman at 6 – Went to Carson by morning train – Got there in good time for Convention – Reported it – telegraphed 3 or 4 times result to *Enterprise* – Stevenson nominated for Governor

. . . took train for home – found wife on board . . . Bed at 1:30, weary –

Sunday, Sept 26 . . . Wife walked to Gold Hill & back, as no 'bus runs Sunday – She paid Jane Noble $30 on account of what we owed her – $100 at first – Owe $45 now – We dined at Chaumond's – Saw her off . . . At 2 PM I attended presentation of a $400 service of silver & gold to Rev Bishop Whitaker at his residence – by several Comstock friends, as he is to leave us to stay in Philadelphia hereafter – Bully good man . . .

Sept 27 . . . Rep County convention – At Pipers Opera House – I reported it . . . Taggart, our new editor, commenced today . . .

Sept 28 . . . Mr Taggart, the new editor on Enterprise, started in yesterday – Dont know as yet whether I like him or not – Good newspaper man . . .

Sept 30 . . . First premonitory touch of Winter . . . Democratic primaries today for delegates to County convention . . . Only one ticket in field – very quiet – Recd complimentary ticket for self & wife to Reno Fair next week – from Secy C H Stoddard . . . My hay fever is passing out of head, nose & eyes, & going down throat into lungs . . .

BOOK NO. *61*

Virginia City, Carson, Reno
Oct 1, 1886 – April 13, 1887

Oct 1 . . . The spurt of rain & snow yesterday operates rather bene-
ficially not only on me but everybody else in the catarrh line – Through
in office at 2 – Home at 3 – Bed at 5 – Was notified by Cohen, Sec'y of
the Enterprise Publishing Co this PM that there was going to be a
"change" – that I was to be superseded by Newton S Rountree of Carson
as local of the Enterprise on Monday – So I am apparently fired out . . .

Oct 2 – Clear & pleasant – Eyes about well – Only used eye shade glasses
short time in sunshine today & laid them aside for a year – Wrote letter
of 10 pages this PM & sent it by evening train to H M Yerington, expostu-
lating against my discharge – Bed at 4 – Been 37 years on Pacific Coast
today – Landed in San Francisco Oct 2, 1849 – Never was so hoarse and
sick with my disease as today – Kept my room most of day – Grand
Republican meeting at Opera House tonight, addressed by Stevenson for
Governor, and Woodburn for Congress – Old Jim Townsend reported
it – After I was through in office I picked up my things, sorted scraps,
etc – Emptied drawers etc into a sack – carried files, chair, sack & everything up to my room – evacuated the premises, as it were – At 5 laid
down on bed to be waked up at 6 for Reno, but didnt wake.

Sunday, Oct 3 – Same – Was called at 6 by Billy Brady, the janitor, but
was too sick & worn out to get up – Slept till 9 – Was down town awhile
and at 11 AM started for Carson by one of Mooney's teams – 2 horses &
buggy – with George Mooney for driver – Made it in 1 hour & 40 minutes – Was about town awhile, & at 3 PM was at railroad office & had
long talk about *Enterprise* – Must be a change throughout to run paper
"out of the old groove" – My talk was with Yerington – Am to be retained in the Enterprise employ at half pay, $15 a week, till Jan 1st, to

report the State Fair, now running at Reno, & do whatever other outside work is required – Took the evening train to Reno – slept all the way, & got off at Reno so sleepy that I didnt know where I was – Wife & Millie took me along – Found everybody all right but myself – Bed at 10 √ – pretty well used up – Too hoarse to talk – Much discharge from nose and throat all night – Slept bad –

Oct 4 . . . Home all day resting & feeling better – Ate but little . . .

Oct 5 – Same – Rose at 9 feeling much better – At 11 took 'bus for the race grounds, about 3 miles out south – Made the rounds of the sheds, taking look at the fine horses, cattle, pigs etc – Saw an Indian pony race, two regular mile dash races, and a sulky race, & rode back to town in carriage. 4 bit fare – Wife was out with Miss Farmer, another school teacher visiting the public schools – as it is a vacation week – At 5:30 wife & I & 2 boys visited the Fair Pavilion – Home in about an hour – Bed at 10 – This PM my 2 boys & I went up the river about a mile & got some "Too-roop" for Louis Hirschburg –

Oct 6 – Same – Left on morning train for Va. At Carson, Yerington made me stop off for consultation with him and Taggart . . . The new arrangement relative to my retention on *Enterprise* . . . was repeated to Taggart – Y gave us each a special pass or permit to ride on locomotives, and at 2:20 PM we left for Va, by a double-header freight train, T riding on head engine & I on the second – Through to Va in two hours & 40 minutes – After dinner I wrote up the Fair, took copy to Taggart in office, and at 12 was there & read proof – Made just a column – Bed at 3 – His name is *Jesse Taggart* –

Oct 7 . . . Wrote another half column of Reno Fair, took it to office, read proof – Home at 1 . . .

Oct 8 – Furiously windy day – Took train at 8 AM for Reno – Slept most of the way . . . races had to be postponed – Many shade trees broken in Reno, and fruit harvested very summarily in the orchards – Fearful clouds of dust . . . Moderated toward evening & wife & I visited the Pavilion about 5 PM for an hour – Very tiresome . . .

Oct 9 – Stormy AM, Windy, cold & threatening – The postponed races & races for today made a huge crowd . . . at race track – Started in at 9 AM & fought to a finish very lively, ending in a snow storm about sunset – Awards will be declared this evening at the Pavilion . . . I left on local train for Va . . . arrived at 7:50 – Went right straight to room –

made good fire & wrote as fast as possible – At little before 10 took my report . . . to Enterprise & gave it to Taggart, editor . . . nearly the whole of it, which would have made a column, was left out by pressure of telegraphic & other matter . . .

Sunday, Oct 10 – Stormy – About an inch of snow on ground this morning . . . Owing to the melting snow, etc & leakage in the roof, the ceiling plaster in my room through which water had been dropping for an hour [or] so fell with a terrible crash about 5 PM – Hunted up the janitor, Billy Brady – a nigger – with his assistant Thompson – another nigger – and got the matter cleaned up . . . Paid my Exempt dues – $4 –

Oct 11 . . . I got my shoes half soled and made new today, $2 – Drew my first half pay, $15 at the Enterprise office – Evening at the Opera House . . . Bought 2 pair of drawers today at Gabriel & Cos, $3 per pair . . . Heavy and "all wool" – The play at the Opera House tonight was "The Unknown," a bit of sensational trash – By the Nellie Boyd Dramatic Combination –

Oct 12 . . . PM about town – Evening at theater – Play "A Case for Divorce" – Very fine – By the Nellie Boyd Combination . . .

Oct 13 . . . Took morning train for Carson – Was about town rest of forenoon – At 1 PM rode in a 'bus, two bit carriage to Sweeny's race track 2 miles north of town. It has been leased by E B Johnson of Chico, Cal who has a lot of horses he had at the Reno fair last week . . . Saw two running races and only a crowd of about 60 people – Wrote account . . . & sent to *Enterprise* . . . Left for Reno . . .

Oct 14 . . . Carson by morning train & in PM attended the races – Went to Va by evening train – Went to room & wrote report . . . Went to theater – "Octoroon" – Very well played . . . All work discontinued on 3200 level from the Combination shaft at noon yesterday – Deepest Comstock mining stopped for first time – Will work from 2400 level up hereafter – *Footlight* resumed – [*Footlight* was an on and off paper featuring Virginia City entertainment news.]

Oct 15 . . . Took morning train for Carson – loafed about town till PM – rode out to the races – very poorly attended – trotting . . . Telegraphed report . . . left on down train for Reno . . .

Oct 16 – Variable – blustering, cold, cloudy, with light showers in the evening – took the morning train for Carson – Hon George W Cassidy on board, also Sam Jones, Dick Dey, et al – bound for Va – I stopped off at Carson – The races indefinitely postponed, and the racers shipped for Winnemucca to Humboldt county fair . . . was about town until 5:20 PM, when I took train for Va – Evening about town – Bed at 1 – Cassidy is up from San Francisco to "shy his castor into the ring" as candidate for US Senator from Nevada in place of Fair . . . It is now decided to shut down the Combination shaft entirely, therefore the regular main shafts of the Savage, Hale & Norcross and Chollar are being put into working order for work separately hereafter . . .

Sunday, Oct 17 . . . Was about town – Home at 10 PM, & sat up all night sorting my scraps . . .

Oct 18 . . . PM & evening I was about town – Bed at 3 – This PM at the invitation of Frank Wyatt who is attending her, I visited the widow of Dennis McCarthy of the *Chronicle* – [erasure] –

Oct 19 – Cloudy & cool – PM about town – Evening grand Democratic ratification meeting at Piper's Opera House – Bonfires in front on B street and in front of International and Gillig's on C st – Opera House well filled of course – I took a front seat – cold & uncomfortable – Hon Geo W Cassidy talked an hour & 20 minutes – band of music etc – I ran with Johnny Trezona of Gold Hill & others awhile – Bed at 2 – Sent letter to Jeff. Hull, Assessor of Lander County . . . this evening, enclosing $2 greenback to pay my tax on old cabin property . . . $1.80 –

Oct 20 . . . Much political buzzing everywhere – I was about considerably – Evening at Opera House – Play the "Two Colonels" – Very funny – Company direct from the East – Includes the Heely Brothers, the "king high kickers of the World" – Wonderful acrobats and contortionists – Bed at 3 –

Oct 21 . . . Play was "Muldoon's Picnic" – Very funny . . .

Oct 22 . . . Evening I got a 2 horse buggy team and driver & went to Silver City to Republican Campaign meeting at Miners Union Hall . . . H Rolfe, Senator J P Jones and Hon W M Stewart addressed the meeting – Home to Va at 12 – Went to office & wrote ⅔ column of report – Bed at 5 –

Oct 23 – Cloudy but pleasant – Rose at noon – A great many people on C st – looks like old bonanza times – Quite a boom in stocks the last 3 or 4 days, owing to reported strike of extensive body of good paying ore on

1400 level of Con. Cal & Va mine, extending into Ophir – C C & Va touched $10, and Ophir $3.65. Lots of political buzzing also going on, & big Rep rally at Opera House this evening – I was about town some – also at room mending, noting, etc. Fried a nice flounder for dinner & ate it all – Evening attended the speaking at Opera House – Big bonfires on C & B streets . . . Brass band – House full – Stewart long & forcible address – Rolfe and E O Leermo spoke – Senator Jones came in amid great applause – Was called loudly for, and forced to speak although not feeling able – He did finely, & carried his audience with him completely – Bed at 1 –

Sunday, Oct 24 – Clear & pleasant – Rose at 6, shaved, breakfast, etc, & took morning train for Reno – Stevenson went as far as Carson, where he met Woodburn, & they went by private conveyance to Glenbrook, electioneering – George Cassidy got aboard train at Carson & rode to Reno with me – I found folks all right – Took walk with my children after dinner – Evening at home – Bed 9 – Stewarts last nights speech, reported shorthand by Chartz, took 5½ cols nonpariel type in this mornings *Enterprise* –

Oct 25 . . . Took the morning train for Virginia – Was about town as usual . . .

Oct 26 . . . Took morning train for Reno – All right there – Took down gallon jar of apricots & 2 pickle jars of gooseberries that I put up in "rex magnus" . . . opened them & found they were no good . . . The process is a failure, and an expensive delusion to me – I am out about $15 on it . . . After dinner went down to Depot Hotel – Met lots of acquaintances – The 8:10 train from the East brought George Tufly, Republican candidate for State Treasurer, J F Hallock for Controller, J M Dormer, Secy of State, J F Alexander, Atty Genl, & W C Dovey Supt of Public Instruction, from their electioneering tour – to address the people of Reno – By some misunderstanding no preparations had been made, & Hugh J Mohan, the young Irish orator, had the Theater, & was addressing a big audience on "The Progress of Labor" – He kindly gave way about 9:30 oclock . . . Owing to the lateness of the hour, however, only Alexander spoke, representing the "gang" . . .

Oct 27 . . . Rode on morning train to Carson in order to interview Sec'y of State Dormer on the way – Succeeded – It was about getting his deputyship in case he is re-elected – [erasure] . . . at 10 took down train for Reno – At 2 PM went on 'bus to the new reduction works about a mile below town, on the river – Will be completed & running about the middle of December – Took notes – found Howell & Carey, the projectors & principals, to be old acquaintances . . . Howell gave me $10 for cigar money . . . Senator J P Jones was on the train with me from Carson to Reno today & gave address in evening . . . I was there – After it was over, I was at Depot Hotel with Jones, Bill Gibson, et al . . .

Oct 28 . . . Took morning train for Va and returned on the evening train . . . free special train to Reno carrying a big crowd to attend Stewarts speaking . . . I attended the speaking awhile – Theater full . . .

Oct 29 . . . Arr at Va on time – It snowed some this morning . . . Politics red hot, & stocks up . . . This PM, J D Chassnell a former Gold Hill Comstocker, now of Nevada City, Cal, . . . gave me a couple of pieces of silver ore from the Greenhorn mine . . . 3 miles south of Nevada City – First silver mine I have yet heard of in the old gold region of Cal – It goes nearly $100 to the ton, about one fourth gold – Has been worked as a gold mine for last 20 years, yielding over $500,000, and only recently realized to be a silver mine – Looks like Comstock ore – J H MacMillan of Humboldt, Democratic candidate for Lt Governor, and W E F Deal spoke at Opera House this evening . . .

Oct 30 . . . About town talking politics all day – Evening I wrote up the Reno Reduction Works . . . J P Jones gave the final speech of the campaign at the Opera House this evening to big audience . . .

Sunday, Oct 31 – Heavy snowstorm this morning . . . I was about town among the political chaps, etc – Took evening train for Reno . . .

Nov 1 . . . Returned to Va . . . Was around among the politicians considerably today & evening . . .

Nov 2 – Clear & pleasant – Grand general Election day – State Election – PM was about town – *voted* – Evening was called upon to report the election in this city – Did so in good style – Had to visit all the wards, from one end of the city to the other – over ½ mile, about twice – Bed at 3 –

Nov 3 – Same – PM about town – Was engaged in getting in the local election returns for *Enterprise* till 1 oclock – Bed at 4 – This PM Harry Johns met me on the street, & we went to the Crystal saloon & had pleasant little talk – He presented me with $20 –

Nov 4 – Same – The 4th Ward, Va & 2nd Ward, GH got through counting last evening, the First & 2nd Wards, Va, this morning, and the 3d

Ward, Va, & 1st Ward G.H. this PM – Grand Republican victory throughout the State – Nearly a clean sweep – Bed at 1 – C C Stevenson, being
found to be elected Governor, his miners from the Kentuck mine, and
other friends gave him a big serenade this evening – Cara's brass band
from here went down – Miners marched, about 200, from the mine down
to his residence – Music, fine spread of good things, speeches etc – On
the way back they stopped at Senator Jones' & had a similar good time –
and better –

Nov 5 . . . Rode down to Mound House on evening train & back –
John Mackay on train, bound for San Francisco – I expected to find
Jones also, but he wasn't there . . . Wrote letter to L P McCarty, San F
tonight –

Nov 6 . . . Rode down on the evening train to Mound House & back –
Jones not on board . . .

Sunday, Nov 7 . . . Found that Jones is going down to SF tonight, so
I took the evening train myself . . . Found good chance to talk with him
as we rode in same seat all way from Carson to Reno – Senator Stewart
also on board . . . Found all right at home – Bed at 10 √ –

Nov 8 . . . About town most of day talking political matters – At 9:30
AM visited the kindergarten school of Misses McCracken and Finlayson
with Alfie and Goodie – Very interesting exercises by the 24 little girls &
boys belonging to it, including Goodie – Was at *Reno Journal* office
couple of times – Evening . . . wife & I visited Mrs Lew Stevenson at
the Golden Eagle Hotel . . . She has lately returned from an 11 years
absence in Colorado & the East, with her son Charlie . . .

Nov 9 . . . The morning train brought me to Va – About town as usual
. . . Evening I rode down to Mound House & back – Bed at 1 –

Nov 12 . . . Tonight I wrote letters to each of the legislators Senatorial
elect, telling them I am candidate for Engrossing Clerk of the Senate –
Bed at 3 . . .

Nov 13 . . . Continued excitement in stocks – Con Cal & Va touched
$16 on improvement in mine – All other stox up in sympathy – Best boom
for years . . .

Sunday, Nov 14 . . . Took morning train at 8 for Reno – Found all
right at home . . .

Nov 15 . . . Rose at 6 – Thermometer showed 9 deg above zero – Pretty dam cold, so to speak, for so early . . . Found a little more snow at Va than in Reno or Carson . . . Wrote letters to R S Osburn, Reno and H Harris, Genoa, both Democratic State Senators elect telling them of my candidacy for Engrossing Clerk . . .

Nov 16 – Clear & cool – Rode on morning train as far as Mound House – found by telegraph communication that Yerington was on the up train – Waited & rode back – got chance to speak with him a few minutes about a chance to report Legislature this session for *Enterprise* – No satisfaction at present – At noon was informed by Pete Myers, a printer, that Young Rowntree had resigned as local of *Enterprise,* because of insufficient pay, & gone to clerking for J R Douglass, the stock broker – He used to be the same with Geo T Marye, stock broker – He was only paid $100 per month as local on *Enterprise* – The result was that I was called to the office & reinstated as local, at my old salary, $30 per week – So I went on to work as usual tonight – Got along well – Home at 1:30, Bed at 2:30 – Cloudy & promising a snowstorm –

Nov 17 . . . Wrote letter to wife enclosing $20 greenback, & sent her a telegram: "I mail you a valuable letter tonight" – Work as usual . . .

Nov 18 – Same – recd letters from John Forbes, State Senator elect from Esmeralda, & from J W Powell, Senator from Elko, in reply to my letters to them for Engrossing Clerk – They will favorably consider, etc – At noon I rode in 'bus to Gold Hill – Got into basement of the Masonic building and saw the 4 boxes of books, pictures minerals etc, I stored there 5 yrs ago, when we left for Austin – Arranged with Adam Gillespie to take them to depot & ship to Reno – Rode back with Dr Manson to Va – Work as usual – Evening fraternal visit from the Knights of Pythias of Reno, Dayton, & Carson – They came in special train of 2 coaches – 70 of them . . . Were met at depot by Va & Gold Hill Knights, with brass band – Marched up Smith st to C & to Sutton Avenue & to Pythian (Pioneer) Hall on B st – Subsequently they marched to National Guard Hall to big banquet – At 11 they marched to depot & gave the outsiders on departure, a good send-off – Bed at 2 –

Nov 19 . . . Mining day – Traveled very considerably from one point to another, whole length of ledge . . . Got up the best report I have written for some time . . .

Nov 20 through 24 [A snowstorm – Mary sick abed & Millie & a friend from one of the Truckee Meadows ranches teaching for her – A visit, at Reno, from Chris Batterman, on his way to take charge of a mill in Candelaria.]

Nov 25 . . . Thanksgiving Day – Took morning train for Reno – Took along a jug of sweet cider . . . also . . . my big square & some other tools . . . Found wife sick abed with continued bad cold – Millie bad sore on her foot . . . Could only hobble around, but assisted mother very materially in getting up Thanksgiving dinner . . . Made a cupboard 8 ft high, with 6 shelves besides the top – in the kitchen – Dinner at 5 PM – 2 roast turkeys, cranberry sauce, mince pie, sweet cider etc – jolly good dinner, with all but Mary at the table . . .

Nov 26 . . . Took morning train for Va . . . Stirred around on mining report . . . wrote <u>mining</u> and a whole lot of local from my notebook. I did not use any scissors, but *wrote* everything I put in the paper. And didnt exhaust my notebook either . . . Never wrote the entire "local" before without outside help somehow –

Sunday, Nov 28 . . . AM train to Reno – Wife better & able to be up & around – Made myself busy at carpentering . . . Evening with family, etc – Sammy learning banjo fast – Bed 9 –

Nov 29 . . . AM I worked at sorting out and sacking my cabinet ores . . . At 11 took them in a dray to the Reno Reduction Works . . . 207 lbs – Not over 20 lbs Comstock – About 120 of it was the richest of Austin ore – ruby silver – rest was base ores . . . mostly from the Reed & Curtis dump, Austin – Staid at the works and saw the whole lot run through . . . Too late for assay . . . Walked to Reno in company with George Ernst . . . assayer there, I think – He used to be compositor in *Sentinel* office, Dayton, over 20 yrs ago . . . Have not seen him since . . . Got to Reno at 4 PM – telegraphed at once to H P Cohen, *Enterprise:* "Couldn't make afternoon train – Will be up in morning sure" – Went home to family . . .

Nov 30 . . . Home on morning train – Cohen got George Warren, local of the *Chronicle,* to localize in my place last night – George owes me $17.50 for last 5 years, so he let the $5 for his services go on that old account . . . The great Stock excitement ran highest yet today – Con Cal & Va touching $40 & all others up in proportion – Streets full of excited folks & sidewalks crowded . . .

Dec 1 . . . The big stock boom continues unabated and stronger than ever . . .

Dec 2 – Clear & very pleasant – Stocks got a little set back today for 1st time by reason of the failure of L B Frankel, stock brokers of this city, & other firms in San Francisco – Frankel failed for about a million – Has been short of stocks, not purchasing & filling orders during the present boom – couldn't either buy or sell so had to bust – great excitement – The Frankels filed petition in insolvency with list of creditors & skipped out for San Francisco – Bed at 2 –

Dec 3 – Same – Mining day – Work as usual – Nothing new in the Frankel case – Received letter from John Howell, Manager of the Reno Reduction Works, enclosing statement of my crushing of ore – 207 lbs – Gross yield $101.88 – Reduction charges, $5 – check enclosed for balance due me, $96.88 – Pretty good days work for me – Got the check cashed at California Bank – Through in office at 1½ – Bed 2½ – The Dalys, in "Vacation," or "Harvard vs Yale" appeared at Opera House tonight – Slim house –

Dec 4 . . . Continued excitement in regard to stocks, the Frankel failure, etc. and in the PM, the alleged failure of McGurn, which was probably not true, but it created big excitement for an hour or so . . . Paid my assessment on Centennial today . . . $40.30 . . .

Sunday, Dec 5 . . . Went to Reno on morning train . . . Wife still ailing a little, headache, etc, but improving and able to run her school . . .

Dec 6 . . . Through to Va on time at 10 AM – Work as usual – Bed at 3 – No stock Board today in S.F. as they are trying to straighten out the brokers – several other failures reported since Saturday among the brokers there – The Frankels are still missing from here – all three doubtless in San F – Street quotations from S.F. carry stocks much higher and still advancing –

Dec 8 . . . Ordered new pair of pants of Hirsch & Co., tailors, C st – $12 – Got hair cut . . .

Dec 9 . . . Got letter from wife enclosing letter from Jane Noble, who wants the $45 we owe her – She is very liable to get it tomorrow . . .

Dec 10 . . . Walked to Gold Hill at 11 AM – Was about town awhile . . . Then called on Jane Noble . . . Paid her the $45 balance due her from the Doten family, and she was glad to get it, as she is cramped in stocks . . . Lively days work – 2 columns of report on mines – Bed 3 . . .

Dec 11 . . . At 7 this evening, Sol Frankel was arrested at his rooms, where he has been concealed, right across the way from mine, since his bust up – He was badly dilapidated, mentally & physically and almost starved – Took him to jail . . .

Sunday, Dec 12 . . . At 8 AM left for Reno . . . Put up couple more shelves in store room – Had good dinner on fresh herring I brought down – dessert of canned plums my wife got in bill of goods sent for to Big Tree Store . . . $30 worth in all, of sugar, tea, beans, canned goods, ham, etc . . . Bed at 10 . . . Had a terrible dream about being in a theater, front seat near orchestra – Stage full of pictures and statuary – One large black & shiny cast iron statue of Venus, naked, suddenly strode forward from the rear, and toppled over upon me, having evidently selected me from the rest of the audience – I held up both hands to fend her off but the great weight was crushing me down – I grunted and tried hard to yell for help. Just then my wife woke me, in time to save me from total destruction – About 2 oclock woke again out of a troubled slumber and found my [four-line erasure] – Awful cold night – Got nearly frozen & took me long time in bed to get warm again . . .

Dec 13 . . . [In Va] Was introduced to Col Pat Quinn of the old Quinn mine below Silver City this PM by Col E D Boyle, Supt of the Alta mine – Had a short talk, & Quinn made me a present of 50 shares of Quinn stock, quoted on the Board at $1½ today – Am expected to write up the mine in the paper –

Dec 14 . . . Meeting of Centennial Trustees this PM . . . I presided – Passed bills to extent of $1300 – Letter from Supt says have sunk 15 ft deeper on the new resumption – & got through lava strata into black sand, loam & white clay – Very encouraging –

Dec 17 . . . Mining day – PM rode with Archie McDonell, Supt of the Bullion, in buggy to the Bullion mine, Croesus shaft, & took look at the new hoisting works recently erected there to get after the good ore on the 300 level & below . . .

Dec 18 . . . A young man named Flannagan shot his sister, a Mrs Murphy, this afternoon in Gold Hill – He was drunk – shot her in right temple and she died in 2 hours – He is in the County jail – Should be hanged . . .

Dec 21 . . . Rode down to Gold Hill on the 'bus at noon – Coroner's inquest had been held in case of young Michael Flannigan . . . Preliminary examination before Justice Cook at 2 PM . . . prisoner held to answer before Grand Jury without bonds . . .

Dec 23 . . . Con Va got down as low as $18 this PM board – Creates quite a break –

Dec 24 . . . Being Christmas Eve there was much jollification about town – with turkey lunches in the saloons, etc – Found some of them . . . Was at Bob Patterson's house short time, corner F & Taylor streets to see his little daughter Elva's . . . Christmas tree – fine – Had lots of egg-nog, lunch . . . & singing & music . . .

Dec 25 and 26 [AD works through Christmas, sleeps through morning train to Reno, "cruises," sleeps through evening train too, & can only wire Christmas greetings to his family.]

Dec 27 . . . Wrote letter to G W McHardy, Austin, returning his manuscript of long communication on cause of present depression in stocks etc – Not thought worth publication . . . Took the 8 oclock train for Carson – Was there all day looking for Engrossing Clerkship – Interviewed Yerington – Must get out of Enterprise this week . . .

Dec 29 and 30 [Mary comes up to Virginia City, fixes up a new vest for AD & sews buttons on his overcoat.]

Dec 31 . . . Many drunken men about – Great ringing of bells, blowing of whistles at midnight . . . Pistols popped lively all along C street for about half an hour – Lots of noise, but luckily nobody got hurt –

Jan 1, 1887 – Clear & very pleasant – Work as usual in the office till 2 – Closed out in office, taking my clip, old Lynch scissors, etc, evacuating the premises, as my time is up and Frank B Mercer takes it – Bed at 4 –

Sunday, Jan 2 – Same – went on morning train to Carson – quite a crowd of men on board, as Legislature convenes tomorrow – Worked to best ability in electioneering for my desired position of Engrossing Clerk of the Senate – Evening, caucus was held by the Republican members elect of each house – There being a candidate for the same position from Eureka, and Eureka claiming nothing else, the Caucus felt compelled to give it to Eureka. My successful competitor was Paul V Roux – So I got left – Slept at the Ormsby House – The caucuses nominated all the officers and attaches for the Senate and Assembly –

Jan 3 – Clear and pleasant – Governor, Lieut Gov, 3 Supreme Judges & all the State officers sworn in this AM – At 12 M both Houses convened, and I was in my chair at my desk in the Senate as reporter for the *Enterprise* – Swapped reports with Sam Davis of the *Appeal*, he giving me the Assembly & I him the Senate – Full organization effected of both Houses – I took evening train for Va with my report – Slow trip – Nearly 8 when I arrived – Went to room & wrote up my report – little over a column – Home at 2:30 from reading proof at office – Bed at 4 with clothes on –

Jan 4 – Cloudy & cool – Legislature convened at 11 AM – I reported as before – About 1½ hour's session but gave me big report that took all the PM to write up – Think it nearly 2 columns – Sent it on evening local train to Va – Evening, joint caucus of Republican members of both Houses held in the Assembly room for nomination of US Senator – Only one ballot taken, resulting: Stewart 34; Wren 9; Powning 1 . . . I walked out to the Railroad depot very lively, found an operator and telegraphed the caucus result to *Enterprise* – Was about town some – Bed 1 – at the Ormsby House –

Jan 5 through March 4 [AD continues to report the Legislature, sleeping in various Carson hotels when he finishes in time to send his report by evening train, going up to Va to write up when he can't, and spending most weekends with his family – Routine and highly repetitive entries, with little detail – Of interest:]

Jan 5 . . . Evening at Opera House – Play of "On the Rio Grande" by the Lamb-Jordan-Price company . . . Good house but not much of a play except as a blood & thunder sensational racket – Bed at 1 – at the Ormsby House –

Sunday, Jan 9 . . . Did several little jobs of carpentering etc – Not a drop of whisky today . . . The children showed me all their Christmas & N Y presents from East & from Eunice – Some for me & Mary, Millie & mother –

Jan 10 . . . Evening cruised about town, concert saloons etc – Bed at 11 in Circe's Hotel next north of the Mint –

Jan 11 . . . US Senatorial election in the Legislature today – He [Stewart] received the entire Republican vote, 46 out of 60 – Cassidy received the complimentary vote of the Democracy . . . Got pass renewed for self & wife till March 5th – by Yerington . . .

Jan 12 . . . At noon the Senate & Assembly in joint convention confirmed the election of Wm M Stewart as United States Senator from Nevada – lots of ladies, & big crowd present – He made a nice speech – An hour later another joint convention elected Frank J McCullough, of Ormsby, State Prison Warden – for next 2 yrs term – Kept me very busy . . . Stewarts speech, etc, will make 3 columns . . .

Jan 13 . . . Evening at Opera House – Play of "Faust and Marguerite" by the Morrison-Alsberg Dramatic Co – Very fine – Big house – A *Hell* of a good play – *Devilish* good – After the play went up to Hon W M Stewart's residence to grand reception and congratulation – Big crowd of everybody – Big table spread with choice salad, sandwiches, cake, etc – Hot coffee, punch, etc – Bed at 1 –

Jan 14 . . . Did not complete report but took evening train for Va . . . The Morrison-Alsberg Co at Opera House in "Faust and Marguerite" . . . Big house . . .

Jan 15 . . . Paid Odd Fellows dues . . . Paid Marshall for fixing my clothes, all I have – $6 – Bought 2 undershirts $1 each – Evening . . . saw the Morrison-Alsberg Co play "Under the Gaslight" . . . Office & wrote obituary notice of Frank Moore, old pioneer 62 yrs old . . .

Jan 19 . . . Got report off on evening train . . . Went to Theater & saw three acts of Uncle Tom's Cabin by Horace Ewing's company from San Francisco . . . I went up to reception of Gov Stevenson & wife at their residence in NW aristocratic part of Carson – Everybody there – Nice lunch of salad, cake, nuts, sandwiches etc, and some very thin punch or claret lemonade – very harmless – Staid half an hour – Down town again . . .

Jan 25 . . . Wrote out a bill to introduce tomorrow regarding presentation of Pioneer Cabinet etc to the State – Also put local in Enterprise to same effect – Bed 4 –

Jan 26 – Clear & pleasant – Morning train to Carson – Work as usual – My bill No 55 – Society of Coast Pioneers – got up a bill providing for transfer to the State Cabinet, Carson, of the great Pioneer cabinet, etc. Bill passed both Houses and will be signed by the Governor tomorrow morning – My report was so voluminous this PM, Pioneer speeches etc, that I had to go to Va to finish it – Will take about 2 columns – Was at Opera House a short time – Hermann the magician – Good Houses last evening & this evening – Was at office & read proof – Bed at 1½ –

Jan 27 . . . Met Lieut Gov Davis, & had to go to dinner with him at his residence – Had a big turkey, 16 pounds, from Ogden – fine, fat and juicy – Splendidly cooked – Company present – Davis & wife, Mr Hardy from Tuscarora, Doten, Miss Davis, sister to the Gov, Rev Mr Davis & wife & Col H G Shaw – Had very pleasant time, & had to tear myself away & take cars for Reno at 6:55 . . . Met Powning & had a little talk on newspaper business . . . On the train with me tonight were most of the members of the Assembly, Speaker and all, they having adjourned over till Monday – Taking a run on free passes to San Francisco . . .

Jan 29 . . . Evening [in Va] at Piper's Opera House – Joseph R Crismer, Miss Phoebe Davis & a good stock company – Play was "The Field of Honor" – Military drama – North & South – This company is playing to good houses . . .

Sunday, Jan 30 . . . Reno on morning train . . . Sammy appeared on the stage at a school exhibition festival Friday evening – 2 bits admission – in a banjo and harmonica duet with Charley Stevenson – They did finely and were highly encored, more so than all other performers of the evening – Sam made a decided hit . . . Charley Stevenson is son of Lew, son of the Governor –

Jan 31 . . . Morning train to Carson – Went to Dr Southworth, dentist, & got three teeth filled, on the starboard side of my mouth . . . Silver filling . . .

Feb 1 . . . Heaviest gale for last 16 years – Did considerable damage at Va, smashing windows etc & prostrating small houses – Blew in a window or two in State Capitol . . . from the SW & a genuine *"Washoe Zephyr"* –

Feb 2 . . . Went to Dr Southworth and he filled or capped three more defective teeth . . . Returned to Va on evening train . . . The new paper, daily, the *Evening Report,* made its first issue this evening – By Alf Chartz and D L Brown – I visited their office this evening – 24 column paper – Democratic –

Feb 3 . . . Jerry Schooling, prominent old resident of the State, formerly State Treasurer for 8 yrs, died in Carson at 4 PM from apoplexy – I wrote him up tonight in the local . . .

Feb 4 . . . Both houses adjourned over at noon till Monday, each adopting resolutions of respect relative to the death of Hon Jerry Schooling, formerly State Treasurer and also member of the Legislature from Washoe County, who died in this city yesterday . . . He was a native of Missouri, aged 54 years, and leaves a wife & 2 or 3 children – Body sent to Reno tonight for funeral tomorrow . . . After supper took evening express train for Reno . . .

Feb 5 . . . Wife & I took morning train for Va . . . I was about town tending to various matters – also at Pioneer Hall awhile – The cabinet etc being packed up for transmission to Carson . . . Wife & I dined at Rotisserie . . . Evening at home – Wrote an item relative to old Tom Hanbridge who died this morning in this city – 59 yrs old – heart disease – Old member of the old Fire Dept . . .

Sunday, Feb 6 . . . Excursion train from Carson took down over 50 to the Jerry Schooling funeral, which was a big one notwithstanding the inclemency of the weather . . .

Feb 7 . . . Evening train to Va – Finished my report at room – Also wrote item obituary of "Salem" Andrews, an old 49'er, Comstocker etc . . . His real name was William Andrews – 53 yrs old – from Salem, Mass, Came 'round the Horn in '49 – Member of the Exempts – & will be buried from their Hall at 2 PM tomorrow – He was one of those who came on the " 'Liza ship," "Bound for the Sacramento with my washbowl on my knee" – He came over here in 1861 – Bed at 3 – [The ship *Elizabeth,* with the small Salem Mining Company, left Salem April 5, 1849, and arrived on September 17.]

Feb 8 . . . Class A, Va High School, came down on morning train on visit to Carson – 15 young ladies & 1 young man – Prof J E Bray with them – They took a look at the Public Schools, Orphans Home, State Prison, Capitol, State Printing House, etc, & went home on evening train – I went also – Lots of singing – Snowed all the PM in Carson & Va . . . George ("Pike") Allen, my next room neighbor, got badly hurt night before last in the Con Va mine – Was unloading 12 x 12 timbers from a cage at 1500 station – Had one in his arms when another fell over on him & down he went on the floor. Head badly bruised, but worst injury to left thigh & groin, where timber got across him – He is in his room, well cared for . . .

Feb 11 . . . On train coming up met Frank Brown, [illegible] "little Brownie" of Gold Hill – He is just up from San F, where he has been in the hack driving business for last year & a half – Come up on a visit to his folks in Gold Hill – Told me about the big snow in SF last Saturday – 3 inches on a level – Great time snowballing – made quite a big excitement pelting everybody in sight – Street car windows smashed in and D—l to pay generally . . .

Feb 12 . . . Evening wrote short sketch for the *Enterprise,* about my lassoing Horace Greeley . . .

Feb 13 through 17 [Heavy snows, two feet on level in Carson & Reno, more in Virginia City, delay V&T and block CP RR in the Sierra entirely, cutting off the Pacific mails.]

Feb 18 . . . The train from Reno arrived at 10 AM, bringing the delayed passengers, mail etc from California – including three members of the Senate, & some of the Assembly – Been delayed at Colfax since Sunday . . . John Mackay and Dick Dey were with and among them . . .

Sunday, Feb 20 . . . Sunshiny but freezing all day – 7 deg below zero last night and 9 night before – Coldest of the Winter . . .

Feb 22 . . . Evening attended theater – Play "Zitka" by a travelling troupe – miserable damfool of a play, miserably performed . . . Made six good "fig leaves" . . . out of heavy toweling . . . ["fig leaves" – pads to absorb dribbling and catheter bleeding now that heavy drinking is increasing the trouble.]

Feb 23 . . . Frank B Mercer who has been in as "local" on the Enterprise since Jan 1st, left on Monday to take similar position on Reno *Gazette.* Willie Nicoll is local on *Enterprise* – A Gold Hill boy – used to go to school to my wife – Don't think he will amount to much as a local –

Feb 24 . . . Snowed all day pretty heavily – Reported as usual – Homeward had only 4 passengers, myself included – D B Lyman, Ed Harris, and a woman – We bucked into several snowbanks about the Am Flat tunnel – Had to back down to the Haywood switch, a mile and leave 2 big carloads of lumber, after which we got along pretty well . . . Met Ike Stith on the morning train, bound for Hawthorne – Have met him several times of late – He was the "preferred" lover of Mary McDonald, my Como schoolmarm, but I don't think he ever got into her right – Anyhow he "knocked me out" and somehow said I was right and [illegible] –

Feb 26 . . . At the *Enterprise* office getting in report etc – Dan De Quille to go on Monday, after a shut off for 2 yrs – By orders of John W Mackay – who is ½ proprietor of the concern . . .

Sunday, Feb 27 . . . Morning train to Reno . . . Evening down town – at Depot Hotel etc – Saw the electric lights for 1st time in my life – About a dozen of them in saloons and hotels, & 2 or 3 on street – Bright white light transcending all others – Even made the moon look yellow and gas lights & coal oil lamps looked like "pumpkin lanterns" . . .

Feb 28 . . . Reported as usual – The Assembly holds its first evening session tonight – At Va I went to Opera House & saw the burlesque opera of "Methusalem" by the Pyke Opera Co from San Francisco – Jennie Winston leading lady . . . Dan De Quille on local today –

March 1 – Cloudy and Springlike – Thawy – Went to Carson as usual – Sent up my report by evening train conductor – Staid to the Pioneer reception and banquet – Big lot of the "Old Boys" arrived on the down train – Met by Legislative Committee with brass band, escorted to the State House – Hon Bob Briggs of White Pine acted as master of ceremonies – Dispersed, & met again at 8 PM at Carson Opera House – Big banquet to the Pioneers by the Legislators – the members & not the Legislature as a body – Splendid time – Collation, with champagne etc – Fun over at 12 – Was at Circe's Carson Exchange with many of the Comstock crowd – Slept there – Bed 2 –

March 2 – Same – Rose at 8 – At 9:30 was with the rest of the Pioneer crowd & had our picture taken, standing on the Capitol steps, South side – Big group – about 30 in it – Took evening train for Va – Wrote up the Pioneer banquet – Nearly 2 columns – Bed at 5 – [See Appendix for AD's 1899 write-up of the Pioneer Society and banquet.]

March 3 – Variable – Sixtieth and last day of the Session – Both houses industrious so that they recessed at 4 PM – Evening session, both houses – Assembly at 7, and Senate at 7:30 – lots of spectators – "Third House" occasionally in the short recesses which were taken while waiting for messages from either House – Bob Briggs of White Pine and Sharon of Storey were the presiding officers of the 3d House – by turns – Very funny – At 12 the gavels fell and the 13th Nevada Legislature adjourned sine die – I went up to Lieut Gov Davis' house to reception of legislators, State officers etc – Collation, punch, wine, etc – Big crowd – Left there at 2 – Bed at Circe's Carson Exchange at 3 – Lively slogging match at that time in a room over Cohn's dry goods store near Sweeney's – 2 matches – 1st between Avery and Jack Campbell, champion light weight of the Pacific Coast – 13 rounds – Queensbury rules – Hard fought battle – Boxing gloves, but stuffed back so is about same as the naked fists – Campbell victor – Both young men less than 30 yrs old – 2nd match was between Brady & Trembly – same sort – Both light weights and about 20 yrs old – Carson boys – 13 rounds – Brady victor – Both bloody battles, especially the last – The first match took the gate money ($5 admission) – Second – purse made up – About 50 persons present including quite a number of legislators – Speaker McDonell, Boyle, Egan, Briggs, Poujade et al –

March 4 – Clear & pleasant – Rose at 8 – Was at depot and saw the morning trains come in – on time – Went to the Capitol at 10 – Wrote most of day on report of wind-up of the sessions – About 2½ columns of it – Legislators busy cleaning out their desks etc – & getting out homeward – I bundled up my desk contents to take to Va – & left it at Harry Summers' saloon near the depot – Sent my letter to *Enterprise* by conductor Jerry Bray – Took evening train for Reno – Met George Stenhouse at Reno depot – He gave me a book just issued by his mother, "An Englishwoman in Utah" – Had long chat with him – Home – found all right there – Bed at 10 –

March 5 . . . Yerington extended my pass ten days – To Va on evening train – Went to theater – "Mikado," by the Pyke opera troupe – Fine – Big house – My report in Enterprise . . . cut down to less than a column –

March 6 through April 13 [AD constantly about town, drinking and "skirmishing" for a job or anything that will make a little money – Of interest:]

Sunday, March 6 . . . Evening Frank Ward came to my room & got me to write up report for him on his La Plata Oro mine, Gold Hill, to the President, John H Dickinson, San Francisco – Getting it incorporated & stocked as the West Crown Point Mining Company – Also wrote his opinion to the company, through Dickinson as to the best way to work and develop the mine – Took 4 hours – Went to Enterprise office & had talk with Taggart . . .

March 7 . . . PM I was out on South C street and called in & saw Charley Ockel at his saloon – Has been nearly dead from kidney disease and partial paralysis for the last three or four weeks, but is a little better and able to walk around . . .

March 9 . . . PM and evening wrote letters – One to W S Hobart, S.F. asking a lease for Andrew Lawson and myself of a portion of the Chollar surface workings – 300 ft deep & from 100 to 600 feet long – Took it to train to mail it – Saw Major Tim Storer off on a four months visit to California. Has been clerk at International Hotel for years – Very old and decrepid & liable never to come back. President of the Society of Pacific Coast Pioneers – Also wrote letter to Andrew Lawson . . . Also letter to S T Gage, office of the CP RR, San Francisco, asking for two passes or tickets to Los Angeles – Can sell 'em . . .

March 10 . . . Left for Carson at 8 – Went to State Capitol and made a condensed summary of the principal bills passed by the Legislature, signed by the Gov, those vetoed etc – Only the big lottery bill now in his hands – Will have to pass upon it by Saturday, under the limit . . . got through in time to leave for home on 5:15 . . . straightened out my report & took it to Enterprise office . . .

March 11 . . . The first carload of the Pioneers' cabinet arrived at the State Capitol this morning from Va – Stuffed animals principally – Evening about town awhile . . .

March 14 . . . The last of the Pioneer cabinet was shipped from here Saturday . . .

March 15 . . . PM a meeting of Centennial – I presided – We levied assessment of 2 cents per share . . . This is probably the *last* assessment on Centennial – Got letter from W S Hobart, San Francisco:

> San Francisco   March 14, 1887
> My Dear Doten – I received your letter and showed it to the Chollar people, but do not think they would let contract – Shall be up to Virginia very soon and will see you.
> Yours very truly
> W S Hobart

March 16 . . . About town most of day – Evening wrote letter to Wm Gibson and Mike Finigan, Austin, E K Downer of the *Mountain Messenger*, Downieville, Cal and Andrew Lawson, American Flat – Bed at 5 –

March 17 – Cloudy, cooler, blustering & dusty – St Patrick's Day – No observance other than green ribbons and neckties – About town – Sol Frankel the busted broker on trial in Dist Court yesterday & today for embezzlement, etc – Evening I was busy writing up Pioneer Legislative doings, banquet etc for a pamphlet – Bed at 2 –

March 18 . . . PM I attended 3d days trial of the Frankel case – court crowded – Testimony all in – counsel argued, long charge by Judge Rising – Case given to the Jury at 5:45 PM – Bed at 12 –

March 19 . . . The Jury in the Frankel case came into court at 10 AM and reported total disagreement, standing 8 for acquittal to 4 for conviction, and were accordingly discharged . . .

Sunday, March 20 . . . Had fine big chicken stew for dinner – Paid 7 bits for one yesterday . . . Evening at home – writing up the Pioneer banquet, etc – Bed 2 –

March 21 . . . Busy most of day and evening in fixing up the roll of the Pacific Pioneers Society – About 500 members – Had Dr Delavan helping me . . .

March 22 . . . About town – Evening wrote long letter to Yerington . . .

March 23 . . . PM I met W S Hobart at Wheeler, Hall & Cos hardware store & had quite a sociable chat with him – Cannot get my desired lease of a portion of Chollar upper workings – Evening at home working on my Pioneer pamphlet . . .

March 25 . . . I finished my Pioneer pamphlet tonight – Bed at 4 –

March 26 . . . Wrote Introductory and Valedictory to my Pioneer pamphlet – took all night . . .

Sunday, March 27 – Clear & very pleasant – Bed at 7 AM – Rose at 11 – About town – At the Crystal saloon this evening was introduced to George H Bump just in from Bodie on short visit – going to SF & Los Angeles – He is an engineer or [illegible] at the Standard mine works Bodie for several years – About 45 yrs old & about my size & weight & shape – Brother to Minnie Warren and Lavinia Warren (Mrs Tom Thumb). Their real names were Huldah and Lavinia Bump – 8 children of them – Born in Middleboro Mass. He knew me well by reputation, etc – Tonight I fully revised & completed my pamphlet – 43 pages – Bed at 3 –

March 29 – Clear, warm & pleasant – Went to Carson on morning train – My pass having run out, I had to put up for my passage – Bob Patterson went along – I had my pamphlet manuscript along, and we went to Att'y General Alexander's office in the State Capitol, where we met with W C Dovey, State Sup't of Public Instruction and I read my pamphlet copy to them – They highly approved it – Also was at State Printing House with it, getting the ideas of the State Printer as to the style of its publication, etc – We saw the Pioneer cabinet being put in order, so far as specimens were concerned etc, by Dr Delavan, the Mineralogist of our Society – The big cabinet case and 2 smaller cabinet cases were placed in position last week, grained, etc, and Doc Delavan commenced putting in the specimens yesterday – Evening train to Reno – Found all right at home – Bed at 10 √ –

April 4 . . . [Va City] Finished my transcript of the Pioneers' register today – Avoided the big dust storm in so doing – 14 page large legal cap – Bed at 2 –

April 5 . . . Dr Delavan returned from Carson last evening, called on me this morning, telling me the Pioneer cabinet was all completely rehabilitated & in place . . . He got $150 . . .

April 6 – Cloudy, blustery, very dusty and disagreeable – PM Dr Delavan came to my room & helped me complete my list of Pioneers by comparing the old register, etc with what I have prepared to print – Corrected spelling, etc, and found several missing names – The list may not be considered fully completed and contains 502 names – Evening I attended the second performance of the McGibeny Family – Small attendance – Fine performance – Home – Wrote letter for my next door neighbor, George Allen, ("old Pike") to his sister Rachel Johnson, Dawn, Livingston County Missouri – Bed at 2 –

April 7 . . . Evening at first performance of Baird's Minstrels at Opera House . . . Best performance of its kind I have seen for years – Everybody enjoyed it . . .

April 8 . . . Wrote letter to Harvey Blood, (Bear Valley,) Murphy's, Calaveras Co, Cal, for Bob Patterson, asking him to get a medium sized grizzly for the Pioneer cabinet – Send it to S.F. & get it stuffed etc, all at Pattersons expense . . . Baird's Minstrel troupe brass band paraded at noon today as well as yesterday – 14 pieces up C & down D . . . fine band . . .

April 9 . . . Fred Klempfer, an old Comstock contractor, builder, plasterer etc came this PM & did several jobs . . . in Douglas building – Among rest he patched the place in ceiling of my room where it fell last Fall – Gave me more trouble attending to it, cleaning up, etc – Frankel's second trial . . . went to the jury at 3:30 PM yesterday . . . at 10:30

AM today brought in verdict of "not guilty" – He is still held to answer on three or four other similar indictments.

Sunday, April 10 . . . Several light snow squalls . . . Evening wrote letters to Hon C E Laughton, Ex Lieut Gov, Carson – and to Secy Cal Pioneers, SF for a list of his Society . . . Spent my last two bits this evening – *Busted* –

April 11 . . . I was busy most of the day fixing up and getting printed for Bob Patterson a list of the group of Pioneers taken at Carson at the Capitol steps . . . Several inserted since to make picture more complete – 52 in all – Done at *Evening Report* office – under my supervision at Bob's expense . . .

April 12 . . . I negociating for sale of some of my Centennial stock – Bed at 2 –

April 13 – Variable – A few light snow & rain squalls, just enough to keep the dust laid – Evening the Carlton Opera Company – About 40 of them, women and all – Very good performance & good house – I was there – They run two more nights and Saturday matinee – They played the comic opera of "Nanon" – Tomorrow night "Erminie" – Wrote a puff for Joe Mallon, grocer, this PM, to insert in the Enterprise – He paid me $5 for it – When I was [at] the Opera House this evening, while I was in Piper's box office, getting a deadhead pass, Ed Swift of Gold Hill got at me and gave me $10 not to "give him hell" on the street sprinkling in view of the present stormy weather – I won't do it. After the theater I was about town awhile – Bed at 1:30 – Weather still threatening –

BOOK NO. *62*

Virginia City and Reno
April 14, 1887 – Dec 31, 1887

April 14 . . . A few light drizzles of rain during the day – I was about town, and in the evening attended Piper's Opera House – 3 act Opera of "Erminie" . . . very good indeed – good house . . . Dan De Quille got drunk again today for the first time since he has been back in his old position as local of the *Enterprise* –

April 15 . . . About town – Evening at theater – "Drum Major's Daughter" – Very good . . .

April 16 . . . Frankel's case was called in Dist Court at 10 AM today, on indictment No 4, embezzlement in having taken in $360 from Mrs Burke the afternoon before his failure was announced – The Dist Atty refused to prosecute – The Evening *Report* says:

> State vs Frankel—District Attorney stated he had engaged an expert to examine the books with reference to indictment No. 4 and had failed to obtain necessary evidence, . . . and in addition . . . the prosecution witness had no desire to prosecute; therefore he asked that a nolle prosequi be entered. So ordered. That disposes of all the indictments against the firm of L. B. Frankel & Co.

As soon as the case was dismissed, about 10:30 AM, Sol Frankel was taken from the County jail, where he has been since Dec 2, and taken in a close carriage out over the Geiger Grade by Chief of Police Henderson and officer Austin – Another carriage in waiting took him to Reno or elsewhere in that direction, and he probably will be in San Francisco tomorrow . . . PM I attended the theater . . . "The Mikado," and the best rendition of it I have yet seen – by far – The Carlton Opera Company left on the evening train . . . A big crowd saw them off . . .

Sunday, April 17 . . . Was about town, watching points as usual – At

11 oclock Dan Fahey, an old Gold Hiller, met me in International saloon – He was exceedingly drunk – I could not get rid of him and had to take him up to his room on B street and see that he got to bed right – He was the drunkenest friend I ever assisted home . . .

April 19 . . . John Yule, my old time friend of Gold Hill and subsequently of the Hussey mine, Cornucopia, Elko County, called upon me about noon – He is now superintendent of the Atlantic mine, Silver City –

April 20 – Early morning a big snowstorm . . . Speculating – Evening I wrote a notice of the great Pioneer Group picture for Bob Patterson, to go in the Va Chronicle tomorrow . . .

April 21 . . . Tom Johns paid me $300 this PM for 500 shares Centennial . . . I got a check on Wells Fargo & Co at Joe Douglass' for $100 and enclosed it in letter to my wife . . .

April 22 . . . Comstock Division No 3, Knights of Pythias, was instituted this PM . . . The Reno Uniform Rank Division . . . came up on a special train . . . At 5 PM the newly organized Rank & Reno paraded publicly with band of music . . . About 7 in all – looked fine – Had a big ball in the evening at Opera House . . .

April 23 . . . Paid my Centennial assessment today – $40.30 –

April 24 through 26 [AD writes to his wife, attends a Centennial meeting, & is "about town" with Hugh J Mohan of Reno, canvassing for the Reno papers – On the 26th AD says:] Mohan gave me some of the powder or snuff he is taking for catarrh – It is pulverized borax & pulv. Soyas equal parts – Only snuff or catarrh preparation that I ever took that did not make me sneeze – He originated it – It is very good – Also gave me a recipe to take next September to stave off the hay fever – 4 oz syrup of rhubarb, 20 grains quinine, pulverized, mix. Commence Sept 1 taking 1 oz every three hours, until it operates – Then cease its use till next day, and repeat – "cure inevitable" – Got it from his mother –

April 28 . . . Slept an hour or so in the evening, then sat up and wrote a piece for my pioneer pamphlet entitled: "The Bowers of California" – introducing the old song of "Joe Bowers" and adding two more verses to it by way of sequel – Bed at sunrise –

April 29 . . . In overhauling my old stocks today I found 100 shares Pioneer, which I have had for about 10 yrs – It is now in the stock list at 30 cts – Took it to broker Douglass & told him to sell it –

April 30 . . . Sold it at 10 cts a share – cash to me $7.50 . . . Moral – never throw away a piece of old stock –

Sunday, May 1 . . . May day – Street looked lively with everybody in their best clothes, going to or from church etc . . . Wrote all night on article for my pamphlet, entitled "Monumental" –

May 3 . . . Rose at 4 AM & went to writing for my pamphlet – Wrote 2 fine articles "Executive and Legislative," and "An Interesting Pioneer Group" . . . Got letter from wife telling me of the death of Joe Weston at Los Angeles, Cal, a week ago Sunday – of consumption – 32 yrs old – His father, Joseph Lewis Weston [and I] went to school together in old Plymouth, at the old schoolhouse down the lane, Tim Berry, teacher, and Emily Brown, subsequently little Joe's mother, was the last girl I kissed when I left Plymouth – She gave me a kiss in the entry of our old home . . . saying "take this to Josey from me" – I found him lying sick in Stockton, Cal, when I arrived . . . He subsequently went home, married her & little Joe was the result – a new chapter opened and closed –

May 4 – Cloudy but pleasant – Rose at 11 AM – PM about town – Evening at Opera House – The Roland Reed Dramatic Co in play of "Humbug" – Not much of a play & ditto house – Looked in at the keno game at the International – Old Bob Patterson suggested that we try a card – did so and immediately I won a pool of $5 – Tried 2 more cards without success and quit – Bed 2 . . . The *Enterprise* changed its style this morning back to what it was before Taggart put everything on the 1st page – Also adopted the ready set matter for 1st page – 3 columns – Very good improvement – Bed 2 –

May 5 . . . PM about town – Evening home at 11 – Slept 2½ hours & then worked at copying for my pamphlet rest of night . . .

May 6 . . . Concluded to go to Reno . . . found all right at home and all happy to see me again after so long an absence . . .

May 7 . . . Sent a letter to Frank M Huffaker, Va, to send me my bunch of keys which I left in my desk lock & which I much need here to unlock my tool chest etc – After breakfast I took my little ones out to walk up on the Powning Addition, west part of town – got home as soon as I could on account of my weakness of bowels . . . Evening banjo and songs . . . At 8 I was at depot . . . took a lot of brandy & ginger & also a little flask of it home . . .

Sunday, May 8 . . . The electric lights showed brilliantly tonight –
three of them on tall masts 60 or 74 ft high . . . My bowels all right
today – Brandy and ginger did it – This PM visited the first National
Bank . . . just removed to a new & better location on Virginia st near
the bridge . . .

May 9 . . . Was at home most of the day building a crib bed for Goodie
to sleep in . . . Evening at home – Wife finished reading Dickens "Great
Expectations" to us – Children all take great delight in her reading . . .

May 10 . . . Worked hard at carpentering . . . Evening down at the
depot short time . . .

May 11 . . . PM about town, at *Gazette* office, etc . . .

May 12 . . . PM rode out to the Insane Asylum with Charley Legate –
Great investigation . . . of grave charges against Dr Bishop, the Sup't,
of maltreatment of patients, malfeasance in office, etc – Conducted before
State Board of Insane Commissioners consisting of Gov Stevenson, State
Controller Hallock & State Treasurer Tufly – Strong legal talent on both
sides – Investigation only organized today . . . I reported it for the Reno
Journal and also sent short telegram of it to the SF *Chronicle* – Evening
down at Depot Hotel – Bed at 10:30 –

May 13 . . . Witnesses examined and cross examined all day – Took
lunch at noon with Dr Bishop's family, the Commissioners, Alf Chartz,
the official shorthand reporter & 1 or 2 others . . . Rode back to Reno
on Asylum wagon with Hugh Mohan – Gave him some of my notes –
Found the *Journal* could take but little of my report . . . Bundled the
whole in a big envelope and sent it to the SF *Examiner* . . .

May 14 . . . Prosecution rested their case at noon . . . I took lunch
with the Bishops et al . . . PM wrote good report & sent to *Examiner* . . . Was down town & saw the trains arrive & go – First section
from the East had Sara Bernhart & troupe on board for San Fran . . .

Sunday, May 15 . . . After dinner took all my young ones out to
walk . . . Evening at depot – Met Mohan, Stevenson, Hallock et al . . .

May 16 . . . Was at Asylum at 9 o'clock . . . Noon, dinner with the
employes – Back to town before 6 PM . . . Then fixed up whole testimony . . . and put it on the west bound evening train for the San F
Examiner . . . Governor Stevenson visited us in the evening, before I
got home, & chatted with wife for an hour or so –

May 17 . . . At Asylum & saw close of investigation at 4:30 PM – Dr Bishop wiped out every charge against him . . . He will be perfectly exhonerated by the Board . . . if they have the proper amount of back-bone against public opinion or partisanship – Sent the last batch of my report to the SF *Examiner* . . . has not published a line of my Asylum report thus far & will probably not –

May 18 through 20 [Makes a bedstead and four screen doors.]

May 21 . . . In Carson train stopped an hour & 15 minutes so I had time to visit the State Printing office, the Gov's office, etc – The State Printer wants the copy on my Pioneer book forthwith – At 2 PM today the Board of State Insane Asylum Commissioners decided unanimously . . . that "the charges nor any of them are sustained by the evidence adduced on the hearing." . . . Arrived at Va on time – Was about town – got some much needed grub, etc – Bed at 1 –

Sunday, May 22 . . . Rain about 3 oclock, which soon poured down lively & kept at it for a couple of hours or so – streams flowed every-where . . . at 7½ PM attended regular monthly meeting of the Society of Pacific Coast Pioneers at our hall – 8 of us present – At conclusion I read synopsis of my pamphlet copy and a resolution was passed unani-mously indorsing it as the true and correct version of the cabinet property presentation, acceptance, banquet etc . . . S D Baker, Vice Prest, took the chair this evening in place of Prest Storer, who is still absent in Cali-fornia, & Dr Delavan acted as Secy – Bob Patterson, Chas Rawson, Alex Coryell, Otto Ecklemann, Lee McGown also present –

May 23 . . . PM I commenced copying off my pamphlet . . . Eve-ning ditto – got asleep in my chair a few times during the night, so I did not go to bed at all – But I got a bad cold thus sleeping in my chair –

May 24 . . . I took the 7:20 morning train for Carson . . . Wrote couple of items for *Tribune* in Lieut Gov Davis office . . . I went into the Governor's office and finished copying and straightening out my copy – Took it to the State Printing office and left it . . . Slept all the way home on the evening train – Went to my room, got asleep in my chair & got more cold – Bed at 10 exhausted – very troubled feverish sleep – [Six-line erasure, probably concerning bowel trouble]

May 25 . . . Morning I felt so sick and feverish, lame and exhausted that remained in bed . . . till 2 PM . . . Evening I went down to the Capitol Restaurant and got a little roast beef, dry toast and tea – could eat very little – Was in Gus Gross' cigar shop seeing a new weighing machine – Drew crowds of people – for a nickel 5 ct piece I was weighed – 200 lbs exactly – Went into Patterson's keno room & at his suggestion we played a couple of cards – I won the first one – $4.25 – We divided and quit – I went home . . .

May 26 . . . Down town in the PM – Had not eaten a morsel of grub for a couple of days when at 4 PM . . . I took a good hearty dinner at the French Rotisserie – Felt so full and comfortable that when I returned to my room at 8 o'clock I sat in my chair, read myself to sleep & staid with it firm & good all night . . . Sent short note to Powning this evening, enclosing an item about the Reno public schools – Taggart has leased the Enterprise and will commence on that layout June 1 – Cohen goes out as business man –

May 27 through 29 [AD spends two days in Carson, watching his pamphlet go to the printer & getting the speeches made at the Pioneer Banquet, then, in Virginia City, begins to read proof.]

May 30 – Clear, & 86 deg – Memorial Day – Flags at full mast all over the city – Lots of people in from around – Procession formed on B st & went out & decorated the soldiers' graves in cemetery with flowers – Procession started at 11 AM – Gen R P Keating & staff, Emmet and National Guards and Uniform Rank K of P – Grand Army etc – out B to Junction and through C st north – Cara's band did the music – After they returned, had exercises at Opera House – Oration by J A Stephens, music, etc – I was busy most of day fixing up my pamphlet proofs, & got them off by the evening mail for Carson . . .

May 31 . . . Busy with the State Printer today – Got all the speeches & pamphlet pretty well straightened out . . . Home on evening train . . .

June 1 . . . Att'y Gen'l Alexander got his banquet speech remodeled for me by 11 AM & I took it to the State Printer, that being the last of the "copy" for my pamphlet – PM I was there & read proof . . . Home on the evening train . . . Will probably be published next week – 1200 copies –

June 2 through 10 [AD describes (June 3) a sharp earthquake, which makes "cocktails" out of bottled goods in bars & grocery stores and frightens occupants out of the larger brick buildings – Corresponds with the State Printer about his pamphlet, gets a first copy of it, writes it up in the *Enterprise* – eats a sirloin steak cooked with green peppers and onions in his room, attends a performance by a Negro minstrel troupe, Lew Johnson's "Mamma's Black Baby-Boy Combination," "very good indeed" – Wins a $12 keno pool, notes that his neighbor, "Pike" Allen, is 52, and spends a day "fixing up my newspaper file, political scrap book, etc."]

June 11 . . : Big picnic of the Public Schools over to the Bowers Mansion in Washoe Valley – 8 flats & 4 coaches left at 7:20 AM . . . Many carriages went from here with people to the picnic, via Ophir grade, & across Washoe valley – 4 car-loads from Gold Hill & as many more from Carson and Reno – Must have been about 3,000 people there . . .

Sunday, June 12 . . . Dined at the French Rotisserie (Allen & Chaumond's) – About 10 o'clock news came of a bad accident on the Geiger Grade about a mile north of town – Chaumond thrown from a wagon and killed – Billy Allen, his partner started out at once with a team to see about it – Found it a fact – Old Chaumond was brought in as soon as possible to Conboie's undertaking place . . . He & 2 others were returning from Steamboat Springs – ran up on the steep west side of the Grade and turned over . . . I saw the corpse at Conboie's – Only injury to the head – About 60 years old & evidently a native of France – Unmarried . . . Member of the Society of Pacific Coast Pioneers – My Horace Greeley sketch in *Enterprise* this morning –

["A Lassoing Lesson" nearly fills the lead editorial column with a fictitious, though ostensibly true anecdote about AD, while out to rope some stock in the Santa Clara valley in 1859, meeting "a queer looking gentleman, of medium stature, with a gray coat, light felt hat, white whiskers away under his chin, and a peculiar look generally." – The stranger asks diverse questions about the region and about the lasso, asks for some instruction from AD, and ropes himself by the left leg and right shoulder – This feat is greeted jocularly by AD, only to discover that the dude is Horace Greeley, down to give a lecture in San Jose.]

June 15 . . . At noon I was at Con Virginia office & presented John W Mackay with a copy of my pamphlet – He left for Europe by this evening's train – At 1 PM the funeral of E Chaumond took place from Pioneer Hall – Myself & all the old Pioneers attended . . . Long procession of carriages – Evening down town – Bed at 12 – Chaumond . . . was ·buried in the Pioneers' cemetery –

June 17 . . . At 2 PM I walked down to Gold Hill to meeting of the Centennial trustees at Gold Hill Assay office . . . We audited a lot of bills, etc – I paid $20 on account of assessment . . . Home at 6 on 'bus – Bed at 1 – At Gold Hill today Frank Folsom, storekeeper, gave me four nice little trout – They were from a private fish pond near Washoe City, and of the New Hampshire brook trout variety . . . genuine "speckled beauties" –

June 18 . . . Wrote an item for Bob Patterson, & saw it all right in Enterprise, about his wife's style of farming etc – Won a $9 keno pool . . . Ate my trout at home –

Sunday, June 19 . . . Took 7:20 local train for Reno – During the 30 minutes we stopped at Carson I went to the State Printing office & got 50 copies of pamphlet . . . Found all right at home – Heat about 95 in the PM . . . At 8 was at depot, watching & interviewing people – distributed quite a lot of pamphlets – They take well – Met Gov Stevenson, Lieut Gov Davis, Mohan et al . . .

June 20 . . . Took train at 7:10 AM for Carson – Dovey came from Silver City in the morning train from Va – I met him at the depot – I went to the State Printer and got a lot of pamphlets and gave them to the four printing offices, *Appeal, Tribune, Index* and *Union,* and to various individuals – At 10:30 went to Dovey's office, Supt of Public Instruction, the room in which the Pioneer cabinet is placed, and there we worked hard all day fixing up the pamphlets for mail . . . We mailed about 500 . . .

June 21 . . . Dovey & I completed our pamphlet job at 4 PM – Had 300 left – He helped me pack 200 to the depot . . . I left on the 5:15 local train for Va . . . Took 40 to Bob Patterson . . .

June 23 . . . About 7 PM met Taggart on the street and he got me to fix up the local department of the *Enterprise,* Dan being too drunk – He has been drinking heavily the last few days, & other parties have had to do his work occasionally – I sailed in at once . . . bed at 3 –

June 24 – Clear & pretty warm – PM about town – Shortly after 7 PM fire discovered at 1500 level station of the Gould & Curry mine – All the miners got out but 5 on the 400 and 6 in the 1500 – The 5 on the 400 tried to escape by the old drain tunnel which runs out near the Mint mine below the city, but couldn't make it, the fearful smoke & gas catching them – They were found about 11 oclock, by a rescuing party, & some were yet alive. But all soon were dead – Joncy Morgan of Gold Hill was one – Efforts are being made by drifting from the Con Va or Best & Belcher to rescue those on the 1500 – Small chance for them – Taggart called upon me to stand in & manage the report of the thing, Dan being on his beer – Frank Wyatt also employed – We got up a staving good account of the affair – Bed at 3 –

June 25 . . . Nothing new in the mining calamity situation – Dan being still on his beer, Taggart put me to work . . .

Sunday, June 26 – Clear & pleasant – Rose at 8:30, washed etc, & at 10 was at depot to meet wife . . . we went to room – About 1:30 we were on street to see Joncy Morgan's funeral – The longest I ever saw here – Firemen, Mining Union, Shooting Clubs, Odd Fellows – 540 – 72 carriages . . . 828 people – Before last carriage left Odd Fellows Hall the 1st of procession was in cemetery – About a mile long – Crowds lined the street – Wife & I returned to room √ – went to French Rotisserie to dinner & I saw her off on the 5:25 . . . Returned to C street in time to see funeral of Trounce, and Bean from the churches – 2 hearses – Miners Union et al on foot, 356 – carriages, 43 . . . Carpenter was shipped to SF last night – Bruce was buried in Gold Hill this PM – Big day for funerals – regular funeral picnic jamboree – No news yet of the men on 1500 – Strong efforts continue to reach them by winze and drifting from the Con Va – Evening down town – Bed at 1 –

June 27 . . . Taggart paid me $12, what I asked for my services as "local" the last 3 nights – Nothing new from the imprisoned miners . . . Was about, getting items, but Dan was sober enough to work tonight, so I was not needed – Bed 1 –

June 28 . . . Evening was down at the Con Va and the Curry works with Billy Pennison, Chief of the Fire Department –

June 29 . . . No news from the entombed miners, but it was thought that chances were favorable for communication by morning –

June 30 . . . Graduating exercises of Public Schools at Opera House . . . Ball in evening . . . by the Schools & school authorities, for benefit of the suffering wives & families of late disaster – The connection from the Con Va not completed yet & don't know when it will – Situation getting desperate in case of the men being alive – *may starve to death* – [six-line erasure about illness]

July 1 and 2 [AD writes letters to J P Jones, J G Fair, J Poujade and Adolph Sutro, & sends a Pioneer Pamphlet to Sutro.]

Sunday, July 3 . . . Nothing new about the entombed miners . . . Lots of crackers, etc popping this evening and flags being put up for the

4th – Big keno game at the International saloon rooms – Biggest pool $50, ordinary pools from $10 to $17 – The mining pay day yesterday made things flush – Bed at 1 –

July 4 . . . Left on 7:40 excursion train for Reno . . . Had four coaches crowded from GH & Va – Picked up passengers all along the route & took on 2 coaches & 2 excursion flats at Carson, all densely crowded . . . At Reno I went directly home . . . We attended the parade, Balloon & all other propositions – Home on the train at 6 PM . . . Wrote up a column account of the Reno celebration for *Enterprise,* also couple of other items . . . It was a very hot day in Reno . . . 96° in the shade . . . About 4:30 PM gathering clouds . . . sent a warning gale . . . thunder showers followed – On the way home, those to go on the two flats behind having crowded into the 6 coaches out of the rain, all the standing room was occupied . . .

[Clip, *Enterprise:*] True American patriotism was at fever heat to-day, and even the thermometer got up to about 96 degrees in the shade. The people of Reno put their best foot foremost, determined not to be outdone in this annual celebration of Uncle Sam's birthday, and succeeded to their full satisfaction and the approval of everybody else. [The sidewalks and saloons were crowded, everybody seeking a shady, cool place. Flags and evergreens decorated the buildings and streets. The parade included politicians, bands, the military, "young girls dressed in white, with red and blue sashes and liberty caps," two steamers from the Reno fire department, families in carriages, and wagons and drays from local businesses.]

THE EXERCISES,

Conducted at the theater, were well attended by a densely packed, sweltering crowd, and passed off excellently. Bartine's oration was rather longer than requisite, but was a masterly effort nevertheless, and the poem, by Hon. C. C. Goodwin, read by Miss Marie McIntosh, of Reno, could not fail to be approved. The reading of the Declaration of Independence was effectively given by Colonel R. H. Lindsay, and the singing was a fine, particular feature of the occasion, Dickey Jose, Reno's favorite tenor, participating. In response to encores and vociferous calls he sang "Grandfather's Footsteps" in his clearest, sweetest, most sympathetic voice, and was rapturously applauded.

BALLOON ASCENSION.

About 2 o'clock Professor Monroe, from over in California, a professional balloonist engaged for the occasion, performed his contract to ascend through the upper strata of the hot sunshine, and he did it in gallant style, too, in the presence of the assembled thousands who had patiently waited in the shadiest and most eligible places to see his big balloon inflated and himself go up—or down and break his neck, so long as he did no damage to property beneath. It was a great white cloth bag, shape of a California fig with the big end up, gradually swelling to thirty feet high by twenty feet thick. He inflated it by means of a furnace supplied with burning pitch pine, coal oil and other approved combustibles, and when the thing was cut loose from strings and stakes it shot suddenly and rapidly upward, the Professor himself appearing in the tights and spangles of a circus rider, sitting securely in a neat little swing at the lower end of the aerial outfit. At the hight of 186 feet he let go a bundle of 2700 posters, a foot or two square, for a liquor firm in Reno, inviting everybody to go there and take a drink at his expense, and kept on to the hight of 634 feet, when he struck a cold blast from the Sierra Nevada and concluded to come down for his overcoat. The light wind had blown him to the northwest, and over 3,000 of the audience ran pell-mell in that direction, hoping to fish him out of the town reservoir. But no, in four minutes from the time he started up he landed comfortably in the crotch of a sour apple tree, in the outer edge of town, coiled up his drag rope, rolled up his balloon and sent for an express wagon. He got $400 for the job—$100 a minute. Nobody can say he didn't do it in spendid style.

July 5 . . . Was with Sam Davis of the Carson *Appeal* – Visited the Con Va and the Gould & Curry works together – The air compressor was stopped yesterday morning, it being ascertained that the pipe had been broken by the cave at the 1500 level of the shaft – The air blower still working . . .

July 7 . . . Got letter from Col Jas G Fair, San Francisco, saying he had received no pamphlet & wanted one – About noon went with Dr Delavan and put up our Pioneer flag on the flagstaff over the old Hall on B st – This was in honor of the anniversary of the acquisition of California, and the day when the American flag was first raised on the soil of that territory – It was also in token of our regular annual meeting . . . for the election of officers – Evening I attended the meeting – About a dozen present – Election resulted as follows: [A clip from the *Enterprise* lists the new officers – AD is president] . . . I made a nice little speech in acknowledgment of the honor conferred in electing me President . . .

July 8 . . . PM responded to letter of Jas G Fair with a pretty lively one enclosing three pamphlets . . . The much desired connection in the mines not completed –

July 9 – Cloudy but sultry – A very light shower or so in AM & PM – The long desired connection was made this morning of the rescue drift from the Con Va with Best & Belcher and Curry – Drill ran through into crosscut about 4 AM & at 8 a hole 3 ft wide was blown through – Exploring parties failed to find the entombed miners . . . but got on their track – They had removed a bulkhead 150 feet north of the Gould & Curry shaft & gone into an old drift that leads to a winze incline 550 feet further north – This winze runs down to the Sutro Tunnel level – It has closed, from the swelling of the ground etc, & also bulkheaded at lower end – So no hope for them – they must be in that incline winze – Air pipes were being put in today and the bulkhead at lower end removed – Bodies will probably be brought out tomorrow – I sent a telegram about it this evening at 7:40 to the Reno *Journal* – Evening down town – Bed at 2 –

Sunday, July 10 – Clouds & Sunshine – in PM about town – Those bodies were found this morning, but owing to pretty extensive trouble in getting at them, bad air etc, they were not brought to the surface until late evening – About 11 oclock I was with Frank Trezona & we [went] to Conboie's undertaking shop and saw all the corpses – They had evidently been dead many days and came apart at the joints unless care was taken in the handling – They were rolled onto canvass sheets which were bound around them and tied securely in order to bring them up the shaft – The stench from them was simply fearful and I had to cover my nose and mouth with my handkerchief – Could not recognize one of them – Their clothes had been removed and all were of a dark brown color almost black – ham rind – as though they had been baked or roasted brown in an oven, the flesh being shriveled & dry – Tregallis' head dropped off in handling, in the drift, In fact he came apart in two or three places – Their names were John M Kennedy, Foster Hamilton, Edward B Jeffrey, Martin Tregallis, Peter Eddy and Charles Dougherty – This PM, on C street, in conversation with others on the subject of the day, I was accosted by an oldish looking man about 49 yrs of age, plainly dressed, who asked me which of the crowd was Mr Doten – I told him and he said he was Moses Simmons of Plymouth, youngest son of George Simmons who used to keep the coal yard – I did not remember him or recognize him in the least, nor he me – We had a long, interesting chat together – also some beer . . . Mose Simmons used to go to school to Eunice – He arrived here this morning and is looking for a job, in a mill or in mining works – Seems like a wide awake, pretty good man –

July 11 . . . Met Mose Simmons again, and saw him off on the evening train for Carson, en route to Glenbrook, Lake Tahoe, where he expects to get a job in a sawmill . . . has been up in Washington Territory and about Puget Sound last five years, engaged at sawmill and lumbering work . . .

July 12 – Clear & pretty warm – The funerals of the 6 mining victims took place today – Kennedy's from the Catholic Church in Gold Hill – He was buried in the Catholic Cemetery, G.H. – The others were all buried here – Eddy first by the K of P before noon – At noon I rode with Charley Legate to Gold Hill in his one-horse, two-wheeled cart – Funeral of Foster Hamilton and Martin Tregallis took place from Masonic Hall – Immense crowd occupied the town – The funeral procession to Va was big – brass band at head – Charley & I were in the line of carriages and it was a *double* line, with the two hearses abreast, and the miners & others on foot, 4 abreast – First time this double hearse & carriage arrangement was ever seen on the Comstock – Made very imposing appearance passing down C st & out to the cemetery – At 5 PM funeral of Jeffrey and Doherty took place from Odd Fellows Hall & was the largest of all – Miners Unions 500; AOUW 130; IOOF, 120; Pall bearers, 16; Band, 14; in 60 carriages 240 people – Total over #1,000 people, making the largest attended I ever saw on the Comstock – The mines mostly shut down today – business houses ditto & flags all at ½ mast – Very populous day on the streets – Evening about town considerably – Bed at 12 – Tired –

July 13 through 18 [AD is about town daily, meets an old friend, Owen Fraser, back from Washington Territory to stay – "Weighs 318 lbs & looks as vigorous as ever" – "Financiers" $25 and pays the rest of his Centennial assessment & transfers 500 shares to Harry Johns, leaving himself 1,515¼ shares – Financiers $100 from "Matt Rider, my old Plymouth friend, who works at the Con Va assay office" & pays off $70 in recent small borrowings.]

July 19 – Variable & very pleasant – About town – Evening took Harry Johns to Piper's Opera House & deadheaded in to see Mrs Langtry & her company in "Pygmalion and Galatea" – Big house with high rates of admission – We enjoyed the play very much, but the "Jersey Lily" is growing too stocky, too much of the turnip order for continued good shapeliness – She is a pretty good actress, and has excellent lady support, the men not amounting to much, not even Mr Morton Selten as "Pygmalion" – A great crowd assembled at the depot when the morning train arrived, to see the famous English beauty arrive, but she didn't arrive – She & her company came from San F in her own special eating & sleeping car to Carson, but being 74 ft long, Yerington decided that it would be injurious and unsafe to pass around the short curves of the road, so it staid in Carson, & she & Co came through in carriages, arriving at 2 PM –

Her engagement here was only for this evening – The theatre was not very crowded – not as large a house as Emma Nevada had – Bed at 1 –

July 20 . . . Mrs Langtry left for Carson at the close of the show last night, by a 4 in hand carriage to sleep in her own private car – Her Co followed her by this morning's train – About noon Andrew Lawson found me on the street – we went to my room & had long talk about our knowledge of the Chollar upper workings & how to take advantage of it . . .

July 21 . . . My 58th birthday – No unusual circumstance marked the occasion except a letter from Hon Jas G Fair, San Francisco, in response to my last letter . . . and enclosing a $20 and a $5 greenback – I sent the $5 to Reno by evening train to wife, with strict instructions to take the children to the big Robinson Circus from the East . . .

July 23 . . . Old John Robinson's big circus from the East arrived this morning in good style . . . Got free ticket at *Enterprise* office and went in evening – Circus in old place in Alexander's cow-yard, ½ mile below C st and three half miles coming up back – Big crowd, fully 5,000 . . .

Sunday, July 24 . . . The regular monthly meeting of the Pioneers . . . Only five present including myself – I presided for the first time . . . Did a little unimportant business and when we adjourned Otto Eckelmann, of the Capitol Rotisserie, one of the members present, took us to a saloon & treated us, then to his rotisserie, where he treated us to hot coffee and baked beans . . . The Resolute base ball club of this city went down to Carson today and played a match game with the Amateurs of Carson for $500 – They scooped our boys in – also the money & loose friends of the principals . . . Resolutes 10 – Amateurs 19 –

July 25 through Aug 4 [AD writes to Mary, to Fair, a twelve-page letter to his sister Rebecca Talbot of Plymouth, several letters to others about his pamphlet – Also orders more catheters, gets a letter from his brother Sam & a birthday card from his sister Cornelia, "affiliates" with a couple of old timers, offers to settle an old $160 debt to druggist John Jones Jr by selling him 500 shares of Centennial for only $150, wins $10 and four pool tickets at keno & notes that his neighbor, "Old Pike," has gone to San Francisco for surgery on his leg.]

Aug 5 – Clear & very pleasant – 85 deg – Evening attended the Finlayson-Jose musicale at Piper's Opera House – Thoroughly crowded as long as a live soul could get in – Very good indeed – Bed at 2 – Miss Flora Finlayson and Dickie Jose were both brought up in Reno, and now come from there to their field of triumph – Dickie has a peculiarly beautiful tenor and alto voice – a mezzo tenor, as it were, and she is a rich contralto, "sympathetic" etc – Both are young – She about 19 or 20 & he a little older – Good team –

Sunday, Aug 7 . . . Wrote nice, 2 page letter to Bro Sam, relative to annexed clipping from the *Memorial* of July 28 – [The clip says Major Samuel H Doten has been thrown from a buggy – collarbone broken] – Bed at 2 –

Aug 9 . . . Lively watermelon war in town – Plenty of them – McGurn knocked the price down to *one cent a pound* – Everybody buys 'em . . . Wrote three pages of a letter to Eunice . . .

Aug 10 . . . PM down to Gold Hill & back on 'bus – Found Sam Jones at the Crown Point office & had good interview relative to my Chollar proposition . . .

Aug 11 – A little cooler – About 78° – PM met Lawson, & we had consultation relative to our Chollar proposition – Told him about my Sam Jones interview etc – He was in with a buckboard & 1 horse – rode with him out to the Divide – We left the team, & walked up to the Lima shaft – found it all caved in at the surface for about 15 feet down to the cribbing – Shaft 216 ft deep, single compartment – about 4 or 5 ft square – drift south at bottom 75 feet in $20 ore – Crosscut east from bottom of shaft 20 feet, cut rich vein – Had to quit because the Chollar company made them do so – It was the Lima Co, ½ dozen men, trying to make a location back of the Chollar and steal Chollar ore – About 450 ft north of the Sharon shaft and 200 ft west or about 600 ft northwest – on the line – Evening at home – Bed 12 – The Lima shaft was sunk nearly or quite 12 years ago – 3 or 4 years before I left for Austin –

Aug 12 . . . At noon met Sam Jones and Leon Hamilton at Wheeler, Hall & Cos hardware store and we had private consultation relative to Chollar – I rode with Sam Jones up to the Lima shaft in his buggy, & he took a look at the situation – Will re-open the shaft and investigate the ledge at bottom . . . Evening was up to Opera House awhile at parting reception of T W Booth & wife – The elite were there & filled the house in dancing – Good music etc – Extra fine party, select & invited – Tom was presented with a fine, gold headed cane by the telegraph employes here – He has been manager of the telegraph here for some years past and is now promoted to the management of the office at Ogden . . . James A Brown, an old sport generally known as "Long Brown," committed suicide today – He was a tall, slim, gentlemanly man, sandy complectioned, quiet – [three-line erasure] – getting painfully around on crutches – could do nothing and had no money and was going from bad to worse so he thought he had better die, so he took morphine successfully –

Aug 13 . . . Morning at 10 met Oramel Evans, a well known old resident Comstocker and complied with his oft repeated request . . . to take items for his obituary as he was liable to die at most any time . . . Wants to be buried in the Pioneers' cemetery – I agreed to it as President of the Pioneers and he seemed to feel relieved – First time I ever wrote a genuine ante mortem obituary dictated by the subject thereof, personally . . . Went to Crown Point office & had short interview with Sam Jones about our Chollar proposition – Flags at half mast for Bob Marshall, who died last evening at his residence in Crown Point Ravine, of miner's consumption . . . When I got back to Va met Joe B Marshall, his brother, and he gave me points for obituary on Bob, which I wrote this evening and gave to *Enterprise* – Am getting to be an obituary sharp . . .

Sunday, Aug 14 . . . PM finished letter to Eunice – 6 pages in all . . .

Aug 15 . . . Major T B Storer, my immediate predecessor as President of the Pioneers returned from Benicia today, looking much improved in health – About 10 oclock this evening Duncan Cameron, employed as blacksmiths helper at the Chollar works or mill, lay very dead drunk on the sidewalk just below McGurn's on C street – Some of the police whom I was with, got a buckboard and carted him up to the jail for the night . . . Belongs to the Good Templars society here, but has been on a drunk for the last 3 or 4 days . . .

Aug 16 . . . About 4 AM, two miners, John McLane, and Robert Clemmo, quarreled in a saloon on C street as to who could talk the best Spanish – The whisky in them spoke the loudest and they fought on the sidewalk – Clemmo got badly beaten, but McLane got a bad stab in the breast from Clemmo's pocket knife & is likely to die – C is in jail . . .

Aug 17 through Sept 1 [Mostly drinking & "skirmishing" – Attends Centennial meeting, visits the Lima shaft, sees *Old Lavender* played by Edward Harrington & his New York Theater Company, writes to Sam Jones and appropriates some sample gravel from the Centennial.]

Sept 2 . . . Wrote letter for Bob Patterson to manager of Woodward's

Gardens, San Francisco for a taxidermist to stuff a grizzly bear which Bob has contracted to be killed by a hunter in Alpine county for the Pioneers' Cabinet . . .

Sept 3 . . . PM borrowed $40 of Bob Patterson & sent it, greenbacks, in letter to wife . . .

Sunday, Sept 4 . . . Miner's Union Picnic at Steamboat Springs – Five coaches and five flats, loaded, and a commissary car pulled out from here – Took on one coach & a flat in Gold Hill – Many also went by private conveyance over the Geiger Grade . . . all hands half frozen – Bad picnic day, and not a good place for such a crowd – Much fighting on the grounds as well as in the cars . . .

Sept 8 . . . Evening Beaumont Comedy Co at Opera House in "Harbor Lights" – Good house – Taggart, editor & publisher of the Enterprise, not feeling well, & wishing to attend theater with his wife, got me to run the editorial department for him tonight –

Sept 9 . . . Evening at Pioneer banquet given by Otto Eckelmann – About 50 Pioneers, invited guests, etc present . . . Dan De Quille being drunk tonight I had to stand in on local . . .

Sept 10 . . . Evening attended the Opera House . . . "Harbor Lights" . . . was about town & at 12, met Taggart & he made me write some editorial . . .

Sunday, Sept 11 . . . At home all day – Wrote to wife as usual – Evening at theater – Sleight of hand, pretended spiritualistic medium show by Alex Hume and wife (Kate Eddy) – Densely crowded house at 50 cts admission – Most of the tricks, rope tying etc, in and out of the cabinet, were done pretty slick, but the whole thing as judged from the advertisement was a strongly flavored humbug – Bed at 1 –

Sept 12 through 20 [AD writes ads for midwifery & lace making, and some local, stands in for Dan again, & for Taggart, receives 2 musical instruments, "Kazoos," he has ordered, orders cuff-holders, notes that work has begun at the Lima shaft "on my account," that his annual hay fever has begun & he is treating it with "Santa Abie" and California "Cat-R-Cure," and that Governor Bartlett of California has died (Sept 12) and the stockboard is closed for his funeral (Sept 16) – Otherwise, weather & about town.]

Sept 21 . . . Took excursion train at 8:25 AM for Reno & the State

Fair . . . \$2 round trip . . . I got off at the fair ground, short distance south of Reno and took items – Saw one race and at 3 PM rode to town & home & wrote letter to *Enterprise* . . .

Sept 22 . . . I rode out to Fair grounds in 'bus with Hugh Mohan – took items on cattle & horse exhibits, races etc – back to town on 'bus at 3 – visited the Pavilion & took items on the showing there – Home & wrote my letter to Enterprise & got it off all right by the excursion train at 5:10 . . . Meet many Comstockers here at the Fair – Gov Stevenson attended today –

Sept 23 – Cloudy & cooler – Heavy rain storm in morning . . . At 1 PM rode in 'bus to race grounds – saw ladies' equestrian tournament exhibit – 7 entries – also three running races and a bycicle race – Wrote my letter in the entry clerk's office at the grounds and sent it by the up bound excursion train when it came along at 6:15 . . . Evening wife & I went to the Pavilion – well crowded – Splendid exhibit . . .

Sept 24 – Clear & very pleasant – Got shaved and rode out to the Fair at 11 AM on 'bus in time to see the stock parade – At noon Prof Monroe's balloon ascended from the grounds with a man on the trapeze in tights and spangles like a circus rider – about 1000 feet – Up 4 minutes and descended just outside the horsesheds on the west side of the grounds, near the gate, about 300 yards from where it started – No breeze – During the PM pacing & running races, etc – Got on excursion train when it came along and arrived at Va at 8:10 – Wrote up report of Fair for *Enterprise* took it to the office, staid & read proof – Bed at 2 –

Sept 25 through 27 [AD spends Sunday in Virginia City, misses the excursion train on Monday, & gets his Fair report from Powning by telegraph, gets down to Reno on Tuesday with Comstock miners, who have a day off to go, sees "Ladies riding, Indian pony race, other races" & notes that "The balloon failed today, only going up about 50 ft."]

Sept 28 – Clear & very hot – The excursion train brought 2 carloads from the Comstock & 5 from Carson, the business men closing in Carson & Reno today for the Fair – The attendance was therefore double what it has been . . . I went through the Pavilion in AM, taking notes – Met Sam Davis & wife & little daughter – Went to Lake House & had lunch or dinner with them at noon – The excursion train ran out to the grounds at 1 PM taking all who wished – I went – Ladies riding, successful balloon ascension – Big bicycle race with twelve entries from the Carson & Reno clubs, won by the Carsons in 3:34 – single mile dash – Indian pony race & other races – Excursion went back at 5:15 as usual – Evening at Pavilion with wife – crowded – brilliant time, with music, electric lights, etc – Bed at 11:30 – I got my letter off to Enterprise by excursion as usual – About a column of it – The Carson brass band came down with the excursion this AM & played alternately with the Reno Band on the Grand Stand at the races – this PM – Today and yesterday were as hot as we have had it this season – sweltering hot –

Sept 29 . . . Took look at cattle in the sheds, particularly Gov Stanford's of Cal, Holstein-Friesian cattle . . . Met John Piper on return to town & he took me to dinner with him at the Palace Restaurant . . .

Sept 30 . . . AM visited the bottling works of Wieland's lager beer, just below the railroad depot – Interviewed J B Francis, agent, had sundry glasses of cold lager from the ice-house and secured a $10 ad per month for the *Enterprise* . . .

Oct 1 . . . Last day of the Fair . . . stock parade and award of premiums – blue ribbons put on the winners – Wrote up part of my report . . . took the excursion train for Va . . . Went to room & finished report & got it to *Enterprise* office at 10 – Wrote out ad for the Wieland Lager beer . . .

Sunday, Oct 2 . . . At home most of day, fixing, washing and mending up . . . My regular hay fever catarrh has troubled me but very little thus far . . . Have used 2 bottles of Santa Abie and the California "Cat-R-Cure" – also 12 grains of quinine –

Oct 5 . . . PM about town – Evening attended theater – The Osbourne & Stockwell company from the Alcazar theater, played – The play was "Shadows of a Great City" – good house . . .

Oct 6 . . . PM about town – Evening at theater – "The Golden Giant" by same company, who are to play rest of week –

Oct 7 . . . About town – Evening, theater – Play "Ranch 10" . . .

Oct 8 . . . Went to Carson on morning train . . . At noon 4 passenger coaches arrived with 250 passengers from Reno to respond to Carson for her attendance at the State Fair – I rode in carriage to the Fair grounds, a mile or two north of town – John Sweeney's place – Very good attendance & very good time . . . Fair about same as Reno . . . only less of it . . .

Oct 10 . . . PM about town – Evening at Opera House – Webster-Brady Dramatic Co – Play – "After Dark" – Of the sensational order, after the style but inferior to "Under the Gaslight" – Bed at 2 – Finished & sent to SF Examiner an 8 page letter about Carson Fair –

Oct 12 . . . PM worked at "fretting" my big old Jim Henley banjo – Evening down town – Met Frank Doten, my cousin, who has been engaged in the freighting & teaming business for several years between Carson & Bodie . . . Here on business . . . Bed at 2 –

Oct 13 . . . At 10 AM footed it to Gold Hill, to attend meeting of Centennial Co . . . by reason of letter rec'd from Supt Richards, telling about big strike of water flooding the mine – Decided to tell him to keep the pump running for a few days, or till could definitely ascertain if it is a big pocket of water or a permanent flow . . .

Oct 14 . . . PM wrote & mailed letter to Sam Jones, San Francisco, striking him for $350 or $500 – Evening at theater . . . "Round the World in 80 Days" – good house – Bed at 1 –

Oct 15 . . . PM about town – Evening theater – "Pavements of Paris" – Bed at 1 . . .

Sunday, Oct 16 . . . Met Joe Grigg's ("Wildcat Joe") today – He is about my age and is keeper or watchman at the Wells Fargo mine 2 miles north of this city – Quite an original character . . . old timer on the Comstock – Engineer by profession, and the first employed by the Savage Co – He wanted to know how to telegraph to Reno on Sunday, inquiring about George W Nelson, another old Washoite, 61 yrs old – I showed and helped him out –

Oct 17 . . . Met Wildcat Joe & he showed me telegram stating that his friend Geo W Nelson died last night – chronic liver & kidneys, at Washoe County hospital . . . Evening I wrote a nice send-off for him and gave it to the Enterprise – Bed at 1 –

Oct 21 . . . Tom Johns passed me $100 in $20's this morning, as a loan which I have asked of the Johns Brothers . . . Met W P Bawden, Gill and others just in from Austin – The old place is gone to the devil, under the new proprietorship of the mines, and all hands who can get out are doing so . . .

[The Austin *Reveille* of this period clarifies that, after an abortive attempt to put silver on a par with gold by paying wages and bills in silver certificates, the Manhattan Mining Company of Austin was attached by Chicago creditors and had to suspend operations late in September.]

Oct 22 . . . The Bazaar held by the ladies of St Paul's Episcopal Church, which has been in successful run through the last 4 or 5 evenings, finished up this evening with a social dance . . . Andy Subtovich, the winner of $7,500 in the Little Louisiana Lottery last week gave a big blowout at the Sazerac saloon tonight – Barbecue of pig & oxheads, beans, etc – Free drinks – Well patronized . . .

Oct 23 through 30 [Fixes up his "big old banjo," presides over a Pioneer meeting at which only two other "old stiffs" appear, pays "last and present" Centennial assessments, writes about a dozen items and an anniversary account of the big fire of '75 for the *Enterprise* & another reminiscent feature about General Batterman & the Gould & Curry shaft for the *Chronicle* – Mary visits him & they go through the Fourth Ward School.]

Oct 31 – Same – I did nothing and accomplished nothing today, therefore it was one of the very latest blank 24 hours of my existence – *a day lost* – Evening down town – The gambling law being suddenly enforced, all licensed gambling games have to close & stay closed after 12 o'clock midnight, *Keno* and all – The faro, stud-hoss poker and Keno ran very lively – I was around, and took items on the business – Bed at 1 – No more licensed gaming for the present or until legally arranged –

Nov 2 – Same – Dave James, who has been working at the Lima shaft, and boss of the thing, has kept me posted the last week and tonight – 95 ft down, they found a drift north 60 feet, with short cross cuts east & west showing low grade quartz – Found bottom of shaft 212 ft from the surface – 6 ft less than I had it – found no south drift, and only 15 ft east drift instead of 20 as I had it – Samples were taken from the face of this drift, and operations suspended this evening – So now comes the solution of my 8 years Chollar cathop – Gaming being knocked out, the Catholic fair which commenced tonight had all its own way – Well patronized – I was about town during the evening – Bed at 12 –

Nov 3 – Same – Judge D O Adkison died at San Francisco this morning – One of the oldest & best known residents of this city – I wrote his obituary in the *Report* this PM and in evening for *Enterprise* – Read proof etc for *Enterprise* & bed at 3 –

Nov 4 – Cloudy but pleasant – PM rode to Gold Hill with John Briggs, in his buggy – Went to Crown Point works & had interview with Supt Sam

Jones – Says my Chollar Lima shaft proposition is a dead failure – no ore at all being found in that east crosscut at the bottom of the shaft – Has the men working there yet to try it a little farther, but it is not even in quartz – So after 8 years persistent effort to that end I find myself completely humbugged – and Lawson too – Went down to Jack Long's saloon in Lower Gold Hill at lower end of the 'bus route – Jack an old friend – He treated me very hospitably & presented me with a ½ gallon jar of pickled onions, a bottle of tomato catsup and 9 fresh duck eggs, all of which I took home with me on the 'bus – Evening at home and at *Enterprise* office – Bed at 3 –

Sunday, Nov 6 – Clear & pleasant – Train arrived 2 hours late, at noon, with remains of D O Adkison – also wife and daughter – Delegation of Odd Fellows took corpse from the depot to Odd Fellows Hall, where it was placed in state amid the finest floral decoration I ever saw – At 2 PM the funeral took place – Odd Fellows from Reno, Carson, Dayton, etc – He being prominent member of the Exempts, we were given the lead under marshalship of J C Harlow – County Commissioner Bart Burke & myself marched ahead & led off – Long procession on foot besides many carriages – Went to IOOF cemetery – On return we were left at our hall, roll called, etc – I was made Committee on Resolutions, with Charles Rawson and Pete Smith, on death of Bro Adkison – Evening at home – Bed at 1 –

Nov 7 . . . About town most of day – Evening attended Dan Morris Sullivan's "Mirror of Ireland" show, at Pipers Opera House – Panorama, and incidental Irish songs, dances, acting etc – Pretty fair show – good house . . .

Nov 8 . . . George Warren of the *Chronicle* paid me $5 more on his old account – still owes $5 – Bed at 1 –

Nov 10 . . . Jack Stephens died in Gold Hill today of pneumonia – My old friend Jack with the heavy chest and most powerful lungs – Has kept saloon there for the last 20 yrs – The funeral of Hop Sing, an old resident of the Chinese quarter of this city, merchant, man of property and great influence among the Chinese, took place this PM at 2 o'clock – About a dozen carriages loaded with Chinese – Hearse, pall-bearers, etc – Passed up Union street & south along C street to burial ground beyond the County Hospital – Chinese band of 6 or 8 pieces . . . got upset by a balky team . . . on Union st, just below C street, coming up the steep grade – Knocked them out of time, tune and funeral – Nobody hurt –

Nov 11 . . . Evening down town – Dropped in at grand social of the High School Literary Society at National Guard Hall short time – Nice party, fairly attended – Bed 1 –

Sunday, Nov 13 . . . PM attended the regular monthly meeting of the Exempt Firemen's Association – I reported resolutions on D O Adkison's death which I wrote at noon today – Were unanimously adopted – Jack Stephens' funeral took place from Pythian Hall this PM & he was buried in the cemetery, north of town – Had big funeral – Knights of Pythias, and Sons of St George jointly . . .

Nov 14 . . . Evening at Opera House – Bill Emerson's Minstrels from SF – 20 of them – Fine troupe & performance, & big house . . . A D Bullard, formerly of the Vesey House, Gold Hill, but now resident of Virginia got badly hurt about 5:30 PM – He was very drunk and got into a quarrel with Jack Wolfe, a teamster – They were having a small bit of a fight in Young Bros saloon when Bullard was thrown or fell down backward striking on the iron threshold of the door – He was made insensible and paralyzed all over – He is liable to make a die of it –

Nov 15 . . . [Learns of death of J D Pollard, who once kept a hotel at the head of Donner Lake] – Read my "3 days at Donner Lake" – When Dan & I went "way over in Excelsior" over 20 yrs ago –

Nov 16 . . . Stocks up quite lively – Bullard died at 9 AM. This evenings Va Chronicle says [Bullard died of apoplexy after a saloon fight – AD calls it "whiskeyplexy"] – Received a letter today from wife, enclosing an essay she has written for the State Institute . . . Sent me for inspection . . . "Language Teaching in the Public School" – Very able, well written document –

Nov 17 . . . Got letter from Fred Stevens, Ontario mine, Park City, Utah, about killing of "Bullion Pete" of Gold Hill out there recently by a saloon keeper, Richard Grant – Made item of it for *Enterprise* – Bed at 1 –

Nov 18 . . . Sent a $1 greenback to Austin . . . to pay my tax . . .

Sunday, Nov 20 . . . Evening wrote a long 7 page letter to H M Yerington . . . offering to sell him some of my Centennial stock . . .

Nov 23 . . . Wrote a long 8 page letter to Hon J P Jones, San Francisco, & copied it . . . didn't go to bed at all –

Nov 24 . . . Took 8 AM local . . . for Reno, this being Thanksgiving Day . . . Had roast mutton for our dinner, stuffed, with cranberry sauce – cauliflower, etc – About dark furious hail & snow squalls set in . . .

Nov 25 – Clear & cold but pleasant . . . I busy at odd jobs about home . . . During this week a State Teacher's Institute has been held at the Public High schoolhouse . . . Wife attended all through, closing this PM – Evening she attended a sort of reception or Teacher's Reunion at the home of Prof Brown, the principal of the State University . . .

Nov 26 . . . Visited the *Gazette & Journal* offices – Did some carpentering jobs about home . . .

Sunday, Nov 27 . . . Was down town two times – AM & PM – but briefly each time, merely watching the arrivals & departures of the trains . . . At home most of day, enjoying society of my family – Bed at 10 – OKF –

Nov 28 . . . Took morning train . . . for Va . . . PM about town – Evening ditto . . .

Nov 29 . . . Wrote another letter to Yerington –

Dec 2 . . . About 6 inches of snow this morning – grocery wagons on runners . . . Evening . . . Play "Natural Gas" by the Gilbert, Donnelly & Girard farce comedy company . . . no plot – only lots of good fun . . .

Dec 3 . . . Evening the electric light was exhibited for the first time for public use in this city – In the Delta saloon, and also sidewalk lamp in front of the Old Magnolia saloon – Attracted much attention – Been in use for about a week at the new Chollar mill & the Chollar, Norcross and Savage works – Received letter from Yerington . . . declining my offer to sell him some Centennial stock –

Dec 5 . . . Several more electric lights . . . in business houses along C st . . . Frank Mayo & most excellent Dramatic Co in "Nordeck" tonight . . .

Dec 6 . . . Mayo & Co in 6 act drama of "The Royal Guard" – Excellent . . .

Dec 8 . . . Taggart today paid me $10 as compensation, in full, for my services in reporting the State Fair . . . Almighty mean – Evening about town – Bed at 2 –

Sunday, Dec 11 – Clear & pleasant – PM I attended funeral of Vincent Elliot, an old Comstocker – Italian – About 60 years old – from his residence on South F or G st & the Catholic church – About a dozen carriages – I rode on the driver's seat of 1st one with his wife & 2 daughters inside following the hearse – Evening about town – Bed at 2 – PM Exempt election – I attended – [AD was elected first vice president.]

Dec 13 . . . R K Allen, manager of the Bankers & Merchants Mutual Life Association is in town – Offers me the agency for this State – May take it –

Dec 14 . . . About town a little on Insurance . . .

Dec 17 . . . Received this morning my official Contract as soliciting agent of the Bankers and Merchants Insurance Co for and throughout this state –

[Two clips are pasted into the journal here – One, from the Plymouth *Old Colony Memorial* of December 8, tells of the death of AD's fellow forty-niner Winslow B Barnes – The other is from the *Daily Evening Report* of Virginia City:] Alf. Doten, the old pioneer and stalwart war horse of journalism, and for many years proprietor of the Gold Hill News, which stood by the Virginia papers in the dark days of the great fire, has been appointed from the head office in San Francisco, soliciting agent of the "Bankers' and Merchants' Mutual Life Association of the United States," for and throughout the State of Nevada. No better selection could have possibly been made.

Dec 19 . . . At noon, in the Fountain Saloon under the Fredrick House, corner of C and Union streets, I wrote my two first applications for insurance – for Hiram Crandell and Alfred McCansland – the first for $2,000 & the other for $3,000 – Took & left them respectively with Dr Packer and Dr Webber for examination of the subjects . . . Evening down to Gold Hill & secured other insurance . . .

Dec 20 . . . Wrote application of Michael Albert Crane . . .

Dec 21 . . . Around on the "biz" lively, good & effectively – Got Bill Bowden & saw him entirely past the Doctor . . . This was my 1st fee – "1st blood" on my new business –

Dec 22 . . . PM at Gold Hill – Wrote the applications of Wm Henry

Eddy, and Henry Goetz . . . At Fred Burke's Arcade Saloon this evening I saw a *dressed* turkey for Christmas lunch, weighing 25¼ pounds – He was fat and slick, and the largest & finest turkey I ever saw or heard of – Was from Mason Valley . . .

Dec 23 . . . PM Gold Hill, canvassing etc . . . Allen left for San Francisco evening train –

Dec 24 . . . Borrowed $20 from Louis Hirschberg & took 3:45 for Reno . . .

Sunday, Dec 25 – PM & night blustering – At home – AM Mrs Batterman called – she is visiting the Lindsay's – Children have received lots of presents from the East & a letter from Eunice says she sends some . . . We had a nice turkey dinner, & celebrated Christmas in good style – Evening Mary & I visited the Lindsays – Millie & her beau, Ruel Waggoner, sparking in the parlor – she works at Jamisons, next door, helping at housekeeping, at $12 per month – Bed 10 –

Dec 26 – Snow squally – Off by morning train – Stopped at GH & attended to Insurance . . . Evening about town . . .

Dec 28 – Snow squalls most of day & settled down to regular business toward dark – nearly or quite a foot falling by midnight – Met my cousin Frank B Doten, about noon, on C st, & ran with him more or less during the PM & evening, to the neglect of insurance – He got very drunk, and about 9 o'clock I took him to my bed . . . at 1 went home to bed myself – Frank . . . has now turned out his teams for the season & come to Va to collect moneys due . . .

Dec 29 – Heavy blustering snow-storm all day – Over 20 inches this morning – I was about town on insurance – Frank on his own business – RR connections east & west demoralized – The regular V&T left Reno at 10 AM with no East or West mails and owing to the heavy drifts in Am Flat got stuck there about 3 hours, arriving at Va at 4 PM . . . It brought up Maud Granger & good theatrical Company – Frank & I went – Play "The Creole" – very good – slim house – Bed at 12 – Still snowing . . . Frank slept with me again, duly sober . . .

Dec 30 – Moderating, with sunshine and stray snow in the air . . . Fully 3 ft must have fallen this time – [AD sends in another policy application & receives eight completed policies from Allen.] . . . Frank slept with Joe Douglass in next room tonight – Bed at 2 –

Dec 31 – Same – Wrote application of Wm Naileigh for $5,000, but he was too drunk to pass Dr Webber – PM at Gold Hill – Snow too deep for *good* sleighing – Recd by express a full supply of new circulars and blank applications, receipts etc . . . Delivered Gregory and Kritzer's policies – Evening about town – Bell of Corporation House rang the New Year at 12 – Lots of New Years fun & mutual connubiation generally – The mail got through about 2 PM and went back on time – 3:45 PM – Frank left on the train for Carson, and San F – Evening about town – Bed at 2 –

BOOK NO. *63*

Virginia City and Reno
Jan 1, 1888 – Dec 31, 1888

Sunday, Jan 1, 1888 – Cloudy, but moderate and pleasant – PM & evening, about town tending to business . . . Bed at 1 – An unusually quiet "New Years" – Turkey lunches at the various saloons, but little heavy drinking or boisterous hilarity – Snow 2 ft deep –

Jan 2 – Stormy & thawy . . . Fierce winds in evening – My hat blew off, went 1737 feet high & soared off over the Sugar-Loaf down toward Fort Churchill 20 miles distant – I had to get a new one – about town as usual – letter from Bro Charley in letter from wife . . .

Jan 3 . . . Over a foot of additional snow this morning . . . not good traveling for man or beast in any direction . . . Evening at Opera House – "Monte Cristo" by Horace Lewis and company, and a very poor company at that and they deservedly had a very poor house – This Co is just from the East and a scrubby crowd at best – Bed at 2 –

Jan 4 . . . Had a 2 square, $5 ad in *Enterprise* this morning of my insurance agency . . .

Jan 5 . . . A friend arriving from San Francisco today brought me a cane from George W Allen, "Old Pike," who used to be my next door roomer – He was nearly or quite recovered from his injury and keeps his promise to give me his cane – Good stout crook-necked hickory stick –

Jan 6 – Occasional snow squalls . . . colder – Delivered the policies of H Crandell – $2,000 – receiving $18 therefor, Alex Crane $2,000 – $18 – and A McCansland $3000 – $24 – Total $60 – my commission 50 pr ct $30 – Paid my rent $8, and Odd Fellows dues $7.50 – Evening at Opera House – Good house – Campanini Italian Opera concert for this night only – Very good indeed – Special train from Carson brought about 60 to attend concert & returned – Ran with old Deacon Parkinson awhile after the show – Bed 1 – Thermometer 8° below Zero –

Jan 7 . . . Made up my statement of account with Ins Co & sent it with check for $42 . . .

Sunday, Jan 8 – "Pogonip" hazed the air most of the day – Shoshone Indian word, meaning frozen fog, such as gave the White Pine pioneers so much fatal pneumonia – air full of fine floating sleety frost particles, glinting in the sun-light and collecting on tree twigs, bushes, horse hair and human beard – coldest fog in the world, and not often found on the Comstock – The thermometer this morning, at 7 oclock stood at or a little above zero and was not above 10° during the day & dropping to below zero during the evening – Coldest of the season so far – PM I attended regular monthly meeting of the Exempts & was installed as 1st Vice President with the rest of the officers elect – Had a very amusing time, collation of sandwiches, beer, whisky, cigars etc – Evening down town awhile – Home – good fire – wrote etc, Bed at 5 – My thermometer outside of my window showed 2° below zero –

Jan 9 through 14 [AD is about on insurance & notes a brief thaw, a blustery storm & a return of the cold.]

Sunday, Jan 15 . . . According to thermometers at the Utah, Sierra Nevada, Combination & other mines the real temperature, outside of local town influences, was 20 degrees below Zero during last night – Coldest I have ever seen on the Pacific Coast – Received my new commission as agent for the Bankers & Merchants Mutual Life Ins Co – Gives me 60 pr cent instead of 50, since Jan 1 . . . Water works frozen up somewhere so it was shut off all day – I saved up a 5 gallon can of water last night, so have a good supply – About noon today John Henderson, Chief of Police treated me to a nice sleighride along C & D sts . . . Most froze our ears off –

Jan 16 through 24 [The weather warms up to a thaw & even a little rain & AD hikes all over Virginia City & Gold Hill on insurance business with little luck.]

Jan 25 – Clear & pleasant – Springlike – I about as usual – Evening at theater – 2nd and last appearance of Neil Burgess and company – They played "Vim" last evening to a good house, and "Widow Bedott" this evening to about half a house – He plays the leading female character in each piece – Very funny indeed – Each evening concluded with most excellent acrobatic feats by Bowler and McVeigh – Bed at 2 –

Jan 26 – Cloudy but very springlike – Snow going off fast – C st slushy & very bad for travel – Evening I attended meeting of Comstock Degree Lodge No. 1, IOOF and received my first degree in the order – I took the initiate degree Aug 25, 1866 (see Book No 32) Never have attended Lodge since – hardly ever – There was a large attendance, and at close of my initiation responded to call with best speech I ever made – much applauded – Bed 2 –

Jan 27 through Feb 1 [Weekend visit from Mary – AD looks in on a Leap Year Ball given by the "high-toned" ladies, and "runs" with Lieut Gov Davis.]

Feb 2 – Clear & pleasant – cooler – I put advertisements of my insurance Co into the *Chronicle* and the *Report* – this evening published – Evening at 8 I went down to St Paul's church to the marriage of John Randolph Vail to Miss Susie Rising, second daughter of Judge Rising – Church crowded – Altar surroundings finely decorated with evergreens, holly, smilax, oranges, etc – Music fine, & everything lovely – Awhile after, I was up to the Rising residence on Howard st – Grand reception, wine, cake, music, dancing, etc – Staid ½ hour – About town awhile – Bed 2 –

Feb 3 . . . PM was at train & saw Vail & wife leave on wedding tour to Los Angeles . . . Lots of friends at the depot . . . Evening . . . entertainment by Va High School Literary Society, for benefit of piano fund – songs, recitations music, etc, closing with a dance . . .

Feb 4 . . . About as usual on life insurance, but accomplished nothing – Evening at regular meeting of Mount Davidson Lodge No 3, I.O.O.F. . . . After Lodge I was at theater & saw last act of "Passion's Slave," by Miss Nellie Boyd and Company – very good –

Sunday, Feb 5 . . . Evening at theater & saw closing acts of "Unknown" by the Nellie Boyd company . . . Wrote letter to Frank G Newlands, S.F. –

Feb 6 . . . The following I cut out of the Virginia evening *Report:*

[Short clip reporting that Isaac F Stith, formerly of Esmeralda County and Lake Tahoe, was stricken with paralysis January 29 and died in Reno Thursday night.]

Ike Stith cut me out in the affections of Mary MacDonald the schoolmarm at Como – my rival is dead –

Feb 7 through 14 [AD gets two dozen more catheters, takes his second degree at Lodge, attends an Exempt Firemen's meeting, writes a $5000 insurance application, runs to see two buildings burn in Chinatown during the Chinese New Year celebration, looks in on the AOUW ball, "Nearly or quite 2000 people present," and buys 400 lbs of Wellington coal.]

Feb 15 . . . Evening down town – at 12 met Hy Crandall and Evans the banjo player – Had been out playing somewhere, Hy with his guitar & Evans with his banjo – Went up to my room & we had a regular concert for nearly 2 hours – One of the best banjo players I ever heard & the very best banjo . . . Met Joe King on the street today – He was *police* of Austin when I was there, and had charge of my old log cabin etc after I left – Joe is on the lookout for something to do here . . .

Feb 18 . . . Left on the 7:45 . . . for Reno – At Carson took short opportunity to call on Major Garrard, Supt of the Mint . . . Folks all right . . .

Sunday, Feb 19 . . . Home all day – Evening banjo & songs, also reading of Dickens' "Our Mutual Friend" – Bed 9 –

Feb 20 . . . AM about town – Got more material for history of Sandy Bowers for Dr Bishop – Started in at noon writing it up . . .

Feb 21 . . . At 9 resumed writing Bowers & kept steadily at it all day & evening not even stopping for lunch . . . wrote till 1 & finished the job . . .

Feb 22 . . . Took the train for Va . . . Laid over at Carson – Interviewed Garrard & he gave me lots of documents relative to reporting Comstock for Gov't statistical work . . .

Feb 23 . . . Evening in Degree Lodge, I & Jimmy Harris & —— Pascoe took the Third Degree & became full Odd Fellows – I was called on & made real good little speech which was well received . . .

Feb 25 . . . Arranged for certificate of my membership to be sent to Nevada Lodge No 7, Degree of Rebekah, Reno, with application for my wife to join it . . .

Sunday, Feb 26 . . . Met Henry Shaw Smith . . . He is recently from Sydney, where he is engaged in the hardware business & rich – Been there last 10 years – Old timer here – Used to be part owner and in charge of the Ophir Grade toll road – I cruised about town with him . . .

Feb 29 . . . The first case of genuine smallpox for several years developed today – Man recently arrived from Grass Valley, Cal, where they have several cases . . . General Mathewson fell down the stairs from the 2nd story, leading out onto F street, broke his left arm near the wrist – Cut his head badly on an iron railing in falling & rolled onto the sidewalk insensible – Mike Heney of Gold Hill, a miner called to see me at my room about 8 oclock, relative to a mean article, which might get some believers, in the *Evening Report* on the 16th and which had been attributed to me – We parted amicably . . .

March 1 . . . Toward evening a lively snowstorm set in . . . More cases of smallpox are reported in lower south part of the city – The first case, Mr Frazier, was taken to pest house this PM . . .

March 5 . . . 6 inches snow & good sleighing . . . Evening at Opera House – Play "Ivy Leaf," by a company from the East – Very good – Heard the Irish bagpipes for the first time in my life – The theater was densely crowded . . .

March 6 through 11 [AD to Lodge meeting in Gold Hill & on insurance business in Virginia City, Carson & Reno, where he spends Sunday.]

March 12 – Clear, warm & pleasant – Took morning train – Laid over at Carson – Met Frank Doten & we ran some together – Was at the Mint & fixed up things with Garrard on the required Comstock statistics for the Treasury Department – Bureau of US Mint – I wrote out my proposal in the matter with charge put at $350.00 – He forwarded it to Washington by evening mail – I got to Va at 6:30 – attended the "Campobello Grand Society Concert" at Pipers Opera House – Very good company – Mostly Italian Opera, lots of piano, some extra fiddling and rather of a slim house – Wrote an item or two for *Enterprise* – Bed 2 –

> [A clip from the *San Francisco Post* accuses Governor C C Stevenson of Nevada of having gained complete control of the Kentuck mine by way of a dummy board of directors & of having robbed the stockholders & gutted the mine. Another clip, from the *Virginia Chronicle,* states that Stevenson's libel complaint against the *Post* has been ignored by the grand jury, "which was equivalent to an indorsement of the *Post's* charge."]

March 13 through 17 [*Our American Cousin* plays at Opera House, & AD attends opening of Emmet Guard Ball, writes an insurance application, attends Lodge, notes that there is no observance of St Patrick's day and writes to Senator Jones in Washington for "certain Pub[lic] Doc[ument]s relative to the Comstock."]

Sunday, March 18 . . . Composed a seven page Comstock variety sketch for S H Blakely, a brother-in-law of Dave & John Crosby, grocers, which he wishes to publish as his own in a weekly paper in his town, called the *Bad Axe Democrat* published at Bad Axe, Michigan – Bed at 4 –

March 19 . . . Haverly's Minstrel troupe arrived – paraded the streets, & in the evening had very big house – I was there – Minstrel, acrobatic, clog dancing, etc – One of the most amusing as well as interesting entertainments I ever saw . . .

March 20 . . . Rec'd short letter from Garrard saying . . . "Last night I received the following telegram: Information proposed relative to Comstock not what is wanted – Have written" – Evening was at Opera House & saw latter half of the Haverly performance . . .

March 21 – Clear & cooler, but pleasant – About town as usual – The Haverlys left and Abbey's Uncle Tom's Cabin Troupe arrived – Their big band of music paraded about 4 PM – Fannie H Robinson of Gold Hill died this morning, aged 26 – She was one of the GH public school teachers – Worked herself to death, not being constitutionally strong – I telegraphed it to wife – Evening attended theater – Good house – Play of Uncle Tom's Cabin very well rendered with assistance of the two Hyer sisters, colored, who are great in song, dance, etc – They were here several years ago, when I saw them at Piper's old Opera House – Much improved since then – When I came out of the theater I learned of suicide of Dan B Sohl at Salt Lake – Met his wife on C st about 4 this PM & we spoke to each other – I went to Enterprise office & learned full particulars from telegrams – Wrote a few words as windup to the account – Bed at 2 –

March 23 – Cloudy and dusty – very disagreeable – Rose at 7 – fixed up, cleaned up etc ready for wife – Train delayed, & she arrived at 12:20 – We ate together at room – She intended to have been to Fanny Robinson's funeral this PM, was not feeling well, so didnt – It was a big funeral, with many from here – Buried in the Masonic Cemetery, Gold Hill, *at sunset,* according to her expressed desire – Evening at home with wife, she resting in bed – I wrote a 3 page letter to Dave Monroe Tyrrell, Silver Reef, Utah, in response to one from him asking me all about my life insurance proposition – Explained it pretty fully – enclosing circulars and an application blank – Bed 2 √ –

Sunday, March 25 . . . Wife & I went to French Rotisserie to breakfast . . . Home rest of the day till I saw her off on the 3:45 . . . Rufus Ford, about 29, driver of Keller & Batchelder's grocery delivery wagon shot a pistol bullet into his brain at Silver City this PM – either by design or accident . . . But the grand principal act was the rather abrupt announcement that seven fresh cases of smallpox were discovered this PM on the Divide . . . Also another at the north end of the city – Wife's 44th birthday – We were married July 24, 1873 –

March 26 . . . Wife being gone I felt like a grass widow – AM sent telegram to my wife: "Extensive concealed smallpox – Zangerle arrested – Devil to pay" . . .

March 27 . . . Recd letter today from Garrard enclosing one from Director of the Mint, Kimball declining my proposition as not being the desired information relative to the Comstock –

March 28 . . . Evening at Opera House – Conried English Opera Co – for this evening only – Good house and very good performance – Opera "The Gypsy Baron" – About 40 people or more in this Co, & over half women – The march of the Hungarian Hussars in the last act was finest I ever saw – all women – 22 of them – very shapely & well drilled . . .

March 29 through April 3 [AD buys a new pair of pants, leaves his old banjo at the Fountain Saloon to be raffled off, gets 300 lbs of coal from Smith & Co of Gold Hill – Attends Lodge, notes that April Fools' Day is not observed because it is also Easter, & that the Knights Templar attended St Paul's in uniform, that smallpox is still on the increase, that a benefit by the Virginia Amateur Dramatic Club draws a slim house & that he has received an answer from Senator Jones.]

April 4 – Clear & pleasant – About town as usual – More cases of smallpox reported – guess it's got loose & getting promiscuous – Evening at the Opera House – Royce & Lansing Comedy Co & Swiss Bell Ringers – ½ doz or so of them, including two women – Very good variety music performance, including bells, banjos, violin, zithers, ocarinas, etc – Lansing played six instruments at once – banjo, accordion, harmonica, cymbals, bass drum, triangle and shook a lot of bells on his head – Very good performance, but the smallpox scare only allowed about ¼ of a house – Bed 2 –

April 6 – Same – PM at Gold Hill – Evening at Opera House – Grand ball of the Uniform Rank K of P – Big affair – Fine drill at the commencement – Bed at 2 – Got a letter from Garrard dated 5th stating that he had received that day following dispatch from the Director of the Mint: "For what amount will Doten work up Comstock as per my letter of nineteenth ult" –

Sunday, April 8 . . . Got a letter off by the 3:45 express, to Garrard – I offer to do that Comstock statistical job for $250 . . .

April 9 . . . Telegraphed: "If Kimball still rejects ask whats most will pay. Can promptly suit him and on time . . ." Evening was at regular bi-weekly meeting of the Irish Land League in lower hall of the Miners Union – Music, ballads, recitations, etc – Bed 1 –

April 10 . . . Mose Simmons called in – going to old Plymouth tomorrow to see to the settlement of his father's estate – deceased – We dined together at Otto's & had some beer at The Arcade Saloon and bade each other good by – I wrote a nice 2 page letter this evening & sent it by Simmons to brother Samuel . . .

April 11 . . . Rec'd letter from Garrard . . . containing acceptance by Jas P Kimball . . . of my offer to furnish the desired Comstock statistics for $250 – Evening down town – Saw the "lightning tooth extractor" perform on the street in front of the International – Must have pulled a hundred or more teeth, free of charge – Big crowd . . .

April 12 . . . Rec'd by mail today a bag containing 12 books, weighing 50 pounds or more – It was from Senator J P Jones, Washington – "Pub Docs" – the 4 big ones were Powells survey of the Pacific coast and rest were reports of Director of the Mint on the Gold & Silver production of the United States . . .

April 13 . . . Streets very dry and very dusty – Storekeepers howling for the sprinkler –

April 14 – Same – Evening at my Lodge – No initiation – only regular work – Big car 64 ft long came up today – Painted up in fine style and labeled *New York Aquarium Car* – Took station near depot – Had a steam calliope for attraction – I paid 2 bits admission – Full of live rare birds, monkeys, etc – big boa constrictor, big vampire bat, nine crocodiles in a big tank amidships – largest 60 yrs old, 12 ft long, big as my body – the smallest 4 or 5 ft – good show – This PM I took ride with Chief of

Police Henderson in his buggy about town, down 6 mile Canyon and out on Divide – Saw the quarantined smallpox people – Two houses of them will be released tomorrow, all cases in them being cured – 2 other houses have a few cases convalescing – Bed 1 –

April 15 through 17 [The street sprinkler starts its rounds – AD does business in Gold Hill, makes some visits there, comes away with a present of eggs and walks the two miles home in ¾ of an hour – "not bad for a cripple."]

April 18 – Same – At noon rode on 'bus to Lower Gold Hill to see Ed Swift – Didnt see him – rode back at 4 with Ed Boyle in his buggy – Edith Rising & Hugh Vail were married this PM at St Paul's church – High-toned wedding & well attended – church beautifully decorated inside with flowers etc – No reception – They left on evening train for wedding tour in California – Evening I attended Degree Lodge – Saw Jack W Plant of the *Enterprise* take his 3d Deg and 9, including Harry Johns, put through the 2nd Deg – The largest batch yet in that Deg – Bed at 1 –

April 21 – Same – Grand excursion to Reno got up by Powning to boom auction sale of lots in his "addition" west of town, by the riverside – 3 big passenger coaches left Va crowded, at 10 AM – I went – Jammed in a few Gold Hillers, but a hundred or two couldn't get on – At Carson 3 more crowded coaches joined – Fully 100 on each car, men & women – I had to stand up all the way – Made Reno in 2:40 . . . Met wife at depot – The sale of lots took place on premises this PM – I didn't attend – Only 7 lots sold, at from $185 to $410, I heard – I busied myself about home fixing up front gate, side steps, etc – Evening down town short time – Met lots of acquaintances – Bed 10 –

April 22 through 27 [AD spends three days in Reno, carpentering & visiting about town and at the depot, then returns to Virginia City and writes a letter to Senator Jones, thanking him for materials sent and requesting more – Sends letters to Almarin B Paul & W H Watson in San Francisco requesting further Comstock information.]

April 28 – Clear & cool . . . Mackay and Fair arrived from San F together – came by private carriage from Reno – another change being made in affairs of the Nevada bank brings them here – Primary election this PM for delegates to the Rep State Convention at Winnemucca on the 15th of next month – I voted in 3rd Ward – Light vote & no opposition – Evening at the Opera House – McKanlass' colored Specialty Co – Song, dance & variety, & good brass band, which paraded streets – McKanlass is one of best banjo players I ever heard – Rest not much – About ½ a house – Bed at 1 –

Sunday, April 29 . . . Recd [a letter] today from Dept of the Interior, US Geological Survey . . . stating that a copy of the Comstock Atlas was mailed to me . . . at request of Hon J P Jones . . .

April 30 . . . PM fierce blustery Washoe zephyrs, whirlwinds of dust . . . The smallpox has entirely disappeared, and the last house was fumigated today – Wild night –

May 2 . . . 1 PM walked to Gold Hill & skirmished on insurance pretty diligently with little success – When Jack Harris came off shift at 3 PM from Crown Point he assisted me more or less & made me go up to his house to dinner at 6 PM – Lives on Ft Homestead . . . footed it home . . . Jack escorted me with a lantern by a new trail back of the Imperial works up to the main road – I noticed today that a barber now occupies the Gold Hill News office – Has his pole out in front, yet the fine large old sign still adorns the front overhead –

May 3 . . . PM walked to Gold Hill – Skirmished – walked back before dark . . .

May 4 – Cloudy & cool & pleasant – About 12:30 PM John L Black killed his brother Sam J in basement of their well-known building, corner of C & Taylor sts, in pursuance of an old quarrel about their property – created some excitement – He went up to jail & surrendered himself – I was sold out of Centennial by Sheriff at sale yesterday – 1515 shares – Evening at home – Bed 12 – Samuel J Black was about 70 & John 67 yrs old – natives of Alabama – Old citzens of Va, well known & law abiding – only vicious to each other – The murderer was perfectly cool, showing no excitement or remorse, & when he went to Sheriffs office merely told Deputy McGown he wanted to surrender himself as "I have killed my brother in self-defense" – He has a wife & four sons in California – He shot his brother just below left nipple and then smashed in his skull, middle of forehead, above eyes with a big machine wrench, making a hole big enough to put a boy's fist into – Worst I ever saw in that way – Also broke his left arm between wrist & elbow –

May 5 – Clear & pleasant – Received by mail today the Comstock atlas from the Dept of the Interior – Wife arrived about 10 AM in 4 in hand with 8 other teachers from Reno & attended the convention of the Nevada

Educational Institute at 4th Ward schoolhouse – Evening I attended with her – Crowded house – music, singing & other exercises & address by S Summerfield on Pacific Coast Characteristics – Very good but very long – Bed 11 √ – Sent letter today to D A Bender, Genl Fr't & Passenger Agt V&T RR Carson, asking him to give me a ½ fare permit to travel over the road – Democratic primaries today for delegates to State Convention – Miles Finlen and David Pine had a fight over it on the Gould & Curry dump, below D st – Dave was knocked down & so badly hurt that he subsequently became partly paralyzed in left limbs, & may die – Finlen under $200 bonds –

Sunday, May 6 . . . About 10 AM wife & I walked to Gold Hill – She visited Mrs Chubbuck – I visited Bill James about my Centennial at assay office . . . About 4 PM she & her crowd left for Reno in their conveyance – I saw them off – Saml J Black's funeral took place from undertaker Brown's – Preacher and man in buggy, followed by hearse, corpse & pall-bearers was all – Met Bob Lindsay – He is up from Reno, called as counsel in defense of J L Black . . .

May 7 . . . At 1 PM annual meeting of Centennial, at Gold Hill Assay office . . . Company passed resolution restoring my stock on paying up assessments in full – Old board of Directors re-elected, including myself . . . Rec'd letter from A B Paul, & from D Bender with ½ fare permit till December –

May 8 . . . Frank Sperling, a general agent of the Bankers & Merchants Insurance Co arrived from San F, drumming up business for the Association – I was about town some with him . . .

May 9 . . . PM Frank Sperling & myself took a walk out on the Divide prospecting on insurance . . . J M Douglass came up stairs to his room next to mine about 12 – Visited me 2 hours – pretty drunk, & told me whole lot about Stevenson, to the effect that he was *busted,* etc – Owed Douglass $178,000, & was *"gone"* – Jewett Adams owed $48,000 and also was *gone* –

May 10 . . . AM wrote 7 page letter to wife about Stevenson, Adams etc . . . At 12 was getting ready for bed when old Joe Douglass came in, rather tight, as usual, & I had to play the banjo & sing "Susanna" for him . . .

May 12 . . . Frank B Doten arrived about 4 PM with his big team, from Bodie, bringing the boiler engine & other machinery of the Booker mine at that place to the West Con Va mine, western part of this city . . .

May 13 through 16 [AD writes a $5,000 policy, sees Sperling off, notes that the funerals of Andrew Fahey, Secretary of the Miners' Union and Mrs Tom Kelley, wife of the US Marshal, were well attended – Learns from Judy, the Piute woman who used to work for them in Gold Hill, that Mary is sick, takes the train for Reno, noting that there are quite a number of "delegates, lobbyists, etc" for the Republican Convention aboard, stays with his family a day & returns to Virginia City with delegates to the Democratic Convention.]

May 17 – Clear & very pleasant – Democratic State Convention here today – Opera House – Well attended by delegates from all parts of the State – Temporary organization at 1 PM adjourned to 7 PM – reassembled then, committees reported etc, G W Cassidy nominated for Congress and W M Sewell for Supreme Judge – Through at 9 – About town – Bed at 1 – Republican delegates to State Convention returned from Winnemucca today – Rec'd letter from son Sammy written last evening, saying wife no better –

May 18 through 31 [AD chiefly busy gathering & corresponding about Comstock mining statistics, doing insurance business, including making an inquiry into the death of one Gregory, & attending IOOF instructions & initiation – Of additional interest:]

Sunday, May 20 . . . Rec'd . . . an invitation to Fourteenth Annual Reunion of El Dorado County Society, California, to be held at Placerville next Friday . . . Evening I wrote a neat reply . . . Dave Pyne died this morning at Sisters Hospital –

May 21 . . . Miles Finlen arrested this morning and jailed for murder, no bail –

May 22 . . . Evening theater – Daniel E Bandmann in "A Strange Case" – "Dr Jekyll and Mr Hyde" – Bed at 2 –

May 23 . . . The Grand Jury in session today found a true bill of indictment against Miles Finlen for murder in killing Dave Pyne . . .

May 25 . . . Major T B Storer left International today, where he has been stopping since return from Benicia . . . and went over to the County Hospital to stay – went this morning or last evening – Gone to the Poorhouse at last –

May 29 . . . Major Downie arrived from California last evening & is stopping at the Beebe House – Has come to canvass for one of Mark Twain's books, & thinks of getting up a book of his own – Has recently returned from Alaska & that section & proposes settling for good at Downieville, Cal with his family – Met him & had quite a talk – He is fully as deaf as ever – Little Maggie Ryan fell down a shaft 80 feet deep this PM [suffered only a broken rib] – The first new apples of the season in market today . . .

May 31 . . . Letter from wife says Millie is to be married to Ed Cochran tomorrow evening . . .

June 1 – Cloudy & cool, with light showers – About town as usual – Left on the 5:10 PM train for Reno, taking along a box of cherries – $1.25 – 10 lbs – fine – Arrived home at 8 & found a small wedding party assembled consisting of my family, Cora Ferguson, Chrissie and Ben Anderson, Mrs Powell, Mrs R H Lindsay, Miss Lindsay, Mrs Ayer, & daughter, Frankie Dolton – and Rev Wm Lucas and the bridegroom, Edward Everett Cochran – The ceremony took place in the parlor, after which collation in next room, cake, fruit, sandwiches, lemonade, etc – then banjo and singing etc till about 11, when Mr & Mrs C left for the Golden Eagle Hotel near by, Goodie & I throwing an old shoe after them for luck – Bed 12 –

June 2 through 27 [AD at work on his Comstock statistics, "skirmishing" very hard, & with considerably more success, all about Virginia City, Gold Hill & Silver City on his insurance business & attending Lodge & Exempt meetings. Of additional interest:]

June 2 . . . Received letter from my old Gold Hill carpenter friend, W R Litchfield, now of Santa Cruz, Cal, enclosing an old photo of myself taken at San F about 1862 or 3 –

Sunday, June 3 . . . Wrote & sent a letter to Jas O'Leary of *SF Journal of Commerce*, transferring to him from Sperling the mining statistics job . . . wrote letter to Judge James Walsh, San F, for early Comstock Ophir statistics, etc, Almarin B Paul, Middle Creek, Shasta Co, Cal on same thing . . .

June 5 . . . Evening at performance of the Original Comstock Minstrels, at Opera House – Very good and very full house – Gross receipts $528 – Bed at 1 –

June 11 . . . Morning train at 11 AM brought the A R Wilber Comedy

Co and a lot of delegates or members of the Grand Lodge, R.A.M. which convenes here today – I met from Austin, C W Hinchcliffe, A D Vollmer, Wm Foster and Hopkins . . . Was about town some with the Austin boys, & to bed at 1 –

June 14 . . . I rested today, being very tired – Sent check for $44.40 to my Ins Co, also Jake Wyckoff's application – Dr Manson today refused to pass Barnaby – too heavy a drinker . . .

Sunday, June 17 . . . The SF papers which came this morning brought news of the death of Oramel Evans from paralysis or apoplexy – He got me to write his obituary on the 13th of August last, expecting to die as he has done . . . I completed it for publication – Bed at 2 –

June 18 . . . Gave my Evans obituary to the *Enterprise* . . .

June 19 . . . Made a nice big table – 28 x 60 inches – in my room today for use in my mining statistical work – easily taken apart & put out of the way when not in use – Received by mail a package from wife containing five clean collars and a cabinet size photo of herself, just taken . . .

Sunday, June 24 . . . PM with Mr Lowell Secy of Con Cal & Va mine at his office, on statistics, etc . . .

June 26 . . . Searched records of the County assessor on mining statistics – Evening made out a lot of hektograph blanks for the purpose – Bed 2 –

June 28 – Cooler, very blustering, dusty – I worked all day at the County Recorder's office getting statistics for my Govt job – At noon Bob Patterson got me to work a couple of hours taking inventory of tags, Jewelry, etc, received at bar or at the Faro game etc . . . Evening grand Rep. ratification at the Opera House – brass band – Big time – Meeting addressed by J A Stephens, C E Mack, Hon David McClure of Cal, and H F Bartine – Good speeches all – great enthusiasm – I reported, Dan being on a big drunk – made about a column – Bed at 1 –

June 29 . . . Dan on deck again . . . The Enterprise donned a new dress of body type . . . this week – been needed for several years –

June 30 – Clear & pleasant – Took morning train to Carson – Met lots of Jolly acquaintances – Went to Controllers office in the Capitol at 11 AM & commenced the big task of overhauling and gleaning from the reports of the Assessors of Storey, Lyon, Ormsby and Washoe Counties for statistics as to mining production, ores, tailings, cost, etc, by calender years since beginning – Worked hard at it all day, till 6 PM without stopping for lunch – Evening about town a little, but went to bed at John Wolmerding's lodging house at 10:30, tired – Sent a postal card to wife by train this evening, telling her where I am, etc – Carson is looking beautifully at present, Capitol Square especially, with luxuriant trees, shrubbery, flowers, etc – One big picnic ground – Capitol Square the most beautiful spot of its size in the State of Nevada –

Sunday, July 1 – Clear, warm and pleasant – Started in again at Controllers at 10 AM & worked very diligently without cessation till 6 PM – Slept at Wolmerdings again at 11 –

July 2 – Same – Commenced again at 10 and at 4:30 got through – Left on 5:10 PM local train for Va, arr at 7 – good dinner – Went to Opera House – About ⅔ of a house – Very good entertainment – Mrs Bowers seems as good as she was a dozen years ago when she was here last – Bed at 1 – US Marshal Thos E Kelly died suddenly at noon at his home on A street from heart disease – About 50 years old – Wife died of same disease a few weeks ago – Leave 6 children, youngest about 4 –

July 4 – Same – Odd Fellows picnic left at 8 AM for Treadways Park, Carson – 10 cars well filled – Took on 4 or 5 more at Gold Hill – Reno Guard came on a special train at 10, with quite a number of others from Reno & Carson – Town full of people – Procession moved at 11 out on B st & back on C, Nationals, Emmets, & Reno Guard – Liberty Hose & Engine Cos Gold Hill, Divide Hose Co & Paid Fire Dept Car of State, Ship of State & ½ doz carriages – Very fine, what there was of it – Exercises at Opera House – Bob Lindsay Orator of the Day – I was about town – Evening at room – Bed 12 – Rear of procession was packed mule, a la '49, labelled "Yuba Dam," with Charley Sullivan & Jack Curry on foot as old '49 miners – mule packed with cooking utensils, camp equipage, mining tools, etc –

July 5 through 9 [AD working very long days, & once all night, on his statistical report – Mary arrives in Virginia City to help him on the weekend – AD goes to Dockstader's Minstrels.]

July 10 – AM clear & hot – PM cloudy, with a few sprinkles of rain in the evening – finished copying the narrative of my report just in time to take the morning train for Carson – Called on Garrard at the Mint short time – Went to State Capitol & about town & at 3:30 PM was at the Mint again – Delivered to Garrard my completed report filing bill for $250 –

It will leave for Washington tomorrow – Home on evening train – Soon went to theater & saw play of "The Cattle King" – Blood & thunder border equestrian drama of 5 acts – Very good – 2 fine trained horses and a jackass on the stage – James H Wallick in the title role – Bed at 2 very tired – Good house at theater –

July 11 . . . PM rode on bus to GH & back – attended meeting Centennial trustees . . . Evening . . . got to overhauling my copy on Ass'ts and Divs & found had made bad job of report in that respect – Slept 3 hours in my clothes . . . worked rest of night on new table of Ass'ts & divs –

July 12 . . . Got my asst & div statement corrected in good form & tried to make morning train for Carson – got left – telegraphed to Garrard . . .

July 13 – Clear & pleasant – Morning train to Carson – Went to Mint, corrected and fixed up my Comstock report all right and it was forwarded for Washington by this evening's mail – Was about town some with John Allen et al – Home on evening train – Bed 12 – Today I took with me and delivered to the Pioneer cabinet in Carson the old big book of Constitution & By Laws and autographic list of members from commencement – also my pamphlet pasted into it, etc – It forms a pretty good history of the Society, & will remain so –

July 14 . . . PM was at Jack Long's, Lower Gold Hill – Borrowed $10 from him – Evening at Opera House to Scenoramic show & lecture . . .

Sunday, July 15 [Erasure – doubtless bowel trouble] – Was not on the street at all today – Evening ditto – Bed at 12 –

July 16 . . . Felt much better today – Evening at home & wrote one of my longest letters to wife – Bed at 4 –

July 17 . . . 2nd day of Miles Finlen's trial for killing Dave Pyne – Evidence for prosecution . . . PM received telegram from wife: "No letter for five days. Is anything wrong? Answer immediately" – Didn't answer, as she will get my letters tonight –

July 18 . . . Evening heard arguments in Finlen case – Went to Jury at 8:30 – Bed 12 –

July 19 . . . Jury in Finlen case came into court at 10 AM – 10 for acquittal and 2 for manslaughter – discharged . . .

July 20 . . . Evening at theater – Mrs Jeffreys Lewis & Co in "La Belle Russe" – Very good – Slim house – Bed 1 –

July 21 – Cloudy, quiet & sultry – very threatening, but no rain – My 59th birthday – About town – Got letter from Cornelia, with birthday card – Evening Mrs Jeffreys-Lewis ended her engagement with "Chlotilde" – Very fine – About a $40 house – Match fight at Simon Fraser's saloon, between Matt Riehm's bull slut Susie, and Billy McKeighan's wildcat, caught in a trap in 6 mile canyon – I visited the cat in the PM – It is a young lynx – At the fight it was given no show – Its hind claws had all been pulled out and it was almost choked to death by a strap round its neck before the dog was let at it – It was not much of a *fight* – The dog chewed its flanks for about 15 minutes till it died – Dog not much hurt – The contest was a brutal fraud on the cat & its abettors – Bed at 1 –

Sunday, July 22 . . . Evening total eclipse of the moon about 10 oclock . . .

July 23 . . . A lodge of United Order of Honor instituted here last week, by Alexander Rothenstein, from San F – Insurance association – Very cheap – SF Chronicle makes it out a fraud – Over 100 members – Quite a stir –

July 26 . . . Big fire at 2 PM – Rosenbaum's furniture store on east side of C st short distance north of Taylor st – completely gutted and adjoining wooden buildings on D st badly scorched – Whole loss $15,000 or more – My new son-in-law, Ed Cochran, came from Reno this PM in a carriage, bringing advance people of a circus . . . We were together during evening about town . . .

July 27 . . . Morning I showed Ed the city, as he was never here before . . . At 3 PM he left for Reno – Sent bundle of dirty clothes, etc – Evening theater – Play of "She," by the Webster Brady Co – Very trashy – Miss Laura Biggar leading lady . . .

July 28 . . . Evening same company closed in "Lynwood, or the Blue & the Gray" . . .

Aug 1 through Sept 3 [AD on insurance business, about town & at theater. Of interest:]

Aug 1 . . . Trial of John L Black for murder of his brother Monday & Tuesday – Jury retired last evening, & at noon today discharged, unable to agree, standing 6 for acquittal, 5 for manslaughter and one for murder in the 2nd degree . . .

Aug 2 . . . By mail today I received an official letter from the Treasury Department, Washington, to the effect that my bill had been allowed . . .

Aug 6 . . . Evening theater – Rentz-Stanley Novelty & Burlesque Co – Big legged women, etc – "Adam and Eve" the principal play . . . Flags ½ mast all over town today in token of the death of Gen Phil Sheridan . . .

Aug 7 . . . My expected check arrived from Washington by today's mail – $250 . . . I got it cashed at the California Bank – Bought a check for $100 & enclosed in letter to wife, & another for $46.40 & enclosed it with statement of acct to Bankers & Merchants, which squares me in full – Settled lots of small bills, borrowed money, etc. & feel more easy . . .

Aug 11 . . . PM at Gold Hill – stockholders' meeting of Centennial – Letters read from the mine – Operations discussed – also the present condition of my stock, as I owe $191.80 – It is to be advertised tomorrow in list of delinquents – Was down to Lower Gold Hill . . .

Aug 14 . . . Wm Davis Pres't of the Exempts fell sick from a touch of heart disease this morning in Burke's shop on B st, where he works as a horse shoer – Chief Wm Pennison of the Fire Dept & myself visited him at his rooms in the Chapin House, South C st this evening – He is improving, but very sick – Nick Tredennick shot his son by accident with pistol last evening . . . Bad wound – Nick in jail – Works in Chollar mine . . .

Aug 18 . . . PM rode in buggy with Col Pat Keyes to the Keyes mine in 6 Mile Canyon – Took a look at ore on dump, works, etc, & home – Evening made ¼ column report of it in the *Enterprise* . . .

Aug 20 . . . Got an assay made at Dowling's of an average piece I selected from the Keyes ore dump, & it went: Gold $62.35; silver $176.00 . . .

Aug 22 . . . Telegraph news of drowning of J C Hampton & wife, et al, by a steamer collision in SF bay this morning, rec'd about 3 PM – We put up flag on Exempts hall at once, as he is Treasurer of the Association – The news created much sensation about town – The regular daily . . . train arrived exactly on time this morning, for the first time in 3 or 4 months . . . The trouble, however, has always been on the CP . . . short of rolling stock, locomotives etc, sufficient for the great and increasing overland traffic –

Aug 24 . . . P J Keyes of the Keyes mine has been occupying my attention the last few days doing newspaper work for him on promise of stock or money . . .

Aug 25 . . . Morning train brought Mrs Hampton's body – Received by the Knights Templar of which Mr H was one & taken to the Hamptons dwelling – Evening train brought my wife – She was at Carson today, visiting Mrs Gov Stevenson . . . Went to dinner at Fitzmier's, then to the Opera House – T J Farron's Comedy Co, in "A Soap Bubble" – Very funny – Good house . . .

Sunday, Aug 26 . . . Saw wife off on 7:20 . . . Met Bob Lindsay about 9 AM, just up from Reno, to attend Black trial tomorrow – At 2:30 PM we rode together in his buggy to funeral of Mrs Hampton, which took place from St Pauls church – Very big funeral – She was deposited in vault at cemetery for the present . . .

Aug 27 . . . P J Keyes signed promissory note or order in my favor for 300 shares Keyes M Co or $500 in coin – Bed 1 –

Aug 28 . . . Evening brought my big old banjo back from Al McCansland's saloon . . .

Aug 30 . . . PM showery . . . 10:30 AM was at Dist Court – Jury in Black murder case came in declaring they were impossible to agree & were discharged – New trial set for Oct 8 . . . The 2 women Evangelists on street this evening – Big crowd – Front of *Enterprise* office – Exhorting, singing, etc – Mrs Elizabeth R Wheaton, about 60, & Miss Mary J Moorman, about 45 – Americans – Claim to be "Prison Evangelists," Christianizing the world, etc, & no connection with Salvation Army – They visited the county jail this AM & prayed & sang with or to the prisoners, old J L Black, et al –

Aug 31 . . . Met Col Pat Keyes at noon & he went to my room, & got me to sketch off a statement from him to the Board of Directors of the Keyes Silver Mining Co, relative to the various Superintendencies & managements of the mine . . . A young man of name of Preusch, shot another named John Doyle about 7 PM at a blacksmith shop on North C st, north of Sutton Avenue, in breast and thigh – Not necessarily fatal, but very bad – Family matters . . . R M Daggett arrived from California last nights train – Come to engage in the political campaign –

Sept 1 . . . Busy most of day with Keyes' statement . . . Hamptons body found this morning floating near Vallejo st wharf, San Francisco . . .

Sunday, Sept 2 . . . I finished my Keyes job at noon & met him & we took it to D H Brown of the Evening Report to print . . .

Sept 3 . . . Evening at Opera House – Lew Morrison and Company in "A Dark Secret" – Big house – pretty good play – Had a big pond or tank of water in the stage, with boats, steam launch, swans, etc – Whole width of stage & 7 ft to 2½ ft deep – Heroine thrown into it to drown, but is rescued by brave lover, who dives boldly in . . .

Sept 4 – Clear, windy, a little cooler – The body of Hampton arrived on train at noon & was taken to Masonic Hall by delegation of Knights Templar . . . I was busy most of day at the Report office attending to the printing of my Keyes job – D W Baily the printer who set it up worked at it yesterday PM & started in again at 6 AM today – at 10 he had set all but about a dozen lines when he went down to the *Chronicle* office, got a razor & cut his throat – Taken over to the County Hospital at noon – Horrible gash 6 inches long, straight across, deep each side of windpipe, but razor too dull to sever the windpipe . . . Been drinking very heavily last week or two – Brown finished up the job, I read proof, etc – He printed about 40 copies – Keyes took most of them to SF tonight – Saw him off on train . . . Took a sheet 6 x 15 inches to print Keyes statement – solid piece –

Sept 5 . . . PM at 2:30 I was at Exempt Hall & subsequently joined in Hampton's funeral with about 20 other fellow members, H being a prominent member of the Association – Footed it out to the cemetery & back – One of the biggest funerals ever seen in Va – Evening Opera house – "Faust" – Very fine – Old Deacon Parkinson of the Carson Tribune sat with me . . .

Sunday, Sept 9 . . . AM I drafted a series of resolutions on the death of Hampton, & at 2 PM I introduced them at regular monthly meeting of the Exempts . . .

Sept 10 . . . Maud Harkin a young girl of 17 suicided with strychnine about noon at her parent's residence – Cause not stated – love & consequent trouble probably – I put up the Pioneer flag today in honor of Admission of California to the Union . . .

Sept 11 – Clear, sultry – 86° – George Warren, local of the Chronicle called on me at 7 AM, before I was up, & engaged me to take his place as he is sick, & going away to recruit – I went down & stood in – Took 2 PM 'bus to Gold Hill, borrowed $30 from John Huss & paid my present assessment $45.45 on Centennial, this being sale day – Evening cloudy, with some light showers – The hay fever has caught onto me the last 3 or 4 days – nose plugged, hoarse in throat, and eyes getting weak & watery & itchy – Bed at 1 – Helped localize on the Enterprise also this evening, read proof, etc – Got in good item on John Huss –

Sept 12 through 30 [AD working as *Chronicle* local, selling insurance, attending Lodge & Centennial meetings – Mostly very short entries, no detail – Of interest:]

Sept 13 . . . Evening at Opera House – Political Republican speaking commencement of campaign, by Bartine for Congress, and Murphy for Supreme Judge – Big crowd – Bed at 1 –

Sept 14 . . . After paper to press I visited Geo Warren who lies sick at lodging house on B st, with diarrhea and whiskey . . .

Sept 17 . . . Warren still sick abed – I visit him daily . . .

Sept 20 . . . Barney McGear shot in leg this morning – Bed 1 –

Sunday, Sept 23 . . . Received by mail today a package of . . . campaign documents for distribution from the American Protective Tariff League of California, headquarters, San F – W W Montague Pres't, J J Scoville Sec'y –

Sept 24 . . . Warren not yet able, although about town . . . Met Miss Fannie J Work, formerly of Austin, schoolmarm, now book agent – "Museum of Antiquities" – Introduced her at *Chronicle* office & gave her a puff –

Sept 26 – PM lively thunder shower – muddy – Evening called on widow of C B Gregory . . . relative to the insurance policy on his life . . .

Sept 28 . . . After paper I got off long 3 page letter to Company, about the Gregory matter – Bed 12 –

Sunday, Sept 30 . . . Evening about town politically – Bed at 12 –

Oct 1 – Variable and cool – 57° – Cold day & I got left – George Warren resuming his place on the *Chronicle* – Republican primaries today for County Convention – I was about town – Bed 1 –

Oct 2 . . . The Neil Warner Dramatic Co at Opera House this week – Played Othello last eve & "Time the Hour" this eve – I attended this eve – Very poor house . . .

Oct 3 . . . Got telegram from SF, saying that C M Gregory had been paid his half of his father's policy – $2500 – Evening I wrote a note to Mrs G to that effect – Rep caucus for tomorrow's convention – Bed 1 –

Oct 4 . . . Reported Republican County Convention for Chronicle – Dan De Quille & I walked up home together . . .

Oct 6 – Clear, cool & pleasant – Reported Dem County Convention today in Gold Hill, at Miners Union Hall – Through at 6 PM – Rode home on wagon – At 7 met wife at local train from Reno – Room – Took her to theater – Neil Warner troupe's last night – "Othello" – Not very good – poor house – We left at close of 2nd act – Went out to supper – Bed at 11 –

Sunday, Oct 7 – Same – slept late – rose at 10 √ – Took our meal at home today – canned corned beef & soft boiled eggs – fresh doughnuts, etc from the bakers – tea with milk – apples, etc – PM took walk about town – Train at 5:10 & saw her off for Reno – Evening at home writing etc – Bed 2 –

Oct 8 through 16 [AD about town a great deal, attends Lodge, writes to his brother Charley, to J M Dormer, Secretary of State of Nevada, and to his wife.]

Oct 17 – Clear, cool & pleasant – Bed 12 – Senator Stewart, from Washington, received & spoke in Carson last evening, & in Reno the evening before – R M Daggett took editorial charge of Enterprise 1st of this week for campaign – Paid by Rep Cent'l committee – Frosty night –

Oct 19 – Same – Hon J G Fair unexpectedly arrived from S.F., registered as a voter, paid visit to Con Va mine, etc, & left on PM train for SF again – May return to vote & may not – Evidently looking ahead politically – Hon G W Cassidy Dem aspirant for Congress spoke in Gold Hill last evening & was in town today – speaks here tomorrow night – I saw squaw "Maddie" & daughter on street today – from Austin last day or two – says Austin no good place now & have come to stay – Evening about town – Freezing cold – Bed 12 –

Oct 20 . . . Evening attended speaking of George W Cassidy . . . at Opera House – Bonfires – Big house – I on stage at reporter's desk – Good speech . . .

Oct 22 . . . Evening had Bob Evans up in my room, giving me lessons on the banjo – he restrung my small banjo with new steel wire strings – We played together, big & little banjos, flute etc – Bed at 1 –

Oct 23 . . . Evening at Opera House – Play "A Tin Soldier" – by Eugene Canfield, Jesse Jenkins, Chas F Raymond, Miss Kate Davis, Isabel Coe, Marie Cahill, et al – 13 in all – Very funny – good house . . .

Oct 24 . . . Senator Stewart addressed a crowded audience at Opera House this evening – I attended – Very satisfactory – Bonfires in streets – Bed at 1 –

Oct 25 . . . This morning's *Enterprise* has following:

> [Clip, *Enterprise* – At request of the fire chief the bonfires for the Cassidy rally were built with kerosene-soaked bricks rather than with the usual and more dangerous cordwood.]

Oct 26 . . . Evening at Opera House – Largest audience I ever saw there – between 1300 & 1400 [Twentieth-anniversary concert put on by the Ancient Order of United Workmen.]

Sunday, Oct 28 . . . Evening regular monthly meeting of the Pioneers . . . Made arrangements for supper or banquet celebration of Admission of Nevada into the Union, on the 31st – Bed at 1 –

Oct 29 – Clear & pleasant – AM about town – PM took train to Reno – Found folks all right, but typhoid fever next door – Dalton died of it day or 2 ago, & 16 yrs old daughter Ida nearly dead with it – J P Jones arrived on train from the East – Quite a number came down on train with me to receive him – He spoke at the new theater, McKissick's Opera House – crowded utmost capacity – Was there with wife – At 11 attended Jones Banquet at Depot Hotel – Grand affair – About 80 present – No ladies – Boned turkey, and champagne, etc – Toasts etc – I responded to "The Press" – Through at 1:35 – Home – Bed 2 –

Oct 30 – Cloudy – AM about town some on life ins. PM took off screen doors & stowed 'em away for the season – also put a slide window into pantry – Evening I & wife visited the Lindsays – Bed at 10 √ – Jones left for Gold Hill and Va by morning train –

Oct 31 – Same – Morning train to Va – PM about town, arranging for banquet [for Pacific Coast Pioneers] at Capitol Rotisserie . . . In honor of Nevada's admission into the Union – Nice layout – About 30 present [Jones invited but not able to attend – AD wrote and read a letter of excuse from him.]

Nov 3 – Stormy – AM cloudy – at noon a rain storm gradually set in, washing things nicely – middle of PM changed to snow & kept up its lick – Evening J P Jones addressed big audience at Opera House – cannon, bonfires, etc – I was on the stage with rest of them, & afterward was in International B st parlor with J P, his bro Sam, Daggett, & several others – had wine & lots of stories, etc – a very pleasant party – Bed 2 – Still snowing lightly – about 2 or 3 inches –

Sunday, Nov 4 – Cloudy & wintry – Fully 3 inches of snow on the ground this morning . . . PM Col Wm Sutherland gave a nice little reception at his new job printing office in the Black building . . . beer, whisky, sandwiches, cake, etc – Evening about town – Much political buzzing – Bed 2 – freezing hard – I bought from Jake Baumann, agent, on Friday evening last, a ticket in the big Louisiana Lottery for $1 and one in the little Louisiana Lottery for 50 cts . . . Am now waiting for the lightning to strike me –

Nov 6 . . . Cloudy but somewhat pleasant – General election – Very lively of course – Bands of music, etc but no bad fighting, etc – I ran with it all day & till past midnight – Bed at 1 – tired – all quiet . . . great crowds during evening in front of the Enterprise and Chronicle offices reading the bulletin returns from the East – special electric [lights] placed for the purpose – much excitement, whooping, yelling & betting –

Nov 8 – Clear & pleasant but cold in the shade – Plenty of lively election talk & discussion – The Republicans are conceded to have made a grand sweep and regain the Administration by large majorities everywhere – Even carry West Va, thus making the first break of the Solid South – Reps very jubilant and both parties astonished – J K Estep for County Commissioner, Dennis Kehoe, Justice of the Peace & Coroner, Virginia, and Frank McKenney, Constable, Gold Hill, the only Democrats elected in Storey County – also 2 Legislators – Bed at 2 –

Nov 9 through 14 [AD makes another long-range correction in his Comstock mining report, gets the Gregory insurance difficulty settled, Mrs G accepting the $2500 and surrendering the policy, does some more writing for the Keyes Mining Company, attends an Exempt meeting and sees "Virginius" at the Opera House.]

Nov 15 – Cloudy – PM at Gold Hill – sale day at Centennial – I got it postponed till Dec 10 – Evening about town – Light snowstorm for an hour or so – Got an item or two into Enterprise – Bed 2 – Capt Harry Symonds one of my best friends, Supt of the Como-Eureka, (old Monte Cristo) mine, Como, came to town today with his 2 horses & spring wagon on business – Got pretty drunk – I was with him a little & when in Gold Hill saw him leave for Como – Was thrown out & fatally hurt –

Nov 17 – Cloudy & stormy – AM about town – PM went down to see north extension of the Daney mine – rode down on buckboard with Bill Trudgen & Jim Hardwick, the other partner rode horseback – Took good look – Rain set in & had to get back – stopped at Silver City awhile – Va at 5 PM – Evening at Fred Burke's Arcade Saloon – turkey feast – played the banjo short time with Bob Evans & Josh Ely (guitar) – Bed at 2 – Snow 2 inch –

Nov 18 through Dec 2 [AD attends usual meetings, does some more writing for the Keyes Mining Company, is about town more than a little, and joins his family for Thanksgiving. Of interest:]

Nov 21 . . . PM I wrote a letter to Hon W M Stewart, San F, for Josephus Bath, about the Daney north extension discovery –

Nov 26 . . . Evening at Opera House – Big densely crowded house to see Haverly's Cleveland Minstrel & variety show – Bed at 2 – Had an excellent Japanese troupe – acrobats etc – with the show –

Nov 28 . . . Financiered for trip to Reno tomorrow – sent $5 to wife & a telegram that I was coming – Bought new hat for $3 . . .

Nov 29 . . . Took morning train for Reno . . . At 2 PM we all sat down to Thanksgiving dinner – Ed and Millie with us – 9 in all – Fine, big turkey & all the fixins – Mighty good dinner – Evening down town short time – Met Billy Henry & took him home – Home myself at 7 . . .

Nov 30 . . . PM down town on life insurance – Evening wife, Bessie & I visited Ed & Millie at their rooms, across the street . . .

Dec 1 . . . AM I boxed up the water pipe in the cellar against possible heavy frost this Winter – PM down town . . . This PM got shaved at Morris' barber shop – Old Jim Killeen, whom I followed in the chair walked off with my cane – I took his, and after dinner at Millie's, took it back to barber shop & left it – mine not returned, so I walked home without any – It is the cane Gallup, of Gold Hill gave me when I broke left knee cap several years ago – Have another at home to use –

Sunday, Dec 2 . . . AM at home patching up attic windows, etc – PM & evening down town . . .

Dec 3 – Clear & fine – Took morning train at 7:35 for Va – Hallen & Hart troupe on board, & an extra lot of passengers made cars pretty full – Through on time, arriving 10:20 – About town – Evening at theatre – Hallen & Hart's Musical farce comedy Co in "Later On" – queer, variety, no plot thing – Very amusing – good house – [three-line erasure – probably on bowel trouble] – Mrs Murtha Porteous formerly of this city leading lady in troupe – 6 other ladies – The Virginia *Evening Report* suspended publication this eve indefinitely – Published by D L Brown last 2 or 3 yrs, daily – During the past week, dynamo electric energy has been applied to running the new Nevada mill at the Chollar – partial success so far – 6 dynamos at Sutro Tunnel level –

Dec 4 through 31 [AD skirmishing on insurance & attending meetings, but obviously spending a great deal more time keeping up the holiday spirit – Of interest:]

Sunday, Dec 9 . . . PM regular meeting Exempts – annual election of officers – I elected President . . . Ran with the boys awhile . . . I am now President of the Society of Pacific Coast Pioneers and also of the Exempt Firemens Association – *Chief of all the old stiffs* –

Dec 13 . . . Evening attended Degree Lodge – Biggest crowd yet . . . 1st of new paraphernalia, costumes etc under the new work – Very grand & sublime . . .

Dec 17 . . . Sent 30 letters through the Postoffice – 20 to all the members of the State Senate & 10 to the Storey County members of the Assembly – on my candidacy for the Engrossing Clerkship of the Senate . . .

Dec 18 . . . 3 PM Dr Kirby's funeral – About 300, Societys etc on foot, 33 carriages etc – Dan De Quille (Wm Wright) & myself joined the procession, behind the Odd Fellows & ahead of the Chosen Friends & walked from Taylor st to Mill st & dropped out . . .

Dec 19 . . . Evening at theater – The Dalys in "Upside Down" – The funniest thing of all . . .

Dec 20 . . . PM at Gold Hill – Postponed sale of Centennial a month – Walked up – Bed at 2 –

Dec 22 . . . Wrote & sent three page letter to Hon J P Jones, Washington D.C. . . . Charley Legate died at Woodland Cal yesterday, of dropsy – Charley Rawson very sick & likely to die tonight . . .

Sunday, Dec 23 . . . Evening presided at meeting of the Pioneers . . . at club room in rear of Patterson's International Saloon . . . Elected Byron Isaac Turman of Dayton as a new member – he paying $10 entrance fee – He came from McLane County, Illinois, across the plains in 1850, when he was only seven years old, landing at Placerville, Cal . . .

Dec 24 . . . I put up the Pioneer flag at 9 AM . . . In token of funeral of Charley Legate, which took place this PM – I rode out & back with Bob Patterson, Doc Delavan, and S D Baker . . . Considerable snow fell during evening – Being Christmas Eve, the city looked gay & lively – Markets, fine showing of meats etc –

Dec 25 – Christmas Day – Morning 4 inches of snow on the ground – Cloudy and variable all day – melting & sloppy – Egg nog at all the saloons, and free lunches of turkeys, pigs, etc – Fred Burke at his Arcade saloon set up 200 lbs turkey with pigs on the side, cranberry sauce, celery, salad, etc, and Louis Hirschberg turned out free, six dozen champagne, opening & serving the same himself – Very festive day – At 3:25 took train for Reno – Arrived 6:30 – Found all right at home, except wife *alarmed at possibilities* – Children having circus over lots of fine & desirable presents from East & West – Bed at 9 –

Dec 26 . . . Occasional snow & rain during the day made it very muddy & sloppy – Reno the nastiest place imaginable . . . Ed and Millie breakfasted with us, having broken up housekeeping, as they go below tonight – He takes good employment at San Francisco . . . I & Bessie & Sam went to depot with them and saw them off about 7 . . .

Dec 27 . . . About town – Met Lieut Gov Davis, Bob Peacock et al – Also P K Faulds, special agent for the Bankers & Merchants operating in Reno – Long & interesting talk with him on Life Insurance – At barber shop found my cane . . . Visited the *Gazette* office, met Powning of the *Journal* . . . Home after trains had arrived and departed . . .

Dec 28 . . . Left on morning train – Carson at 9 – Cruised about town – Met A F Bartine, Congressman elect & had talk about my being

Supt of the Carson Mint . . . At 5 PM left for Va . . . About town some – Bed at 1 – foggy –

Sunday, Dec 30 . . . Evening wrote a 2 page letter to Hon W M Stewart, Washington D.C. similar to the one I wrote Jones relative to Carson Mint Superintendency . . .

Dec 31 . . . AM cold and regular "Po-go-nip" . . . prevailed . . . Was about town as usual – Sent off the letter to Stewart, also one to Lieut Gov H C Davis, Carson, about Engrossing Clerkship, and letter to wife as usual – Evening about town – Lots of turkey free lunches & at 12 guns & pistols popped lively to the music of the bell . . .

BOOK NO. *64*

Virginia City, Carson, Reno
Jan 1, 1889 – Dec 31, 1889

Jan 1, 1889 – Morning cloudy – Cleared off fine, clear by 10 AM –
Total eclipse of sun about noon for about an hour . . . Almost total –
only a little rim of ½ inch or so left of the sun . . . one bright star was
plainly visible in the sky (Venus) – Very peculiar light at time of greatest obscurity, some like electric light – Chickens got fooled & went to
roost – The eclipse totality was north of Reno – belt of 90 miles width –
Winnemucca in the total belt – Everybody out observing with smoked
glass etc – even the Piutes took particular interest – Evening at Opera
House – Lydia Thompson & her English Burlesque Company – Big leg
show but not so good as the Rentz-Santley Co in August last – About 40
women – Pretty good show & good house – Bed 1 – Coldest night yet –
17 above Zero –

Jan 4 . . . PM at Gold Hill – Crown Point Office – borrowed $100
from Sam Jones, giving my note therefor . . . Called on Jane Noble at
her room at Mrs Fraser's – She had bad cold, but recently recovered from
a light touch of paralysis in one side of face and head – looking older
than ever – Footed it back to Va, paying some of my bills as I came –
evening theater – "Chip O' the Old Block" by a variety company . . .

Jan 5 . . . Left on evening train for Carson – Quite a lot of legislators
and expectants on board – At 10:30 bed at Circe's Carson Exchange –

Sunday, Jan 6 . . . Did my best political skirmishing – Evening at 7,
Caucus – I got left . . .

Jan 7 – Clear & pleasant – Went on morning train to Va – diarrhea
bad – Wrote up Caucus, etc for the Va *Chronicle* – contracted to run the
Legislature for $15 per week – Borrowed $10 of the office and left on the

3:25 train – Loafed about Carson & wrote up 2nd letter to the Va Chronicle – Bed at 12 –

Jan 9 . . . No session of the Legislature today on account of funeral of State Treasurer Tufly's wife – Many from Va attended – 85 carriages . . .

Jan 10 . . . Got duplicate key today to room of Dovey, State Supt of Pub Instruction, in State Capitol & have good place for doing my writing . . . Got through at 10 – went to Opera House & saw last act in "The World Against Her," by the Grismer-Davies Dramatic Co – Very good house . . .

Jan 11 – Same – Work as usual – Succeeded in getting a pass from Yerington, over the railroad, for the session – Back to Virginia this evening – At theater short time & saw last act of "Forgiven" by the Grismer-Davies Co – good house – Bed at 1 – Letter in Carson Postoffice today told the following, from the *Memorial:*

> [A clipping reports the death of AD's eldest sister, Rebecca H Talbot, who was stricken on Forefathers' Day and died in Plymouth at age 74.]

Jan 12 . . . This AM mail rec'd bound copy of "Production of gold and silver in the United States – 1887 – Kimball" – 375 pages – from the Director of the Mint, Washington – It includes my report of the Comstock and my name is printed – "Alfred Doten" as the author of it –

Sunday, Jan 13 . . . PM, funeral of James Livingston, foreman of the Crown Point mine . . . Took place from Gold Hill & came up here to Masonic burial ground – Big funeral – Masons and Chosen Friends & Exempts on foot – 86 carriages besides the hearse – I walked with Exempts . . .

Jan 14 through March 13 [AD reports the Legislature for the *Virginia Chronicle,* then for both the *Chronicle* & the *Enterprise,* returns to Virginia City most week nights, spends many weekends in Reno – Mostly short entries, no detail – Of interest:]

Jan 17 . . . [AD learns of the death of John Black, from illness, in county jail.] He was 68 years old, native of Alabama, & killed his brother Sam, a year or two older, on the 4th of May last – Sleighs were out by 9 this evening – The first sleighing of the season –

Sunday, Jan 20 – Cloudy – PM adjourned regular meeting of the Exempts – Newly elected officers installed in good style and I took the gavel as President – A fine collation followed of cold meats baked beans and Boston brown bread cake, Swiss cheese, beer and other drinks – One of the best enjoyed feasts I ever saw – Evening about town – Home – Wrote up Exempts for both papers – Bed at 1 – George I Lammon was chosen Secretary in place of Charley Rawson deceased –

Jan 21 . . . Sent $15.45 to Gold Hill to pay for one of my Centennial certificates & will let the rest go at the sale today . . .

Jan 22 – Clear & pleasant – When I returned from Carson this evening I met Frank B Doten in the International Saloon – Has turned out his teams for the season & is going over to California for 2 or 3 weeks – We went to theater – M B Leavitt's "European Novelties" consisting of Marionettes, song, dance, acrobatic, Japanese jugglers, etc – Very good show, and bully house – We went & got oyster stew – I wrote up my Chronicle letter – Bed 4 –

Jan 25 – Same – morning train to Reno – all right there – Grand excursion of the Legislature today to Reno to visit & inspect State University, Fair Grounds of State Agricultural Society, State Insane Asylum – 2 carloads . . . They left Carson at 9:15, & returned at 5 PM – I did not follow them around, but wrote them up all the same – PM was about town awhile – Evening at home – wrote Chronicle – Bed at 2 – Very tired –

Jan 26 . . . PM our neighbor, Mrs Jamison took wife, Bessie & I out to ride in her carriage . . . Rode out to Lake's ranch on the Virginia road & about town some . . .

Sunday, Jan 27 . . . Morning train to Va . . . PM about town awhile – Saw 4 funerals pass down C st – One of them the younger son of Thomas C Johns, brother to Harry, my old Austin Comrade . . . I thought lots of little Tommy Johns . . .

Jan 28 . . . Second issue of *The Comstock Miner* this morning – Weekly 24 column paper – Old *Report* resurrected – M W Sills runs it – was formerly local of the Report –

Feb 1 . . . Attended Georgia Minstrels at the Opera House this evening – Good troupe – 16 of them, various shades of nigger people – all blacks – good house –

Feb 5 . . . Reported Legislature for both Carson & both Va papers today – Very busy – Bed 2 –

Feb 6 . . . Reported for both Enterprise and Chronicle – Bed 1 –

Feb 9 . . . Evening at Opera House short time – Camilla Urso – 25 years ago [she had a] big musical festival of one week, in S.F. – I was there – Had 5,000 audience then, but not 500 now – Bed 1 –

Sunday, Feb 10 . . . Wrote resolutions on death of Chas Rawson and James Livingston, and at 2 PM went to meeting of Exempts . . .

Feb 11 . . . Special election day called for to get up a State Lottery – I got up the returns for Enterprise – had to go to Gold Hill, & walk back at 12 with the returns, & then get the Va wards – 6 in all – Hard job but made it . . . [The lottery amendment was defeated.]

Feb 13 . . . Ormsby House Carson dosed with ½ doz cases smallpox, in family of the proprietor – Boarders, legislative etc all got out in a hurry after discovery last evening – Two daughters, one 21 and other 16 died this PM & evening – Great excitement – Evening I attended Billy Emerson and Katie Putnam Co at Pipers Opera House – Played "Old Curiosity Shop," with Billy Emerson between acts in his specialties . . . Got in Enterprise report – Wrote up the Chronicle, and bed at 3 . . .

Feb 15 – Light snow storm most of day – 7 or 8 inches this morning . . . Carson as usual . . . No increase in smallpox – scare subsiding – Reported both Va papers as usual . . . Splendid sleighing in Va & GH –

Feb 16 . . . Evening at Enterprise office – Read proof of communication written by M.S.D. (My wife) from Reno, commenting on some legislative points . . .

Sunday, Feb 17 . . . Staid in Va – Fixed up 60 of my Pioneer legislative pamphlets of 2 yrs ago for distribution among members . . .

Feb 18 . . . On return from Carson this evening had two cars crowded, special excursion to Pipers Opera House to see the great Conried English Opera Company . . . Opera was "The Kings Fool" – Very fine – big house – Bed 2 –

Feb 21 . . . George Keyser, the 13 yr old son of D Keyser of the Ormsby House, Carson, died at noon today of smallpox . . .

Feb 25 . . . Got in my bill for $250 for Pioneer Pamphlet – Introduced by Frank P Langan, in Assembly . . .

Feb 27 . . . Capt Avery developed . . . as a genuine case of smallpox about noon today, & is quarantined at his room on King street – He was bar keeper at the Ormsby House . . . My bill passed Committee on Claims all right at noon today . . .

Feb 28 . . . Gov Stevenson of Idaho arrived in Carson this morning & was in the Senate with his brother, our Gov –

March 1 . . . Today it was announced that Keyser and 3 more of his children had the disease, also a colored woman who has been doing washing for the Keysers . . .

March 4 . . . Capt Avery died at 5 PM yesterday, of smallpox – was buried before midnight from the pest house . . .

March 5 . . . Both Houses holding night sessions – I staid & reported . . . Bed at Arlington House at 1 –

March 7 . . . Last day of the session . . . My bill passed Senate this PM, only Emmitt of Reno voting against it – Hard days work and at it till 1 at night, as the session adjourned a little before midnight . . .

March 8 . . . Was in governors office most of day, getting up summary of the bills approved, for Chronicle – Evening train to Va – Got in last report for Enterprise . . .

March 9 . . . Got my summary of bills approved in PM Chronicle – Took PM train for Reno . . . I found Alfie sick with earache . . .

March 11 . . . Morning train to Carson – Had to pay regular passage $3 to Virginia . . . Found my bill signed by the Governor – Got it certified & fixed up, and put in hands of the State Controller . . .

March 13 . . . PM wrote and sent 3 page letter to Senator J P Jones . . . relative to Superintendency of the Carson Mint . . .

March 14 – Cloudy – variable – Morning heavy snowstorm – 4 or 5 inches – Took morning train to Carson, in response to Hallock's telegram – Got my $250 in gold & silver coin of the United States – Letter from G W McHardy of Austin rec'd asking me to send him a copy of the proceedings before Assembly Committee on Elections relative to the contested seat from Lander County for the Assembly, of Geo W McHardy vs Geo W Dickson – I worked 4 hours at it & finding I couldn't finish, got some of the original documents to take along – Back to Va on evening train – No snow below Mound House – Copious rains in Carson last night & this morning – Evening about town – Bed at 1 – cloudy –

March 15 . . . Sent $100 check to wife . . . Paid Joe Josephs $15 . . . which he advanced for my IOOF degrees about a year ago – Also paid Fredrick the jeweler $11, & got my porcelain sleeve buttons and pearl scarf pin out of soak –

Sunday, March 17 – Cloudy & threatening – Took morning train to Reno – Found Alfie still sick with apparently a slow fever – About noon I went to Depot Hotel & telephoned Dr Bishop of Insane Asylum to come up – He came with his wife – took out a tooth that was bothering Alfie, left medicine etc – Wore my porcelain sleeve buttons and pearl scarf pin for first time today – Found that Mary had received a letter from Sam, enclosing a check for $100 in settlement of sister Rebecca's death, he being the executor of her estate – About $300.00 more to come – He also sent a lot of silver spoons, etc, that she had, as my dividend of that class of her property – In consideration of the aforesaid check from Sam, wife paid me back $50 of the $100 sent her – Evening at home – Bed 10 – Heavy storm threatening – Last evening I was in the Chronicle press room & saw the edition running off – The press at its regular rate ran 36 copies a minute and on speeding it up ran 41 a minute – 24 a minute was the Gold Hill News, and 30 its utmost safe capacity – Enterprise runs about 17 –

March 18 . . . Forty years from home, as I left old Plymouth March 18, 1849 – Wore my maritime jewelry all day in honor of the occasion and we had a trout dinner – I packed and fixed up Millie's banjo & shipped it to her . . . Also sent the drum of Sammy's banjo to Kohler & Chase, San F, to have a new and better skin put to it . . . Bessie Tahoe Doten . . . has become a *woman* during the last three months – Will be 15 yrs old in July next – Taller than her mother now . . . Evening wife joined Rebekah Degree No 7, Daughters of Rebekah – Initiated . . .

March 19 through 30 [AD returns to Virginia City, completes & mails the legislative evidence to McHardy of Austin, returns the documents to the capitol, writes out a pension application for "Valentine Ritchie, the barber," orders steel banjo strings & new catheters, sends a life of Charles Sumner & a puzzle to Alfie and attends Lodge & Pioneer meetings. Also buys "a pair of eyeglasses and a pair of spectacles . . . $1 each," writes a long letter to his brother Sam, asks a pass renewal of Yerington, and receives one, takes in Janauschek, "the great tragic actress," in *Macbeth* and *Meg Merrilies*, an adaptation of *Guy Mannering*, pays a couple of small debts and visits Jane Noble.]

Sunday, March 31 – Clear & Springlike – warmest – Morning train to Reno – Found all right but Alfie – His fever appears to be broken, but inflammatory rheumatism supervenes, making his left wrist draw up & hand bend over in front, at about right angles – Very sick boy – Evening down town – Met E T George of Lewis, Lander Co, who is one of the 3 Regents of the State University, & put a flea in his ear, as to the additional teacher required for the State University – He positively agreed to stand in for my wife for that position & Fish, the Washoe Co Commissioner is all right, so it looks like a *dead thing* for her – Bed 10 –

April 5 . . . The other Carson Mint officers being nominated, I telegraphed Jones today: "Melter and Refiner, Alfred Doten" –

Sunday, April 7 . . . AM train to Reno – Found Alfie much better and able to be about, and out of doors – Evening I killed & dressed a young pullet for him, sent by a friend – Bed 9 –

April 8 . . . About town most of day, house hunting, as our landlord wants his house – PM Bessie, Sam & I went to Opera House – McNish, Ramza, & Arno's Minstrels, just arrived by evening train from the East – good house – good show . . .

April 13 – Cloudy, cool, blustering, dusty and disagreeable – PM and evening snow and hail squalls laid the dust – PM Bob Evans was with me at room, and we strung up Sammy's banjo and had some practice music together – Evening at Lodge and I did up the Warden business all right – Afterward was at Opera House awhile & saw greater part & windup of big glove contest to a finish between Jack Sullivan of Sacramento and James Morrissey of San F – Good house – Fought 3¼ hours, closing at 1:15 – Sullivan gave it up – Purse $250 – Bed 1:40 . . .

April 15 . . . Wrote letters to Stewart, Jones and Bartine, relative to Govt building, Carson, Superintendency . . .

April 16 . . . Wrote a letter from Sam Pidge, (her bro-in-law) to Mrs J C Williamson formerly Maggie Moore . . . Made item for tomorrows Enterprise regarding it –

[The article recalls "festive little Maggie Moore, whom most of us Comstockers remember in the prosperous past of Virginia theatricals . . . one of the finest and most popular of comedians." A letter from her to Sam Pidge, quoted in the clipping, says: "I am going to pay 'Frisco' a visit; then, 'God willing and the roads dry,' I am going to see dear old Virginia. I have never forgotten it and the happy times we have had there."]

April 17 . . . Letter from McHardy with Silver note for $2, & a promise of $3 more on 5th of next month – Got a round, pine curtain roller 5 ft long by 1¼ diameter at Frederick's for my walking staff as the Old Warden – Took PM train . . . for Reno – Found Alfie & the rest all right – getting ready to move – Evening at home – Wife out at Opera House rehearsing scholars for a school benefit . . .

April 18 . . . PM down town – interviewed Hoffman, the owner of our house & others – evening at home – got out my old fiddle & had some of it – Brought Sammy's banjo to him yesterday, so we had music together . . .

April 19 . . . Morning train to Va – Odd jobs . . .

April 20 . . . Evening, Lodge – Charley C Bowman and [blank] Cameron initiated – I did the Old Warden, for 1st time, and pretty successfully – Afterward went up to Opera House – Grand Reunion of Order of Chosen Friends – Supreme Councillor H H Morse of N York & C M Arnold, Grand Councillor of California present – Speaking, and literary exercises, & dance wind up . . .

April 21 through 29 [AD plays flute and violin with "Spanish" friend Jose Salinas, is about town, returns to Reno, where he does some house hunting, fixes Sammy's banjo, mends an old trunk for Bessie – Returns to Virginia City, where he is warden at Lodge, receives a letter from Wells Drury, interviews Evan Williams, superintendent of the Nevada Mill, presides at a Pioneer meeting at which the Masons propose unification of the cemeteries of the two fraternities – & notes that "a few prominent agitators" have been stirring around to have a celebration of the centennial of Washington's inauguration.]

April 30 – Clear & very pleasant – Centennial anniversary of the inauguration of Washington as President of these United States – Grand Celebration thereof throughout the US – Here the National and Emmet Guards and Uniform Rank, Knights of Pythias, paraded, also the Va & G Hill Fire Depts, Grand Army & Mexican Vets, some of the Miners Union, Young Mens Literary Institute & some other societies – Nearly 400 in all – Paraded the streets in grand procession, with 2 bands of music, 10 pieces each – City full of people from outside, even from Reno and Carson – City profusely decorated with flags, all same as 4th of July – Evening entertainment of Young Mens Institute at Opera House – Overtures, solos, quartettes, choruses, recitations, duets, etc – The theater was crowded as long as a live soul could get in – Wound up with a big dance – I put up the Pioneer flag on the flagstaff of the old Hall on B st this morning . . .

May 1 through 7 [AD returns to Reno & busies himself with insurance & negotiations for buying the house his family occupies.]

May 8 . . . On the house buying proposition today again – telegraphed to Sam for $500, & to Eunice for $300 . . .

May 9 . . . Telegram from Seth said: "Have no money outside of my business. E will write." Telegram from Sam said: "No telegraph of money from here. Three hundred by mail" – Was about town most of day on house negociation . . .

May 10 . . . Concluded negociation with Hoffman for house – Evening at home – Sam & I played fiddle & banjo together . . .

May 11 – Clear, warm & pleasant – Morning at RR depot – Saw Pete Jackson the famous colored pugilist – just arrived from California, on way to Virginia where he gives sparring exhibition tonight – he is very black – attracted much attention – I brought my house negociation to successful issue today – Had the $100 received from Sam March 17 and Bender of First National Bank, Reno, loaned me $300 on Sam's telegram, making $400 my share of Rebecca's estate – same bank also loaned me $200 on note from self and wife, indorsed by Justice of the Peace W H Young. Deposited the $600 in the Bank of Nevada, which loaned me $1000 on mortgage, so that at 2 PM the whole $1,600 was paid for our house which we live in and William Hoffman deposited the deed therefor, made from himself to my mother-in-law Sarah A Stoddard – Williams the County Recorder will have her sign note and mortgage on Monday – Evening at *home* – very tired – Bed at 9:30 in our own house –

Sunday, May 12 . . . At home most of day fixing up things again – unpacking, re-hanging pictures, etc . . .

May 13 . . . Worked hard splitting wood, repairing fence, hanging gate, etc . . . Mother signed note and mortgage this morning – Williams came with them & took them to record –

May 14 through 20 [AD receives the $300 from his brother Sam, and takes up his note, hears from sister Eunice that sister Lizzie will be passing through Reno with her friends, the Willards – goes to Virginia City, finds his $3.00 balance from McHardy and an insurance policy to Lew

Stevenson there, buys a new hat, coat & vest, on credit – returns to Reno to see Lizzie, who doesn't come, returns to Virginia City and is prevented from going back to Reno for two days by a bad attack of diarrhea, then goes down on Monday evening.]

May 21 . . . Barrett's and Sell's big circus and menagerie came down from Carson early this morning & performed here this PM & evening to big houses, out on Powning's Addition, west of Reno – We did not attend, but all hands were out and saw the trains unload . . . 100 wagons, chariots, vans, etc – over 200 horses, good stock – Made best street parade I have ever seen on this coast . . .

May 23 . . . Letter from Lizzie, Palace Hotel, San F, says she will pass here in morning & for us to meet her at depot . . .

May 24 – Clear & pleasant – Lizzie came on 8:30 AM train from California – She was accompanied by her friend Mr Willard – Wife & 4 children & myself were at depot & met her in good style – She & I recognized each other at once – Pleasant interview for 20 minutes, the time of stoppage of the train, & we saw her off – She is the only one of the Doten family who has ever seen this branch of the family – appeared much pleased with us all – I was about town most of day – Evening wife was at ball at Nevada Theater, given by the young gents and ladies of the State University – She went with Chrissie Andrews – Sam & I had fiddle & banjo together – Bed at 10 – I wrote up my Lizzie interview in the Reno Gazette this PM – Headed it "After Forty Years" –

May 25 . . . AM odd jobs about home, trimming the front locust trees, repairing the screen doors, etc – Had a good sweat – Took the 1:40 PM local train for Va . . . Went straight to Odd Fellows Hall . . . Stood in as Warden, in good style – Under "Good of the Order" we had a very pleasant time, good talk, etc from several – I made my best talk yet . . .

Sunday, May 26 . . . Letters from Wells Drury and Congressman Bartine . . . Evening, presided at meeting of P C Pioneers in club room of International saloon . . . Indorsed and ratified the action taken by the Committee . . . and the Directors . . . in conveying the right and title of the Society to its cemetery to the Masonic fraternity in this city, the Masons to keep the whole property fenced in with their own cemetery adjoining, & the whole to be used by both Societies . . . Big fire in Reno this evening – Depot Hotel, whole block opposite and all east destroyed –

May 27 . . . Took evening train to Reno – took look at ruins of fire – Bed at 10 – √ *1,000*

May 28 . . . Met Senator J P Jones as was leaving on Va train . . . Had just a word or two with him, & will see him later, in Gold Hill – PM busy at home putting up a set of shelves in wife's bedroom . . .

May 29 – Clear, very warm and pleasant – Found Sam Jones going up on the 8:30 AM train, so I rode up to Va & talked with him most of way to Carson – PM about town – Bed 11 – Sam just up from the Mariposa grant, 44,000 acres, recently purchased by J P and Sam Jones, owning one half, and J W Mackay, Hobart and Hayward, owning the other half –

May 30 . . . Memorial Day – Observed as usual – Procession out to Cemeteries & decorated graves, & had appropriate exercises at Opera House . . . Procession best of its size & kind I have yet seen in this city . . . PM rode with Lawson on his buckboard & 1 hoss to G.H. & interviewed Senator & Sam Jones – Evening about town – Bed 1 . . .

May 31 . . . Johnstown Penna destroyed by flood today . . . 12,000 to 15,000 lives lost – Greatest disaster in history of this country.

Sunday, June 2 – Same – PM, funeral of Frank Wallace, Grand Secretary I.O.O.F. in this State, who died last Friday of cancerous condition of the stomach and bowels – as shown by autopsy – Old timer, here, & old friend of mine – Band of 15 pieces; Patriarchs Militant 36; Order on foot, 200; carriages 23 – Finest floral pieces I ever saw, were borne on foot, one a grand bed of flowers representing top of grave 6 ft long – Many Odd Fellows from Reno, Carson, Dayton & elsewhere – Evening about town – Bed 12 – Tom Alchorn killed at Belcher works today –

June 3 – Clear & very warm – 86° – At noon I rode to Gold Hill on bus – got off at Senator Jones' residence – Had interview with him on something for me – could get nothing definite . . . rode back in a one horse cart with Con Ahern – Got a 50 ft string of garden hose at Gillig's for $7.50 and took it with me by 5:20 PM train to Reno – Found all well – Evening saw Jones off for SF by 10 o'clock train – Bed 11 –

June 4 through 11 [AD works in the yard & garden, returns to Virginia City for Lodge & Exempt meetings, notes that "Seattle W.T. burned yesterday PM, totally – loss over $15,000,000," that a Johnstown relief committee is collecting in Virginia City & that the Red Men are having a

Sunday picnic at Treadway's – Writes a letter to his brother Sam & returns to Reno – About town a good deal in both Reno & Virginia City.]

June 12 – Clear – 92° in PM – Clouded up & cooled off about 4 PM with breeze, but no rain – Renewed the $200 note at First National Bank for #60 [days] longer . . . with Justice W H Young's indorsement – Was about town – Sam Jones went up on morning train, with Haggin's private traveling car to take his old mother and members of his family to Santa Monica, Cal – It was so long and 3 big wheels on each side of the tracks – 12 in all – that it spread the track in rounding a curve just below the Eureka switch – When the evening local train went up two box cars became derailed at that point . . . & it took several hours to clear & repair the track – The down evening express train had to wait & didn't arrive at Reno till 2 next morning – Evening down town – Bed 11 –

June 13 . . . At 7 AM went down to RR station and visited Sam Jones in his car – Met and conversed with his old mother, 86 yrs old, blind . . . left on train for Va at 10 AM . . . about 5:30 the Uniform Rank K of P & Reno paraded streets . . . escorting the Grand Lodge, now in session . . . Masonic Grand Lodge been in session here the last day or two . . . Evening about town . . .

June 14 . . . Morning train to Carson – About town, State House etc – Home on evening train – Evening called on Johnny Noe, my old photo operative friend . . . Very sick with apparently consumption or something like it – Don't think can live much longer – Mother attending him . . .

June 17 . . . Evening attended show of the "Drummer Boy of Shiloh," . . . Mr A R Carrington – A sciopticon show and wearisome lecture about the battle of Shiloh – Did some wonderful drumming . . .

June 18 . . . About town as usual – Big toe of left foot very sore from ingrowing nail . . .

June 19 . . . Evening train to Reno . . . R M Daggett who has been here for 6 or 8 months past, left for his home in California last evening – Was in Reno today in affiliation and consultation with Tom Fitch . . .

June 20 . . . Limped about town some with sore toe – Paid first interest on my mortgage . . . Thatcher, Primrose & West's Minstrel Co from the East arrived . . . Street parade at noon – 30 on parade – white silk plug hats, etc – fine brass band, with a miraculous little drum major . . .

Evening I bummed into the show through John Piper, manager – Took
Sammy along – Very excellent – Big house . . .

June 22 . . . Back to Va by morning train . . . PM I wrote letter to
Hon W M Stewart, San F. . . . Evening at my Lodge and did the old
Warden in 1st class style – much commended . . .

Sunday, June 23 . . . PM wrote & mailed a letter to J P Jones, San F –
about my appointment . . . Mrs Matilda Dam died a few days ago . . .
at Oakland Cal, aged 72 – She used to be Mrs Lynch of the Gold Hill
News, when I was on it –

June 28 . . . Morning train for Reno – At Carson I had short talk with
Sam Wright the new Supt of Mint – No show for me there . . . Evening
Sammy and I had fiddle & banjo concert on the front porch . . .

July 1 . . . Morning train to Carson – Was about town all day – Saw &
talked with Senator Stewart – accomplished nothing – Back to Reno . . .
My railroad pass expired . . .

July 3 . . . PM went to Chinatown with Sam & Alf & bought $1 worth
of fire crackers . . . Evening took Sam & Alf to theater – Ben Cotton
company – Played "Irma the Waif" – Very excellent . . .

July 4 – Clear & hot – 98° – Big celebration – Fine procession, fire dept,
trades, Cars of State . . . Novel wagon machine – 1st I ever saw – Used
for hauling logs by the Verdi Lumber Co – Afterward the "Horribles"
paraded – Town decorated with flags, etc, & full of people – I put up all
our flags on our house porch, & children had lots of fun with fire crackers
etc – Mrs Andrews & daughter Crissy & Mrs Powell dined with us – Evening good fireworks in public square, front of theater – McKissicks Opera
House . . . I went with the children . . .

July 5 through 20 [AD hangs about the depot waiting for a chance to
see Jones, does see Mackay, goes to a big fire at 2nd & Sierra streets, notes
that there is "much interest" in the Sullivan-Kilrain fight, won by Sullivan in 75 rounds – writes a column called "Riverside Reflections" for the
Enterprise, which is reprinted in the *Nevada State Journal* in Reno –
Returns to Virginia City, where he writes two more "Riverside Reflections" & an article about the third issue of the *Enterprise,* published at
Genoa on Jan 1, 1859, notes that the Nevada Mill has shut down &
attends Lodge & a picnic of the Chosen Friends – "Not a very sociable

sort of a crowd . . . I didn't spend a cent – got two or three drinks &
not a morsel to eat."]

["Riverside Reflections" clip, *Enterprise,* July 9:] Both Reno and Carson have taken the lead of the Comstock, recently, in the matter of public
conflagrations. It has been years since a destructive fire has visited either
Virginia or Gold Hill, but within a month or so whole blocks of buildings
have burned here and in the Capital city. When the big Depot Hotel was
blazing good and the neighboring blocks were subsiding into smoldering
ruins, here came a gallant company of Carson firemen to the rescue as
fast as an extremely nimble locomotive could propel them, and they
landed their fine steamer, ready for instant action, right in the midst of
the fray, assisting very effectively in checking the further progress of the
flames and saving much valuable property. Those Carson boys made a
very bright mark for themselves in the estimation of the appreciation of
the riverside population. The other night, when the Corbett block burned
in Carson, Reno firemen would have willingly responded had they been
called upon or needed.

Last Friday night another block of wooden buildings, right in the heart
of Reno, burned to ashes. Brick buildings on one side and wide streets on
the other favored the hemming in of the fire, and fortunately there was no
wind. The bucket brigade covered itself with glory on this occasion, pre-
venting several buildings already smoking with intense heat from breaking
in flames. The steamers were somewhat slow in getting to work, but did
splendidly when they got into effective action.

All three of these fires are alleged to have been created by incendiaries,
and with good reasons therefor, human cussedness and insurance being
mentioned among the inducing motives. Of course much household, mercantile and other property was destroyed, yet much was covered by insurance, and the actual loss in buildings was more extensive than real, as
many of them, especially in the last two fires mentioned, were dilapidated
old shanties of small value, which will be replaced by better buildings,
more in accord with present and future progressional requirements. The
Pollard House, destroyed at the Depot Hotel fire, is being rebuilt of brick,
three stories high, and Cooper's Pioneer Hotel will soon make a good
showing of brick construction above its foundations. Other buildings are
being restored in brick, and the whole will soon be rebuilt, in far better
style than ever. No move is yet being made toward reconstructing the
Depot Hotel, there appearing to be some hitch or disagreement in the
matter. A union depot, inclosing the tracks, like that at Sacramento, and
also locating it further west, are hinted at, but nobody seems to know.

SOMETHING NEEDED.

Meanwhile, Reno sadly needs a properly organized, encouraged and supported fire department. She possesses one excellent "La France" steam
fire engine, procured from the East; also that formerly belonging to Monumental No. 6, on the Divide, the most powerful in the State, and as good

as any on the Pacific Coast. With six or eight well experienced firemen properly organized as a paid fire department like we have in Virginia, with suitable horses, these machines could be playing effective streams on a fire in one-fourth the time it takes now—in fact, either of these recent fires might then have been knocked out at the very commencement. A further improvement would be adequate sized water pipes or fire mains, separate from the public domestic supply, with suitable hydrants. A few more such fires will work the Renoites up to a true conception of the economy of these propositions.

GOOD WATER.

Reno used to be supplied with the meanest water in Nevada, all on account of the sawdust nuisance in the Truckee river, but the Water Company, at the expenditure of much labor, time and expense finally succeeded in proper filtering arrangements, and now the citizens are plentifully supplied with good water through the pipes, as are the people of the Comstock.

Sunday, July 21 – Clear & pleasant – 85° – John S Noe, my old photographer friend died at 2 AM, at his home on E st – Belongs to my Lodge – Death from continued, long practiced overindulgence in alcoholic drinks – alcoholism – a real disease – Plain case – I became 60 years of age this day – Celebrated it by being about town some, after 10 AM, writing some newspaper items in the PM, and going to theater in the evening – "Lilly Clays Collossal Gaiety Company" – about ⅓ of a house – Very good performance indeed – 14 women – Scenic 1st part – "Beauty in Dreamland," etc – Interlude of acrobats, dances, songs, etc, Hilton the wonderful contortionist, Burlesque "Robinson Crusoe" – negro act, etc, & concluding with grand Amazonian march – Many ladies present – Most talented troupe of choice shaped ladies I ever saw – They left for Reno & the East by special train at midnight – Met Jim Garrity & his friend Dempsey, both of the California pan mill, just off shift, and was with them for an hour on street & at Dempsey's room, corner of Sutton Avenue and C st – Went & took supper with Dempsey, at Tom Heffron's American Rotisserie – Bed at 2 – 60 years old and poorer financially than I ever was in all my life – Weight 196 pounds –

July 22 . . . Letter rec'd from J L Stevenson . . . for me to come down to starting up of electric plant at Insane Asylum Wednesday or Thursday – Replied to it, also wrote letter to Yerington to get pass renewed . . . Evening wrote up another "Riverside Reflections" . . . also wrote up good obituary notice of Johnny Noe . . .

July 23 . . . Tom Clark who has been engineer for the regular mail, passenger & express train for many years past, died at Rubicon Springs, near Lake Tahoe last evening, where he went for health – Spinal disease, diarrhea, no stomach, etc – Whisky principally – Johnny Noe's funeral this PM from Odd Fellows Hall – Not very well attended . . .

July 24 . . . AM mended up & fixed up – borrowed $10 from Joe Guggenheim and took 5:20 train for Reno – Big distress all the way from a sort of cramp colic from an *overdose* of peppermint, taken this morning for benefit of loose bowels . . . Dr C L Mullen . . . took me to Pinniger's drugstore & got me a dose – 2 teaspoonfulls paregoric, a dash of Jamaica ginger in 1 ounce good brandy – It did relieve me . . . in 15 minutes as the Dr said it would – Before I reached Asylum, however, was struck with violent reactionary chill which lasted over an hour, & I was all right again . . . Wife there with the rest of the big crowd . . . 1st plant of the kind on Pacific Coast – I took look at the storage batteries & all else, leaving dancing, supper etc to run itself . . .

July 25 . . . Was at Lew (J L) Stevenson's office awhile – Met there Frederick Reckenzaun, the electrician of the Pacific Electrical Storage Co, & got all information I could from him . . . Evening at home – slept couple of hours in the big chair – Commenced at 10 to write it up for the *Enterprise* – Rather difficult bit of writing – Had to study up some also – All night job as I expected . . .

July 26 – Clear & hotter – 96 in shade . . . Finished my writing about 9 AM . . . Was down town to see Lew Stevenson . . . Paid me $10 . . .

July 27 . . . Left on 1:45 train for Va . . . Got my MSS into Enterprise . . .

Sunday, July 28 . . . My article makes nearly 2 columns in Enterprise today . . .

ELECTRIC PROGRESSION.

A numerous party of representative citizens were present Wednesday evening at the State Insane Asylum, to witness the starting into practical operation of the large electrical storage plant just completed for lighting that institution. It being something new in that line, and the first established on the Pacific Coast, beyond the small plant exhibited in San Francisco, much interest naturally attaches to its success, not only here, but everywhere else, and the gratifying result last evening was fully up to the requirements and what was expected. . . .

THE LIGHTING CONTRACT.

A few weeks ago the Board of Directors entered into a contract . . . to procure and establish this plant at a cost not to exceed $6,000. A capacity of 70 incandescent lights of 16 candle-power each was called for,

100 lamps to be placed in circuit and distributed throughout the Asylum building, residence, laundry, barns, etc. Any portion of the whole number can thus be used, as may be desired, to the extent of the 70 light capacity. . . .   THE MOTIVE POWER.

The steam engine is eight horse-power, with boiler sufficient for double that capacity, and is placed at the bank of the river, 1,000 feet east from the Asylum. The dynamo, which is an ordinary shunt-wound incandescent light machine, capable of either running the lights direct or by charging the storage batteries, is situated near it, also the turbine water wheel. This arrangement is in order that the power derived from the Truckee river may be utilized during the time the water is sufficient, and when it is not, as at the present time, the steam engine is brought into requisition, or if the conditions are favorable both water and steam power may be used together, dividing the work. Coal is burned under the boiler, and the energy evolved through heat and steam moves the engine and drives the dynamo, which in turn converts the mechanical energy applied to its pulley into electrical energy. Thence the current is transmitted by wire to   THE STORAGE BATTERIES.

These wonderful arrangements are situated in the basement of the Asylum, and consist of two sets, of 28 cells each, placed upon convenient tables. These cells or jars are square in form and are of heavy plate glass, quarter of an inch thick, placed in double rows, like a lot of coal oil cans. . . . Each of these cells contains a series or electric "pile" of prepared lead plates immersed in diluted sulphuric acid—20 per cent. acid, the rest water. . . . The cells are all electrically connected, forming the two batteries of 28 each, or 56 in all, each battery capable of delivering a current of 35 amperes at 50 to 56 volts pressure. . . . These storage batteries are, in an electric machine, what a gas holder is to a gas plant; they permit of using light during any or all hours of the twenty-four without necessitating the running of the dynamo or generator of the supply. . . . The entire system is a low pressure one, and a baby may handle the wires or any other metallic portions and attachments with perfect impunity—in fact, scarcely the least shock is perceptible.

THE ELECTRIC LIGHT.

The lamps used are the Sawyer-Mann incandescent lamp, very similar to but an improvement upon Edison's. All the necessary and convenient switches, instruments and controlling devices are provided, and when light is required the lamps are made to glow instantly by merely turning a little key, when any number required within the circuit may thus be used. The current sent from the storage battery has to overcome in these lamps the high resistance of the wire-loop-like carbon filament, in doing which the carbon is turned to a white heat, producing the brilliant white light desired. The combustion or destruction of these filaments is prevented by the vacuum within the pear-shaped lamp bulbs. The entire 100 lamps of the Asylum were lighted at one time Wednesday night, showing the capacity of the plant. . . .

Electric lamps for private dwellings have never been obtainable away from connection with some central system until this storage discovery and application, and a ten horse-power engine would waste its energy at times in running one lamp. By this system the entire ability of any steam engine can be utilized to the most unlimited advantage, storing up all its own power in transmitted energy, to be drawn upon at leisure; in fact, drawing from the electric storage battery is the same as drawing from a tank of kerosene—one lamp or forty can be supplied with the same facility. It is merely electricity "on tap" and both demand and supply easily governed and most economically regulated. It is the only current that will not fluctuate in the lighting of steamers, railroad cars, etc., and which can be depended upon for absolute safety from conflagration in case of accident, and possesses many other advantages besides what are here enumerated. The plant at the Asylum is believed to be a measure of advantageous economy, as being cheaper than gas and furnishing a far better light. It is a bold step forward in the progress of electric lighting, and Nevada takes the lead of the Pacific Coast therein. The system is plain and simple enough when one understands it, and all visiting and inspecting this plant cannot fail to be interested, instructed and profited in so doing.

July 29 . . . About the hottest yet – C street average thermometer made it about 94° – Con Va and Ophir offices 100 & over . . . PM about town – Evening at Enterprise office fixing up report of Pioneer meeting . . .

July 30 . . . Busy at room most of day fixing up journal clippings from file, etc – PM & evening downtown . . .

July 31 . . . Evening met brother to Jack Harris of Gold Hill, whom I insured a year ago for $2,000 – Said he had died at 7 oclock this evening . . . of a bad cold, and general letting down – lungs used up, etc – Bed at 2 . . .

Aug 1 – Clear & from 86 to 90 deg in shade . . . AM copied off my "Educational Nevada," University article & put it in mail with letter to wife – PM about town – Evening ditto . . .

Aug 3 . . . PM wrote & sent letter to Lew Stevenson, relative to bill Enterprise $30 for printing my electric article, $20, and 100 copies paper, $10 – Also letter to Wm Glassman Real estate ag't, Salt Lake City relative to a mutual endowment or dividend insurance Co, such as I propose getting up – Evening attended my Lodge – Then I went to Opera House –

"Old Jed Prouty" – New England Yankee Comedy Co . . . Richard Golden as "Jed" – Very good company & play . . .

Sunday, Aug 4 . . . Evening at Opera House – J B Polk and Comedy Co in "Mixed Pickles" – Poor play, $30 house, and no extra good acting – I could hardly keep awake . . .

Aug 5 . . . Evening theater – same Co in "The Silent Partner" – Very good indeed . . .

Aug 6 . . . AM met R K Allen on C st – We had much Life Insurance talk & compared notes etc . . . Got short note from Yerington today, enclosing free pass for three months . . . Letter read: ". . . My Dear Sir – Altho the grass is indeed very short with us I have concluded to renew your pass as you will note from enclosed. Hoping it will be a source of both pleasure and profit to you, I remain Truly Yours, H M Yerington" . . .

Aug 8 . . . Evening at Degree Lodge – All three degrees conferred to accommodate 3 from Carson . . . Through at 11 – Collation in front hall of sandwiches, salads, melons, etc, hot coffee, & other beverages & cigars – Wrote it for *Enterprise* –

Aug 10 . . . Went on Caledonian excursion train to Carson – Was on grounds all day . . . Wrote up, read proof – Bed at 2:30, very tired –

Sunday, Aug 11 . . . Wrote resolutions for Exempt Society on death of Wood Knight – Regular meeting of Exempts at 2 PM – I presided – Resolutions adopted . . .

Aug 12 . . . Evening Theater – single night engagement of Robert Mantell & good dramatic Co in the 5 act romantic drama of "Monbars" – Very good play & good house – About 7 oclock fire alarm from little girl of Crockwell the photographer running out on B street covered with flames from coal oil explosion –

[Clips from both *Enterprise* and *Virginia Chronicle* – Ten-year-old Ada Crockwell was burned to death by an explosion of some coal oil which had accidentally been left on a stove – Three others badly burned.]

Aug 13 through 17 [AD reports a meeting of the State Board of Reclamation and Internal Improvement in Carson, settles the Harris insurance claim, writes resolution on death of John Noe for the Lodge, corresponds with Glassman of Salt Lake on the Crockwell tragedy, which has scotched his new insurance company, apparently Crockwell's original idea, and with New York agents wanting an evaluation of the Chase ranch on Walker River.]

Sunday, Aug 18 – Clear & cooler – 80° – AM busy at room, patching, mending, etc – also patched carpet – PM about town – Evening copied & fixed up some visionary sketches for W P Bennett of Gold Hill – that he has written from time to time – Bed 2 – coolest night of season – About 7 oclock last evening Steve Gillis, printer in Chronicle office had a row with George Warren local editor of that paper on account of an article he put in a week ago about the "Brown-Sequard Elixir," making Steve the subject of ridicule – Steve beat Warren about the head with a loaded cane, cutting his forehead, blackening his eye & breaking the cane – This was in front of the office – This morning they met again inside the office & Steve presented a Colts revolver saying, "shall it be peace or war?" but further trouble was avoided for the present –

Aug 19 . . . Evening benefit to the Crockwell family – Volunteers in songs, recitations, etc, & a social dance – I attended – Very good – Big house –

Aug 21 . . . Letter received by Eckley & shown to me about canceling the policy of P H Ford – $5,000 on acc't of drunkenness – Bed 12 –

Aug 22 – Clear & pleasant – Eckley & I got Ford into conference at California Bank – Ford felt very bad about his policy, & we could do nothing at present but tender the amount of assessments he has paid in, amounting to [blank] – I wrote & sent letter to the Co this evening's mail asking them to rescind their action – Evening about town – Bed 2 – The Senatorial Irrigation Committee with Senator Stewart as Chairman arrived in Carson today & came up & went back on special train – Senator Jones also along – They arrived at 5 PM, took dinner at Chollar office, & left on return at 8 – Will go over to Lake Tahoe tomorrow morning – About 10 AM today Lieut Gov H C Davis fell dead from heart disease in his front yard at Carson, while running a lawn mower – 42 yrs of age – Evan Williams, President Pro Tem of the Senate, succeeds him as Lieut Gov . . .

Aug 23 through Oct 3 [AD becomes, all at once, much busier with his insurance again, and it and Lodge & Exempt meetings make up greater part of entries – Of additional interest:]

Aug 23 . . . Copied & finished up those Visionary Sketches for W P Bennett – 14 pages foolscap . . . After Lodge was at room of Marco

Medin on floor above mine, in front room – Bob Evans, the banjo player, Senor Gonzalez, violin, Frank Mayer and Marco Medin, guitars, and I on big banjo – Bully concert . . .

Aug 27 . . . Morning train to Carson – About town – PM attended funeral of Lt Gov Davis – Back on evening train – Wrote up – read proof etc – Bed 2 –

Aug 30 . . . Morning train to Reno . . . Found all right home – school recommenced Monday, with wife as *Assistant Principal* – My Kirby squashes doing finely – some big ones growing – Worked awhile fixing up things in front yard – Evening down town with wife – Bed 9:30 –

Sunday, Sept 1 [Va City] . . . Benny Jenkins shot his wife about 5 PM yesterday at their residence on A street near Sutton Avenue – Put 6 bullets into her from his revolver – Jealousy – She will probably die – The shots seem to have been from behind – He has been working in the Chollar mine till recently – Been drinking some, but did not seem drunk on this occasion – Is said to have had cause for jealousy, and they have quarreled considerably of late –

Sept 2 . . . Took evening express train as far as Mound House, expecting to find Senator Jones on board . . . Didnt, so I returned on local . . . Went to Opera House – Edward Harrington and good company in "Old Lavender" – Good big house – Nearly 100 came in special train from Carson . . . Very good play . . . Benny Jenkins' wife died at 5:20 this PM – One bullet having penetrated the bladder was the immediate cause of death – He is still in jail, of course –

Sept 3 . . . Took evening train for Reno – Senator Jones got aboard at Gold Hill, with Hamilton, Gosham & other relatives & friends for San F – Got a small chance to talk with him . . .

Sept 4 . . . Returned on AM train to Va . . .

Sept 5 . . . Funeral of Mrs Jenkins and J P Flanningham this PM – Both buried here – He died in Gold Hill Tuesday of diarrhea and typhoid fever – Good man & friend – Evening I got in a batch of items, entitled "Along the Railroad" . . .

Sept 7 . . . Went with excursion train to Carson & back – Evening wrote up picnic . . .

Sept 9 . . . Met W P Bennett – took him to my room & delivered him his "Visionary Impressions" job – Much pleased with it – Paid me $5 on acc't . . . Rose Coghlan and dramatic Co in play of "Jocelyn," at Opera House –

Sept 10 . . . Evening at theater – Karl Gardner, German Comedian & singer with company in "Fatherland" . . .

Sept 12 . . . Saw last act of "Karl the Peddler" – with Chas A Gardner in the leading role – His third night, with 3 slim houses, this the poorest of all – Dont amount to much, the whole crowd . . . Got postal card from wife this AM saying . . . Millie had a baby on Monday, a daughter – She & baby doing well – So I suppose I may be considered a step grandfather –

Sept 13 . . . Evening at Enterprise – Got in "Along the Railroad" notes, nearly a column, & other items . . . No Western mail today – Big bridge burned yesterday near Cascade on the CP . . .

Sept 14 . . . Rewrote an article from wife on the Reno public schools and State University – Took it to *Enterprise* . . . Bob Lindsay to father it . . . waited till delayed mail train arrived from Reno at 1:45 AM – Went down & got items . . . Work actively commenced rebuilding the burned bridge – No freight to be transferred across the chasm . . .

[The *Enterprise* of the 15th prints the school piece, signed "Diogenes," as the lead editorial – "Diogenes" complains it is "a notorious fact" that:] Whenever a scholar becomes dissatisfied with the teacher or fails of promotion from one grade to another [in the Reno public schools] because of his own shortcomings, he is admitted to the University, received in fact with open arms, the idea of numbers—quantity, not quality—seeming to predominate there. A farce of an examination is gone through with, but the applicant is never refused admittance.

Sept 16 . . . Took train to Reno . . . Evening the Reno Guard out on drill – Nearly 40 – full uniform – Reviewed by Brig Gen Booton – Bed 10 – Sammy commenced as messenger boy for the W U Telegraph Co today – $20 per month – 14 yrs old in December next –

Sept 17 . . . Evening, at 6, the first through passenger train across the repaired bridge arrived . . . Blockade raised and country safe . . .

Sept 19 . . . Very smoky & hazy . . . morning train to Carson . . . About town on life insurance, etc . . . Back to Reno . . . Saw more butterflies on the streets of Carson today than I ever before saw – They were of the migratory kind, perhaps driven out by the forest fires of the California slope of the Sierra – Were in Cisco and about Lake Tahoe last two days –

> [The *Enterprise* notes that "neither the Regents nor Faculty of the State University" seem to have taken notice of "Diogenes," but prints a letter from "Comet" in Hawthorne who calls the editorial "an unjust presentation of a man piqued by a professional jealousy." – Comet reassures everyone that admission standards are established and observed, and says] "Diogenes" has been fighting the University from purely personal motives . . . and [by his diatribe] has sent to California schools forty Nevada students. . . . The management of the State University is now, and ever has been, above reproach.

Sept 20 . . . AM to Carson . . . Butterflies all gone – eastward, said to be . . .

Sunday, Sept 22 – Clear, cool & pleasant – About 3 PM went on the street, & down town – At 8 PM went with a party to Chollar shaft, & down among the Dynamos on the 1600 level & through Sutro Tunnel level to C&C shaft, & to Combination shaft, & to the new Yellow Jacket shaft, Gold Hill – Nearly 3 miles in all – Gold Hill section d––d hot – Sweated 11 lbs apiece – Back to town at 12 – Over 3 hours underground – Bed at 2 – tired –

Sept 23 . . . Evening wrote more "Along the Railroad," Pioneer meeting report, and second "Diogenes" communication for *Enterprise* . . . also wrote up our Sunday evening trip . . . Read proof . . . Bed at 4 – very tired –

> ["Diogenes" feels that "Comet"] evidently must have willfully allowed the overpowering weight of some unexplained personal animosity to sit upon and addle his callow brains . . . "Diogenes" is no verdant carpet-bagging pedagogue, but a long-time, prominently well-known, responsible married citizen and taxpayer of Reno. . . . Go to, "Comet;" bag both thy head and tail. . . . [The *Enterprise* forestalls continuation of the contest by saying "we are strongly of the opinion that short communications, over actual names, will be much more satisfactory and convincing to the public. No anonymous letters . . . will get the slightest attention."]

Sept 24 . . . Complimentary season ticket rec'd today for self & wife to State Fair . . .

Sept 27 . . . Indian Summer weather – PM walked to Gold Hill & presided at Trustees meeting at Centennial Co – Henry Richards, the Supt of it was there, just arrived from Nevada City . . . Agreed to

resume work at the mine . . . to hold the claim from being jumped –
Levied a 3 cent assessment . . .

Sept 28 . . . PM was a witness in Justice Kehoe's court in case of
O'Brien, or "Butt Murphy," for . . . fisticuffing with another hoodlum
on the sidewalk, front of the US Saloon . . . Fined $10 . . .

Sept 30 . . . On Friday last when on my way to the Hill I stopped at
the Divide scales & saw the big team of grays weighed, belonging to one
of the Fire Dept hose carts, both weighed in the same notch – exactly
1,527½ lbs each –

Oct 4 – Clear & very pleasant – Morning train to Reno – All right – PM
took Bessie out to race track & grounds of State Fair on a 'bus – sent her
up on grand stand, while I slopped about looking at the races, gambling,
drinking, etc – Great big crowd – biggest Reno ever saw on such occasion – Fully 5,000 people on the grounds – I rode down on the local
train, on which was quite a number, but on the excursion train which followed at about 10 there was 521 from Va & GH – Ten coaches & 7 flats
left Carson en route, carrying over 1,000 – Evening I was at the Court
House & heard address of Frank G Newlands, before State Agricultural
Society on irrigation, etc – He is an aspirant for U.S. Senator – Pretty
good address – ½ an audience – Went to the Pavilion, & saw the big
showing of vegetables, manufactures etc – Bed 12 √ *

Oct 5 – Same – About noon rode out to Fair grounds with Bob Lindsay
& wife & my wife in their carriage – Saw ladies' riding & racing tournament, they picking off rings with poles, going around the track on mile
dash, etc – race between a man and a horse 40 yards & around a stake –
horse winner by a foot or so – Indian pony race, mile dash, 29 entries, &
regular running & trotting races – Very good attendance – Rode in with
Capt Joe White of Gold Hill on cart behind his black mule Jack, in gay
style at 6 PM – Evening took Bessie to Opera House – Margaret Mather
and her dramatic Co in Romeo & Juliet – Densely crowded – all that
could get in – Very good – Bed at 12 –

Sunday, Oct 6 – PM cloudy & cooler – Morning train to Va – Louis
Hirschberg of the Crystal, sold out to Con Ahern last Thursday – Louis
had the liquor stand privilege at the Fair, & made from $1,500 to $2,000
out of it – PM about town – Evening at Opera House – Isabel Morris and
dramatic Co in "Gwynne's Oath" – Very poor house – Bed at 1 – Nose
still bothered & eyes sore, but recovering from my annual hay fever –

Oct 7 – Stormy – Took morning local train to Carson . . . Cloudy, windy, threatening and fearfully dusty – Bad day for commencement of the District Fair, which consequently didnt amount to much this day – I was on business, & took the regular passenger train back at 10:20 . . . PM about town – rained lightly most of the PM, laying dust well . . . 1st rain since June 7 last, I think . . . The Isabel Morris Co played "The Great Divorce Case" to a very scarce audience – A Meekins says Louis Hirschberg took in $1,460 on Friday & about $900 Saturday at the Reno fair bar –

Oct 8 – Cloudy & cold, with occasional light snow storms . . . Sent letter to A W Bishop, Secy of Mutual Endowment Association, Oakland Cal asking for agency – Evening wrote a humorous sketch for Enterprise about wind-up of State Fair, Cap Joe White's mule, etc . . . Nellie McHenry & dramatic Co at Opera House tonight, in "Sweet Charity's Sake" . . .

Oct 9 . . . Evening train to Gold Hill – went to Ed Swift's residence on life insurance – Capt Kent, another agent there – walked back to Va . . .

Oct 10 . . . Two gymnasts, Davidson Bros, had a rope stretched across from Black's building to the old Bauer or Gillig corner on C st at Taylor – 40 ft above street – Did some very fine tight rope walking, etc, and collected what they could from the immense crowd of spectators – Evening at Degree Lodge . . . Old Joe Douglass got very drunk last evening, & been so all day also – Been abstinent & sober for about a year –

Oct 11 . . . At Carson all day & attended Fair, races etc – Took application of Danl H Pine to be member of Society of Pacific Coast Pioneers – also his $10 therefor . . .

Oct 12 . . . At Carson Fair as yesterday – Was at the Pavilion, & not at the grounds . . . wrote "District Fair Wind-up" . . .

Sunday, Oct 13 . . . By mail today I recd a package of supplies, etc, and a letter from L A Kelley, Genl Manager of the Mutual Endowment and Life Association – making me agent . . .

Oct 14 . . . To Carson – Was about town – Frank Doten getting loaded up & ready to leave for Bodie – Took his $10 with application to join the Pioneers Society . . .

Oct 15 . . . To Carson again . . . Saw Frank Doten pull out for
Bodie at noon, 12 horses & 3 wagons with assorted cargo 24,500 lbs –
Home on evening train – Wrote up "Capital Notes" for Enterprise – Saw
Edison's phonograph at Appeal office & Sam Davis worked it for me –
Wonderful instrument . . .

["The Wonderful Phonograph," clip from "Capital Notes" in the *Enterprise* of Oct 16:] Sam Davis was enterprising or curious enough to import
a genuine Edison phonograph for the benefit of visitors to the Pavilion
[at the Carson Fair], and operated it himself quite successfully in the
presence of admiring crowds. Yesterday I visited him at his office, and
was treated to a private seance with the instrument. It looks some like a
sewing machine, and is similarly operated with a treadle. Sam has about
a dozen cylinders belonging to it, about the size of a rolling pin, and made
of a waxy composition, each representing a different subject, including
stump speeches, instrumental airs, popular ballads, etc. With the ear quite
close to the outlet of sound, words or music could be faintly but plainly
heard, but with the sound conductors from it placed in each ear, the
sound vibrated loudly on the ear drum, just as though the instrument
playing or the persons singing or speaking were immediately present.

MUSICAL GYMNASTICS.

The first cylinder he worked was a piano solo and could not be mistaken, notwithstanding sundry discordant whirrings and sputterings, like
fresh butter on a frying-pan. Some new beginners on the piano or violin
give more nefarious results. Another cylinder represents a puff for the
machine itself, given in Sam's own vigorous style, his voice and bad spelling being unmistakably recognizable even by his worst enemies. But the
best cylinder, a grand concert by Patrick Gilmore's famous brass band,
was unfortunately broken in removal from the Pavilion. Sam tied the
pieces together as well as he knew how, and turned her loose, but owing
to having got some of the pieces in wrong end first the effect was intensely
ludicrous. The cornet got crossed with the tuba, and the trombone and
clarionet jumped several bars at a lick, leaving the bass drum and cymbals
away behind in chaotic confusion. Some of the finest passages were split
diagonally and agonizingly, while others got in wrong end first, and
Gilmore cursed fearfully. Anyhow, the phonograph is really a most wonderful instrument. It throws spiritualism entirely in the shade, giving
communications in a natural, easily-recognized voice years after a person
is dead—as though speaking from another world beyond the grave. Davis
brought this phonograph from San Francisco, and it is the first introduced
and exhibited in this State.

Oct 18 . . . Evening at literary entertainment and ball of Chosen
Friends – 65 came on special train from Carson . . .

[Clip, *Enterprise:*] S. B. Emerson, one of the earliest settlers of California, died in San Francisco Monday. He was a renowned horse breeder of Santa Clara.

Sunday, Oct 20 . . . [In Reno] PM a light steady rain . . . At 11 AM special excursion from St Louis arrived with the Old Reliable Railroad Conductors Life Insurance Association, Wives, daughters, 168 members – all bound for California . . . heavy showers set in, lasting most all night . . .

Oct 21 . . . Morning took box of baby clothes to CP RR depot, & shipped it to Millie . . . Took 1:45 [to Va] . . . Evening at office & wrote "Riverside Reflections" . . .

Oct 25 . . . Evening big crowd at Opera House – ball for benefit of Matt Hogan who lost a leg by jumping from a wagon runaway a year or so ago on South C st – Auspices of the A.O.U.W. –

Oct 26 . . . The Frank Daniels Dramatic Co arrived from the East, at Opera House tonight – was there – good house – Fantastic comedy entitled "Little Puck" – Very amusing – Harry Courtaine, one of the actors – Not been here for 17 years – Too drunk to appear tonight – much disappointment to his old friends here –

Oct 28 – Cloudy – Mail from the West arrived at 2:10, brought Dick Allen to settle the Harris loss – I got a buggy & went at once to Gold Hill & got Mrs H, took her to the California Bank & saw her get check for her $2,000 – she drew $200 & left $1,800 on deposit in the bank – Cost her $5 for exchange of check, it being drawn on California (SF), & $2 for carriage I brought her in – She gave me $10 for my trouble in the matter – Wrote letters to Senators Fair & Jones and Congressman Bartine – they in SF & he in Carson – inviting them to banquet of Pioneers next Thursday evening, & sent them by evening train – Rode down to Mound House & back on cars – Dick Allen on down train bound for Salt Lake – quite a chat with him on my life insurance proposition – Returning from the Mound House found old Jim Townsend on board – He was in from Mill Creek or Lundy, where he has been for last 3 years running the *Homer Index* & mining – Evening was about town with him some – Wrote some items [for] Enterprise – read proof etc – Bed 3 – Jim is on his way to London on account of mining trouble at Lundy –

Oct 29 . . . Mrs Hall [who died today] was one of my lady friends before I was married, and the one I was "paired off" with at the Jim

Gladding party in Gold Hill and to whom I paid that filopoena dress in consequence – Her name was Colburn then –

Oct 30 . . . Got letter . . . from Bartine saying he would try to be at the banquet . . .

Oct 31 – Clear & pleasant – The funeral of Mrs Hall this PM from the Episcopal Church had 83 carriages, one of the biggest in that respect I ever saw – I was busy considerably today arranging for the Pioneers banquet tonight – Collected $20.50 – Good time – About 35 present – quit at 11:30 – I wrote it up, read proof, etc, Bed at 3:30 –

Nov 1 . . . Rode in the evening train to Mound House with Bartine in order to talk with him . . .

Nov 2 . . . Took evening train for Reno . . .

Sunday, Nov 3 . . . Thalia Mitchell, niece of Gen Batterman, with her sister Patty arrived this last week from South Britain, Conn, with Mrs Batterman, who went on to Oakland, Cal, leaving them here, guests of Bob Lindsay & wife – Miss Thalia visited us this PM & I made her acquaintance – About 24, & a fine smart girl . . .

Nov 4 – Clear, cold & pleasant – Miss Thalia Mitchell rode on train with me this AM to Va – I to show her the Comstock – Got permit from Supt Lyman and after lunch at the French Rotisserie we went down the C&C shaft with Dennis Goyette, foreman – Went through the 1650 level and descended to the 1750 or Sutro Tunnel level – Went into the Tunnel enough to realize its appearance – Then we walked out to the new Nevada Mill, at the Chollar – Went through it, & I saw her off on the evening train at 5:20 feeling very tired but gratified with what she had seen – I rode with her to the Mound House & back – Bed 12:30 –

Nov 7 . . . Frank Mayo and Company in "Davy Crockett" – Good house – better than the play deserved –

Nov 8 – Same – About town, & much with R K Allen General Manager of Bankers & Merchants Mutual Life Association, of which I am the agent here – Also with Capt Kent and P K Faulds two traveling agents for the same concern both doing business therefor on the Comstock – Evening Enterprise – Bed 2 – In a controversy this PM about the B & M, agencies etc, Manager Allen fired Kent out as an agent – Evening received a pass from Yerington till end of year –

Nov 11 . . . Evening at theater – Patti Rosa and Company in play of "Bob" – Good house – fair entertainment but nothing extra . . .

Nov 12 . . . Letter from Bessie says Millie & her baby arrived Saturday – Evening was at IOOF Hall at consolidation of Olive Branch No 12 with Nevada Lodge No 7 – Big crowd from all the Comstock lodges, also few from Reno – Splendid collation afterward in National Guard Hall . . .

Nov 13 . . . PM walked to Gold Hill to see Jack Long, a member of the Exempts – In a bad fix with inflammatory rheumatism – just able to walk – gave him $20 on his interest in the Association – He will receive $7 per week sick benefits from now on – He was glad to know that he was looked out for and said he would vigorously stand the devil off – I fooled away an hour or so about the saloons, walked back & didnt go down town . . .

Nov 16 . . . Evening train to Reno – Found Millie & baby there . . . a little very red headed girl – Looks most like Ed, especially in the bluish gray eyes –

> [Clip, *Enterprise:*] The residence formerly occupied by Alf Doten and family, back of the *News* office, in Gold Hill, was sold a few days ago to Mrs. Fraser, who owns the Comstock lodging house near by, for $300. It was erected by Mr. Doten fifteen years ago, in the prosperous days of Gold Hill, at a cost of over $8,000, being the best constructed wooden building in the town, and the comparatively insignificant price it has now been sold for is a good indication of the decline of values in that locality. Gold Hill . . . has seen more prosperous days.

Nov 18 – Light steady rain set in about 2 this morning & kept at it all day – Took train for Va . . . About town – Found letter from Wells Drury, on the Examiner, SF enclosing a scrap or clipping he wrote in that paper, last January, in which he speaks of me and Baldy Green the Pioneer stage driver – also enclosed photo of his little 7 mos boy – I wrote letter in response, also wrote letter to wife enclosing Drury's letter etc . . . Evening at Opera House – Play of "Little Lord Fauntleroy" by company arrived today . . . Had a very good house, considering the storm – Was about 2 inches of snow, commencing early this morning & still going it, with furious winds . . . Wrote "Along the Railroad," & got it into the *Enterprise*, Read proof etc, Bed at 2 – Still snowing and 6 or 8 inches deep . . .

Nov 19 – AM sunshine a time or two, with snowstorm sandwiches – PM

furious winds and snow – blew blazes out of awnings, loose signs, etc –
one house on north C st blown to ruin, also windows on C st, blown in, &
some stovepipes prostrated . . . Evening dropped in at National Guard
Hall to first dance of the "Bijou" Club comprising the best of Comstock
folks . . .

Nov 21 . . . Was with Capt Kent awhile – he up from Gold Hill – on
B & M Insurance matters –

Nov 23 . . . Took evening train to Reno – Senator J P Jones on board –
Sat in seat with him clear through – chatting all the way . . . Home . . .
Millie & baby still there . . .

Nov 25 . . . Morning train to Carson – Was at State Controller's office
& filed objections on part of the B & M against the New York Mutual
Reserve Fund Association doing business in this State as they pay no $200
license – Home to Va . . .

Nov 26 . . . State Teacher's Institute commenced session here today –
teachers from all parts of the State arrived – Prof Ring from Reno, et al –
My wife didn't come . . . Evening wrote "Along the Railroad" . . .

Nov 28 . . . Thanksgiving – Plenty of turkey everywhere – Went to
Reno . . . Millie still there, & baby – Evening down town awhile – Saw
bogus Salvation Army, 8 of 'em, parading streets on way to masquerade
ball at Pavilion – Jolly . . .

Nov 29 . . . Back to Va . . . Evening at Opera House to grand banquet ball of teachers institute – Big crowd & success . . .

Nov 30 through Dec 23 [Heavy snows delay the mail & bring out the
sleighs – AD writes more "crankiness" for Bennett, two "Along the Railroad" pieces and reports on an Exempt meeting & an Odd Fellows literary
& social entertainment for the *Enterprise,* a letter to Senator Jones asking
to be appointed Consul to Australia & a long letter to Eunice – Notes
death & funeral of Andy Patterson, brother of his friend Bob Patterson,
proprietor of the International Saloon – Reads *Don Quixote,* attends performance of Lew Johnson's Refined Minstrels, a Negro troupe, which he
finds good, "but real negro minstrels are not as good as white imitators –
Don't come up to the old SF Minstrels by a long chalk" – About town
often.]

Dec 24 – Steady, quiet snowstorm all day – About 2 ft deep – Mail about 6 hours late – Took evening train for Reno, with 2 Christmas tur-keys 8 lbs each I bought of McGurn, also a quart of olives etc . . . Millie left with her baby and things for San F last Thursday –

Dec 25 – Snowed steadily and lightly most of day – Very fine sleighing, best Reno has seen for years – Snow 15 inches deep on a level – Christ-mas Day – staid at home all day & didn't have a drink of whisky, egg nog or anything in that line, *for the first time on the Pacific Coast* – I chalk this down for a singular circumstance – Our children had lots of presents from both East & West – Mary & I got some also with the rest – Good Christmas dinner – Mrs Powell dined with us – Evening Charley Steven-son here – had games, music, singing, etc – Sam still works as telegraph messenger – Bed 9:30 √ –

Dec 26 through 31 [AD remains with family – Weather, "about town some" & early to bed every night.]

BOOK NO. *65*

Virginia City and Reno
Jan 1, 1890 – Dec 31, 1890

Jan 1, 1890 . . . Was about Reno awhile during the day, taking observations, etc – Times very dull – Day observed about as usual, people visiting, etc, & little business being done – lots of sleigh riding . . .

Jan 3 . . . PM heavy snowstorm for hour or so . . . About town some – Evening wrote a sketch for the Reno Journal entitled "A Reno Character" – "Twenty-one years on his knees – A long, yet hopeful pilgrimage" . . .

Jan 4 . . . Owing to the big snows in the Sierra no train got through either way – none from the East either – Va train left, therefore, on time – I went . . . Evening at my Lodge – officiated as Warden for last time as this was last meeting of the Lodge – Next Monday evening we consolidate with Virginia Lodge No 10 . . .

Jan 6 . . . Evening the Helen Blythe dramatic Co from San F played "A Mother's Love" to a fair house – I attended the Lodge consolidation, & wrote it up for the Enterprise . . .

Jan 7 – Clear & very cold . . . reported to be about 20° below Z at Dayton, Carson, Reno & along Carson river . . . Evening at theater – Helen Blythe Co played "Cora the Creole" to a very poor house –

Jan 10 . . . Mail arrived late . . . owing to the local train getting off in Washoe Valley near Franktown – Letter from Wife says: "Monday & Tuesday 20° below Z in Reno, and Wednesday morning 22° below, and Thursday 24° below . . . Same all over town. Water pipes froze, including ours, and plants froze in the parlor" – This evening Archie McDonnell gave a nice kettledrum party at National Guard Hall – I was there & saw it – About 60 couples – High-toned – Archie did it all himself – wine,

lemonade, punch and collation – gave each gent a little drum, & the ladies
each a nice fan . . . Sent my letter to Jones . . . about the Australian
consulate which he proposes for me –

Sunday, Jan 12 – 34° – Light snowstorm most of day, closing with a
furious blizzard at dark . . . Evening express train did not leave till
7:45 – waited for the local to come up with snow plow . . . At 2 PM
attended the regular monthly meeting of the Exempts – Presided for last
time – E A Pottle installed as President, & also the other new officers
elect . . . Had a fine collation with invited guests – Only 39 members
now in good standing – commenced several years ago with 150 members – died, scattered & dropped out since – Evening about town some –
"Wild night on Treasure Hill, & poor Mulligan busted" – Bed 12 – Got
letter & documents from Bankers & Merchants – commencing to insure
women –

Jan 13 . . . Sleighing on C st very billowy from so much being shoveled
off the houses & awnings – The express train for Reno last night waited
[at] Mound House till 3 this morning . . . for the narrow gauge train
which was stuck in the snow between there & Dayton . . . I was about
town most of day – Evening at my new Lodge, Virginia No 3 – Slim
attendance – Was at Enterprise & wrote lots of items, etc, read proof etc –
Bed at 2:30 – snowing again – The roads are demoralized in all directions – The Nevada mill had to close down, not being able to transport
ore from the mines – Most of the mills on Carson river shut down for
same, & also from freezing up –

Jan 14 . . . W P Bennett of Gold Hill found me this PM & took away
the second lot of crank sketches – gave $2 more –

Jan 15 through 17 [Snow & high winds – Railroads blocked – Pneumonia prevalent.]

Jan 18 – Variable – Morning, snowstorms – with a foot more snow accumulation from last night . . . Trains all abandoned, in all directions –
Snow on the railroad summit of the Sierra 30 ft deep or more – was about
town – Jack Plant, foreman of Enterprise, has the popular disease, the
influenza or "la grippe" – had to lay off last night, as well as today –
pretty sick . . . C street merely a wavy lot of deep snow – Impassable
for wheeled vehicles – People on one sidewalk cant see those on the
other . . . More snow water stored on that street than I ever saw there –
settled & compact – Telegraph communication west to California entirely

cut off today – All right East & locally – No trains, or expectations of trains –

Sunday, Jan 19 . . . Snowstorms & sunshine . . . 5 locomotives with a snow plow left Carson at 4 AM & got through to Va at 3 PM . . . At 5 PM left for Carson again, followed by another train of one passenger and a baggage car, with 2 locomotives . . . had about 20 passengers – 1st outgoing train – no mail since last Tuesday from anywhere . . . last night about 20 or 30 feet of the firewall of the Odd Fellows Building fell into Smith st, from pressure of snow on roof, sliding down against it . . .

Jan 20 . . . About town – Evening I visited Jack Plant at his residence on B st north of Carson st – Very bad & slippery trip – He was abed, but getting better . . . wife & 4 children, oldest 8 yrs youngest 6 mos, with strong croppings for the 5th – Bed at 12 – 14° above Z – The local train got through from Reno at 8:30 this evening with all the delayed eastern mail and about ten passengers . . .

Jan 21 – Clear – Train to Reno and back for passengers and Eastern mail – Nothing from the West – Still blockaded . . .

Jan 22 – Clear, & from 20° to 30°, but very blustering . . . a snow storm whirling from summit of Mt Davidson all day . . . This big wind played hell with the railroads in all directions, filling up the cuts etc . . . No train from Reno at all – Was busy at room most of day copying MSS for W P Bennett about the early staging of Washoe and the Comstock . . . The roof of the stone building on D st, corner of Taylor, rear of Nevada Bank, fell in this morning from weight of snow . . . Other roofs about town suffering . . . also some awnings . . .

Jan 23 . . . About town some and writing some for Bennett . . . gave me $5 . . .

Jan 24 – Storming . . . 5 PM I telegraphed wife: "Burn woodshed, all fence, and front or all upstairs floor" – Never saw so much snow, or was much more completely cut off . . .

Jan 25 – Snowstorm all day . . . Snow shoveler busy and in great demand – Wrote for Bennett . . .

Sunday, Jan 26 – Clear & very pleasant . . . North side of Piper's Opera House roof caved in . . .

Jan 27 . . . Same as yesterday – Everybody feeling a little better . . .

Wrote for Bennett . . . principally . . . George Francis Train's famous trip over the Geiger Grade Aug 24 1869 – (See my personal journal)

Jan 28 . . . John Cavanaugh funeral today – Member of the Exempts – Delegation attended . . . fuel getting short on the Comstock – Cavanaugh's funeral about 100 of the Miners Union on foot, a dozen Exempts, & 12 sleighs, besides the sleigh hearse – Catholic burial ground – This is the first time that potatoes, or such, were shipped to Va through Sutro Tunnel – Very useful now, even for passengers –

Jan 29 – Clear and not very cold, but PM & evening high winds . . . Wrote for Bennett and gave him a batch of over 50 pages today – Paid me $5 more, & owes me $5 yet – Evening was about town & at Enterprise – Got in a few items . . . Much sickness about town . . . Coal all burned, but wood continues – Fuel famine imminent –

Jan 30 . . . The natural and shoveled drifts along C st are from 10 to 15 ft high, and the main track of the street, from Wells Fargos to the International is from 6 to 8 ft deep – solid snow – No wheeled vehicles can get along . . . All along, on each side of the street are to be seen steps cut in the snow at every crossing, and they are not many yards apart – Lots of cross cuts . . .

Jan 31 . . . Trains still blockaded, and sleighs beginning to run to Carson and Reno with passengers and express – but no mail . . .

Feb 1 . . . Strong warm breeze – thawy – snow settled fast – Several carloads of wood through to Gold Hill & Va from Carson last evening & this PM, but road blocked again by drifting snow on Am Flat . . . CP RR open across the Sierra and delayed trains all moving . . . Mooney's sleigh, Bob Grimmon driver, took local passengers etc to Reno this morning & returned this evening – brought SF papers . . . first since Jan 15 . . . No coal for sale in town, & wood supply getting short – I have been out of coal for a week – use what odds & ends of boxes & lumber I can get hold of – Had no fire yesterday & today – About all mines & mills shut down . . .

Feb 3 – Clear, pleasant and very thawy – The regular mail & express train over the V&T got in from Reno about 2:30 PM, nearly on time, with all the delayed mails east & west: West since Jan 15, and East since Jan 20 – I got letters from wife & sent postal card by return mail – also letters from sister Eunice, S A Jones, President of the State University, Dick Allen, et al – At room most of day, writing "A Warning Fiery Phantom," for Bennett – Was about the burning of the steamer Belle of the West, on Ohio River in 1850 – about 1,000 lives lost – Bed at 12 –

Feb 4 . . . Wrote long 6 page letter to wife, enclosing S A Jones' letter & copy of my reply . . .

Feb 5 . . . Thousands of cattle in the eastern part of this State died from cold & starvation during the storm, and thousands are being rushed forward over the railroad to California or wherever hay or feed can be got at – Carson river swollen so that it backed up & stopped the Mexican & Morgan Mills yesterday, & caused suspension of work in Crown Point & Belcher mines again today . . .

Feb 6 . . . Evening at theater – Jos R Grismer and Phoebe Davis and their own Company for this one night in a very good play entitled "The Tigress" – Good house – Bed at 2 –

Feb 7 . . . Busy most of day getting off a lot of proxies for Dick Allen from members of the Bankers & Merchants, for the annual election next Tuesday – He sent me 75 blanks to be filled – Sent most of them in envelopes, with small hektograph note enclosed, Reno, Carson, Empire, Dayton, Silver, etc & here in Va & Gold Hill . . . I attended to 11 here in Va . . . Dayton stage on wheels again, as sleighing is spoiled beyond the Divide . . .

Feb 8 . . . PM rode to Gold Hill & back on bus sleigh which only runs down as far as the old Vesey House . . . as below there is no good sleighing . . . I paid old Jane Noble a visit . . . Old & much broken down . . .

Feb 11 . . . Evening I wrote about ⅔ of a column on "Notable Comstock Winters" – Took it to Enterprise . . . I got Dr Webber to examine me this PM on application for 2,000 in the B & M – Passed a splendid examination –

Feb 12 – Cloudy, windy & threatening – Evening it consummated in the wildest fiercest snowstorm I have yet seen here . . .

Feb 13 . . . Adam Gillespie brought me 400 lbs more coal today, making 1,000 lbs in all this Winter –

Feb 14 – Clear & more moderate – Thawy . . . T A Washburn called on me at my room, & I took notes for an item for him about a patented device of his for amalgamating pans – Evening I wrote it up & put in paper . . .

Feb 15 . . . Evening wrote Railroad Notes for Enterprise . . .

[A ¾-column piece entitled "The Impertinently Inquisitive Tourist Takes Notes" appears in the Sunday *Enterprise* – Recounts a journey on the V&T smoking car from Reno – "On the seat ahead of us was a peculiar looking individual, with small round-top hat, side whiskers, eye glasses and tourist style. Nothing escaped his eye in passing, and he took frequent lead pencil notes in a little book." – He frequently and "impertinently" interrupts the conversation of the two locals, asking them about the Newlands irrigation project, the state prison and its prehistoric dinosaur tracks, the Morgan quartz mill and the Comstock method of extracting ore, and jots down their answers – The locals decide to "steamboat" him a little, and tell him the trout in the Carson loose their teeth because the effluvient quicksilver "salivates" them, the sagebrush is ceasing to produce its usual apples, and that a party of Italian woodchoppers singing and drinking in the forward end of the car is an opera troupe hired by the railroad to entertain its customers – "Then we saw him note down, 'Worst singers out of h—ll travel this road; also, two of the d—dest liars.'" – Later they meet the tourist in Virginia City, right after the snow blockade has been lifted – He had been in Carson, and asks them how provisions held out:]

"Very well. Potatoes got scarce, but we soon got a supply from Dayton through the Sutro tunnel and hoisted up the C. & C. shaft."

We slyly glanced over his shoulder, and saw him make the following note in his little book: "Only use made of Sutro tunnel is transporting potatoes from Carson river to the Comstock. Met those two infernal champion liars again."

Sunday, Feb 16 – Heavy snow blizzard all day . . . John Capurro member of my lodge, who died on Thursday evening of pneumonia had his funeral this PM from IOOF hall – Services largely attended by Odd Fellows, Knights of Pythias, Italian Benevolent Society, & friends – Hall full . . . but the storm & traveling too bad for anybody to march, so widow & chief mourners in ½ doz carriages accompanied corpse out to cemetery & put him in a vault for future reference – The snow of today's storm drifted terribly . . . No mail from the west – CP RR blocked . . .

Feb 17 – Steady light snowstorm all day, with some blustery winds occasionally . . . Trial of Benjamin Jenkins for wife murder commenced today . . .

Feb 18 – Big snowstorm all day, with more or less furious wind especially in the evening . . . Evening went with Wm Pellow & visited his wife who has been trying to get divorced from him – out on South C st beyond the Savage office – Wrote his application for $2,000 – Afterward at Enterprise office helping out Jack Plant the foreman, reading proof, etc . . . .

Feb 19 – Light snowstorm about all day . . . Snow so deep on C st that I can walk along middle & look [at] top of porches on each side . . . CP blockaded –

Feb 20 – Same . . . no Western mail . . . Jenkins case submitted to the Jury at 9 this evening . . .

Feb 22 – Morning sunshiny but before noon clouded up again & in the PM & evening light snow storms – 3 days of the delayed western mail arrived but [none more recent than] the 19th . . . Washington's Birthday – Flags up all over town – Jury in the Jenkins case brought in a verdict of manslaughter at 12:30 last night . . .

Sunday, Feb 23 – Clear & pleasant, but cold – Mail arrived about 3:30 PM – 3 days mail and all up to date – David Nagle the Deputy US Marshal who killed David S Terry came from San F. I met him on C st – Knew each other – Evening about town – Bed 1 – Old Joe Douglass, my landlord, fell down stairs at the International Hotel evening before last & got a big cut on back of head & lots of bruises – Badly busted but will recover –

Feb 24 . . . Air full of sleety snow from Mt Davidson & the roofs . . . I wrote a letter to C D Allen Secy of the B & M enclosing the applications of Mrs Boland, Wm Pellow & myself – $5000 in all . . .

Feb 25 – AM fierce blizzard with light snow from sky & more from mountains – PM more moderate, but snowy – The Express train got through to Reno last night, but the local, which passed it at Haywood switch below the Am Flat tunnel got stuck at Scales, on Am Flat & got snowed and drifted in so that it is there yet . . . Owing to the big drifts obstructing the various side tracks, and the Am Flat blockade shutting off the ore trains the principal mines are shut down again . . . The public schools reopened yesterday after a weeks shut down – Evening about town – Enterprise etc – Bed at 2:30 – 12° above – quiet but snowing lightly . . .

Feb 26 – Clear & cold – No trains today – The local still at Scales and 100 shovelers trying to dig it out . . . Evening wrote "A Chapter on Cats" – Took it to Enterprise . . .

March 1 – Cloudy but moderate, thawy & pleasant – Trains, mails etc all on time – Big break in the Water Cos flume, near Marlette lake, caused

shutting down of electric works & lights & Nevada mill . . . Got letters
from B & M today to the effect that Mrs Bolands application is accepted,
but mine & Pellow's refused – Send a letter in response . . .

Sunday, March 2 – Clear, warm & very pleasant – PM I went out &
visited Dr Jas Delavan . . . He accidentally slipped & fell last Wednesday, wrenching his right arm & shoulder very seriously – He is confined
to his bed . . . about 76 yrs old, so can't stand such things very well . . .

March 3 . . . Rewrote & added to my "Bowers of California" for Bennett – Jane Noble died at Gold Hill yesterday – our old nurse – 63 yrs
old . . .

March 4 – Rainy – A light drizzly rain at intervals most of the day –
AM wrote application of William Cuff, for 2,000 – miner – in Con Va
mine – At noon rode to Gold Hill on 'bus, on *wheels* – Snow melting &
running off very fast – No good sleighing south of the Divide – Very
muddy & sloppy – Attended funeral of Jane Noble – body taken from her
rooms in the Comstock, (Mrs Fraser's lodging house) to the Episcopal
church, where the services were conducted by Rev Mr Ridgely of Va –
About 50 people present – I rode out to the cemetery on seat with driver
of chief mourners carriage, in which were Mrs Fraser, Mrs Fox, Mrs
McMartin and Mrs Robinson – Pall bearers were March, Welch, Wyckoff, O'Donnell, McDonald & one other man I didnt know – Very bad
walking indeed for them – 6 carriages – Rode back to Va on my carriage, Mrs McMartin and Mrs Fox also, Mrs Fraser & Mrs Robinson
getting off at their houses in Gold Hill – It rained all way to Cemetery &
back quite hard, so we all got a little wet – Evening I wrote application
of Dan'l Tierney miner, Yellow Jacket mine, for $2,000 – Dined at French
Rotisserie with Matt Callahan – Was about town & at Enterprise – Bed
at 2 – Sent off my letter to Eunice, also one to wife – by evening mail –

March 5 – Clear, warm & pleasant – About, as usual – Train on time
brought "A Postage Stamp" Comedy Co – with their Black Hussar Band –
The band paraded up one sidewalk & down the other, on C st, about 2
PM – 14 of them in elegant uniform – Excellent – One of the best bands
ever visiting the Comstock . . . Evening I was at Opera House to their
performance – Good house – Variety, musical & very amusing performance, entitled "A Social Session" – One of the best ever here in that line –
I as well as everybody, enjoyed it very much – Bed at 2 –

March 6 . . . I attended anniversary reunion of the Daughters of Rebekah – They made me make a speech . . .

March 7 . . . Evening attended performance of the Casino Burlesque Opera Co from the East . . . about 60 of them women & men – Opera of "Erminie" – Very good – Big house . . .

March 8 – Stormy – A fierce snow blizzard prevailed for 2 or 3 hours this AM . . . light snow with more or less squally winds rest of day . . . Opera of "Nadjy" – Fair house . . .

Sunday, March 9 . . . Snow squalls . . . Not much snow fell, but what fell drifted badly on the railroads – so that we got no western mail though the V&T was on time . . . PM was at regular monthly meeting of the Exempts . . .

March 10 – Stormy – Snow squalls at intervals – PM rode to Gold Hill on 'bus, (wheeled) – Found Bennett at his room – delivered "Joe Bowers" to him – Paid me $2 on acct – Was about town some, & rode back on McGrath's grocery delivery wagon . . . Evening at Opera House & reported meeting, on stage, cold –

[An *Enterprise* clip explains that between 400 and 500 ladies and gentlemen weathered the chilly Opera House to "listen to speeches against religious interference" and draw up resolutions against the "Blair Sunday Rest Bill," a proposed constitutional amendment prohibiting work on Sundays and allowing state and national governments to prescribe the "fundamental and nonsectarian principles of Christianity" to be taught in the public schools.]

Bed at 12:30 – clear – 21° above – No mail from the West last 2 or 3 days owing to big snowslide and snowshed destruction – got a copy of New York Times of Feb 28 today, from W W Austin my editor on News – His name was marked on the margin therefore I presume he is employed on that paper – That railroad sketch of mine about the inquisitive tourist in Enterprise Feb 10 was copied into it and he had marked it in blue pencil –

March 11 through 21 [The weather is good and AD is chiefly about on insurance business in Virginia & Gold Hill – Of additional interest:]

March 17 . . . St Patrick's Day – Lots of green neckties, ribbons & shamrocks to be seen on streets . . . Was up to the Emmet Guard St Patrick ball couple of hours – Bed at 3 –

March 19 . . . Evening at Opera House – "Monte Cristo," with James O'Neill in the dual character of Edmond Dantes, & the Count of Monte Cristo – Big house – $413 – Good play – I reported it for Enterprise –

March 22 – Cloudy – PM was at Gold Hill – Delivered Wyckoff his policy, & he gave me $2.50 for my trouble – Evening, about town, etc – Bed 1 – Windy & threatening – Gold Hill streets dry & nice – Va streets very muddy near the Divide – snow and ice 3 or 4 ft deep in places along C st in city – track had to be cut in Taylor st from B to D, & carted away – C st very rough wheeling over the billowy snow – No heavy loads can be hauled over it – Rode to GH & back in the bus – Getting back about sunset I got off at J C Werrin's store out on South C st – found him pretty badly banged up from a brutal assault by Dennis Sullivan, son of Con Sullivan the policeman – dispute about a lot near by, where Werrin is about building a house – Was knocked down & kicked insensible about head & shoulders – right eye blacked, 2 teeth broken, right arm bruised & lamed, etc – Sullivan was arrested –

March 24 . . . Went to Dr Webber & got him to take my respiration over again for insurance – He made it 15 this time against 11 before – Evening Opera House – Good comedy Co from Cal for the East, played "A Hole in the Ground" to the biggest house for the last year or two – Variety performance . . .

March 25 . . . Evening about sunset a lively snowstorm set in . . .

March 26 . . . Dennis Sullivan was fined $250 by Justice Kehoe this PM for beating J C Werrin so last Sunday . . .

Sunday, March 30 . . . Evening a heavy snow blizzard prevailed for an hour or two . . .

March 31 . . . G W Prentice was shot & killed by John Taylor about noon today in 6 Mile Canyon – Was brought up to C M Browns undertaking shop where I took a look at my old acquaintance – Got long letter from wife enclosing Reno correspondence for publication . . .

[A clipping from the *Enterprise* of April 1 – Taylor bought the building in which Prentice had been squatting, and an argument ensued when Taylor tried to take possession – Prentice made a threat, and Taylor retaliated with a smooth-bore shotgun: "the charge of buckshot . . . leaving a gaping wound that no one would think anything less than a cannon ball would effect. The same old sinister smile that Prentice has worn since 1863 still suffused his countenance . . . he looked no dirtier than usual." – Townspeople suspect Prentice of several other "dark and bloody night deeds," most notably the killing of old man Pollard and his aged wife – The *Enterprise* is disgusted that Taylor is being held in jail for the grand jury, rather than being released immediately and given an award of some kind.]

April 2 . . . Wife's Reno Correspondence in paper this morning –

April 5 . . . The Nevada (new Chollar) electric mill was in full blast today again – Has been idle most of last month & this till today by reason of the big snow & land slides in the main Sierra Nevada making breakages in the flume or ditch of the Water Company thus cutting off the water power that runs the dynamos –

Sunday, April 6 . . . Easter services at churches well attended – Knights Templar . . . marched from their Hall to Episcopal church to attend service . . . All in full uniform . . .

April 9 . . . Play "The Great Metropolis," by the Rial & Morris Dramatic Co – Pretty fair . . .

April 11 . . . Lawyer M N Stone who has had his office rooms above mine in this Douglass building for the last 6 or 7 years is packing & boxing his books & furniture for removal to Salt Lake with his family . . . By today's mail I received policy of 2000 for J S Hardwick, and a letter from Eunice, enclosing a letter from Bro Sam with final documents for signature, closing up estate of sister Rebecca – $160.53 balance due me – Evening at Opera House – Literary & musical entertainment, & ball for benefit of John Bennetts, a member of the Chosen Friends, got up by the Order – Pretty fair house & show – Wrote it up for *Enterprise* – Bed at 1 –

Sunday, April 13 . . . PM at Exempt meeting . . . By this evening's mail I forwarded to Major S H Doten, Plymouth Mass those final documents in settlement of Rebecca's estate – I being the last of the heirs to sign it –

April 14 . . . Hon J B Williams paid me $2.50 for writing a complimentary notice of his departure for Europe, which takes place tomorrow – Was at office – read proof etc – Bed 2 –

April 15 . . . Evening visited J S Hardwick & family . . . on D st, opposite Savage office, couple of hours – treated me to lemonade, whisky & mince pie – Delivered him his policy . . .

April 17 . . . PM I reported trial in Justice Kehoe's court of J M Campbell for violation of State lottery law in publishing advertisement of the

Juarez lottery (Mexican) – Jury trial – Jury went out at 3:45, and failed to agree . . .

April 18 . . . Franklin Ward went to County Hospital at 5 PM yesterday & died at 4 this morning – Member of Pioneers – 60 yrs old . . .

April 19 . . . Went down with Welch, the Pub[lic] Ad[ministrator], to his residence on Taylor st & I helped go through Frank Ward's trunks for papers & valuables – found very little value . . . The last of the snowbanks so long infesting C street has gone – A few snowbanks still remain on some of the shaded crossstreets –

Sunday, April 20 . . . Evening attended Spiritualistic seance of Miss May Howard, and husband at the Opera House – Frank Fielding & myself were committee on the stage, and tied the lady in the cabinet, after the style of the Davenport Bros – Gave pretty much same performance only slicker . . . Wrote letters to . . . brother & sister of Frank Ward . . .

April 21 . . . About town collecting money to bury Frank Ward . . .

April 22 – Cloudy – a light sprinkle or two in morning – At 2 PM attended funeral of Frank Ward – Walked with hearse from Brown's undertaking establishment down to Episcopal church – Rev Mr Ridgely officiated at services – Choir sang – Rode in carriage with Otto Eckelman & Abe Coryell behind the hearse – Six carriages in all – I wore Frank's old Pioneer badge with the gold bear on it – After burial service at cemetery I presented the badge to Robert Logan Supt of the Brunswick Mill, Carson river, who came around Cape Horn to Cal in '49 with Frank – Evening about town & at office – Bed 2 –

April 23 . . . Evening at theater – Hyde's Star Specialty Co in play of "Way Down South" – Very good – good house – Bed 2 – Paid Charley Brown the undertaker, $40, this evening, of what I have collected toward paying for Frank Wards funeral expenses –

April 26 . . . Letter from Wife . . . had rec'd letter from Bro Sam with check for $160.53, in final settlement of Rebecca's estate . . .

Sunday, April 27 . . . Evening meeting of Pioneers . . Rec'd letter from Mrs E G W Tilton, Los Angeles, regarding her dead Brother, Frank Ward –

April 29 . . . Recd letter from wife with $100 check in it from Sam . . .

April 30 . . . Cashed my check for $100 at Nevada bank & paid several of my old bills about town – to extent of about $50 – Evening was at ball of the "Jack Rabbit" club at National Guard Hall – at Enterprise office . . .

May 1 . . . Sent check for $45 to Bankers & Merchants Co settling up my dues to the Co – Also sent letter to Mrs J C Williamson (Maggie Moore) No 4, Sanchez st San F, enclosing my photograph – She & her husband with Miss Grace Riehm & little Nellie Riehm leave for Sydney, NSW tomorrow . . .

May 3 . . . Evening excitement of prize glove fight between Wm Keough and James Fell for $500 a side, kept biggest crowds on C st I ever saw here on such occasion – I was at Opera House & saw the fight – Was on stage – Big house – Fight began at 11:35 – 27 rounds, ending at 1:20 in favor of Keough . . .

Sunday, May 4 . . . Wife arrived on morning train . . . Took her to room √ – At 4 PM we dined at New York Bakery, on South C st – took long walk . . . Tommy Morgan died 7 PM – Received by mail today letter from Maggie Moore Williamson S.F. accompanying three fine cabinet photographs of herself . . .

May 5 . . . Wife visited the 4th Ward schools all day today . . . She left on evening train . . . My bowels bad from strawberries, oysters etc we ate for breakfast & lunch . . . Theater in evening – Hallen & Hart's Variety Company – Very good – Fair house – Wrote "In Memoriam" on Tommy Morgan for *Enterprise* . . .

May 6 . . . PM Tommy Morgans funeral had 53 carriages behind the hearse – About 160 Odd Fellows and Miners Union escort on foot . . .

May 10 . . . This PM Mrs E G Ward Tilton called on me at my room – Arrived from Los Angeles . . . to see after the effects of her brother Frank Ward –

May 11 through July 3 [AD undertakes an extensive correspondence about the affairs of Frank Ward for Mrs Tilton, bustles about on insurance, works at correcting and bringing up to date his Comstock mining report, spends a few evenings at the *Enterprise,* notes that his wife has been too ill to teach for some time, is troubled for several days himself by an infected toe & attends his usual meetings – Of additional interest:]

May 20 . . . Members present from all parts of the State attending meeting of the Rep State Central Committee, held at Odd Fellows Building . . .

May 23 . . . Evening at Opera House – Mrs Scott Siddons in recitations – Very slim house – Bed 2 – Received prize $2.50 in the Little Louisiana lottery . . . Bought $2 more tickets – Also received pass renewal from Yerington for 3 months . . .

May 27 . . . Prof Ring with his graduating high school class arrived from Reno in a 4 horse 'bus about 11 AM – 13 of them – Bessie not along by reason of her mother being sick – They visited schools, & saw sights, & left at 7 PM . . .

May 29 . . . Went to Carson by morning local train – Attended State Silver Convention – Delegates from throughout the State – Used my pass, but convention met at 2 PM, Opera House, but closed at 5:30 – too late for my train – Bought ticket for $1.50 on special train taking folks generally and the Young Men's Institute (Catholic) particularly . . .

June 2 . . . Took evening express for Reno . . . found all right but wife who is still sick, although able to attend school – Bed 10:30 –

June 3 . . . AM put on the screen doors, & did other odd jobs about the house – Planted some of my big squash seeds etc – At 1:45 PM left on local train for Va . . .

June 5 . . . Evening attended Opera House – Play, "Paul Kauvar," with Haworth in lead – Very good . . .

June 7 . . . Took morning local for Carson to report Chosen Friends picnic . . .

Sunday, June 8 . . . Got letter from W H Virden and also one from Ben H Miller, Bridgeport, Mono Co, Cal, telling me that Frank Doten was severely and perhaps fatally hurt on the 2nd inst. by his team running away, & that was now lying insensible at Bridgeport – Want me there . . .

June 9 . . . Morning train to Carson – Went to Elrod's hay yard & saw him about Frank – Back on Express . . . Tried to get a telegram through to Bodie or Bridgeport this PM but couldn't, there being no telegraphic communication –

June 10 . . . Wrote a humorous sketch for Enterprise, entitled "On the Picnic Train" . . .

June 11 . . . Sent following telegram this PM – "To H M Yerington, Hawthorne, Nev. I have to go to Bridgeport tomorrow. Will you kindly give me pass at Mound House for Hawthorne & return" – Got reply in evening: "Alf Doten Passes over C&C not in order. To aid you will grant half fare. Apply to Virginia office." . . .

June 12 . . . Latest reports say that Frank not so badly hurt, & liable to come out all right . . .

June 13 . . . Evening attended a benefit of Miss Rose Sommers, a young lady of this place, at Opera House – It commenced with a literary business, songs, recitations, etc – Operetta of "Cinderella" by 20 young ladies – Wound up with big dance . . .

Sunday, June 15 . . . Wrote & sent letters to W H Virden, Frank B Doten and Ben H Miller, Bridgeport, Cal . . .

June 19 . . . Went on morning train to Carson – Was at Mint and then at Secy of States office, then at State Controller's, where I went through the quarterly statements of the mines for last 2 yrs, to add to my government report . . .

June 24 . . . Evening at Jingler Concert Co, colored, at National Guard Hall – ½ dozen of them including 2 women – Singing with Piano accompaniment – Very good – Jubilee singers, etc – Good house – Was at Enterprise – Published piece written by wife about Sagebrush . . .

June 26 . . . Evening theater – Play, "Held by the Enemy" – Good company – good house . . .

June 27 . . . Was at the Chollar, & works, & mill – got last returns from there & from Boyle of the Alta of the Comstock mining statistics I have been after for the last 2 wks or more . . .

Sunday, June 29 . . . Evening annual meeting of Pioneers held at hall – I presided – Only a quorum: Myself, Delavan, Baker, Haist and Eckelmann – Reelected all old officers – I again President . . .

July 1 . . . My report of the Pioneer meeting was published in full in morning *Enterprise* – as annexed – PM I copied it in writing, & mailed it to Senator Jones . . .

[Clip – Besides election results and claiming "the Society is in a very flourishing condition, although . . . the fact becomes more and more apparent that 'there's only a few of us left,' " AD reports a Pioneer resolution drawn up to applaud the efforts of Jones, Stewart, and Bartine on the silver question, and to advise them that if unrestricted coinage is not possible to insist that Congress at least provide for the monthly purchase of no less than 4,500,000 ounces of silver for dollars or certificates.]

July 2 . . . Met W H Messerve that used to keep saloon in Gold Hill when I was running the *News* – He is running the Indian store for Gov't on the Walker Lake Reservation, & now in on a visit for health . . . I took dinner with him at Fitzmier's – Toniest dinner I have eaten for months – had claret, etc – Figured all night at my statistics –

July 4 – Clear, warm & pleasant – 85° – Big celebrations in Va and Reno, but none in Carson – Rode in local passenger hitched to excursion train to Reno – 6 carloads including National Guard Va and Liberty Hose Co, Gold Hill – Big crowd from Gold Hill and lots got on along route and Carson – The flat joined at Gold Hill with Liberty hose cart on it was also crowded with the boys – Must have had nearly or quite 400 on the train when arrived at Reno – Big reception, military, firemen etc – Was about an hour before I got home – Found all right, flags & lanterns up, etc – Children all went with me to view procession about noon, and about 3 PM to see the "Horribles," also in the evening to see the fireworks on the public square, front of theater – Accidental explosion of a box of fireworks hurt 2 or 3 boys badly also a man, and other people trampled & hurt in the panic – Nobody killed – We also had juvenile fireworks in front yard – Bed 11 –

July 5 . . . About home most of day – trimmed trees, etc . . .

Sunday, July 6 . . . Left . . . on regular Express for Va . . . Tom S Fitch was orator in Reno on the 4th, and Frank G Newlands at Va –

July 7 . . . Evening wrote "Outside celebrations" for Enterprise . . .

July 8 . . . Jack Long died this AM at Hospital from injuries received 4th while putting up decorations in Lincoln Hose house, Gold Hill – Fell about 18 ft from a ladder, broke leg, some ribs & ruptured his bowels – 70 yrs old – Bed 2 –

July 9 – Same – On my statistics – 4 PM funeral of Jack Long – I rode out to cemetery & back with John Connerton, he driving his 'bus loaded with women attending the funeral – About 20 Exempts in line – Only a few of us left – Evening at Enterprise awhile – Wrote all night on "narrative" conclusion of my statistical Comstock –

July 12 . . . Delivered my Comstock report to S C Wright, Supt Carson Mint . . . Wrote resolutions on death of Jack Long for Exempts – Bed at 1 –

Sunday, July 13 – Went to Carson to see Sam Wright, Supt of the Mint – Found him – My Comstock report was mailed for Washington last evening – I gave him my bill to send after it . . . $150 – 2 PM attended meeting of Exempts – Introduced my Jack Long resolutions – unanimously adopted – Bed 1 –

July 14 – Same – Hotter – 87° – About town, at Con Va office on statistics, etc – Took evening train to Reno – Bob Evans, R S Evans, on board – Been out to Aurora working in milling concentration business, & now on way to experiment on the famous old time black sand deposits of Gold Bluff and Klamath river, Gold Beach etc – Thinks he can make the gold amalgamate, and otherwise achieve the success that everybody has failed in for the last 40 years – We rode together in the smoking car and he having his banjo along we had it turn about on the instrument much to the enjoyment of the mixed crowd of passengers, Chinese, Indians, niggers, Dagos, Jews, wood choppers, gentlemen etc – Arrived at Reno at 9 oclock – looked very dull – Bob walked up street with me & I bade him good by as he had to take the west bound train at 10:30 for Sacramento, there to take the Cal & Oregon for Yreka – Found all right at home – Bed at 10 √ –

July 15 . . . Very hot – Back to Va at 1:15 –

[Obituary of John C Frémont clipped from the *Chronicle* – Reviews Frémont's explorations and calls him "the pioneer of the civilization west of the Rocky Mountains" – The travels revealed the grand features of Upper California, "in the conquest of which Fremont bore an honorable part."]

Fremont was an honorary member of our Society of Pacific Coast Pioneers –

July 16 . . . Busy at room all day on statistics for the Treasury Dept, Washington DC – William Windom, Secy – A C Pratt, Comm, Examiners for this State . . .

July 19 . . . AOUW excursion & picnic . . . Visited picnic ground about an hour . . . Evening wrote up picnic . . .

Sunday, July 20 . . . PM had Charley Mathewson at room interviewing him on statistics . . .

July 21 . . . Horrifying tragedy at Savage mine at midnight last night –

Wm Nicholls murdered by Pat Crowley on the 1300 level – Saw corpse at Brown's – terrible – Bed 1 – Only 61 years old today –

[Long clips from the Virginia *Chronicle* and the *Enterprise* – Since a pick-axe killing in the Yellow Jacket 25 years before, all such altercations had been settled "on top," because concern for mutual safety ruled in the mines – At 11 Sunday night Nicholls, the shift boss, had reprimanded Crowley and two others for not getting enough work done, as they were all being lowered to the 1200-foot level – At the station Nicholls followed Crowley off and said something to him, and the 29-year-old, 6'3", 220-pound miner hit his boss with a pick – The three miners then went to the 1100-foot station, where, for an hour, the "men simply knocked their knees together while Crowley stared at them." – Crowley then returned to the 1200-foot level, and the two men started to climb out by the ladders, then contrived to ring the cage up to them, cut the bell rope to prevent Crowley from signalling a stop, and got to the surface – Police took Crowley without resistance at the 1200 level, but he had thrown the body down the shaft in an effort to make it appear an accident, and men had to be lowered by ropes to the 1300-foot level, where the vertical shaft changed to an incline – "The body was taken to Brown's undertaking rooms, where it was viewed by hundreds . . . The left side of the head was all crushed in, and there was nothing left from which to recognize a human face on that side, except that it lay at the end of a human trunk." – The popularity of the dead Nicholls, eleven years on the Comstock, sober and industrious, with a wife and five children, led to rumors of a lynching, and Crowley, a member of the Emmet Guard and "a very quiet, unobtrusive man," was taken to Carson at night, and would offer no explanation.]

July 22 through Aug 30 [The weather turns very hot – AD suffers a severe attack of diarrhea which is probably part of a plague of dysentery & typhoid fever which kills several people in Virginia City, but carries on busily with his mining statistics until he has completed them, does a little on insurance, a good deal of special reporting for the *Enterprise,* attends shows & meetings and is about town as usual – In the course of his business, works in several brief visits to his family – Representative and of independent interest:]

July 24 . . . Funeral of the murdered Wm Nicholls from Odd Fellows Hall this PM, a big one – Miners Union, IOOF, K of P, Chosen Friends etc – on foot 450 – 58 carriages – Band of music 10 – also *silent band* – over 700 people in all –

July 25 . . . Over 90° along C st – some said 95° . . . [two-line erasure] – Felt better & slept some hours . . .

July 26 . . . Took 7:20 train for Carson, having been up all night writing – Was at State House all day writing . . . Have not eaten a morsel of food since day before yesterday – ate a plate of soup with dry toast and tea this evening . . . [erasure] – Bed at 10, plum wore out –

Sunday, July 27 . . . I am losing flesh rapidly, & getting weak . . . slept till 1 . . . went to work once more on statistics for rest of night – I am using a diarrhea mixture of A M Cole, druggist . . .

July 28 . . . Diarrhea now a general complaint, among the miners & everybody – quite a number of funerals from it of children and others . . . Took what copy I had written down to morning local . . . I enclosed private note to Pratt, explaining that I was too sick to come down . . . Emanuel Nye, old timer here died yesterday . . . Was taken to Sacramento for burial – Pioneer, so I was invited to be a pall bearer – Too sick and weak to even do that for my own funeral –

July 29 . . . Went to Carson & worked with P on statistics . . . Think the diarrhea is checked – Very little appetite though . . .

July 31 . . . Carson & back again . . . Ate nothing today till I returned, when I took a pretty fair meal at Heffron's, roast beef ribs, pudding etc – most I have eaten for a week –

Aug 1 . . . Have got my appetite again apparently – Made out duplicate bills in Carson for my Mint job & gave them to Sam Wright . . .

Aug 2 . . . Lively fire at 8:30 – Lonkey's lumber yard – $1000 damage or loss – at 12:30 fire in front part of Odd Fellows building below sidewalk – from a man sleeping there putting his pipe away in his pocket still lighted – caught clothes afire & gave good start for a fire – detected it from outside – He nearly smothered to death when rescued by Alex Coryell, of police – Bed 12 –

Aug 7 . . . PM cloudy with 2 or 3 light thunder showers, which laid the dust & purified the air finely – sagebrush fragrance . . . Evening got "A Truckee Meadows Angel," sketch written by wife into paper . . . William Kemmler executed by electricity yesterday morning at Auburn, N.Y. – First case of the kind – Made bad job of it – Papers all condemn the experiment –

Aug 11 . . . Had a very bad spell of nightmare about 2 from lying on my back – Joe Douglass heard my miserable attempts at outcries and waked me – Worst I ever had –

Aug 12 . . . Evening at Opera House . . . Comstock Minstrels –

About 20 mostly local talent – Usual minstrel show, acrobatic, solos etc –
Pretty fair show for amateurs . . .

Aug 13 – Cooler – PM cloudy with good steady rain showers . . . Evening wrote sketch about the Douglass building for Enterprise . . .

The Douglass building is one of the most populous and popular structures for business and sleeping purposes in this city. What is not occupied for saloon, office or club-room arrangements is fully and completely utilized by a pretty good class of roomers, especially on the second and third floors. The entrances from B street, as well as from C, furnish ample facilities for ingress or egress at all times, and away in the past midnight and dark morning hours somebody is liable to be moving about. . . . Harmonious peace pervades the establishment, and the general rule long since squarely promulgated by the festive proprietor is always carefully respected: "Gentlemen, quarrel in your rooms, if you take a notion, but no fighting in the hallways or on the stairways."

The roomer who gets home after midnight, in compliance with the early-closing law, and plays his banjo or fife awhile before going to bed disturbs nobody but himself, and so long as he don't get into the wrong room he is all right. . . .

The other night the proprietor, who frequently sleeps in the building, heard a stranger noise than usual, and bounced out of bed to see about it. The noise came from a room near by, and sounded as though somebody was strangling to death or being murdered.

He banged at the door and gently shouted: "What the devil's the matter? Got the death rattles or the jim-jams?"

"Ugh! ugh! Come quick! Ugh, ugh! Ah, wah, wah! Ugh, hoo, oo!"

"But your door's locked: where's the key?"

"Ugh! Wow, wow! Ugh, ugh! It's on the inside. Come quick!"

"All right my son, you just keep your key on the inside and go on rasslin' with the devil; I'm going back to bed. Stop that thing now, or I'll raise your rent."

The noise ceased, and next morning they met and explanations were in order.

"No use you telling me about your having a fit of the nightmare. I know what it was, you'd been gorging yourself with 'sheep-dip.' Can't fool me—not for Joe. Been there and know all about it. 'Sheep-dip' straight, according to the unmistakable symptoms. But young feller you just quit that now, its hung onto you too long."

Aug 16 . . . Republican primaries today for delegates to State Convention . . . Very small vote cast – Bed 1 –

Aug 18 . . . Finished my statistical job & took on morning train to Carson – Steve Gillis was along & treated me to a good breakfast, drink, & cigar – I went to State House – Wilkinson, a type writer, type copied my MSS and I read & corrected it – So ends my statistical job – most of it forwarded to Washington last Saturday by Pratt – He paid me $2.50 more, making $42.50 in all . . .

Aug 21 . . . T B Storer died at Hospital, Va night before last –

Aug 23 . . . Dan Donovan died at 5:20 PM – room on my floor – front on C st – Evening wrote "Outside Notes" . . .

Aug 25 . . . PM 3 funerals – 2 yesterday – Many deaths last 2 or 3 wks from Typhoid fever, bowel complaint, diphtheria etc . . .

Aug 27 . . . Wrote up "Magpie Chatter" for tomorrow's Enterprise – staid with it – read proof etc – Bed 2:30 –

> A family down in Reno has a pretty good specimen magpie. He was captured a couple of months ago by one of the children before he was old enough to fly, and in less than a week made himself a full member of the family. His appetite was fine, and he kept all hands busy shoving hunks of bread and meat down his capacious throat, squawking very energetically whenever he was hungry. "Jack" has a free run of the premises, and the house dog stands in mortal fear of his strong, sharp bill. At first the old cat regarded him with a speculative eye, licking her chops as she fondly contemplated what a nice chicken dinner he would make, but a few sociable jabs of his bill between her eyes directly changed the current of her thoughts, and she gladly avoids his aggressive company. He whistles splendidly and talks three or four different languages, repeating very readily most any word he hears, and nothing delights him better than to sit face to face with one of the children and chatter and whistle uproariously to whatever is said to him.
>
> Down at the Mound House—junction of the C. & C. with the V. & T. railroad—is another lively young magpie. He belongs to Dave Pitman, conductor on the C. & C., and makes himself at home in and around the depot. He especially enjoys flying into the open door or window of some temporarily stopping passenger car and having a garrulous chat with the passengers. The other morning, for instance, when the local passenger train stopped there, as usual, "Barney" flew in through the rear door, perched himself on the back of one of the seats, and astonished the ladies and gents present with the volubility of his linguistic powers. He volunteered more information than anybody had heard or he knew himself, waiting for no introduction to those who didn't know him. Everybody liked him and listened to him like an oracle. One familiar gentleman addressed him:
>
> "I say, Barney!"
> "What?"
> "Are you there, Barney?"

"Ah there, pretty good; ah there, ha, ha, ha; dammit, get out; dry up, rats."

"Where are you going, Barney? Are you a deadhead on this train?"

"That's what, hurrah; ha, ha, you bet, rats, rats."

"What's the news in politics, Barney? Who's getting in?"

"Barney, Barney, ha, ha, whoo, whoo; dammit, rats."

"But who's going to be next Congressman?"

"John Mackay, John Mackay, ha, ha, John Mackay."

"But which party is going to win, Republicans or Democrats?"

"Rats! rats! rats! ha, ha, dammit, rats!"

"You observe the intelligence of this wonderful bird, ladies and gentlemen, and how readily he answers that the Democrats are going to win. But now Barney ——"

Just here Jerry Bray, the conductor, stepped in from the baggage-room.

"Get out o' here you long-tailed rascal, whoosh!" and with a wild derisive squawk Barney flitted out of the back door, flying back toward Mound House. "Oh, what a pity, now," some of the ladies exclaimed, "he'll be lost."

"Never you fear for him, ladies," responded Jerry, "he's all right. Have to run him out of this every day. Never allow him to deadhead any further than the Eureka dump." The trainmen, freight-handlers and everybody about Mound House station know Barney and handle him familiarly, yet have to be on their guard lest he should take a sly notion to nip a small chunk out of their finger or back of their hand with his stout beak.

Three or four days ago at the boarding house near the station he was having a little concert with a pet canary, when out of pure rollicking fun he gave his musical little friend a jovial poke with his bill under the left ear. Directly after Barney stood over him watching his death struggles with his head cocked contemplatively over one side muttering "dammit, rats, rats, rats." Barney was arrested and caged, but for the two days that he languished in the Bastile he never spoke a word or even squawked.

Aug 30 . . . I sent letter . . . to Yerington asking renewal of pass . . . Was weighed at Mallon's today – 196 lbs . . .

Sept 1 – Clear & pleasant – 76° – George Warren of the *Chronicle* being on a drunk, the management put me on the paper in his place, with directions to stay on till told to quit – Started in at 9 AM – Got along well – Evening about town – Bed at 1 –

Sept 2 through Nov 30 [AD very busy on *Chronicle* local, insurance & doing free-lance pieces for the *Enterprise* – Mostly short entries. Of interest:]

Sept 2 . . . Pass renewed for 3 mos . . .

Sept 3 . . . Evening attended prize fight & reported it . . .

Sept 4 . . . Rep State Convention . . . I reported . . .

Sept 5 . . . Localized as usual & rep convention & County Commissioners – Convention through about 4 PM – Got full report in Chronicle – Most of delegates, etc, left by evening train . . .

Sept 9 . . . Sent wife a $20 greenback . . . Gov Stevenson very sick & liable to die –

Sept 11 . . . By today's mail I received a treasury draft for $100 from Washington DC – Paid Douglass $62.50 of it rent to Oct 1 – $10 to Williams & Prater, borrowed money . . .

Sunday, Sept 14 . . . Went to W S James, Gold Hill Assay office, Secy of the Centennial & paid my last two assessments, $15.45 each . . . about town – WCTU own and occupy the old *News* office . . .

Sept 15 . . . The hay fever has hit me as usual . . . Bowels troubled me bad today . . . Much sickness prevalent . . . many deaths – Richard J Thomas 18 yrs old died of fever & was buried this PM – Big funeral – Battery A of which he was a member turned out in full – delegations other Cos –

Sept 18 . . . John H Dennis came up from Reno today – Going on as editor of *Chronicle* tomorrow . . .

Sept 19 – Clear & cooler – Dennis started in as editor today – Both of us writing in same room – 35 yrs ago we were at Ft John together – I was lying helpless from a mining injury & he nursed me – God bless him – Bed 12 – Wrote & sent letters this evening to C H Stoddard Reno, acknowledging receipt of Fair ticket – letter to wife enclosing her the ticket – letter to B & M – Catarrh bad –

Sunday, Sept 21 . . . Governor Stevenson died this morning – flags ½ mast . . .

Sept 23 . . . Evening at theater – W J Scanlan & Co in "Myles Aroon" – Very good – Very full crowded house – Bed 1 – Hay fever, etc, very prevalent –

Sept 24 . . . Scanlan & Co in the "Irish Minstrel" – good play and good house – Met Scanlan after the show, at International – Pretty good sort of a fellow – Like him – Bed 1 –

Sept 25 . . . Thomas Keene, a very good tragedian from the East with a good Co played Richard III – Very good house . . . This PM I telegraphed: "Samuel B. Doten, Reno, Nev. Tell Piper to admit couple of you to theater" – Alf Doten –

Sept 26 . . . Grand Military day at State Fair . . . Emmett guard got the prize for best attendance . . . [Mary publishes a poem about Governor Stevenson in the *Reno Evening Gazette.*]

Sept 27 . . . Went to theater – "Black Hawks" with "Arizona Joe" in leading character – Sort of Buffalo Bill, cowboy piece, horses, dogs etc, on stage – Big St Bernard dog "Jumbo," 195 pounds . . .

Sept 29 . . . Only good solid rain since last Winter – Helps out the hay fever vastly . . . Last evening . . . I suffered much from cough, congestion of lungs, difficulty in breathing, etc, more than ever before – so much so that I had to take a walk down town – The fresh, damp air benefited me some, but three or four drinks of whisky did much better and I went to bed feeling all right and had a good night's sleep – Think liberal and frequent doses of whisky good for *pneumonia,* a light touch of which I had, in my opinion . . .

Sept 30 . . . Evening at theater & saw last of engagement of "Arizona Joe" . . . Played "Little Violet" . . . to about a $30 house – It is simply a dime novel crowd without a good actor except the dogs – plays the same – trashy & no merit – excepting the fine rifle shooting of A.J. – That was the best I ever saw, unless there was a trick in it which I think not – apple target . . .

Sunday, Oct 5 . . . Evening the McMahon circus arrived – Big she *"Jumbo"* – elephant the "largest in the world" . . .

Oct 6 . . . McMahon's circus paraded at noon – Band chariot, cavalcade of performers in knightly uniform – long string of horses led by grooms – 2 biggest elephants ever on the Comstock – Evening I walked down to circus – at old grounds – Audience all that could crowd in – I think about 4,000 – Very good single ring circus . . . Sent $20 to wife . . .

Oct 9 – Snowstorm from earliest morning all day at intervals – Republican County Convention at National Guard Hall – I reported it . . . John S Werrin died of typhoid pneumonia . . . Got in 600 lbs Pleasant Valley coal today . . . so I feel well fixed on a starter for the Winter –

Oct 11 . . . Democratic primaries casting for County Convention on Monday – No opposition tickets & no excitement – Evening at Opera

House reporting big Rep meeting – Powning, Newlands, Colcord et al spoke – Was at Enterprise office afterward reading proof, etc . . .

Oct 13 . . . Reported Democratic County Convention – No very great stir or excitement . . .

Oct 16 . . . Got letter from J P Jones . . . who will be here in a day or two . . .

Oct 17 . . . Evening attended a called meeting at National Guard Hall to make arrangements for reception of J P Jones – Visited Mechanics Union Ball at Opera House, for benefit of the striking Iron Molders' Union of San Francisco – Crowded and having big time . . .

Oct 18 . . . Evening, Senator Stewart spoke at Opera House – Big crowd – Afterward he had a reception at W E Sharon's house – 2 bands of music – I was around – Bed at 1 – I was on the stage as one of the Vice Presidents tonight . . .

Oct 20 . . . Evening attended the reception of Senator Jones, at Opera House – Big crowd, etc – Bed 1 –

Sunday, Oct 26 . . . We got over a barrel full of pears from our big pear tree at home in Reno – some still on the tree . . .

Oct 28 . . . Evening I walked down to Gold Hill & back to hear Geo W Cassidy's political talk at Miners' Union Hall – Brass Band, bonfires etc – Spoke 2 hrs – I at the reporter's desk on the stage, with Alf Chartz . . . Went through Orphan Asylum . . . St Mary's this AM & wrote it up – Orphan's Fair tomorrow commences for a week –

Oct 30 . . . Evening reported Bartine-Cassidy joint discussion at Opera House – Big affair – Bed 1 –

Oct 31 . . . Evening rode to Gold Hill on train . . . attended meeting at Miners Union Hall – Newlands, Colcord, Judge Wells, Egan and John E Jones spoke . . .

Nov 1 . . . Evening speaking at Opera House by C C Powning, J A Stephens and Senator J P Jones . . .

Nov 3 . . . Politics stirring pretty lively . . . The paper delayed by election matters etc for over a week, getting to press late, etc . . . this eve . . . got to press nearly 6 oclock – Press ran at usual rate of 33 per minute, and Coleman, manager of the paper, who is an old newspaper folder and carrier, stood in, folding them just as fast as the press ran them – 33 a minute – fastest newspaper folding I ever saw by hand – Evening at Opera House – Carleton Opera Co in the "Brigands" . . .

Nov 4 . . . AM worked lively, & got through at 2 PM, as desire was to get paper out early, being election day – Very lively election day – Music, carriages with placards, etc . . .

Nov 5 . . . Busy getting returns of the elections – Reps have made a clean sweep, apparently . . .

Nov 7 . . . Got in last of election returns, 3d Ward, 3 PM . . .

Nov 11 . . . Colder – As usual – Bed 12 – Undressing for bed I discovered my right leg between knee and ankle considerably swollen – Not painful but enlarged and firm – Is it dropsy? Dennis off the paper – Through Sat night – Was only on for the campaign – Paid by the Central Committee Dem –

Nov 17 . . . Trial of Pat Crowley for Killing Wm Nichols in the Savage mine on 20th of last July was commenced in the Dist Court this AM before Judge Rising – Day used up trying to get a jury – 11 out of a venire of 100 but more yet challanged . . .

Nov 18 . . . Exhausted another venire of 50 in Crowley murder case this PM . . .

Nov 24 . . . Jury secured in Crowley case, this PM and trial of case begun –

Nov 25 . . . Rose at 6 – shaved etc – wrote & sent letter this morning train to Yerington asking influence to secure US Marshalship for Nevada for me – Also sent letter . . . to Powning on same subject – Sent one yesterday . . . to US Senator Stewart . . . The Crowley murder case with full jury in Dist Court today at 10 AM – I reported – Evidence all in this evening . . . [The papers show Crowley's plea to be the usual self-defense – Not only had Nicholls called him a "s—n of a b—h," but he had seemed to be threatening Crowley with the pick he was carrying.]

Nov 26 . . . Heard most of the arguments of counsel in the murder trial – The 4th & last, Stephens, was fairly started when paper was going to press . . . I took evening train to Reno . . .

Nov 27 . . . Thanksgiving Day – AM down town – Had Thanksgiving dinner at home – Only the family – Roast pork, cranberry sauce, sourkraut, peanuts, cake, etc – PM train for Va – At Carson 1 h & 10 m – Met Yerington at his office & had short interview – Found turkey at Harry Summers' saloon etc – Arr at Va at 7:15 – About 9:30 went to Chronicle office, went through the exchanges & got good start for tomorrow – At 11 visited ball at National Guard Hall, for benefit of 4th Ward School – Closely crowded with young folks mostly – Very fine & successful ball – Left it at 1, still going on – Bed at 2 – The murder jury came to a verdict at 1:25 this morning, were called into court at 2:10 – rendered verdict of *murder in the second degree* & were discharged – Sentence, Saturday at 10 AM –

Nov 28 . . . Major J H Dennis reported for duty this morning and is to supersede me after this week . . . Wrote & sent letter to J P Jones, Palace Hotel, SF . . . also telegraphed Jones at noon "Powning will confer with you on Marshalship Nevada – Please answer" –

Nov 29 . . . Judge Rising . . . sentenced Crowley to the State Prison for life – Big crowd – I saw Crowley leave in carriage for Prison about 1 PM . . .

Sunday, Nov 30 . . . Sent letter to Yerington . . . for pass renewal – About town considerably – Bed 11 –

Dec 1 . . . I helped on the *Chronicle* some, to get Dennis started in right . . . About town mostly – Evening at *Enterprise,* helping, reading proof etc – Bed at 2 . . .

Dec 2 . . . Dr J B Zangerle died Sunday evening . . .

Dec 3 . . . When I got up at 8 AM was about 4 inches of snow & still snowing lively . . . Bed at 12 – Nearly a foot of snow on ground & still snowing . . . This PM I sent following telegram & got no answer: "C C Powning, Reno – When will Jones Reno – Must consult you both Marshalship – Answer" –

Dec 5 . . . Sleighing good – Gold Hill bus on runners & lots of grocery & other vehicles same way – About town as usual . . .

Sunday, Dec 7 . . . Got out the type written headings, etc of my US Marshalship application from Alf Chartz . . . Wrote & sent various letters on small propositions East –

Dec 8 . . . Made a big quail stew this evening – 8 California valley quail – cost a bit apiece –

Dec 9 . . . Carson on morning train – About town – got some signatures to my Marshalship application – Recd by mail today 1 doz catheters . . .

Dec 10 . . . At Carson same as yesterday . . .

Dec 11 . . . Getting signatures as yesterday – Tried to get my pass renewed, but Supt Yerington refused – Evening to Reno . . .

Dec 12 . . . A female ghost has been seen about the big Congregational Church on the next street west of our house the last 2 or 3 evenings – creates much talk and excitement –

Dec 13 . . . Met the Piute chief, Johnson Sides this PM down town, & he gave me a good fill about the Indian "Messiah," etc – I took copious notes – Bed 10 –

Dec 15 . . . Evening Piper passed Bessie, Sam & I in to see Adelaide Moore in Juliet . . .

Dec 17 . . . Morning train for Va . . . The Adelaide Moore Co at Opera House in Pygmalion & Galatea – Good House – I was at my room – Wrote "Along the Railroad" – Took it to the Enterprise . . .

Dec 19 . . . Went to Carson morning train – secured couple more signatures – At Secy of State office I wrote letter to Congressman H F Bartine . . . asking his assistance to Marshalship and letter to Hon W M Stewart on same subject, enclosing my application & note to President – So now my bark is launched . . .

Dec 23 . . . Today I wrote up a Christmas advertising review for *Chronicle* – Column & a half of puffs – Coleman the manager paid me $5 for it . . . Had my Reno ghost story in morning Enterprise –

Dec 24 . . . Wrote "Piute Messiah" for the *Enterprise* – Staid with it, read proof etc – Bed 3:30 – Lots of Christmas cheer at the various saloons tonight –

Dec 25 – Clear & pleasant – Christmas Day – About town – Everybody enjoying the occasion, nicely – Plenty of turkey everywhere, so I got some of it at Joe Marshall's – Evening theater – John S Lindsay as "Ingomar the Barbarian," supported by Miss Luella Lindsay his daughter, as "Parthenia" & a pretty fair Co from the East – About ⅓ of a house – Pretty good show – He, 1st rate – Show out at 11:20 – Went to N G Hall &

saw annual ball of the National Guard – Excellent party – Bed 2 – Had my "Piute Messiah" sketch in the morning's *Enterprise* –

[A half-column clip, consisting mostly of quotes from the interview with Johnson Sides, "the well-known Piute chief representative and interpreter," who is put out with a vile woodcut from the *Police Gazette,* showing "a ghostly white cadaverous-looking dude with a light moustache, scanty frizzle bangs and no shirt, holding in one hand a sort of mop like a horse's tail tied onto a broomstick," which the *Gazette* claims is Sides – He is tired of his "Messiah" notoriety, and says:]

"This whole story was begun by a Piute over in Mason Valley they call Jack Wilson. Everybody knows him, and he was raised there. He's about 40 years old and his Piute name is 'We-vo-cah' . . .

"He tells everybody he got sick and died two years ago last Winter and God made him alive and said he must preach to the Indians, and so he does ever since. He tells 'em that all what's dead will come to life again and get all their country back, and the whites will have to leave, so they'll be better off than they ever was before, with plenty of game and whatever they wants.

". . . There used to be much more Indians that believed in him, but he's gettin' played out.

"It's a dam lie 'bout I was at Salt Lake and the Mormons put me up to be Messiah. . . . I was up to Idaho a couple of years ago visitin' the Bannocks about Fort Hall; that's the nearest I come to it. There isn't been no trouble . . . and no need of the Governor sending guns and powder and soldiers out in Nye county. The only trouble has been whisky, and I think damn bad whisky at that. The Piutes are all good folks if you give 'em a chance. . . .

"But this makin' a Jesus Christ out of me don't go . . .

"That story troubles and makes fun of me, and I don't like it. Sam Davis and Bill Nye got it up, and they think it's funny, but I don't cause it hurts me. They're newspaper men and ain't got no character to lose, but I have. . . . They should let me alone."

Dec 26 . . . Evening at Opera House – "Damon & Pythias" by the Lindsay Co – Very slim house . . .

Dec 27 . . . Paid W S James, Secy of Centennial $15.50 assessment, which squares me to date, & took up my piece of stock . . . Evening went to theater – Play "Miralda" a Cuban Spanish piece by same Co – Poorest house I ever saw for so good a Co – Not over $40 I should judge . . .

Sunday, Dec 28 . . . Evening and night at room straightening out & fixing up my Insurance accounts & records – At it all night . . .

Dec 29 . . . This PM, Mike Conlon an old Irish mining friend of mine presented me with a nice new hickory cane – Took me to Harris' cigar store where there is a fine assortment & I selected to suit, & he paid for it $1 – It is the best one I ever had, and I am proud of it –

Dec 30 – Morning about 3 inches of snow on the ground – light storms during the day – not enough for sleighing – Was about town . . . Evening about town, & at the social of the Bijou Club at N G Hall – They had the O N O club from Carson to entertain & did it big – Special train, carriages & all that sort of thing – 11 o'clock, presentation of tin whistles, trumpets & toys to all the crowd – at 12 big lunch on little tables set all around the hall – Carsonites returned on their special about 2 oclock – I bed at 1 – still storming – I received a box by mail, from Reno, containing Xmas presents – Book "Standish of Standish" and a fine silk handkerchief from Cornelia – A fine cabinet-size picture of Charlie from himself, a little pocket match box, from "Steve" and a nice neck-tie from Millie . . .

Dec 31 . . . The usual saloon festivities went on this evening, with egg nog etc – people generally hilarious, but quiet and not disposed to be belligerent – Bed at 5 . . . At midnight the mining and milling work steam whistles blew in the New Year very vociferously – No other demonstrations – And so ends Journal Book No *65* – To be continued in Book No 66, if I continue to live –

Alf Doten.

BOOK NO. *66*

Virginia City
Jan 1, 1891 – June 30, 1891

Jan 1, 1891 – Variable weather – sunshine and cloud – thawy and muddy – A.M. busy at room till noon– By mail received B & M proof blanks from San F to give to C E Mack, atty in Zangerle death case – W P Bennett of Gold Hill met me – We went to my room, and I examined and corrected a lot of manuscript for him, for the book on pioneer reminiscences he is getting up – Took a couple of hours, and he paid me a couple of dollars – At 3 PM went to John Connerton's residence, corner of E & Washington sts, & dined with him & wife – Turkey, etc, & pleasant social time for 3 hours – Evening, about town – quiet for New Year – Bed at 1 – Clear & pretty cold –

Jan 2 – Same – Busy at room most of day, tailoring, sewing and fixing up my daily costume, etc – Evening down town – Met John H Dennis, editor of the Chronicle, & we dined together at the City Bakery – After that, we met Fred Clough who was born at Fort John, Amador County, Cal, after Dennis & I left there – His father, Orson Clough kept the store where I was taken at the time I got caved on and so nearly killed at Ft John in 1854 – We had a long and very interesting chat together about those old times – Clough is an engineer at the Alta – His father is still living in the Ft John section – We three the only Ft Johners in this vicinity that we know of – Bed at 1 –

Sunday, Jan 4 . . . Jim Jewell fell dead on C street about noon, from hemorrhage of the lungs . . .

Jan 5 . . . PM rode to Gold Hill on bus, was [at] Crown Point office, etc – walked back – went to room & wrote letter to J P Jones, Washington D.C. about my Marshalship . . .

Jan 6 – Light snow storms most of day – cloudy & coldest of season – PM attended special meeting of the Exempts – called to attend funeral of Jim Jewell – Only 8 present out of the 37 of us left – concluded not to turnout as a body & detailed 2 pall bearers – Light funeral – 5 carriages – About 50 Odd Fellows, Chosen Friends, Miners Union, Exempts etc on foot – Bad day for funeral excursions – Evening about town – at room wrote up or fixed up sketch for W P Bennett – "Downie of Downieville" – Bed 2 –

Jan 7 . . . Evening at N G Hall to Dr Clark's specialty entertainment – a medical lecture with song, dance, dog show etc as attractions – Paid 15 cts admission to seats – standing room free – Advertised to run for two weeks commencing last Monday – Full houses . . .

Jan 8 . . . Mailed tonight letters to Geo B Van Emon, and W R Mc-Fadden assemblymen from Linclon County, Pioche, notifying them I am candidate for Sergeant-at-arms of Assembly . . . letter from wife enclosing one from Rozzie, brother Sam and a little well written sketch from Sammy: "The Fate of an Indian Doctor" –

Sunday, Jan 11 – Clear & pleasant – PM attended funeral of Miles Goodman from Pioneer Hall – About 60 Exempts & pioneers etc & about 20 carriages – I walked out & back in the circus – ain't going to do it again – "hardly ever" – Rec'd letter from Bartine this PM – Nothing in it for me – Bed 1 –

Jan 12 . . . On Chronicle today in place of Major Dennis who was in Reno . . .

Jan 16 . . . About town – Evening do – Caucus held at 8 of the Storey Co Assembly delegation – at N G Hall – Jimmy Williams of Gold Hill agreed upon as nominee for Sergeant-at-Arms . . .

Jan 17 . . . Evening I got in Sammy sketch, properly fixed up . . .

Sunday, Jan 18 . . . Went to Carson on morning train to watch the starting in of the Carson Congress, or more properly speaking the Nevada Legislature – and most especially to get in as Engrossing Clerk of the Senate – Worked best I knew how on it . . .

Jan 19 – C[lear] & P[leasant] – Morning train to Carson – Legislature convened at noon, both houses – attaches sworn in etc . . .

Jan 20 . . . Reported Legislature for the Enterprise – Campbell got me a pass from Yerington for the session –

Jan 21 – Same – Carson & back, as yesterday, reporting the Legislature – Read proof etc – Bed 1 – In the Enterprise of Tuesday I find the following [clip] among the death notices:

> MORTON—In Eureka, Nev., January 15, E. E. Morton, a native of Plymouth, Mass., aged 72 years.

Now the above most assuredly must be Ellis H Morton – E H, instead of E. E. – my old friend and schoolmate "Morton the Ciderman," whose place I made my home in my early days on the Comstock – B st – I dont know where his wife now is that he then had – my "little mother."

Jan 22 through Feb 23 [AD reporting the Legislature days & reading proof evenings – No detail – Of interest:]

Sunday, Jan 25 . . . At room most of day – got bad cold & *both* legs swelled . . . Bed at 12 – with both legs wrapped in alcohol –

Jan 28 . . . Yesterday both Houses elected Senator Jones to succeed himself, and today in Joint convention ratified & confirmed the same – also reelected Frank J McCullough Warden of State Prison . . .

Jan 29 . . . This PM Theodore Winters who got the complimentary vote of the Democratic legislators (6) for US Senator yesterday gave a champagne blowout at the Arlington Hotel . . . At 8:30 big banquet in honor of Jones at Arlington – I was invited and present – Grand time – Bed at Circe's Carson Exchange . . .

Sunday, Feb 1 . . . I staid at home most of day, fixing up a pair of drawers, mending, writing etc – Wrote obituary resolutions for Jim Jewell, Virginia Lodge No 3, I.O.O.F. and for Miles Goodman, member of Exempts – Evening at theater – The Eunice Goodrich Company played "Little Emily" (from "David Copperfield") – Very good entertainment but rather a slim house . . . Bed at 3 –

Feb 4 . . . I went to Theater – Goodrich Co in "Innocent Salt" – Rather amusing – good house for the last night – Each of audience had 2 tickets with numbers on them given to them on entering, & at conclusion drawing for a gold watch took place – A little boy held the winning number & got the watch . . .

Feb 7 . . . Evening at Theater – "Corinne" – Good house – Bed at 2:30 – Very good show – in fact extra good – The play was "Carmen" by the Kimball Opera Comique and Burlesque Co – A sort of Spanish piece in 3 acts – Big crowd of actors – about 40 – "Corinne" was the prin-

cipal character – as "Carmen" – One of the prettiest, most dashing sou-
brettes in the world –

Feb 9 . . . Evening at theater – Goodyear, Elitch & Schillings Minstrels – Big full house – Big 1st class show . . .

Feb 12 . . . Both Houses . . . adjourned about noon to attend the
funeral of Mrs Parker, late Matron of the State Orphans Home – I got
my report all written up . . . left at 7:50 for Reno . . . Found all
hands all right – Bed – 10 √.

Feb 14 – Cloudy with fierce gales all day . . . did some damage blowing down awnings, signs, fences etc . . .

Sunday, Feb 15 – Big snow storm all day – 6 inches . . .

Feb 16 . . . Met Frank B Doten in town today . . .

Feb 17 . . . Evening at room, Enterprise etc – Long report – nearly 2
columns – At room had good fire, wrote & read & didn't go to bed at
all . . .

Feb 18 – C & P – About an inch fresh snow on the ground in morning –
Same in Carson – On way back met remains of W H Meserve at Mound
House, coming in from Schurz the RR station of Walker River Reservation, where he has been Sub Agent, or Post Trader for Indians last 3 or 4
yrs – Died of general break down consumption, etc – 62 yrs old – His
wife was along – Bill Gibson came up from Carson with me – At Va the
remains taken to C Brown's undertaking shop, to be buried tomorrow by
the P C Pioneers of which he was a member – At Enterprise etc – Bed at
3 – very tired & sleepy – Sleighing still pretty fair on C st – Swedish lady
concert at Opera House – 8 of them – Very good indeed – Fair House –
Cold clear night – All the members of the Bankers & Merchants M L
Ass'n in this section received notices today from the home office, San F,
of closing out business of the B & M, and proposed transfer to another
Co – In other words the B & M has *busted out* – I received this evening a
letter from G W Pease, clerk at the Indian Agency, Schurz where Meserve
was & died – Wants me to get Meserve's place –

Feb 19 – Cold, sleety day – AM at room – PM attended at funeral of
W H Meserve – I presided – made a few preliminary remarks – Rev Mr
Witter did the religious part – I rode out to the cemetery in 4 seat car-
riage, with Doc Delavan & 2 others – Very cold raw time – Got legisla-

tive report from Carson in Tribune – Fixed it up, with addition of my
own for Enterprise – read proof etc – Bed 3 –

Feb 20 . . . Jos Grismer & wife, Phoebe Davies, & Co played "Beacon
Lights" this evening at Opera House to good audience . . .

Feb 21 . . . Evening I wrote report of the Senate from the Carson
Tribune and from what Senators Boyle & McDonell told me . . . The
Grismer-Davies Co played "Lights & Shadows" . . .

Feb 24 – Very snow stormy all day – About 2 ft of snow on deck this
morning – and 6 or 8 inches in Carson – Very slippery and bad – Morning train about an hour late on account of snow obstruction with an
up-bound ore train – I got to Carson in time however, to get report – Evening got my report into Enterprise all right, but about 11½ oclock was
going down from Douglass building to finish up report, when I slipped &
fell in front of Mallon's store, spraining my left leg at the knee joint very
badly – May be a broken bone on the outside – Got up to room, splinted
leg and staid there – Bed at 1 – Very sore and painful – Think I am
knocked out for the present –

Feb 25 . . . Was alone all day till 4 PM when I called my next room
neighbor Jerry Hurley & sent him for Dr Manson – Manson found no
bones broken, more a very bad strain and tear of ligaments which will
lay me up for a few days – Gave me a linament or lotion to dope it with –
Keep it well toweled – Evening Several of the boys, including Plant and
Zimmer visited me, with aid and comfort –

Feb 26 . . . My leg grows stronger, but can only walk on it with cane
and chair . . . Got dinner sent me from restaurant – Evening Zimmer
was with me an hour or two – Brought me bowl of soup from Joe Mar-
shalls saloon . . .

Feb 27 . . . Can walk all about room with only a cane – Had several
visitors today – Zimmer especially – Evening mostly – He brought me
clam chowder from Marshall's saloon – John Connerton about noon
brought me chicken fricassee . . . The sun looked sideway and very nar-
rowly into my window this PM for the first time this year –

Feb 28 – Stormy . . . can walk all about room with no cane – Plenty
of visitors . . .

Sunday, March 1 – Stormy – A heavy wet snowstorm prevailed AM &
most of day, with occasional high winds . . . Got out through the hall-

way as far as privy . . . Evening Zimmer & another gent called – I played banjo, and Z my tin flageolet – together very well . . .

March 4 . . . Worked at patching my carpet where it was badly worn into holes – Got down to it very well, considering my lame knee . . .

March 5 . . . Plenty of visitors – Evening Fred Clough & John H Dennis, my 2 old Ft John boys visited me . . .

March 10 – Variable – very thawy & mild – As usual till 11 PM when I got on my breeches for the 1st time & went down stairs & out on the sidewalk to where I fell 2 weeks ago – Sidewalks being all clear & passable & having the same rubbers on, I walked down to the Enterprise office, & to Joe Marshall's saloon & got a plate of stew & a glass of beer – Got along 1st rate – At 12 got back & up to Room 29 in Douglass Building, next floor above me, to room of John H Dennis, my old pard, and now editor & local of the *Va Chronicle* – He got his right arm broke about 7 PM by a tumble off sidewalk corner of C & Sutton where Joe Stewart fell & broke his ankle, about a year ago – Bed at 1 –

March 11 . . . Down to the Chronicle office before 8 – offered my services in place of Dennis, but Al Mills had been selected . . . Evening was at *Enterprise* awhile – reading proof, etc, & got in a couple of items – Bed at 3 – Visited Dennis for an hour or so this evening – He is having a pretty hard time – much pain – helpless etc . . .

March 13 . . . L Guggenheim, Treasurer of the Exempts, paid me $6 this PM, benefit for my lame knee – 2 wks benefit – $6 deducted for dues to Jan 1 . . . Evening I was at home mostly, cooking a nice chicken I bought of McGurn – 90 cts – Bed at 2 –

March 17 . . . Col Pat Ford received his policy this morning's mail from the Mutual Benefit Life Association of America, being the first I have seen from the B & M transfer . . . got $40 from Campbell this evening –

March 18 – Morning a heavy snowstorm – Walked down to the RR Depot, with a darkey friend assisting me down Union st . . . Reno nice and pleasant – Found folks all right . . . Had a mean, restless night, the bed and my leg troubling me . . .

March 19 . . . Morning train to Carson . . . Last day of the Legislature . . . Evening train to Va – Was at Enterprise & about town awhile – Bed at 1 – A C Pratt paid me $10 today – Owes me still $2.50 –

March 23 . . . Too slippery to venture out much . . . Lent Major J H Dennis my best overcoat today to get on the street in . . .

March 26 – Stormy . . . At room most of day – Quite a boom in stocks last few days – Con Va up to $13 – Improvement in quality & quantity of ore said to be the cause – All stox up proportionately – Overman $5 today . . . Much sickness from la grippe, etc – many deaths . . .

March 28 . . . Wrote & sent letter to Mrs M N Morton, San Francisco, speaking of her husband's death in Eureka Jan 15 – Dont know even if she is still alive, but wrote to her anyhow . . . Don't know anything of her since I was in S.F. last – a dozen years ago – Also wrote to wife as usual – PM Kinzle and James came to my room, & we held meeting of the Centennial Trustees – levied asst of 3 cts, & called annual meeting for May 4 – Evening I got advertisements of each, with local notices, etc, into the Enterprise – Also wrote and fixed up about ½ column of acct of annual banquet of New England California Pioneers in Boston with bit of poetry – furnished by Bob Patterson . . .

Sunday, March 29 . . . Easter Sunday – Special train from Reno & Carson, etc, brought several Knights Templar – Made a fine show in their fine uniforms marching to & from church service . . .

March 30 . . . Evening at the Opera House – "Social Sessions" company, with the "Black Hussar" band – Fine music & amusing play . . .

March 31 . . . Evening Opera House – Cleveland's Minstrels – Big house – Best performance of the kind I ever saw –

April 3 . . . Got my regular shoes on today – been wearing "arctics," with slippers inside . . . Looked in at ball of Wenonah Council I.O.R.M. at National Guard Hall – Fine party – special train from Carson brought about 60 to it . . .

April 4 . . . Campbell of the Enterprise paid me $20 more today, so I squared up my standing in IOOF – $3 to April 1 – paid room rent $8, sent $3 postal order to Wakelee & Co – $1 PO Box – $1.50 granite iron po' – etc $2 – & have $1.50 left – Evening attended Fell-Wilson prize fight at Opera House – Big fizzle . . .

[Clip, *Enterprise,* April 5 – One of the fighters held out for $100 more than had been put up – No fight – Only a few of the audience recovered their money – Police broke up ensuing brawl.]

April 6 . . . At dark, heavy snowstorm . . . Evening staid at room –

too much chance for slipping – Visited Dennis, who is still unable for duty – Bed 1 –

April 7 . . . Dave Morgan of Gold Hill died this morning –

April 9 – C & P – Campbell of the Enterprise paid me $10 more this PM – John W Mackay arrived by noon train, from San F & the East – Had his eldest son along – Evening I called on Prof Thos Cara at the International – He is just recovering from "la grippe" – Dave Morgan's funeral this PM was attended by 100 miners on foot, and 60 carriages – came from Gold Hill, & buried in the cemetery north of this city –

April 10 . . . PM about town – Evening was up to Opera House awhile, at big masked ball of National Guard – Biggest I ever saw here – many from Carson, etc – Bed 1 –

Sunday, April 12 . . . Attended regular monthly meeting of Exempts – & was allowed 4 weeks more sick benefits – $24 – Then I went to John Connerton's by invitation to dinner – Dr Delavan also there . . . Clam chowder, fish balls, oyster stew & custard – oranges etc . . .

April 13 . . . The "Si Plunkard" (J C Lewis) Yankee Comedy Co arrived by noon train – Their fine band paraded at 3 PM up & down C st – Very excellent music – Band rigged up as farmers, etc – Hard looking lot – Evening I attended their show at Opera House – Big audience, & very good performance of the amusing character – Bed at 1 –

April 15 . . . Stocks booming, Con Va 14½, etc –

Sunday, April 19 . . . W P Bennett of Gold Hill got onto me in the PM, and piled a big job of cranky writing about a book he is going to print before long . . .

April 20 . . . Was talking hilariously with Dan Davis in the International saloon only about 20 minutes before he went up home and died – Showed no sign or inclination of dying – [Died of heart failure]

April 23 . . . I was about town as usual – Evening at theater – "Shenandoah" – Biggest house for years – Good play . . .

Sunday, April 26 . . . Was at room most of day writing for W P Bennett – "Some Fast Trips" – Bed at 1 –

April 30 . . . Delivered to Bennett his writings done by me . . . As compensation for my work to date he agreed to pay $15.50 to Bill James Secy of Centennial, my present assessment, delinquent last Monday . . .

May 1 . . . Yesterdays S F *Examiner* & the *Chronicle* brought up from Reno over the Grade by single horse cart this morning arriving at 3 AM . . . before the *Enterprise* was out . . .

May 2 . . . About 6:30 AM I dreamed I was asleep in the old house at home. 2 persons, one of them a tallish young lady, & a relative came in from another room weeping and she said to me: "She has just died" – I understood this to be my sister Cornelia, who was sick. I awoke feeling very sad. The letter I wrote to my old friend Mrs M N Morton March 28, directed to San F, returned to me today marked officially, "Unclaimed" etc. Guess she must be dead . . . Stocks stronger today on the new boom, Con Va being $19 – higher than for years . . .

May 4 . . . Con Va got up to $21 – PM I 'bussed to GH & attended annual meeting of Centennial at GH Assay office – Old Board re-elected – Stock dividend declared . . . Evening attended my Lodge – My case was called up & I made a statement as to my standing at time of accident – was $3 behind on dues then – Voted to donate me $20 – Wrote up the Centennial meeting for Enterprise, etc – Bed at 2 – [AD now owns 993 shares of Centennial stock out of the total 100,000.]

> Pursuant to published notice, a regular annual meeting of the Centennial Gold Gravel Mining Company was held yesterday at the office of the company in Gold Hill. Over three-fourths of the stock was represented, being held principally by influential Comstockers and residents of this State.
>
> The report of the Secretary W. S. James showed the financial state of the company to be good—out of debt and no assessments needed for the next three or four months, and perhaps none further if the present good prospects ahead properly materialize, as expected, into a dividend proposition. . . .
>
> A letter from Superintendent Richards at the mine, which is situated in Nevada county, California, about fourteen miles above Nevada City, stated that the new tunnel was in over 1,400 feet, running in the bedrock beneath the gravel probabilities, from which he was making frequent upraises, another of which he has just started. The face of the tunnel is in tough dry rock at present, having passed through the wet stratum beneath the front gravel channel in which gold was found, but not in paying quantities. None was expected before cutting through to the main back channel already developed by adjoining mines, in which good pay is found. The long continued and costly previous explorations of the company directed the location and direction of this new tunnel, and ultimate success is pretty well assured.

May 6 – Clear & fine, but windy – Evening listened with crowd on the street to 3 fakirs in a wagon – Had banjo & organ & singing, etc – One a great talker and characterist – selling "Franklin oil," a wonderful pain-killer & other medical notions – front of Postoffice – "Petrified woman" also on exhibition in a room across the street from Douglass building – Purported to have been found on Jan 7 last, in Tuolumne County, California. White woman, good ordinary size & shape, naked – light stone color – entire. Found by 2 miners 5 or 6 ft beneath surface – Very interesting – But I think she is artificial, and made of some sort of stony composition – Very neat fraud – Whole surface of body rough and seamy, like confluent small-pox –

May 9 . . . Evening attended Thatcher's Minstrels at the Opera House – Dickie Jose with them. Crowded house – Splendid performance – Bed 1½ –

Sunday, May 10 . . . AM I walked out & visited Charley Ziegler, on the Divide, as member of Visiting Comm of the Exempts – got his left leg broke a week ago last Wednesday by his horse falling with him . . . PM monthly meeting of Exempts – I got 2 wks more benefits – makes 8 weeks in all – total $48 – Whole lot better than nothing . . .

May 12 – AM cloudy – PM a copious rain prevailed for some hours, washing off the dirt, flushing out the sewers, etc – lots of angle worms made their appearance crawling on the streets and sidewalks – evidently rained down – clouds must be wormy – I have been engaged the last 3 or 4 days, getting material and information for F C Robins, Pres't & Genl Manager of the Golden West Investment Company, headquarters at Winnemucca, as to how many millionaires the Comstock has produced, their names, amount of millions of each, present whereabouts and commercial doings, etc – Also the amount and variety of Nevada's traffic with the East for general merchandise, supplies etc – Quite a job – Wrote it up today and this evening in pencil – 24 pages – Bed 2 – Rec'd letter from D A Bender, Genl Freight & Passenger Agt V&T RR, Carson, in response to one I sent to Yerington last Saturday applying for ½ fare pass over the road – Enclosed ½ fare pass for Alf Doten & wife, good until Dec 31 1891 – Stox broke some today – Con Va down to 15¾ – but rallied to 16¼ after the PM board –

May 14 . . . I copied most of my Winnemucca article – G W Pease, clerk at the Walker Lake Indian Agency was in town & presented me with a very nice greasewood cane from that locality – made item of it for *Enterprise* . . .

May 16 . . . Finished my Winnemucca job in good style . . . Evening about town . . .

May 18 . . . Great break in stox today – Con Va from 14 this morning down to 9 in PM – Market demoralized . . .

May 20 . . . Letter from F C Robins, Winnemucca, enclosing $10 for my job – He was much pleased with it – Was at room most of day repairing, sewing etc . . . Stocks have rallied a little to $12 Con Va –

May 21 – Morning snowing heavily with about 4 or 5 inches accumulated except on street where it melted down to mud & sloppiness – Snowed more or less till past noon – PM cleared off – At room most of day sewing, repairing etc – Evening much excitement relative to prize fight – $10,-000 – in California Athletic Club San F, between Peter Jackson and James Corbett – Each round, commencing about 10 oclock, telegraphed to the Crystal and the Magnolia saloons – Crowds gathered to hear them read – 34th round last telegram – supposed to be received before 12 when the early closing law was enforced – Neither of the combatants seemed to have the best of it, & fight likely to continue several rounds longer – I went to bed at 1 –

May 22 . . . The Jackson-Corbett fight lasted till about 2 this morning, 61 rounds being fought in 4 hours & 4 minutes – Both were so exhausted that they could fight no longer and it was declared "no contest" . . .

May 23 . . . Within the last week good pay gravel has been struck in Centennial – $1 to the carload of 1,000 lbs – 12 ft above the new tunnel which should run into it in 100 further – Evening at Enterprise reading proof etc – Bed 2:30 –

May 25 . . . Made a Postoffice hole through my door this AM for the Enterprise, to be delivered free hereafter – PM, Bennett of Gold Hill came and I wrote for him to G H Morrison, S.F., Mountain Democrat Placerville Cal, and Mrs Dr A Slade, S.F. – also took notes on a spiritualistic interview with Dr Schlesinger at the International Hotel in this city March 16 . . . Bennett paid me $2 . . .

May 27 . . . Rec'd by mail a copy of the *"Cyclone Occasional,"* Vol 1, No 1, Reno, Louis Stevenson, publisher – 24 column paper [actually a four-page section from the Carson *Morning Appeal,* boosting Reno and advertising "Cyclone" windmills and farm implements].

May 28 . . . Got off a 4 page letter to F C Robins, Winnemucca, including a millionaire sketch of W M Stewart . . .

May 30 – Cloudy with rain and snow & hail squalls occasionally – enough to lay the dust & create a little mud – Decoration Day – Nice little parade of the National & Emmet Guards and the Artillery & the Canton War and Mexican Veterans etc – About 300 on foot & in carriages – Flowers by the bushel and carloads just swamped the cemeteries – Found postal from wife saying she was coming up in carriage with Janitor Clark of the schoolhouse – But she didn't arrive . . . Weather looked too bad probably – Copied off a written up "Spiritualistic Seance" for Bennett & met him & delivered it to him – Evening about town some – Bed 1 – I put up the Pioneer flag on the flagstaff at 7:30 this morning. But I had a bad time getting it down about 6 PM – It had got around on wrong side of staff, and halyards wouldn't work – Had to go up on top of building twice, by a long, shaky, unsafe ladder at rear of building, outside – a hard and very dangerous doing for *anybody* –

June 1 . . . Evening at Lodge – Election of officers . . . Then went to Enterprise, wrote report of election, account of Kimball's funeral, etc . . . cremated the last ragged & dirty remnants of those shirts I sent East for from Austin . . . Cooked my breakfast with 'em –

June 4 . . . Took noon bus to Gold Hill – Was up to W P Bennett's room for an hour or so, writing etc for him – Paid me $2 for it – Was at assay office – got my new stock on the stock dividend arrangement, 500 shares in one piece and 493 shares in another . . . got also a small sack full of the gravel recently sent over from the new strike . . .

June 5 . . . Busy at room most of day fixing up big boxes etc . . . The old *Alta California* newspaper, San F, suspended on Tuesday last for want of nourishment –

June 6 . . . Evening I was at Opera House – George C Staley, Dutch dialect comedian with a fair stock company in "A Royal Pass" . . . Enterprise awhile . . .

Sunday, June 7 – Finest day of season and quite an eventful one – About noon McGurn's 4 horse team just in with a load of freight from Reno, discharged cargo at store and ran away down street, dumping driver & turning the wagon over on side – Was stopped opposite Postoffice – Little damage – At 3 PM the following took place, as per advertisement in *Chronicle* and *Enterprise:*

A CHANCE FOR SPORTING MEN.

I, the undersigned, am willing to wager from $100 to $500 that I can shoulder an eight-gallon keg of beer, not to weigh less than 105 pounds, and pack it to the flagstaff on the top of Mount Davidson, and return, from the corner of Union and C streets without any artificial means of support or any rest. My weight is 146 pounds. Should I slip or fall without outside interference, so that the keg touches the ground, I lose my wager. Man, money and keg can be found at the U.S. Saloon, Virginia.

LEO. HECHINGER.

A big crowd saw him off from the International corner at C st. He passed up C & Taylor sts & returned same way & made it in 1 hour & 20 minutes to flagstaff on the summit of Mt Davidson, & 2:25 the round trip – Quite a number were along up the mountain to see fair play etc – and a crowded, enthusiastic street full harrahingly accompanied him down C st to his goal, landing the keg where he took it from . . . And he didn't seem much worried over it either – He is regularly employed by the Electric Light Co, taking care of the lamps, wires, climbing posts, etc – Height from C st to flagstaff about 1780 – Total distance about . . . 3 miles the round trip – There was much betting, $4000 or $5000 changing hands on the result – A funeral passed along during the PM, and a young man about 20 yrs of age, Fred Boegle was found dying under the railroad trestle bridge near the cemetery at north end of town – strychnine and love, etc – I was about, more or less – Bed 1 –

June 8 through 14 [Showery weather – AD writes up the Yellow Jacket fire of 1869 for Dr Delavan, reads proof etc, at *Enterprise,* is about town, and goes to Reno on his new half-fare ticket.]

June 15 – Clear & pleasant – warm – 82° – 1st real summer day of the season – I worked at odd jobs about home, hanging screen doors etc – Everything green & pretty about home & Reno generally . . . Bessie plays finely on my old violin – Been taking lessons . . .

June 16 – Same – 84° – Fixed bedstead, front gate, etc – hard day's work – Evening down town short time – Bed at 10 – Sammy has got a photographic outfit from the East, suitable for amateurs, and is already taking lots of meritorious pictures – The magpie continues to be a prominent member of the family.

June 17 through 30 [AD works about the house & in the garden, gets a haircut, takes Sam & Alf to a show & attends Reno High School commencement with Bessie – Back to Virginia City and his usual activities – Of interest:]

June 22 . . . Arr at Va at 7:10 PM – Attended Opera House – Play "The Twelve Temptations" – Big crowded house – 1st class variety show – lots of women, ballets, etc . . .

June 24 – Same – As usual – Con Va touched $5¾ today – The boys are all busted . . .

June 25 . . . PM I attended funeral of old man Houghton from Pioneer Hall – Rev Mr Witter did the services – Funeral consisted of hearse & 2 carriages – Officer Coryell fell dead on B st at 1:30 AM, after making an arrest – heart trouble or blood vessel rupture . . .

June 27 . . . 11 AM I attended the funeral of Alex Coryell, from the Episcopal Church – Many others attended the services – 25 carriages followed the hearse to the Exempts cemetery where he was buried by side of his brother William – Evening I was at theater – 1st night of Russell's Dramatic Co's engagement – Play "Black Flag, or Brother Against Brother" – Very good indeed – Slim house . . .

June 29 . . . PM at room fixing up & washing the only good shirt I now have for every day wear – It is a light flannel that I can wash myself, & I have it arranged for detached collars, etc – Evening at theater – Play: "Lynwood" by the Russell Dramatic Co – Very good – fair house – Bed 1 –

June 30 . . . Evening theater – Play "Night Shift" – Pretty good – slim house – Bed 12:30 –

BOOK NO. *67*

Virginia City
July 1, 1891 – Dec 31, 1891

July 1 . . . Pretty warm for the Comstock – 85 degrees in the shade – Stocks continue depressed . . . Evening at theater – Fourth night of the Russell Dramatic Co – Played the "Octoroon" to a very slim house – Played it very excellently – Bed at 1 . . .

July 2 . . . Evening, Play of "East Lynne" by the Russell Co at theater drew a very slim house – I was at Enterprise, read proof on my much deferred "Along the Railroad" . . .

July 3 . . . Wm Meadows of the Wm Tell House, opposite where I live . . . died at 6 AM . . . Old timer – 59 yrs old . . .

July 4 – Clear & pleasant – One of the best celebrations ever on the Comstock – I rode with Doc Delavan and old Klink in a carriage – 4 in hand – black horses – provided for the occasion – Subsequently, at 2:30 PM was at exercises at Opera House – Evening at ball – Bed at 12 – Excursion train from Reno & Carson was eight passenger coaches well filled – brought Reno Guard and Carson Guard & lots of folks beside – arrived about 11 AM – Procession formed on B st after guests had lunched etc and started about noon – Nationals, Emmets, Reno and Carson Guards, Battery A Artillery, Fire Depts of Va & GH, Goddess of Liberty etc – Several young ladies on horses among the aids in advance – Cara's Artillery band – and Silver State Band – 40 girls and 30 boys of 4th Ward high school – all in uniform, on foot – finest feature of the procession – principal streets – Divide and back, & dispersed in B st – At 3 PM exercises at Opera House – Crowded – Powning of Reno, orator, Miss Freethy Giles Poet – George Noel Reader – good singing, music, etc – I was in audience – All passed off finely – I raised Pioneer flag in morning & took it down in the evening – Ball biggest & best I have seen here on such occasion – Drill of the school girls on ball room floor just splendid – Whole city a wilderness of flags – Everything passed off gloriously with no trouble, etc –

July 7 . . . Evening annual meeting of the Pioneers . . . I re elected President – Old officers re-elected – Only 8 of the old boys present . . .

July 11 . . . PM I labeled & fixed up a lot of specimens accumulated during the last year or 2 at the International saloon for the Pioneer cabinet: aluminum, copper and silver ore, crystals, etc, and a Japanese cane – Bob Patterson will take them to Carson tomorrow & place them in Pioneer cabinet in State Capitol . . .

Sunday, July 12 . . . I wrote 4 letters to parties in California for W P Bennett – Took me 2½ hours, & he paid me $2 – At 5 PM dined at Zimmer's residence . . .

July 14 – Clear & pleasant – Bed 12 – Met J W Haines, one of the State University Regents, in town today & had quite a chat – He came up on the noon train from Carson, and returned on the evening train – Borrowed $10 of Campbell of the Enterprise today and paid my room rent to Joe Douglass – Got the two worst snubs of my Nevada life today – J W Haines told Bob Patterson that my wife's application before the Board of Regents for a position in the State University was hanging fire on *my* account – *She* was considered competent enough but she had a *"drunken husband"* – Haines however left with his mind disabused of that idea – Guess Lew Stevenson has been getting in some *revenge* work down in Reno – About 5 PM [met] Nelson, a friend of mine, on C st – He had a drunken friend along named George Pease, a miner, of Gold Hill – Introduced me to him and George incidentally remarked that he had known me a long time, but said he: "You never amounted to much" – Two such snubs in one day is rather discouraging, but I guess I'll worry through all the same and nevertheless –

July 15 – Same – Pretty warm – 85° – Bob Gracey told me of a dream he had last night – He found me *dead* somewhere & shipped me in a coffin to my folks in Reno – He said it was natural as life – A fitting windup to yesterday's *"Terrific Snubs"* – *Knocked clear out*. Was about town – Got in item about Centennial – Bed 12 –

July 16 . . . Been last two days engaged in effecting a negociation of 500 shares Centennial for $300 . . . with John H Hitchcock the Pioneer Laundry proprietor – Papers all fixed, but he failed to bring in the money . . . Kept me watching & waiting all day . . . Washburn of Lower Gold Hill is buying the News office property for a residence – This evening Fred Clough brought me face to face with his old father on C street opposite *Enterprise* – He was at Ft John when I was hurt . . . Haven't seen him since . . .

July 17 . . . Completed my Centennial negociation with Hitchcock today – He loans me $300 on 500 shares for 12 months . . . to bona fide own it at expiration of the 12 months if I don't come to time – I owed him $20 already, so he paid me $280 – $100 in gold and rest in silver – PM I went about paying lots of small debts, etc . . . Guess I am the only Centennial man who has made it pay – $1700 cash so far – Stocks down – Con Va sold as low as 4½ today . . .

July 24 . . . Paid the last of all my saloon borrowed money and whisky bills – some over two years old – About $150 in all paid since I got the coin from Hitchcock . . .

Sunday, July 26 . . . Many went to Steamboat today to the horse races, baseball & other sports . . . By evening mail I sent letter to wife with another $5 greenback enclosed – also asked her to write me a list of desirable groceries, etc, in order that I might ship her some from McGurn's . . .

July 27 . . . Evening wrote & got into Enterprise "Memorial Sentiments" on Alex R Coryells death . . .

July 28 . . . Dined with Major John H Dennis at the City Bakery at 5 PM –

July 30 . . . Got letter through Gold Hill Postmaster from Hudson Wilson, President Citizens National Bank, Faribault, Minn . . . George Pease, cashier . . . inquiring the whereabouts of Granville W Pease . . . Family not heard of him for 4 or 5 yrs, & fear he is dead – It is my old friend Pease, of Schurz station . . .

Aug 1 . . . Wrote reply to Hudson Wilson, also wrote to Granville W Pease, Schurz, Walker River Indian Agency enclosing Wilson's letter . . .

Aug 2 through 19 [AD writes more for Bennett, dines at Zimmer's again, sends another $5 with a letter to his wife, reports the Caledonian picnic & gets in a piece on the Pine Nut district, attends an Exempt meeting and a Centennial meeting, gets a reply about Pease's whereabouts – Many days with nothing but weather & bedtime.]

Aug 20 . . . Jerry Hurley, my next room neighbor was groaning with pain this AM – Had to come off shift, Con Va Mine at 3 AM – Big boil on each arm, and big swelling in right groin – I doped the swelling with Franklin oil and gave him a tonic of 1 table spoonful of paregoric, 1 of whisky, to 3 of water . . . By my directions he made a flaxseed poultice for the swelling . . . Evening I was at theater – Benefit of Mrs B F Layton – Farewell benefit, as she goes to Reno shortly to be teacher of music, etc at the Bishop's school . . . Met W S James Secy on street this PM & paid him my assessment (No 42) Centennial – $14.90 –

Sunday, Aug 23 . . . 11 AM Dr Manson came and I assisted him to fix up Jerry Hurley – He stuck his exploring needle into abscess in right groin, over an inch but got no matter . . . Opened out the boils on his shoulder and arm for better issue – This PM Jerry was taken to the Sisters' hospital, as he is liable to be laid up for several days – Evening I boiled a lot of walnut shells, about a gallon, four hours – got about a pint of dark brown liquid – for what I think good remedy for diarrhea . . .

Aug 24 . . . PM I wrote long 6 page letter . . . for W P Bennett . . . Evening at theater – Pawnee Medicine Doctor troupe of variety performers – very good indeed – Big house – free show – best I ever saw here . . .

Aug 27 . . . About 10:30 this evening, Dr James Delavan, returning from the . . . Pawnee Dr show slipped & fell in front of his residence near the 1st Ward school-house, spraining his left hip so badly that it was thought to be dislocated or broken – I walked out there with Dr Harris – examined under chloroform – no break or dislocation – Bad sprain – Will lay him up awhile – 76 yrs old –

Aug 28 . . . This evening about 9 I noticed lights down at Chinatown & walked down there alone – Met Billy Pennison, Chief of Fire Dept there & we kept company – It was annual celebration of the Chinese Masons – Small but brilliant candle lights stuck in ground 8 or 10 ft apart, clear around & through two blocks – lanterns etc – We got into the Temple & saw the starting of the ceremonies – Transferred to ground in front – 12 dishes or bowls for the Apostles, I guess, filled with sweetmeats, etc – placed in two rows, with plenty of candles – liquors passed to cups to east of the 12, with hot tea for a windup – Then a big bunch of peculiar paper was burned in front of each bowl – Meanwhile an old chap in a long black dress and a red bandage round his head, standing at one end of the outfit gave a lecture in a sing song Chinese and there was considerable bowing and scraping by others – The band, three or four gongs and drums also occasionally broke loose quite vigorously – Quite a number of white spectators, including a few women and girls – When the paper was burned, the bowls, table, etc were taken back into the temple & the fun ended – Pennison & I walked up town –

Aug 29 . . . The telegraph today brought the news of the success of the revolutionists in Chile – Valparaiso taken and President Balmaceda getting away for safety – This doubtless ends the six months war, the Congressional insurgents coming victorious – I met my old friend Jose Salinas and we had quite a little celebration over it – Bed 12:30 – Dr Delavan was taken over to the County Hospital yesterday PM – On re examination by Drs Harris and Webber it was decided that his left thigh bone was broken, near the hip – neck of the bone –

Sunday, Aug 30 . . . Evening was up to the house of my Chileno amigo, Jose Salinas, lawn tennis court, Taylor st bet A & Howard sts – for about 2 hours talking Spanish, relative to the Chilean revolution . . .

Aug 31 . . . At noon W P Bennett came . . . & I wrote a letter . . .

Sept 1 . . . Big fire at Winnemucca Sunday PM destroyed all the business part of the town – loss $300,000 . . . Evening at room – made 8 fig leaves . . .

Sept 2 . . . Bennett caught me on the street at 10 AM, and took me to my room and made me take notes for 2 hours, & afterwards 5 hours writing out the same . . . Series of his visionary sketches to some friend . . . he paid me $2 on account – He is 73 yrs old today – Evening at the Pawnee Doctor show – Still running free show to big houses – Bed at 1 –

Sept 3 through 14 [AD has dinner at Zimmer's twice, visits Dr Delavan at the hospital, is dunned by the Bancroft Company for notes from 1885, notes that the Miners' Union Picnic has a very small turnout & is a financial failure, gets $100 more from Hitchcock for his Centennial stock & pays $35 worth of his bills, puts in a few hours at the *Enterprise* & a great many about town, and goes every evening to the Pawnee Doctor show, which continues to play to full houses – No detail.]

Sept 15 – Cloudy & cool – less than 70° – Sent a short letter . . . containing a $5 greenback to wife – Evening showery – Fred Clough and his father came to my room by invitation and we had a big old interesting talk about Fort John . . . Read my journal of that time to them – played the old banjo, etc – Afterward down town with them – Steady pouring rain for hours – Bed at 1 – still raining – Mrs Theresa Fair the divorced wife of Jas G Fair died in San Francisco Sunday PM – 46 yrs of age – worth $6,000,000 – Divorced from J. G. Fair about 9 yrs ago –

Sept 17 – Clear, cool & pleasant – W P Bennett called on me about noon relative to more writing he has for me to do – Paid me $2 more – Evening at Pawnee show – Big house as usual, and extra good performance – 2 bits admission – closing of its months run – It has had the greatest success of anything in that line ever on the Comstock – Two doctors, brothers, named Burgess & excellent Company of performers, in varieties, song, dance, juggling, acrobatic etc – free show except Saturdays and this evening – when 2 bits admission charged & extra good show given – Consultations free to public every day at theater, with crowds of consultors, men women & children – Sold bushels of "Pawnee" medicines – "Too-re," "Pain Balm," "Magic Salve," "Worm Destroyer," etc – Show goes to Gold Hill for next two nights, then to Reno – I ought to be having my regular annual hay fever, but have it not as yet – Damp weather stands it off probably –

Sept 18 – Same – Bennett called on me again, and I wrote four letters for him . . . including one to the SF Examiner enclosing 3 sketches of "Fast Trips" across the Sierra Nevada in early days – Bought $16 worth of groceries, hams, clams, jams etc at McGurn's, & shipped them to wife by McGurn's Reno stage which goes daily at 3 PM – Evening principally at room, reading, writing etc . . . Play of "Incog" at theater this evening, by the great Charles Dickson Comedy Co from the East – I didnt care to go – Received yesterday from C H Stoddard, Secy, season ticket for self & lady to State Fair at Reno all next week – sent it in letter to wife this evening –

Sept 19 . . . Busy most of day on a job for P J Keyes – Itemized statement relative to suit now pending for his wages as Supt of the Keyes Mining Co – 5 pages of legal cap . . .

Sunday, Sept 20 . . . Campbell of the Enterprise engaged me to report the State Fair at Reno . . .

Sept 21 through Oct 4 [AD reports the State Fair at Reno and then the District Fair at Carson – Mostly repetitious entries with little detail – Of interest:]

Sept 22 . . . Evening at home – Wife read me to sleep with a long original story . . .

Sept 23 . . . Evening took Millie & Bessie to theater – The Burgess troupe – same as was with Pawnee show, but now under Piper's management for Fair week – We got in free, & Sam got in afterward, free & sat with us – (75 & 50 cts admission charged) – Slim house & not very good show for the money . . .

Sept 25 – Clear, warm & pleasant – The big day of the Fair – AM at 10 went with Alfie to the grounds in 'bus – Met Wells Drury just before we left, just over from Sacramento to the Fair – At Grounds some pretty good bronco riding in the big enclosure inside the race track – a big alfalfa field – ½ doz or so of rather unruly horses, half breeds or otherwise, mostly American I think – but they acted mustangish and filled the bill as "broncos" very well – 3 or 4 riders – One after the other was stirred up and started out and some very eligible bucking was done – one white rider was squarely & fairly bucked off – A Piute Indian was the best stayer – lots of fun – PM three running and one pacing race, and Theodore Winters' famous racer "El Rio Rey" was galloped and speeded around the track to show him to the spectators – the most famous race horse of Nevada – Has made $80,000 for his owner, in this & other States – Got my report, about a column, off on the excursion train at 5:20 PM – Telegraphed result of last race, 10 words to Enterprise: "Frank C won fourth heat and race in two twenty." Evening at home – Bed at 10:30 –

Sunday, Sept 27 . . . Morning train to Va . . . Wells Drury also – He is right over from Sacramento, where he is editor & proprietor of the *Sacramento News* . . .

Oct 3 . . . Reported fair at Carson as usual – Big fire there this morning – Old Theater block . . .

Oct 5 . . . Got $20 from Hitchcock, paid $12 borrowed money etc and my Odd Fellows dues . . .

Oct 6 . . . J B Marshall sold out of his Louvre saloon this PM to Dan Hanifan, his barkeeper this PM. In the windup Joe presented me with the biggest apple I ever saw, which he has had on exhibition in the saloon for last 3 weeks – It is from Smith's valley, Esmeralda County, & weighs a strong *pound & a half* . . . I obtained the address of Mrs J W Mackay today for my wife from John Donahue, clerk at the Con Virginia office. It is: Madam J W Mackay, Carleton Terrace, London S.W., England –

Oct 7 . . . Professor Louis Zimmer has been living in Gold Hill the last week or so, residing with his sister Mrs Lutjens and family, being separated from his wife, who has sued for divorce on grounds of failure to provide, extreme cruelty, drunkenness etc – She will retain charge of their little son Eddie, between five & six yrs old –

Oct 8 – Clear & pleasant – About as usual – Evening "Mass meeting" of the citizens of Storey County on the irrigation question at the Court House – I went up at 8 oclock – Nobody there except Harry Sutherland and Under Sheriff Joe Bleakley – I called the meeting to order, made Harry secy & Joe audience, appointed all three as delegates to the Mississippi Congress on Irrigation to be held in Omaha on the 15th instant – adjourned – Bed 1 – But there had been half a dozen or so others at the hall before we were and they made up a similar meeting which was more legitimate and reported in the papers – W E F Deal President, & Alf Chartz Secretary –

Oct 9 through 20 [AD mails a letter to his daughter Goodie, is paid $40 by Hitchcock, examines a new cross-cut in the old Daney Mine in Spring Valley & writes it up in *Enterprise* and is much about town.]

Oct 21 – Cloudy – Evening attended services at Catholic Church – Some sort of a Mission going on, to last till next Wednesday – Discourse by Father Shaw – Very good – Subject – "Hell, or Punishment after Death" – Strong ceremonies as usual – First time I have been to church for several years – Was at Enterprise afterward, items, proof, etc – Dr Delavan reported dead at the County Hospital – He has been getting very low for last few days – Billy Ash has bought half interest with Bob Patterson in the International saloon for $800 – They gave a big turkey etc lunch this evening in honor of the new departure –

Oct 22 – Same – Dr Delavan died at the County Hospital about 3 oclock this morning – I joined with his son in making arrangements for funeral, etc – from old Pioneer Hall 2 PM Saturday – The son is a young man about 21 or 22 yrs old – works at slaughter house business here – Evening wrote up Doc's death, etc, & was at Enterprise, read proofs etc – Bed at 2 – The District court report in *Evening Chronicle* contained the following: [clip saying Zimmer's divorce is final] – Orlando E Jones, whom we have known in times past, on the old Va *Daily Union* as "Dan" Jones, printer, etc, and in the circus ring as "Dan Conover," clown, has been in town the last 4 or 5 days – He left last evening – He lectured Monday evening in the Methodist church, and in Gold Hill Tuesday evening on "The Delights of Drunkenness" – Nobody better qualified than he on the subject – Used to be the most drunken swab I most ever saw – For last dozen years or so has been in the newspaper business over in the Bodie section, editor of the *Bodie Miner,* etc – His lectures were very poorly attended, though good enough in their way – He took up collections to pay expenses . . .

Oct 23 . . . I indorsed Hitchcocks 500 share price Centennial today, so its *his* now –

Oct 24 – Clear & pleasant – 2 PM funeral of Doc Delavan, from the old Pioneer Hall, B st – I presided made a few preliminary remarks, followed by the Episcopal services by Rev Mr Hyslop – Everything went off fine, singing, organ, etc – Rode in a carriage to the Odd Fellows cemetery, where he was buried by side of wife & a son – About 20 carriages – Evening at Enterprise awhile – Wrote up funeral & other items – Bed 1 – John H Coleman, manager of the *Evening Chronicle* closed his connection therewith this day and left for San Francisco tonight – Mr Stevers a relative of the McCarthy family will probably succeed him, as the paper belongs to the McCarthy estate –

Oct 25 through Nov 2 [AD writes a memorial on Dr Delavan, sees it and other pieces into *Enterprise,* constitutes himself & R C Hardy a Pioneer meeting, gets $50 for his reporting of the fairs, visits with Ed Plank, once a printer on the *Gold Hill News,* notes that Admission Day has been observed with flags and a National Guard Ball & that Coleman has returned to the *Chronicle,* attends an amateur spectacular, "The Interviewer," writes for Bennett, buys a new coat & vest on credit ($18) to go with pants already paid for, and is about town a good deal.]

Nov 3 – Clear & pleasant – PM attended funeral of Jim Donovan killed by a blasting accident in the Ophir mine last Friday – I rode in carriage with Major F A G Gearing, Mark Feeny and John Brady – Took a ride out on Geiger Grade as far as the summit afterward – Evening about town – at room, writing, reading etc – Bed 3 – I had a real nice old time dream last night – I had struck it somewhere in a "prospect" of a gold vein – picked out chunks of gold in $1 $2 & $3 and bigger ragged quartz gold pieces – more than $100 worth – hated to wake up to the scrubby reality – Yet 42 years ago I was on my way from Stockton to the California gold diggings – footing it for Woods' creek on the Tuolumne – Left S Nov 2 & got there on the 6th – But this dream was so good and naturalistic that it made me feel rich all day afterward – "The days of old, the days of gold, the days of Forty Nine" –

Nov 4 through 9 [AD writes for Bennett, and for H W Bracken about a new device for safety cages, gets $20 more from Hitchcock, attends Centennial & Exempt meetings, pays dues, is around with his divorced drinking friend Zimmer and writes a long letter to his sister Cornelia, in which he asks for an old violin bequeathed to him by his father.]

Nov 10 – Same – Evening at theater – Benedict and company of 2 or 3 – slight of hand, illusionists & delusionists – very slim house – fair performance – Bed at 1 – Was disturbed before getting to sleep by noise of a rat in my room foraging around – Got up twice & rummaged around trying to get him or run him out – Finally I found him in upper drawer of bureau and jammed him as he was trying to escape over rear part of drawer – Held him fast, got him by the tail, jerked him out & banged him dead – ½ grown rat – Got in last night by the janitor leaving my door open inadvertently – Troublesome pest well rid of – That rat did squeal well when I had him jammed – Bed finally at 4 oclock –

Nov 14 . . . Evening attended lecture of Patrick Henry Lynch at Opera House on "The Past Present and Future of the Republican Party by an Irish Roman Catholic Republican" – Very slim audience – Not much of a lecture . . .

Sunday, Nov 15 . . . Evening I visited Bob Patterson at his residence – He is laid up with a gouty foot and his daughter Elva is just recovering from the scarlet fever . . . very prevalent in Va & GH – probably 200 cases –

Nov 17 . . . Goodyear, Elitch & Schillings Minstrels arrived on morning train & paraded the streets with fine band of 9 pieces – About 25 in the crowd – Evening I was at theater & saw them – big house – $530 – Performance splendid . . .

Nov 18 through 30 [For three days AD, dressed for the first time in his new brown suit, attends as a witness at the Carson suit of P J Keyes against the Keyes Silver Mining Co (Keyes awarded $1,015.40) – Then he sends wash to his wife, gets a letter from Eunice, misses train to Reno, finds plenty of Thanksgiving turkey in the Virginia City bars, attends a ball of the Young Ladies Institute, gets a $5 advertising commission from the *Chronicle,* goes to Reno, where he renews the note on the house, does chores, is about town & has a concert with Bessie & Sammy – Returns to Virginia City.]

Dec 1 . . . By express this day arrived a box to me containing my father's old violin and packages of Christmas presents for each and all of my family, even to Millie – That violin is a very interesting old relic – over 100 years in our family I think – Bed at 3 –

Dec 2 through 11 [Snow puts the Comstock on runners – AD writes a Reno letter for the *Enterprise,* a letter for Bennett, letters to Mary, his son Sam, & his sister Cornelia – Pays his Centennial assessments, goes to another ball, and to a very good but poorly attended variety show by the Noss family.]

Sunday, Dec 13 – Cloudy & thawy – PM took my old father violin up to Jose Salinas to straighten up the fingerboard, cure a crack in the belly and rub it up generally – 2 PM I attended regular monthly meeting of the Exempts – Had a hot argument with Charley Bowman, regarding the cabinet of the Society, comparing and he referring to the Pioneer cabinet detrimentally – After adjournment he wanted to fight me, and in fact threatened to slap my face, applying some very insulting remarks – But he didn't *do* it – Evening I went to the Methodist Church services to soothe my feelings – Then to my room & staid there, reading, writing, etc – Bed at 2½ – At 4 PM I dined with Mr & Mrs John Connerton at their home –

Dec 14 through 23 [AD cuts himself chopping wood, writes nine letters for Bennett, has an evening of drink & music with Jose Salinas and two Italian friends, notes Forefathers' Day and sees Wilber Dramatic Co play *The Planter's Wife & Streets of New York.*]

Dec 24 – Light snowstorms occasionally – Variable, cold & decidedly Wintry – Streets lively with people preparing for Christmas – Toys and turkeys doing good business – Morning bad bowel trouble & all the AM – PM about town some – Met George Hymers of Reno – He came up with a rockaway, bringing a District Judge Talbot and wife of Elko who had missed the train and desired to be here Christmas Eve to visit friends & relatives – He insisted on my riding with him back to Reno – I went to McGurn's & got a nice 11 pound turkey, and in the bag with it packed those presents from Cornelia – We left Mooney's stable on B st at 4:50 – Extremely cold, but I was well coated and had plenty of comfortable wraps about feet & legs – Good sleighing all over the Grade – 11 miles – we on wheels – Zero weather – Mighty cold ride. Arrived at home at 7:45 . . . Found family all right and passed pleasant evening. A box of fruit, nuts & presents from Eunice had arrived – After children got to bed, wife & I filled & hung up their blessed little stockings – Bed at 11 – coldest yet – 10° above Zero –

Dec 25 – Christmas Day . . . At home all day, except about an hour down town – Looked like Sunday, all the business houses being closed, & nobody on the streets – Even the saloons did not seem to flourish – certainly not like those on the Comstock which were all full of Christmas cheer, free turkey & pig lunches in profusion. Services in a church or two, but most people were housed with their turkey – Dinner at 3 PM with family and Mrs Powell . . . Evening we had *good* music; Bessie on violin, Sam on banjo, & I on flute . . .

Dec 26 . . . PM I was about town some . . . but Reno is dull . . .

Sunday, Dec 27 . . . I left on morning train for Va . . . PM about town some . . .

Dec 28 . . . Evening at room – good fire – Wrote *Outside Reflections* for Enterprise . . .

Dec 30 – Steady snowstorm all day – PM about town some – Evening also . . .

Dec 31 . . . PM Jose Salinas was with me at my room & we took off the back of the old violin of my sire – Found about a teaspoonful of dusty, cobweby dirt & nothing more – scraped out lots of extra glue, etc & cleaned & sandpapered it all right, glued up old cracks in the belly & put in a few small cross pieces across some of the cracks by way of reinforcement – Evening at Enterprise awhile – read proof on my "Outside Observations" etc – Bed at 2 –

BOOK NO. *68*

Virginia City
Jan 1, 1892 – Dec 31, 1892

Jan 1, 1892 . . . Streets lively with people out making New Years calls or enjoying the usual salutations and festivities – Snow 20 inches deep, finest kind of sleighing and many sleighing parties out. Saloons all setting forth good cheer and everybody cheerful and hopeful – PM I dined with John Connerton & wife at their home, corner Washington & F streets – turkey, etc – Evening about town some . . .

Jan 2 . . . More like a holiday than yesterday was – Col Thomas B Woods died today. I wrote notice of him for Enterprise. Got the letters HOPF on back of the old violin of my sire retouched . . .

Sunday, Jan 3 . . . W P Bennett came and I wrote a couple of letters for him . . . Evening wrote a three page letter to Hon J P Jones, San Francisco, striking him for $5,000 . . .

Jan 5 . . . Met Jose Salinas . . . and we glued the back onto father's old violin again . . .

Jan 7 . . . An evening or two ago Prof Zimmer, on his way to Gold Hill slipped and fell on top of his violin, badly cracking it. This PM I repaired it for him . . .

Jan 8 . . . Zimmer played his violin at a dance tonight, my repairs proving to be effectual . . .

Sunday, Jan 10 . . . Attended regular monthly meeting of the Exempts . . . installation of officers . . . Then came the banquet usual on such occasions – baked beans, sandwiches, beer etc . . .

Jan 12 . . . PM met Bennett on C st, & he paid me $2. Jose Salinas was with me at room awhile and we cleaned up and finished up the old violin so that all is needed is the running rigging and consequent musical extraction . . .

Jan 14 . . . At 4 I dined with the Connerton's . . . Evening attended performance of the "Combination Minstrels" – Comstock amateurs . . . Chas A Jackson from Reno played mandolin and banjo very good with fancy points, swinging in the air, etc. He also did some very expert and fancy rifle shooting at a target. He was the best of the lot . . .

Jan 15 . . . Wrote letter to Frank Delavan, Reno requiring him to return the Secretary's books of the Pioneers which he took away with other effects of his father after his death & burial . . . Put the strings, tail piece, bridge and pegs onto the old violin just before going to bed . . . didnt tune it, only set up the strings a little to stretch them – rosined the bow, which is new.

Sunday, Jan 17 – Clear & cool – PM down town short time – At room and completed the stringing up and fixing up of the old violin. At 4:30 PM, having got her in 1st class tune, with Billy Brady the colored janitor of this Douglass Building I struck out on the first tune I have played on that old violin for about 43 years, as I left home the 18th of March 1849. And the tune I played was "On the Road to Boston," one of the most familiar of father's old tunes on this jolly old instrument. It sounds out splendid, especially in the bass or lower notes. Evening Professor Zimmer called and he played the old violin for all of its merits. Says it is a very fine & valuable instrument, and in the bass or lower notes it is really *phenomenal*. Bed 1.

Jan 18 through 22 [AD writes half a dozen letters for Bennett, works an evening at the *Enterprise,* plays the "old violin" and has it examined by Prof Frank Reichel.]

Jan 23 – Clear & pleasant – PM about town – Evening, theater – Robt Gaylor and excellent company in "Sport McAllister" – "one of the 400." About 20 in the company, from East, en route to California. Sort of a variety humorous comedy show with little or no plot to it, but extremely amusing. Best I have seen for the last 3 or 4 years – Gave big satisfaction – Had a big house – entirely full – Bed 1 – This PM I met C W Craig, editor & prop'r of the *Inyo Index,* away down in Independence Inyo county Cal. Have known him for years but never personally before. On a visit to the Comstock. . . . Big Betsy, a huge rifled gun for the new coast defence ship, Monterey, at San Francisco, passed through Reno Wednesday morning . . . Biggest gun ever made in America or transported across the continent, therefore attracted much popular attention.

Jan 25 . . . The mail today brought me a copy of the *Free Press* a weekly . . . published at Plymouth, Mass. It was marked on margin in pencil, *S M Burbank* (Cornelia's husband). Democratic paper, I think – Gives account of a banquet in honor of commencement of the Plymouth and Middleboro RR . . . Also the accompanying clip about the old '49ers from Plymouth to California – This is mainly correct, but not wholly – Eight names omitted from the Yeoman's list, viz: Capt J M Clark, John Clark, Seth Blankinship and Tom Brown (from Sippican) and Nathan Churchill, —— Gifford, George Bradford, —— Montgomery (Plymouth) . . .

Jan 26 . . . The mail brought me a ½ fare pass over the V&T RR for self and wife for present year, from Yerington . . . Pretty good – Evening wrote nice obituary article on death of Thomas Burke, who died at 1 AM today at Sisters' Hospital from an accident in the Utah mine, where he was at work last Thursday, both legs being very badly broken by the upsetting of a car of ore or waste . . .

Jan 28 . . . PM met W D C Gibson, Sup't of the State Indian School near Carson – He came in light wagon with 2 of his Indian pupils, who were introduced to me – Very intelligent young Indians . . .

Feb 1 . . . Evening foggy – I went to theater – Edwin Barbour Dramatic Co – engagement for a week – good Co, with little Gracie Beebe in song, dance, etc – Play tonight was "A Legal Document" – Very good – highly amusing – Good house . . .

Feb 2 – Dense frosty fog – "pogonip" – all day. Very cold & disagreeable – good sleighing throughout the city – PM I was about town – Evening at theater – "Black Diamonds" – ½ a house – very good performance – Bed at 12 – Received a very nice, well and correctly written two page letter today from Sterling Price, the Shoshone Indian boy, in complimentary acknowledgment or recognition of the item I put in the *Enterprise* relative to him Jan 29 . . . Old Pioneer Brother Klink invited me, Col Bob Patterson, Otto Eckelmann and a few other fellow members of the Society of Pacific Coast Pioneers to his residence this evening where he proposed a nice little banquet festival in honor of his arrival in San Francisco, 42 years ago today. But the fog was so dense, the night so dark and the way so slippery, off the main street and to where he lives, near the

Savage works that we all backed out of the really dangerous proposition –
not enough in it to pay for risk of life or limb. So I wrote this item which
was published in next morning's *Enterprise,* just to apologetically please
the old boy:

> [Clip – J G Klink's party written up as if it really had been held, pork &
> beans, liquor, songs & stories.]

Feb 3 . . . Fred W Clough left this evening for a short visit to relatives,
friends in Tulare County Cal . . . I saw him off on train – borrowed
$10 of him – Evening at Theater – "Shadows of a Homestead" – Very
good – Good house – At Enterprise awhile . . . Terrapin stew at free
lunch at International saloon this evening – fine –

Feb 4 – Moderate snow storm all day – PM about town – Evening at
theater – "Joe the Waif" – Pretty good – Slim house . . .

Feb 5 . . . Evening at theater – Play dramatization H Rider Haggard's
famous story of "She" . . .

Feb 6 . . . Evening theater – Played this PM matinee "Peck's Bad
Boy" to big lot of children, women . . . evening "Chips From Old
Blocks" . . . Was at Enterprise afterward, reading proof etc till 3
oclock . . . This was last of the Beebe-Barbour Co . . .

Feb 7 through March 3 [AD mostly about town & at the *Enterprise*
office & meetings – He is invited to dinner five times by the charitable
Connertons and dines along the street with other friends – Of added
interest:]

Feb 12 . . . Evening grand ball of the Jack Rabbit Social Club, at
National Guard Hall – crowded and one of the best and liveliest parties I
ever saw – At midnight refreshments – sandwiches, cake, coffee & ice
cream was passed around – At 2 when I left, Virginia Reel, the 1st dance
after supper was going it fast and furious . . .

Feb 13 . . . Professor Frank Reichel brought an old violin to me at
room this PM for me to fix – He took mine home with him to adjust the
bridge department, fastening of tail-piece, etc.

Feb 14 . . . Evening at room – Repaired Prof Reichel's old violin . . .
It is marked STAINER, on the upper edge of the back . . . where mine
is marked HOPF. Reichel says this is an old violin, but whether it is a
genuine "Stainer" or not he dont know . . . Stainer, like Hopf, was one
of the famed old violin makers.

Feb 16 . . . AM Prof Reichel brought to my room my old violin in full order . . . and took his . . .

Feb 19 . . . Evening at Opera House – Conried's Comic Opera Company for one night – "Poor Jonathan" . . . Very good indeed – Had big house . . . 30 or 40 people in this Company –

Feb 20 . . . PM I localized on the *Chronicle* for Al Mills . . . who had to go to Reno . . .

Sunday, Feb 21 . . . PM John Connerton & wife visited me at my room and brought a small platter of baked pork & beans – also an apple – Entertained them with all the instruments I have – the old fiddle, banjo, flute, flageolet, fife, and harmonica . . .

Feb 22 . . . Met my old friend Almarin B Paul, arrived on train today – Had quite a talk with him – Wrote him up *Enterprise* – Also Ernst Zimmer deceased . . .

March 3 . . . Evening theater – Play of Uncle Tom's Cabin . . . Big house – Don't like their rendition of it – seems like a burlesque . . . Their Gold Band, 9 pieces, paraded sidewalks up C & down B sts – Very good music – fine uniform . . .

Sunday, March 6 – Clear & pleasant – At 2 PM went down to Connerton's by invitation and took lunch with them – Baked beans and pork, etc – At 3 I attended funeral of John T Brady . . . commenced at hall of Comstock Council No. 1, O.C.F. [Order of Chosen Friends] of which he was a member, in Odd Fellows Building about 2 PM. After usual ceremonies of the Order were over, procession, headed by 50 or 60 C.F.'s and others on foot, including about a dozen lady C.F.s, passed thence down to the Catholic church, where the religious part of the ceremonies were conducted by Rev Father Lynch. About 3 PM the procession, in same order passed up Taylor & out C st to the Catholic cemetery, 70 carriages following the hearse. I rode with Bob Patterson & daughter Elva, and Sol Noel – At the closing of Father Lynch's ceremonies a shovelfull of earth was handed to him by undertaker which he threw down upon the coffin. Then, each of the Chosen Friends having a small sprig of evergreen, about a dozen were cast into the grave, as is usual with most Orders, when Father Lynch abruptly raised his hand exclaiming loudly: "Stop! We dont allow that here. This ground is consecrated to the Cross." Then, addressing George Thomas, the CC of the CF's he said: "The Chosen Friends shall never enter this ground again as a body. I wish it distinctly understood that they shall never enter this ground again as a body. There are no more ceremonies to be performed here; the performance is over." Then turning again to Mr Thomas, he said in a lower tone of voice: *"You knew better than this."* Mr Thomas replied: "Father Lynch, if there was anything wrong, it was a misunderstanding and I hope to be excused." Father Lynch replied: "We excuse nothing." Col Robt Patterson, standing near, said: "Father Lynch I wouldn't have spoken as you did. They meant no wrong. You should have warned or instructed them beforehand. It would have been much better to have passed this little mistake over quietly and said nothing to them at this time." Father L. made no reply, the filling of the grave was proceeded with, and everybody dispersed. Evening about town – By mail today I got a letter from my old friend Almarin B Paul, Gen'l Manager Calumet Gold Mining Co, Middle Creek, Shasta County Cal. . . . for my kind notice of him recently in the *Enterprise,* when here, and enclosed a $2 greenback, to buy cigars with. Bed at 12.

March 7 through 18 [AD writes letters for Bennett & Patterson, enters clippings on the commitment of Sarah Althea Terry to the insane asylum at Stockton, happens to meet James & Kinzle on C street, so the three men construe the encounter a meeting of Centennial trustees & levy another assessment, dines with the Connertons & visits Connerton & Jack Plant when they fall ill – Prof Zimmer gives him a violin case, & he attends a Chinese funeral, *The Burglar,* presented by the Grismer-Davies Company, & a St Patrick's Day ball – About town & at the *Enterprise.*]

March 19 . . . John S Clark, aged 46, native of Pa, shift boss at the Oest mine, west of Silver City was killed about 7 oclock last evening in the shaft of that mine. He was at the 126 ft level and in attempting to cross to the other side of the shaft by means of the wall plates he was knocked down by a descending cage, falling 82 ft to the bottom . . .

March 21 . . . Meeting of State Central Committee, Republican –

March 22 – Variable – cold – PM & evening I visited Connerton and Haist – Bed 12 – Clear and cold – Frank Sullivan, about 19 yrs old, with a one horse buckboard brings the San Francisco *Chronicle* and *Examiner* up from Reno over the Geiger Grade for Murray & Davis the newsdealers, etc. Goes down in the evening & comes back in the morning after the arrival of the East bound train from California, thus getting ahead of the mail and express over the V&T RR several hours. This morning Dick Whalen, about 17 yrs old, was with him, having gone down with him for company & pleasure of the trip last evening. This side of the toll house and near the Philadelphia Brewery, the horse took fright at something and ran away. Sullivan was thrown out and badly bruised. Shortly afterward Whalen was also thrown out, striking on his head against a rock, smashing the skull and killing him. The hind axle broke at that time by contact with a rocky bank projection, releasing one wheel, and the horse dashed on with the crippled buckboard into town where he was arrested. Sullivan walked in, passing Whalen's body without seeing it owing to his own dazed condition, and subsequently Whalen's body was brought in.

March 23 through 31 [AD dines twice with the Connertons, writes letters for Bennett & Patterson & a Memorial tribute on John Clark, the miner killed in the Oest shaft, for the GAR, for which he is paid $1 – "About $9 less than it was worth."]

April 1 – Cold and variable, with considerable snow squalls – Wintry day – "April fool day" – PM about town – Bed 12 – clear & freezing – About 8 oclock last evening August Bouheben, brother-in-law of A Laigneau the coffee dealer on South C street was fatally shot by Jerry Barry, a miner in the Yellow Jacket mine. It was at Laigneau's store in a dispute or discussion about money matters, between Barry and Laigneau. Barry drew a pistol and Bouheben, in trying to prevent his shooting Laigneau by wrestling with him for the pistol, got shot in the head, from which he died this PM. Barry ran home to Gold Hill, but subsequently came back to Va and gave himself up by advice of his wife – Barry was somewhat under the influence of liquor. Both were young men –

April 2 . . . The Georgia Minstrels, (colored) arrived on noon train and had band parade on C st sidewalk – Evening gave performance at Opera House – Very good indeed – Good house . . .

Sunday, April 3 . . . PM dined at Connerton's . . . wrote three letters for Bennett – Received a nice one from my son Alf . . .

April 4 . . . At the Enterprise office I found a copy of Sunday's Reno *Journal* with a column & a half communication in it from my wife entitled "Two Pictures – Woman in the Dance House, and Woman in the Salvation Army."

April 5 – Clear, warm & tolerably Springlike. PM wrote couple of letters for Bennett & he paid me $1. My old Chileno friend Jose Salinas got very badly used last evening – Nearly killed on the street, going home, by some scoundrel. He was found by Bob Gracey and Bill Sutherland who informed the police & he was taken to the Court House where he was properly cared for, surgically & otherwise, and about noon today taken to the County Hospital. Evening about town – Bed 12 – Jose sent word to me this PM . . . that he would like to see me. I am his special friend with whom he always talks Spanish. He is a native of Chile, Valparaiso, about 65 yrs old, & I have known him here about 25 yrs –

April 7 . . . PM I footed it over to the County Hospital, via Washington st, etc about 2 miles – and had interview of an hour or so with Jose Salinas . . . Most he wanted was to talk Spanish, he being a very poor English talker . . . Looks as though he had been having a lively fistic discussion with John L Sullivan . . .

April 8 . . . Considerably lame & stiff from my walk yesterday . . . About 2 miles to Hospital & 3 miles back . . .

April 11 . . . Legs . . . badly swollen from knees to ankles . . . since my hospital walk – Of a dropsical nature – Dont admire the symptoms – Had it more or less for a year or more.

April 12 . . . PM funeral of Jake Nicholls – I was in attendance, etc – Evening at the Opera House – John Dillon & Company in: "Wanted, the Earth" – Good house but poor play . . . Poorest for its pretensions I think I ever saw . . .

April 13 through 30 [AD comments upon the unusually windy weather, "Washoe Zephyrs," and upon earthquakes which have done extensive damage in Dixon and Vacaville, California, and been felt on the Comstock, writes a letter for Patterson & several for Bennett, and a few of his own, attends "Cul" Hall's funeral, notes that the Knights Templar have turned out for Easter as usual, & that the Republican primaries have taken place, & looks in upon Chosen Friends, Bijou Club & Odd Fellows balls, finding them all smaller & less spirited than usual. Of additional interest:]

April 20 . . . Mrs Maria James, wife of Zephaniah James, a miner, of Gold Hill, hanged herself to death in an out-house to the rear of their dwelling. Cause, natural dementia or suicidal cussedness. Leaves a husband and 3 children.

April 27 . . . Evening at the Opera House – Mr & Mrs Sidney Drew and good dramatic Co played "That Girl from Mexico" to a fair house. I was there – Cranky sort of a play but ridiculously laughable . . .

April 28 . . . Bennett received 27 copies of his book, the "Sky Sifter" today – showed me a copy and will give me a copy tomorrow, or next day – 85000 words – Thinks his next book, the "Knights of the Whip" will make 62000 words – Recd letter today from sister Eunice . . .

April 30 . . . PM attended Republican State Convention – Evening about town . . . Met many old friends from all parts of the State. Philip A Doyle Chairman, Wm Sutherland Secy and Wm Oates, Sgt-at-Arms . . .

Sunday, May 1 . . . Most of the outside delegates left . . . Evening wrote a nice two page letter to Alfred H Phillips, Austin – He was the devil of the Reveille when I was its editor – He is now the editor. He came in here as delegate . . . but he had so grown out of my recollection that I did not recognize him although he did me. Therefore I apologetically send him this letter. Bed at 2 –

May 2 . . . Gold Hill to attend the annual stockholders meeting of the Centennial . . . Only Kinzle, myself, and W S James of the directors present, and a couple of other stockholders, but over 80,000 shares were represented, out of the 100,000. We examined into the accounts . . . and re-elected all the old officers . . . Evening I visited ball of Jack Rabbit Club at Opera House – Finest & most elaborate decorations I ever saw – Was at Enterprise . . .

May 4 . . . Met Jose Salinas on street – just over from Hospital for 1st time since he was hurt . . .

May 9 . . . About 3 PM the Reno *Elite Minstrels* . . . arrived . . . in carriages . . . About 40 of them . . . They gave a fine street parade at 4 PM – Band of 16 pieces, all the Company on foot, preceded by three gaily dressed cavaliers or heralds, horseback – Evening at Opera House – I was there – Very good minstrel and variety show – crowded house . . .

May 10 – Cloudy and variable – PM about town some – wrote a 2 page letter for G M Ardery, section agent and watchman down at Baltic switch on the V&T RR, Gold Hill – letter was to A J Sielaff about his son throwing stones at a board fence beside the RR track. Paid me 50 cts. Also wrote a business letter for W P Bennett – His Sky Sifter books have all come up from Oakland – 1,000 copies, and he is now engaged in placing them for sale . . . Charley Chatterton, killed about noon today at the Nevada mill, was friend of mine, & contemporary over in Como, & I have known him well ever since.

May 11 . . . Evening was at masquerade ball of National Guard awhile – Very amusing – funny costumes and incidents – Grand crowd of spectators in the gallery . . .

May 13 – Variable but generally pleasant – Met wife on C st about 11 AM. Went to room and found Bessie playing the old Doten violin & Sammy accompanying her on my banjo – Decidedly a surprise party for me – They came up with Reno school excursion – Only visited me short time, as they had to run with the crowd – We four dined at French Rotisserie & they & rest of Reno crowd left on return about 6 PM – I saw them off – PM I took notes for a letter for G M Ardery – Evening I was at theater – Carroll Johnson & dramatic Co from the East, in "The Gossoon" – Very good company and play, and a big audience – Bed 2 –

May 14 . . . Wrote out & delivered letter No 2 from G W Ardery to A J Sielaff, Gold Hill . . . Democratic primaries this PM for delegates to State Convention . . .

Sunday, May 15 . . . PM about town some – Evening same, with Prof Zimmer – We had a game or two at Cards – "7 up," I beat him, went to a shooting gallery on C st, near Sutton Avenue, and I beat him – rang the bell – Bed 1 –

May 16 . . . PM I re-haired the bow that came with fathers old fiddle from Plymouth – I had lent it to Professor Zimmer – he wore it out . . .

May 18 . . . Evening wrote item about father's old fiddle – was at Enterprise . . .

May 21 . . . Evening attended the big silver convention meeting at Opera House – Was on stage as one of the Vice Presidents – Bed 2 –

May 23 . . . Bought me a new pair of shoes this AM to take the place of those I bought in Austin of Bob Hogan about 8 years ago . . .

May 24 . . . Took evening train for Reno. Took the old fiddle of my sire along for Bessie – Sam and Alf met me at the depot . . . Evening, Bessie, & Sam & I had music, she on the old violin, I on my old '49 fiddle and Sam on banjo . . .

May 25 . . . Busy about home all day with screen doors, windows & general repairing etc . . . Looked both violins over carefully, glueing a crack in each of them. Both now in perfect order. Bed at 11 √ –

May 26 – Clear, warm & pleasant – At home most of day trimming trees, glazing windows etc – Evening down town awhile – Saw Salvation Army on street – Two women and 7 men including a nigger. One woman beat a tamborine and a stout man lustily pounded the glory of God on a bass drum. And they sang lots of jolly songs, related experiences, etc, and a crowd followed them down to the "barracks" near the Virginia street bridge where the same sort of a show continued – Bed at 10 –

May 27 – Same – Wife extra busy at school exercises. PM I rode on 'bus out to State University. "Field day." Students had athletic games, sports, foot racing, etc. Large crowd of visitors, spectators etc on the grounds. I visited the library for an hour or so, overhauling the bound file of the *Gold Hill Daily News,* which Mrs Gov Stevenson presented to the University a year or two ago – after the Gov died. PM wife received following telegram: Woodland, Cal, May 27, 1892. Mrs Alf Doten. Arrive Saturday morning. Wait few hours for special. Tell Alf. C C Doten. Sam, Alf & I went to work & cleaned up the yard & premises generally. Evening at home. Sam & I practiced violin & banjo. Bed 10 –

May 28 – Same. 78°. We all rose at 6 getting things ready for reception of Charley. Train arrived at 11 AM, 3 hours late. Charley & wife, Mary, arrived. Sam & Alf & I were at depot. Sam detected them first. Knew Charley by his photographs. I had not seen him, personally, since March 18, 1849 – over 43 years. Recognized him, knowing he was coming, otherwise I should not. 3 yrs & 8 mos younger than myself. His wife a nice looking old home body about his age. PM I took Charley about town – across the bridge, around by the schoolhouse, etc. Visited *Gazette* office, introduced him to lots of my friends, including Major J H Dennis. Dennis is stopping in Reno yet, journalizing, etc. Evening Bessie on the old violin, Sam on banjo, & I on flute gave them a concert in the parlor, playing "On the Road to Boston" & lots of other old home tunes that Charley knows. They were very much pleased, and we got them a good place to sleep at Payne's across the street. Bed at 10.

Sunday, May 29 – Same. Up at 6. Breakfast. Train from California 2 hours late. I & my boys went with Charley & wife to depot. Their special cars, 4 of them, were attached to rear of the second section, which pulled in as the first pulled out. Charley introduced me to several of his traveling editorial comrades. They left for the East at 10:30. PM & evening at home – Bed 9 – This morning Sam took photos of our entire crowd, including Charley and wife, on front porch, also of Charley & wife by themselves. Charley presented me with a scarf pin composed of a small square (⅓ inch) of Plymouth rock – the rock on which the Pilgrims landed in 1620 – gold setting.

May 30 – "Memorial Day." Flags all displayed at ½ mast in Reno, but nowhere else. Train over an hour late. Morning, Sam took pictures on front porch, of our band – he, Bessie & I, banjo, violin & flute respectively, instruments in laps. Also of myself alone, standing and sitting – hat on and off, etc. At 9:20 left on train for Virginia – Arrived just after noon, just in time to see the parade . . . pass down & out along C st to the cemeteries north of town to decorate the graves – Very good. Prettiest procession I ever saw for size, kind & occasion – National and Emmet Guards, Battery A artillery, Canton Silver State IOOF, Fourth Ward school girls & boys . . . two brass bands, Phil Kearney Post No 10 G.A.R. and carriages with officers of the day, etc. The battery fired guns while decoration went on. On return, usual services and exercises were held at Opera House. Evening about town – Bed 1 – I brought my old violin with me back to Virginia today – It is the good fiddle I brought around Cape Horn in '49 from old Plymouth, and which has traveled California and Nevada with me ever since. Bessie has been playing it . . . since she commenced – but now I have swapped with her, letting her have the old Doten fiddle *of my sire –*

May 31 through June 10 [AD reports the Republican national convention and spends a good deal of time "about town" – Half the entries nothing but weather & bedtime – Of interest:]

June 1 . . . Evening at room writing up my Reno trip . . .

June 2 . . . PM I finished up writing my Reno trip "Outside Observations" and staid with it on Enterprise this evening . . .

June 8 – Variable & cold – Saloon stoves fired up . . . Only stirring news is Rep National Convention at Minneapolis . . . Only got as far as McKinley for Permanent chairman & adjourned . . . Bowels bothered me badly yesterday & today – kept me washing etc . . .

June 9 . . . The dispatches from Minneapolis the excitement of the day – The convention wrangled till way past midnight over report of Committee, on Credentials . . .

June 10 . . . Several light snowsqualls . . . Wintry cold – Harrison was nominated on first ballot this PM: Harrison, 565; McKinley, 183; Blaine, 175; Reid, 4; Lincoln, 1. Whitelaw Reid was nominated for Vice President – Convention adjourned . . .

June 11 – Variable – a little warmer – 1 or 2 light sprinkles of rain or snow – About 10:30 AM a 'bus arrived from Reno with 15 young ladies and gents, students of the State University on a visit to the Comstock – They dined at the International and in the PM visited the C&C shaft &

down into the mine – some of them – They returned to Reno, over the grade about 6 PM – The morning train . . . brought a special Pullman car attached, loaded with about 60 men, women & children from Truckee, consisting of Knights of Pythias, wives, etc, and infant drum corps of 12 little girls – They attended the Grand Lodge of K of P at Carson yesterday, and rolled up here to see the Comstock people & brethren – They marched up from the depot to the International, the drum corps at the head – dined, rested and cruised about town seeing the sights etc – visiting the Chollar works, mill and mine etc & at 5:20 PM left on return to Truckee, very well pleased – The drum corps of 12 little girls neatly uniformed was finest feature visiting us ever, in that line – Only been drilled a month and only play "taps," but didn't miss a tap or evolution in drill – At leaving they marched up C street couple of blocks & back, and immense crowd of children, women & men followed down to the depot & saw them off with hearty cheers – Among the Knights, all of whom were in full uniform I met for the first time with C F McGlashan of the *Truckee Republican,* Mr Mayers, who helped build my house in Gold Hill, Mr Schaefer, Truckee lumber dealer, Mr Dolan et al – Evening about town – Bed 2 –

June 14 . . . Rec'd box by express from wife, enclosing supply of clean collars, also 2 dozen photos from Sammy, of myself and the rest of us including Charley & wife . . .

> [Clip, *Territorial Enterprise,* June 14:] At the regular monthly meeting of the old Exempts, Sunday afternoon, in the usual business routine, the invitation from the Virginia Citizens' Executive Committee on the coming Fourth of July celebration was duly considered. It was decided that, like the old Pioneers' society, there's so few of us left we couldn't make an adequate show as a distinctive feature in the procession and general exercises, therefore the invitation had to be declined with appreciative thanks.
>
> But it was agreed that the old machine, Virginia No. 1, should be placed at the disposal of the citizens' celebration committee for the occasion, also certain other relic emblems of the old volunteer fire department, to be properly cared for and returned. . . .
>
> Brothers Jake Young and Alf Doten were of the opinion that with supplementary efforts in that line, all hands putting their shoulders to the wheel, we can carry a cabinet to the World's Fair that will beat even the Presidential Cabinet of the nation, and redound to the honor and glory of the Sagebrush State and the Exempt Firemen's Association.

June 15 . . . It was June 13, 1888 that I was at J C Caldwells house, in Gold Canyon, just above the Devil's Gate and saw his little imbecile, crippled daughter Bessie, of whom the annexed clip from the Enterprise relates. Henry Collier, arrested Sunday morning and now in jail on charge of rape upon her, I never saw. Her father tells me that she is five or six months gone in pregnancy. A very beastly, *damnable* case.

June 16 . . . McGurn's stage, coming in from Reno got tumbled over the Geiger Grade this side of the toll house, by old Jones the rancher from Truckee Valley trying to pass it on the upper side with his 2 horse rig . . . claims his team was running away. Judge Whitcher, a passenger, got his head badly cut, and a boy got arm broke . . . the coach rolled over three or four times – The driver got bruised, cut and strained some, but came out all right. So did the horses. Some of them got loose and with Jones's horses stampeded toward town. On the way they demoralized a horse & buggy in which was Mrs Williams and daughter, of Silver City, smashing the buggy badly – Mrs W had her hand cut & mashed some, both being thrown out, but girl not hurt – Much stir about the bad accident –

June 18 . . . PM attended funeral of Tom Keig a member of my Lodge, also of Chosen Friends . . .

June 20 . . . Evening theater – Tyndall, "Mind Reader," "Mystifier" etc. Very slim attendance. Performance rather tiresome & not devoid of suspicion of humbug. Bed at 1.

June 21 – Clear & warmer – a little more breeze – Grand Lodge IOOF convened at Odd Fellows Hall . . . Al Mills, local of the Chronicle being a member he got me to localize for him – I was on hand at 7 AM at office & stood in good all day – did well – Had to walk out to the Divide to get suicide of old lady Hoskins, but got chance to ride back – Evening at the Opera House short time to I.O.O.F. ball – Bed at 12 – very tired – The parade of the Reno and Virginia Cantons in their fine uniforms at 4:30 PM on the streets was a splendid feature – headed by Hoskins' Juvenile Brass Band, of Reno.

> [Clip, *Virginia Chronicle* – The lonely widow Hoskins, about 70 years old, in a fit of despondency cut her throat with a razor.]

June 23 . . . I localized on *Chronicle,* as Al Mills went down to Sutro to play in band for picnic of public school children from Dayton, at Horseshoe Lake near Sutro . . . The national Democratic convention at Chicago finished business . . . yesterday – Grover Cleveland was nominated for President and Gen J E Stevenson of Illinois for Vice President, each on 1st ballot –

June 24 . . . Graduating exercises of High School this PM and ball in evening . . . Splendid party, full and good – I wrote up George Cassidy's death in Enterprise . . . [Centennial directors] Levied 1½ cts a share on Centennial today.

June 25 . . . Evening attended a lecture at N G Hall on Free Thought by Samuel P Putnam, a lecturer from the East – Slim audience – good lecture . . .

June 27 . . . I took dinner with Jack Plant, foreman of the *Enterprise,* at his home on Stewart st near Union – Cottontail rabbit stew – very fine . . . Letter from Nicholls today not accepting Centennial proposition – Replied to it by return mail . . .

June 30 . . . Drew up and mailed some Centennial agreements to Andrew Nicholls, Los Angeles – Evening at Opera House – Reed & Collins comedy variety troupe in "Hoss and Hoss" – lots of general fun and whimsicalities but little real merit . . .

July 1 . . . Was called to work on *Chronicle,* Mills . . . being disabled by piles . . . Got along all right . . . Evening about town – Bed 12:30 after getting in an item or two into *Enterprise* –

July 4 . . . Had a $900 celebration here – Procession & usual exercises, & PM the "Horribles." But a big crowd went to Carson . . . a bigger celebration by far than we had here . . .

July 6 . . . I was at theater – "Lights O' London" – McCann, Lizzie Kendall & good Co – good house & play – They are playing all this week – Wilber Dramatic Co . . .

July 7 . . . Rec'd long letter from Bro Charlie through my wife . . . Wants Bessie to come East & be in his family, etc – Evening at theater "The Two Orphans" . . .

July 8 – Clear & pleasant – At 10 AM took 'bus to Gold Hill, being subpoened as witness in Collier-Caldwell rape case – in Justice Cook's court. I was to testify to writing a letter for or introducing J C Caldwell to Dr G H Thomas, Supt of the State Insane Asylum Reno, as showing that he was trying at that time – Feb 27th last – to get her into the Asylum as a helpless imbecile. The examination took place with closed doors . . .

Bessie told her sad story, how her ravishment was accomplished & followed up at numerous subsequent times by Collier – She being now about five months gone in a family way – Yet she seems to be totally unconscious of the fact or her condition . . . Her father testified as to Collier's frequenting the premises and his having frequently left her in his charge when obliged to be absent from home . . . Dr Harris testified as to the girl's condition – Collier declined or waived his right to make any statement or introduce testimony in defence. The court considered that there was sufficient evidence to justify holding defendant to answer before the Grand Jury, therefore bound Collier in the sum of $500 to appear . . . Collier failing to furnish the $500 security was remanded to the custody of the sheriff and taken back to the county jail – I was about town some, and returned to Va on 1 PM 'bus. Evening theater – "The Child Stealer" – Very good – Slim house – Bed 1 –

July 9 . . . Evening theater – "Muldoon's Picnic" – Big house – Trashy performance – Bed 1 –

Sunday, July 10 . . . Letter from Nicholls returning Centennial documents – I replied by evening mail . . . Evening Theater – last of the Wilber Dramatic Co – Three small plays: "In honor Bound," "My Uncle's Will," and a farcical windup entitled "Penelope Ann." Slim audience . . . Very good show . . .

July 12 . . . Letter from wife with one from Eunice proposing to have Bessie come over and live with her & go to Normal School, San Jose. I replied at once with letter of approval . . .

July 13 . . . Bessie's 18th birthday . . . Evening sensation was a one-legged strolling gymnast or acrobat performing on C st, front of post-office – horizontal bar, etc – Very good . . . passed the hat . . . Dick Hicks one of the old time young Comstock printers arrived from Reno & elsewhere today . . . He used to be one of the *Gold Hill News* compositors, under my jurisdiction . . . About 50 years old – noted as one of the fastest & best compositors on the Pacific Coast – He looks seedy & wants a job. He will probably go to work on the Va Evening *Chronicle* tomorrow or next day, so he tells me . . . subbing for Steve Gillis, for a couple of days . . .

July 15 through Aug 3 [Mostly about town – Letter from Nicholls concerning Centennial – Letter to Eunice with some of Sam's family photos – Is photographed with his Lodge, talks with Frank Newlands, candidate for Congress, puts in a day "prospecting" in Carson, attends the funeral of Jake Becker, an old Gold Hill friend, & writes a notice for Caldwell, putting Bessie Caldwell's newly born son up for adoption – Of additional interest:]

July 18 . . . Evening at Opera House – Thatchers Minstrels and Rich & Harris Comedy Co in the musical farce "Tuxedo" – Dickie Jose with them – Crowded house and most excellent & satisfactory entertainment – Bed at 1 –

July 23 . . . Surprised by a letter from wife at 842 West street Oakland, Cal, with her aunt, Mrs Batterman, her residence – She went over there Wednesday to attend funeral of Mrs Gov Stevenson . . . thinks she will stay in Cal a week or two more, and visit Eunice . . . Never was other side of the Sierra Nevada before.

Aug 4 – Clear & cloudy by turns, but pretty hot – 86° – Evening attended the Weaver-Lease reception & speaking at Theater – Densely crowded with gents & ladies – I got a good seat on the stage – Powning presided & made best little introductory speech I ever heard him, lasting 15 minutes – Genl Weaver [People's Party candidate for president] followed with a first class well delivered speech of 1½ hours – Then Mrs [Mary E] Lease [of the party's national committee] spoke an hour, giving one of the best if not the best and most eloquent address I ever heard from a woman. Splendid style, voice and elocution – All well applauded – I was at Enterprise afterward, reading proof etc – Bed 2 –

Aug 6 . . . I attended Caledonian picnic – Tom Dick gave me a ticket – Rode on a flat each way . . . Returned at 8, very tired & sorefooted – Found letters at the P.O. from Wife and Sammy, from Reno . . .

Aug 10 . . . Evening I was at Opera House – A pleasant entertainment entitled "The Little Tycoon" by well drilled members of the 4th Ward School . . . About 5 PM I visited Jack Craze, an old friend, keeping a saloon and lodging house on South C st, opposite the Savage office – He is very sick from pleura-pneumonia and sent for me – He is generally known among his brother "Cousin Jacks," as "Blackwater Jack" and a mighty good man.

Aug 11 . . . Harry Nye was badly if not fatally hurt this morning about 8. He is a member of the Fire Department. Fire alarm at that time . . . In dashing out for the fire, down the steep grade south from the Corporation house, the cart got off over the steep embankment . . . Harry got beneath the cart and has his right thigh and knee badly broken and both wrists broken and dislocated. Also has his nose broken – His right leg was so badly smashed up that it had to be amputated about midway of the thigh . . .

Aug 13 . . . The funeral of P H Ford was the feature of the day – Largest I ever saw here. 103 carriages followed the hearse, and 200 men on foot preceded it. Artillery Band, the Emmet Guard, detachments of the National Guard and Battery A of the Artillery, societies, etc – Took place about noon from Catholic church . . . [Ford, a local grocer, was a long-time resident and a former county commissioner.]

Sunday, Aug 14 . . . I wrote a brief letter to Hon C C Goodwin, editor Tribune, Salt Lake City, Utah, enclosing clips . . . about Lannan – H P Cohen who used to be business manager of the *Enterprise* went from San Francisco out to Salt Lake a few days ago to have some employment on the *Tribune* . . .

Aug 16 . . . About noon received following telegram from C B Noe, Ashland Oregon: "Alf Doten, care Virginia Enterprise, Please send me twenty dollars, by telegraph until I come" – I replied: "Would accommodate, but been flat broke for a year." . . .

Aug 18 . . . Evening at theater – Comedy Co from the East producing "Little Tippett" a 3 act farcical comedy – Very good & funny & well played . . .

Aug 20 . . . Regular Republican Primary Election, for delegates to the State Convention . . .

Sunday, Aug 21 . . . Evening attended the M E Church, as Mrs Prisk was announced in the Enterprise to sing there this evening. Crowded house – She was with the rest of the singers but kept seated in the 2 first acts . . . After the sermon . . . got up & sang a solo, with organ accompaniment. Sang "Nearer My God to Thee" in different tune & style than I ever heard it. Had same good voice as [when] I heard her last in Austin. Simply glorious . . .

Aug 22 . . . At 5:20 AM took train for Reno – At Treadway's ranch, Carson, passed the annual encampment of the State Militia . . . First under law of last Legislature . . .

Aug 23 . . . I came down to see Bessie off. She left on train at 10:45

for Eunice's, & will attend Normal School, San Jose the next 3 years . . .
Evening, Sam, Goodie, & I attended Salvation Army services . . .

Aug 24 . . . Sammy is employed at $25 a month, or 15 cts an hour
skirmishing for butterflies, bugs and worms, etc, for Prof Hillman of the
State University – Alfie telegraph messenger, $25 a month – Both to quit
on the 1st, for school –

Aug 25 through Sept 14 [AD remains in Reno, & is about town most
of the time, meeting politicians, watching the Reno Guard receive the
Tuscarora Guard after the Militia encampment, attending the telegraphing
of the Corbett-Sullivan fight, the State Fair and the Republican Convention, which splits through the emergence of the "People's" or "Silver"
party – Notes, with a slight touch of indignation, that his wife has
chosen to sleep alone in order to get "uninterrupted rest" – Says that the
CP snowsheds on the Sierra summit have burned, his whole family has
returned to school, a Gold Hill schoolhouse has burned, and the Democratic Central Committee meeting in Carson has split, with the "regular"
portion of it nominating the ticket – No details.]

Sept 15 – Borrowed $20 and at 1:45 PM left for Va – Arr at 7:00 – Got
in work on Enterprise, and bed, at 2:30 – Hay fever starting in onto
me . . . On my arrival at Va today I found in my Post office box among
other letters one from Fred Clough . . . enclosing a souvenir badge of
the Native Sons of the Golden West, of which he is one – Very fine &
appropriate badge: gold bear on top and silver medallion beneath about
size of silver dollar, appropriately inscribed, connected by a short red
white & blue ribbon arrangement –

Sunday, Sept 18 . . . Politics hot – Stewart in town – I put an ad in
Enterprise, announcement that am candidate for County Recorder . . .

Sept 22 . . . County Republican Convention at National Guard Hall –
I was Secretary, but knowingly got left, on the Recordership proposition –
Evening, about town among the old boys . . . Got $15 for my Secy
work today . . .

Sept 24 . . . Stocks booming higher than for last 3 or 4 years – Good
ore strikes in Belcher the cause . . . Belcher up above $6 yesterday . . .
All stocks "sympathize" – Newlands and Stewart addressed the people
on the political situation at Opera House this evening – Big crowd – I
there –

Sunday, Sept 25 . . . Evening much caucusing by the Weaver Silver Party at room in the Doylan building . . .

Sept 26 . . . Big Silver Weaver Convention today – Opera House in PM & evening – *"I was with 'em"* – Bed at 2 –

Sept 29 . . . Pat Keyes paid me $10 on his judgment in the Keyes Mining case, and Charley Mack his attorney $8.20 fees & mileage . . .

Oct 1 – Clear and much cooler – 70° – About town – Evening Opera House – Big speech of William Woodburn Republican candidate for Congress – 2 hours – I was on the stage reporting for myself – Bed at 2 – Woodburn had a big, well-enthused audience and made a splendid, well-applauded speech – Silver State Band of 10 pieces, bonfires on the streets, etc –

Oct 3 – Cloudy but pleasant – About town as usual – Evening took supper at Jack Plant's residence with he & family, sang songs & had pleasant time – Then went to Theater – Georgia Woodthorpe Company – engagement of a week – Play tonight was *Little Lord Fauntleroy*, with Georgie Cooper in the title role – A wonderful juvenile actor, & good troupe – Bed 1 –

Oct 4 through Nov 8 [AD gets in a few licks at the *Enterprise*, attends meetings, writes several letters to J P Jones &, upon inquiry, offers to bring his Comstock mining report up to date for $100 – In the main, however, he is about town, once for five days running with nothing else recorded, more often with summary comments on politics – Of interest is the following, signed by AD:]

[Clip, *Enterprise*, Oct 9:] Carson City never looked cleaner than at the present time, which includes yesterday. . . . The dust is very effectually laid by the late rains, and the river itself, which cuts such a prominent figure in Comstock ore milling, has experienced a rapid rise, which, if properly followed up by further rains, will soon give ample water power for the ore reduction mills.

MILLING AND MINING.

The Morgan mill, run by steam, is the only one running at present; but the Brunswick, Mexican and others are in complete order and condition ready to resume active and lucrative work as soon as sufficient water gets onto their wheels. Water power is a whole lot cheaper than steam. Meanwhile the mines have not been idle, exploration and developing work goes right along, and ore production will come up to the milling and resultant bullion requirements during many months of a prosperous run. The additional miners being put to work of late is not a political election proposition altogether by any means.

POLITICAL.

Some of the Weaverite dudes of Carson wear a silver collar, not around their necks, but as a hat-band. That mild attack of political cholera will be summarily suppressed and forgotten about election time. Weaver weevils won't be in it. John T. Jones of the coinage department, Carson Mint, just returned from a three months' visit East, came up to the Comstock last evening. He says Weaver is not considered worthy of special mention, politically, outside of Nevada, his greatest notoriety at present consisting in being rotten-egged down South. He visited the principal cities of the East, and found the straight Republican element on top—New York is for Harrison.

MISCELLANEOUS NOTES.

Johnny Jones occupied two or three days looking through the World's Fair arrangements at Chicago. The buildings in course of construction and completion each cover not only acres but farms of ground, and will be noted and recorded as the largest anybody in the world ever saw. . . .

Bicycle riding is very fashionable in Carson, and universally adopted except at funerals.

The pasturage on the islands in Carson river at Empire, continues good, and the cows, who have all become web-footed through swimming from one island to the other the last thirty years, are in fine condition.

Oct 10 . . . Evening at Opera House – Gen Paul Vandervoort, Ex-Chief Commander of the G.A.R. addressed a big audience on the political situation, Silver or Peoples Party standpoint – Talked an hour & 20 minutes – Good speaker but he simply asserted and declaimed, without argument – Silver Quartette, 2 gents & 2 ladies from Reno sang several campaign songs, rather poorly – Stewart was announced to speak but wasnt there . . .

Oct 13 . . . Stewart made his big speech in Gold Hill this evening – Many from here to hear it . . .

Oct 15 . . . H F Bartine, candidate for US Senator, successor to Stewart spoke at Opera House this evening to big audience – I was on the stage – Got my clothes from Marshall the nigger clothes repairer etc this evening – Been there nearly a year – Coat, over coat & vest – Bill $8 – promised to pay the first of the coming month –

Oct 18 . . . Frank G Newlands and Thos Wren spoke on the political situation . . . Big house – After that Newlands took a run of the town – Hooped her up – I saw some of it – Bed at 2:30 –

Oct 21 . . . Columbus Day – Big celebration of 400th anniversary of his discovery of America – Best celebration I ever saw on the Comstock – 2000 in the procession – 1400 school children, Va & Gold Hill – Simply grand and phenomenal – Exercises at Opera House – Senator Stewart spoke for 15 or 20 minutes – all the rest was music by the band, elocutionary efforts & singing by the youngsters, etc – Evening about town, Bed 12 – Cold freezing every night now – We the Directors have concluded to shut down the Centennial for the Winter and only call in one half of the present assessment of 1 ct a share. [A clip from the *Enterprise* of Oct 23 says:]

CENTENNIAL GRAVEL.

As has been stated, the present assessment of one cent per share, levied by the Centennial Gravel Gold Mining Company, is the least and last of all. It is merely to square up accounts and pay for the requisite washing sluices. Over 600 feet of pay gravel have been developed during the last year's exploration, and most certainly that is enough. The company does not ask the earth but goes for what gold is obtainable therefrom in the Centennial ground—several hundred acres. There's no discount on gold, therefore the Centennial folks feel happy, and will continue that way henceforth. The Centennial is well worth five dollars per share right now, and will be worth double that or more during the coming season, with straightforward dividends.

Oct 27 . . . Newlands and Wren spoke at Gold Hill this evening – Quite a crowd went from here, brass band, glee club etc – I didn't – Bed at 1 –

Oct 28 . . . Evening at Opera House – speaking by Hon Thos Wren, B F Leete and Hon W M Stewart – 2 hours in all – Nearly a full house – no bonfires – not much enthusiasm . . . Received letter from Maggie Moore Williamson, Adelaide, NSW –

Oct 29 . . . Evening at room writing a campaign song entitled "Up Salt River" . . .

Oct 31 . . . I delivered my campaign song, "Up Salt River" to Henry Baglin of Gold Hill, who wanted it . . .

Nov 1 . . . Speaking of Hon C C Powning, and W E F Deal – Big crowd – Bed 1 –

Nov 3 . . . Dan Sully & good dramatic Co in *"The Millionaire"* – Good house and exceedingly good play – Bed 1 –

Nov 5 . . . Evening at Opera House on the stage hearing Woodburn on the political issues . . .

Nov 7 . . . Everybody up & down the street studying and discussing the political situation . . . Evening at Opera House – Senator Stewart made his wind-up speech – 1 hour – Big audience – brass band, glee club, & good enthusiasm – Saloons ran most all night – I was at *Enterprise* . . . Got in my letter from Maggie Moore – Bed 2 –

Nov 8 . . . The Grand Election day – Bands of music and all sorts of transparencies, mottoes etc traveling up & down the street, goat wagons, etc – Very badly mixed election – I was about town generally . . .

Nov 9 – Cloudy & cold – Election returns getting in – looks like Cleveland be next President – Much interest displayed – Everybody wants to know, etc. Australian ballot system, adopted by Legislature put into force for first time and proved a grand success. Bed at 1 – Returns not all in, but Republican party generally left –

Nov 10 . . . Bob Patterson very sick with pneumonia – Went down and saw him at 11 in the evening – made item in *Enterprise* of him . . .

Nov 11 . . . Sent three *Enterprises* to Maggie Moore . . .

Nov 12 . . . Wrote & sent a nice 4 page letter to Mrs Maggie Moore Williamson . . . Evening excursion train took about 100 to big Stewart ratification meeting in Carson . . .

Sunday, Nov 13 . . . Bob Patterson died about 3:30 PM – He was attended by Drs Manson and Webber – They cupped him this AM, to the extent of ½ pint of blood – His right lung had become solidified so that he was running on the one lung. Could get off a small hacking cough, but too weak to raise off any relief. So he had to die. I went up and raised a flag at ½ mast on Pioneer Hall . . .

Nov 14 . . . Visited Mrs Patterson, and at her request telegraphed to the Secy of the California Pioneers . . . Wrote up Patterson for Va Evening Chronicle and later on for Enterprise . . .

[Clippings from the *Enterprise* and *Chronicle*, virtually identical – Patterson, 66 years old, born in Scotland, was brought to Boston when 18 months old – Went to California in 1849 via Cape Horn, mined on the southern lode – In 1865 or '66 he "gravitated naturally toward the Comstock and Virginia City, where he has remained, engaged in mining and sporting speculations, saloon business and being a first-class all-around citizen."]

Nov 15 – Cloudy & cooler – At 3 PM attended religious services at Patterson's residence – Many friends present – I, acting as President of the

Pioneers appointed pall bearers, etc, and at 5:45 we escorted the remains to the RR depot, I acting as one of the pall bearers myself. At Carson several Pioneers & friends met us & with myself stood in as pall bearers to the residence where we left the corpse. This was after 7 PM. After that I ran with the undertaker, Conboie, eating & drinking, & at 12 got to bed at the Arlington House – By mail today rec'd Maggie Moore photos –

Nov 16 . . . Funeral of Patterson at 3 PM from his family residence – I attended again as pall bearer as far as the RR depot, where we all – eight – got into a carriage provided for us and rode out to the Cemetery a mile north-east of town – Usual services at the grave by Rev Hyslop – Back to Va on evening train . . . Was at Enterprise awhile and wrote up Patterson's Carson funeral . . . [clip]

> . . . All the available members of the Society of Pacific Coast Pioneers here and in Carson, including Alf. Doten, President of the Society, joined in giving their brother old boy a good send off, and a longer line of carriages is seldom seen . . . Prominent citizens were the pall-bearers, and a few shovelfuls of earth soon closed the last shuffle and deal in the life and death of our old-time friend, Uncle Bob Patterson. May he rest easy in the eternal hereafter, for, like the rest of us, he will be a long time dead.

Nov 17 . . . Evening at Theater – Clara Morris and fine dramatic Co in "Claire" – Splendid emotional play – good audience – She & Co came on her own car . . . Rec'd today . . . letter from J P Jones, New York, regretting very much his inability to help me . . .

Nov 19 . . . Evening visited Mrs Robt Patterson 2 hours . . .

Sunday, Nov 20 . . . Was sent for and interviewed by Mrs Patterson in the PM . . .

Nov 23 . . . At noon commenced snowing & did so all the PM & evening . . . I gathered up all my big accumulation of newspapers in my room the last 7 or 8 years. Bundled them up for sale – 4500 of them –

Nov 24 . . . Thanksgiving Day – Turkey at saloons all about town and everybody had the bird at home, or enjoyed it somewhere. The day was very quietly observed, very few seeing much to be thankful for . . . I wrote and sent a letter to Bessie – 2 page – with 5 of Sammy's photos . . .

Nov 25 . . . Evening wrote a 4 page letter to Sister Cornelia . . .

Sunday, Nov 27 . . . Wrote Memorial Tribute on Bob Patterson for Pioneer Society – and meeting that should have been held this evening – regular night. I was alone at Pioneer meeting tonight

Nov 28 through Dec 24 [Heavy snowstorms & wind disrupt trains & mail & make it hard to get around town – AD sees a juggling & song & dance team named Albini & Maguire, the Hatch & Trader Comedy Company in *The Convict's Daughter, Rip Van Winkle, My Mother-in-law, Stricken Blind,* and Minnie Seligman Cutting & W F Owen in *My Official Wife,* looks in on a National Guard Ball, visits Mrs Patterson again, places another order for catheters &, despite the weather & little mention of the fact, is evidently about town most of the time – Of further interest:]

Sunday, Dec 11 – Cloudy & cold – A light snowsquall about 10 AM – PM I attended regular monthly meeting of the old Exempts – Declared a dividend of $40 each – 31 members – from the big surplus in the treasury – Elected officers for ensuing term, as follows: Bart Burke, President; John Piper, Vice President; Fred Plunkett, Secretary; Joe Guggenheim, Treasurer – Bed 12 – Clear & dam cold –

Dec 13 . . . Evening visited Mrs Patterson for couple of hours at her residence. When I left she presented me a bottle of whisky from old Bob . . . Con Va assessed 50 cts today – 1st for several years.

Dec 14 . . . The assessment of 50 cents on Con Va yesterday and the gas trouble knocked the stock down to $1.50 today. All other stocks were depreciated also and accordingly.

Dec 15 . . . Got my Exempt dividend this PM, $40 . . . Paid my Odd Fellows dues, $7 to Jan 1 – also several other bills – Going up to my room this evening about dark I slipped & fell up on the winding stair almost fracturing a rib or two on left breast.

Dec 16 . . . This evening I took the Pioneer Group picture, 24 x 30 in size from the International Saloon where it has hung the last 2 yrs and brought it to my room – Was presented to me by Mrs Patterson . . .

Dec 24 . . . Steady rain most all day – Very sloppy – Many people out getting holiday goods regardless of weather or hard times . . .

Sunday, Dec 25 – Cloudy & thawy – Evening a few good rain showers – Christmas Day – Generally observed – Everybody ate turkey – All the principal saloons served free lunch to their patrons, roast turkey, pig, salads etc, liberally – Egg-nog and Tom & Jerry everywhere – By invitation I dined at Jack Plant's, away up on Howard st, near Union – Present: Jack & wife & Miss Martha Rooney, Zeb Day & wife, Mr Bishop & wife & 2 children, Geo Kritzer, 10 children including Jacks 4 – 19 of us in all – Excellent turkey dinner – After that, Christmas tree in the parlor – fine tree about 8 ft high, well hung with presents etc, lighted with little wax candles, etc – Children happiest of the happy – I had banjo along and there was plenty of singing, dancing, etc – Party broke up at about 9:30. I left banjo there for Jack to bring down tomorrow for the streets are so slippery I did not dare take it along with me – By slow and extremely careful travel I managed to get down Taylor st safely to C – Was about town awhile, then at room – Bed 1:30 . . .

Dec 26 – Cloudy & thawy . . . Rivers and creeks all booming – A wash-out or flooding of the track near the Brunswick mill delayed the mail train . . . letter from wife . . . Floods throughout California . . .

Dec 28 . . . The International saloon was closed by the Sheriff about 4 PM on an attachment by J B Dazet and Sam Pidge et al for liquors furnished and barkeeps salary, etc, total $1,500.

Dec 30 . . . Evening I was at annual ball of Battery A artillery at Opera House awhile . . . Mrs John Piper who has been in the Nevada State Insane Asylum at Reno for the last two years was returned to Virginia Friday morning, being considered cured or about so. This was *last* Friday morning – a week ago – She seems to be getting along all right, though a little flustrated by the change, but has calmed down all right *apparently* –

Dec 31 – Clear, cool & pleasant – At midnight, guns, pistols, crackers, bombs & other explosives, all sorts of trumpets, mining whistles and salute by Battery A of the artillery ushered in the new year 1893. Bed at 2 –

BOOK NO. 69

Virginia City and Carson
Jan 1, 1893 – Dec 31, 1893

Sunday, Jan 1, 1893 . . . Was about town considerably – New Years Day – generally observed after the usual style – Turkey, egg-nog, etc at saloons, visiting parties, church services . . . it being Sunday . . .

Jan 2 . . . H P Cohen, who used to be bookkeeper of the *Enterprise* arrived from San Francisco today to be head clerk or bookkeeper of the V & GH Water Co.

Jan 3 . . . Evening I was at a surprise party at the William Tell House given to Charlie Meadows mail agent on the Southern Pacific RR now on a holiday visit to his mother . . .

Jan 7 . . . The Countess Magri, widow of Genl Tom Thumb together with her husband, the Count Magri, Baron Magri, his brother, three very small dwarfs, with 2 usual sized men & a woman, comprising the Mrs Genl Tom Thumb Company, arrived on passenger train at 10:45 today – A grand big crowd of youngsters & women & men were at the depot to see them arrive. They rode in their own little hack drawn by 2 little ponies & with a dwarf driver to the Opera House via Taylor & C sts, several hundred youngsters leading & escorting them. They gave a matinee in the PM which was densely crowded mostly with children & women. Evening they again performed, & I was there – Another big house and same excellent show. Was at Enterprise office afterward, writing, reading proof, etc. Bed at 4.

Sunday, Jan 8 – Clear, warm & very pleasant – About noon I called on the Tom Thumbs at their rooms in the International Hotel – All three dwarfs and Bump & wife present. Jolly little fellows. Had a long and interesting chat with the little countess and brother George about our Massachusetts home – She knows Lizzie and has one of her books – "Poems From the Inner Life." Has traveled all over the world . . . PM attended regular monthly meeting of Exempts – Installation of officers – Fine collation – baked beans, cake, boiled ham, beer, whisky etc – several invited guests – songs, recitations, etc – Then I visited the Thumbs again & walked down to the train with them & saw them off at 5:20 for Carson where they appear tomorrow evening. Another huge crowd at depot – Bed 2 – J M Campbell severs his connection as lessee and editor of the Enterprise – Don't know yet who takes his place.

Jan 10 . . . Alfred Chartz is now editor of the Enterprise . . .

Jan 11 . . . Yerington was up today, and evening train took away Campbell & wife, of the Enterprise . . . going to start a paper in San F – I was down to the train & saw him off – Evening I got in an item or two in the paper . . . Indications point to a total suspension of the Enterprise – Not a paying thing for last 10 yrs or more –

Jan 12 . . . Evening I attended installation banquet of the Red Men, at French Rotisserie – and in response to call I made quite a talk – Wrote it up for Enterprise . . .

Sunday, Jan 15 – Took morning train to Carson – Cloudy & cold, and PM very rainy – Met many members of the new Legislature, from all parts of the State – convenes tomorrow – Much caucusing among them this evening, till midnight at the State House – The only trouble in the Senate was with the hold overs who are Republicans – Two of them however, Stearns of Eureka and Williamson of Lander, went over to the Silverites at last, giving them the majority – House all Silver – This fixed organization for Silver in both Houses – Bed at 12 at the Arcade lodging house – John Wolmering's – Still raining and very muddy . . .

[A clip from the *Enterprise* announces its suspension with the present issue, and says that its legal advertisements will be continued in the *Chronicle*.]

Jan 16 . . . In response to a telegram I reported telegraphically to *Reno Gazette* the organization of the Legislature . . .

Jan 17 through 21 [AD reports for the *Gazette* & is "about town" – Notes on 18th that flags are at "½ mast" and Legislature adjourned because of the death of "Ex President R B Hayes."]

Sunday, Jan 22 . . . PM I met Frank Doten . . . Got in from Bodie with his big team yesterday, & will pull out on return tomorrow with load of freight – Was about town awhile with him . . . Reno Gazette having made other arrangements for reporting, lets me out with the one weeks work for $15 –

Jan 23 – Reported for Carson *Appeal* and *Tribune* . . . Evening I attended reception of Gov Colcord at his residence – Big crowd . . .

Jan 24 . . . Wm M Stewart re-elected US Senator by Legislature to-day . . . Only business transacted . . .

Jan 25 . . . At PM session, Frank Bell was elected State Prison Warden . . .

Jan 26 . . . Reported as usual – Evening, commencing at 10 attended Stewart banquet at the Arlington House – About 150 guests at the 3 tables fully occupying the big dining room – Fine collation, wines, etc – good talks, toasts etc till 2 . . .

Jan 27 . . . Quite a little stir about meteorites or aerolites falling from the sky during last few days – several picked up – saw some of them – finally traced them to the RR foundry source of supply for young kids with snap shot rubber guns – granulated bits of iron from residue of furnace melts –

Feb 1 – AM clear & pleasant – PM very blustery & barometer indicating storm. Reported as usual – Furious wind from the west – and about 5 PM as Senate adjourned wind blew in one of the big lights of a front window & later on still another – Evening blew over a chimney on the northern section – Assembly Chamber – The Assembly was in session & the mass of bricks falling on the roof created general consternation – Gale subsided after midnight – Wind blew today as high as 70 miles an hour according to State Weather Observer Friend's record – Bed at 11 – still blowing furiously by spells – In the Assembly this PM the following bit of fun took place – Resolution introduced by Bob Hammill of Elko, the funny man of that body – Resolved – That when the socks now under course of construction in the Assembly are completed they shall be sent as a present to Hon Jerry Simpson of Kansas. Pike moved to amend by presenting them to the Speaker. Speaker declared the resolution out of order. Explanatory – Miss Annie Martin, editor of *Carson Morning News* is an old maiden resident of Carson, with but a few months newspaper experience – Reports the Assembly for her paper, and to utilize the intervals of rest she has her knitting along. She enjoyed the joke and kept on knitting more ostentatious than before – (But she left her knitting at home after this) –

Feb 2 . . . Reported as usual – $20 from Williams . . .

Feb 7 . . . Evening attended prize fight at Opera House between Abe Meyers of Va and Ben Tremblay of Carson – $500 a side – Big house – special train from the Comstock brought 150 people, & many were up from Reno – Tremblay was settled in 22 rounds – neither much damaged – Bed 1, snowing lively –

Feb 10 . . . Long sessions of both Houses – Big crowd from State University . . . cadets etc – over 100 – Visited Legislature, etc – Uncle Tom's Cabin troupe also came . . . Evening I was at show, at Opera House – Some good dancing and banjo, Topsy and Eva tolerable, and a fair orchestra – otherwise rather of a poor show & badly cut up . . .

Feb 13 . . . Both Houses off on special visit to State University, & State Insane Asylum . . .

Feb 15 . . . The Chinese celebrated their New Year very strongly today & tonight – fusillade of crackers and bombs very lively all day and especially spiteful tonight – Bed 12 – Hell still a popping –

Feb 17 . . . Legislative ball at Opera House tonight . . .

Sunday, Feb 19 – Fine & Springlike – Finest of season – Evening was at Friend's observatory with Senators Cousins and Williamson & Asst Secy Davis of Senate – Saw the new moon, also Jupiter & his 4 moons through the big telescope – Bed 12 –

Feb 20 . . . Elrod, clerk at Mint, received dispatch from Director of the US Mint, Washington, saying: "Your report received. When will Doten forward *his* report" – I told Elrod to answer that I would do it in a week . . . Evening, excursion train to see & hear Bill Nye, at Reno . . .

Feb 21 . . . Evening at Opera House – Richard Foote & Miss Annie Plunkett, his wife, & a good Co played "Hugo the Hunchback of Florence" – Good play, good Co & good house . . .

Feb 22 . . . Washingtons Birthday – No session – Flags up – Carson Guard paraded – Evening at theater – Same Co – Plays: "A Happy Pair," "The Bells," "The Old Guard" . . .

Feb 23 . . . AM I reported as usual – PM I went off on my Mint Comstock report – Evening at Theater – "Othello" . . .

Feb 24 through March 5 [AD reports Senate in AM, works on Comstock report PM and weekends and all night the final Sunday in the office of Orvis Ring, Superintendent of Public Instruction – Hears John Mackay was shot in San Francisco – Sees *Don Caesar de Bazan* and *Richelieu* at theater – No details.]

March 6 – Variable but pleasant – AM reported Senate as usual – PM completed copying Comstock report and delivered it to Elrod at the Mint at 4 PM. Evening both Houses held session this being the last day and close of the Sixteenth Session. Had "Third House" fun as usual, but it didnt amount to much – Few good hands at it – Lieut Gov Poujade laid down the gavel in Senate at 12 oclock & both Houses closed. After that I went with others to Lieut Gov Poujades reception at his residence – Good crowd, refreshments and social time – Bed at 2:30 very tired & sleepy. *16th Session Closed.*

March 7 through July 2 [AD remains in Carson, doing nothing most of the time, and not recording much in his journal either, in part because he doesn't have his journal with him and is just keeping notes for it – Of interest:]

March 7 . . . Filed my bill, $100, with Comstock report and both started by the evening train for Washington . . .

March 11 . . . Evening at Ring's room or office writing up Poujade's valedictory speech for *Chronicle* and *Gazette* –

March 13 . . . Wrote & sent letter to J P Jones . . .

March 14 . . . Wrote & sent letter to A Nicholls . . .

March 15 . . . Evening at theater – Marie Heath & Co in "A Turkish Bath" . . .

March 18 . . . Rec'd $15 from the Reno Gazette for that first weeks reporting . . .

Sunday, March 19 . . . PM met Frank B Doten – Took him to Ring's room and he signed the old roll of the Pacific Coast Pioneers . . .

March 22 – Variable – Snow about all gone again – Bed at 11 – About 5:30 PM Miss Sadie Scheffer, a waiting woman at the Arlington House, met Ed Parkinson editor of the Carson Tribune on a cross street going home and threatened to cowhide him for something in his paper which she thought referred to her – quite a sensation – She made a fool of herself, and was the only one hurt.

[Clippings say that Bessie Caldwell, principal witness against Henry Collier (who was acquitted), was committed to the Insane Asylum – "The law recently passed allowing imbeciles to be cared for at that institution will no doubt add to the number of habitues of the asylum."]

March 30 – Cloudy & cooler – blustering day – Bed 11 – When I came to Virginia City from Como & went to work on the old Daily Union as "local," Dr Henry de Groot was there and was, I think, connected with the paper as a writer – I became quite well acquainted with him – Killed at Alameda, Cal, day before yesterday – accidentally run over by a railroad train – One of the earliest pioneers of California and Nevada – Was deaf and did not see the train as he was crossing the track on foot –

March 31 . . . PM wrote letters to wife and to sister Cornelia – got letters from Wife and Bessie – Millie at home in Reno for the last week, but will soon go East with her husband . . .

April 3 . . . Received letter from Director of the Mint . . . enclosing US Treasury warrant for $100 . . . Wrote Sam Baker's obituary today – He is an old pioneer, living here and wanted it written so he could read it before he dies, like old Uncle Dave Evans.

April 4 . . . Got my $100 warrant cashed at the bank – paid bills and had about $30 left – Bed at 1 –

April 6 . . . PM wrote letter to President Grover Cleveland asking appointment as Supt of Carson Mint . . .

April 12 – Variable & blustering – Evening at Opera House – Prize fight, $500 a side – Allen and Turner – White and colored – 143 & 160 lbs – Big house – I on stage – square fight – Allen knocked out by the floor in the 7th round . . .

April 13 . . . Jake Young died 4 PM, Va [Young was an early Comstocker (1860) and prominent Odd Fellow.]

April 14 . . . Went to railroad office, and after consultation with Yerington and Bender, got my half fare pass renewed till next New Years day . . .

Sunday, April 16 . . . Special train of 2 cars took big crowd from here to Jake Young's funeral – Many also came on train from Reno – One of the biggest funerals ever seen on the Comstock . . .

April 17 . . . Letter from wife says Millie & Ed & baby left Wednesday night last for his parental home in the East – Decatur, Ill . . .

April 18 . . . Letter received from Lizzie, via Reno informs me of death of Sister Laura, on the 10th – Brights disease of the kidneys complicated with other difficulties – Evening Mrs W J Florence and Company in "The Mighty Dollar" . . .

April 24 – Cloudy – an inch of snow this morning – Evening about 8 oclock false alarm of fire brought out the machines – At 9 a real alarm brought them out again. This time it was Sweeney's corner – I happened close by and saw it all – after it started. Incendiary set fire at south side of rear end – Fire did little damage, but water did, and the firemen & others tore down and destroyed all they could – The Dairy Restaurant next door, and shops adjoining did suffer considerably in that respect – Worst handled fire I ever saw – Bed 11:30 – cold night –

Sunday, April 30 . . . Big target shooting done by the Carson Guard teams, at Treadway's Park range, claimed to be the best in the world . . .

May 4 . . . Evening prize fight at Opera House – Reported it for Reno *Journal* . . . Judgment affirmed in Trolson case [Sentenced to five years in state prison for embezzlement while an agent of Wells Fargo.]

Sunday, May 7 . . . Wrote Memorial Tribute of Va Exempt Firemen's Association on death of Jake Young . . .

May 8 . . . Evening at Opera House – "The Prodigal Father" and "Carmencita" by a good dramatic Co – good house . . .

May 12 – C & P & warmer – 82° – sultry weather – Evening, by special complimentary invitation I attended entertainment given by Piute Tribe No 1, Improved Order of Red Men, at Odd Fellows Hall, in honor and observance of St Tammany's Day – Fine time – Dancing till 11 – then fine collation, banquet at which 120 were seated at a time – speeches, recitations etc, and in response to call I made a nice little speech – anyhow I had lots of applause – Bed at 1 – Sent my Jake Young tribute up to Va by this evening's mail, to the Exempts –

Sunday, May 14 – Same – letter from wife, inclosing one from Ed Cochran to her – Millie and her child, Sara, got back home to Reno Friday morning, absent East just a month – She couldn't get along with his folks – He will come back also shortly – Bed 11:30 –

May 15 . . . Trees leaving out finely last 3 or 4 days – lilacs getting into full bloom in Capitol square . . . George Humphrey of Reno, newly appointed US Marshal for Nevada sworn in today here . . .

May 25 . . . Extra heavy frost this morning – About all the fruit about here thought to be killed . . . Carson Mint ordered closed as to coinage . . .

May 26 . . . Judge R S Mesick died this evening at the Palace Hotel, SF – aged 70 yrs . . . [Mesick was an attorney for Flood, Mackay and other mining moguls, and for Nagle in his trial for killing the notorious California duelling judge, David S Terry.]

May 29 – C & P – 70° – Sent following telegram to Hon J P Jones US Senator, Hoffman House New York: "Telegraph me six hundred dollars – Financial emergency – Please don't fail me now – Respond. Alf Doten" – Bed 11 – A bycicle party of 5 arrived yesterday from Reno in five hours – 31 miles . . . Returned today – Names: Charley Jones, Gus Gottschalk, W A Moore, Chas Nash and A C Helmold –

[Clip, *Nevada Tribune:*] Superintendent T. R. Hofer received orders from the Secretary of the Treasury this morning to suspend coinage entirely at the Mint on June 1st and dispense with the services of the entire coinage force . . . and reduce the pay of the watchman to $3 a day.

Gold and silver will be received and paid for as heretofore, and parting and refining of gold and silver bars continued.

Out of a force of sixty employees only about 20 will remain. This is a hard blow to Carson, as it means the taking out of circulation in Carson of at least $5,000 a month, and all in the interest of "free and unlimited coinage of silver."

May 31 – Same – Gen Wade Hampton and party arrived this evening – Staid in his car and did not show himself to the eager public – Fighting at Buckeye, placer diggings about 30 miles SE from here, by contesting claimants. Bed 11 –

June 1 – The Mint drop takes effect today – Bed 11 –

June 2 . . . Got after Evan Williams at the bank in the PM and he promised me an order for stock to assist me . . .

June 3 . . . Found the following at the bank for me: ". . . W S James, Gold Hill, Nevada. Friend Bill – I believe that my Centennial stock is still on the book in your possession. Should Alf Doten want any of my stock, give him up to one thousand shares and oblige, Yours truly, E Williams." . . .

Sunday, June 4 . . . Sent letter to James enclosing Williams' order and calling for 1,000 shares in 2 pieces 500 each . . .

June 5 – Clear & pleasant but hot – 84° – Considerable warlike trouble has existed at the Buckeye placer diggings, some 30 miles southeast of here in the pine-nut range for some weeks past, owing to opposing claimants for ground and water right – Culminated the other day in resort to armed force – several shots were fired, but no one hurt . . . These diggings appear to be of the good old California style, rich and good & worth fighting for – The gold is both fine and coarse and worth $19 an ounce – Bed 11 –

June 6 . . . M Kinzle, Vice Prest Centennial arrived from Va and puts up at my lodgings . . .

June 7 . . . Evening mail brought my new stock . . .

June 9 . . . Wrote & sent letter to Nicholls . . . Sharon-Crosby shooting at Va yesterday –

Sunday, June 11 . . . Letter to J P Jones . . .

June 12 . . . Kinzle left for Nevada City this evening – Sontag and Evans [famous California railroad bandits] captured today . . .

June 16 – C & P – 84° – Evening, ball of Warren Engine Co at Opera House – looked in short time – Sammy Doten graduated at Reno today – Bright & Reynolds' faro bank at Dempsey's saloon got busted last night ($60 did it) and in consequence there is no faro game running in Carson tonight – closed permanently – This is the first time in the history of Carson that such has been the case – Yet there are one or two faro games running in Chinatown, lower side of the city – Bed 12 –

June 19 . . . Odd Fellows gathering in to Grand Lodge . . . Bought me a new pair of pants – $7 . . .

June 20 . . . Grand Lodge elected officers, etc – Evening at Opera House was Cantata of the "Flower Queen" – Crowded – Odd Fellows attended and at close all marched to Odd Fellows Hall, where we enjoyed a fine banquet . . .

June 21 . . . Got letter from wife saying she was going to take a run over into California and would come home with Bessie . . .

June 22 . . . Senator and Ex-Gov Stanford dead . . .

June 23 – C & P – Prof Zimmer's ex wife with their little son Eddie came down on evening train – I met her at the depot and directed her to the Ormsby House – Later on in the evening I called at Ormsby House parlor

& paid her and the Professor a visit of an hour or so – They have concluded to marry over again tomorrow – Bed at 12 –

June 24 . . . At 5 PM Zimmer married his former wife, at Ormsby House parlor – Justice Hawthorne did the ceremony, and J M Holbrook and myself signed as witnesses . . .

June 26 . . . Made Centennial item in all three Carson papers, *Appeal, Tribune,* and *News* – Letter from Kinzle rec'd . . .

> [Clip, *Appeal,* June 27:] On the Jefferson ridge leading up from Nevada City, California, are situated several prominent gravel gold mines, some of which pay regular dividends. A rich strike of pay gravel, recently made in the Lupin mine, yielding over $17 to the carload, as well as another in the San Jose mine, showing a goodly amount of coarse, heavy gold are creating quite a lively sensation in that quarter. Both mines adjoin the famous Centenniel on the West and South, and are doubtless developing the same big gravel channel. Some Carsonites and several Comstockers are the principal owners of the Centenniel.

July 1 . . . Sweeney's corner reopened in popular style – faro, "stud," "craps" etc – big free lunch – ran big all night . . .

July 3 – Clear – 86° – People preparing to spend the 4th somewhere – To be no celebration here, but at Va and Reno. The cannons of Battery A, Va, and hose carriage of Liberty Hose Co, G.H. passed by train to Reno. I took evening train to Va in response to note from Al Mills asking me to come up & report the 4th for him in Chronicle – Been absent nearly 6 months but found my way about town among old friends as usual – Old Joe Douglass had me locked out of my room, but was persuaded to give me bedroom on same floor, next to front, where Joe Stewart used to bed. Bed at 12 –

July 4 through 31 [The weather remains hot – AD reports two days for the *Chronicle* and is paid $7.50, attends an Exempt meeting & a Chosen Friends meeting, is about town with Jose Salinas and Fred Clough, writes another begging letter to Jones, pays for catheters – notes that Miss Laura Tilden has been admitted to the bar, the first woman lawyer in Nevada, & that the remains of A Laigneau have been brought to town, that he is sixty-four years old & has received a birthday letter from his sister Cornelia, and that his friend Harry Johns has been seriously hurt in the Chollar – He visits Harry several times – All short entries, half of them nothing but temperature and bedtime.]

Aug 1 . . . The Crown Point mine started up again today after about a months shut down. Great depression in both stocks and mines at present & for weeks past. Less than 300 miners working on the Comstock – Many saloons & places of business closing, people moving away, etc. Silver mines shut down throughout the State. All on acct of low price of silver – Comstock ore averages about 60 pr ct gold. Great combined move among the mine owners of the Comstock to reduce wages, salaries and mine expenses. Gold Hill bus ceased running 2 or 3 weeks ago from lack of patronage.

Aug 3 – C & P – Bed 10 – Trouble in the *Chronicle* office – Manager Coleman threw up his position Saturday last and left for San Francisco that evening, leaving Joe McCarthy in charge – Joe got drunk as usual and said so, licked his wife & got arrested – He left also for SF Tuesday night –

Aug 4 . . . Went to Gold Hill by morning train at 7:45 – Skirmishing . . . Evening at Opera House – "Virginia Mastodon Minstrels" . . . One of the best amateur variety entertainments I ever saw here . . .

Aug 5 . . . Denis Donahue was drowned in Washoe Lake yesterday AM by the upsetting of a small canvas boat – He was alone in the boat – about 150 yards from shore – could not swim – he sank in 10 ft of water – parties hastened to his rescue and got within a few feet of him when he sank for last time – Body recovered three hours later and brought to his home on the Divide – Native of Grass Valley, Cal, aged 22 yrs – A well known good young man –

Aug 7 . . . Congress convened in extra session today on the silver & financial question –

Aug 9 – C & P – Bed 11 – A Seven-Day Second Adventist preacher and a woman supposed to be his wife gave an open air discussing and singing entertainment on C st in front of the Wm Tell House this evening – He predicts and figures out the second coming of Christ and the destruction of the world by fire six years from now. Only good Christians will be saved, therefore exhorts all to get in to Christ as soon as possible.

Aug 10 through 20 [Very brief entries – "Same – Bed 10" and so on.]

Aug 21 – C & P – 80° – Big trouble with Va C & C hoodlums down at Nevada brewery, 6 mile canyon – 2 of 'em got a charge of No 6 bird shot each. Pd Douglass $20 this evening – Then he & I ran together on drinks and oyster supper awhile – he paying all – Bed 1 –

Aug 22 . . . Yesterday I stove cremated a linen shirt which I have worn daily for about 8 months & none other, except at night – Too rotten to hold together any longer – Hard times – About town as usual . . .

Aug 23 . . . Sent 2 page letter to Cornelia . . .

Aug 24 . . . Sent following telegram to J P Jones . . . "Eloi, eloi, lama sabacthani" – Cost $1 . . .

Aug 25 . . . The Va Chronicle came out this evening with a half sheet supplement from mining sales – *18 columns of them.* The longest and biggest lot yet since I ran 24 columns on the same layout in the Gold Hill News – Wonder if such patronage now will end as disastrously as it did with me? Looks like big prosperity for the *Chronicle,* but we shall see.

Aug 26 . . . [Clip on the death of H B Loomis in Stockton, Calif.] This came in the SF Chronicle today – Loomis was reporter on the papers here, Va Chronicle, Sutro Independent, etc and for some time on the GH News – Must have been over 50 yrs old & leaves wife in Stockton –

Sunday, Aug 27 . . . Matt Rapson's funeral this PM from Odd Fellows Hall – Belonged to my lodge – 100 on foot, and 26 carriages . . .

Aug 28 . . . Wrote out some Centennial agreements . . . Repeal of the Sherman Bullion purchase law today in the House at Washington by 129 majority created a profound sensation –

Aug 30 . . . Centennial negociations . . .

Aug 31 – Clear & pleasant – As usual – Evening Douglass let me back to my old room, No 7 – Removed all my traps to it at once, from the front room I have been occupying while locked out the last 2 months – Slept there happy & at home once more – Bed at 11 –

Sept 1 – Clear & pleasant – 80° – Busy at room most of day fixing and arranging my traps generally – Over 20 more miners drafted from the different mines – Only about 200 miners employed, in all, along the Comstock – Great depression in all business – Miners Union holds full meetings at their regular weekly meetings, Friday evenings – Have come to no conclusions as to reducing their wages – Bed at 11 – Took a bath in my old room this morning – sponge bath [several lines erased, apparently having to do with how badly he needed that bath] – By evening train to Reno I sent my old '49 violin to Bessie . . . because she says father's old fiddle is busted.

Sept 2 . . . Around all day, and, as so happened, only two bits expenditure – Wrote and sent a letter to S E Stivers, proprietor of the *Va Chronicle,* Irvington, Alameda County, California – suggesting that I be manager, editor or reporter . . .

Sept 4 . . . Coleman, manager of the *Chronicle* quit again 3 or 4 days ago and is now in San F – Left Joe McCarthy in charge – Joe been drunk last two days, Abusing wife & family – This evening she swore out a warrant & had him sent to jail for threats against life. Staid in jail tonight, no bail being accepted – Bed 11 . . . I did quite a heavy washing of dirty clothes this AM [two lines erased]

Sept 5 – Cloudy with several heavy thunder showers . . . Stivers & wife, proprietors of *Chronicle* came by today's morning train – Joe McCarthy was bound over in the sum of $500 to keep the peace, for 6 months this morning – Had to "swear off" drinking to get bondsmen –

Sept 7 . . . Snowy whiteness on the summits of the Palmyra or Como range this morning – and all day was pretty good overcoat weather – Bob Sage of Reno came up today to probably take business management charge of the Chronicle in place of Coleman – I have suffered greatly last 2 or 3 days from a bruised tooth in lower jaw . . . chin and throat much swollen & sore . . .

Sept 8 . . . Evening with good fire in room, I wrote letter to wife and a ¼ column item from Nevada City for the Chronicle – Toothache much better . . . Met Harry Johns on the street this PM, for first time since he got hurt . . . gains strength slowly . . . and will not be able to work for some time –

Sept 9 . . . Morning and evening writing up this Journal from notes taken in Carson – Badly behind by nearly 6 months . . .

Sunday, Sept 10 . . . Jack W Plant, formerly foreman of the *Enterprise* has got position on the SF *Examiner* as proof reader, at $43 a week . . .

Sept 11 . . . Al Mills was superseded today as "local" of the *Chronicle* by W Scott, for awhile local of the *Enterprise* before it died – Joe McCarthy stays as foreman and S E Stivers business manager – Evening at room writing up this Journal . . .

Sept 14 – C & P – cool – Sent letter to Sam Davis, Carson, enclosing three photos of Major Pauline Cushman, which she gave me twenty years ago – still have four left – Evening I was at train and saw Mrs John Connerton off on a visit to friends in California – Went to Opera House – Comedy farce in three acts entitled "Jane," by Jennie Yeamans and good company – Very funny – good house – Bed 12 – clear & cool –

Sept 15 . . . Just one year today since I was in Reno . . .

Sept 16 . . . Miners Union decided by vote today not to reduce wages from $4 per day. 206 to 85 –

Sept 19 . . . Gold Hill Miners Union today voted to reduce wages to $3.50 . . . 49 to 47 . . . Remains of a woman and a horse found in an old abandoned shaft a mile or so below Silver City today . . . been there many years – perhaps 20 or more . . .

Sept 21 . . . The Fair special train took about 60 from here this morning, 20 from GH and pulled out of Carson with nearly or quite 300 in all – This is the boss day of the Fair – "Comstock day" –

Sept 23 – Clear, warm & pleasant – J H Coleman, manager of the *Chronicle* returned from San Francisco today – Stivers & wife & baby left for their home at Irvington . . . last Wednesday evening – Coleman returns to resume the management . . . This evening, at my room I burned a big lot of old letters, etc, and among them about forty which I have kept in a sacred little package in my trunk, being all the letters I received from my first love, Martha B Atwood – Yes I burned all those old love letters at last after carefully preserving them about forty-five years – 45 years! – And so ends that sweetly romantic chapter of my earlier boyhood life. I read a few of them, but the old feeling did not come over me – they didnt read or seem natural – the ink was faded like my boyish love, and scarcely legible – 45 years! – Ah well, the love of Mary is far better than that of Martha, and has possessed my entire heart. Good bye Martha. She married long ago, and has half a dozen grown up children to bless her advanced age. So I retired to my lonely couch at about 2 oclock in rather of a pleasant state of mind. And slept well – No hay-fever as yet – eyes rather sore – J H Coleman of the *Chronicle* left again this evening, very abruptly, for San Francisco. "Quien sabe?" –

Sept 26 – Clear & pleasant – Bed 12 – PM was about town with Judge Cook of Gold Hill – The Mechanics Union of Storey County held an election here this PM on the wage question resulting as follows: for reduction, 70; against reduction, 14; scattering, 2 – The Gold Hill Miners Union takes another vote on the proposition tomorrow, giving all members a chance to vote who are not in arrears for dues, etc, for over a year –

Sept 27 . . . The Gold Hill Miners Union vote . . . for reduction 107; contra 37 . . .

Sept 28 . . . Cutting & contriving as usual . . .

Sept 29 . . . Fair at Carson closed today – hasn't amounted to much – Bed 11 –

Oct 3 . . . PM Pat J Keyes was with me at my room, and we got up a letter to Frank Shay, San Francisco – 3 pages – about Keyes' lawsuit . . . & his chances (and mine) of getting some money out of it . . .

Oct 5 . . . Letter from wife, wanting my "Age of Fables or Beauties of Mythology" by Bulfinch – Sent it to her . . .

Oct 6 . . . "Hard Times" ball given at Odd Fellows Hall, by the National Guard . . . Very good party – didnt look like hard times –

Oct 11 . . . PM I wrote & sent 2 page letter to J P Jones . . . Evening wrote letter to Andrew Nicholls . . . and one to M Kinzle, Nevada City, Cal, at the Centennial mine . . .

Oct 12 – C & P – The Miners Unions of Va & GH took a vote jointly at Divide Hose house this PM on the wage question – got through counting, about 9 this evening – 416 votes cast – 41 majority for the old rate – $4.00 per day – Bed 11 – Freezing weather every night now, ice forming – Days of the Indian Summer type.

Oct 17 – Clear, pleasant & cold – Considerable stir in Con Virginia stock last few days – owing to circumstances connected with annual stockholders election – For months it has stood at 1.20 to 1.30 or 1.40 but last Tuesday . . . it got up to 2.90 – yesterday it was 2.20 – This AM it was 2.50 but dropped in the PM to 2.05 – Annual election took place yesterday – John H Coleman the old manager of the *Evening Chronicle* returned from 2 or 3 wks absence in San F today and resumed management of the paper – Was much needed.

[Two clippings entered into journal here – The San Francisco *Daily Report* for the 16th notes "The firmness of Consolidated California and Virginia shares imparted a better tone to the Comstock market this morning." – At the annual stockholders' meeting the directors authorized a James Rule to continue explorations in the upper levels of the mine, above 1100 feet, where Rule claimed a large body of good ore could be found – Both Mackay and Flood, after careful investigation of Rule's offer, consented – Rule to get no pay except $10,000 from the bullion of the new ore body when found – And from an unidentified newspaper:] Although a retrospect of the year discloses little that is satisfactory . . . this is not the first crisis through which the Comstock Lode has passed. In 1870 the market value of the entire lode, as represented in shares, was about $4,000,000, while in 1875, after the discovery of the bonanzas . . . it appreciated to about $275,000,000. In 1882 it had again declined to about $3,000,000, but on the discovery of the new ore body in the . . . Consolidated California & Virginia . . . in 1886, the market value again rose to about $36,000,000.

Sunday, Oct 22 – Same – colder – Bed 11 – W J Rippey the old crank that shot John W Mackay in San Francisco, on the street, wounding him severely was sentenced yesterday, in S.F. to pay a fine of $250 or go to jail 125 days – Mackay did not prosecute, and jury recommended utmost mercy of court –

Oct 23 . . . Stocks strong – Con Va touched $3.00 – Neighboring stocks sympathise much . . .

Oct 25 . . . About ½ past 7 this evening fire discovered in 3d story of O'Donnel & Ryan's building on C st – House flooded – Damage $2000 – more from water than fire.

Oct 27 – C & P – Indian Summer weather – Bed 11 – Work started up in the old Con Va shaft repairing etc getting ready for the Jim Rule bonanza discovery proposition – Charles Harper, the new foreman under Rule came up yesterday and took command today . . .

Oct 28 . . . Stox up – Con Va touched $3.10 . . .

Sunday, Oct 29 . . . Vale! International saloon, kept by Dolph Shane closed out today – Harris' Cigar store did so day before yesterday – Whither are we drifting? . . .

Nov 4 . . . Tried to sell Keating, et al some books but couldn't – Con Va touched $3.95 – Monthly Comstock pay roll $57,949.75 – smallest for years . . .

Sunday, Nov 5 . . . 3 funerals in Gold Hill today – Matt Rowe, Tip Woodcock & another – only a couple here – Plenty funerals nowadays – miners consumption, grippe, etc –

Nov 7 . . . Evening Joe Douglass locked me out but made up by treating to the oysters – and etc . . .

Nov 8 through 24 [Weather, which toward the end of the period turns cold and windy, with a little snow, bed time, and repeated citations of Con Va, which reaches 5¾ at its highest, and does not get below 3.95.]

Nov 25 . . . Jim Rule, H Zadig, Spring of the SF Report and other mining notables arrived today from SF – H M Yerington and D L Bliss came up from Carson, and a meeting of the Enterprise Publishing Co was held to wind up the business of the concern – The paper will start up again in a few days.

Sunday, Nov 26 . . . The Jim Rule crowd left by this evening's train on return to San F. They were down the Con Va mine about noon with the Chief Supts of the Comstock and christened or inaugurated Rule's project for discovering a new bonanza or body of pay ore in that mine, above the 1,000 level – or on it –

Nov 27 . . . Got a letter from H Freeman, St Paul Minnesota – about selling his stock in Centennial – authorizes me to sell on reasonable commission . . . Worst catheter difficulty yet – Not able to introduce effectually today – Only blood results –

Nov 30 – Variable – Moderate & pleasant – Thanksgiving Day – Church services, two or three funerals, plenty of turkey feeds in saloons and restaurants, and ball in the evening at N.G. hall by Young Ladies' Institute, which was very fully attended and a very fine & agreeable success – Bed at 12 – I dined by special invitation with Billy Pennison and wife at their residence on Howard st above the Corporation Fire Dept house, he being chief of the Fire Dept – She is a Mexicana, so we talked a little Spanish – Fine turkey dinner and very agreeable time – Evening I took a look in at the ball, and got to bed at 12, sober and all right – Pennison's wife used to be known in the early days here as *"Sailor Jack."*

Dec 2 . . . Evening I was at Enterprise office some – Work going ahead lively for resumed issue tomorrow morning –

Sunday, Dec 3 – C & P – The Enterprise appeared again this morning, resuming publication after an interval since Jan 15, when it suspended – It looks fresh, fine and prosperous – Very much improved typographically, etc – Everybody glad to see it again – [New lessee, John E McKinnon.]

Dec 4 – C & P – Evening at theater – Richard Foote and select Company, 2 nights for benefit of the Nevada exhibit at the Midwinter Fair,

San Francisco – "Don Caesar de Bazan" and "The Old Guard," with interludes by throat humming and violin playing artist who is very excellent at it, in fact a big novelty – Bed at 12.

Dec 5 . . . Took morning train to Gold Hill – Was at James' assay office on business . . . also about town among the deserted relics . . .

Dec 8 . . . Paid old Joe Douglass $20 this evening on lock out –

Dec 9 . . . Was at Gold Hill getting Centennial stock transferred . . . Evening wrote a Gold Hill cow sensation item for *Enterprise* – Bed 12 – Sent letter to Freeman –

A CRAZY COW.

Day before yesterday a cow being driven with other cattle toward the slaughter-house on the Ophir Grade, near Gold Hill, became desperately belligerent at the idea and broke away from her fated companions. She made a wild, plunging dash down Crown Point ravine, declaring war on everything in sight.

McGurn's grocery wagon was first in her way and she went rabidly for the two men who had sacked flour and boxes of things on their shoulders delivering to customers. They dumped their loads lively and climbed out of her way while she amused herself for a moment with the provisions.

Directly a lot of the ravine kids rushed from all sides to the rescue, stoning her into increased cussedness. She plunged and bellowed in various directions with one horn broken and an eye knocked out, and rushed up the back street from the Kentuck works toward the railroad depot. After that she held the whole upper part of town in holy terror. Even the locomotives and freight cars on the track trembled with emotion, and the dismayed population scrambled to places of safety.

Finally the Town Constable summoned a brave posse, provided with ropes, pitchforks, clubs and other weapons and they made a bold advance upon the enemy, who was still sloshing about with tail erect, seeking whom she might destroy. They succeeded at last in lassoing her around a telegraph pole, got another rope around her hinder end and dragged her in triumphant procession down to Baglin's corral, the population accompanying, including 500 noisy kids.

There she remains, in durance vile, and will be duly slaughtered when she cools off, but meanwhile she created the greatest sensation which has been known in Gold Hill since the big fire.

Dec 11 . . . Putnam paid, and got his 200 shares – Letter from wife about paying note $75 and $350 on mortgage, from Stevenson money – Bed 12 –

Dec 12 through 17 [Only weather, including a snowstorm which produces sleighing, and bed times.]

Dec 18 – Cloudy, thawy, muddy – Wrote and sent letters to A B Paul (4 pages) Wife, M Kinzle and A Nicholls – Evening about town as usual – Bed 12 – Kinzle and Richards, who have been working Centennial quit last Wednesday and the mine is closed for the Winter – Two weeks ago yesterday they struck good *free washing* gravel in an upraise about 10 feet above the main tunnel, 800 ft from the mouth – It gives good panning results in heavy gold, and they consider it the best and most important strike ever yet made in the mine – The Va Chronicle of this evening gives the following: [Discovery of a piece of float containing considerable free gold starts prospecting boom on the Carson River.]

Dec 19 . . . This evening Ernest Werrin took a big dose of morphine with suicidal intent – guess he succeeded, but was hopelessly alive when I went to bed at 11 – Stocks showed much of a break today – Con Va down to 2.70 . . . [Werrin died later that night – no explanation.]

Dec 21 . . . Wrote and sent a six page sketch to the SF *Examiner* about Major Pauline Cushman's lecture at Pipers Opera House 21 years ago . . .

Dec 22 . . . Received a letter from Oscar T Shuck, lawyer, 509 Kearny st, San Francisco making inquiry as to the whereabouts of William Miller, son of Lawrence Miller formerly a watchmaker in Gold Hill . . . mother died in San F a few days ago, leaving him some thousands of dollars – I got run of William's whereabouts this evening and think I will find him tomorrow –

Dec 23 . . . Everybody preparing for Christmas – McGurn selling turkeys at 15 cts a pound – cheaper than ever before . . .

Sunday, Dec 24 . . . Letter from wife with one from sister Lizzie . . .

Dec 25 – Clear & pleasant but freezing in the shade all day – *Christmas* – usual church services – Turkey in the saloons & at homes about the only luxury most people seemed to be able to indulge in these hard times – Toy and clothing stores had very little extra rush of business . . . but the grocers, McGurn especially, did. People must eat, drink and be merry anyhow when appropriate – Evening about town – Telegrams to Enterprise speak of big fire in San Francisco this AM near Clay & Sansome sts – Valentine & Co & printing block – $250,000 – Bed 12 – Clear & cold –

Dec 27 . . . Evening wrote an article about the " '49 Theater" at the Midwinter fair, & took it to the Enterprise –

THE PIONEER THEATER.

In a recent number of the San Francisco *Chronicle* was given what purported to be a picture of "The Theater of Old Time Pioneer Days." The descriptive item accompanying it stated that it was "one of the features lately added to the exhibit to be made in the '49ers mining camp" at the Midwinter Fair. The cut represents a much dilapidated old stone or adobe building, with a flat roof and crumbling walls. Six windows adorn the front, and over the door is the sign: " '49 Theater," with a big cross above it. On the roof is a lot of palm trees, ferns and other shrubbery and a huge windmill of the most modern type.

As a caricature or a burlesque the picture may be tolerated, but as an intended representation of any theatrical building of those early days, either in the mining camps or anywhere else, it is totally devoid of correctness or common sense. No pioneer ever saw its like, especially in the mines, where all structures, from the tent to the log cabin, were new, and nowhere in the country were gardens or orchards growing on housetops, to say nothing of windmills, which were a scarce commodity, and not one was to be seen throughout the mining region. If such a theatrical structure should be erected at the Fair the designer and perpetrators ought to be arrested for slander or lunacy.

Perhaps, however, the ideal proposition of this '49 mining camp is to burlesque the pioneers. If so, they will no doubt represent us as a fearfully rough, uncouth set of border ruffians, loaded down with revolvers, big knives, rifles and shotguns, ready to slaughter each other or anybody else on any kind of a pretext.

They will ignore the fact that the forty-niners, as a class, were good, enterprising citizens from all parts of the country and the world, men who made their mark in the organization of society and the State. There were roughs and villians, but most of that element got in afterward. The management of the Midwinter Fair should allow no willful misrepresentation in any respect, especially of our own people or our own institutions, ancient or modern.   ONE OF THE OLD BOYS.

Dec 29 – Clear & very pleasant but cold – Wrote & sent a letter to M H De Young, General Director of the Midwinter Fair San Francisco, inclosing my Pioneer Theater item from the Enterprise – with further comments & inducements – Bed 12 – Got letter from wife today, inclosing a nice long letter from Bessie, and a beautiful silk handkerchief from Sister Lizzie to me –

Dec 30 . . . Letter from wife, inclosing a nice silk handkerchief . . . from Cornelia . . . By McGurn's stage this PM I sent a nice turkey – $1.75 – to my family –

Sunday, Dec 31 – Clear, warm & pleasant – Churches well attended and everybody hoping the new year will be better than the old – About 4 oclock this morning, old Joe Douglass, being drunk, tried to get into his room – next to mine – through a side window, not being able to unlock his door – He fell nearly 20 feet to lower floor, breaking through it. Badly hurt, but no bones broken – Bed 12 – whistles & bells for the New Year. Wrote & sent to the Crown Point office a letter to Harry M Gorham recommending my old friend Harry C Johns for position of watchman at the Combination works made vacant by death of Uncle Joe Eddy – The manuscript of the sketch I wrote for the *SF Examiner* returned to me today with a filled out printed blank thusly: San Francisco 12–29 1893 – To Alf Doten, Virginia City, Nev. The Editor of the Examiner regrets that the manuscript herewith returned is not available   G.S.P.

Carson City, looking southwest from the capitol dome in the early 1880s.

The state capitol
in the early 1880s
as seen from the
Ormsby House.

The Arlington House in Carson City in the 1880s.

The U.S. Mint in Carson City, circa 1889.

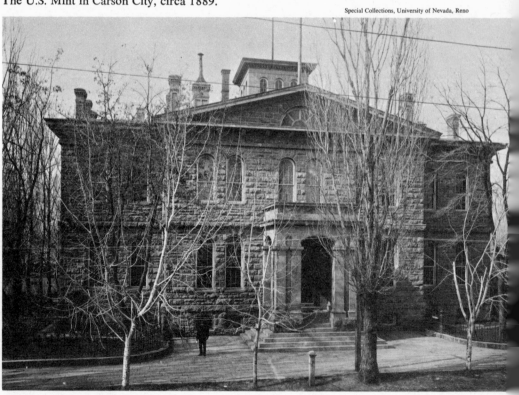

Carson City, July 4, 1892, looking west on Musser Street.

The Fitzsimmons-Corbett
fight in Carson City
on March 17, 1897.

Carson City decorated for
the arrival of Theodore
Roosevelt, May 19, 1903.

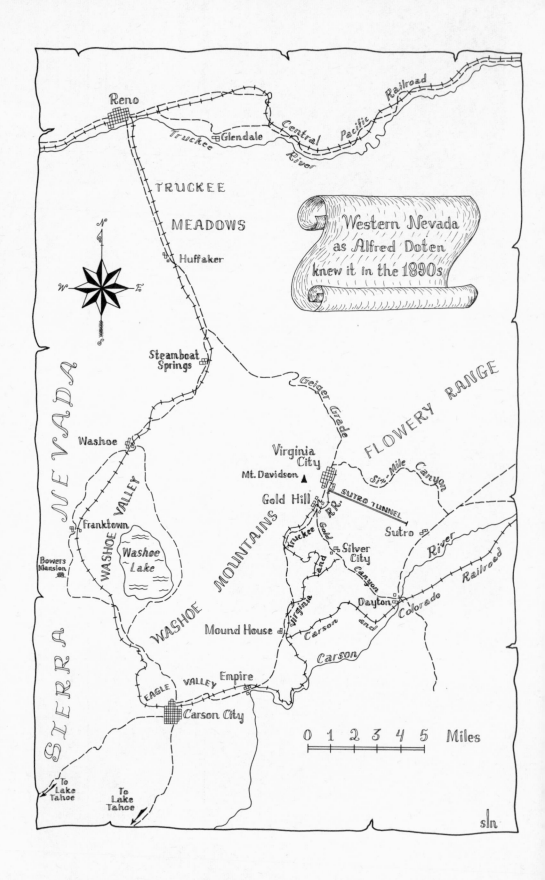

The Riverside Hotel in Reno, circa 1885.

Commercial Row, Reno, in the 1880s.

Standing: Mary S. Doten and her mother Mrs. Stoddard, Bessie and her little sister Goodwin, Alf and son Alf Jr. Seated: Charles C. Doten (Alf's brother) and wife. May 29, 1892.

Mary S. Doten in
the late 1890s.

Alfred Jr. (seated) and Samuel B. Doten, circa 1898.

Goodwin S. Doten in 1903.

U.S. Senator John P. Jones, 1889.

One of the Reno Wheelmen
(Al Helmold) in a Reno
photographer's studio.

Stewart and Morrill Halls, University of Nevada, Reno, circa 1895.

State Insane Asylum,
Reno, circa 1895.

Office of the *Nevada State Journal* in Reno, circa 1900.

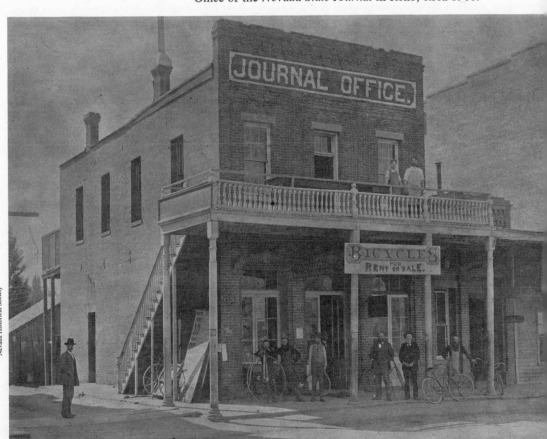

[1901]

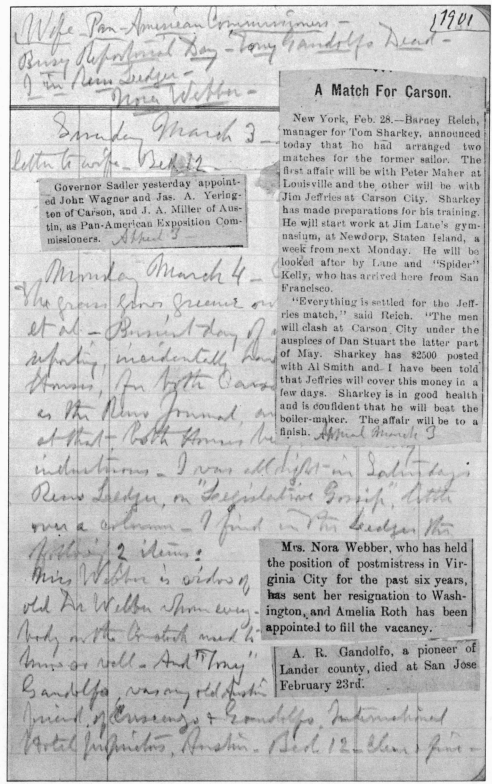

Wife Pan-American Commissioners —
Busy Reportorial Day — Tony Gandolfo Dead —
? in Reno Ledger —
Nora Webber —

Sunday March 3 —
letter to wife — Bed 12

> **Governor Sadler yesterday appointed John Wagner and Jas. A. Yerington of Carson, and J. A. Miller of Austin, as Pan-American Exposition Commissioners.** Attend 3

Monday March 4 —
The grass grows greener on
et al — Busiest day of
reporting, incidentally how
Houses, for both Carson
as the Reno Journal, on
at that — both Houses be
industrious — I was all right in Saturday's
Reno Ledger, on "Legislative Gossip", little
over a column — I find in this Ledger the
following 2 items:
Mrs Webber is widow of
old Dr Webber whom every-
body on the Comstock used to
know as well — And "Tony"
Gandolfo was my old Austin
friend of Krusengo & Gandolfo, International
Hotel Proprietors, Austin — Bed 12 — Clear & fine —

A Match For Carson.

New York, Feb. 28.—Barney Reich, manager for Tom Sharkey, announced today that he had arranged two matches for the former sailor. The first affair will be with Peter Maher at Louisville and the other will be with Jim Jeffries at Carson City. Sharkey has made preparations for his training. He will start work at Jim Lane's gymnasium, at Newdorp, Staten Island, a week from next Monday. He will be looked after by Lane and "Spider" Kelly, who has arrived here from San Francisco.

"Everything is settled for the Jeffries match," said Reich. "The men will clash at Carson City under the auspices of Dan Stuart the latter part of May. Sharkey has $2500 posted with Al Smith and I have been told that Jeffries will cover this money in a few days. Sharkey is in good health and is confident that he will beat the boiler-maker. The affair will be to a finish. Attend March 3

> **Mrs. Nora Webber, who has held the position of postmistress in Virginia City for the past six years, has sent her resignation to Washington, and Amelia Roth has been appointed to fill the vacancy.**

> **A. R. Gandolfo, a pioneer of Lander county, died at San Jose February 23rd.**

A page from Doten's journal for 1901.

The International Hotel
in Virginia City, circa 1895.

The Florida Hoisting Works in Virginia City.

C Street in Virginia City circa 1895.

Composing room of the *Territorial Enterprise* circa 1895.

Gold Hill in the 1890s, looking south toward Silver City.

Doten paid assessments on this stock for years.

Tonopah on April 1, 1901, five months after work began on the mines.
Doten included the district in his last mining reports.

BOOK NO. *70*

Virginia City
Jan 1, 1894 – Dec 31, 1894

Jan 1, 1894 – Snowstorm set in about daylight and continued at intervals most of the day . . . Good sleighing and many parties out enjoying it. New Years Day. Observed after the usual style, calls and general good cheer, all wishing the New Year would be more happy and prosperous than the last. Egg-nog and turkey at most of saloons – Old Joe Douglass . . . was able to hobble about his room, etc for a few minutes this noon – Wonderful escape . . .

Jan 2 . . . Evening I wrote 9 letters, to William Miller, Butte City, Bozeman and Helena, Montana, and the postmasters of Butte and Bozeman, also to Candelaria, Hawthorne and Bodie. Also one to Oscar T Shuck . . . all of them about the aforesaid William Miller . . . The Va Chronicle of this evening gives this on death of J B Marshall. Good bye Joe.

[Clip – Marshall, who died of "quick consumption," kept a bookstore in Gold Hill for years & later ran the Louvre Saloon in Virginia City.]

Jan 4 . . . According to the Enterprise of this morning the entire working force in the mines of the Comstock, including miners, carmen, engineers, foremen and shift bosses sums up to 259 . . .

Jan 5 . . . Joe sent for me this evening and at his request I put a short item in the *Enterprise,* making the first newspaper notice of his accident & condition . . .

Sunday, Jan 7 . . . Got a letter from Oscar T Shuck telling me he had got the wrong Miller . . . It is *Charles* . . . So this evening I wrote . . . 6 letters . . . all on the Miller subject . . .

Jan 9 . . . The sketch about Major Pauline Cushman which I sent to the SF Examiner Dec 21 & which was returned declined, I put in *Enterprise* this evening . . .

Jan 10 through 17 [Writes to Mary & to a Miller in Anaconda, Montana, receives three letters, puts "three good items" in the *Enterprise,* is about town with Billy Virden, once his business manager on the *Gold Hill News* and now superior judge of Mono County, California, and attends the installation meeting and bean feed of the Exempts where he is appointed to both the Finance Committee and a committee to revise the constitution.]

Jan 18 . . . Barlow Brothers Mammoth Minstrels, 25 or 30, arrived on train – Paraded . . . Evening at Opera House – Very good minstrel, acrobatic and variety show, and very good house . . . I was in a stage box with parties from Mason Valley . . . I received today by mail, a copy, No 2, of the *Midwinter Fair Appeal*, published by Sam Davis in the "Forty Nine Camp" at the Fair – Small, about size of *Carson Appeal* – Spicy, etc, but not natural – Dont like it –

Jan 22 . . . Saloon keepers, butchers & others who use ice & snow in Summer, have been and are busy shoveling and packing liberal supplies of snow into their cellars . . .

Jan 23 . . . Recd letter from *Lawrence Miller* Silver Lake, Montana . . . Says . . . he is the Lawrence Miller, watchmaker in Gold Hill from '75 to '81 when he and his son William went to Montana leaving the other son, Charles, with the surveying party of the Carson and Colorado Railroad.

Jan 24 . . . Wrote & sent letters to Lawrence Miller and to O T Shuck . . .

Jan 25 . . . Big prize fight at Jacksonville, Florida, between Jim Corbett and Charley Mitchell – Mitchell was whipped in 3 rounds . . . Much excitement in town over the telegrams . . . A few hundred dollars changed hands . . .

Jan 26 . . . The International saloon (Sol Noel) had to close again, after a months run, from lack of patronage – Times getting no better fast –

Jan 27 . . . Frank F Fielding, assayer at the Con Va office reported to be down with the small pox . . . First case for years in this city . . . Contrariety of opinion among the local Drs as to whether it is genuine or no . . .

Sunday, Jan 28 . . . The Fielding case of small pox turns out . . . to be merely severe blood poisoning from acid fumes in assaying – he has had it so before –

Jan 29 . . . The Sunday editions of the San Francisco papers, arriving today were very unusually good – Midwinter Fair editions – very voluminous and interesting –

Jan 30 . . . Sent letter . . . to Yerington, Carson asking renewal of half fare pass . . .

Jan 31 . . . Rec'd half fare pass . . .

Feb 5 . . . China New Year, which commenced last evening with great popping of crackers, firing of bombs, etc, in the Chinese quarter was followed up lively today and evening – feasting & general enjoyment among them . . .

Feb 7 – Furious winds before daylight blew up a few snowsqualls during the day – Cold & disagreeable – Funeral of Pat Rippingham this PM was well attended . . . About 50 men on foot, band, Red Men, pall bearers – 25 carriages – Rippingham died of heart disease last Sunday in Grass Valley, 67 yrs old – Been on the Comstock longer than I have – mechanic – musician – Band leader, cornet player, etc – Leaves wife here and grown up family of 3 daughters & 2 sons – Native of Galway, Ireland – Was about retiring for the night at 12 when Johnny McKinnon, lessee and manager of the *Enterprise* came to my room – said his "local," George Warren was on a drunk & wanted me to fill in – Went on at once at office. Stood in effectively – Bed at 3 –

Feb 8 – Very blustering, cold and snowstormy day . . . Got letter from Mrs Batterman . . . giving me address [of] C. S. Batterman . . . I wrote & sent a letter to him forthwith asking about Charles Miller, who was with him in survey of the C&C Railroad – Wrote letter also to wife . . .

Feb 9 . . . Fiercely snowy & blustering all day – Telegraphic communication interrupted . . .

Feb 10 – Clear & cold . . . 10° above Zero – The mail & express train from here last evening was robbed just after leaving Carson by one man – He got into the express car, forcibly took possession of pay-master Mills' tin box with a couple of thousand dollars in it – skipped off and not seen since – This is the first V&T RR robbery and creates quite a sensation . . .

Sunday, Feb 11 . . . The storm still continues – PM attended . . .
Exempts . . .

Feb 12 . . . Looks like our boss storm of the Winter is over. Old man
Harvey Harris, 80 yrs old, died at his residence in Gold Hill, about noon
today [Harris was a Gold Hill assayer] . . . He was at our wedding on
Lake Tahoe – Vale –

Feb 13 through 18 [Snow & high wind – Copies a poem for a friend,
notes the death of Colonel Jonathan D Stevenson, "military pioneer," in
San Francisco & of Annie Pixley, actress, in London.]

Feb 19 – Heavy snowstorm most all day – Over a foot of new snow fell –
nearly or quite three feet of snow all over the country – C st pretty well
snowbanked – Good sleighing through to Dayton – Hard times and everybody poor – Tom Heffron had to shut down his restaurant yesterday
because he couldn't feed non-paying patrons – No mail train from Cal
yesterday, and it only succeeded in getting to Gold Hill this PM, & the
mail was brought from there by sleigh. No mail went out from here last
night nor tonight. All on account of the "beautiful snow" – The CP is
totally blockaded and chances are against it for a week – Bed at 1 –
Moderate but cloudy, with light snow – Saturday nights storm did quite
a lot of damage – About a dozen windows blown in at International, etc –

Feb 21 . . . RR between here & Reno clear, but on the CP, across the
Sierra, all trains abandoned still . . .

Feb 22 – Clear & cold – The delayed California mails arrived about 2:30
PM, also Jim Rule – I wrote up a nice article or sketch of old man Harris . . . to be in *Enterprise* tomorrow . . . Got the points from Ed
Harris who was in town yesterday looking about 5,000 insurance on old
man's life . . . This was Washingtons Birthday – No public observance
or parade . . .

[Clip, *Enterprise,* Feb 27:] Austin, Lander county, twenty years ago was
one of the most flourishing mining districts in the State. At that time ten
thousand people thronged its streets and jostled each other in the race for
riches. The Manhattan Mining Company at that time was shipping tons of
bullion monthly, produced from that property, and gilt-edge prices were
charged for the necessaries of life.

The population of the town now does not exceed 400 and the bullion
output from the mines does not exceed $10,000 monthly. Some of the
highest grade silver ore produced in the State was from that district, a
three-hundred-pound sample of which was on exhibition in the grocery

house of J. C. Hampton & Co. of this city for several years. The sample referred to showed wire and ruby silver and was valued at $1,500.

There is a vast amount of low-grade ore in the mines of that district, and if silver is ever placed on a parity with gold Austin is likely to again become a flourishing town.

Feb 28 . . . Evening got item into Enterprise on three letters rec'd from Kinzle, Nevada City . . . about matters & things there and Centennial particularly . . .

March 1 . . . At 4 PM the old sun made out to peep into my room for a minute or two as he was disappearing behind Mt Davidson . . . 19 more drafted from the Con Va mine yesterday from scarcity of ore – 9 more were drafted from Best & Belcher having completed the connection from that mine with the Rule drift – A very important strike is reported in the east crosscut from the Rule drift today – 6 ft of $80 ore – found in cutting out for an upraise . . .

March 2 – Frequent sunshine and snowstorm . . .

March 3 – Cloudy, cold & snowsqually all day . . . The strike on the 1,000 level of Con Va, Rule drift – east crosscut, don't seem to amount to much as yet – Stock jumped $1 on strength of it yesterday, but receded today to $3.50 –

Sunday, March 4 . . . Got letter from Charley H Price formerly of Gold Hill Bank Exchange day or two ago . . . Leadville, Colorado – Stranded there – lost wife & 1 child – would like to come back here – Sent him 3 page letter tonight – stay there – all of us stranded here . . .

March 5 – A Very blustering snow-storm all latter half of the day – Very Wintry – Sent a letter to R E Preston the recently appointed Director of the Mint, Washington, D.C. asking if he wants report of Comstock from me . . . M Gilligan's Boot & Shoe store in the International building burned about 3 AM. Goods well destroyed – $2,000 insurance – well covers the loss as far as Gilligan is concerned – The building injured $1000 or more – Evening about town – Storm ceased about 10 – 3 or 4 inches new snow – Bed 1 – Among the fixtures destroyed by the fire was the famous big mirror 8 x 10 ft in size in the clear, of French plate glass, introduced by Barney Clark after the big fire in fitting that same place up as a high-toned 1st class saloon – Times went back on him, so he went under – Subsequently Jim Killeen kept the saloon, the fixtures belonging to Hancock, proprietor of the Hotel – One day Mike McGowan the "man eater" being refused a drink threw a heavy bar tumbler at the barkeep and hit the glass, smashing and cracking badly its lower half. It was quarter of an inch thick, full – The front windows were French plate glass about 6 x 10, with doors & adjuncts to match, the glass of which was ¼ inch – Fire and water shattered all.

March 6 . . . Sent letter this evening to wife calling for $100.00 –

March 8 . . . Letter from wife on the financial proposition – replied to it by evening mail . . . Assessment of 50 cents levied on Con Va – the first for some months – Had to be, for mining production and prospects are looking worst I ever saw on the Comstock – Not much over 200 miners at work.

Sunday, March 11 . . . This morning half dozen young 24 yrs old hoodlums, "C & C gang" tried to run the town, drinking and eating where they pleased & having hilarious time without putting up – Officers finally combined on them, had a fight on Union st about Chinatown – All arrested & taken to jail – Pat Hanifan resisting and running away from Deputy Sheriff Burke, got shot in the kidney region – Bad wound – & sent home to his folks in Lower Gold Hill –

March 13 . . . Rec'd $100 from wife by mail – Paid up much of my indebtedness – Evening sent for to go on *Enterprise,* Warren being drunk, etc . . .

March 16 . . . Evening I attended St Patrick's ball, given by the Emmett Guard – A 2 coach special brought about 70 from Carson, including the Lieut Gov, Poujade. I never saw the Opera House more crowded at a ball – I counted 180 couple in the grand march – Began with the "Bayonet drill" and other evolutions by 30 members of the Guard – Very fine – Theater splendidly decorated electric lights for second time, the other being at ball of Battery A, New Years night . . .

March 17 . . . Received following telegram: . . . Would be glad to have a review of the Comstock to date, but the appropriation is very limited. What would be your charge . . . R E Preston, Director of the Mint. I replied as follows: "Same as to your predecessor – one hundred dollars. . . ."

March 21 . . . Evening at theater – good house – Ole Olson and good variety Company – Very amusing and satisfactory entertainment – Swedish in the lead, with lots of funny things dances, songs, etc – Bed at 1 – The stock board quotations today, for the first time in Comstock history were given in fractions of a dollar less than five cents.

March 22 – Letter from wife says she and Sammy go to California on a trip tomorrow . . .

March 23 . . . This PM, with Capt Harry Trewella, I visited Uncle Bill Dunn, north end of town – Old Cornishman – used to keep saloon in Gold Hill in the palmy days – popular favorite, and great admirer of me & *Gold Hill News*. Old man badly crippled with the rheumatics last few years – Waiting to die . . .

Sunday, March 25 . . . Easter Sunday – Letter from Alfie with PO money order for $5 . . .

March 27 – Cloudy & cooler – Dr R Webber died at San Jose this morning – Known him personally and well on the Comstock ever since I have been here – He was the last survivor of the old time doctors – Bryarly, McMeans, Bronson, Kirby, Hiller, Green, Guffin, Cleburne, Gaston, Atchison, et al – all dead but Dr J U Hall now in San Jose, who removed from Gold Hill there several years ago. Webber left some weeks ago with his wife for S.J. for his health – 72 yrs old – breaking down from long use, etc – Dr Harris still here – one of old timers also, so he may be termed the last survivor – Dr P Manson, a later old timer yet here in Va – also Dr Packer – Bed 12 –

March 29 – Cloudy, cooler and fiercely blustering. Fearful clouds of dust – Cleveland vetoed the Bland silver coinage or seignorage bill today – His veto message occupied 2½ columns in the *Va Evening Chronicle*. It also had the following items: [clippings on the appointment of Jewett Adams as superintendent of the Carson Mint, and Dr Webber's funeral] – Evening at Opera House – Freeman's Funmakers in "A Railroad Ticket" – About a dozen male and female variety actors – General melange of funny acts, scenes & incidents with comic singing and funny, loud and shapely dancing, etc – Good house – Bed at 12 – Weather cloudy but moderated – Con Va and Ophir each touched 2.15 today – Con Va has gone a little below Ophir two or three times in last few days – first time in many months – Prof Thomas Cara left Va for Grass Valley Cal this evening to reside hereafter – He has been chief musician, band master, organist at St Paul's Episcopal church and music teacher for last 25 yrs or more – I and others were at depot to see him off –

March 30 . . . Evening at Theater – Effie Ellsler, C W Couldock and good dramatic company in "Doris," a very interesting, well-written play – Well rendered – Good house.

March 31 through April 3 [AD does a big wash, attends a committee meeting on revised Exempt constitution, is told by the director of the Mint that he doesn't want a Comstock report, hears from Mary & Kinzle & attends a lodge meeting.]

April 4 – Same – Bed 12 –

April 5 –   "   "

April 6 –   "   "   Evening attended lecture of Mr Crittenton, evangelist, at Presbyterian Church – good house – mostly women – Greatest *talker* I ever heard – talks more & said less than anybody.

April 7 . . . Localized on the *Chronicle* today in place of Scott . . . Louis Reick, one of the oldest Comstockers and a Pacific Coast Pioneer, & proprietor of the Nevada Brewery, Six mile Canyon, died at 1:30 this morning at his residence near the Brewery – 75 years old – Wrote him up in good style – Leaves no wife or child, but about $50,000 property – Inveterate bachelor –

Sunday, April 8 . . . Meeting of the Exempts – Made final report on Constitution & Bylaws . . . Report accepted . . .

April 9 – Clear, warm & very pleasant – Bed at 12 – Last Friday night I dreamed of finding some very rich ground or decomposed quartz or ledge matter, just "lousy" with gold both coarse and fine, and all ragged and rusty & dirty – mixed up with reddish dirt – but *so* rich – a pound or two of pure gold to every pan – coarse lumps from an ounce down and large pieces of rock, ten pounds and less, yellow with gold. Waked up feeling awful rich – the richest dream of my life in that line. Saturday night I had a continuation or second edition of the same dream but little modified – Last night I dreamed I was in California, somewhere, flat broke and making my way to the Midwinter Fair on foot – When I got there I didnt like it – considered it a foggy, soggy, unpopular sort of an affair and in fact got so disgusted and exasperated with the whole snide outfit and the foggy, cold weather and my own impecuniously uncomfortable condition and situation that I waked up feeling anything but rich, and not happy except in knowing it was but a dream – Wonder what I'll dream tonight? Mr Crittenton, the evangelist, had a crowded audience last evening – all the church could possibly hold. McGurn and Crampton completed clearing the Geiger Grade of remaining snow drifts.

April 10 . . . The Geiger Grade being cleared . . . McGurn's stage resumed running between here and Reno . . . About 3 weeks earlier than usual.

April 11 – Clear & pleasant but cool – Freezing in shade all the AM – M B Leavitt's "Spider and Fly" comedy Co arrived on morning train – Big crowd on street witnessed their arrival – Evening I was at Opera House – crowded – Best house & best entertainment for many a day. Big troupe, with 15 or 20 women – Not much of a *play* but lots of incidents – Splendid dancing & lots of it – all *high kickers* – high as can be, yet in long skirts, & no lady in that big audience could see anything indecent or at all objectionable – That and the acrobatic interlude – the acrobats were the features . . . best and slickest anybody here ever saw – March of the Amazons was splendid – Bed at 12 – John Church, who first introduced me into newspaper business on the Comstock is dead, according to the *SF Chronicle* of the 10th – God bless him and the devil miss him . . . Got letter from wife – Returned to Reno . . . Sam still at Oakland . . . Having good time – Wife inclosed letter from Bessie, Santa Clara – Seth in bad state of health & on last legs – Bessie was with Sam and their mother at Oakland, Sausalito & Midwinter Fair . . .

April 12 . . . Evening at Methodist church – Crittenton revival . . . Church well filled –

April 14 . . . J F Egan, State Treasurer, died in Carson this morning . . . Evening I wrote a letter from Kinzle for tomorrow's *Enterprise* – Dont know if it will get in or not – Bed at 1 . . .

April 16 – Wintry – Variable – Most of snow melted off, but good overcoat weather – Funeral of State Treasurer John F Egan – Escorted from his residence to St Mary's (Catholic) church at 10 AM by detachment of Emmet Guard, of which he was an honorary member – and 15 carriages – Solemn high mass for repose of his soul. At 12 big funeral – preceded by Artillery band – 14 pieces – Emmet Guard, 50; National Guard, 25; Artillery (Battery A) 20 – State officers etc 12 – Citizens etc on foot 80 – Pall bearers 12 – Total 213. Carriages following the hearse, 47 – Bed 1 – Clear & Cold –

April 17 through May 5 [The "Kinzle letter" of April 14 appears in the *Enterprise,* and AD writes to the Nevada City *Transcript,* corresponds with Centennial members about their proxies, expresses disbelief at the news that Mark Twain is bankrupt, receives word of the death of Granville Winchester Pease, former Walker River Indian Agent, makes a

Chronicle item of it, & sends the item & a letter of condolence to Pease's sister, records windy, dusty, snow squally weather, and reports that a new discovery on the 1650-foot level has sent Consolidated Virginia stock as high as $8, & others up with it.]

Sunday, May 6 – Clear, warm & pleasant – Big base ball game at Recreation ground, below town, between National Guard team and Young Mens Literary Institute team – Latter won – George Warren resigned or was fired as local, etc, of Enterprise yesterday, and Frank Wyatt of Reno came up today to take his place – He was local on the *Chronicle* here several years ago – The International saloon reopened today after a rest of about 3 months – Eugene Holland, lessee, with Tom Buckner to run his faro game in the rear. Bed 12 –

May 7 and 8 [AD attends the annual stockholders' meeting of the Centennial where he is elected vice president, & sees Charles Gardner & Company in *The Prize Winner*.]

May 9 . . . Trouble between me & Enterprise McKinnon . . .

May 10 . . . Frank Wyatt don't fill the bill on Enterprise – too dissipated & unreliable – So he was let out today – short career . . .

May 12 . . . Big lot of folks left this PM for the Midwinter Fair – Excursion trip – $7.50 for round trip from Reno . . .

Sunday, May 13 . . . McKinnon, lessee of Enterprise got me and directed that I take hold and assume the position of local editor and reporter of that paper commencing tomorrow morning. I consented . . .

May 14 . . . Took chair, scissors & paste pot down to office – went through exchanges – Myself and Geo R Paynter, the editor in chief work in same room, front office – Wrote lots & got up good local. Through reading the proofs & left office at 1:30 . . .

May 15 through 22 [AD localizes, receives a letter & $5.00 from Pease's sister, writes to Kinzle, pays Douglass $20 on rent and notes that Fred J Norris has come from San Francisco to replace him as local.]

May 23 . . . My successor, Mr Norris, started in on *Enterprise* this day . . .

May 24 . . . Sent a nice letter to . . . Pease's sister – acknowledging receipt of the $5 . . . Sent with letter this evening 2 copies of Va *Chronicle* of April 24 containing Pease's obituary, and 2 copies of the Enterprise of the 23d with a small item about Pease, to Mrs H. M. Lyman, his sister . . . Into these papers I inclosed a couple of fine sprigs of sage-brush . . .

May 28 – Cloudy – The only sensation of the day was election for School Trustees, which took place at Fourth Ward school-house. The last Legislature took it out of politics, making it a special election by the people, but this put it into religion. So it was that the Catholics made it their special business to win the day and control the public schools. They had but one ticket in the field while the Protestants had half a dozen or so. Counting the votes got through after midnight. The Catholics won one out of five – Fieley.

May 29 – Clear & warm – very pleasant – I was busy at room most of day – moving into Room 5 having to vacate this room No 7 which I have occupied for the past 9 years, because Con Ahern of the Crystal saloon down stairs wants the three rooms, en suite, 6, 7 & 8 – Worked hard making partial removal of my accumulation – books enough to start a bookstore – Bed at 11 –

May 30 . . . "Memorial Day" was observed fully up to the average . . . I was busy at my removal to room 5 . . . Not as good a room as No 7, being an "inside" room, darker, with no look at out-doors. Wrote a nice long letter to wife . . . Was so busy moving that I was not on the street at all, merely stepped down to the C st door in time to see most of the procession . . .

May 31 . . . The Jim Rule 6 month contract ends with this day – Has not found even low grade ore – A dead failure . . .

June 1 . . . AM cloudy, windy & very dusty . . . The authorities say can't afford to sprinkle the streets . . . I got my traps all stowed away in my new room . . .

June 4 . . . Wrote quite a long letter to Mr Pease, Banker Faribault, Minnesota, brother to my deceased friend G W Pease . . .

June 5 through 8 [AD sends letter to Banker Pease with clips and sprigs of sagebrush, corresponds with Kinzle about reopening the Centennial mine, and notes that workmen have been busy cleaning & refinishing the 3 front rooms.]

June 9 – Clear, cool & pleasant – rather dusty – Only bad incident was the shooting of Wm Cocks on C st front of Wells Fargo & Cos old office by Ernest Herting – at 11:30 – It came out of an attempt to collect a bill from Cox, who was somewhat drunk. It was in the Arcade saloon, it commenced by Cocks striking H – Both were put out, and resumed the trouble on the street – H fired 2 shots from navy revolver, one taking effect in left cheek of Cocks, ranging downward and out. The other shot did not hit him – Quite an excitement – Cocks is about 22 yrs old and H over 60 – Bed 1 – He fell in middle of the street, & was taken to rooms of the National Guard in Odd Fellows Building, near by – Afterward to his home on the Divide –

Sunday, June 10 . . . Herting was captured at his home in Seven-mile Canyon north of town early this morning & taken to jail. He resisted, firing 3 or 4 shots without hitting anybody . . .

June 12 . . . The street sprinkling cart started for first time this season, the Water Co having made reduction in charge . . .

June 15 . . . Got letter from M Freeman, 967 Euclid st, St Paul, Minnesota, asking all about Centennial – Sent him a 3 page reply, also sent a letter to wife.

June 16 . . . Young Cox, or Cocks died at 2 AM . . .

June 18 . . . Funeral of Cocks this PM from N G Hall, he being member of the N.G. – Well attended – Artillery Band, 14; Nationals, 40; Emmetts, 30; Artillery, 30; Carriages 16 . . .

June 19 . . . Grand Lodge IOOF . . . about 100 delegates . . . Daughters of Rebekah also . . . Evening I attended a little blowout of the Artillery at their hall – Nice time – liquid 'freshments . . .

June 20 . . . Stuart Robson and good dramatic Co in "The Henrietta" – Pretty good play about stock dealing, mining brokers etc – but rather dry . . .

June 21 . . . I attended graduating exercises of the public schools . . . 10 girls & 3 boys graduated . . .

June 23 . . . Stocks down lower than for 6 mos . . . Con Va $2.70, & all the rest in proportion . . .

June 28 – Clear, warm & pleasant – Bed 12 – No mail or passengers from the west today, although the San Francisco papers and some express matter came – Grand boycott declared & put in effect by the American Railroad Union against all Pullman cars on all railroad lines in the United

States. Trainmen refuse to handle any train with Pullman sleepers attached. The RR Cos refuse to run without them as they are under contract – Greatest RR strike ever known – Passenger trains not allowed to leave Oakland – All this is because of reduction of wages by the Pullman Company – About 6 PM yesterday old Joe Douglass, being drunk, had a fall at the rear of his office, dislocating his right shoulder – took 2 doctors & chloroform to get it into place –

June 29 . . . Strike more extensive & absolute – No mails east or west – only from Reno & way places, the V&T still running – No SF newspapers

June 30 . . . Strike continued . . . Bad on the fruit interest, fish & all perishable commodities . . . The Midwinter Fair closed by limitation today . . .

Sunday, July 1 . . . V&T train on time . . . reduced to 2 cars . . . had only two passengers – down to hard times basis.

July 2 . . . Pay days for the miners . . . no money to get from SF to pay off with, got it from Carson mint in silver – good enough . . .

July 4 . . . About 60 went to Carson to IOOF celebration, but tendency was to stay & celebrate at home – Procession military, etc, not very extensive but good – exercises International balcony, C st . . . Lots of crackers, bombs, & other fireworks till a late hour, as usual –

July 5 . . . Two byclicists from S.F. leaving there Sunday, arrived today – First to break blockade – Henness Pass route –

July 6 . . . A man arrived with copies of Sacramento papers, via the Placerville route . . .

Sunday, July 15 – Cloudy some and pretty warm – A mail train from the East reached Reno at 9:30 AM – 10 cars, including 2 Pullman sleepers, well guarded with 30 US soldiers – will go on to Cal in morning – This train had 5 or 6 cars of delayed mail – Our V&T noon train brought some of it up. This is first overland mail since the 28th of June – At 3 PM a train bound East reached Reno from California, heavily loaded with mails and soldiers & few passengers . . . Looks as though the blockade was being raised. Soldiers are scattered at all principal points as well as on the trains – The grand organization of strikers still holds out firmly – A few travelers and some fruit get across the Sierra by stages and private conveyance, also a few letters & papers. Enormous amounts of fruit lost and the blockade is strongly felt – Must soon break up or there will be much suffering & privation – Rioting still indulged in at Sacramento & Oakland, but the troops are conquering & martial law fixing things in Cal as well as Reno & elsewhere . . .

July 16 . . . Big delayed mails from the East and West bulldosed the Postoffice – Trains running both East & West from Reno, which place is placed under martial law, much to the indignation of the citizens – about 100 US soldiers stationed there . . .

Sunday, July 22 – Same – 87° – Hot day – The strikers at Sacramento yesterday PM declared the strike off and the first through express train came last night to Reno & here, with yesterdays SF papers – Bed 12 – All trains running as usual on SP and V&T –

July 23 . . . Herting on trial in Dist Court for killing Cocks – Jury hung all night –

July 24 – Clear & 87° – Trains on time for first time since the strike – mails from both west & east – Strike broken in East & Cal & here, but said to be strong as ever in & about Chicago – PM I visited George R Evans at the American Exchange Washington Street – Old prospector & friend of mine – Considerable of an inventor of mining mechanical arrangements and processes – Comes over from San Francisco occasionally – Now at the Exchange badly bunged up with erysipelas & other ailments – Have visited him several times in last week or ten days – This PM drew up a bill of sale of Judie mine, out at Pine-nut, adjoining the famous Zirn mine on the Southwest to Charles Cousins for $10 – from Evans – He has his big bitch "Judie" with him. Evening at the Opera House – Chas A Gardner & good company in "Fatherland" – Good show and good house – Been here twice before – Bed 12 – Verdict manslaughter this morning in Herting-Cocks case –

July 26 . . . Herting given 10 yrs in State Prison for killing Cocks . . .

July 27 . . . Senator M D Foley shot & killed by Mrs Alice M Hartley at Reno yesterday PM . . .

Sunday, July 29 . . . Senator Foley's funeral today at Reno – Several went from here . . .

Aug 3 . . . Took John Briggs to interview Evans . . . Evening I went on Enterprise in place of Norris who left for SF on short visit . . .

Aug 4 – Clear & pleasant – worked on *Enterprise* as yesterday – At noon was with John Briggs to see Evans – effected sale of right to use his amalgamating compound and riffles, etc, also four silvered copper plates – 12 x 24 – for $30 – $10 of which I am to get – I wrote the agreement of sale & witnessed it. Bed at 2:30 –

Sunday, Aug 5 – Same – Wrote a card for Marshall Hatch: "A Cruelly Foul Injustice."

> [Clip from *Chronicle,* Aug 6 – At the private society reception in the Opera House the preceding Friday, "a well-known and popular young gentleman who naturally brought along his preferred young lady companion" was told his invitation did not include the girl – "Like a true, chivalrous gentleman" he withdrew with his "fair lady":] . . . why this flagrant outrage? Why this exceedingly distasteful attempt to cast a foul stain upon the character of an irreproachable young lady? It is true that she is not of wealthy parentage and family, yet if that be a crime, it is the only one of which she can be accused, for all who know her indorse her as a quiet, well-mannered, homelike young lady of irreproachable reputation, and well qualified and deserving to consort with and circulate among even higher toned circles than would seek to exclude her on the Comstock . . .   JUSTICE

Evening visited Evans – Bed 12 – Was introduced by L Elrod of the Carson Mint this AM on C street, to Butter and Braddock, two experts from Washington who are attending to the annual cleanup and report of the Carson Mint – Very pleasant gentlemen – Complimented me very highly on my Comstock reports – Making a Sunday visit to the Comstock –

Aug 6 through 22 [Pays Centennial assessments, goes off local, votes in Republican election of convention delegates & notes that the Silver party voting is causing more excitement – Letters to Mary & to Kinzle – Visits often with Evans, helps him make up a batch of his amalgamating compound, brings notable mining men Dazet & Col E D Boyle to see him & effects a trial of the compound in Dazet's Silver City mill – Dreams that a return to "the rule of the grand old Republican party" has so strengthened American prestige abroad that messages of congratulation are coming in from many nations, and is so moved by the dream that he gets out of bed to record it at length – The messages are astonishingly empty & pompous.]

Aug 23 – Same – 88° – With Evans AM & evening awhile, learning amalgam & sluice – Evening Opera House – Concert by Bistolfi and Montanelli – 2 Italians – One played a huge guitar with an extra side rig of ten strings and a neat little whistle arrangement attached, which he played with his mouth – The other played mandolin with his hands, and a small organ with his feet – treadle and pedal – He also played the banjo at times for a change – The mandolin was attached to the organ by a flexible cord, size of ones finger purporting to be an electric combination with battery near the organ and connection made by the mandolin frets, thus regulating the organ notes to correspond – They played about a dozen popular and select pieces – various nationalities – with excellent skill and effect – Fine entertainment – good house for the times, ½ a house – Bed 12 . . .

Sunday, Aug 26 . . . A detachment of the artillery Co from Reno passed through here this PM enroute for the State military encampment at Carson . . . They had one gatling gun, with caisson, etc – half a dozen soldiers riding thereon, with captain horseback – all in uniform – Came through this way to show themselves & see the sights . . .

Aug 27 . . . Our local military Cos . . . went to Carson by usual morning train . . . The cannon of Battery A left here at 4 AM, overland – Big crowd saw the soldier boys off . . . at depot – Evening I was with Evans . . .

Aug 28 through Sept 16 [Centennial and Exempt business & family letters – Learns that his "6th or 7th" cousin, Frank B Doten, has died, and writes him up – Notes that Bessie has returned to normal school, that Mrs Hartley is making a strong case for self-defense in her murder trial, that the Silver party convention is being held in Carson and that one of the delegates to it is Frank Francis, "boy compositor" for the *Reveille* while AD was editor and now editor & proprietor of the *New Era,* and that Dr Webber's widow has been appointed postmistress for Virginia City – Discusses at length the fact that someone has made public the effectiveness of phosphorous as a delayed incendiary device, something AD had discovered while he was ranching – Injures his thumb, writes a letter for a friend of William Thomas, who has served his sentence for incest, asking the influence of Congressman Bartine in restoring Thomas's citizenship, notes that Evans's health is failing rapidly and is with him almost every evening – No detail of interest.]

Sept 17 – Clear, warm & pleasant – Bed 12 – Wrote 4 page letter to wife this evening, and also drew a rude pencil & pen cartoon to send to John H Dennis, representing him burying his Democratic political enemies, O'Toole, Adams, Harris and Keating. Four graves side by side with names on crosses at head of graves – over them the words "here lies" and beneath

"Victims of the Keating Cure" – Over top of picture: "My Name *is* Dennis; What's *yours now?*" – At right hand side is Dennis standing in the doorway of an undertaking shop with a shovel in his hand, looking at these graves – sign on front over his head says: "John H Dennis, Sexton, Political Coffins made to order."

Sept 18 . . . Major John H Dennis in town . . . gave him my cartoon – PM Jose Salinas visited me at my room and we celebrated the anniversary of the Independence of Chile . . .

Sept 22 . . . PM at Evans', testing some Silver City tailings . . . Excursion to Reno . . . taking about 130 Republicans to hear A C Cleveland, nominee for Governor, and H F Bartine, for Congressman . . . Artillery Band went along . . .

Sunday, Sept 23 . . . Evening with Evans – Caucus of the delegates to Rep County Convention held this evening at Odd Fellows Hall – I was chosen Secy . . .

Sept 24 . . . Storey County Republican Convention . . . Made all the nominations . . . Receipts from all candidates $130 – Paid the brass band, Sgts at arms, hall rent and other charges and I got $15 for my part . . .

Sept 25 . . . County Convention of the Silver party . . . Wrote out . . . my report as Secy of the Rep Convention . . .

Sept 26 . . . Evening attended the big Republican meeting at Opera House . . .

Sept 27 . . . Met Cleveland several times about town . . . Bartine & the rest left last night or this morning . . .

Sept 29 – Stormy – AM Cloudy & blustering – 4 PM light rain set in, mixed a little with snow – Evening at Opera House – Big Silver party meeting – bonfires – F G Newlands, Tom Wren and F M Huffaker talked – Va Glee Club of 7, dressed in Summer uniform of white pants, dark coats and light brown caps with black bands and a silver dollar paster in front did several good topical songs & choruses – All three speakers did well by the old Republican party and in fact it seemed more like a Republican meeting than anything else – House jammed full – Bed 1 – still raining & snowing quietly & lightly – Very muddy – 42° –

Oct 1 – Cloudy, variable and chilly – White frost everywhere this morning. Our old friend Judge E C Cook died at 12 oclock last night at his own little cabin in Gold Hill, aged 78, a native of Kentucky – Been Justice of the Peace in Gold Hill over 20 yrs – and now renominated on the Silver ticket & would have been re-elected – He attended the big Silver rally at Piper's Opera House Saturday evening, walked home over the Divide in the snow and rain, feeling first rate. But his clothes were wet and he went to bed chilled. Lived alone, nobody to care for him properly – Pneumonia got him, neighbors and Dr Manson got onto his case Sunday PM & evening & did their best to thaw him into renewed existence but he died serenely – poor and no relatives, but lots of friends. Good bye old boy. Evening with Evans – Bed 1 – Clear & cold –

Oct 5 . . . Sent letter to H Freeman . . . St Paul . . . posting him all about Centennial . . .

Oct 6 . . . Miners Union Picnic at Sisters Hospital grounds, lower part of town – Big time, music, games, dancing etc – Busses running all the PM from town & from Gold Hill . . .

Oct 8 . . . Many men being put to work in the mines of Gold Hill, also in the middle mines, for election purposes – They will all be discharged after election.

Oct 11 . . . Letter from wife inclosing one from Bessie. She says Seth died Oct 4 at 6:30 PM quietly – Dropsy, old age, etc . . .

Oct 12 . . . Found George R Paynter, editor of the Enterprise at the office – We went to the room of Evans and he, Evans, completed sale to Paynter of right to make & use his amalgam compound, sluice riffle, and grizzly for $30 . . . I fixed up all the writings . . .

Oct 13 – Clear, warm & very pleasant – Been a pretty fair stock boom last week or two – Con Va got up to about $7 week ago – Receded since to $5 today – Mine full of big promise – 1650 & 1700 levels – Nothing new in any of the other mines, yet of course all sympathize . . . Evening with Evans short time, then to Opera House – Big blow out of Silver party – Procession with band of music – Artillery Band – transparencies – Young mens Silver Club etc – bonfires, etc – Jammed house – Powning & Bergstein spoke 1 hour each & spoke well – Cutting, candidate for State Supt of Pub Instruction closed with a short, sick speech – Band played, and the Glee Club of 7, in uniform, sang lots – good meeting, but little enthusiasm – After the show was over the Sharon ran the whisky shops with the boys for awhile – The Crystal, beneath my room ran with a jolly crowd, singing etc rest of night – Was there awhile myself – Bed at 3 –

Oct 14 through 18 [AD visits Evans, attends Exempt meeting, writes to his wife, sends Eunice a letter of condolence & makes music with Jose Salinas.]

Oct 19 – Cloudy, cold & variable – Evening big Silver rally at Miners Union Hall, Gold Hill – Newlands, J E Jones et al, speakers – quite a lot went from here – Same crowd at Silver City last evening – This evening I at Opera House – Murphy, Post and Stewarts comic variety combination in *"U and I"* – Very good performance and good audience – Bed 1 – Miss Truly Shattuck a leading lady in the show tonight – Her mother shot and killed a man on her account a few weeks ago in San Francisco & was put into State Prison for 10 years & is there now.

Oct 20 . . . Evening at theater – "Peck's Bad Boy" . . . Grand Silver Party rally at Carson . . . The registration of voters for the coming State election . . . closed at 6 PM today . . . Total for Storey county 1859 names . . . In 1876 2200 were registered in the Second Ward, Va, alone.

Oct 23 . . . Evening Populist rally at Theater – Dougherty, Manning and Curler spoke – Not much enthusiasm – about ⅔ of a house . . .

Oct 27 . . . Hon C C Goodwin came on noon train – Met him during the PM and affiliated after 14 yrs – Evening big meeting at Opera House – Bonfires in streets – Brass band – Excursion train from Carson brought 100 or more, also the Carson Glee Club . . . Splendid meeting . . . Goodwin spoke 1 hour & 10 minutes – Very interesting – After that I was about town, etc – got item or 2 in *Enterprise* – Comstock Glee Club about town also, in the saloons – big singing etc – Bed 2 . . .

Oct 30 . . . 10 AM saw Evans off for Silver City – was down at his lodgings & went with him and his valise and dog "Judy" up to Dazet's store on C st, where he left his valise, and he & Judy walked down to Silver, his valise to be taken down by Dazet's delivery wagon. Evans goes down to start up work on Dazet's mill tailings for he & I as partners – I gave him a letter [of] introduction to Matt Bay, to show him eating and sleeping place – PM with Pat Keyes, and evening writing up a statement relative to the Keyes mine to be used in coming lawsuit . . .

Oct 31 . . . Evening big Rep rally – Bonfires, music etc – Opera House – Cleveland and Bartine – Crowded house – Norris the Enterprise reporter attended and reported and I filled in the regular business of the office for him . . .

Nov 1 . . . PM General A J Warner, from Ohio, who came from the
East with Senator J P Jones, addressed a grand full audience at the Opera
House . . . He spoke for nearly 2 hours – Fine looking, 6 ft 3, old man
of about 67 years . . . I filled in on the *Enterprise,* Norris working a
minstrel performance for the benefit of the Episcopal Church . . . [War-
ner was a prominent opponent of the "demonetization" of silver from
1873 on, and a leading figure in the various national silver conventions.]

Nov 2 . . . PM wrote out a statement, of Chas E Nuttall for Keyes . . .

Nov 3 – Clear, cool & pleasant – Evening at Opera House – Biggest rally
of the Campaign of the Silver party – Bonfires, 5 on C st & 1 on B, opposite the theater – Brass band, Comstock Glee Club, etc – One of the
largest audiences I ever saw in that building. It was jammed full and many
had to go away unable to get in. There was not less than 1700 people –
the full capacity of the house, standing room, boxes, stage and all – I was
at reporter table on the stage – but not reporting for anything – Frank
Newlands spoke first, for an hour, followed by Senator J P Jones for about
1½ hours – Both principally on the silver and monetary problem – Both
did better than I ever heard them – Jones arrived at Gold Hill Thursday
and has staid there till brought or escorted up this evening by several carriage loads of citizens to the theater – After the show was over, Con
Ahern of the Crystal Saloon had the band playing in front and shot off a
lot of fireworks, rockets, etc, and after closing, had the glee club, Newlands, the Sherms etc inside singing, dancing, drinking etc for couple
of hours – I was with them awhile – Bed 2 – Fixed up my statement, 3
pages, and another for Charley Nuttall for Pat Keyes and swore mine
before Charley Mack, Notary and atty for Keyes – Shook hands with
Jones after lecture –

Nov 5 – Same – All getting ready for the big election tomorrow – I fixed
up the sample ballots of Jose Salinas and Janitor Wm Brady – Evening
about town some – Populist speaking from a stand erected front of the
Enterprise office. Speakers were Doughty, Curler and [blank] – Bed at
2 – "Just Before the Battle" –

Nov 6 – Clear & pleasant – Grand general election – Liveliest I have
seen for years – 2 bands of music all day, from 9 AM till polls closed at
6 PM – Carriages with flags etc rushing wild – little boys, dogs, goats,
etc placarded, traveling the streets, etc – Got in my ballot about 4 PM –
Pretty straight Republican with exception of Court Clerk and Dist Atty
and Dave Lazier for Co Commissioner – Considerable excitement during

the evening over the returns from the East, etc, especially New York. Bulletins posted in front of some of the saloons, and in front of the Crystal they were read aloud every few minutes as received – Looks as if the whole East has gone big Republican – New York unexpectedly so. Bed at 1 –

Nov 7 . . . Only excitement [was] over election telegrams and local returns . . . Senator Jones left . . .

Nov 8 . . . PM I wrote & sent a three page letter to Senator Jones, Palace Hotel San Francisco . . .

Nov 9 . . . PM was at office of Gotth Haist mining & civil engineer and fixed up his statement in Keyes mining suit . . . Evening at Theater – Ezra Kendall and comic specialty company . . . Pretty good and amusing – Good house . . .

Nov 10 . . . Helped out Keyes with more of his statements . . .

Sunday, Nov 11 – Same – "Indian Summer" weather for the past week – Wrote a congratulatory letter to Adolph Sutro on his election as Mayor of San Francisco – Also sent him one of my Pioneer pamphlets. also sent letter to wife, telling her that Prof Orvis Ring's re-election as State Supt of Public Instruction is conceded at headquarters of the Silver Party in this city – The only Rep on the State ticket elected – Evening about town – Bed 11:30 –

Nov 12 – The same clear "Indian Summer" weather . . . Streets dry and dusty, as not been sprinkled this month as County cant afford street sprinkler any more. About town as usual – Bed at 11:30 – George R Paynter, heretofore editor of the Enterprise, having quit about a week ago, Fred J Norris, local reporter now fills both departments. Paynter goes into mining and chicken ranch business in Six-mile canyon. George Brown, ex sheriff of this county, and lastly Deputy Supt of State prison, died there this morning of pneumonia – 55 yrs old – Was here knocking around lively election day, being a registered voter here – rode home that night in a carriage, contracted his death.

Nov 13 through Dec 31 [AD records the coming on of winter, & a long series of earthquakes, none of which does any damage, writes many business letters, many letters to his wife, and almost as many to Senator Jones, stands in for Norris several times as the latter is playing with the Oriole Minstrels in benefits for the Episcopal Church – Attends the

Exempt election meeting & becomes a Trustee, and is much about town –
Of further interest:]

Nov 15 – Variable & cooler – clouds of dust – Bed 12 –

[Clip, *Virginia Chronicle:*] Mrs. Alice M. Hartley, the slayer [July 26] of
Senator M. D. Foley, gave birth to a boy baby this morning.

Mrs Hartley was found guilty of murder in the first degree and sentence
deferred till Dec 1, or till her baby was born.

Nov 16 . . . Dan Sully and good Comedy company of about a dozen
in "O'Neill, Washington DC" – Very good play of the Irish-American
character. Sully is a first-class Irish-American comedian . . .

Nov 21 . . . PM rode in light wagon – 1 horse – with G R Paynter &
his little son George (about 15) to Silver City – visited the Red Jacket &
other mining works, & took look at things generally – I hadn't been there
for a couple of years or so – We finally found Evans, at Mrs Monckton's
residence, where he is rooming . . . Evening at Theater – Jas A Reilly
in his comedy drama "A German Soldier" supported by a fair company –
He was the poorest of the lot – Poor play, poorly played . . .

Sunday, Nov 25 . . . The annual target shoot of Battery A, Nevada
Artillery took place this PM at their range a mile or so north of the city –
cannons and rifles – Lieut Gov Poujade was up from Carson with others
and attended – good time and some good shooting – Evening I wrote a 4
page article on *Nevada Earthquakes* for the *Enterprise* on which I take
Norris's place tomorrow as he goes to Carson with the Oriole Minstrels
tomorrow where they give a benefit performance tomorrow evening . . .

Nov 29 . . . Thanksgiving Day – Dullest I ever saw on the Comstock –
Turkey in only 2 or 3 saloons – Very little general hilarity – Everybody
too poor, and mightly little to be thankful for . . .

Nov 30 . . . PM was with Prof Thos Cara awhile, and we visited St
Paul's (Episcopal) Church, where he officiates as organist & he showed
me all about the organ, which is one of the finest on the coast –

Dec 8 . . . Wrote "A Chapter on Organs" this evening for the *Enterprise.*

[Clip, *Enterprise,* Dec 25:] With Christmas, the most religious time of the
year, come sweet musical remembrances of Christmas carols and of the
grandly accompanying music of the church organ which fills the souls of

all who hear with inspirations of peace and good will toward men, all of which suggests the following:

The fine organ at St. Paul's Episcopal Church in this city is the best in the State of Nevada and has been in use for over eighteen years. It is situated in the gallery over the front or west entrance, and a desire has been expressed by prominent members of the congregation to move it to a more advantageous and appreciative position adjoining the chancel. This expensive proposition, however, has been overruled by the vestry and the organ will remain where it is.

This organ is an excellent instrument of its size and capacity, and is the best of the few church organs in the State of Nevada. It has 1,100 pipes, the principal, or largest and loftiest, being sixteen feet tall and fifteen inches in diameter—room enough for a reasonable-sized boy to crawl inside. It is a fine, rich, full-toned organ, well adapted to the capacity of the church.

The famous organ in the old Mormon Temple at Salt Lake City has 5,280 pipes, varying in length from the chief or principal, 32 feet, down to two inches, in accordance with the varied notes and tones required.

The organ, recently completed, at Grace Church, Episcopal, San Francisco, has 2,924 pipes, the largest 32 feet long or high. It is spoken of as a noble instrument. . . .

The Centennial Hall organ [8,800 pipes, in Sydney, Australia], is the chief artificial musical instrument on earth. Its front is 90 feet in width—15 feet wider than the front of the International Hotel in this city—100 feet high and 25 feet in depth, from the front to the back. It takes a cyclone, driven by steam, to run even the main pipe, which is 64 feet high and big enough to contain a mass meeting of four or five men.

Sunday, Dec 9 . . . About 2 PM, James R McKay, living with wife & 3 children near the Ophir works committed suicide – About 44 yrs old – Native of Nova Scotia – working steadily in the Ophir mine – sober industrious good citizen – Had spat with wife on religious matters, probably, as they have had before, she being Irish Catholic and he Protestant – Anyhow he went out and around into the wood cellar under the house, sat down, cut a two inch gash in his throat with a pen knife, severing the jugular vein and died very speedily.

Dec 11 – Morning light snowstorms – PM Variable – Moderate – Bed 12 – Received a copy of the *Boston Daily Globe* of December 3 today, containing a double column article on Plymouth Odd Fellows celebrating the 50th anniversary of Mayflower Lodge, of which Brother Sam is the only surviving charter member – A cut of the Hall building is given and also a very good picture of Brother Sam. Mayflower Lodge was instituted Dec 3, 1844, with 5 charter members, including Sam.

Dec 12 . . . Cal Press Association unexpectedly visited us today – I met several of them – Most of them from around the Bay & some never in snow country before – Had lots of sleighriding, coasting, etc, & visiting mines, etc – Some of the women especially were especially exhilarated coasting down Union st from C – one young woman having more fun than anybody at it – This crowd seemed to enjoy their visit to the Comstock better than any I have seen.

Dec 17 . . . Fire took in Heffron's old place, from cooking range at the rear, burned up through roof and badly damaged roof of the restaurant & bakery adjoining on the south . . . Big smoke & big alarm – Damage $2,000 or more –

Dec 20 . . . Recd short letter from Adolph Sutro in acknowledgment of my congratulatory letter of Nov 11 – Rec'd copy of *The Index* from Plymouth, containing a very interesting Reminiscence of *The Old Town Pump*, written by Bro Charlie I think – Wrote a 1 page letter to Charlie in response . . .

Dec 22 . . . *"Forefathers Day"* . . . Recd letter from *Lizzie,* Waverley House, Charlestown, Mass. 5 pages real nice home letter inclosing a $2 greenback to buy "popcorn and peanuts" for Christmas . . .

Dec 25 . . . Very quiet Christmas – Found turkey, roast pig etc at principal saloons – Evening at Opera House – "Charley's Aunt," by a very good light comedy Co . . . Bed at 2 . . . Wildcat Joe Christmas –

Dec 27 – Cold, snowy, pogonippy and decidedly Wintry – very slippery – brussels carpet tacked on heels of shoes, boots or rubbers, big thing to prevent slipping . . . Letter each to Jas G Fair and Adolph Sutro – $300 . . . The Cliff House near San Francisco totally destroyed by fire about 7 PM Christmas Day – loss $28,000 – Belonged to Adolph Sutro the last twelve years . . .

Dec 29 . . . J G Fair died at San F early this morning . . .

Sunday, Dec 30 . . . I attended the AM service at St Paul's . . . slim house, but interesting performance, to one who attends church as seldom as I do . . .

Dec 31 . . . At midnight the Old Year was blown out and the New Year ushered in with a very lively racket of fire crackers, bombs, steam whistles – notably the Gould & Curry – guns, pistols etc and the fire bell rattled joyously – *Vale.*

BOOK NO. *71*

Virginia City and Carson
Jan 1, 1895 – Dec 31, 1895

Jan 1, 1895 . . . Lots of New Year's visiting, sleighing parties, etc – Turkey plenty in various saloons. Everybody trying to feel happy and hilarious, but economically so, with apprehensive lookout for the coming times ahead . . .

Jan 2 . . . Letter from Adolph Sutro, declining, etc . . . Julius A Huntoon, County Clerk and Ex-officio Treasurer of Lyon County for last 12 yrs suicided at Dayton New Years Eve – by pistol ball through his heart. Shortage in his accounts and surety of detection was the cause.

Jan 3 . . . The most ferocious zephyrs for years, from the SW, swept down the cross streets, especially at the International corner on C st – made crossing Union st very perilous – Many people were blown off their feet in crossing to the Postoffice, and sleighs were blown around sideways like straws. Much damage was done throughout the city to houses, roofs, windows, chimneys, stovepipes etc . . .

Jan 4 – Snowing very heavily from earliest morning all day. Nearly two feet fell – C st piling up big. Express train 5 hours late – most of the trouble this end of the V&T RR . . . The SP yet kept open by the effective rotary plows . . . Letter from wife says Millie's new daughter, born a week before Christmas, is a "tiny little mite, with dark hair, and I think may look like Millie. I have named it Esther Armorel and shall have to help it along." I got a letter from Oscar T Shuck, San F. with $5 greenback in it . . .

Jan 5 through 7 [The weather clears, many people pack their cellars with snow for summer use and AD writes Shuck and Senator Jones.]

Jan 8 – Variable – thawy – PM lightly rainy – At 2:30 PM I attended the marriage of Dolly McCone to Dr T P McDonald. St Mary's Catholic Church was densely crowded – nine-tenths women and girls. Father Tubman officiated – Altar, etc, beautifully decorated with roses, lilies, smilax, etc, and illuminated with numerous candles. Good music – splendid affair – Reception held at her home on the Divide, and they left on evening train, at 5:40 for a honeymoon trip to California – A big crowd at the depot saw them off. Bed at 12 – Partially clear – big thaw – streets slushy, uneven and bad.

Jan 9 . . . PM I searched the mortuary records at the County Recorder's office, for Shuck . . .

Jan 11 . . . Sent a letter to wife, with pamphlet of "Student's Songs," with a written copy of "Glendy Burk" – darkey song – copied by myself. She says she has use for these songs.

Jan 12 . . . AM I visited Miss Nellie Manning at the American Exchange – About 17 or 18 yrs old – Daughter of Mrs Kate L Welch, a lady O T Shuck writes to find out about, on account of some property involved . . .

[A clip from a Reno newspaper says that Mrs Hartley has been sentenced to eleven years in the state prison, a heavier sentence than was expected, but the general opinion is that justice has been done – Her lawyers will appeal to the Supreme Court.]

Sunday, Jan 13 . . . PM I attended the regular monthly meeting of the Exempts . . .

Jan 15 . . . Evening I attended free lecture of Dr John M Byrne on the Keeley Institute at Carson, from whence he is a recent graduate. He also treated on the tobacco and opium habits, etc. Pretty fair house – good lecture – Several men from here have gone through the treatment since the election, including A Lernhart, and Mott Reihm and come back cured and looking better than ever . . .

[From the *Enterprise* of the 16th:] The Doctor . . . proved conclusively that drunkenness, morphine and opium addictions are as much diseases as . . . diphtheria. . . . His remarks on the cigarette craze were novel. He gave the modus operandi of the treatment in the Carson City Institute. . . . He painted a harrowing picture of the wretchedness of the inebriate and of the amount of misery necessarily existing in his home. . . . The audience went home thoughtful, but satisfied.

[The *Reno Evening Gazette,* reporting Dr Byrne's similar speech in Reno on the 19th, gives more detail on the famous "Keeley Cure":] The patient is given four hypodermic injections each day and sixteen ounces of tonic to drink, and is also given all the whisky he wishes to drink. The liquor does not make you sick at the stomach, as is generally supposed, but in a day or two the taste of the stuff changes, and about the third day you no longer relish a drink, and in a day or two more you despise whisky as much as you liked it before. . . . In the end you lose absolutely all desire for it and cannot bear the sight of it. . . . There is no pain whatever. [The Dr claims the cure works for 95 percent of the patients, and had some 250,000 to its credit already.] He came here a skeptic . . . but he leaves believing it a God-send. . . . There is no wonder, he says, that saloon men decry it and say the patients come out with shattered senses. [The piece closes with a tribute to Dr Lee, the physician in charge of the Carson Institute.]

Jan 16 and 17 [Heavy snow – AD writes W S James, Secretary of the Centennial, about 493 shares, certificate lost, he has sold to Dan Hanifan.]

Jan 18 . . . Snowstorm all day . . . Trains blockaded on the Sierra . . . I started in today as agent for the Associated Press, S.F. – telegraphic reporter . . .

Jan 19 – Clear and pleasant – Passenger train arrived from Reno at 3 PM – 3½ hours late – Brought three days delayed California mails, and all from the East. Quite a lot of passengers, including the Young Ladies' Cadet Corps, from the State University, who gave a pretty good drill and variety and musical entertainment at the Opera House this evening. Over 50 of them, with an excellent brass and string band of about a dozen pieces including two young lady violinists. Good entertainment and heavily crowded house. I was there. The young lady cadets were quartered around among friends about town tonight, by previous arrangement. I received a letter by this mail from Hon Andrew Nicholls, Los Angeles. Bed 12.

Jan 21 – Variable, with occasional light snowstorms – Mail late . . . owing to the drifting snows of last night's wind, filling the cuts and track – toughest of all to shove, drag or push through. At 4 PM I went to Union Brewery saloon and found G R Evans and his dog. They came up on the Dayton stage today from Silver City. He sent all over town for me. He goes below to S.F. on a milling proposition – proposing to return in the Spring. I went with him and his Cuban bloodhound bitch Judy, down to the train and saw them off. Sharp jolt of earthquake at 5:30 PM – Got telegram from John H Dennis at Carson to come down there. Telegraphed back that I would be down tomorrow, and for him to report Legislature, which commenced session today, to the Reno Journal for me, in my name or his, as I am engaged for it.

Jan 24 – Clear and cold . . . Took the evening train to Carson . . . Met most of the legislators et al at the Arlington House – Visited Dennis awhile where he rooms, at Harry Day's. Bed at 12 at the Arlington.

Jan 25 – Same – Telegraphed to *Journal* in morning: "I am here – will report – shall I continue?" Reply came: "Yes. Be sure mail report on evening train. Kelly & Webster." I reported in Senate, and Dennis in Assembly and we exchanged, or copied from each other, thus each getting complete report of both Houses. Got along finely. Lieut Gov Sadler, President of the Senate, and Lem Allen Speaker of the Assembly. Both Houses made their regular hours for opening session at 11 AM and 2 PM. Got my report off as desired. Dennis reports for *Enterprise* and Reno *Gazette* – $10 a week each – I get $10 – Bed at 12, at the Briggs House, where Frank Doten died. Paid for my bed, 50 cts, in advance, lest I should die before morning. It being China New Year there was much cracking of bombs and booming of crackers and beating of gongs etc, with illuminations, etc, in the Chinese quarter.

Jan 26 . . . Both Houses having adjourned over till Monday, most of the members got out of town . . . PM I wrote "Capital Notes" to the *Journal* – 3 pages – and sent by the evening train – Bed at 12, at Briggs House . . .

Sunday, Jan 27 – Snowstormy – Wrote letters to Manager Coleman of the Va *Chronicle* and to Norris, local of *Enterprise* – Tried to get reporting for *Chronicle* but couldn't. To F J Norris I wrote telling him to run the Associated Press reporting. I have the same privilege in the room or office of the State Supt of Public Instruction in the capitol that I have enjoyed heretofore having a key to the door, so I do my writing and fixing up my reports there. H C Cutting is the new Supt, elected by the Silver Party. Was about town this PM. Very dull. Bed at 12 – at Briggs House as usual –

Jan 28 through March 25 [AD reports the Legislature for the *Journal* during the week, writes up "Capital Notes" on weekends, writes his wife frequently, corresponds about the Centennial and the Keyes suit, enjoys his usual dead-head privileges at Piper's Carson Opera House and is about town – Of interest:]

Jan 28 . . . I give my report letter to Joe McCormick, conductor of the passenger train, at 6:30 when it arrives from Va – and he sees it delivered to the *Journal* – Put it in a big document envelope, sealed, tearing off a corner, and using no postage stamps – Bed at 12, Briggs House –

Jan 30 . . . Evening at Carson Opera House – The Carson Minstrels Benefit of the High School organ fund – Crowded house – Splendid orchestra . . . Minstrel Variety show – 15 in the first part, including 7 ladies – all "black face" – acrobatic interlude, small comedy, songs, choruses, solos, etc, concluding with beautiful Indian Club drill, by 12 ladies in costume, aided by magnificent scenery effects, colored lights, etc . . .

Jan 31 . . . Resolution indorsing the career political of Hon J P Jones introduced into Senate by Boyle, passed both Houses today . . .

Feb 1 . . . Old man Eaves, grandfather of Harry, Gus and Alice Nye (now Mrs Col Lord) died in Sacramento Tuesday, aged 87 years. He was one of the old time Comstockers, and at one time Mayor of Virginia City . . .

Feb 2 . . . Sent a copy of the Journal containing the Jones resolutions to Senator Jones, Washington D.C. and one to Sam Jones, Gold Hill . . .

Feb 4 – The Harden-Francis contested seat in the Assembly settled today – Francis winning by *one* majority. The County Clerk of Humboldt County was brought in, by orders of the Assembly, by Sergeant-at-arms Flannery, together with the ballots used or cast at the last election, and this afternoon were canvassed by the Assembly in Committee of the Whole . . .

Feb 5 . . . Evening at glove contest between Beals and Brown at the Pavilion – Reported it – Lasted over 3 hours – Very cold time of it, there being no fire in the house – Bed at 2 –

[Clip – $50 a side – After 37 even, cautiously fought rounds, the referee stopped the fight and called it a draw.]

Feb 6 . . . Had a surprise party at my room this morning – just out of bed in my shirt when a lady servitor who was doing up the rooms came in with a broom – Scared me much under the circumstances, but she left as suddenly as she came, and I *recovered.* My door was not locked or fastened, the bolt being out of fix.

Feb 8 . . . About 30 of the girls and boys of the Gold Hill High School, with Principal Storey came by morning train – Visited the Legislature, Orphans Home, Prison, Mint and other public institutions & went home again . . .

Feb 9 . . . Evening at train I found Tom C Johns, wife & son on board bound for South Africa. Went to theater – Play, "Two of a Kind" – Comic sort of a jumble – By the Truly Shattuck comedy crowd . . .

Feb 13 – Clear, warm, thawy Spring day – Letter from *Journal* with bill to Tim Dempsey $6, for 1 year subscription . . . to collect and keep – did so. Bed at 12 – About 9 AM I was reading paper at Dempsey's with feet on fender of stove. Had just left my chair to go out, when a big 45 caliber bullet crashed through the lathed and double plastered partition from the drugstore adjoining and lodged in the opposite wainscoting. A line drawn from one place to the other showed that if I had kept my seat, I would infallibly have got the ball right in the neck or under the ear. It was a very narrow escape indeed – And it was the same old story of a boy examining a gun and finding it was loaded – When some of the parties in the saloon went in drug store and asked about it, he smilingly assured them there was no harm done – only a bottle of paregoric, etc, smashed, and the hole in the wall was nothing.

Feb 18 . . . Morning, Dennis telegraphed me from Reno that he had got left by the train and would come up on the PM local, and for me to fill in for him on the *Enterprise* . . . Gave me a lively days work . . .

Feb 22 . . . Too muddy for the Carson Guard to parade – Flags on Gov't buildings only sign of holiday. Dullest I ever saw – Most of legislators gone . . .

Feb 25 . . . E D Kelley of the *Journal* came up from Reno to attend the grand Inaugural Ball . . . paid me $20. Evening, on a special invitation from Committee I attended the Inaugural Ball, at the Opera House. Seat in the gallery. Bed at 2.

Feb 27 . . . Bishop Manogue died at Sacramento this morning.

[Clips from the *Enterprise, Virginia Chronicle,* and *San Francisco Examiner* – Manogue emigrated from Ireland – Went to the Comstock in 1862 after being ordained – Was a unique and necessary combination of godliness and toughness – As the *Chronicle* put it:] From the good old days in Virginia City, where this man was frequently obliged to preach Christ with his fist . . . down to the present, this great-famed, great-hearted son of the cross has been a true exemplar . . . has . . . combined so happily in his brave and gentle nature the lion heart and the virgin soul that his life might not inaptly be termed a daily epitome of the Sermon on the Mount. . . .

Sunday, March 3 . . . The horse racing this PM was between Jack Furlong's bay horse, "Barbed Wire Tim," Bagwell's sorrel mare "Mod-

esty," and Raycraft's sorrel horse "Sontag." Purse $100 – single dash of
⅜ of a mile. B. W. Tim won by 60 feet – time, 40 seconds – Some scrub
preliminary racing.

March 4 . . . Assembly held evening session on Washoe, Lyon, Ormsby
and Storey Counties boundary bill – to give the other counties each a slice
of Washoe. Big crowd of ladies, Senators, State officers, etc, present – I
reported. A two hours wrangling session amounted to nothing. Bed at 1 –
(This and all other County boundaries bills were subsequently defeated.)

March 7 . . . Evening I was at Opera House. "Jolly Nellie Henry in her
Cireo-Comedy: *A Night at the Circus"* – crowded house and excellent
entertainment . . .

> [A clip from the *San Francisco Examiner* of March 7 reports the death
> of AD's old California friend Captain J C Morrill – He was one of the
> earliest miners at Sutter Creek, and had resided at Santa Clara since
> 1856.]

March 9 . . . Evening at the Opera House – *University Cadet Corps,*
of young men in general variety show. Drill good and acrobatic interlude
especially good. All the rest, plays, etc, not much good. Show not as good
as that given by the Young Lady Cadets . . .

March 13 . . . Both Houses ran evening sessions . . . Charley E
Laughton died at Tacoma, Washington State, this evening –

> [Five clips, local & from Spokane & Tacoma – Laughton had been auditor
> of the V&T RR and lieutenant governor first of Nevada and then of
> Washington – A notable violinist, who found politics a "curse."]

March 15 . . . I went to Opera House – Play was "Fritz in a Mad
House," by J K Emmett, son of old Joe Emmett deceased. Nothing like
his father – Not very good play or first-rate company . . .

March 16 . . . Last day of the session, and the hardest & liveliest for
the reporters – The gavel fell at 12 in both Houses . . .

March 18 . . . PM I worked at getting up a list of the acts or bills
approved by the Governor . . . and sent it to *Journal* this evening – 84
of them . . .

> [From the *Virginia Chronicle* of Mar 19:] There is a mysterious shortage
> of $70,000 or thereabouts in the value of the bullion on hand at the U.S.
> Mint at Carson, which the Mint officials are unable to account for. The
> shortage was first discovered some weeks ago. It was discovered by Chief
> Melter and Refiner Hirsch Harris, who noted that . . . the amount of

fine gold and silver bullion returned from the refining department did not tally with the amount charged on his books. On taking office he had retained as his chief assistant J. E. Jones, who had occupied the position for several years, as Assistant Melter and Refiner. Mr. Jones was familiar with the work of the department and Mr. Harris asked him [and his assistant, James Heney] to explain the discrepancy noted. Mr. Jones told him there was nothing to worry about, as the matter was a common occurrence, and that the missing gold and silver would be found in the slag which formed the refuse from the bullion put through the melting and refining process. Although frequently thus reassured by Mr. Jones, Mr. Harris about six weeks ago decided to make a clean up and test the matter. The clean up was made and showed a shortage of about $70,000 in the amount of gold and silver on hand.

As soon as the certainty of the shortage was ascertained Mr. Harris notified the authorities at Washington. In response to the notification Mr. Mason, Superintendent of the U.S. assay office at New York, was dispatched to Carson to investigate the matter. He is in Carson at present engaged in that labor.

Melter and Refiner Harris and the Mint officials generally are unable to say how the shortage occurred. Several theories are advanced to explain it, however. One theory is that mistakes as to the fineness of some of the gold bullion received at the Mint were made by the Mint assayer; another is that a fraud was at some time committed in the melting and refining department and spurious bars of bullion substituted for genuine ones. . . .

The disappearance of $70,000 worth of bullion is a very grave matter, and it is to be hoped that Mr. Mason's investigation will reveal how it occurred, and that those who are guilty of the crime or negligence which caused its loss will be held accountable. . . .

March 21 . . . Wrote letter to wife, and one to *Journal* on Mint trouble . . . [AD reports the Mint trouble and subsequent trials for the *Journal,* covering them daily and at length.]

Sunday, March 24 . . . PM and evening at Cutting's office writing & fixing up this Journal to date . . .

March 25 . . . I see by newspapers that Aunt Lucy A Batterman died at Oakland last Saturday . . .

March 26 – Variable, but warm and pleasant – Completed writing up my Journal in this new book this PM and evening, to date. Have been keeping it jotted along in my reporters book in lead pencil. Bed at 12 – The Mint shortage mystery continues. Andrew Mason, the Government expert, from New York, is doing his best to solve it, but never even hints at how he is succeeding. Everybody in and about the Mint are also dumb as oysters. The whole concern is being fearfully raked over by the SF *Chronicle,* the

SF *Argus* and other papers. Received a letter from wife via Virginia, about her Aunt Lucy's death. Aged 79, but stated at 76 – Died of la grippe & pneumonia. 79 the 6th of next month. "For family reasons she is to be considered three years younger." Died Saturday *morning* at 12:07, "passing away as peacefully as a child goes to sleep." Neither of her children with her, but Miss Lindsay was. She has been living with her for some time past. Wife writes that Sam is sick with what the Dr says is the first stages of pneumonia. I finished at Cuttings room writing this by the good gaslight at 8:30 – Was up to the Arlington & elsewhere afterward. Bed at 12. The trouble about Hon J G Fair's property division among his heirs still continues and more actively than ever. He yielded a numerous crop of "last will and testaments," fresh ones springing up quite frequently. And several women claim to be his latest wives and quite a number of children claim him as their father – one a child of his deceased son Jimmy, Jr –

March 27 – Light rain most of day – wet down the dust good. PM I wrote "In Memoriam," on death of Mrs Batterman and sent it to *Enterprise* on evening local, at 5 PM. Also wrote and sent letter to wife by evening down passenger train at 6:30. Evening very blustering and some rain. Bed at 12 – The Board of Orphans Home this PM appointed A M Beebe of Reno and wife as Supt and Matron of the State Orphans Home, superseding Bob Grimmon and wife. Plainly a political proposition, and not for any other cause. A very wrong act for they have been the best possible father and mother of those children for years, giving perfect satisfaction – Politics should never be allowed to interfere in that proposition. This act on part of the Board creates general dissatisfaction. It is too coldly and politically mercenary, without honest cause. Summerfield's Income Tax bill was vetoed by the Governor this PM – $20 from Journal today –

March 28 . . . Sent "Capital Notes" to *Journal* . . . Half fare pass renewed today –

Sunday, March 31 . . . PM I was busy tracing a map of Carson river, & especially the milling sections of it, Brunswick, Merrimac, Vivian, etc – Worked in the rear part of the Assessor's office – about 4 hours – made good job of it . . .

April 1 . . . Put on my new $6.50 pants this PM, that I bought at Abe Cohn's a few days ago . . . Bought a pair at same place 2 yrs ago, & worn them ever since . . .

April 2 . . . Secured my old room – No 7 – at Tim Dempsey's, formerly Wolmering's where I was two years ago . . . dropping my room 7 at the Briggs House . . . So I feel somewhat at home once more . . .

April 8 . . . Carl Smith and Beatrice Lieb dramatic Co, in "Herminie, or the Cross of Gold" – Not very good Co or play. Rather prosey . . .

April 9 . . . The theater Co played "Infatuation" to small audience – I wasn't there –

April 10 . . . Evening at Theater – Played "The Old, Old Story" . . .

April 11 . . . The "Salvation Army" from Reno, about 5 men & 3 women, in their regulation uniform, flags and bass drum paraded on street short time in evening, and held meeting at Odd Fellows Hall after usual style – crowded all could hold . . . Met the 2 Honsucker brothers . . . Hadn't seen them for nearly 20 yrs, but recognized them . . . Had another old Tahoe fisherman J M Coe along with them, going over there – We all had a drink together.

April 13 . . . 3 PM John T Jones assistant Melter & Refiner of the Carson Mint was arrested on charge of embezzlement – Mint shortage $77,000 all charged upon him – He gave $25,000 bonds – I wrote the matter to the *Reno Journal* . . . Professor Zimmer and Andy Cavanaugh came down yesterday and started in on the "Keeley Cure." Zimmer told me this PM that he already had lost desire for liquor – He will take the full treatment for a month – $130 –

April 17 . . . Orders by telegraph rec'd from Washington to the Mint to purchase no more silver, and to ship the bullion etc on hand to San Francisco –

April 18 . . . AM at 10 I attended the starter of the J T Jones Mint investigation – Evening sent short account of it to *Journal* – Further hearing postponed till next Tuesday – Mrs Hartley's case in Supreme Court argued and submitted yesterday & today . . .

April 19 . . . Shipment of bullion from the Mint to the US Sub Treasury, San Francisco commenced last evenings train – $500,000 gold – This evening $40,000 unparted bullion –

April 20 – Springlike & bland – PM wrote & sent letter to *Journal* – $78,000 more unparted gold bullion sent from the Mint to the SF Mint this evening – I attended theater – "Damon and Pythias" by an amateur company from Reno, under management of E S Laurie, his wife and daughter, "little Lizzie," appearing in the cast – He recited "The Money-less Man" – The whole was of unusual excellence even for professionals – but had rather of a slim audience, ½ a house – Bed 12 –

April 23 . . . The Johnny Jones Mint case came up today – "closed doors" – But I reported it very fully and correctly all the same & sent it to *Journal* . . . [Report based on interviews with people at the hearing.]

April 24 . . . Second day of preliminary examination of J T Jones . . . I reported it *in full* . . . regardless of *"Closed doors"* . . .

April 25 . . . Reported the Mint-Jones Examination again today – on the outside . . . The attorneys had a big wrangle . . . over the whole proceedings being reported . . . without any reporters being allowed inside . . .

April 26 through 30 [AD reporting the Jones hearing, hobnobbing with Bill Gibson & Farmer Treadway, also Pacific Coast Pioneers, and noting that snow & a "strong frost" have damaged fruit blossoms.]

May 1 . . . Orders recd from Washington to discharge quite a number of the Mint employes – about 15, next Saturday – Looks like a close.

May 3 . . . Got letter from John Piper, relative to Henry Piper and Mint trouble . . .

May 6 . . . Took morning train . . . to Gold Hill – Centennial annual meeting . . . Got reissue of my lost 493 shares . . .

May 7 . . . Evening at theater – Play *"Columbus up to Date"* – Carson Amateur crowd – Over 80 in it, little and big – Best variety performance I have seen for years. Big house . . . Grand success . . .

May 8 . . . PM attended lecture of W E Smythe Editor of the "Irriga-tion Age," on Nevada colonization – at District Court room – About 50 present –

May 9 . . . Mrs Sarrman murdered yesterday PM at ranch on Carson river, 14 miles above here, by party unknown, but I think by her hus-band – Head split with a hatchet, and afterward her corpse put on a bed and bed set afire – Husband working in the field saw the smoke & put out the fire, so *he* says . . .

May 10 . . . Train late . . . so the Jones examination was not re-sumed till 2 PM – I was about – J H Dennis helped me and I got good report [Dennis was US Marshal on duty in court] – Evening theater –

"London Gaiety Girl" Comedy Operetta – Pretty good company from San Francisco – Variety, leg and high kicking show . . .

May 11 – Clear & pleasant – Jones examination came to abrupt conclusion in ½ an hour this AM by Jones being held in $25,000 to answer before the US Grand Jury – gave bonds – Bed at 12 – Jones got 10 bondsmen, five from Va City, who gave $6,000 more than called for – $31,000 – Met Joe A Miller of Austin, the always County Clerk, etc, yesterday – He is here to take the Keeley Cure – He took his first "shot" this morning. Too drunk the PM or evening before.

May 14 . . . A young druggist clerk named D J Ashbury brought yesterday to room 13, opposite mine, very sick, delirious, with 3 men to forcibly care for him troubled my rest some last night . . . Fred Sargent in room 8, is nearly dead with whooping cough and old age.

May 15 . . . The young druggist . . . worse – Said to have typhoid fever – groaning much & evidently suffering much – delirious & stupefied with morphine injections . . . requiring constant attendance . . .

May 16 . . . Evening, following the express train from Va came a 4 coach special, with over 200 APAs on board bound on a big fraternal visit to Reno – Had brass band – played 2 or 3 pieces at depot – Hitched on 2 more coaches & took about 100 more APAs from Carson . . . [The American Protective Association, founded in Iowa in 1887, was strongly anti-Catholic and antiforeign.]

May 17 – Clear & very pleasant – The APAs last evening at Reno marched from the RR depot through Virginia and Sierra sts to Masonic Hall, with band at head – Quite an army in all – over 100 new ones initiated at the Hall – Susan B Anthony and Dr Anna Shaw, both big lecturers on Woman Suffrage, from the East, also arrived there & will lecture there this evening. Ex-Governor Peter H Burnett – the first civil Governor of California, died at San Francisco at 3 PM yesterday – My sick neighbor, David J Ashbury, . . . shows some improvement, but is still delirious or wrong-headed most of the time, but much weaker – uses no opiates now, but has one or two men in constant attendance, night and day. Bed 12. The late frosts have done no injury to the young fruit, which is fast becoming too large and strong, and with increased foliage is past all danger – Will have the biggest fruit crop Nevada ever saw.

May 21 . . . Ice thick as window glass formed about town last night – did no damage – only nipped some young vegetables, etc – Got letter from Kinzle, Nevada City – was up to the mine Sunday with W S James – More promising than ever before – good strike in SE crosscut – Wrote private letter to E D Kelley of *Journal* . . .

May 22 . . . My sick neighbor . . . suffered a relapse about 4 PM from injudicious feed of beef steak . . . took 2 men to handle him . . . More or less noisy during the night and still wilder demented this morning, singing bits of operetta, loudly, and whistling like a calliope and frequently trying to dance, or beat about with his arms – All his attendants could do was to pile onto him and let him howl . . .

May 23 . . . Tried a stock trade with John Wolmering and got fooled. "Many a slip," etc – The Reno *Journal* of this morning has the following: [The Supreme Court sustains the district court's conviction of Mrs Hartley for murder.] Mrs H has 15 days, under the rule of the Court to file petition for a new hearing. She has said that she will not go to the State Prison. Perhaps she will suicide, or skip out and leave her bondsman to pay . . .

May 24 . . . Evening attended Patriotic Concert at the Presbyterian Church, in aid of the church – 25 cts admission – All patriotic and national songs & music . . . Crowded house – Very good . . .

May 25 . . . Oscar Wilde was found guilty and sentenced today, in London, to two years imprisonment, at hard labor . . . My good old friend – and Lizzie's – dead . . . Joe Griggs – Was a strong spiritualist –

[Clip from the *Chronicle* – "Wildcat Joe" Griggs, also known as "the hermit of the Wells Fargo mine," is found dead of natural causes in his isolated cabin two or three miles east of Virginia City.]

Sunday, May 26 . . . The streets and sidewalks were covered with green leaves, twigs and branches this morning, thrashed off . . . by the fearful wind of last night . . . much young fruit also – The Silver Stars of Va beat the Carson BB club by a score of 34 to 3 . . .

May 27 . . . Day opened with heavy snowstorm . . . PM David J Ashbury was removed . . . in a buggy to more eligible and convenient quarters in town . . . Removal had effect to make him delirious and bad, again, requiring 2 men to hold him, for 2 or 3 hours . . . Evening a very heavy snowstorm . . .

May 28 . . . This heavy snow lodging on the thick foliage, broke down many shade and fruit trees . . . This PM I copied off a portion of the *"Ritual of the A.P.A. Virginia City, Nevada"* – merely the *oath* portion, etc – Rough on Catholics – copied it from a printed pamphlet ritual, surreptitiously obtained and loaned to me –

May 29 . . . Strong frost this morning – 27° – did considerable damage to plums, etc . . . 2 of the tramps arrested [and] charged with the murder of old Mrs Saarman, up Carson Valley, arrived in Carson this PM, having been discharged on examination at Genoa from lack of evidence – No one else suspected except her old husband. If not he, it will evermore be one of the mysteries.

May 30 . . . 10 AM the procession went out to cemetery north of town and decorated the graves . . . Drum corps, Carson Guard, G.A.R., Orphans Home children, Indian boys and girls from the Stewart Institute Indian School – about 200, each carrying bouquet of natural flowers – Sang "America" as they passed along . . .

May 31 . . . Snowing hard – Wintry wind-up for May – Most of the small fruits are destroyed by the late frosts and some of the big fruits also . . .

Sunday, June 2 . . . Joe Miller's wife arrived from Austin to visit him during this, his fourth and last week of the Keeley cure . . .

June 3 . . . Attended & reported Mrs Hartley's case in Board of Pardons. Denied pardon . . . A big movement being made among the Comstock mines to work the Brunswick lode, a mile east of the Comstock, from the Sutro tunnel level . . .

June 4 . . . PM great excitement about bullion being found in possession of Wm Pickler of the Mint, supposed to have been stolen from there – Sam Davis & I investigated & reported – I sent letter to *Journal* . . .

June 5 . . . Pickler was arrested by Govt officers today on charge of grand larceny, and filed bond with US Commissioner Edwards to appear before him for examination next Tuesday in sum of $1,000, with Otto Schultz and Ed Burlington securities . . .

June 6 . . . Heney arrested in Arizona yesterday – $10 recd from *Journal* – Borrowed $10 from the *Tribune* – left on the 5 oclock local train for Va – Was at *Enterprise* office and wrote an item on Heney . . .

June 7 . . . Rode to Gold Hill on morning local – paid my Centennial assessments – $14 . . . Back to Va on noon express – Found old Joe

Douglass had removed some of my room fixings – Left on 5:10 . . . for Carson . . .

June 8 . . . I applied to Yerington for a free pass, and he gave me one for a month . . .

Sunday, June 9 . . . Heney surrendered himself at Leadville, Col, yesterday and is on his way to Carson in charge of US Marshal, Humphrey . . .

June 10 . . . Heney was thought to have arrived at Reno, and this PM Mrs Heney, with their Attorney, Bill Woodburn were driven in a rock-away to Reno to meet him . . .

June 11 . . . Heney arrived about 2 AM in the rockaway, he & wife on back seat, Major Dennis, Deputy US Marshal, on front seat with Jim Raycraft, the driver – drove to his residence & left him & wife – Remains in custody of the Marshal till next Saturday, when his bail bond will be fixed. He was about town considerably in the PM – I met him – He is an old acquaintance – Used to work as a miner in Gold Hill when I was there – Looks fine, & feels so . . .

June 12 . . . Heney's bond was fixed at $25,000 this PM . . . failing to procure more than $15,000 of which, he was put in the county jail for safe keeping . . .

June 15 . . . Preliminary examination of J H Heney, before the US Commissioner Edwards – open doors – I reported & sent to *Journal* – Heney held in $15,000 to appear before Grand Jury . . .

June 17 . . . Preliminary examination of Bill Pickler for stealing bullion from the Mint . . . Mrs Alice M Hartley was taken to State Prison today, from Reno, sentenced to 11 years . . .

June 19 . . . Sent "Carson Mint Juleps" to *Journal* this evening –

June 20 – Clear, cool & pleasant – Bed 11 – Some of the "middle" Comstock Cos, Chollar, Potosi, Hale & Norcross, Savage, etc having bought the Brunswick lode, a mile east of the Comstock, are just starting in to develop the same on the Sutro Tunnel level basis – Probably a new stock deal scheme.

June 21 through Aug 15 [AD continues writing "Capital Notes" and "Observations" for the *Journal* in Reno, and receives and writes many family letters – Corresponds about the Centennial and for Shuck, about

Kate Welch – Meets many old friends passing through town and continues to badger Senator Jones – Mostly short entries with little or no detail – Of interest:]

June 26 . . . Evening theater – Palmer Comedy Co in "Our Boy" – Good variety show – good singing, high kicking, etc . . .

July 1 . . . Met Wm R Jones of Gold Hill – Has been foreman of the Crown Point mine, but came yesterday to go through the Keeley cure for drunkness – Took his first shot last evening – Been pretty drunk all day, & went home to his room at the Arlington at midnight tonight, pretty full – Will begin to do better tomorrow – He is about 45 yrs old, and nephew of J P Jones . . .

July 3 . . . Evening about town – jolly singing party at Dempsey's – Bed 3 . . .

July 4 . . . Big crowd and celebration – nearly 1000 from the Comstock section and 600 from Reno . . . A.P.A.'s materially assisted, had their own flag in the procession – "A.P.A." . . .

July 11 . . . Annual Great Council of the "Red Men" at Odd Fellows Hall . . . banquet at the Briggs House – I was invited & attended & made a little speech . . . About 100 at table, the three Tribes of this State being represented: – Piute, Pocahontas and Apache –

July 12 . . . Got me a new coat & vest today – $5.00 . . .

["A Power Bicycle," from the *Daily Nevada Tribune* of July 13:] A tandem bicycle from the Motor Cycle Company of Courtland, N.Y. arrived from the East this morning for Harry Brown of this city. The cycle is similar to other tandems excepting the wheels, which are very low, but wide, having a five-inch pneumatic tire. It has a compact gasoline engine attachment, presumably of considerable power. A small tank some three inches in diameter and about sixteen inches long hung under one of the coupling rods, and is the reservoir from which the gasoline flows down into cylinders on each side of the rear wheel where it is exploded by an electric spark, the explosion being powerful enough to move a piston and crank connected with the sprocket. The flow of gasoline is controlled by a thumb screw on the handle bar, and the speed is regulated by the dropping of the fluid into the cylinders, the rapidity of the explosions causing the pistons to move slowly or rapidly at the pleasure of the operator. One pair of pedals on the machine serve to start it, or the wheel can be used with the pedals alone. A small electric battery is a part of the outfit and the whole weighs about 180 pounds. It is said that on a fair road a speed of from twenty to twenty-five miles an hour can be attained.

Sunday, July 14 . . . 91° – Jim Rule the old Comstock mining boss died in S.F. yesterday . . .

July 18 . . . Mrs Hartley's baby boy is named Vernon Harrison Hartley . . .

Sunday, July 21 . . . My 66th birthday – Was at the train at 10 AM – J P Jones and family on board bound for Gold Hill – I had quite a chat with him during the 10 minutes the train stopped . . .

July 23 . . . Took morning train to Gold Hill, on my half fare pass, Yerington refusing me renewal of *free* pass – Visited Senator Jones 2 hours, $5 – Back on evening train – Bed 12 – Met S W Chubbuck, my old Gold Hill Confrere, this evening at the Arlington Hotel – Haven't seen him since we left Gold Hill . . .

July 24 . . . Miss Lily Snyder, my best assistant when I was Engrossing Clerk, returned home to Carson yesterday from a 3 years absence in New York where she has been employed editorially on the New York *World*, and the *Sun*. Smart, talented young woman . . .

Sunday, July 28 . . . Evening I met Miss Lily Snyder at her house & had quite a pleasant chat with her on when she was my ass't Engrossing Clerk –

July 29 . . . Great base ball game yesterday at Dayton, between the Silver Stars of Virginia and the Dayton club – Over 1,000 people from Va & around – $150 a side – Stars won . . . 24 to 6 . . .

July 30 . . . Will R Jones took his last "shot," or hypodermic injection last evening in completion of his 4 wks term of Keeley cure, and left on evening local train for Gold Hill, *cured* and in fine health & condition – Out of 116 graduates from this Carson institute only 6 have fallen from grace – gone back on it. Sheriff Kinney sold 14 head of horses, mares & colts at public auction today for $26.25, from the public pound . . .

July 31 . . . Bill Pickler died about 3 o'clock AM in bed at his residence, of heart disease – Wrote it to *Journal* . . .

Sunday, Aug 4 . . . By mail today I received from wife a neat little book of 363 pages entitled "The Story of the Pilgrims," by Morton Dexter – It was sent to me by Cornelia as a birthday present –

Aug 10 . . . Senator Jones came down on the evening train . . . He stopped off for the night at the Arlington hotel – I met him short time . . .

Sunday, Aug 11 . . . Senator Jones left on morning train for San F – I met Jones at depot . . . & had talk – $20 –

Aug 13 . . . Frank M Pixley the noted San Francisco *Argonaut* editor, politician and writer died at San F evening before last – Good all around American . . .

Aug 15 – Clear & pleasant – 86° – The US Grand Jury was drawn today in open court – US Dist – which will have the Mint cases of James Heney and Johnny T Jones for alleged stealage or embezzlement of Mint bullion, creating the shortage of $77,000 – George Metzger left this evening for Butte, Montana – Evening I completed my 6 page "Wildcat Joe" letter to sister Lizzie, Waverley House, Charlestown, Massachusetts – Bed at 12 – Sent short letter to *Journal* this PM, with list of Grand Jury – received a letter . . . from Dan J Hanifan, Virginia City . . . acknowledging receipt of the 493 shares recovered Centennial stock which I mailed to him last Sunday –

Aug 16 – Same – Recd letter from Shuck inclosing $5 and 50 cts in 2 ct stamps – letter from wife – Bessie left for Cal Wednesday evening as her school opens next Monday – I sent letters to Shuck, wife, Billy Flaherty and Lizzie's Wildcat Joe letter – Bed 12 –

Aug 17 – Same – 90° – Received a letter from Mrs Emily Pickler Crow, Kirksville, Missouri, mother to Wm A Pickler of the Carson Mint rascality – Acknowledges receipt of my letter & papers, etc – Kind old motherly letter, thankful for my favor to him & her, etc – Bed 12 – Met Mrs McLeod at train this evening, from Va, bound for Grass Valley, Cal. Her son, William McLeod, well known on the Comstock as "Fatty" McCleod, leg broken in Merrimac mine, Grass Valley, likely to die from blood poisoning and amputation just below the knee. And he did die last evening. She was much in distress. Had short talk with her with consolatory & hopeful remarks, etc. But as stated, he was already dead, while I was talking with her, dying at 6:17 oclock. The Va Chronicle this evening says he had to be buried there & not here as hoped.

Aug 19 – Clear & pleasant – 88° – Quite a number from the Comstock & elsewhere arrived as US Grand Jurors – attended US District Court & reported for *Journal* – Met Wells Drury at train on visit to Carson – His family in Reno visiting her parents – Dr Bishops family – Also met old Jim Townsend, on his way from SF to Lundy – Bed 12 – George Neimeyer, aged 18 of Virginia City fell out of a boat in Washoe Lake this morning & was drowned. Sent letter to the Journal this evening's mail.

Aug 20 – Same – Grand Jury finished consideration of 9 cases of selling liquor to Indians, 4 of counterfeiting and one postoffice burglary . . . and found true bills of indictment in each and every case . . .

Aug 21 . . . The US Court today disposed of the indictments found by the G Jury . . . Jury engaged on Mint cases . . .

Aug 23 – Same – Grand Jury indicted Jones, Heney and Piper, coming into court with final report at 5 PM. Having no more business before them they were discharged and paid off – $2 per day, and 5 cents mileage both ways – Letter to *Journal* – Bed 12 –

Aug 24 through 28 [Early frost and a little snow – AD reporting US District Court for *Journal* – No detail.]

Aug 29 – Same – This cold snap holds on well – Frosty night at Lake Tahoe and other mountain resorts sends the campers in very lively – I reported US Dist Court – The *Tribune* contempt case occupied the day – Bed 12 – Cold – Editor H Lemmon fined $50 and 10 days in jail and his partner, Dunn $25, for contempt of court by Judge Hawley, today, for publishing an editorial intitled "The Third Act," in last Saturdays *Tribune* ridiculing the Court, calling the proceedings a farce, etc, using language and assertions calculated to prejudice or influence the minds of the Jury.

Aug 30 . . . I reported the Court as usual – Arguments to quash the indictments in the Mint cases took all day – Taken under advisement till Monday . . . McGurn's stage runaway on Geiger Grade yesterday PM and Mrs Gerrans of Va killed . . .

Aug 31 . . . Reported US Court – B S Richardson on trial for having counterfeiting implements in his possession – Took all day – Jury brought in verdict of not guilty at 9 PM . . .

Sept 2 . . . Evening Salvation Army detachment of 6, 4 men & 2 women were on street with drum, banjo, cornet, & guitar – good singing, praying, exhorting, etc – Then went to IOOF Hall – 10 cts admission & took up collection besides – audience nearly 100 – singing, dancing, praying etc . . .

Sept 3 . . . Reported Court – Case of Chris Gross for having counterfeiting implements in his possession – The Judge exercised clemency in

Editor H A Lemmon's case, remitting ½ of fine and imprisonment – so he is out again . . .

Sept 4 . . . Case of Chris Gross concluded, he on the stand all day nearly – Went to the Jury, which after being out about 20 minutes brought in verdict at 5 PM of "not guilty." Trial jurors all discharged & paid off . . .

Sept 7 . . . Frank Jennings, the counterfeiter States evidence withdrew his plea of guilty this morning and pleaded not guilty – Trial set for Nov 25 . . .

Sunday, Sept 8 . . . PM I went home with Parson Davis, Sam's father & dined with him & wife – Pleasant little family time – Letter from wife inclosing one from Bessie – She commenced teaching her school last Monday . . .

Sept 13 . . . Rec'd letter from Shuck about Wilson Butler and wife Julia who used to be in Aurora, Esmeralda in 1872 . . . & before – She committed suicide one night in bed, shooting at him first, then into herself – He was Registrar of the US Land Office there – Is now in Bodie, blacksmithing – I got all the information Shuck desired, from M R Elstner and Judge M A Murphy and sent in letter to him this evening . . .

Sunday, Sept 15 . . . My regular hay fever started in *on time* this morning . . .

Sept 17 . . . Evening attended Methodist Church reception of new pastor, Mr J M Wilson . . . Sent letter to Powning – $30 –

Sept 18 – Clear & pleasant – 11 cases of smallpox among the scholars at the Indian School, 2 miles south of Carson – developed during last 2 or 3 days and removed to pest house yesterday – one other with symptoms – Brought, it is supposed, by pupils returned to school, after vacation, from parents etc at Long Valley – Whole school vaccinated – Bd of Health attending to it today – Bed – Letter recd today from Powning, declining, etc – Frosty night –

Sept 19 . . . Sent letter to Shuck about State Prison record regarding the James Smiths – only 2 . . . I received a season ticket to the State Fair . . .

Sept 21 . . . Sent letter . . . to Powning acknowledging receipt of Fair ticket . . . *My hay fever is evidently well* . . .

Sept 23 . . . Recd letter from Lizzie in reply to my "Wildcat Joe" letter – 5 pages – nice letter – sent it to wife . . . Big tent show came to town . . . Vivian DeMonto's Superb Company, dramatic, variety, song, dance, aerobatic, medicine selling, etc – 15 cts admission . . . 2 more cases Indian School smallpox – 14 –

Sept 24 . . . One more case of smallpox reported . . .

Sept 25 – Same – 80° – Carson Day at the State Fair – 2 full coaches came from the Comstock, joined by 3 more from here . . . I was about town – at State House, State Printing office, etc – At 3 PM I telegraphed wife: "Am coming on evening express – Shall go direct to Pavilion" – Bought new pr drawers etc . . . Met Sam on sidewalk when got to Reno – Hardly knew him in his University Cadet uniform. He & Alf commenced there a week or two ago. Went with me to Pavilion – Big crowd – Met Alf and sent Sam home to bring Goodie – We took a look at the agricultural showing in lower hall, then to upper Hall, where Roncovieri's Great American Brass band was playing, and giving stereopticon views, illustrating the same with music – Very fine – Senator J P Jones gave short address – Crowd dense – suffocating – Home at 10 – met wife once more after 3 yrs – Bed at 11 in her bed, she and Goodie sleeping up stairs . . .

Sept 26 – Same – AM about town – This was "Virginia Day" – 6 big carloads from the Comstock, & 2 from Carson – PM I was out to the race track – Big crowd – good races – The band played, and all was gay – Home to supper – I played several tunes on father's old fiddle – Then Sam & I went to Pavilion – Big crowd music, stereopticon, etc – Speech by Rev Mr McGill – Bed 11 – Jack Furlong badly kicked by a horse out at the track today –

Sept 27 . . . About town – PM was at Riverside Hotel, and had quite a little talk with Senator Jones on the porch – with others – Evening was at Opera House with Goodie & Sam . . . Leavitt's All-Star Specialty Co . . . Miss Birdie Brightling, the "Banjo Queen" – Best banjo playing I ever heard or saw . . . Millie and husband and little Sara, & the Baby . . . spent afternoon & dined here . . .

Sept 28 . . . Visited Jack Furlong at the Arcade – Wife & son attending him – Likely to die – Sam walked to top of Peavine Mountain . . . and back, 20 miles – after bugs, etc for his collection – Evening took Alf to Pavilion . . .

Sept 30 . . . Jack Furlong died last night at Carson – His bowels were found to be badly, fatally ruptured –

[A newspaper clipping says the Sutro Tunnel is closed down.]

Oct 1 . . . AM about town – Left on local passenger train at 1:45 PM for Carson . . . saw Jack Furlong's funeral coming back from cemetery as I arrived . . . Ormsby District Fair commenced here today . . .

Oct 2 through 5 [AD reports Carson Fair for *Journal,* largely a duplication of the Reno Fair without Pavilion shows – Notes the death from cholera morbus of Dr J C Hazlett of Dayton, whom he has known ever since the 1860s.]

Sunday, Oct 6 – Same – About town – Sam Davis had a sort of a blowout at his Holstein ranch this PM, entertaining the Nevada Press Association, Agricultural Society officers, etc – I was invited but missed the carriage provided, and wouldnt walk three miles . . . The band and the tent show left on the evening train, together with many gamblers, Fair followers, etc. Big crowd at depot saw them off.

Oct 10 . . . Bowels bad last 2 or 3 days – cholera morbus . . . John Mackay passed up to Va & I shook hands with him at the depot –

Oct 11 . . . Letter from Joe Miller, Austin, declining and returning the 200 shares . . . Met at the 10 AM train from Va Chas H Fish, Prest of the Con Va & Cal, on his return to SF . . .

Oct 12 . . . At evening train met L W Getchell returning from short visit to the Comstock – On his return to Silver City, Idaho where he is engaged in mining operations – His son Noble nearly 21 yrs old is there with him . . . The "Carson Home Mission," opened this evening next door to Tim Dempsey's saloon – I attended – Got up by Ed Lee, a colored evangelist resident of Carson – was assisted by Rev Mr Nash of the Presbyterian church and Rev J M Wilson of the Methodist church – Sort of Salvation Army connection . . . About a hundred present . . .

Sunday, Oct 13 . . . Evening I wrote and copied a long four page letter to J P Jones, Gold Hill all about Como and the "mines" of Palmyra Dist . . .

Oct 14 . . . The sale of the Buckeye placer mining property, some 35 miles southeast of here, last Saturday, consummated – creates quite a sensation – Lane, Hayward & Hobart of California bought it for nearly

$250,000 . . . C D Lane here attending to the matter – He is ⅓ owner in the famous Utica mine, Calaveras Co Cal.

Oct 15 through 24 [AD sends Jones another long painstaking letter, writes up a fake footrace and fake prizefight at Carson Fair for Carson *News,* notes that more mining sales are going on at Buckeye and that a work party has gone out there, sees *Jane, The Lost Sheep* and *The Colonel's Wives* at the Opera House, writes a letter for Tim Dempsey, one to Mary & one to Kinzle, notes that John Mackay's son, John Jr, has been thrown from a horse & killed near Paris, that the Keyes lawsuit is coming up shortly and that the Corbett-Fitzsimmons fight is off – Suffers exhausting chills, which he treats with hot punch and the warmth of Tim Dempsey's stove.]

Oct 25 – Clear & very pleasant – cooler – no chill – Bed 12 – Met Thomas Zeimetz this PM, from Como, or Palmyra. Has been equal partner with Bob Logan in the Reno mine at Palmyra, but has just sold out his half interest to Tom Hully, the millman of Six-mile canyon for $1,000. He got part cash, and came to Carson today in order to get a deed in perfection of his title to Hully . . . The tunnel of the Reno mine shows a ledge from three inches to three feet wide – Five test runs of ore have been worked from it at the Taylor mill, Silver City, the last a year ago – about 200 tons in all – which averaged about $30 per ton, principally gold, the bullion being worth from $3.50 to $5.50 per ounce. Zeimetz and Logan still jointly own the "Golden Chariot" and the "Columbus," the north extensions of the Reno – Zeimetz with 2 or three others will probably work there through the Winter – Nobody working there just at present . . .

Oct 26 – Same – Plenty of white frost this morning – Quite a number of men have been visiting Silver Lake Mining District 35 or 40 miles from here, where the Buckeye gold placers are, prospecting, locating, or looking out for their interests in that section – Oliver Roberts came up from SF day before yesterday & went straight there with Fred Sargent, looking out for their claims – they returned this PM. Another load of supplies, with ½ a dozen men went out there day before yesterday – Quite a stir in the Buckeye boom – I was not troubled with chills this PM nor yesterday, & feel better – Bed at 12 – frosty. The smallpox is officially declared cured & gone from the Indian School – There were 24 cases in all – Today is 20th anniversary of Big fire at Va, Oct 26, 1875.

Oct 28 . . . Evening attended Consolidation of the two Carson lodges

I.O.O.F. – About 100 present, many from Va, Silver, Dayton, etc – was at banquet afterward, & made little speech among others . . . I had a sweet dream of wife and home tonight –

Oct 29 . . . Got letter today from E H Mangus, Oakland . . . Printer who used to work for me, & also on *Enterprise* – Has a small newspaper plant, & wants to go in with me & publish a weekly somewhere, he to do the mechanical, & I do the rest . . .

Oct 30 – Same – PM I was with Zeimetz awhile & he gave me more Como or Palmyra items: The tunnel of the Reno mine is 330 feet to the ledge – drifted, each way, about 400 feet in all following the ledge – About 130 ft to surface croppings at the tunnel intersection and about 200 feet at highest point of croppings – Col E. D. Boyle's tunnel, started this season, is now in about 100 feet – 2 men now working in it – It is about 140 ft below level of Reno tunnel – Evening I gave Morning *News* couple of items – Bed 12.

Oct 31 . . . PM I wrote letter to E H Mangus . . .

Nov 1 . . . Evening I attended concert or recital of Miss Lily Leale Snyder at Opera House – Local talent assisted – very good – About $200 house . . .

Nov 2 – Cloudy & variable – Bed 12 . . . Quite a newspaper change took effect here yesterday – Dunn & Lemmon of the Evening *Tribune* have ended their lease of that paper and bought the *Morning News* – Miss Annie Martin who has been editor & proprietor of the *News* for nearly 4 yrs retiring to private life – The *News* will be issued hereafter, commencing next week – Monday – as an evening paper. The *Tribune* continues by Billy Taylor, until E J Parkinson, proprietor, at Seattle, can be heard from. Big fire at State University at 2:30 PM. The Mechanical building with little quartz mill-smelter adjoining were destroyed – also a haystack or two to the eastward and a big row of sheds at the race track, by flying cinders, the wind blowing furiously.

Nov 3 through 10 [Two light snowstorms – AD attends another Haverley Minstrel show and the autopsy on & funeral of one M O Maynard, who has committed suicide because he was "out of employ, drunk & despondent," and writes several letters, including three to Senator Jones, who finally responds, "Will, in a few days, do what I can to meet your request."]

Nov 11 – Clear & pleasant – US District Court in session at 10:30 AM –

Venire of 75 trial jurors came from Storey, Washoe, Lyon, Douglas &
Ormsby – Jas Heney put on trial for Mint shortage – Jury of 12 selected
& sworn in to try the case – I was there & reported for *Journal* . . . Evening about town – Bed 1 –

Nov 12 through 23 [AD reporting Heney trial for the *Nevada State
Journal* – Short entries, usually brief notes of events reported in more
detail in the paper – Trial opens with Judge Hawley warning the news-
men (especially those from Carson) to be fair and impartial – The prosecution is out to prove Heney stole $23,000 in bullion while foreman of
the Melting and Refining Department from 1891 to midsummer 1893 –
Various witnesses explain mint processes, and Mason, the man sent from
the New York mint to investigate, explains how the loss was traced back
through mint records – Attack centers on Heney's having brought some
peculiar-looking granulated gold in sacks to the Reno Reduction Works,
which changed it into a $5,500 gold bar in late 1893 – On the 20th the
defense opens, calling experts to try to disprove that gold of such appearance could come only from a mint process, and other experts to prove
that sloppy methods at the mint could easily account for the amount missing – Furthermore the defense thinks Mason's honesty questionable, along
with that of the current foreman, and suggests that any bullion stolen in
those melts must have been taken by the now-dead Pickler.]

Sunday, Nov 24 . . . On way to the train at 7 PM I got news that
smallpox appeared at the State University, in the boys' dormitory – One
genuinely developed case and two others apparently developing. A telegram to Dr S L Lee brought the news, telling him to come down at once,
which he did. Sam and Alf are both attending University but eating and
sleeping at home, so I suppose they will quit the University at present . . .

Nov 25 – Clear & pleasant & cool – The prosecution rested . . . at
11:30, all testimony on both sides being closed – Recess till 1 PM when
US Dist Atty Jones opened argument for the prosecution, followed by
Coffin for defense, who was followed by Woodburn for defense who got
about half through when Court adjourned . . . Got letter from wife . . .
says the public schools close for a week . . . Everybody has to be vaccinated. The sick cadet is known as Long Tom Smith – 6 ft 7 high –
Bed 12 –

Nov 26 . . . Rice, "The Cowboy Preacher" and wife arrived on AM
train from Reno where they have been holding forth the last few days –
They sang and prayed and spouted religion during PM & evening on the

streets, doing good business – Woodburn closed his argument to jury at 11:30 – recess till 1 – Then Genl R M Clarke closed for prosecution in a 3 hours speech . . . Judge Hawley's charge to jury took about ½ an hour, and at 5:30 jury retired to deliberate – Still out when I went to bed at 12 . . . .

Nov 27 . . . At 10:15 AM the jury . . . came into court, reported impossible to agree and were discharged for the term . . . Judge ordered new trial of Heney, to commence next Monday . . .

Nov 28 . . . "Thanksgiving Day" – I ate turkey in regal style at my French restaurant in Hotel, next to the Opera House – Met Harry Gorham at the AM train and he told me Senator Jones *passed through Reno today for the East*. So I get *"cold turkey"* in that respect . . .

Nov 29 . . . Recd a brief pencilled letter from Senator Jones . . . on eve of departure for Washington – Has to be there at organization of Congress, so couldn't pass this way . . .

Nov 30 . . . Went to Va on train – Attended to Jones business . . .

[In the *Journal* AD reminds readers that Heney hasn't yet testified, nor has the amount stolen by Pickler been clarified – Also reports that an important witness for the prosecution, one Charley Langevin, was mysteriously missing at the time of the first trial – Rumor has it that Langevin drove Heney from Carson to Reno one night and they stopped at a clump of sagebrush a half mile out of town where Heney got off, saying he had to get some concealed "ammunition" for a friend who was leaving in the morning – Langevin saw him carry two small sacks, apparently heavy, and 2 revolvers – Langevin let him off not far from the Reno Reduction Works – "Anyhow here's the story and what it is worth."]

Dec 2 . . . New trial of Heney – Exhausted old venire remnants, 32, only securing five – Marshal ordered to get the others required on an open venire of 20 . . . Letter from wife with documents transferring our Reno home from Mother-in-Law Stoddard to a *homestead* . . .

My dear Husband:
    You will receive from Judge Webster in a day or two, perhaps with this mail, a Declaration of Homestead on this property to sign, in order to make it complete. The reason for this step I will now explain: I wrote you some time ago that I had received $600.00 from Theresa Stoddard to apply on the mortgage that was on the place; that cancelled the mortgage with the exception of $50.00 which is still on.
    Mother and I gave our note to Theresa, and she already held our note to the extent of $200.00.

Within a few days, we have learned in a roundabout way, that Theresa is dead. Those notes will be among her assets, and the heirs-at-law will doubtless try to recover their value. In order to prevent this, Mother has deeded the place wholly to me, and I am having a homestead made of it. Your signature only is lacking; then I do not see but we shall have the home,—and in such a form that it cannot be wrested from us.

I wish you would attend to it at once, then I shall breathe more freely.

How Theresa died or just when, I do not know; but she is dead; and we shall receive from her no more dog eared bundles of papers, old letters, nor silver spoons. About the last thing she sent me was a half dozen silver "five o'clock" tea spoons . . .

I fully believe that she never expected to call for the money; all she cared for was a good rate of interest, and that she punctually received. Now, I am going to make strong efforts to pay off the $50.00 still due then I shall feel that I am a woman of property.

I was anxious to have mother deed it to me long ago, but did not like to press her; for she is growing quite old and in case of her death, which must come some time, I could not hold it without a will, probate, etc.—I trust you will do your part at once, then I can get it recorded, and all will be done.

I have had the insurance transferred this afternoon. It is costing something but not so much as it would to lose all we have put in.

All are well, small pox scare about over.

We obtained certificates on the ground that *we had all* had the small pox in Gold Hill.
                                                    With love as ever,
                                                        Mary S. Doten

Dec 3 . . . Two more jurymen secured out of the open venire of 20 ordered, and which were picked up by the US Marshal about town – Another open venire of 30 talesmen ordered . . . I executed & signed the Doten homestead document, & sent it to Judge Wm Webster this evening . . .

Dec 4 through Dec 20 [Stormy weather – AD covering second Heney trial, but with little or no detail, badgering Webster regularly for his money – corresponds with wife, Keyes and the Centennial people and writes to Senator Jones – Of interest:]

Dec 5 . . . Evening at Opera House – Mahara's Colored Minstrels . . . Street Parade at noon was extra good – fine band – Very good performance . . .

Sunday, Dec 8 . . . Letter from wife says Ed Cochran leaves for Chicago this morning, where he has a chance for good employment.

My dear Husband:

Your letter duly received. The Declaration of Homestead came the day before. I have had the deed and Dec. both duly recorded, and begin to feel quite swell. The old house looks quite different in my eyes, now that I feel it is in a way paid for. It cost me ten dollars nearly to get it all arranged, but I think the money well spent. At the end of this month, I hope to take up the mortgage, then we shall be proud!

Ed Cochran leaves this morning for Chicago . . .

Millie and the children will remain in Reno until such time as he can send for them.

He leaves them in the house on the Addition where they have lived for the past year and more. I hope and pray that the move will prove a permanent one, and that Millie can soon go; and they may prosper. In the meantime, if she falls short, I shall be obliged to help out.—

Now, here is the train from the West, and this must go.

All are well, but it is cold and looks like snow.

Yours with love from all,
Mary.

Dec 10 . . . Prosecution closed with Langevin sensation – adjourning at 3 PM . . .

[Joseph (called Charley) Langevin, a "most voluble and excitable type of Canadian Frenchman," whose English could scarcely be understood, took the stand and testified as rumor had had it – He also admitted that he took $1,000 from Heney to stay hidden during the first trial, plus $400 to send his boy, who was in the wagon that night, to Quebec, and had wanted $1,000 more to stay away again – The defense questioned this behavior:] "You seem to like to get money that way, and you took a little at first in order to get more later on?" "Yes, sir-r-r, sacre! I want all the money I can get." . . . The large audience enjoyed it very much, the jury was hilarious, the judge's eyes twinkled and Marshall Humphrey tried hard to look fierce as he thumped order. . . .

Dec 11 . . . Defense on deck – Langevin impeached – Heney on the stand – Very lively & interesting . . . Letter from A B Stoddard, Secy of lodge, rejecting – with $12 I gave him when last at Virginia –

[The report to the *Journal* shows Heney attempting to undo Langevin's testimony – He claimed the gold he took to the Reno Reduction Works was obtained from his brother in Folsom, California, and that the night ride was so he could deliver some of it to the brother again when he came through Reno on the eastbound train – The brother, unfortunately, was in Ireland now – Heney didn't know where.]

Dec 12 . . . Prosecution gets lively on the defense – "Quien sabe" . . .

Dec 13 . . . Defense working along – Pickler bullion steal got in this PM . . .

Dec 14 . . . Prof Price on the stand most of day . . .

[The Court having ruled the Pickler matter irrelevant, the defense returns to Price as the leading expert and repeats the effort to demonstrate that the loss could occur through inefficiency in processing.]

Sunday, Dec 15 – Big snow storm . . . The following editorial item appeared in this morning's Reno *Journal:* [Complaints from Carson City that AD is not reporting the trial impartially.] This evening I sent a two-page letter to editor E D Kelley on the subject, and one to Judge Wm Webster . . .

Dec 16 – Stormy and very wintry . . . Sent letter to *Journal* as usual – also a note with it on *"Impartiality"* . . .

Dec 17 . . . The Va Enterprise came out this morning printed by *linotype* – The first in this State . . .

Dec 19 . . . Rebuttal going ahead and toward wind-up – Court held evening session from 7 to 9:30 – The Langevin family made the evening session very interesting and enjoyable . . .

[Further testimony begins to implicate the defense attorneys in Langevin's earlier disappearance, while they counter with assertions that such a man could not be believed, under oath or not.]

Dec 20 . . . Testimony concluded briefly, and at 10, arguments of counsel commenced . . . concluding at 4 PM . . . got letter from Judge Webster of *Journal* with $10, from E D Kelley the editor . . . and from Pat J Keyes, S.F. . . . Says our suit put off till January 22, 1896 – Evening wrote up some of tomorrows report of arguments of counsel. Bed 1 –

Dec 21 – Quite a good snowstorm early this morning . . . Clarke concluded argument for defense at 2:45 PM – The charge of Judge Hawley to the jury then occupied till 3:30 PM and jury retired to deliberate – and court took a recess at call of jury. Court called in at 8:40 and at 8:50 rendered the verdict of *"guilty as charged."* Being too late for the Western Union Telegraph office, which closes at 8, I went to RR depot. All closed, but other desirous had got Miss Hattie Humphreys the W U operator from her dancing at a ball near by – Armory Hall – and I got in with them in waking up the depot, and Miss H took command of the telegraphic department – So I got my telegram to *Journal* of verdict – Bed 1 –

Sunday, Dec 22 – Forefather's Day . . . Sent a letter to editor Kelley of *Journal* – Bed at 2 . . .

Dec 24 . . . Heney was sentenced in court this morning at 10 to 8 years in the State Prison, at hard labor and a fine of $5,000 – taken there at noon by the US Marshal – Bed 1 – Christmas . . .

Dec 25 . . . Christmas Day – Took morning local . . . for Reno . . . Found all right at home, except that Bessie had not arrived . . . Letter from her says ". . . be with you at New Year." . . . Millie and her two babies dined with us and went home in evening – Sat with Sam and Alf in kitchen telling them old '49 stories – and bed at 10.

Dec 26 . . . Down town most of day – Evening, new coat and vest – $12 – and at home – Bed 10 – very cold – Lizzie's package arrived – box of candy, and a little book pamphlet entitled "Anna Malann" – In her letter she said she would rather have written that little book than preached the best sermon ever listened to. Annie Trumbull Slosson was the author. It certainly was the best little story of its kind I ever read.

Dec 27 . . . Sam is 5 ft 10½ inches tall – 2½ taller than his daddy –

Dec 28 – Clear & cold – Bessie arrived on evening train, an hour late – at 10 – No sleeping room for me, so I went to *Journal* office – wrote item of her arrival and went to bed at 11 in lodging place over Ledbetter's store – 50 cents – Room 8 ft wide & 30 ft long – dam cold & lonely – Barney Brule sent to jail today –

Sunday, Dec 29 . . . Turkey dinner at 12:30 – 2 hen turkeys – Millie & her 2 kids, wife, self, Bessie, Sam, Alf, Goodie, and our good old mother-in-law, Mrs Sarah A Stoddard – 10 of us in all – Had to hurry up to leave on the 1:45 local . . .

Dec 30 . . . Bed 2 – Rec'd letter from Col P J Keyes – at Va City . . . wants to see me –

Dec 31 . . . Evening at [Carson] Opera House – Louis James in "Macbeth" – Miss Alma Kruger as Lady Mac . . . Quite a noise at midnight, getting the new year started in properly – a church bell rang, and Curry engine tooted her steam whistle on the street, and squirted a stream of water – Bed at 2 –

BOOK NO. 72

Carson City
Jan 1, 1896 – Dec 31, 1896

Jan 1, 1896, through March 1 [AD has New Year's dinner with friends, continues "Capital Notes" & special reports to the *Journal,* writes to Kinzle & others about the Centennial, to Keyes & Shay about their several-times postponed suit, to Bessie, Mary, sister Cornelia & Senator Jones, gets his half-fare V&T pass renewed for a year, notes that Governor John E Jones of Nevada is seriously ill in San Francisco and that Carson has had another day of earthquakes, suffers a couple of brief illnesses himself & sees Gracie Plaisted & Dramatic Co in *Tina* & Palmer's Dramatic Co in *Trilby* – Of additional interest:]

Jan 4 – Met Bill Zirn of the Zirn mine, Pine-nut, in town today . . .

Jan 11 – Attended & reported examination of Joseph Langevin for insanity before a board of Carson physicians – at the county court house – They pronounced him sane . . .

Jan 17 . . . PM I visited Acting Gov Sadler in his office – Gov Jones reported improving a very little, with a single chance of life – Sent letter to *Journal* . . .

Jan 18 . . . I attended trial of Parkinson contempt case in the Justice's court and reported it for the Journal . . .

[Parkinson admitted his newspaper remarks about the Court had been written inadvisedly and the matter was dismissed after a caution from the judge that he confine himself in the future within the "lines of decency."]

Jan 20 . . . D Circe filed affidavit in US Court today upon which Coffin will be arrested . . .

[Circe, landlord of the Carson Exchange Hotel, swore that Coffin had given him $100 to give to Langevin to keep out of sight.]

Jan 23 . . . *Uncle Tom's Cabin* played at the Opera House tonight, by the Cook Twin Sisters Company, from the East – Good house notwithstanding boycotting of the newspapers for not advertising – The papers at Va where they played last evening burned them up for not giving them free passes, though they advertised and paid for it – I tried to get in free, as a newspaper reporter, and was refused for first time in my life, so stayed out. The manager told me if any newspaper man came around he wanted to kill him . . .

Feb 3 – Variable – cooler – Usual health again – Sent letter to Kinzle, also a copy of Enterprise to wife, giving account of discharge of Prof R C Storey, Principal of the Gold Hill public schools, last Saturday, for lack of tact in getting along peaceably with the teachers under him – Been trouble last year or two from it – The schoolboys had a jollification over discharge Saturday evening, firing guns, ringing bells & whooping her up – Salvation Army established in Carson Hall next to Dempsey's saloon –

Feb 4 . . . Visited the State Fish Hatchery, 3 blocks west from the main st today – Fred Boyce manager – Wrote it up & sent to the *Journal* with note to Webster . . .

Feb 5 . . . Met E H Mangus, printer, today, from S.F. Used to work for me on the *Gold Hill News* – Got a job now in the State Printing office here –

Feb 6 . . . Letter from wife says Bessie left for Santa Clara Monday night – also that our pet magpie we have had for last year or two disappeared. "Two weeks ago Sunday last, he went out of sight utterly and completely. Whether he was stolen, or some of the wild cats about caught him, is more than I know, but I am inclined to the latter belief – We miss the little fellow" . . .

Sunday, Feb 16 . . . Sick and troubled from bad cathetral trouble – unable to introduce at all for last three days, from stricture, inflammation or something similar, near the bladder – Most of time in bed . . .

Feb 17 . . . Succeeded with catheter at 5 PM, after four days – longest ever yet – Bad, sick time of it – Bed at 2 –

Feb 19 . . . Truckee Ice Palace carnival in progress, but a failure owing to the warm weather not allowing of good ice forming . . . About 20 people from the Comstock and here went down tonight to San F to see Padarewski, the great pianist – Bed at 1 –

Feb 25 . . . Miss May Williams took charge of my lodging house today as landlady – notified me . . .

Feb 27 . . . Unwell, & dizzy-headed, so much so that in the evening when I was downtown awhile I got Bill Woodburn to walk home with me . . .

Feb 28 . . . Got off a letter to Journal giving list of venire of 50 trial jurors for next week to select from in Johnny Jones case . . .

March 2 – Snowstorm most of day – about 2 inches – First day of Johnny Jones trial in US District Court for stealing from the Carson Mint when he was employed there as Assistant Melter and Refiner – I reported – 10 Jurors selected exhausted the venire of 50, and open venire ordered for 12 more – at 1 PM court adjourned till 10 AM tomorrow – Sent letter to *Journal* – Recd letter from Kinzle – Bed 12:30 – light snow, & very cold – 16° –

March 3 – Same – Snowsqually & very cold & wintry . . . Jury completed this AM, & Genl Clarke, assistant US Dist Atty made opening statement to the Jury for the prosecution – Warren Noteware, Chief Clerk of the Mint, occupied the PM with expert testimony on the books etc of the institution – Comstock payroll for February, $64,313.16 – $5,000 short of last month – Evening about town – Bed 1 –

March 4 . . . Noteware occupied the stand all day – Letter to *Journal* – Sousa's famous band passed up to Matinee at Va this PM in a two Pullman special – 50 pieces – Quite a number went up from here . . .

March 6 . . . Hirsch Harris, Melter & Refiner testified for prosecution – Letter to Journal – Bed 1 –

March 7 . . . Fred Sargent, the express & job wagon man, got thrown out of wagon this evening by horses running away, & was very badly hurt – insensible for an hour – Head badly banged, and jaw broken in two places – Also hurt internally judging by the blood flowing from his mouth – Nearly 60 yrs old – rooms at my lodging house –

March 11 . . . Letter . . . from P J Keyes, Va – Our suit laid over till April – Fred Sargent died at 2:30 PM today – Been under morphine since last evening . . .

March 13 . . . Prosecution in Jones case through at 11 AM . . . Defense only occupied rest of day till 4 PM and quit . . .

March 14 . . . Witnesses on both sides in rebuttal . . .

Sunday, March 15 . . . The new management of Hale & Norcross came up yesterday, put in new Superintendent, J W Tangerman, and the miners all quit, refusing to work under him – He is an old Comstocker whom the boys all know too well – The mine shut down –

[The *Enterprise* clarifies – The previous superintendent, Joseph Ryan, was very popular, and J W Tangerman is objected to by the union for his failure to pay two surface men the wages he had promised if they found ore underground, in 1894, in the Western Consolidated – The change in management was the result of a long legal squabble during which, says the *Enterprise,* both Tangerman and the new "figurehead" president of the Hale & Norcross, Jeremiah Lynch, showed they knew nothing about mining, Lynch "nothing . . . further than he has observed gas pipes being laid in Pine Street," in San Francisco – William Pearce, foreman for twenty years, was fired too, and Tangerman is to fill both positions – Rumors have it that the mine will be worked by nonunion men with guards, and trouble is anticipated.]

March 16 . . . In the Jones defalcation case arguments of counsel came up. Charley Jones, US Dist Atty, leading off for the prosecution, followed by Jas F Dennis for same . . .

March 17 . . . Court room crowded, many women present – Woodburn for the defense spoke 2 hours in the AM, and Genl Clarke for prosecution 2½ hours . . . Met J W Tangerman the obnoxious new Supt of the Hale & Norcross this PM, together with Jerry Lynch, the new President of the Co . . .

March 18 . . . Jones case concluded, and submitted to the Jury at 11:45 AM – Recess –

March 19 . . . Jury came in about noon, saying could not agree – Judge sent them back – At 7 PM they came in again in same fix & were discharged – 7 for conviction & 5 for acquittal – Got all into my report to Journal . . . Letter from wife & Bessie and one from J P Jones, Washington, D.C. . . .

March 20 . . . Evening at theater – Katie Putnam and good little dramatic Co in "The Old Lime Kiln" – Very lively & amusing – Good house – Bed 1 –

March 21 – Variable & cooler – Evening a great APA meeting – Didn't attend – This PM the Va Miners Union ran Tangerman out of town, over the Geiger Grade, making him promise never to return –

[The *Enterprise* gleefully reports Tangerman was plucked from a barber's chair, lathered face and all – The sheriff attempted to deputize enough men to control the 150 miners, but all refused, and he did not interfere – The mine reopened the next day under Pearce.]

Sunday, March 22 . . . Met Tangerman this PM. He went below with Lynch, and McDonald of the H & N, who came down from Va. by evening train –

[The new management asked for the state Militia, which the governor refused, and retaliation was confined to another suspension of operations.]

March 24 . . . US Grand Jury reported finding indictments in about a dozen cases of selling whisky to Indians, etc, and adjourned till next Monday – Sentence was passed in some cases today – rest tomorrow . . .

March 25 . . . In US Court, AM more Indian whisky cases disposed of – PM the case of Henry Piper, indicted for stealing $50 worth of crude bullion while he was employed at the Mint 2 or 3 yrs ago, came up and he was convicted after the Jury had been out exactly one hour – Bed 1 –

March 26 . . . Evening Opera House – Nellie McHenry and good dramatic Co. in "The Bicycle Girl" – Very lively and good variety entertainment & good house . . .

March 27 . . . Indian whisky cases occupied court today, and the jury on one of them, "Buttermilk Jake," was out all night . . .

March 28 – Variable but pleasant – The "Buttermilk Jake" jury came into court this morning with eternal disagreement, and were discharged – Henry Piper was fined $300, which he paid immediately, was discharged with good admonition from the judge and went home to his family at Berkeley, Cal tonight – His brother, John Piper, furnished the money to pay the fine –

March 30 . . . Coffin indicted and Grand Jury discharged . . .

March 31 . . . Bed at 1 – Fire alarm, and big light north of town – Was too tired to go out to it – Said to be Sweeney's ranch –

April 1 – Clear & pleasant & warmer – Johnny Sweeney, one of the best known men of this section was burned alive in the fire last night at his Carson Dairy ranch, half a mile north of town – He was alone in his house – wife on visit to San F – Cause of fire unknown, but probably from coal oil lamp broken or upset – Indications were that he was trying to save whatever he could belonging to his wife or himself & got overpowered by heat & smoke – Body was recovered, badly charred & disfigured – In court today, "Buttermilk Jake," otherwise W N McNamara, of Va. had jury trial & was convicted of selling whisky to Indians – Bed 1 –

April 2 – Same – "Buttermilk Jake" (Cardiff Giant) sentenced to 18 months in the State Prison, and fine of $25 – Ah Jim, 10 months in the Storey County Jail and $10 – The 12 jurymen in Jones panel were discharged & paid off – The 15 remaining of the venire were excused till the 20th inst. Coffin's case came up on demurrer, and motion to quash the indictment – Argued & taken under advisement, & court adjourned to Monday next at 10 AM – Bed at 1 –

April 3 . . . John Sweeney's funeral took place from the hall of the Knights of Pythias, of which he was a member – 37 Knights on foot, and 64 carriages – Biggest funeral in Carson for a long time –

Sunday, April 5 . . . James Cronan, new Supt of Hale & Norcross M Co passed up to Va, todays train, with Jerry Lynch – Comstock payrolls for March . . . $5000 less than February, which was $5000 less than January . . .

April 6 . . . Coffins demurrer sustained, and indictment quashed in Court this morning . . . The *Daily Nevada Tribune*, Parkinson's paper, so many years in Carson suspended publication with its issue of yesterday – Sold to a Reno party, & going there.

April 7 . . . Letter from wife & Bessie – 1 from Webster, with $10, & to have no more reports till further notice – PM letter to Webster – and 3 page letter to J P Jones, Washington, D.C. . . .

April 10 – Stormy – Several snowsqualls – PM cleared off some – A telegram from San F says that Governor Jones died there at 5:50 PM – Flags on State Capitol and all over town displayed at half-mast – Vaughn at Reno, found guilty of murder in the first degree by Jury at 9 AM – At 1:30 PM, when Deputy Sheriff went to the Jail for Vaughn to receive his sentence in court, he found him insensible from morphine – Doctors couldn't save him and he died at 9:45 PM –

[The *Journal* explains that Alpheus Vaughn, 24 years old, was convicted of killing two reportedly unarmed Lister boys in Boone Canyon, near Austin, in 1893, in what was apparently a sort of family feud – Two trials in Austin had been reversed by the supreme court for irregularities, and the third was held in Reno in an effort to get an impartial jury – How Vaughn got the morphine was not made clear.]

April 13 – Variable and very blustering, closing with misty rain – Governor Jones' remains arrived and were escorted to the State Capitol by Carson Guard and citizens on foot – Remains placed in state in Governor's office with a military guard of honor – The Virginia Chronicle this evening announced change of programme: Lessees – J H Coleman, J W Scott, E D Blake, W H Kearns, J H Sullivan – Coleman manager, Scott editor etc – rest printers – Leased from the McCarthy estate, proprietor –

April 14 – Stormy – Some sunshine, with frequent snow or hail squalls and fierce westerly winds – Blew off the flag on State Capitol – Many, myself included visited and viewed the Governors remains lying in state – His face turned aside considerably, from transportation – Sealed up & cannot well be remedied – Five months today since he left Carson –

April 16 . . . Lieut Governor Sadler was sworn in this morning . . .

April 17 . . . PM was at State Printing office awhile – got some paper cut for my old note book –

Sunday, April 19 . . . Freezing hard – Fruit already damaged by frosts of the last few days . . . Met Jimmy Kneebone from Virginia at the train this evening, bound for Sacramento and elsewhere to try & better himself – He is an old familiar Comstock miner & one of the best –

April 20 . . . Second trial of Johnny Jones for Mint larceny called up – Everybody on hand – Exhausted the 18 remnants of the old venire without securing one juryman – The US Marshal, George W Humphrey, was *ordered* to get a new venire of 50 – an open venire of talesmen, returnable Wednesday at 10 . . . letter to *Journal* – letter from wife and Bessie –

April 22 . . . Out of the 50 talesmen, all from Washoe County, a Jury was obtained at 12:30 for 2nd trial of Johnny Jones – PM occupied by General Clarke . . . *The Nevada Tribune*, formerly of Carson, made its first issue . . . in Reno as a daily morning paper – Independent – C A Norcross & Co, pubs – 50 cts a month –

April 23 . . . Warren Noteware, Mint clerk, only witness on stand today – gave additional and still stronger evidence than ever against Jones . . .

April 24 through 30 [Cool, rain & snow – AD reporting Jones trial to close of prosecution evidence, with Hirsch Harris, Andrew Mason, Crandall and Ives on the stand – Receives notice that there will be no annual meeting of the Centennial.]

May 1 – Stormy – Strong, cold westerly wind and a few light snow squalls – Snowing heavily in the Sierra – In the Johnny Jones case this morning, the atty for defense made no defense whatever, but merely submitted their case on the testimony of the prosecution – US Dist Atty Charley Jones opened for the prosecution, arguing an hour & 25 minutes, till noon recess – PM Woodburn for the defense argued 2 hours, closing at 3:35 when court adjourned – I reported to the *Journal* as usual –

May 2 – Variable & cold – Genl Clarke for prosecution argued 3¼ hours – Judge Hawley's charge occupied 50 minutes, and at 3:45 case was submitted to the jury, which then retired for deliberation and the court took a recess – At 4:20 the jury came in with verdict of "guilty as charged in the indictment" – They took only 2 ballots – first, 11 to 1, and second unanimous for conviction – Court adjourned till Monday at 10 AM, when Jones will receive his sentence – Was taken to the County Jail by the Marshal and from there to the State Prison at 10 – Evening at Opera House – Ezra Kendall in "A Pair of Kids" – He very good & funny – rest not much – play ditto –

[AD's report to the *Journal* clarifies – Jones was convicted of making, as assistant melter and refiner from 1891 to 1894, false entries in the Mint's books to cover the theft, now reckoned at over $75,000.]

May 4 – Variable – The only business in court this morning was the sentence of Johnny Jones to eight years in the State Prison and a fine of $5,000 – Accompanied by the US Marshal he visited his home, wife and children, bade them good bye, & about noon was taken to the Prison in a carriage with Warden Henderson and the Secretary of the prison – Johnny took it apparently in good spirits, bade all the boys a festive "good bye, and come and see me," but looked a little thoughtful as he turned & left for the enforced quietude and retirement of his prison home – I met Webster in street & he paid me $10 – still owes me $10 for last week – Town trustees election today – Republicans and Silverites – Repubs won – highest majority, 112 out of 424 votes cast –

May 5 . . . Chas H Fish, my old time Comstock friend, now Prest of the Con Va mine passed up to the Comstock this morning – I met him at the train – Bill Sutherland, printer, Va, came down here this morning and started in on the "Jag" cure at the Keeley Institute . . .

May 7 . . . Andrew Mason left for the East this morning – I saw him off – US detectives Gallaher and Barker left last evening . . . so I guess mint matters are to take a rest for the present – I moved into room No 13 this PM, from my room 7 . . . Evening about town – Bed at 1:30 in my new quarters, that *unlucky number 13* . . .

May 9 . . . Republican State convention held at Va today to elect 6 delegates and 6 alternates to the National Convention at St Louis June 16. Delegates chosen, A C Cleveland, Enoch Strother, J B Overton, C H Sproule, W D Phillips, G F Turritin – Sent "Capital Notes" to *Journal* . . .

May 11 – Variable – light snow or rain occasionally – Sam T Shaw and Jessie Shirley Dramatic Co, about 20 including an excellent brass band & orchestra were at Opera House tonight – I attended – Admission 10, 20 & 30 cents – Jam crowded house – comedy of "Farmer Stebbins" – Very good & amusing, with song varieties – Played at Va all last week to crowded houses, the biggest last Friday night, over 1,000 present – Biggest Piper has had for years – Bed 2 –

May 12 . . . Band drill of the Shaw Co at noon on the street . . . very fine and attracted crowds of people – They are here for the week – Evening they played "La Belle Marie" to crowded house – Excellent – Fine orchestra . . .

May 13 . . . "Fogg's Ferry" – another tremendous well pleased audience . . . the boss orchestra – The daily band drill at noon is a very popular feature –

May 14 . . . Letter from wife, inclosing . . . a telegram from Alfred S Burbank, Plymouth, Mass, 13th . . . "Father died quite suddenly this morning" – Cornelia's husband, Stevens M Burbank – Sent 3 page letter to Cornelia . . . Evening, theater – "Caprice" – very good – full house . . .

May 15 . . . Evening at theater – "A Texas Steer" . . . at Va drew the biggest house of the week – Same here tonight – Every inch of room occupied – Biggest audience ever seen in Carson – Not much of a play . . . Poorest of the week –

May 16 . . . "In Old Mizzouri" – Very good play and house, and last of the engagement . . .

May 22 – Letter from wife telling of a bad spell of apoplectic nosebleed she had last evening – came on suddenly while she was writing at desk and was so copious and persistent that had to call physician to check it and care for her – letter inclosed one from Bessie – I responded to wife by return mail – Also received letter from Kinzle, Nevada City, Cal. Evening, Prof Ed McAlister called on me and I wrote a letter for him to Dr B M Woolley, Box 387, Atlanta, Georgia, relative to cure for the morphine habit from which McAlister is suffering, and too nervous to write –

May 25 . . . School trustees election today – I voted for first time in Carson – voted Republican ticket, Augustus Cutts and Charles Stewart, who won – The Keating wing of the Democratic State Central Committee held meeting here today . . .

May 26 . . . The School Trustees elections held yesterday throughout this section were hotly contested, the A.P.A. element getting in its work very effectually – making a clean sweep so far as heard from – PM I composed a long political letter to Hon J P Jones, Washington, giving the meat of the situation . . .

May 28 – Variable – sultry – 83° – At 2:30 this morning a very sharp & heavy clap of thunder waked up all Carson, accompanied by a light shower of rain – At Va it was a small cloudburst, washing the streets, flushing the sewers, etc – More showers there, here and all around, this PM & evening – Recd letter from wife, telling that Millie and her two children, Sara and Esther, left Monday night for the East, to join her husband, Ed E Cochran, at Decatur, Illinois, their future home – Also that Bessie's school closes next week – Sent wife a responsive letter – Also wrote & sent 2 page letter to Kinzle – Evening at theater – "Miss Jerry," a stereopticonally illustrated lecture – pretty good – small audience . . . The Ryan or Dennis wing of the Dem State Central Committee met at Va today, Joseph R Ryan, chairman, presiding – Great talk in Carson about Harry Brown, the absconded clerk of the Bullion & Exchange Bank here. He is supposed to be hiding somewhere in Cal, leaving his wife & family here – Said to be defaulter to a large amount from the bank, and many other creditors –

[A clip from the Carson *Appeal,* speculating on the reason for Brown's financial troubles, says:] His expenditures were very large and he invested money in anything that pleased his fancy. Any new fangled thing that came along, no matter what it cost, he bought as if he had Mackay's money behind him. At this rapid pace the end could not be far off and he simply struck the limit of his string.

May 29 . . . Frequent thunder storms with big coarse hail . . . New mint employes selected today – wrote & sent it to the *Journal* . . . The Carson river is flooded and the old Merrimac dam was washed away tonight – Big cloudburst at Empire –

May 30 – Clear & very pleasant – Decoration Day – Procession of Carson Guard and citizens with band went out to cemetery at 10:30, held exercises & decorated graves – letter to *Journal* . . .

Sunday, May 31 . . . PM & evening I wrote a four page letter to Hon J P Jones, Washington, D.C. . . .

June 4 . . . Yesterdays San F Examiner, under the head of "Played Too Much Poker," says:

> Less than two weeks ago Harry Brown was removed from his position as accountant in the Bullion Exchange Bank of Carson because he played poker. Since then he has disappeared without taking the trouble to inform all the gossips of the town; consequently their tongues are a wagging. . . . [At his dismissal some directors wanted Brown's accounts checked, but they were all correct, and Brown still had a considerable sum of his own in the bank, so his disappearance remains a mystery – One rumor is that he, too, was in the mint shortage affair, and that the missing bullion, now quoted at $100,000, was on deposit in San Francisco under Brown's name – "This, however, can scarcely be true, or Brown would long ago have been in the hands of the Federal officials."]

June 6 . . . Bill Zirn, the discoverer of the famous Zirn mine at Pinenut, was killed this PM in his mine by a big rock caving upon him – I telegraphed it to the Journal . . .

Sunday, June 7 . . . An excursion party of forty or fifty wheelmen were expected from Reno, and 26 came down from Va to help receive & entertain them – but only 3 came – Some sort of a disagreement among them –

> [Clip, *San Francisco Bulletin,* June 8 – Heney, after conviction for embezzlement from the US Mint, secretly assigned mortgages on San Francisco property worth over $9,000 to his lawyers, Coffin & Woodburn – Their attempts to cash in on the holdings have been stopped by US Attorney Knight, who seeks recovery for the federal government.]

June 10 . . . Democratic Mass Convention at Reno – Ryan-Dennis faction got away with it –

June 11 . . . Letter from J P Jones, & sent him one in return . . . Saw a dressed cubic foot of Walker river marble weighed today by Lindsay the stone cutter of Carson – weighed just 165 pounds –

Sunday, June 14 . . . At evening train I met Jim Townsend just from Bodie, bound for San F – Very rheumatic, but jolly as usual – Says he was born Aug 4, 1823 . . .

June 15 . . . At evening train I met Bart Burke bound for California, leaving Virginia for good – Been there as long as I have, and now dont want to stay any longer and die with it . . .

June 18 . . . Republican National Convention at St Louis closed to-day – Nominated William McKinley of Ohio for President and [blank] for Vice President . . .

June 19 . . . Wife reelected [assistant principal at the Reno high school] last evening –

June 20 . . . The Silver party State Central Committee today in Reno appointed or elected 15 delegates to represent the Silver party of Nevada in the National Bimetallic Convention at St Louis July 22 . . . [A] clipping from the San F *Chronicle,* June 20, gives me my first knowledge of the death of my old time mining and ranching friend [Henry W Coe] – First on the Rich Gulch of the Mokelumne in 1853, as a miner, and sub-sequently as a hop and fruit rancher near San Jose in 1860 – Good bye Coe –

Sunday, June 21 – Clear & warm – 86° – About 5 PM a 12 horse team with 2 wagons, loaded with grain in sacks was run into at RR crossing on the main street side track south of the depot by a switching train – one wagon badly smashed & load demoralized – nobody and no horse hurt – About 40 cyclers, boys & girls, wheeled to Va, returning by 10 PM, some loving couples being 2 hours on the road –

June 24 . . . Met Fred Hart on the street – arrived from San F this morning – Had long, old time chat with him – looks aged, seedy and unhealthy – Letter from wife says Bessie has come home for her vaca-tion – Steamer Tahoe launched at Glenbrook, Lake Tahoe about noon today . . .

Sunday, June 28 . . . A big base ball game brought 60 or 70 from the Comstock – Va Silver Stars beat Carson nine 21 to 6 – Great time . . .

[Clip, AD's "Capital Notes," *Journal,* June 30:] J. R. Eckfeldt, Govern-ment Mint Inspector, has been here during the past week attending to the regular annual settlement with the Carson Mint. He will conclude his labors in a day or two longer. During the prolonged investigation lasting over a year ferreting out the discovered shortage rascality, the whole business of the institution got very thoroughly ciphered down to cases and perfectly straightened out. So Mr. Eckfeldt has found it, and everything is running along as smoothly and correctly as could be desired in any mint. Twenty-seven employes, including the officials, work and manage the concern, and since the resumption of work in the melting and refining department and the purchase of silver bullion the business has very materially increased, public confidence is re-established and the former good character of the Carson mint redeemed. . . .

A telegram was received to-day from the management of the proposed Corbett and Sharkey prize fight, asking Marshal Humphrey if he would interfere in case they should conclude to pull off the fight in this State. He replied that it was against the laws of Nevada, and he would attend to his sworn duty and prevent such a fight from taking place.

The new steamer Tahoe did not make her trial trip yesterday as some papers announced. She simply took a spin about the lake, regulating and adjusting machinery, bearings, etc., and not speeding over fifteen miles an hour. Her trial trip will not be made until everything is found to be all right and in first-class working order.

July 2 – Clear & pleasant – Hotter – 84° – E. J. ("Lucky") Baldwin, the famous old millionaire of San Francisco, was lucky enough to have a shot taken at him this morning by a woman, and lucky enough to escape without a scratch – She should have used her claws . . .

July 3 – Same – 88° – Extensive preparation being made for Fourth of July celebration on the Comstock, at Gold Hill especially, where the anti APA spirit runs high – And it naturally is that way among the miners of the Comstock, largely composed of Catholics – In fact this celebration, so far as Gold Hill is concerned, comes in the light of a rebuke to the A.P.A. of Virginia, where it is stronger in the State – Therefore a celebration is on in both places, in rivalry of each other, and Gold Hill will have the best of it, as all the Miners Unions, Virginia, Gold Hill & Silver City, will combine there in fullest force, assisted by the Catholic church – Has not been a separate 4th of July celebration since nearly 20 years ago, when I was President of the Day – Carson and Reno do not make special celebration tomorrow – but all go to the Comstock – Excursion rate from either place $1 for the round trip –

July 4 – Same – AM clear, PM cloudy – Went to Gold Hill on the morning excursion train – Big crowd from Reno and Carson – I got off at Gold Hill at quarter to 12, in good time to see the procession – The old town profusely decorated in the good old time style – But the *News* office wasn't – I passed down from the depot, shaking lots of hands on my way to the News office – The front iron doors were thrown open, showing the empty, ruined inside – Streets lined with people – women and children in gayest holiday attire, etc – Soon the big procession came marching down from the Divide – I stood on the sidewalk platform in front of *News* office, same old notebook in hand, taking notes after old time style and received many shouts and cheers of recognition from my passing friends – It was a really fine, large procession and celebration, and everybody understood the incentive of it – After it passed, I passed through the old *News* office, feeling like "Byron's rooster" – After procession everybody enjoyed what they could find to enjoy – I found lots of good companionship, good eating and good drinking everywhere – lots of free tables, freely spread & bountifully supplied in Miners Union Hall, the engine houses and other places about town – and everybody ate, drank and made merry as possible – At 2 PM I quietly folded my Arab tent and silently stole away from the festive scene, footing it up over the Divide to Virginia, arriving just in time to see the grand "Bicycle Parade" pass down C st from the Divide – Only 25 or 30 decorated wheels and riders – all over in five minutes – City finely decorated, as usual on the occasion, but not much of a celebration there as compared with old times – all in Gold Hill . . . I visited everywhere, & shook everybody's hand – dined with Mike Conlon and left at 6 on return – Rained good in Carson this PM, & was still raining when I arrived – Town decorated – was about some in · evening – Bed at 1, very tired –

July 7 – Clear . . . National Convention at Chicago today –

> [Clipping from the *Daily Nevada Tribune* – An A J Stacey, about 42, was found dead at Clark's Station on the Truckee River – "He had almost severed his head from the body with a razor." – A man of "good education" and a capable mechanic, Stacey had been working for the McCormick Harvester Company until his drinking led to his discharge the previous Friday.]

The young man, A J Stacey, referred to in these clippings was in Carson a few days ago. I met him at the Arlington. He scraped acquaintance with me, and I found him a well behaved, gentlemanly, intelligent man, but too fond of drink, as he said himself – Otherwise I was well impressed . . . A letter from daughter Goodie says wife left for Oakland, Cal this morning for vacation –

July 8 . . . Lake Tahoe season in full flourish – Hotels etc overcrowded with tourists and health & pleasure seekers –

July 9 . . . Sent letter to Webster to borrow $20 –

July 10 . . . The Chicago convention nominated Wm J Bryan of Nebraska, for President on the fifth ballot –

July 11 . . . Arthur Sewell of Maine nominated for Vice President on fourth ballot . . .

Sunday, July 12 . . . Harry Day . . . received his commission today from Washington as the new Carson Postmaster . . .

July 13 . . . I wrote & sent following to the Reno *Journal* this evening in *"Capital Notes"* – [Clip on the sudden death of C C Pendergast, cashier at the Carson Mint.] – Pendergast won $25 last evening at the Arlington in a prize key bar patronage contest –

July 14 . . . Letter from wife, Oakland . . . I dined with my good old time Fort John coadjutor and true friend Major John H Dennis, at the Arlington . . .

July 15 – Cloudy & sultry – Evening some light showers and thunder – PM funeral of Pendergast, from the Catholic church – buried in the cemetery – 25 carriages – Met his brother Sam from Salt Lake – used to be in Virginia – Many from Comstock in special car – Harry Day took charge this evening as Carson Postmaster – Letter from Webster, with $10 loan rec'd today – The *Daily Nevada Tribune* after a brief career since its recent removal from Carson to Reno, with C A Norcross & Co publishers, died this morning, publishing its own obituary – Went down with Bryan and Sewell fluttering at its masthead – died from lack of support – Not sufficient field in Reno –

July 17 – Clear & hot – 94° – Letters to wife, and to Goodie, & to Webster – Tom Woodliff killed Tommy O'Rourke at Va this PM – Woodliff clerk in his father's drugstore, aged 30, and O'Rourke 44, a telegraph operator. Had been paying attention to Woodliff's sister for several months – She willing but father & brother opposed & had forbidden him the house – Young W found him in front talking to her, she at window, and after very few words shot him in left breast & lung – lived but few minutes – The murderer arrested shortly & jailed – much excitement & bad feeling against W, also his sister, talk of lynching, etc for awhile . . .

July 20 . . . Found an old horseshoe with three nails remaining in it, & fastened it up over door to my room, *No 13 –*

July 21 through 24 [AD notes his 67th birthday, writes to his daughter Bessie, now 22, gets a letter from his wife, now back in Reno, and a birthday greeting from his sister Cornelia.]

July 25 . . . The Silver Convention at St Louis yesterday nominated Bryan & Sewell, and the Populists nominated Bryan & Watson . . .

July 29 – Morning, big thunderstorm . . . It was a very heavy hail storm at Virginia, hail an inch or two deep . . . Evening I was in trouble and *homeless –*

July 30 . . . Borrowed $10 of Yerington & squared up and re-arranged things at *Room 13* – Bed at 11:30 very tired and unhappy –

Aug 3 . . . Evening I attended first meeting of the National Republican Club of Ormsby County at the county court house – Good crowd – McKinley and Hobart – 122 signed the roll . . .

Aug 5 – Fair & fine – 78° – Hon Frank G Newlands came down on the evening train from Va – Dynamite guns resounded, and bonfires blazed along the street in honor of the occasion – Grand mass meeting at the Opera House – Sam Davis chairman – Newlands rendered account of his stewardship in Congress, experience and working of the recent conventions, etc – Spoke an hour & forty minutes. Remarks well received, as usual – The Comstock Glee Club quartette enlivened the occasion by some choice songs – and afterward at the Arlington, sung some more – festive time – Bed 12:30 – breezy & cold –

Sunday, Aug 9 – Bicycle relay race at the race track this PM, between the Reno and Carson clubs – 50 miles, for fun and glory – Five mile relay heats – whole time, 2 hours & 40 minutes – Best 5 miles in 13:50. Martin Simas of Reno made best single mile in 2:38 – Carson won by nearly a mile – Then followed horse and foot racing, etc – wrote & sent letter to Bessie, Reno – Bed 12 –

Aug 13 – Fair and warm – 89° – The old *Daily Territorial Enterprise,* Virginia, came out this morning with Norris & Blake as lessees – No other change – Norris has been editor, reporter, etc, ever since I was on it, and Frank Blake, chief printer – They have a linotype machine now, run by Blake, and only a boy apprentice to assist – Small force, but very poor paper as compared with what it has been – General Robt P Keating died this evening at Virginia, of typhoid fever, resulting from his recent political convention experience amid the fearful heat at St Louis – He came home very sick all the way, and was too far gone to recover – Remains to be sent to San Francisco accompanied by his family to the residence of his wifes mother Mrs O'Sullivan – He was one of my longest known residents of Virginia, Supt of the Hale & Norcross and other mines, a very energetic politician, good citizen and a leading man among men – His loss will be severely felt by many – Native of Ireland about 60 years of age –

Aug 17 – Fair and 80° – Little old Mike Conroy was found dead on the railroad track, a short distance below the depot early this morning – lying on his face, with both hands in his pockets – He was about as usual last evening and was walking home to his cabin when he evidently fell forward and died at once – probably from a sudden attack of heart disease of which he frequently complained – He was an old well-known resident of Carson about 70 years of age, US army pensioner, native of Ireland, single, etc – Used to be about Dempsey's considerably – Hon Tom Wren is in town –

Aug 19 . . . Letter from wife says Bessie leaves Friday morning for Cal and her school duties – Wrote letter to Bessie . . .

Aug 20 through 25 [AD writes two "Capital Notes," two political info letters to Senator Jones & a letter for Tim Dempsey – Notes that another of his old friends, Jim Hardwick, San Jose farmer & Como miner, has died, that the local Silver primaries have polled only 96 votes & that the trial of Woodliff for the murder of O'Rourke has begun in Virginia City.]

Aug 26 – Clear – sent another letter to Jones – PM I visited the Keeley Institute, Dr Watson, with Billy Ryan of Va, one of the patients, who commenced day before yesterday – 3 there now – Was shown the concern, modus operandi, and given a sample flask of the whisky used by the patients – best quality – The great bicycle overland relay race across the continent started from San Francisco yesterday, and passed Reno at noon today, 2 hours ahead of time –

Aug 27 . . . In the Woodliff murder case at Va the prosecution rests and defense starts in tomorrow –

Sunday, Aug 30 . . . In the Woodliff murder case at Va the jury brought in a verdict of manslaughter about 11:30 last evening . . .

Sept 1 . . . Thomas Woodliff was sentenced last evening to 10 years in the State Prison – the extent of the law for manslaughter – Sheriff Quirk brought him down this morning in a buggy, and landed him in the State Prison . . .

Sept 3 . . . National Gold Democratic Convention Indianapolis . . . Nominated John M Palmer of Illinois [for] President, and General Simon Bolivar Buckner of Kentucky for Vice President – The Ormsby County Silver Central Committee met this evening together with various candidates & selected delegates to the County convention . . .

Sept 4 . . . Miss Lily Schneider is with her sister Elva in Salt Lake, and is soon to give a grand musicale – Schneider says she has about $1,700 of her own money, already, and is going on to New York and Paris shortly . . .

Sunday, Sept 6 . . . The Populist State Convention at Reno yesterday . . . Thos Woodliff Sr and his daughter Clara visited Young Woodliff in the State Prison today . . .

Sept 7 . . . The Silver party State Convention tomorrow at Elko . . .

Sept 8 . . . The great bicycle overland relay arrived at the *Examiner-Journal* office, New York City yesterday, the 7th, at 3:30 PM – Time 13 days & 30 minutes from San Francisco –

Sept 9 . . . The Elko convention completed its labors . . . Bryan for Pres't, Newlands for Congress, etc . . .

Sept 10 . . . Republican State Convention at the Opera House – I reported it & sent to *Journal* . . .

Sept 11 – Fair and warmer – Evening sent letter to Senator Jones, Washington D.C. – Bert Gafford [who escaped from the state prison by impersonating Warden Henderson] was discovered and captured about 11 last evening at the house at Cradlebaugh's bridge on Carson river a few miles up the valley from Carson and only 8 miles from the prison. Had got lost in the Pine-Nut section, finally wandering to where he was found – Reward of $200 offered for him – He was recognized by a woman of the house from description and finally taken back to prison – She gets the reward – He was in for seven years but now will have to stay much longer – [Harry Brown indicted for embezzling $66,000.]

Sept 14 – Clear & breezy – 73° – Primaries held for delegates to the Silver party County Convention – No excitement – Evening at the Opera House – Elleford's big dramatic & variety Co – weeks engagement – 10, 20 & 30 cts admission – Change each evening – Miss Jessie Norton, singing soubrette, and Little Pearl Landers, song and dance specialties, also Frank Cooley, son of Alice Kingsbury, are part of this company – Played "Love and Money" this evening – Good entertainment, good company and good house – Just completed successful week at Virginia –

Sept 15 through Oct 4 [AD writes an article, "Nevada Mine Developers," for the Carson *News* of Sept 17, and reports the Ormsby County Silver & Republican conventions and the county fair for the *Journal* – He corresponds with Keyes about their suit, with one James about the *Centennial* and with Jones about Nevada politics – Sees the Elleford Dramatic Company in *The Silver King, Pawn Ticket 210, The Volunteer, The Dangers of a Big City* and *New York Day by Day* – Notes that Lily Schneider has made $400 on her Salt Lake concert & gone on to Paris, that Billy Ryan of Virginia City has successfully completed the Keeley Cure, that "My old California ranching, and Comstock friend Sol Noel passed in his checks . . . consumption," that Storey County has nominated a nonpartisan rather than Republican ticket, that Reno has defeated Virginia City 14 to 3 in baseball and that the Reno and Carson City fairs have just concluded.]

Oct 5 – Fine – A few of the horsemen, sports and hobos still here – otherwise town assumed its normal quietude – Wrote and published a string of "Mining Gossip" in the News – Senator Jones, arrived from the East, went up from Reno in a private carriage over the Geiger grade, through Virginia to Gold Hill last evening – accompanied by C C Powning & Harry Gorham –

> To whom it may concern:—The report having been given circulation in Carson that Mr. T. Dempsey conducted and managed the Temple Lodging House, I take this method of denying that Mr. Dempsey has any connection whatever with said lodging house, or that I have during the past seven months, received rent from any person other than the present proprietress, Miss May Williams.
> MRS. M. E. RINCKLE.

Dempsey procured the publishment of this card [in the *Appeal*] to vindicate himself from the charge of his keeping a bad house over his saloon – made to hurt him politically in his aspirations to the Assembly –

Oct 6 . . . Evening the Ladies Relief Corps, & Grand Army Vets came down from Virginia on special cars as guests of their Carson contemporaries – Had grand banquet and reunion, and went home on their special at midnight . . .

Oct 7 . . . Dull campaign under the Purity of Elections law –

[The preceding legislature had passed a bill setting limits on and regulating the type of campaign expenses allowed, and established strict rules for submitting the accounts – The bill also outlawed the time-honored devices of anonymous printed matter, the obstruction of voting lines, and the use, for political purposes, of "any premises . . . where intoxicating liquors are sold . . . or supplied."]

Oct 10 . . . Met Keyes at the train this morning, on way back to Va – Says our suit was continued till after election, as Senator Perkins, an interested party, is out stumping the state politically . . .

Oct 15 . . . The Silver Stars base ball club came down from Virginia on this evenings train, bound for San F to compete for the SF *Examiner* championship prize –

Sunday, Oct 18 – Clear & cool – Dan A Stuart the great pugilistic promoter from Dallas, Texas, arrived this morning to try and pull off the long pending fight between Corbett and Fitzsimmons – The Nevada Stars beat the Alerts of Oakland in a baseball game at SF today – Jack Mulcahy, the "Cowboy Preacher," or "Broncho Jack," and wife discoursed on the street this PM & evening to plenty of people . . . Bishop Grace, successor to Bishop Manogue, held forth at the Catholic church today, and confirmed about 60 young people, about all girls –

Oct 20 . . . Went to Gold Hill and back on train – Good old time chat with several old friends there, and with Senator Jones at his residence – Gjd sladw tjiixrs – Evening showery – bed 12 –

Oct 21 . . . Fall weather – blustering – great falling of leaves . . . The Silver Stars returned from San F this morning, passing up to Virginia much cheered & feeling mighty good . . . PM I called on Mrs Jaqua, with George Keith – She used to be of Dayton, but now resides here, with her daughter, Mrs Joe Raycraft – She owns the old Whitman mine north of Como, and wants me to write a good notice of it so as to induce parties to do the holding work for her . . .

Oct 23 . . . Evening I sent a letter to Jones by Massey, they speaking jointly in Reno tonight . . . The letter contained speaking suggestions, as desired of me by Jones . . .

Sunday, Oct 25 . . . About 7 oclock PM the public schoolhouse discovered on fire in the rear – whole town ran to it, I among the rest – machines soon conquered it – work of incendiary – letter to wife . . .

Oct 26 . . . Visited schoolhouse this morning – Damage $500 from last nights blaze – clearly incendiary –

Oct 27 . . . About 7 PM an incendiary fire among the baled hay in shed at Schultze's hay yard . . .

Oct 29 . . . Wrote and published in the Carson *News* the article on the Whitman mine, desired by Mrs Jaqua – Wrote & sent "Capital Notes" to *Journal* . . .

Oct 31 – Fearful wind storm from the west all day . . . Jones and Stewart arrived in Reno from speaking at Winnemucca and Wadsworth – were to speak in Reno this PM, but weather so bad they came up here with Newlands on the PM local & took a special from here to Va, where all three speak this evening . . .

Sunday, Nov 1 . . . Senator Stewart came down from Va on morning local – Somebody tried to fire the schoolhouse again this evening . . .

Nov 2 – Clear, cool and pleasant – Evening a big Silver rally at Opera House – addressed by Jones, Stewart and Newlands – Bonfires and music on the streets and everybody hilarious, this being "just before the battle" which comes off at the polls tomorrow – I attended the meeting & took notes – The Carson Quartette, the Comstock Glee Club, and the Indian Band were the chief musical features, the Carson brass band doing the regular outside and orchestral music – The Opera House was crowded to its utmost limit, and greatest enthusiasm prevailed – People didnt run very late after the show was over, having in view the political work and electoral battle of tomorrow – Bed 12 –

Nov 3 – Clear & pleasant – Jones went to Gold Hill, Newlands to Reno, and Stewart stayed in Carson – National General election day – A quiet but strongly interesting election – I cast my vote in Carson, and for *William McKinley* for President of the United States – Wrote up the big rally of last evening, for the Carson News . . . Everything passed off smoothly, saloons all closed, politicians working quietly under the new Purity of Elections law, and everybody on his good behavior – Evening the telegraphic returns from all parts of the country came in lively and were received and posted at the Arlington, which was crowded with eager Americans – Senator Stewart was among the most eagerly interested – Bed at 2, at which time the returns strongly indicated a *grand Republican triumph* in the East, notwithstanding the frequent protestations of contrary minded Senator Stewart – *McKinley our next President –*

Nov 4 – Clear and pleasant – Election returns pouring in confirming *Republican triumph* –

Nov 5 . . . Went to Gold Hill and back on the train – saw Jones – Stewart left for San Francisco this morning, still badly salivated politically . . .

Nov 7 . . . P J Keyes passed to San F this evening – met him at the train . . . our case comes up on Monday . . .

Sunday, Nov 8 . . . Nevada Stars got badly beaten at SF today by the Tufts-Lyons BB Club of Los Angeles – 3 to 14 on 9th inning – Another fire at Schultze's hay yard this evening among bales of hay in barn – soon put out . . .

Nov 10 . . . Another attempt to burn the schoolhouse was made last night sometime by setting a fire in Fox's barn near by – burned a hole in the floor and went out . . .

Nov 12 . . . US Grand Jury in court today reported finding five indictments for selling whisky to Indians . . . Sent report in "Capital Notes" to *Journal* . . .

Nov 13 . . . Met Wales Averill, from Lake Valley, at the Arlington this AM – Has come in to be treated for dropsy – from stomach to knees – Dr Lee tapped him this evening – 15 holes – drew off over two gallons of watery matter – also very asthmatic –

Nov 16 – Cloudy and a fearful wind storm all day – Another attempt to burn the schoolhouse by setting fire in Fox's barn . . . was made last night – paper and split kindling was used, but the wind blew the fire out – no coal oil – PM wrote & sent State Capital Notes to *Journal* – Evening, wind died away & light rain set in which lasted all night – letter from wife today says got all paid up and full possession and ownership of our home in Reno – clear of all incumbrance – Thanks to assistance from eastern relatives –

Nov 17 – Cloudy & cold – Nevada Stars returned to Va from SF on today's train – Beaten by the Alerts of Oakland 8 to 5 last Sunday – Got letter from John R White S.F. – Sent letter to Senator Jones, Palace Hotel, S.F. inclosing clip of my State Capital Notes in this morning's Reno *Journal* – Visited Averill this evening at his room in the Arlington – Very ponderous, big man – almost helpless now and hard to handle – Was able to walk and get around when he first arrived and I met him standing on sidewalk – Now he sits in big invalid chair all the time sleeping also that way – Bed 12 – clear –

Nov 18 – Same – About noon today Charles A Jones, US Dist Att'y and Sam Davis, editor of the Carson Appeal had an encounter on the broad pavement in front of the Post office and [Davis had] his head cut and bruised by the pavement and Jones' fist – which cut his face and forehead so he bled considerably – It was mail time, many people passing in and out of the Postoffice, and Sam had an armful of papers, etc – Bystanders pulled Jones off, letting Sam get up – I was just across the street and only saw Sam being led away bleeding – Cause of the row was recent editorials in *Appeal,* by Davis reflecting upon Jones' official integrity – Professor Bristol's "Equescurriculum," or troupe of trained horses arrived on morning train, about 20 of them, including 3 or 4 mules – Paraded in the PM and showed at Opera House in the evening – I attended – 12 on the stage at one time – did lots of tricks, and feats of marching etc – very learned animals – Good house – good entertainment for *one time* – Bed 12 –

Nov 19 through 23 [AD notes the funerals of Judge Black and Vic Muller, & death of Ed Buckingham in San Francisco, writes to Mary, Jones and White, and is about town a good deal.]

Nov 24 . . . PM, in US District Court, Judge Hawley, I attended case of Mrs Hartleys baby boy, sueing for a share in the Foley estate as illegitimate son of M D Foley – jury trial – reported case & sent to *Journal* . . .

Nov 25 . . . The Hartley boy trial got through as far as to argument of counsel . . .

Nov 26 . . . Cold & wintry – Thanksgiving – Got no turkey, but only some cold roast pig at a free lunch table – Evening at Opera House – The Clement Bainbridge Company, in "Alabama" a Southern home piece – sentimental and pleasant but not stirring . . .

Nov 27 – Same – Freezing all day – 20° – Hartley boy case argued and at 3:30 jury retired – Reported to Journal . . . Evening at Opera House – Aiden Benedict's *"Fabio-Romani"* Co – spectacular, lively & good – good players & good house – A five act Roman play – Bay of Naples, Vesuvius in eruption, Palace of the Romani, false wife, treacherous friend – knives, blood, retribution – Between acts 2 & 3 Miss Grace Hunter did her serpentine dance with stereopticon effects, red fire – fine – letter from J R White – Bed 12 – Jury still out – cold –

Nov 28 . . . The Hartley boy–Foley jury came into court at 10 AM – impossible to agree, so they said, & were discharged – Stood 8 for the boy and 4 against – New trial next March . . .

Nov 30 . . . Dined with Congressman Newlands at the Arlington . . . Evening about town with Governor Sadler – Bed at 1 –

Dec 2 . . . Evening, Sharkey and Fitzsimmons fight in San Francisco – Ten rounds – for $10,000 – Decided for Sharkey, on a foul from Fitz in the 8th round . . .

Dec 4 . . . Evening at Opera House – Play of "All the Comforts of a Home," by local Carson talent . . . good local orchestra of 10 pieces . . . Very good, lively & amusing play . . . crowded house . . . Comstock payrolls for November . . . $20,000 less than October by reason of discharges directly after election – The Salvation Army including the Beck family, colored, from Los Angeles – 7 in all, paraded street & gave show . . .

Dec 5 – Variable – Sent "Capital Notes" to *Journal* – At evening train I met Johnny Trezona from Va – Going to San Francisco, accompanied by Dick Bennett and Harry Carah – Johnny badly reduced by consumption and goes below for treatment and to die – The Salvationists gave another show same as last night – Street parade and lively exercises, singing and dancing, & shouting etc in front of the jail – Some of the prisoners inside heard the glorious fun and joined in as best they could, shouting "hallelujah!" etc. Then the Army marched to the old *Tribune* office and gave another 10 cent show for the love of Christ, raising the devil and making war on hell – Great stories among the public as well as in the newspapers about a mythical air ship being seen in the heavens all over the Pacific coast – San F, Sacramento, here, Utah & farther East – even the Salvationists thought they saw it this evening, away high up, steering east – Bed 11 –

Dec 8 . . . Assessment of 25 cts per share levied on Con Va today, first for some years. Not one paying mine on the Comstock – *all* now run on assessments . . .

Dec 9 . . . At 4:30 PM all the trout fish – eastern brook and rainbow trout and one landlocked salmon – 8 of them in all – in Tim Dempsey's aquarium were killed in a few minutes by the water from the town pipes becoming suddenly aerated by reason of repairs . . . Gov Sadler & I & Tim were talking together near the tank when we noticed condition of the water was beginning to affect the fish – Tim dipped them out and placed them in a big tub of water soon as possible, but they would die – Been in that tank about 3 years – Fred Gifford took them home and feasted on them – fine eating – luxurious and noways detrimental –

Dec 10 . . . State Att'y Gen'l R M Beatty died at the Arlington about noon, of pneumonia and heart failure – A native of Illinois, aged 46 years – letter to *Journal* – Abe Cohn presented me with a pair of pants today . . .

Dec 12 – Stormy – strong SW wind – showery & muddy – Wales Averill died at 2 PM, at Judge Hawthorne's residence to which he had been removed from the Arlington some days ago – result of his dropsy, asthma, etc – Genl Beatty's remains taken from Pythian Hall to State House at 11 AM – laid in state till 6 PM, when taken to the train, escorted by K of P, State officers, friends – Went to S.F. – Gov Sadler, Supreme Judge Bonnifield, Secy of State Howell and State Prison Warden Henderson went along as guard of honor – quite a number of friends from the Comstock here & elsewhere also went along –

Dec 13 . . . Averill was to have been buried today, but no casket large enough could be found short of Sacramento, so one had to be sent for – He still in the chair where he died, & not to be disturbed till casket arrives . . .

Dec 14 – Variable, but pleasant – The Carson public schoolhouse fire bug is caught at last – At 5 o'clock this morning, Walter Kermeen was arrested in the act of setting fire to the public schoolhouse, by officer Ullrick, who has been quietly keeping inside watch of the building for several nights – About 16 yrs old, son of J J Kermeen Supt of the Dunderberg mine, near Bridgeport, Mono County Cal – out in the Bodie section – His mother & 2 sisters live here – He is in jail – The funeral of Wales Averill took place this PM under the auspices of the Masons of which he was a member – Very largely attended –

Dec 15 . . . Evening at train I met Harry C Johns, my best Austin and Comstock friend, on his way to see his mother in England – Will probably go from there to South Africa where his Bro Tom is foreman of a big mine – We took parting drink and good bye, perhaps forever – hope not – Visited Harmon Kirchner at his room in Arlington – laid up . . . with very sore big toe . . . result of pared callous . . .

Dec 18 . . . Reported the Kermeen firebug examination in the Justices' Court . . . Bound over in $5,000 to appear before the Grand Jury – Sent report to the *Journal* . . .

Sunday, Dec 20 . . . Evening I visited my good friend Harmon Kirchner – toe and foot very bad . . . I visit him every evening . . .

Dec 24 . . . A telegram from Senator Jones, San F. said to me: "Shall pass through Reno tomorrow morning" – Wrote him a short letter to San Francisco . . . did not think he would do so . . . Told him in letter about parties plotting to defeat him in his election for US Senator – Shall go to Reno tomorrow all the same –

Dec 25 . . . Christmas Day – Took morning local to Reno . . . Found my family all right – PM at home telling stories, etc – Sam and I had banjo and old '49 violin music together – Telegram from Jones . . . said: "Not leave today – be in Gold Hill in couple of days" – Evening down town short time . . .

Dec 26 . . . Evening sent short letter to Jones, S.F. with newspaper clips on Nixon & the situation generally – At *Journal* office I got in an item about Jones . . .

Dec 28 . . . A small box of holiday presents arrived from my folks . . . Harmon Kirchner came down from Carson on evening train, bringing his bad sore foot, & went on the west-bound train, at 10 for SF and the German Hospital for treatment – I stayed & saw him off . . . Met Mrs Zimmer and son Eddie on train, also bound for S.F, summoned by a telegram, by reason of serious and critical condition of her father, John Piper with heart disease – Went to *Journal* office & wrote up these items . . .

Dec 29 . . . Took the morning train to Carson – Jones . . . was along, and I got little chance to talk with him . . . I found a letter at Postoffice from my wife, sent the day I left here, with $2.50 in it to buy me Christmas dinner . . .

Dec 31 – Wintry – A few light snowstorms – very slippery – Took the morning train to Gold Hill – lots of snow there – walked down to Jones' house – we had long & interesting talk – 100 – walked up town & was about awhile among my old friends – very dead old place – walked up over the Divide to Va – Got some new arctic overshoes at Cleators, which helped out my feet very materially in the matter of warmth and travelling over the slippery places – Also got me two pairs of eye glasses, 75 cts each – Home to Carson all right on evening train – About town some – Much New Years noise with bells, whistles & all that sort of thing . . . Bed at 1, tired, and slept first rate . . .

BOOK NO. *73*

Carson and Reno
Jan 1, 1897 – Dec 31, 1897

Jan 1, 1897 – Variable – morning, a few light snowstorms – Harmon Kirchner's right leg was amputated above the knee at the German Hospital, San Francisco yesterday. I sent him a letter of condolence this morning. Was about town considerably during day and evening, making New Years calls, etc, paid up some bills, etc – Bed at 1 – Got letter from P J Keyes, S.F. today, wants $20.

Jan 2 . . . Got my cane feruled and spiked for slippery weather . . . A telegram received 11 AM at Arlington Hotel . . . said Harmon Kirchner was dying . . .

Sunday, Jan 3 . . . By evening train from Virginia I learned that John Piper died in San Francisco at 1:30 PM today – heart disease and dropsy – A telegram received at the Arlington said that Harmon Kirchner died at 6 last evening . . .

[Two clippings on Piper, of Piper's Opera House, one from the *Journal* and one from the *Reno Evening Gazette* – Piper, 63, on the Comstock for 36 years, had been a member of the Board of Aldermen, mayor of Virginia City, Storey County commissioner, and twice state senator – "In the early days of San Francisco he was prominent in upholding the peace of the community and took the same active part in Virginia . . . notwithstanding the loss of two or three fortunes by disastrous fires . . . he never lost hope," and even expanded to places in Carson and Reno – "Among theatrical people his name was as well known as that of Barnum or Tom McGuire."]

Jan 4 . . . Piper was buried at SF today – His wife and family were present . . .

Jan 5 . . . Letter from John R White, SF, confirmed the failure of my Keyes mining pool suit of $52,000 – Case to be appealed . . .

Jan 6 . . . Cold letter from —— Bed 12 –

Jan 7 . . . Great talk in the papers about the new American Flat boom . . .

[Various local newspapers report a new scheme to extend the Sutro Tunnel laterals westward to drain the old mines (the Baltimore, the Knickerbocker, the Rock Island and the American Flat) which had been unable to handle the water struck at shallow depths in the region west and south of the Gold Hill mines – Excerpts from mining reports of 1875–77 show the mines had been in good ore, but were overshadowed by the big strikes at Virginia and abandoned – A combination is now being formed to reopen them – Wm E Sharon, controlling the consolidated Gold Hill mines, is the moving force and signs of a big ledge have been found in a tunnel driven west from the Confidence shaft.]

Sunday, Jan 10 . . . Tried to get a free pass from Yerington but couldn't . . .

Jan 12 . . . Mrs Hartley was pardoned today from State Prison . . .

[Clip, *Journal:*] There were petitions for pardon and remonstrances against pardon from citizens of Reno and other parts of Washoe county presented to the board. Among the petitions for pardon were the foreman and other members of the jury which tried her. Warden Henderson of the State Prison testified as to her good behavior while in that institution, and James F. Dennis made an eloquent plea in her behalf. Her child, now about two years old, has been with her at the prison, and had she not been pardoned would probably be sent to the Orphan's Home. Rumor has it that she will leave the State when the question regarding the right of her child to a portion of the Foley estate is determined by the courts.

Jan 13 . . . Justice Mining Co suit vs the Crown Company, Barkley et al, in the US Circuit Court today brought about 40 persons from the Comstock . . . Paid Yerington $10 I owed him . . .

Jan 15 . . . Legislators and official aspirants gathering in lively from all parts of the State . . . I sent letter to Norris & Blake, lessees of the Va Enterprise asking to be reporter for the coming session – Afterward called on Yerington . . . then sent a telegram to N & B saying "Consulted Yerington – was favorable – told me to write you immediately" – Sent a letter to J P Jones . . . inclosing newspaper clips, informing & posting him up in the situation to date . . .

Sunday, Jan 17 . . . Greatest buzzinest day of all . . . Evening caucuses of both houses made full program of nominations of attaches etc . . . At 4 PM sent telegram to Norris & Blake . . . "Will I proceed to report Legislature . . ." The answer came an hour later "No" – only this and nothing more. Sent a letter to Jones to date . . .

Jan 18 – Fine, thawy day – Reported Senate for the *Journal* – Evening caucus of both houses in the Assembly chamber on US Senator – First ballot resulted Jones 35, Nixon 3 – Through at 9, too late for telegraph – Went to RR depot – got Dempsey with me on the subject – He went after the RR telegraph operator and got off the following message – Hon J P Jones, US Senator from Nevada, Washington, DC – Legislative Joint Caucus tonight resulted: Jones thirty-five, Nixon three. That settles it and we congratulate you. Answer. Dempsey and Doten –

Jan 20 . . . Dempsey received dispatch from Jones acknowledging receipt of our telegram and that letter on way to us –

Jan 21 . . . Change in my reporting, through Sam Davis – Sent letter to Jones . . . Dr Stubbs, Pres't of the State University addressed joint convention in Assembly room this PM on educational and University matters . . .

Jan 23 . . . Took morning local train to Reno in time to eat noon lunch or dinner at home . . . Staid at home and mended up Bessie's traveling trunk . . . She and I & Sam had fine little concert in the evening, with violin, banjo & flute – I gave her sheet music: "The Cat Came Back," and the "Little Alabama Coon" . . .

Sunday, Jan 24 . . . Saw Bessie off on the morning train for California as did also Sam and Goodie . . . Evening wrote sketch article on John Piper for John P Meder . . .

Jan 25 – Sunshiney, but cool – Got back to Carson by morning train – Reported Senate as usual – short sessions of both houses – Evening at theater – Carrie Clarke Ward Company engagement of a week, commencing tonight – play of " '49" . . . Pretty good play & players . . .

Jan 26 . . . Both houses voted separately on US Senator at noon – I wrote & sent following dispatch [to Senator Jones]: . . .

> Senate voted Jones twelve, Assembly Jones twenty eight. Will have forty on joint ballot. Nixon six – Our congratulations.
>
> Dempsey and Doten.

This dispatch cost $1.70 – Dempsey paid for it – Bill to allow prize fighting in this State passed Assembly this AM getting 20 out of the 30 votes –

Evening at theater – play of "Kitty O'Connor" – fair house and tolerable play . . .

Jan 27 . . . Joint convention, on US Senator. The result was merely a confirmation of yesterdays balloting . . . 40 votes out of 45 . . . I was at the banquet on the Jones proposition at the hotel Arlington. Grand affair. About 150 plates – Fine speeches, etc, lasted from 9:30 till 2:30 – Bed – Letter of acknowledgment to me personally from Jones today . . .

Jan 28 . . . The bill to regulate and restrict glove contests in this State which passed the Assembly day before yesterday passed the Senate this AM by 9 to 6 . . .

Jan 29 . . . Gov Sadler signed the Glove Contest, prize fight bill allowing Nevada to be the only State in the Union where the Corbett-Fitzsimmons prize fight can be pulled off on the 17th of March next – Considerable popular excitement over it and great expectations etc . . . Sent a letter to Senator Jones . . . Evening at theater – Play was "Underground," a Pennsylvania coal mining sketch – not much – small audience –

Jan 30 . . . Much snow fell in the Sierra last 24 hours – Evening at Theater – "Ten Nights in a Bar-room" – This is the last of the Carrie Clarke-Ward & Burch Company engagement – They go to Va next . . .

Feb 1 – Stormy . . . Evening attended lecture discussion on Woman Suffrage – Held in Senate Chamber – Crowded – Mrs Williamson, formerly of Austin, made the principal talk – Summerfield of Reno next, against it, and Denton, Skaggs et al all the same . . .

Feb 3 . . . Letter to wife – George Millar, formerly of Austin, in town – drumming for crockery . . . Very drunk . . . been here since Tuesday – Is on a very stupid drunk – Letter from Jones . . .

Feb 4 . . . W K Wheelock, partner with Dan Stuart arrived this morning, says Stuart will be here also next Sunday or Monday . . . Then the final arrangements will be made for the Corbett Fitzsimmons fight – Put George E Millar to his bed at the Arlington about 10 oclock this evening – still keeping up his drunk and getting sick on it . . .

Feb 5 . . . About 9 oclock AM . . . fire alarm – State Printing office – Gasoline tank of the 4 horse power gasoline engine exploded – About 12 gallons in it – flew all over everything in the room & blazed good – 12 printers in composition room, and 7 women in binding room got out lively – Only man hurt was Jim Huling . . . was working a Gordon press within 15 ft of tank . . . so he rushed out like a comet with a fiery tail. Succeeded in brushing off the fire, but both hands badly burned. Whole inside of the room badly charred . . .

Feb 6 . . . Edward G Cook, connected with [blank] Brady, manager of Corbett, arrived this morning . . . Has examined the accomodations of Steamboat Springs & come from there . . . with view to best place for Corbett's training – will see Walley's Hot Springs, Genoa, also, and decide shortly – W W Naughton, the S.F. Examiner famous special correspondent also arrived this morning to stay till battle is over – Evening sent letter to wife – Recd letter circular from Ethan Allen Doty, 70 Duane st N Y City . . . Wants my subscription for copies of History of the Doty-Doten families at $3 each, which he is engaged in the preparation of – Dont think I want it . . .

Feb 10 . . . Was introduced to Harry Corbett, Jim's brother . . . He came yesterday on lookout for business . . . Evening sent a letter to M H DeYoung of the SF *Chronicle* asking chance to report for it on the prize fight campaign . . .

Feb 11 . . . Dan Stuart, Wheelock, Brady and all the others except the fighters themselves . . . arrived on morning train – Settled at noon conference with Stuart that the fight comes off in Carson . . . Sent letter to Sacramento Bee about reporting tonight –

Feb 12 . . . Evening a meeting of citizens – conference as to how to provide for reception and storage of the great big incoming crowd to the big fight – Lots of talk and all left to Wheelock and Gray, arranging committee . . .

Sunday, Feb 14 . . . Letter from SF *Chronicle* saying had sent a man . . . Big lot of strangers already arrived & daily arriving – promoters, fighters, attaches, gamblers, business hunters, detectives, newspaper correspondents, etc – All business places taken – no unoccupied houses, and hotels & lodging places getting filled up rapidly – Boom well started – The fighting arena to be in northwest corner of race track infield . . .

Feb 15 . . . Evening received $10 from Livingston for services rendered . . . Joint convention . . . in the Assembly Chamber . . . to consider submission of woman suffrage bill to the people at next general election . . . Addresses by Mrs J R Williamson, et al – Considered in

Committee of the Whole – Voted to report bill without recommendation – At 10 adjourned –

Feb 16 – Stormy – AM light rain – PM heavy snow storm set in – J J Corbett arrived on morning train with 2 brothers, trainers – Great crowd at the depot to see him arrive – Saw him at the Arlington playing billiards – sized him up – About 6 ft – 180 lbs – 31 yrs but looks about 45 – No good color in face, in fact looks rather pallid & careworn & nervous – keen black eyes & resolute expression – uneasy quick movements – A lot of young hobos and vags were picked up yesterday by local officers & collected into jail – 14 of them, from outside – All shipped to Reno in a box car by local train – cattle & hog train at 10 AM – The woman suffrage bill was killed in Assembly this PM 16 to 14 – Bed at 12 – snow 8 inches & still snowing – Martin Julian Manager for Fitzsimmons arrived this day. Fitz married to his sister –

Feb 17 . . . Nearly or quite a foot of snow . . . Corbett was about the Arlington most of day, & evening quite a crowd, including myself watched him playing billiards with his brother Joe. 2 balls – cushion shots – hit three cushions or more before hit other ball – Jim is a great expert at it. The woman suffrage vote of yesterday PM was reconsidered in Assembly this PM and on final passage stood 15 to 15 – therefore lost and settled for next six years at least . . .

Feb 18 – Heavy snowstorm most of day, piling up additional 6 inches . . . Snow plows kept running steadily all day between here & Va . . .

Feb 19 . . . Sleighing splendid . . . Corbett & his trainers & attaches stay in town mostly, trained some in Opera House this PM, sparring, wrestling, etc – Evening he played billiards . . . Letter from Sac *Bee* reply to mine – Dont need anybody – Coming over here to the fight & report it –

Feb 20 – Snowstorming . . . whole country snowed under . . . Fitzsimmons came on PM local with his trainers, etc . . . Evening was at Arlington House & saw Fitzsimmons playing billiards – Sized him up some – Looks to me to be in better condition than Corbett so far as healthy color and general appearance are concerned – Will train at Cook's Grove on Carson river, just above Empire . . . Big crowd found him at depot, bigger than Corbett's reception . . .

Sunday, Feb 21 – Clear & pleasant, but cold . . . Thermometer this morning at 7 scored 1 degree below Zero . . . Saw Fitzsimmons big dog at the Arlington this morning – Danish mastiff, dark or black color, short hair, like satin. 182 pounds – Was taken out with other dunnage & paraphernalia to Cook's Grove – Neither Corbett nor Fitz about town this day – at their respective training quarters . . .

Feb 22 . . . Letter from wife, with one from Bessie, and piece of poetry – 9 verses in *Latin*. Very good – copied it and sent Bessie and Goodie back in letter to wife – Clearing off snow etc for the fight arena commenced today . . . 8° below Z in early morning . . . Indian killed by a white man at Yerington, Mason Valley yesterday – Indian trouble – troops called for, etc – Adj Gen Galusha went out to tend to it . . . Corbett is training at Shaws Springs, 3 miles north of Carson –

[A clipping from the *Appeal* says that two whites, Silas Logan and Charles Gunzel, killed an Indian – The whites had been following a squaw about, "trying to keep her from going out to the Indian camp" near Wabuska, and when the Indian tried to help her, Logan hit him with an iron bar – The slowness of the justice of the peace in issuing warrants "has caused the Indians to think there is an effort made to protect the criminals," who had departed, unmolested, though officers were now on their trail – Trouble is expected.]

Feb 23 . . . 14° below Zero early this morning – The Mason Valley Indian outbreak amounts to nothing . . . The fighting arena foundation set & marked out . . . Evening at Opera House – "All the Comforts of a Home" . . . repeated . . . Jim Corbett with a lot of outside newspaper friends were in a box . . . He bowed to the audience in response to fond calls – Vernon Harrison Hartley – the Foley Child – died at Reno Sunday of scarlet fever – Another closing page in the tragedy – 2 yrs old –

[Clip from the Carson *News* – General Galusha had returned to Carson, and the Indians were quieting down – The Indian killed was a prominent member of the tribe, a graduate of the school in Grand Junction, Colorado:] Logan and Gunsel, the two young white savages who assaulted the squaw and afterwards murdered her natural protector, were arrested at Winnemucca. They will be taken back to Yerington and tried, and it is hoped punished. In case they are not and the Indians see fit to take the law into their own hands no one can blame the long suffering Piutes. . . .

Feb 24 . . . Fitz & his big black Danish Mastiff, *Yarum,* took a foot run from their training quarters at Cook's ranch through the snow, by way of exercise, & were here at train time to see who arrived – Then they went back – Some of his training companions were along in a buggy . . .

Feb 25 . . . The New York Bloomer and Extravaganza Company came this morning from Reno, where they had good house last night – Paraded at noon up & down street – A dozen bloomer ladies with brass band of 8 men – They played at Opera House tonight. Was there – Big house. Bed 12 –

Feb 26 . . . About 100 men working down at the fighting arena, which is getting up into shape rapidly . . . This morning W A Brady, Corbett's manager, and Charley White, who will be one of the seconds in the ring, arrived, and went out to Shaw's Springs . . .

Feb 27 . . . Warm spring day – 45° – snow went off rapidly . . . Legislature held full sessions . . . Judge Rives of Eureka came in today – Evening I was with him, also Sam Davis, & we had a little oyster supper . . .

March 1 . . . 120 men working on the arena . . . Most . . . are from the Comstock.

March 2 . . . Corbett's wife and his sister came on train this AM, & he took them out to the Shaw's Springs in carriage . . . Senate held AM & PM long sessions and evening from 7 to 10 – gave me lively work . . .

March 3 . . . Got in an editorial to C W Stone – article entitled *"Taxation of Miners."* Rives $10 . . .

[Clip, Carson *News* editorial – AD opposes Assembly Bill No. 74, which proposes that for tax purposes, on ores worth less than $12 per ton, no more than 90 percent of the gross yield may be deducted for mining and milling costs – "This leaves ten per cent which must be taxed, profit or no profit to the miner. What a discouraging absurdity. The great majority of our mines throughout the State are not paying expenses. . . . Let well enough alone."]

Met old Bill Davis at Appeal office, afterward at Dempsey's – He is an old prize fighter of note – used to be at Va on the police. Kept a saloon also – Killed Billy Ash while policeman – Had Japanese wife . . . is watchman down at the arena . . . Evening sessions both houses – Keeps me busy – Bed 1 –

March 4 . . . Inauguration Day – Telegraph says grand affair – Over 40,000 people spectators – Mac is all right and "country's safe" and under *our good old Republican administration* once more.

Sunday, March 7 – Variable, with sunshiny, snowsqually and cold – Letter from wife says she was here with her class Friday. Visited Capitol, schools, prison, Arena and other places – Was in Senate twice, seated behind me, but did not like to call my attention or trouble me, etc, under the circumstances – Wrote her a letter in reply – By special invitation from Sam Davis I rode out to his Holstein ranch about 2 miles north of town to a press banquet given by him to representatives of leading papers East and West – mostly East – About 30 people at tables including Davis, wife & two daughters, and Miss Bessie Mighels – Nice collation of usual good things & plenty of white wine & claret – Howard C Hackett, sporting editor NY World, was toast master, etc – jolly good fellow . . . toasts, speeches, sentiments and jolly fun winding up with some singing – In response to call I made a brief speech – Broke up at 2:30 – Rode out & back with Hal Mighels in 1 horse cart – Bed at 3 – cold & inclined to storm.

March 8 . . . Both Houses . . . held evening sessions – Hardest work of the session for me on my duplicate reporting . . . Last day . . . but they will run till get through – But no salary after today, except for the attaches – Sam Davis $10 – Bed 1 –

March 9 . . . The great arena about completed & fighters in full active training – All sorts of games running all about town & a host of gamblers from all parts of the country . . .

March 10 . . . At noon parade of Makara Minstrel Co – I was at evening performance. Very good. Big house . . .

March 11 . . . Met with Scott Jackson last evening and this evening – 6 ft 2 inches of very black nigger from Australia – a leading member of this troupe – 2nd cousin to Peter Jackson the famous pugilist . . .

March 13 . . . Legislature fought to a finish at 12 tonight – I reported of course . . .

Sunday, March 14 . . . By morning train I sent to Fred D Plunkett, Secy of Exempt Firemen Association Va, *Memorial Tribute,* on death of John Piper, as desired . . . Letter from wife enclosing one from Abbie V Davis, Hyannis, Mass . . . daughter of my sister Euphelia . . . Among the compliments passed in the closing proceedings of the Senate last evening was the following resolution [reprinted here from a newspaper clipping] –

> Whereas the press of the State of Nevada has largely assisted the Legislature in its efforts to enact beneficial legislation, Therefore be it Resolved: by the Senate that our sincere thanks are tendered to the press of Nevada

but especially to Alf Doten for his constant daily efforts to correct and render presentable our many errors of speech and logic: to cover our many faults with a broad mantle of charity as best he can, and extolling such small virtues as in a brotherly way he may have formed in the Nevada Senate during the 18th session. Adopted.

March 15 – Clear & springlike – Every train brings fresh cursedness from outside – Monte Carlo in full blast and pugs, gamblers, newspaper reporters, scrubs, whores and sons of bitches in plenty – Sharkey arrived with lots of them on PM special, 2 cars from Cal, 5 PM – and another lot of 60 or 80 arrived on another special about 10 PM from California – more from Cal, and the Eastern specials will arrive tomorrow – Things are getting rapidly to a focus – Evening I was at theater – "Ida Fuller and her company of all star entertainers." Variety show with Ida Fuller, sister to La Loie Fuller, in her wonderful illusion dances – Really wonderful and prettiest I ever saw in that line – Illusion drapery, gauzy, and colored lights, etc – Big house – Bed at 1 – More gambling games than anybody ever saw – like California in '49 – The Fuller Co for four nights . . .

March 16 – Variable – a little snow in the air and generally not very pleasant – not auspicious for the big coming morrow – Morning trains late – Reporter passenger in at 12:40 – Maggie Moore on board – met and *kissed* her – She is from Europe now, from a visit there to Paris etc – and going back to Australia very soon – Went up to Va with her brother-in-law Matt Riehm, but will return in the morning – About 30 cars of specials arrived today adding a thousand or more to Carson – Lots more *pugs* . . . Sullivan, old John L . . . arrived about 10 oclock from the East – I received $20 ticket to the arena big fight from Al Livingston this PM – Carson plum full, but more coming on the morrow – Bed 2 – Evening at Opera House . . . I met old Capt Dave Numana this PM & took him into Dan A Stuart's office and introduced him – Chief of all the Piute tribe – Wants to get in and see the big fight tomorrow – They arranged it. Cowboy tournament advertised for yesterday & today at Sweeney's race track just north of town – J W Buckley of Idaho, manager – Lassoing & tying wild steers – riding bucking broncos, wild mustangs, cayuses etc, by Scoop Lloyd, Bill Ireland, Jimmy Hayes, Jimmy Martin & other noted riders – Proved a failure from lack of attendance.

March 17 – Clear fine day – St Patricks Day – Special trains from Va, Reno and everywhere – Streets overcrowded with all sorts of people and all sort of moral cussedness – Nate Roff $5 – At 10 AM was seated in the arena, about 50 ft from the ring, among Fred Fairbanks of the Lyon

Co Times, Alf McCarthy, Walker Lake Bulletin & D S Truman, Reese River Reveille, et al – About 6,000 or 7000 or more present, including 20 or 30 women scattered throughout – arena capacity 18,000 – John L Sullivan on stage ring challenged winner, $5,000, Tom Sharkey followed with challenge $2,500 . . . At 12 Fitzsimmons and Corbett entered the ring – Toed the mark at 12:10 – Fitz refused to shake hands and round 1st commenced – with cautious sparring – good exchanges etc – 6th round Fitz bloody from cut lip and downed on one knee, Corbett having a little the best of the fight thus far – 9th round Fitz got in best of it and held his own till the 14th round when he got in a big left lick on Corbett's heart and another quickly with his right on the jaw. Corbett fell on one knee, and sank over to the right sideways, grasping the ropes – Couldn't get up or in on call of time, and Fitz was declared winner. Corbett got over his heart trouble and went for Fitz and everybody else on the stage, in a wildly rattled manner till subdued by friends – Everybody then went home – Two more fights between lesser celebrities, which I cared not to see, later on in the PM. Evening trains took away large numbers, and the most notable fight of the century was ended – Best I ever saw, and more money changed hands – millions – About 9 in evening W F Bradford, a faro dealer at the Magnolia saloon was shot by another gambler, W H Smith. Had small scrap inside saloon, and ended on the sidewalk in front. Smith was arrested and jailed, and Bradford taken to his room down street. Dr pronounced wound probably fatal, as 45 calibre ball passed through, and out at back . . . other events of the day passed very smoothly and satisfactorily – Evening about town – Bed 2 – Met Maggie Moore Williamson on street in company with Matt Riehm her brother-in-law . . . Corbett left for Reno soon after the fight by a special car and locomotive. [Many clippings of the fight from various Nevada and California papers are pasted into the journal here.]

March 18 – Stormy, filthy day, snow, mud etc – Good thing that St Patrick got in ahead and all right . . . Train this evening took 5 carloads or over 300, *L*, Legislators, gamblers, hobos, newspaper men & sons of bitches – big lot of them, and plenty still left – Wrote letter to Judge Henry Rives . . . Bradford shot last evening, died at 6 PM today. Prof Ed McAlister also died about 9 PM . . . Worn out with morphine and other dissipation – Fine piano player . . .

March 19 . . . Sent another letter to Rives inclosing what I left out in yesterday's letter . . . Evening about town with some of the boys and to bed at 2 . . . Fitz & wife & baby left for San F. tonight . . . Billy

Smith, one of the fighters in the arena, Wednesday, was on the train and drew a pistol to shoot a man he quarreled with, & was arrested & taken to jail –

March 20 . . . All quiet . . . Nearly all the gamblers & sports have left, and games closed – Dan Stuart left on evening train . . . Carson settled down to the old groove . . .

Sunday, March 21 . . . Was at the last meeting of the Salvation Army tonight – Miss Van Dyke last soldier remaining . . . She was assisted tonight by other church folks – Good house, but not very profusely benevolent. She only made out to collect $3.25 to help her to get away . . .

March 22 . . . Letter from wife, inclosing booklet, poetical, "By Woodland and Sea," by my niece, Euphelia's daughter, Mrs A V Davis of Hyannis . . . 24 pages – including 6 engravings of Cape Cod scenes – Very nice poetry . . .

March 23 . . . Coroners inquest in the matter of the killing of Bradford . . . ended this PM, in the dismissal of deft on grounds of self defense . . .

March 25 . . . PM and evening I composed a letter to J P Jones . . . Very few people to be seen about streets or saloons tonight – Carson seems almost deserted . . .

> [Clip from a local newspaper:] The Kinetoscope people, who purchased the exclusive right to reproduce the Corbett-Fitzsimmons fight are beginning to realize that their exhibition will be met by opposition on nearly every hand. The appeal of the Women's Christian Temperance Union to prohibit the reproduction has resulted in laws and ordinances in several parts of the country which prohibit the show, while others permit it under heavy license.

March 26 . . . PM had a colloquial row with Sam Davis – got $5 – and got mad also – Bed 12 –

March 30 . . . Sam Davis paid me $5, balance due of $20 for legislative reporting . . . 2 Salvation Army lassies arrived from Reno this morning . . . Started up the works this evening again . . . Mrs Trudell, a French Canadian lady of this place was paid $3,750 today by agent from the Little Louisiana lottery . . . won it on a 2 bit ticket – She paid agent $50 for traveling & incidental expenses, and gave $10 to Willie Clarke, from whom she bought the ticket – A story is circulated that Phillips the agent and telegraph operator in the RR office Reno was caught by his wife evening before last in a room with Mrs Hartley – great row over it – family bust up –

March 31 . . . Camilla Urso, the famous lady violin virtuoso of years past gave three concerts at Golden Gate Hall S.F. . . .

[Clip, local newspaper:] Professor Michelson, of Chicago, has won fame by an important discovery regarding ether. Professor Michelson is a Virginia City boy.

April 1 . . . Was at State Capitol awhile hunting up some old legislative bills of this session . . . for John B Gallagher – about Lyon County bonds . . . May Williams, heretofore my landlady ceased as such and evacuated the premises this day, therefore I am an orphan . . .

April 2 . . . Mrs Rinckle the proprietress . . . came in today and resumed possession . . .

Sunday, April 4 . . . I had this lodging house all alone today – no other lodger, and no new landlady – Take care of my own room . . . In letter to wife I sent for my old trunk –

April 5 . . . Got letter from Henry Rives, Eureka . . . Will hear from [him] again shortly with $35 . . . US Grand Jury in session today – Judge Hawley sat down on Sam Davis of the Carson *Appeal* considerably . . .

April 8 . . . The trial of Logan at Dayton for killing Jim King, an Indian, at Mason Valley Feb 13th is progressing at Dayton this week and creates much interest among the Indians generally, many of them gathering at Dayton and the court room . . .

April 9 . . . Logan's trial . . . concluded today, with a sentence of 30 years in State Prison . . .

[Clipping from the *Journal,* reprinting an article in the *News* – The next day set for the hearing on C A Jones's assault upon Sam P Davis:] Mr. Davis through the Appeal has tried to make this case one of national importance . . . It was a pretty hard dose for a 190 pound heavyweight to be knocked out by a featherweight of 125 pounds, and particularly in so short a time. Some excuse had to be offered for it and . . . Sam dropped on the brass knuckle theory. [After efforts to have Jones arrested by local authorities fail, Davis] proceeds by insinuation to create a prejudice against Jones as having received money from Dan Stuart to quiet any possibility of federal interference at the [Fitzsimmons-Corbett] fight, etc. . . . absurd . . . Yet Sam has pushed this racket until THE NEWS has exposed the whole thing . . . Now Sam you are growing old and consequently peevish. You are not as funny as you used to be . . . Besides, how about the admission you made before a legislative committee that you received $10 for a severe editorial criticism on a certain bill in the last Legislature . . . You had a scrap and got licked, now acknowledge the corn. "A squealing pig never gets near the trough."

April 10 . . . . Wm McCluen, yardmaster at the RR depot lost both legs below the knee this morning by a heavily loaded box car passing over them – He accidentally slipped in adjusting the brake – Dr Byrne who took the Keeley cure here about 3 yrs ago and afterward lectured on the subject eulogistically, and has since resided in San F, returned yesterday to take the cure again – very drunk – Went back on it the last five or six months . . . This PM I attended argument before Supreme Court of petition for mandamus to oust Cronan, Supt of Hale & Norcross mine, and put Joe Ryan the newly elected Supt in his place – Lawyer Baggett of SF, for Cronan, spoke 1½ hours – Deal for Ryan – Case continued till 10 AM Monday –

[A clipping clarifies that this new confusion was the result of a split into factions at a directors' meeting, and a spurious handling of proxies by the Cronan side.]

April 12 . . . . Bundle of 3 copies of the *Students Record,* a monthly little magazine got up by the Students, etc – articles, meritorious, etc, by Sammy and his mother, which interested me much – PM was in Supreme Court awhile listening to Lawyer Baggett . . . He is abnormally long-winded . . . The editors of our two Carson dailies are at war of crimination and recrimination – giving each other thunder every day . . .

April 13 – Clear & spring-like – Wm McCluen who lost both legs last Saturday morning is getting along all right – Mrs Rinckel left for San F tonight – Letter from Kinzle, inclosing one from Andrew Nicholls, Los Angeles – Bed 12 – Quite an excitement stirring at & about Carlin in the eastern part of the State relative to extensive gold placer mines discovered, up the Humboldt river, a little over three miles above or to the east of Carlin – Gold belt reported to be richer and more extensive than any placer deposit ever before discovered in this State – The discovery was made and the claims staked by the Bernard Mining Company, consisting of Messrs Bernard, Moore and others of Carson. Been traced for some miles – Auriferous deposit of red oxide cement and quartz – in high bars and reefs running back from the river – test of 80 lbs sent to Carson mint, went $16 gold per ton – Other tests show all the way from $12 to $16 per ton . . .

April 15 . . . Col P J Keyes returned from S.F. . . . went down March 15 to attend to our mining stock case – Has got it appealed to the Supreme Court of California – I borrowed $10 from Ed Yerington – Paid May Williams $6 I owed her for my room rent . . .

April 16 . . . Found my trunk at the freight depot . . .

Sunday, April 18 . . . In evening I attended M E Church – literary & musical exercises . . . organ accompaniment – Good choir – Mrs A L Smith sang the new piece of "Lake Tahoe Gives not up her Dead" – originated here, & printed at *News* office – Pretty good but not destined to be extensively popular – too sadly sentimental, both words & music . . .

April 20 . . . Sent 2 letters to Hon Henry Rives . . .

April 21 . . . Hale & Norcross Supt Case, Ryan vs Cronan, came up in Supreme Court today . . . About 8 oclock this evening I was at work fixing a bed in Room No 10, & while sitting in a chair resting, I suddenly heard a very distinct voice, as of some one speaking or grunting through a tube – distinguished no words – Only lasted a couple of seconds or so – Don't understand – Guess it was a spook –

April 22 . . . Busy at rooms all day – Am moving from No 13 into room No 10, at the rear end of the building – Prof Tom Cara from Virginia passed on the train last evening bound for Angel's Camp, Cal. where he goes on a visit to his married daughter, and perhaps to stay . . . I met him at the train and bade him the best of luck . . . Johnny Trezona, another good friend of mine on the old Comstock died at San Francisco Monday morning of miners consumption – age 47 yrs . . . Native of Redruth parish, Cornwall . . .

April 23 . . . I completed my removal from Room 13 to Room 10 today at 5 PM when I took down the old horseshoe from above the door and transferred it to over the door of my new room . . .

April 24 through 28 [AD does some mending and washing, works to rid his new room of mice, exchanges letters with his wife, notes that an unknown man has killed himself in Carson with a pistol, that Reno has beaten Carson 17 to 12 in baseball and that his friend Dave Tyrrell, once superintendent of the Imperial mine, has died in Salt Lake City.]

April 29 . . . A strike of rich ore is reported in upraise above the 1650 level of Con Va mine . . . and stocks are up in consequence – Dr Sylvestro Ambrosio Ambroseuf, otherwise known as the "Russian Doctor" left very suddenly this morning for parts unknown, leaving his wife here – The authorities were getting after him for practicing without a genuine legitimate diploma – has been here four or six months, and I have considered him as a first-class fraud . . .

May 4 . . . Mrs Rinckel, my landlady, returned from her visit to San Francisco this morning . . .

May 5 . . . Letter from Henry Rives . . . says will be here Monday next, & cash up . . . Mrs Rinckel visited the lodging house this PM, and we had quite a talk and "inspection" . . .

May 8 – Clear & pleasant – Ice thick as window glass plentiful this morning – Fruit blossoms were extensively killed – Bed 12 – cold as last night – Day before yesterday . . . I received an ultimate notification from Fred D Plunkett, Secy of the Virginia Exempt Firemens Association that my delinquent dues amounted to $9 and that I was liable to suspension from membership. At the bottom he wrote: "Alf, I am instructed to forward this by the Association as the last appeal. Plunk." So, as I am unable to financially come up to the racket, I shall very probably be read out of the Association at the regular monthly meeting tomorrow. The Heney $5,000 fine and mortgage case came up in the US District Court again today – I didn't attend, but the *Appeal* tells the story as follows:

> [US District Attorney Jones states he has proof that Woodburn and Coffin, the defense attorneys in the Heney-Mint trial, meant to enter into a conspiracy to sell the mortgages on the property which, at the eleventh hour in jail, Heney had assigned to them – The principal charge is that the mortgages were granted as a means of preventing the government from confiscating the property in payment of the fine – It is unclear whether the attorneys are under suspicion for giving some of the money from their sale to Mrs Heney, or for not giving her any.]

Sunday, May 9 . . . A double bicycle styled the "Companion" appeared on the street this evening . . . Lady & gent rode abreast, & afterward 2 gents – Very sociable affair –

May 10 . . . Judge Henry Rives arrived . . . Owes me $35 – Shall meet him "a little later on," as he told me . . . J W McCrimmon, about 20 yrs old suicided with big dose of morphine at Washoe City night before last – crossed in love, too much beer, etc – Member of Carson Fire Dept and funeral this PM . . . well attended by the fire boys in uniform . . .

May 12 . . . PM attended trial of DeLamar Co in US Dist Court – Sent letter to *Journal* on it, etc. Trial good for a week or less . . .

May 13 . . . Reported DeLamar case . . . The Enterprise says the Exempts declared a $15 dividend at their regular monthly meeting last Sunday.

May 14 . . . Reported DeLamar trial or case as usual, 10 AM to 5 PM when both sides said no more testimony to produce – To be argued tomorrow . . . At train this evening I met George Warren my old Comstock, Va, friend and at one time newspaper antagonist, he on the *Chronicle* & I on the *Enterprise* – On his way home to New York . . .

May 15 . . . At 11:05 while I was sitting reporting in the US Dist Court quite a strong shock of earthquake . . . The three big chandeliers of the court room swung vibratingly two or three inches east and west . . . The DeLamar case was argued today and at 4 PM submitted to the Judge Hawley – Court adjourned till 10 AM Monday – Most of the outsiders in this case left for home this evening – Judge Rives left – Paid me 15 on acct . . . $20 more still due . . .

Sunday, May 16 . . . Letter from wife inclosing last one from Bessie, also a postal order for $2 for me . . . Fixed up a bottle of *"Berunckum"* Hair Tonic, new & accurately regulated, before I went to bed –

May 21 . . . Fixed good fly netting screens to my window and door transom . . .

May 24 . . . I attended US Dist Court & heard Judge Hawleys decision in the case of the Mill Companies vs the ranchers for right of using the water . . . Two hours & 20 minutes in reading – a compromise decision, each party pay own costs . . . Smiths Big Show Comedy Co commenced this evening for a week at Opera House – Play Jack O'Diamonds – Very good – Good house & good company – Also good brass band – 12 pieces – It paraded street at 11 AM – good parade – Good orchestra in evening – Admission 10, 20 & 30 cts – Sent letter this evening to *Journal* – "Capital Notes" . . .

May 25 through 28 [AD exchanges business letters, writes an advertisement for Circe's Carson Exchange Hotel, and sees the Smith Big

Show Company play *Dad's Girl, La Belle Marie, Too Much Johnson* and *Lady of Lyons* to steadily larger houses, the last two "crowded."]

May 29 – Fair, breezy & pleasant – 87° – Sent a letter to wife – Evening theater – last night – Good house – Play was *"Triss,"* sort of an old '49 piece in the old diggin's but a very bad, trashy imitation idea of it. Lots of funny scenes and incidents, but poor plot and very trashy, unnatural play – even wrung the Salvation Army into it, a very recent sort of a formation – Bed 12 – 20 or 30 Indians, bucks, squaws and little ones filled the two upper stage boxes at the theater tonight – invited – looked jolly –

May 31 . . . Memorial Day observed today instead of yesterday . . . Nice procession – Carson Band, 20 pieces; Carson Guard, 40; G.A.R., 30; 2 carriages officers of the Day, etc, 20; Indian Band from the Indian School, 22; Indian scholars, boys, 80; Carriages 20, average 3 in each, 60; Indian girl scholars on sidewalk together in uniform dress, gray gowns, 50. Total 322 . . . Held usual style of exercises at cemetery . . . After return, each band played awhile in the Capitol grounds . . . Indian Band very good . . .

June 1 . . . Got Circes ad fixed & agreed upon all right & sent it down to Journal tonight – ¼ column, 1 yr, $35, a copy of the paper mailed regularly, gratis – I to have $5 fee out of it . . .

June 2 . . . My son Sammy is reporting the annual commencement exercises at the State University for the Reno *Journal* and he does it well –

June 4 . . . Hale & Norcross suit decided in the Supreme Court yesterday in favor of the Grayson crowd, Joe Ryan Supt – He will take possession soon . . . At San Francisco yesterday the Mayor signed an ordinance prohibiting high hats being worn in theaters – good lick at the women . . .

June 5 . . . Met Johnny Q A Moore, returned yesterday from his gravel gold mine near Carlin & sent what he told me about it to the *Journal* . . .

Sunday, June 6 . . . I attended farewell meeting of the Salvation Army this evening . . . cant make a living . . .

June 7 . . . Salvationists left for Reno this evening, leaving the hard sinners of Carson to go to hell their own way – Bed 11 – Joe R Ryan took possession of the Hale & Norcross mine this morning as Supt . . .

June 8 . . . 3 new Salvation lassies arrived this morning & opened out in the same old hall this evening . . .

June 9 . . . Sent letter to J R White, S.F. on Folsom & Marlette decision . . . Evening big 20 round fight between Sharkey and Maher, New York – Couldn't get telegraphic news of it in Carson –

June 10 . . . The Sharkey-Maher fight in New York last evening was declared a draw in the 7th round – Very little fighting done until last 2 rounds – 6th round Maher was knocked down, and 7th Sharkey was ditto – they clinched – Maher's second interfered and was punched in the nose by Sharkey – cries of *foul,* police jumped over the ropes. All the principals arrested, & referee declared it a draw – great dissatisfaction and disappointment – All fights of any importance will be pulled off in Nevada hereafter – About 6 PM big alarm of fire – General R M Clarke's residence, with office, kitchen, wood house etc connected, destroyed . . . Burned over an hour . . . Visited Salvation Army a little while this evening – They collected $1.15 first evening, $1.25 second, and $1 tonight . . . The Clarke fire occurred about 6 PM, when the water pressure is lowest and the supply the least, throughout the town – Thus the fire had pretty much its own way, aided by a nice breeze from the west. Only one story high, but noted as one of the most homelike mansions of Carson, giving more receptions, socials, lawn parties, evening entertainments etc than any – Fine orchard surrounding it, beautiful grassy lawn, etc – All the furniture, piano, books, paintings, carpets, etc were saved by neighborly assistance – Nothing saved from the attic or upstairs . . . The fruit and ornamental trees and shrubbery around the residence were not materially injured.

June 14 . . . PM I pencilled a good long letter to Brother Sam, Plymouth, in response to his of Feb 24 . . .

June 15 . . . This morning the tops of all the surrounding mountains . . . were capped white with fresh snow . . . Fires in barroom stoves this evening & last evening felt comfortable . . .

June 17 . . . The New York authorities have prohibited all further boxing or pugilistic contest exhibitions since late Sharkey-Maher fight . . .

June 19 – Variable, blustering & cool – *Enterprise* this morning had account of suicide of my old time Como friend and musical coadjutor Henry Fischer, at his home in Dayton yesterday about 5 PM – shot himself through the head with pistol, sitting in a chair and died immediately –

Wife nearby heard report, rushed in & found him dead – Wrote it up for the Appeal in evening, read proof – Henry was 64 yrs old and native of Bavaria – Bed 12 –

Sunday, June 20 . . . Mrs Trudell . . . who won the $3,750 prize in the lottery . . . got divorced last week and was married today at Glenbrook, Lake Tahoe – Reputed to have already gone through with nearly all of her $3,750 in riotous fast living –

June 25 . . . The Jury in the Foley estate case, which has been on trial at Reno last three weeks, brought in verdict in favor of the heirs this morning – The Widow had half of the estate under the law, but wanted the other half also – Notice was given of appeal to the Supreme Court, and Mrs Hartley will have to get that court to decide whether her deceased little son is one of the heirs of Foley or not . . .

Sunday, June 27 – Cloudy, warmer, pleasant – The Charley Jones and Sam Davis fight case came up before US Commissioner Waldo in Reno yesterday on preliminary examination. Several witnesses testified, and Jones was bound over in the sum of $300 to appear before the US Grand Jury on charge of assault – Recd letter from wife, written this morning – She went with 4 horse 'bus load of High School graduates over Geiger Grade to Va Friday morning – They attended graduating of Va High School – wife went to Gold Hill – visited Mrs Fraser, at *our* old home, which she owns now – old McDonald, Mrs F and an old Adventist preacher there, and Mrs Dr Conwell came in, so wife had pleasant visit, and footed it back to Va over Imperial trail – attended graduating ball in evening, and all rode back to Reno next morning – Bessie arrived home from Santa Clara for vacation last Tuesday morning, leaving all well at S.C. – Wife re-elected Vice Principal for another year, of the Reno High School – All the teachers re-elected – Sent wife 2 page letter by evening train – Bed 11 –

June 29 . . . The melting & refining dept of the Carson Mint shut down about 6 wks ago, from lack of work – let seven men out of employment . . .

July 2 – Fair and very pleasant – nice breeze – Letter from J R White S.F. – PM wrote a Kinzle letter dated June 30 – W J Bryan the defeated Presidential candidate is on his way from Nebraska to Los Angeles, Cal, where he is to deliver Independence Day oration – was expected to pass through Reno, arriving at 10 this evening – Committee from Comstock,

Carson, Reno, etc selected to welcome him, take him to a stand front of Court House & have a speech from him during the short time the train stopped – About 2:30 PM news came that his train would be 4 hours late at Reno – The big excursion planned from Comstock & Carson, $1 for round trip . . . was at once declared off, abandoned – But a beautiful silver plate, appropriately engraved, for the Committee to present as tribute from Nevada . . . was taken to Winnemucca yesterday by Judge Bonnifield – So this Bryan demonstration was otherwise a fizzle – immense crowds of Christian Endeavorers are on the way from the East to their grand convention in San Francisco – Will be 40,000 or more from all parts of the country – 2 dozen or so will attend from Carson – John White, in his letter says looks like my Keyes suit is to be quietly dropped, or settled – amount to nothing – Bed 11 –

Sunday, July 4 . . . PM & evening plenty of firecrackers, bombs etc . . .

July 5 – Clear, fine breezy day – No celebration in Carson – considerable decoration, flags etc – Train hour late – 150 or more from Carson got aboard for Va celebration – Indians, Chinese, etc – Curry Engine Co, Gov & staff – 4 extra cars – Arrived at Va 12:20 – city crowded – Procession forming – It started about 1, out B st to Divide – back through C st & by Mill st & B to Opera House – Dr Stubbs of University Orator – I didnt attend exercises – round town – Met Jose Salinas – went with him to his house & saw his new fiddle made of his Tahoe wood by himself – Tried it – pretty good – Took him to dinner at [blank] restaurant, C st – Met Mrs Zimmer on C st & had pleasant chat – Told me Louis had left her again 3 wks ago – failed to provide & shiftless – PM lots of games, athletic, etc, on C st – very lively & interesting – The procession was usual style, military, Fire Depts, Car of State, Goddess, Miners Union, etc – I met lots of old friends – After midnight tried to find a bed, but couldnt – sat in a chair & slept about an hour – About 400 in procession – Va collected $416.75 – A very good celebration, better than usual – Reno had also big celebration – raised over $600 for it – Also celebration at Glenbrook, Lake Tahoe –

> [Clip, paper not identified:] The kinetoscope took 143,000 different pictures during the Corbett-Fitzsimmons fight. The length of the film upon which the pictures were taken is 2⅓ miles long.

July 6 . . . Slept on car all way to Carson – Arrived there at 10:20 feeling tired & demoralized – got off on wrong side of train – got home as soon as I could & to bed, & slept about 5 hours . . . Evening about town – Bed 11 – Got right hand and right shin bruised somehow in my trampings about Va – both quite sore – Didn't get into any fight, and dont think I tumbled down anywhere . . .

July 7 . . . Johnny Carter got pulled for disturbing the peace last evening, in front of Salvation Army Barracks – Kept in jail & in court this PM suing officer Brule for assault & battery – got beaten – Dined with him at Arlington Hotel – Johnny *celebrated* too vigorously – Quite a little excitement last day or two about a newly discovered gas light, which is at Evan Williams' place, Empire. He recently returned from the East with the inventor, where he got it patented – parties from Carson who have visited it last 2 evening pronounce it wonderful . . .

July 8 . . . Johnny Carter was fined $10 this AM for disturbing the peace . . . Took me to dinner again with him . . . Then I took him home & left him to care of his wife . . .

July 10 . . . Letter from Goodie, Oakland, July 8 – at Miss Lindsay's – Mama & she left Reno with a Christian Endeavor train, at their rates of fare – was Iowa Delegation train – Met some of wifes relatives who came on a Connecticut train – They are having a good time – Goodie never was there before – Bed 11 . . .

Sunday, July 11 – Fair & hot – PM wrote 2 page letter to Bessie, Reno – Forgot to mail it at train because I met E Lauzon, from Va en route for Montreal, Canada, to see his old folks whom he [has] not seen for 25 yrs – To return in a month – Told me all about Dan De Quille, his neighbor on A st – Dan will leave for old home in Iowa next Tuesday with family – never to return – All gone with rheumatism – sciatic – Bed 11 – 81° during the night – Hottest for years –

[Clip, *San Francisco Chronicle,* July 13:] The veroscopic reproduction of the Corbett-Fitzsimmons fight, given at the Olympia, formerly the People's Palace, demonstrated that Edison's invention is a most wonderful one. Though it has imperfections, the general result is so remarkable that hearty applause was given throughout the hour and three-quarters' entertainment.

The continuous view of the fight was thrown on a large white screen on the stage with dazzling brightness. At first it was very trying to the eyes, but the inconvenience wore off as the exhibition progressed. Most of the films were clear, though in the first part of the fight some were too light, and at all times the imperfections in the films were apparent.

The views showed the entire ring and the crowd beyond it on the side opposite where the photographic apparatus was stationed. The people in the ring were plainly shown. After the fight had ended Referee Siler could be seen picking his way in front of the ring to Harry Corbett, with whom he had a talk. Muldoon, the timekeeper, was plainly seen all through the fight. Lew Houseman, Fitzsimmons' timekeeper, was also in full view, as well as Billy Madden. The views exposed a questionable tricky action by Houseman, who as the gong was about to sound for the end of a round, would raise his hat in the air to signal to Fitzsimmons and his seconds the expiration of the three minutes. . . .

July 14 – Same – The Christian Endeavorers' Convention at SF closed on Monday in great style, and yesterday Oakland invited and entertained about 15,000 of them, free lunch, free glory, etc – Many are visiting other sections of the State while tickets hold good, and many are pulling out on return home East – Greatest excursion ever known across the continent . . . On board the passenger train this evening I found Dan De Quille (William Wright), wife and daughter Lou – I had talk with Dan during the ten minutes stop – Going to West Liberty, Iowa, their old home . . . He never expects to come back, for he is so terribly broken down with rheumatism and used up generally that he cannot live long anyway – Is racked with it from shoulders to knees, back humped up double and is merely animated skin and bone, almost helpless – can only walk about the house a little, grasping cane with both hands – has not been able to walk down from his residence on A st, Va, to C st & back for nearly or quite 2 yrs – Looks to be 90 yrs old, yet was 68 on the 9th of May last – 2 months & 10 days older than I am – Promised to write to me when he gets home – Poor dear old boy Dan – my most genial companion in our early Comstock reportorial days, good bye, and I think forever personally on this earth . . .

[Several clips pay tribute to Dan De Quille – One from the *Appeal* reprints a tribute from C C Goodwin of the *Salt Lake Tribune*, which emphasizes the large amount of writing accomplished over all those years, his tact in handling volatile subjects, his great knowledge of mining, and his present poverty: "There is nothing left to show for all the splendid work that he has done." – Another clip, unidentified, reprints this from the *Mining and Scientific News:*] If every one whom this veteran writer had delighted were to contribute a penny he would start on his trip a millionaire . . . He was always lavish of his literary treasures and his money—Mark Twain, his former collaborator, knows considerable about that—and his best jokes were oftimes published by and credited to others who better understood how to advertise themselves.

[A third, from the *Enterprise,* after paraphrasing an *Appeal* item that paraphrases the *Mining and Scientific News* piece, proposes a farewell banquet and adds:] He is as one may say almost the last leaf on the tree that bore the old crowd and flourished on the Comstock a quarter of a century ago. Mark Twain, Joe Goodwin, Rollin Daggett, D E McCarthy, Charlie Goodman and Steve Gillis are either off the Comstock or in their graves . . . He has stayed with the fortunes of the ledge since the first shaft was sunk in Cedar Hill, and was one of the first to advocate mining further down the hill and sinking to the east. His advice resulted in the uncovering of the biggest bonanzas the world has ever seen.

July 17 . . . Sent another letter to Rives, Salt Lake – Evening, attended, with half the town, open air concert of Nevada State Band in front of State Capitol building – about 20 pieces – very good – Bed 12 – SF papers give glowing accounts of new gold fields of the Yukon River and Klondyke, just across Alaska line in British Possessions – nuggets & coarse & fine gold in plenty, but hard old country, especially in Winter – hard to get to or live in. Many miners arriving from there with from $5,000 to $65,000 apiece – creates much excitement – estimated that $10,000,000 be yielded from there next season . . .

Sunday, July 18 . . . Letter from Rives with check $20 balance due – Sent him receipt by return mail . . .

July 20 – Same – The Yukon Klondyke gold discovery is creating an excitement throughout the coast and country equal to the California gold fever in '49, or more so – gold comes from there to Seattle and San F by the millions – and thousands of men are going or preparing to go on a rush thither – like old times, and whisky is said to be "four bits a drink" in the new diggins, like as in "the days of old, the days of gold, the days of Forty nine."

July 21 – Same – 84° – Letter from wife says they have returned from Cal to Reno – Says visited sister Eunice – This was my 68th birthday – 68 years old today – good average health and weigh 180 pounds – poor in flesh, poorer in purse, and poor prospects ahead, but still in good hopeful spirits – Bought me new pair of pants for $1.25 today – Tim Dempsey set up ½ bottle champagne this morning in honor of my birthday –

[Two clips from the *Appeal* – "Whisky is 50 cents a drink in the gold fields of Alaska. This news only increases the desire to get there. Where whisky is four bits a drink times are alright." "As soon as Alf Doten heard that whisky was four bits a drink in Alaska he was talking of starting for the gold fields."]

July 22 . . . George Irwin & wife with Mrs Rinckel visited my lodgings this PM – The Irwins talked of taking the [Keeley cure] but didn't conclude to –

July 23 . . . PM busy at room fixing my new pants . . . Parties are starting out from Reno, Va & other places for Klondyke –

July 26 . . . John McKinnon and Tom McCabe were on evening train from Va bound for Klondyke – Both good Comstock miners . . . They are backed by Dave M Ryan, Archie J McDonnell, brokers, and Supt Pat Kervin with money and supplies for 18 months, profits to be equally divided among the five . . .

July 29 . . . Klondyke craze bigger & bigger – one man going to leave on steamer from SF today sold his ticket which he had paid $150 for, on steamer sold it for $1,500, & didnt go – lots of other passengers were offered three times as much as they had paid but wouldn't sell – Bed 11 –

July 30 – Same – 86° – Went prospecting or on the realization of my mining dream of the last 8 or 10 years – of a small but rich gold lead, ledge or lode, running from near the old Merrimac mill and millsite, northerly on this side of the Carson river, up toward Tom Calvert's Half Way House – My ideal locality was less than ¼ mile of the river and the V&T Railroad, in a small ravine showing a small nut-pine tree from the railroad track. Have viewed it always in passing on the train, also a red ledge of something showing prominently on the side of a hill near by, on the west side of a small flat crossed by the railroad. That ledge might be rich in gold, and crossed the ravine next beyond at that little pine tree, and there was my golden dream of a fortune awaiting me – The morning train was late, so I left on it at 11 AM – got off at the Brunswick mill – struck out into the hills – got bothered with cross roads, etc and uncertain knowledge of direction, making much useless travel – Finally got right and arrived at my little pine tree at 12:30 – rested awhile under its shade – the only shade I found in the treeless country – ate my sandwich lunch, took a drink from my flask. Then prospected and observed and saw places where others had dug, picked, prospected and observed in years past without golden realization – inspected the little red ledge at the west side of the little flat with much difficulty from its peculiar steep, rough, sliding location – Found no golden quartz at all – nothing but hard, flinty red agate – put some specimen pieces of it in my pockets, and *this ended my long rich dream* – Climbed the hill and sat on a convenient rock to rest & reflect – Finished contents of my flask and smashed it – picked up an old horseshoe lying by the roadside, pocketed it and left on my return at 2:30, having spent two hours of hard observation and traveling on my prospect. Then I struck out wearily for Empire where I arrived at 4 PM – staid at Andy Todd's saloon, resting, refreshing & observing, and at 6:20 was at depot & took train for Carson – very tired – 25 cts passage each way.

> "The dream is past, and with it fled
> The hopes that once my passions fed."
> Vanished castles in the air.

. . . After lunch I laid down & rested awhile – About town awhile, & bed at 12 –

July 31 – Clear & warmer – 89° – Nevada State Band gave a very excellent musical and amusing street parade at noon, for their minstrel performance this evening – Evening I attended – crowded house – Very good minstrel & variety entertainment under management of Charles Regan an old professional hand at it – Had Jas McCoy also from the Wizard Oil Co which recently performed here a week & disbanded – McCoy specialties drum major baton, indian clubs, and musical glasses, bells and zylophone, etc with Regan in the olio – as well as general acting singing etc throughout – About 20 in the "first part" – The west bound passenger train had a fearful smash up near Verdi, Wednesday, caused by a broken rail – 5 or 6 of our Nevada Indians killed, mostly from the Comstock, including Dick Sides squaw – going over to California to pick hops, as they do yearly – riding free on car platforms – Bed 12 –

Aug 1 through 12 [AD corresponds with Mary, who sends him $2.50, writes business letters for himself and others, suffers an all-night siege of diarrhea, fights bedbugs, comments further upon "Klondyke Komstockers," noting that the rush has slowed down due to the lateness of the season, meets numerous traveling friends & acquaintants at the depot, including his organist friend, Professor Cara, notes that the Salvation Army is attempting another revival and not doing well either musically or financially, that fight promoter Billy Brady of New York has taken a look at the Carson arena, and that Dottie Lee's "Palace," "the most noted resort in the 'Tenderloin' district" in the southwest part of town has burned down, and assembles materials for an unidentified *"light* experiment."]

Aug 13 – Same – The sensation of the day is Senator Stewart's sudden flop from the Silver party, according to New York telegram of yesterday – Tells his friends in the West it is time to turn to face new issues, leaving silver and Bryan to go to grass – Senator Jones does not tumble hard with him, but agrees that prosperity seems to be getting in all right without free coinage – Stewart says he shan't be surprised to see silver go down to 25 cts an ounce and wheat go up to $1 per bushel – Silverites here are disgustedly demoralized and the Republicans quietly smile – This almost beats Klondike sensation – Bed 11 –

Aug 14 – Same – The Stewart sensation of yesterday is authoritatively denied by telegrams from him today from Washington – says story is totally and absolutely false. Gov Sadler's house caught fire this PM – big alarm, but little damage – Bed 11 – Big strike in Trinity County, Cal, attracting much attention & travel. At Coffee Creek, 300 miles north of San F – The 2 Graves Bros took out about $100,000 in 2 or 3 days, including one $42,000 nugget, the largest ever found in California . . . Many prospectors for there instead of Klondike –

Sunday, Aug 15 . . . Letter from Hon J P Jones . . . Two pages about the tariff, all type written . . . Sent Jones a 3 page letter in response . . . Silver is quoted at 55½ cts per oz – lower than ever.

Aug 16 . . . Sent another letter to Jones with clippings inclosed . . . Mrs Rinckel visited my domicile this PM to take a look . . .

Aug 17 – Same – 93° – This is the highest of the season . . . Sent what Jones had to say on the tariff to the *Journal* this evening . . . Mrs Rinckel had parties at work cleaning out my lodging house today – Big job – very dirty – 3 yrs dirt . . .

Aug 18 . . . Senator Jones tariff article was in this morning's Reno *Journal* all right – Sent brief letter to him inclosing clipping . . . All the rooms of my lodging place are stripped, carpets up, hallways & stairways – dirt accumulation of many years cleaned out . . . The famous Utica mine at Angel's, Cal took fire on the 800 level yesterday morning & is still burning – shafts closed & mine being flooded – throws 1,000 men out of employment – principal support of town of 6,000 people – The convent & school of Sisters of Charity at Virginia is closed, & Sisters depart for other fields – lack of adequate support – Sisters Hospital to close also –

Aug 20 . . . Rec'd notification from Mrs Rinckel to vacate my lodgings – notice given by Geo Wilcox, who has contract to tear out some partitions, make more transoms and, in fact remodel and renovate the institution thoroughly – going to have new carpets & furniture, whitening, painting, papering etc . . . I called on Mrs Rinckel & tried to arrange to change into some other room temporarily but couldn't – have to *git eaout* . . .

Aug 21 . . . Geo Wilcox commenced this morning in the front rooms, cutting out partitions . . .

Aug 24 . . . AM I packed all into my trunk and valise, and at noon vacated my room, 10, putting my trunk, valise & overcoat into room 11 . . . Mrs R came, and they moved my bedding into No 14 – Evening I went there and made up a bed on floor of No 12, from my old mattress & bed clothes . . .

Sunday, Aug 29 . . . Evening I finished & copied 4 page article on "Nevada Mines and Miners" – Bed 11 – cool night – Sent 2 page letter to wife this evening . . .

Aug 30 . . . Got my Appeal article in all right . . .

Aug 31 . . . The old *Daily Evening Report* at Virginia, defunct for last 6 yrs was resurrected yesterday by D L Brown, Frank Cox, Jimmy Sullivan & Johnny Considine & Johnny Mahoney, who think they can make a living for themselves out of it – Not a very brilliant looking paper or brilliant prospects – A plasterer got in his work patching up in my lodgings today . . .

Sept 1 . . . Fred Hart died in the County Hospital, Sacramento, day before yesterday – Brights disease, etc – Over 60 years old – leaves a wife & 2 children – Bed 11 –

Sept 2 . . . 4 page letter to Va Chronicle on Fred Hart . . .

Sept 4 . . . My letter returned from the *Chronicle* this morning – Took it to the *Appeal,* read proof of it this evening – Manager Coleman in sending it back, indorsed on it, "Guess will let the Hart matter stay as it is – How are you, old man" . . .

Sunday, Sept 5 . . . My Fred Hart in Appeal – full column . . . [This obituary sketch is reprinted almost verbatim in AD's later article, "Early Journalism of Nevada" – See Appendix.]

Sept 6 – Clear & windy – 75° – Miss Emma Tousic suicided this morning at Gardnerville – About 23 yrs old – used to belong to the Salvation Army here, but left it – Never very sound headed, & got worse of late – Got letter from wife today & sent her 1 in return – Jack Strait nearly 60 yrs old, died yesterday here from immoderate indulgence in cold water drinking – Was Salvation Army convert and joined the Presbyterian Church . . .

[A clip reports that the Court found the assignments Heney made to Coffin and Woodburn "suspicious," but not legally fraudulent – Coffin got half of his $2,000 claim, Woodburn got $2,000 instead of $3,500, and the balance went to the court – Mrs Heney will receive a considerable amount after fines and fees are paid.]

Sept 8 . . . I got my trunk, valise etc out and down stairs . . . About noon was up stairs and gave up my keys to Mrs Rinckel . . . Went to Alta lodging house and paid $4.50 for room 10 till Oct 1 . . .

Sept 9 . . . The Sisters of Charity abandoning Va including convent, school, hospital etc, and the closing of the famous Washoe Club, marks an era in the history and decline of Va and the old Comstock – Rose at 7 AM after a hard bedded nights sleep, disturbed by plenty of bedbugs – I found & killed 2 or 3 dozen – About noon got my landlady in to see the business – induced her to pay me back $3.50, leaving $1.00 for my night's lodging, then took my valise & overcoat back to Dempsey's – Bed 11, at Arlington – Paid $1 for 3 nights, in advance . . .

[Two clips from the *Enterprise* – A short one reports that Sisters Rose and Regina had left Saint Mary's Hospital and its eight or nine patients in charge of "a woman" and left on the train – The Convent school closed in mid-August, and the hospital, originally built by Bishop Manogue and run by the Sisters of Charity for the last twenty years, is expected to close too – The second clipping reports:] The Washoe Club, which has been a landmark in Nevada and a household word throughout the Pacific Coast since the early bonanza days, when mining magnates, millionaires, artists and men of letters were wont to congregate there for social intercourse, is a thing of the past. . . .

Soon after the organization of the club on February 27, 1875, it was incorporated under the laws of Nevada. It then flourished until the more recent decline of the mining prospects of the Comstock. A restaurant was run in connection with the club for ten years . . . and later the club was turned over to Major [James] Cummings, who collected monthly dues of $2.50 from the few remaining members and made what he could out of the bar, but of late the Major has been losing money, and yesterday decided to cease operations. . . . [Only] two charter members . . . still remain in Virginia. . . .

One of the interesting relics of the Washoe Club is its visitors' book. . . . Among the notables who have written their names in this book are General U. S. Grant, and two sons, Jesse and Ulysses, Generals Robt. Sherman and Phil Sheridan, the famous actors, Jefferson, Ward, Booth the younger, John McCullough, Lawrence Barrett, Prof. T. Soule, whose reference work "Soule's Synonims" is classic and standard, D. O. Mills and fifty other millionaires of world-wide reputation. The closing of the Washoe Club marks an era in the history of Nevada, as did its opening.

Sept 11 . . . Borrowed $10 from H M Yerington . . . Bought a new purse today, for 35 cts, to replace the empty one picked from my pocket March 17th, at the Fitz-Corbett fight –

Sunday, Sept 12 . . . Rose at 6 – Excursion special train to Reno – Carson bicycle club vs Reno club – 50 mile relay race . . . **Reno at** 9:15 – express carriage took me for 25 cts home with my valise – Found everybody all right . . . Reno beat Carson by 1⅛ miles – Return train for Carson at 5 PM – Only $1 for round trip, so I saved a dollar without taking the return – Didn't attend the race – Was about town among friends – Supper at home – Bed 10 . . . I slept in son Alf's bed, & he slept upstairs –

Sept 13 through Dec 31 [AD, completely broke, remains in Reno with his family, attending the fair, which suffers from the national hard times and the continuing decline of the Comstock, reading the newspapers in downtown hotels and bars, chatting with passing friends and acquaintances at the depot, writing letters to Jones on the mild, off-year politics, trying to stop drinking, designating each drinkless day by entering 000, doing repairs and painting around the house, fixing himself a small, separate bedroom in the old kitchen, making occasional music with his children and getting to bed much earlier than he does when he's alone – Mostly short entries, much of the substance second hand, from his newspaper reading – Representative or of independent interest:]

Sept 17 . . . H H Beck beat M Cooper terribly about the head this evening with a metal crib board at Elite Saloon – quarreled over a game of "freeze out" –

Sept 18 . . . Rec'd through mail complimentary season ticket to State Fair, holding next week – Evening down town awhile – Salvation Army out, etc – Bed 11 – my boys had two of their mates visiting them this evening – they had peanuts, candy and poker in the kitchen – All other evenings of the week they have been very busy evenings with their studies – Goodie also – No school today –

Sunday, Sept 19 . . . Many people gathering in for State Fair . . . gamblers, horsemen & sports, etc – made town lively – Bed 10 –

Sept 20 . . . Fair commenced – PM some running races out at the track – slim attendance – met my old Va friend Whitcomb, now of Colfax, Cal . . . Evening we went to Pavilion together – very few exhibits in, & no exercises – Hadnt seen him for 15 yrs – long pleasant chat together at Palace over old times – Bed 1 –

Sept 21 . . . Evening I attended the Beck hearing before Justice Linn – He pleaded guilty to assault on Cooper & is to appear again for decision tomorrow evening –

Sept 22 . . . "Comstock Day" – Quite a number came down, via the Geiger Grade principally . . . No special Fair train for this Fair – for 1st time – Yerington says the Railroad Co cant afford it . . .

Sept 23 – Fair & warm – At 1 PM rode out to the Fair grounds & races – largest attendance of the week – many from Comstock & Carson – Reno and Indian bands turn about playing in grand stand – Some good running races – plenty of gambling there as well as all about town – Bus drivers put up rates at noon to double rates – 25c each way, instead of 25c round trip – Paid that going out, but I as well as very many others would not stand the extortion and walked back – wouldn't ride – Evening at Pavilion awhile – music & waltzing – Bed at 11, in wife's bed – Beck was sentenced last evening to pay a fine of $400 – Very tough lot of Fair and race followers, gamblers, crooks and hobos, infest Reno for the time, from Sacramento . . .

Sept 24 . . . Walked out to the track & back in the PM – Busses all displayed placards & streamers "To the Fair Grounds & Return 25 cts" – But I walked, as did others . . .

Sept 25 . . . Last day of fair . . . I did not care to attend . . . Was at the *Journal* office and got in a puff for Circe's Hotel, Carson, as the Ormsby Dist Fair takes place there next week . . . Judge Hawley came down on evening train from Carson, bound for SF – Told me he rendered decision in the DeLamar case last Monday, against DeLamar Co, & in favor of the town site owners – Bed at 11 –

[Clips concerning the case, from various papers and dates, are pasted in here – The DeLamar Company had located claims around which a town grew, helter-skelter, and the main street lay over the Naiad Queen claim, which the company had bought but not patented – When prospects led the company to want to dig up the street, and to apply for a patent, the property owners sued – Judge Powers of Salt Lake City represented the townsfolk, who claimed the street was on nonmineral ground and hence not entitled to a patent, while Judge Rives of Eureka represented the company, claiming the ground was located for mining in 1892, while the townsite wasn't laid out until 1894 – Case considered important as a precedent for such conflicts between mining and private property rights.]

Sept 27 . . . Reno deserted – Two full coaches went up this morning's train, with scattering remnants of the sports, hobos etc for Carson Fair . . .

Oct 2 . . . Met John Mackay at morning train on way from SF to the Comstock – Had quite a little chat with him – We received a box of plums and a box of grapes from Bessie today . . .

Oct 5 . . . John W Mackay went from Va to the Silver Peak mines, Esmeralda Co yesterday, to examine with idea of purchase – I am badly troubled with hay fever – nose & eyes, sneezing, weeping, etc, & bad cough – got it good now . . .

Oct 7 – Variable – Citizens election held under the new city incorporation, on question of whether the city shall construct new water and light works or allow the old Co to keep on as heretofore – Election passed off quietly & resulted in favor of citizens, new water etc by vote of 409 to 130 – Saloons all closed during election, from 9 to 6 – *000* – Bed 11 . . .

Oct 8 . . . On AM west bound train I saw about 150 sailor boys from the East for the US cruiser Baltimore at San F, ordered to Honolulu – Mostly young fellows & rather a fine looking lot . . .

Sunday, Oct 10 – Clear & very pleasant day – Big 50 mile relay race between the Sacramento & Reno clubs, at race track – AM trains brought wheelmen & excursionists from Sac, Carson, the Comstock, etc, & many came via Geiger Grade – 3 coach special from Va full, $1.50 round trip – $1 from Carson – 2500 people at the race – Judge W H Young & I walked out (distance a mile) & back & together – in grand stand – Big crowd – piles of women & children – Hastings brass band did fine music – Race very interesting & well contested & Sac won by about ¼ mile – Began at 1:30 & closed at 4 – Mishaps to Reno boys gave the Sac Boys ¾ mile ahead at 8th relay, & the Renos gained lively in last 2 relays – Mishaps were Snare's bike gave out in each of 2 first heats coming in on home stretch – Johnson tripped against his antagonist in 5th relay & was pitched off heavily – Nash gave out in last heat of 8th relay & had to have a substitute, all losing the time . . . Prize was a beautiful silver pitcher – Evening the Reno boys banqueted the Sacramento boys & sent them home on 10:10 west bound train . . . Bed 10:30 –

Oct 12 . . . John Mackay came in from Silver Peak . . . with his companion, young L J Hanchett Jr, and went on west bound train at 10:10 for San F – I met him and shook hands . . .

Oct 14 . . . Wrote 4 page letter to J W Mackay, Palace Hotel S.F. inclosing my recent Fred Hart sketch . . .

Oct 18 . . . Worked at fixing up rear upstairs window, putting in new lights, etc . . . My old friend Hon W E Price died at his home, old town-site of Ophir in Washoe Valley, yesterday morning, of consumption – About 60 yrs old – My old friend Hon Theodore Davenport died this morning at Price's lake or pond near Washoe Valley, west of Price's residence, consumptive & worn out – over 60 yrs old – Both he and Price were formerly members of the Nevada Legislature . . .

Oct 19 . . . Finished my window job – 10 new lights – & did other jobs about the house . . . The case of Walter Kermeen, the Carson school-house firebug on trial at Carson yesterday & today – Our mother in law, Mrs S A Stoddard 81 yrs old today – pretty old & feeble – I today *000* –

Oct 21 . . . I put in a new 16 x 30 light into wifes bookcase – The Jury in the Kermeen case disagreed . . . 3 for acquittal considering the boy irresponsible, cranky, etc . . .

Oct 22 . . . Wrote note to Jim Townsend, Bodie, inclosing *"Inside Hell,"* for his paper, the *Bodie Miner* – will mail it on morning train – Bed 12 – Today *000* –

Oct 23 . . . Wife bought me 2 suits of underwear & a shirt – $2.65 – Wrote 3 page letter to J P Jones . . . Today *000* –

Sunday, Oct 24 . . . At home most of day – Wife gave front door orders – Bed 11 – This was seventh successive day of *000* . . .

Oct 26 – Clear & pleasant . . . Hard days work fixing steps to side kitchen door – rough job – Bed 11 – 000 (9) –

Oct 27 – Same – (2d) – Bed 11 –

Oct 28 – Same (2) – Hon W M Stewart arrived about 2 PM, on delayed west bound train from Winnemucca, where he spoke last evening – Been speaking all through eastern part of State last 5 wks, getting ready for his US Senatorial campaign next year – Spoke at the Court House this evening – Fair audience – I attended & took notes, & acted as Secy – Introduced by Powning, Prest of Silver Central Committee – Spoke 2 hours, giving account of his stewardship in Congress, lining out policy of Silver party in next campaign – Go in [for] free coinage of our own silver regardless of foreign nations or rest of world – considers present new tariff best we ever had – Go in for Bryan for next President, as greatest man on earth – Bed 12 – Stewart visited University this PM –

Oct 29 – Same – 000 – Stewart visited High School this PM – I wrote a long 8 page criticism of Vol V, No 2 of the *Student Record* to give to Sam, as he was editor of it this time – The Veriscope of the Fitz-Corbett fight on exhibition tonight at Opera House – Good house . . .

Nov 4 . . . Mr Paine building new kitchen and woodshed . . .

Nov 9 – Cloudy, moderate – US Dist Attorney Jones shot & killed in Carson at 4 PM, by Julian Guinan, 16 yrs old son of Dr J Guinan – shot in front of the Guinan residence, all on account of the boys sister Jessie, a fly young miss – shot with a rifle, from an upper window – Much excitement both there & here, where Jones resided with his wife & little son – Today by request I wrote *"A Peculiarly Eventful Night,"* sketch for the *Student Record,* a nice little semi monthly magazine published by the students of the State University – My Sam is associate editor – Instructive and amusing article – Took me 4 hours to copy it off fair for the printers – A colony of Polish Jews arrived yesterday morning here from California to settle near Wellington a few miles southeast of Carson – They took the train for Carson – plenty of children –

Nov 10 . . . Charley Jones body brought to Reno on AM local . . .

Nov 11 . . . Sardis Summerfield recd appointment by telegraph today from Washington . . . as US Attorney in place of Charley Jones . . .

Nov 12 . . . Charley Jones' funeral this PM here well attended – Under charge of K of P . . . State officers et al from Carson . . .

Sunday, Nov 14 . . . Sam went out on a geological exploring trip afoot, with Jason Libbey, one of his student mates, in mountains back of Huffakers – hard trip – went about 30 miles he said – got home way after dark . . .

Nov 16 . . . The Julian Guinan examination on charge of murder was before Justice Stone yesterday and today – Grand Jury also in session – Was held to appear before it and the G J ignored the charge, and young Guinan was set free – popular approval . . .

[A clip from the *Journal* asserts, on the other hand, "The feeling here . . . is very bitter." – Another, from the *San Francisco Chronicle,* indicates the boy's justification was his fear that Jones would kill his father, Dr Guinan, who had earlier warned Jones to stay away from his daughter Jesse – While the daughter and Jones were talking out on the street, the boy trained a rifle on him from a window, and, when the father appeared and the boy saw Jones's hand going toward a pocket, he shot – A storm in court was brought on by a sensational letter which proved Jones was not in that locality on official government business, as his defenders claimed.]

Nov 23 . . . Evening I attended meeting at Court House, addressed by Newlands and Dr Stubbs of the University – on the present and future of Reno, how to improve and advance her natural advantages, interests and prospects – Newlands made good talk of an hour and Stubbs ½ hour – Committee of 5 gents & 2 ladies selected to investigate & study up the whole matter & report at a future meeting . . . The meeting was very well attended, many ladies present . . .

Nov 25 – Thanksgiving Day – Clear & cold – morning ground white with frost and the snow of last evening – freezing in shade all day – No schools – services in churches – At home most of day – Too poor for turkey, so we had roast pork, cranberries, & mince pie for our dinner – Evening I wrote & mailed on train a 5 page letter to Bessie – Bed 11 – dam cold –

Nov 26 . . . PM busy overhauling old file of the *Reese River Reveille* which I brought from Austin – Had a few unfilial remarks from my son Alfred about burning wood . . .

Nov 27 . . . The Berkeley University 11 arrived this morning, and were met by our students with University band, 16 pieces – PM they played lively game of football at the "campus" with our University 11, and beat them 20 to 6 – Evening, minstrel & variety show of our University boys at Opera House – well attended – Pretty good . . .

Dec 4 . . . PM I started in painting the new kitchen, inside . . . Sam went to Wadsworth by morning train to take part in performance of the University Minstrels tonight . . .

Sunday, Dec 5 . . . Sam returned with the rest of the Minstrel Co on a freight train early this morning . . . They had a good house last evening and scored a good success, winding up with a dance.

Dec 7 . . . Sent letter to *Examiner,* S.F. relative to competition for a $100 prize story for Christmas – Painting kitchen . . . Am afflicted with a very sore right eye, from a sort of "stye" . . . similar to that of nearly 3 years ago in Carson . . .

Dec 8 . . . Finished first coat of painting in kitchen . . .

Dec 10 . . . Worked from 8 AM to 10:30 PM on my kitchen painting job – Biggest days work for years . . .

Dec 11 . . . AM, son Alfred helped me and we finished my big painting job . . . PM I was busy painting window casings & trimming doors, mouldings etc . . . Evening I was down town awhile – The gas and incandescent light works out of fix – everybody burning coal oil & candles – dark – no use for reading rooms – Only 4 arc electric street lights and the moon to light the town . . . Orion Clemens, elder brother of Mark Twain, and Territorial Secretary & Treasurer of Nevada, died at his home in Keokuk, Iowa, this morning – old age, heart-failure, etc –

Sunday, Dec 12 . . . AM down town – PM painting door & window casings, moldings, trimmings etc of the kitchen a brilliant blood red, contrasting beautifully with the light olive of the general painting . . . Evening down town – electric lights all right again so I read up the papers, etc . . .

Dec 14 . . . Light snowstorm most of day . . . I painted a cupboard and put in lot of shelves in cellar stairway – Worked till 11 PM – Bed 12 –

Dec 15 . . . Light snow squalls . . . Did hard days work, taking up & putting down linoleum carpet in kitchen – some carpenter work etc – got stove and most everything moved into new kitchen and fixed up for supper . . . Bed 10:30 – completely used up, & so lame I could hardly walk. Had a severe chill on first going to bed, and turned and rolled about all night groaning with severe pains in my back, legs and every bone in my body – worst I ever had – And the Salvation Army seemed with me tormenting me –

Dec 16 . . . Sat by hot fire most of day . . . PM I had to go to bed for 2 hours good sleep – got none last night – was groaning and talking all night, in fact quite delirious at times – Bed 11 –

Dec 17 . . . Feel better – PM I worked a little fixing up our old kitchen for my own occupancy . . .

Dec 20 . . . I got my new quarters in the old kitchen sufficiently fixed up to move in this evening . . . Wife & Goodie moved down from their roost in the garret & into their front parlor bedroom . . . My eye was still worse today – was completely closed & looked horrid – Sam pricked the boil for me this morning & it discharged quite copiously . . .

Dec 21 . . . Eye looked its worst this morning . . . After breakfast . . . Sam with my penknife blade re-opened the boil – ran freely, and he picked out the core . . .

Dec 23 . . . Eye steadily recovering –

Dec 24 . . . Did quite a lot on my job – Door frame, with transom in, and about ½ the partition, also – Bessie arrived on evening train from Cal – Brought grapes and pomegranates fresh from the vines and trees . . .

Dec 25 . . . We had an excellent Christmas dinner, paid for by Bessie, 13 lb turkey, at 17 cts a pound – mince pie, cauliflower, grapes, oranges, pomegranates, dates, nuts, etc – Real home time – Evening I was down town awhile – Evening train . . . brought news of a hold up of Steamboat Springs this evening – 3 robbers stole money and whatever they saw that they wanted & slid out . . .

Sunday, Dec 26 . . . Evening Bessie & Sam with their violins played duets etc in the new kitchen – I chipped in with flute & we had a nice little concert . . .

Dec 29 – Clear & fine – Found telegram in SF Examiner of yesterday of my old Plymouthian Comstock friend Matt Rider, committed suicide by shooting in S.F. Sunday – He was working as helper in the Con Va assay office at time of big bonanza and made 30 or 40 thousand dollars – Quit his job. Told me he would never have to do a lick of work again – Went to S.F. & seems he would try his luck in stocks again, & so this was the end of it – A mighty good man & good friend of mine. Nearly 60 yrs old – Bed 12 –

Dec 31 – Same – Carpenter work completed & got on 1st coat of paint – Worked late in evening & got to bed at 12 – Much noise down town at midnight, firearms, bombs, crackers, etc – Salvation Army paraded, etc, letting the old year 1897 out and letting in the New Year 1898 –

BOOK NO.  74

Reno
Jan 1, 1898 – Dec 31, 1898

Jan 1, 1898, through Feb 15 [Little snow, even in the mountains – Cold, often below zero – AD completes carpentry & painting in his new room, makes a writing desk & footstool and paints them bright red, puts bookshelves in his closet – Other odd jobs – Notes deaths of two more old Comstock friends and the fact that Adolph Sutro has been declared "mentally incompetent" – Letters & gifts from sisters Lizzie & Cornelia & letters to them & to brother Charley – Mary is acting principal of the high school as Prof Bray has typhoid fever – AD is about town and at depot – Has short conference with Senator Jones & keeps close track of his travels – Writes a fifteen-page story, "Manuel Anjere, The Grip Fiend of Valparaiso," which is rejected by the *San Francisco Examiner* – Sends a letter to Wells Drury in San Francisco, asking his advice on writing stories for the San Francisco papers.]

Feb 16 – Variable – telegrams this AM tell of US battleship Maine, blown up & sunk in harbor of Havana, Cuba, at 10 oclock last night – 266 lives lost – Very exciting news in view of hostile feeling between US and Spain on the Cuban question, already assuming a warlike tendency – Supposed to have been done by Spaniards with a torpedo or sunken mine – Morning and evening down town –

Feb 18 . . . PM & evening I worked at remodeling and recopying *Manuel Anjere,* improving it somewhat –

Feb 19 . . . AM down town – met Prof Bray, who is sufficiently recovered to attend to his duties as Supt of public schools . . .

Sunday, Feb 20 . . . Finished Manuel Anjere today and mailed it tonight to M H de Young of the SF Chronicle . . .

Feb 22 . . . Flags still flying at ½ mast for loss of the Maine & her crew . . . *Manuel Anjere* returned from the *Chronicle* today with: "Dear Sir – Your story is a good one but unfortunately there is no market for romance in the *Sunday Chronicle*. Yours very truly, Taliexin Evans, Sunday editor" . . .

Feb 24 . . . Sent *Manuel Anjere* to SF *Bulletin* tonight – letter from Millie says she had nice boy baby on the 10th inst – named same as his father.

Feb 25 . . . PM wrote an editorial for the *Reno Journal,* entitled: *"Poor Railroad Economy"* . . . Sutro's property appraisement filed Thursday at SF – Total amount $2,849,570.10 . . .

Feb 26 . . . PM commenced a big cryptogram story for the *"Black Cat"* magazine prize competition which closes March 31 – Highest prize $1,500 – Over 2 feet of snow fell at Truckee this last storm – Is about 5 ft at the Summit – My editorial . . . resulted in the paper being ordered left by the carrier regularly at our house . . .

Feb 27 through March 19 [More snow, and three more deaths of former Comstock acquaintances – "Manuel Anjere" is rejected again, this time by the *Argonaut* of San Francisco – AD writes and revises a story entitled "Wildcat Joe" and another called "The Golden Crypto-gram" (which draws heavily on his earlier story, "The Living Hinge," written in July, 1867) – He gets his trunk sent in from Carson City, and in response to a note from M H de Young, sends "Manuel Anjere" off to the *San Francisco Chronicle.*]

Sunday, March 20 . . . PM polished off *Wildcat Joe* and both are now ready to ship East – The *Golden Cryptogram* 23 pages – 5,880 words – *Wildcat Joe* 22 pages – 5,815 words . . .

March 21 . . . Lively snowstorm . . . Made a very careful research-ing review of both stories – got postal order for $1.00 to cover two (50 cent) annual subscriptions to the *"Black Cat"* – one for each story – as per advertised stipulations in the competition – wrote private note to go along, also stamped envelope for return M.S.S. Inclosed all in one enve-lope directed to *Shortstory Publishing Co. 144 High st, Boston, Mass.* . . . 40 cents . . . Launched my boat on the postal car of East bound train at 8:30 PM – [Inserted loose in the journal is a small square of lined paper which says, in AD's handwriting:]

Prize. $1,500 –

Bessie	$ 100 –
Goodie	100 –
Millie	100 –
Sam	50 –
Alf.	50 –
Grandma	50 –
Aunt Eunice	50 –
Mama & Papa	1,000 –
	$1,500 –

March 26 . . . My big son Sam went up the river 6 miles, fishing –
caught 37 – all whitefish except 8 trout, one of which weighed 3 pounds –
27 pounds in all . . .

Sunday, March 27 . . . We feasted on whitefish and trout today –
gave some away –

March 29 . . . Dan De Quille died on the 16th of this month at West
Liberty, Iowa. Va *Enterprise* this morning had over a column about it
from the Salt Lake *Tribune,* and the Va *Chronicle* ½ column on it –
Died of la grippe . . . nearly 69 yrs old . . . Evening I wrote his obituary, as I had often promised him I would.

[Clip from *Enterprise,* reprinting C C Goodwin's tribute to "one of the
most useful lives that ever wore itself out for the West":] One week ago
. . . the 16th inst, just after midday, poor, gifted, genial, quaint William
Wright—"Dan de Quille"—died. . . . The work that he did . . . was
never equalled on a newspaper by any one man. He wrote incessantly.
. . . A reporter . . . but in addition, he wrote essays, some of which
were purely and profoundly scientific; others . . . were a burlesque on
science. . . . He wrote winsome stories . . . a learned historian . . .
a gifted geologist. . . . He knew the Comstock lode, with all its peculiarities and habits . . . had much more power than Twain, and was of vast
service to him, for in those days Mark was unseasoned in newspaper work
and more or less uncouth. . . . While there was friction and excitement
on all sides, Wright moved unruffled and untouched among all . . . was
at home when talking with the great Silliman or Agassiz. . . . We hope
the peace that came and lulled the senses of the great hearted man . . .
will remain with him forever.

March 30 . . . Simon Fraser died at Va this morning – effects of a
buggy upset in 6 mile canyon last Sunday, with his wife – She was little
hurt, but he had broken ribs and other injuries internally – 62 yrs old –

Knew him long time in Gold Hill – in business there – Afterward Chief of Police at Va, etc – War news occupies increasing public attention and telegrams in the newspapers and on bulletin boards are eagerly looked for – Looks as though might have war with Spain yet.

March 31 . . . My Dan De Quille obituary appeared in *Journal* this morning all right – Sent a copy of the paper to Mrs William Wright (Dan De Quille) . . . one to Eunice, and a clip of it in a note to M H de Young . . . PM I was at *Journal* office and met Will O Young, son of Judge W H Young, . . . a tall, hearty young fellow, about 34 yrs old, and just returned from Klondike and Dawson – Showed us a pound or two of nuggets, the two biggest about $100 each – Had a long and very interesting conversation – half a dozen of us – Came on visit to his family, etc and will start back again next Saturday . . . [The obituary in the *Journal* appears, except for the facts about Dan De Quille's death, in Doten's piece "Early Journalism of Nevada" – See Appendix.]

April 2 . . . PM, baseball game between the Stanfords of Cal, and our Nevada State University boys . . . Stanfords won, 35 to 1 – Evening I wrote & sent letter to C C Goodwin, of Salt Lake *Tribune*, with Dan's obituary inclosed.

Sunday, April 3 . . . *"Manuel Anjere"* in today's S.F. *Chronicle* in good shape, illustrated with the grip scene in the corral . . . This story crossed the Sierra Nevada nine times in M.S.S. and this printed makes the tenth. Singular bit of journalistic history.

> [The story recounts how a young Chilean peasant rises unintentionally to fame with a bone-crushing grip that righteously whips the sports that come to try it, but money and an affiliation with a beautiful but unprincipled lady of Valparaiso turn Manuel to the boastful bad, until the lady's husband, a professional gambler, uses a dark, windy night to quietly knife the grip fiend in the back.] The brawniest muscle is as nothing against the glittering knife or the leaden bullet. He who poses as master and conqueror of his fellow man will some day find his own conqueror, and he who, in the confident insolence of his overpowering strength willfully tramples with impunity upon the life and dearest rights of others, will be given no show when the hour of revenge cometh. . . . His invincible grip availed him naught against the grip of grim death.

April 4 . . . Wife went on morning train to attend State Teachers Institute . . . at Winnemucca . . . Our youngsters keep house while she is gone – I busy at cleaning up our ranch, trimming shrubbery, etc . . .

April 5 . . . Evening I took look at an acetylene gas plant . . . opposite the depot . . . whitest, clearest, steadiest & brightest of all gas lights . . . half the cost of ordinary gas . . .

April 6 . . . Mended my coat & worked at my ranching job – Wife returned on evening train . . .

April 8 . . . Clear & pleasant – Spain has from the first denied all culpability or responsibility for the Maine disaster. Our naval Board of Inquiry find that an explosion from a submarine mine, from the outside of the ships bottom on the port side, exploded two or more of the ships magazines but unable to fix the guilt or responsibility upon anybody.

April 9 – Same – Finished my home ranching job – letter from Jones – very brief – only thanking me for the full details of information in my last letter – Wrote & sent letter to M H de Young – also wrote to Frank M Huffaker, Va, inclosing *Manuel Anjere* to my Chileno friend Jose Salinas, who told me the story originally in Spanish, and I translated it freely into English now. Read in the Va *Chronicle* this evening that south side of the Douglass building, Va, fell or collapsed at 11 oclock last night – Nobody hurt – 3 story brick – south wall in bad condition for some time, so it went down of its own volition – Old Joe says he will rebuild it – The Washoe Club rooms destroyed but damage did not extend quite to where I used to room – Two or three members of the *Washoe Club* (disbanded some months ago) were there having a little game of cards but being alarmed made a lively escape – The SF papers tell of big avalanche in Chilcoot Pass last Sunday – 100 lives lost.

April 11 – Clear and pleasant – Busy fixing screen doors and windows, in view of approaching fly time – A meeting of Nevada and California cattle men, called by the Governor, was held at Carson today – Decided not to allow the quarantined, starving cattle of California to be brought into this state for feed or pasturage –

> [The *Journal* clarifies that the "Texas" or "splenetic" fever, carried by ticks, had infested the cattle of the San Joaquin Valley, and Nevada ranchers feared that even inspected cattle might carry the disease in a dormant state.]

April 12 . . . President McKinley's delayed and important message to Congress, presented yesterday on the Cuban crisis, he recommending armed intervention . . .

April 14 . . . Bad drought prevailing throughout Cal . . . Severe wrangling in Congress over war resolutions in response to Prest's message – The lie passed, books thrown, etc. They growled fiercely about the Prest's delay in sending them his message, & were almost ready to declare war upon *him* and now they make worse delay, quarreling over it –

April 16 . . . Put on fourth and last of screen doors . . .

Sunday, April 17 . . . First blossoms on our big old pear tree opened today . . .

April 18 . . . Last Thursday evening there was a banquet of the Eastern Star . . . Lisle Jameson borrowed wifes big cactus plant for the occasion, it having bloomed that morning in the full glory of one of the most beautiful flowers I ever saw – most as big as a dinner bell – fine light pink in color, with white trimmings . . .

April 19 . . . Odd jobs, carpentering, etc – Congress agreed last night or this morning, on war resolutions in accordance with Prest's message – Spain must leave Cuba or fight, and the Cuban people to make their own independent gov't . . .

April 20 . . . Fixing water pipes, faucets, etc – President McKinley signed the Congressional Cuban joint war resolutions at noon today and Secy of State Sherman at once telegraphed . . . Madrid . . . Troops are gathering from all parts of the country to the southern coast . . .

April 21 – Cloudy, cooler & very blustering from the West – Lieut Hubbard, sent here some time ago as military instructor to the cadets of the Nevada State University has been officially sent for to rejoin his regiment in New York, so he closed up his affairs and left on this mornings train at 8 oclock with his family. The Cadets with the University band – about 100 cadets – marched in from the University to the depot and saw him off in good military style – He made a short speech bidding them good bye – This is the first war incident for Reno. Spain refused the ultimatum at Madrid this morning, first giving Minister Woodford his passport – He left for France at 4 o'clock PM – The President sent notifications to all other nations that a state of war now existed between the US and Spain, without war being formally declared. The "White Squadron" from Hampton Roads is ordered to Porto Rico to intercept the coming Spanish flotilla. The Key West fleet ordered to strictly blockade Havana, keeping about 7 miles outside, lying off and on. This evening the University students or cadets marched the streets carrying a sort of hay-stuffed ragbaby or effigy marked "Spain" on one side and "Sagasta" on the other, all singing "John Browns Body." They hung it by the neck to a telegraph pole, beside the railroad track, at crossing of Virginia st and Commercial Row amid the shouting hilarity of a huge applauding crowd and left it there for the night.

April 22 . . . This evening the boys let old Sagasta down from telegraph pole, tarred and feathered him, dragged him through the streets to place of beginning and there burned him up with Spain – while a lot of kids got up a lively, whooping war dance around the blazing remains.

April 23 . . . Finished my water pipe work with aid of a plumber – I had a very hard day of it – made me very sore and lame. The "Buena Ventura," a Spanish merchant vessel was captured at sea this morning and brought into Key West as a war prize. The first gun of the war was fired throwing a shot across her bows to make her heave to . . .

Sunday, April 24 – Home all day with lameness and bad bowels – President McKinley issued call yesterday for 125,000 volunteers – Nevada's quota only 138 . . .

April 25 – Clear & springlike – All fruit trees got into full bloom during last week, and now the green leaves are trying to throw a shade – even the locust trees, last of all, show opening buds of green – Kept pretty quiet today – Received check on W F & Co from the SF *Chronicle* for *$14.* for *Manuel Anjere!* Cashed it and paid sundry small bills, etc . . . War formally declared today –

April 26 . . . Some of the University Cadets have sent in their names for enlistment as cavalry men – Among them Emmet Boyle of Gold Hill . . .

April 27 . . . Busy training hop vines, etc – 3 or 4 more sea prizes reported taken today – and one, the "Saranac" an American merchantman captured by the Spanish off Manila, the first prize they have taken . . . Melville Atwood, old time well known assayer, geologist and Mineralogist, died at San Francisco day before yesterday and was buried today – Made the first assay in discovery of Comstock silver, in 1859 in San F. [Atwood's assay was actually made in Grass Valley, California – Some people credit J J Ott of Nevada City, California, with being first.]

April 28 . . . Procured three dozen or so of horseradish slips and set them out today in our yard . . . Three of our cruisers blockading Matanzas, Cuba, being fired upon by one of the forts, responded by bombarding both forts to death in 18 minutes – killing 100 or more Spaniards –

April 29 . . . Busy making a door-step platform 3 ft by 10 – for the two doors on north side of house . . . bowels still troublesome . . . Cardenas, Cuba, was bombarded yesterday by monitor Terror, and gunboat Machias, because they were fired upon from a fort – They silenced all the works in about an hour . . . Commenced horse radish cure for rheumatism today – Also commenced writing up this journal into regulation book for 1898, this evening –

April 30 . . . Bro Charley sole proprietor of *Memorial* since April 1, having bought out his long time partner, Avery –

May 2 . . . Commodore Dewey's fleet engaged the Spanish fleet at Manila yesterday and after severe engagement with both it and the forts, completely conquered the fleet, with great loss of ships and men . . . in the evening Manila surrendered & was taken possession of by US marines. Capt Terrence J Talby died at his home at Virginia . . . Formerly chief of Police and always prominent in Va & Storey County –

May 3 . . . Finished writing up to date – 5,000 troops to be sent to the Phillipine Islands from Pacific coast . . .

May 4 . . . Bowels checked and improving – Enlistment of cavalrymen going on lively at Carson . . . The 30,000 insurgents at Manila put themselves under Commodore Deweys command . . . Devil to pay in Madrid, Spaniards terribly excited over the Manila defeat . . . riot and revolution threatened – Martial law proclaimed . . .

May 5 . . . Commodore Dewey's report received, is reported to say that he lost 50 men and 100 wounded . . . Two of his ships badly damaged . . . Twenty three cavalry recruits from the Comstock went to Carson yesterday, and 16 from here . . .

May 7 . . . *Official* report from Dewey received at Washington this morning – That of Thursday was hasty or premature . . . He reports that he cut the telegraphic cable to Hong Kong for a starter, then went into Manila harbor and totally destroyed the Spanish war fleet of 11 vessels and silenced the land batteries . . . No American loss – half a dozen wounded – no ship damaged . . . Great rejoicing throughout the whole country . . . Here in Reno it was like the 4th of July in flags & decorations – Evening the University Cadets and Company C, NNG,

paraded the streets with band, and there was big meeting at crossing of
Virginia and Third streets – President Stubbs of the University presided
& made speech – also Dr Patterson, Hon S Summerfield, Judge Cheney
and Rev Mr Hudleson – big bonfires on the Plaza and dynamite shooting – Cannon at University fired national salute – Much cheering and
singing of national songs – Everybody felt proud that he was an American – Greatest victory the world ever saw – Bed 12 – University field
day – Athletic sports contest between the Stanfords of Cal and our
Nevada University boys . . . The Stanfords had the best of it, generally – Was held at the race track – Adolph Sutro was removed from his
home by the sea to that of his daughter and guardian, Dr Emma Merritt
in San F, for better and more convenient care and treatment day before
yesterday – taken on a litter in an ambulance – Hopelessly imbecile –
His younger daughter, Clara Sutro, raised big row over removal – threatens to appeal to the law, etc.

Sunday, May 8 . . . PM I commenced . . . rewriting Journal Book
No 72 – 1896 . . . Deweys official report fully confirmed . . . Seems
like a miracle that our fleet was uninjured and we lost no men . . .

May 9 . . . The Reno boys enlisted at Carson were expected home on
a 36 hours furlough by evening train at 8 – Band and GAR veterans were
on hand to receive them – marched through streets and to the armory –
much enthusiasm . . . Dewey has not only been made Rear Admiral,
but received the thanks of Congress . . .

May 11 . . . Carson celebrated Dewey's victory today . . . Sampson
is looking out for the Spanish war fleet, but don't find it – reported to
have gone back to Spain. Embarkation of troops from Tampa for Cuba
reported to have commenced today . . . It is stated that Admiral Mon-
tijo of the defeated Spanish fleet escaped capture by running along the
shore of the harbor with his two sons to Manila – The citizens enraged by
his defeat just pounced on him and killed him . . . The most practical
point for exploration of the Brunswick lode is the Sutro tunnel level.
When the Brunswick exploration commenced, a couple of years ago, this
could not be done, but now the Tunnel Company have come to an agreement in the matter, and the deep merits of the lode will be practically
developed forthwith . . .

May 13 . . . I stayed at home all day journalizing . . . Great official
war news – Sampson's fleet destroyed the principal fortification of San

Juan, Porto Rico, in a three hours bombardment with loss of only one man killed and seven wounded – Fleet uninjured – The place surrendered . . .

May 14 . . . This evening's train at 8, brought down the cavalry company enlisted at Carson, bound for rendezvous at Cheyenne to be attached to a regiment there and probably be ordered to Chickamauga shortly – Big town excitement and reception . . . whole population seemed to be at the depot – A big bonfire blazed on the open square just below the Palace – There being no time for a march through the streets, as intended, all countermarched up and down and around the bonfire, halting at Hunter st, facing the Palace to be addressed from the balcony of the Palace – Professor Bray presided and spoke, followed by F H Norcross and Rev F C Lee – Band played patriotic music, and everybody cheered & felt good. Merrick Booth is one of this accepted troop – 84 in all, including three officers – They boarded the east bound train and left about 9 oclock – Then the people subsided homeward . . .

Sunday, May 15 . . . Met Ed Higgins, from Carson on the evening train and he told me Dempsey is very sick last three or four days, confined to his bed and liable to die shortly – Frank Folsom is running the saloon for him . . .

May 16 . . . At home most of day, finishing my 1896 journal . . . a full week of steady work to do up the year . . . The steamer Gussie which left Tampa on the 10th instant with a load of soldiers and supplies has got back to Key West totally unable to effect a landing on the Cuban coast – The insurgents were not on hand to receive them at any of the proposed points, but the Spaniards were – Owing to the blockade, provisions are extremely short in Havana, and Blanco has seized all supplies sent to the relief of the starving reconcentrados to feed his troops with and has driven the reconcentrados out of the city into a barren part of the country to starve, which they do with the greatest facility – very few being left to fight about or to relieve . . .

May 18 . . . Twelve volunteers from Wadsworth went up on morning train and all were accepted as members of the new Cavalry Company – this making 56, out of the 84 required – Col W H H Pike came in with them . . . I met him. He says a telegram received from Capt Cox of the other Cavalry Co . . . now at their destination, Cheyenne, says the regiment with them will leave there for San Francisco within a week . . .

May 19 . . . The west bound passenger train leaving here at 10 AM jumped the track and two locomotives, four baggage mail & express cars were ditched about two miles above Verdi . . . in a bad place, in a cut – Engineer hurt and two or three Piutes riding on platform of baggage car were killed – All trains blockaded both ways for the day – About 2 PM a big special from the East pulled into Reno and had to stay . . . It was a train of ten pullmans and two box commissary cars – They brought a battalion of four companies of 84 each . . . belonging to the Third Regiment Nebraska Volunteers, N.G. – The rest of the regiment – 1,000 men in all – passed through in two other trains between three & four oclock this morning – all bound for the Presidio, near San F – They claim to be principally farmer boys, and they certainly are a fine looking lot of men, choice specimens of manhood, all robust, well behaved young fellows – They wore the uniform of the regular service & were fully armed & equipped as required – sleeping and eating on the train – Their train occupied the main track in the center of the town, & having to wait, they were allowed to go as they pleased about town – first having a march through the streets for drill & exercise – showing finely – Everybody shook hands with them and affiliated, especially the young ladies, all of whom seemed to take a special liking to the soldier boys – They expect to go to Manila . . . One car in this train, named "Pioneer," was said by the soldiers occupying it to be the oldest and first Pullman car ever built and the car in which the remains of Abraham Lincoln were taken home from Washington after he was assassinated – I as well as many others took a look through it . . . Evening the Reno brass band serenaded the soldier boys and some guns were fired – Fourteen more recruits, principally from Elko, arrived at Carson yesterday and were joined to the new cavalry company, making 68 men in all – Only 16 more required –

May 20 – Variable – warmer – The wreck near Verdi being cleared away, the delayed train of Nebraska soldiers pulled out about 1 oclock this morning and was soon followed by trains arriving from east with balance of their regiment, & others from Minnesota, Colorado, etc, about a dozen trains passing through during the day – Some stopped long enough to let the boys have a drill on the streets, get refreshments etc – and some merely stopped a few minutes, keeping the boys on board – Nearly or quite 3000 soldiers passed through – More coming tonight – Most of the cars today were Wagner sleepers – A Colorado train of 12 coaches & 3 commissary cars passing through at noon had a big flyer on the side of one car – *"Remember the Maine"* – This train only stopped at depot five minutes and had a full band in one car which played "Hail Columbia" in passing – W J Bryan is stated to be raising a regiment, in Nebraska, which he will command – only way he could get into commission –

May 21 – Same – breezy – The Kansas regiment passed through last night for S.F. – About 7 this evening, Batteries A & B, Utah Volunteer Artillery arrived, the boys paraded up & down street briefly and after a stop of nearly an hour passed with whoops and cheers for S.F. One train carried their cannons, caissons, etc, and 8 coaches carried the soldiers – about 250 of them – The cruiser Charleston left Mare Island on her final start for Manila – Bryan's regiment he is raising is the 3d Nebraska Volunteer Infantry – He has been commissioned *Colonel* – So he gets into office that way, if he can't through election – The second cavalry company at Carson was completed today, full ranks – 84 including officers – Bed 12 – cloudy – The Utah train this evening was decorated with flags from one end to the other –

Sunday, May 22 . . . PM a big 50 mile relay bicycle race, out at the track between Olympic Club, S.F. and the Reno Wheelmens Club – Good attendance & excellent race – But the Olympics won by half a mile – The best time made in a relay was the first, Wing (Olympic) making the five miles in 12 minutes, 59 seconds to Stanley's (Reno) 12:59⅕ . . .

May 24 . . . The crack Pennsylvania 8th regiment of volunteer infantry passed through at 6:30 and 7 o'clock this morning . . . Over 1,000 men . . .

May 25 . . . [A clip gives the roster of the recently organized cavalry company] In this list Fred M Linscott of Reno appears in place of F C Lord, of Virginia, who withdrew, preferring to be Captain of a new company of infantry volunteers expected soon to be organized at Carson – This morning the President issued a call for 75,000 more volunteers – The big Spanish war fleet is now definitely reported to be "bottled up" in the harbor of Santiago de Cuba, with Schley's squadron guarding the entrance . . .

May 26 . . . The ladies of Reno held an enthusiastic meeting last evening at the Congregational Church forming The Red Cross Society, No 2, that at Carson being No 1 for this State – 73 signed the roll – The last of the Utah Cavalry volunteers . . . passed through here on a special at 1:30 this morning . . . General Merritt, commander of the Phillipines army of invasion, and staff passed here . . . on the 9 AM west bound . . . The three transports with first troops, 2,500 for Manila, & relief of Dewey . . . sailed yesterday from San F – Big time . . .

May 27 . . . The First Regiment Colorado Volunteer Infantry passed through Reno this PM . . . 1,038 of them – in four sections . . . First one came shortly after 1 PM and last one about 4:30 – Fine looking young fellows, from various parts of Montana, hearty & robust – About half of them uniformed, but will be made all right in that respect at S.F. The Red Cross ladies rushed around lively before they came and treated them to cakes, sandwiches, etc and flowers which they collected into the depot, and passed along the side of the trains presenting to the boys at car windows & platforms, or alongside – Many got out and patronized lunch counters & restaurants & saloons – I met Capt John Hallihan, Capt of Company M – Used to live here, and several of his old friends, Judge Young, Sam Hamlin, Hymers, Barber, et al who knew he was coming, also met him & we had pleasant little meeting at the Palace . . .

Sunday, May 29 . . . PM I was taken with a severe chill for half an hour – got cold – Hot drink and to bed with fever – also introduction barred – bad . . . Bed at 10, relieved – from 7 AM –

May 30 . . . Memorial Day – About 11 AM procession went out to the Hillside cemetery north of town, and afterward to the Masonic cemetery west of town and decorated soldier's graves with flowers, held exercises, etc . . . I had another severe chill about 8 AM, succeeded by fever . . .

May 31 . . . PM & evening I wrote a long 6 page letter to Eunice . . .

June 1 . . . Jason Libbey and Curtis Seagraves, two of our University Cadets, left about 8 AM on bicycles for the Keswick mine, northern part of California, about 300 miles from here, where they seek employment for the vacation, or longer – a pretty arduous trip . . . Sunday working in the Comstock mines was entirely suspended on Sunday last for the first time in the history of the great lode – Sign of the times . . . My two stories . . . returned from the *Black Cat* competition today . . . So I *wasn't in it* – and have lost $1,500 that I didn't win . . .

June 2 . . . The South Dakota regiment went through about 12 oclock last night – with a wild whoop . . . Most business places in town closed to attend University windup today, & big crowds of people went – I footed over there – The exercises were held in the gymnasium – Crowded and interesting – Raising new flag on the new flagstaff – 107 ft high – with dedication exercises very enthusiastic & American – 23 students, including seven girls graduated – My boy Sam, president of the graduating class . . . Schley's big victory corroborated . . .

June 3 – Variable, more pleasant – Just before noon the new troop of Nevada Volunteer Cavalry . . . arrived on the local . . . bound for Cheyenne . . . They marched to the Pavilion at once, where they were lunched and dined by the Red Cross ladies of Reno – were about town as they pleased during the PM, visiting friends, relatives, etc. At 7 PM they were escorted to the open space near the depot by the Reno Guard with band – Big crowd of people – bonfire – exercises on porch of the Palace Hotel – Dr Stubbs presided – Speeches by T V Julien, B F Curler Jr, F H Norcross, Dr Stubbs, Gov Sadler, etc – Swords presented to Capt Linscott, and Lieuts Gignoux and Wright by University cadets and citizens with usual form – High School girls & boys sang patriotic songs from the balcony, band played – much hurrahing and great general enthusiasm – Train from Cal came along at 8:40 – Our boys had two special sleeping cars – train made long wait to say final good bye's, and finally pulled out at 9:30 for the East – The boys had splendid send off – They carried a beautiful little company banner of orange colored silk, etc, presented by citizens of Carson . . . Three of the boys who got drunk & disorderly about town this afternoon were promptly discharged by Capt Linscott, & their places filled by Reno recruits –

June 4 . . . Sam preparing for a camping trip out in the Sierra Valley and Independence lake section with Guy Walts . . . Sampson has joined Schley with his fleet and are making things very uncomfortable about Santiago, bombarding forts, etc – They sent a big collier ship, the Merrimac, and sunk her yesterday morning in the narrow channel of the narrow harbor entrance, thus blocking the Spanish fleet in – Lieut Hobson and 7 other daring men did this under big fire of batteries, then rowed in a boat to Spanish flagship & surrendered as prisoners of war – Brilliant exploit –

Sunday, June 5 – Clear, warm & pleasant – Sam with Guy W Walts, a fellow graduate . . . started out about 7:30 AM on their camping trip – They had a buck-board and black mare belonging to Walts – also a small gray Jennet, led behind – well fitted with grub, utensils, fishing poles, rifle, bedding, etc – Wife rode with them to 2 or 3 miles above Verdi, where they took lunch, transferred their outfit to the back of the little Jennet and took the grade and trail into the Sierra – wife drove back home alone . . . State Orphans' Home management at Carson being investigated – scandalous charges brought by Day, a discharged employe . . .

June 8 . . . About 10:30 the first of three railroad sections with an Iowa regiment passed through . . . cars bore war cry: *"Remember the Maine"* – Much shouting and cheering as they passed through town . . . The armored cruiser Monterey sailed for Manila yesterday from S.F. accompanied by a big collier, Brutus . . . More troops being landed in Cuba for investment of Santiago . . .

June 9 . . . A telegram says that Manila has surrendered to Dewey, as a matter of protection against the insurgents – Sent strong force of marines and took possession – (This turned out untrue) . . .

June 11 . . . After silencing the batteries by the battleship Oregon, et al, the city & harbor of Guantanamo, Cuba, was captured yesterday, 600 marines landed & took possession and the American flag was raised for the first time over Cuba . . .

June 14 – Clear & pleasant – The west bound train at 9 AM, brought our second troop of Nevada cavalry which went from here a week ago last Friday, back from Cheyenne, on their way to San F, and to Manila – Big crowd at the depot welcomed them, and the Red Cross piled a wagon load of lunch onto them, enough for a regiment – Boys looked fine & happy – Only stopped about ten minutes – Had a rancorous discussion this PM in family about my youngest daughter Mary Goodwin Doten taking upon herself to change her name to Goodwin Stoddard Doten – Evening down town – Met Owen Fraser and Ben Higbee, from Va on a trip to S.F. Bed 1 –

June 15 – Same – Evening the High School graduating exercises took place at the Opera House – I attended – densely crowded – The exercises very interesting after usual style – My youngest daughter, Mary Goodwin Doten, graduated with first honors under her assumed name of Goodwin Stoddard Doten – Exercises commenced at 8 & closed at 11 – Bed 1 –

June 16 . . . Fixed up "Wildcat Joe," and shipped him to Hon M H de Young, San Fran *Chronicle* . . . The second fleet of soldiers, etc, for Manila, 3,500, sailed from San F yesterday . . . A full regiment of Tennessee volunteer infantry – 1200 men – passed in three RR sections . . .

June 18 . . . 108 recruits from Iowa, to fill Iowa regiment companies now at SF passed through this AM . . . Red Cross gave 'em lots of good lunch . . . nice looking boys, but poorly clothed – no uniform – I copied Goodie's graduating essay for myself . . . Under the last call for troops, Nevada has been allotted three companies of infantry . . .

Sunday, June 19 – Same – PM breezy & dusty – At 9:30 AM, the noted Astor troop or company of volunteers from New York, arrived and after about 20 minutes stop passed on to SF for Manila – Astor Battery of artillery – 107 total . . . had their cannon, etc along – but no mules or horses for sea voyage – Will get those at Manila – Finest looking and best equipped lot yet – needed & received no lunch or grub assistance from the Red Cross – only flowers & locks of hair – At 12:30 the delayed west bound train brought over 100 more recruits for Iowa and Idaho companies, S.F., not dressed or regularly equipped, same as those of yesterday – At 10:05 AM saw 2 carrier pigeons turned loose from the depot office of W F & Co on opposite side of street – They were sent over here from Sacramento in a nice little basket by a Mr Kinney . . . who makes business of raising them, for a test of ability – Each one [had] its number on a little ring around its ankle – and their basket will be returned to Kinney by express, telling time of turning loose, etc – They rose up in air, circling higher, higher, till out of sight – afterward supposed to get their bearings and strike out on return to Sacramento – PM commenced letter to Bessie – Bed 11 –

June 21 – Clear & pleasant – Wrote two page letter to Senator Jones . . . Evening down town & mailed it – Met . . . Hank Mitchell old time Va friend, lawyer – now of San F – been up to Va & came down this evening – Had long old time, highly gratifying chat together at the Palace, till west bound train came at 11 & he passed homeward – Bed 12 – The Cuban invasion fleet which reached Santiago yesterday, consisted of about 50 transports and war vessels – 16,000 troops – largest armada ever seen in American waters –

June 22 . . . L Guggenheim, Grand Secretary I.O.O.F. at Va found to be a defaulter by Grand Lodge, now in session at Va – He is short from $5,000 to $10,000 in that and other Associations of which he is Secy or Treas – Tried to suicide with laudanum but didn't succeed – left $36, a life insurance policy for $3,000 and a will bequeathing it to the I.O.O.F. in his safe – Is said to have lost all this money on a turn in stocks –

June 23 . . . 180 recruits from Nebraska and Colorado passed on 7 coach special . . . Much hilarious cheering and waving of flags . . .

June 24 . . . General Shafter's big army of invasion . . . effected landing yesterday at Baiquiri, 15 miles east of Santiago de Cuba, and Juragna, 3 miles nearer in perfect safety – Were protected by guns of the warships, and also by 5000 insurgent troops waiting to join them – L Guggenheim's defalcation is now reported to foot up to over $7,000 . . .

June 25 . . . Guggenheim was arrested & put in jail last night – brought before Justice of the Peace Weir today at 1 PM, held in sum of $1,500 bonds to appear Monday at 10 AM for examination on embezzlement . . . Our troops had 1st big battle of the invasion yesterday, 8 miles from Santiago . . .

June 27 . . . About 11 AM a special came along with a lot of recruits from Ohio – were riotous, had a muss with a brakeman – were arrested, 14 of them, & taken before Justice Linn, who released them till evening on condition of good behavior – They left for S.F. on 10 PM train . . .

June 28 . . . Leo Guggenheim before the Grand Jury today, pleaded guilty to embezzlement, waived trial & asked for sentence at once – Judge Mack sentenced him to 5 years in State Prison . . . He is 68 yrs old . . .

June 30 . . . At 3:30 Sam, with Guy Walts returned from their camping trip – Had good time & looked rugged & well & dirty . . .

July 1 . . . The grand American assault upon Santiago de Cuba commenced this morning, by land and sea – Sampson bombarding the forts at the entrance, and Shafter advancing upon the city . . .

Sunday, July 3 . . . Telegram at 9 PM said Cevera's fleet of seven war vessels made a bold dash to get out of Santiago harbor this morning but was met by Sampson's fleet and every ship was sunk except one and they were in hot chase after her – Surrender of Santiago was momentarily expected . . .

July 4 – Clear, fine, warm day – Reno full of people . . . Parade excellent, what there was of it – Governor & staff – Brass band, Reno Guard, GAR vets – about a dozen floats, Goddess of Liberty, States, Red Cross, The Masonic, trades, etc, Uncle Sam & Johnny Bull on a tandem bicycle – carriages – Passed through principal streets – exercises at the Convent Park, corner 4th & Lake sts – President, Hon Wm Webster; Orator, Hon Judge A E Cheney; Reader, W C Lamb; Poet, Miss "Goodwin S Doten" – She recited poem written by her mother – band, quartette, etc – Fireworks in evening, west part of town – Pretty good – I was around & saw everything – Reno profusely decorated and terrible fusillade of bombs, crackers etc all day . . . The news made all feel good . . .

July 5 . . . Shafter concluded to take a rest, now that the Spanish fleet is destroyed and Santiago at his mercy . . .

July 6 . . . The US Senate today passed the Hawaiian annexation resolution . . . Company C, Reno Guard, Capt Stoddard, went to Carson on the PM local train, that being selected as the mustering rendezvous of the new battalion of Nevada infantry . . . Lieut Hobson & his gallant crew were exchanged yesterday at Santiago, and returned to their ship amid great rejoicing – Wife, with other lady school teachers left this morning train for an outing at Oakland, S.F. etc – Sam went fishing up the river yesterday with two other young chaps – went afoot & took blankets along . . .

July 7 . . . Alfred rode on his wheel, up to Laughton's Springs, half a dozen miles above here on the river this morning – found Sam & his party having good time – Brought home a lot of rainbow trout, & we had them for dinner – fine . . . Sam returned . . . about 10 o'clock this evening –

July 8 through 13 [AD loses sleep and eats little because of an infected molar, hears that Mary & Bessie are both at Miss Lindsay's in Oakland, starts packing some pictures to send there, observes infantry companies from Elko & Winnemucca on their way to Camp Sadler at the race track in Carson, and a signal corps company from Utah & Montana and the First New York Volunteer Infantry on their way to SF – Notes that Carson has forbidden the watering of lawns due to a drouth caused by the meager winter snows, Santiago is under bombardment, the Spanish Ministry has resigned, the fleet of Admiral Camara, on its way to the Philippines, has been ordered back to defend Spain from Watson's fleet, and that yellow fever is breaking out among American troops in Cuba.]

July 14 – Clear & hot – Telegram to the *Gazette* that Santiago has surrendered, received at noon, set the town crazy – Bombs, crackers, etc fired in profusion on the streets – and much increase of congratulatory drinks – Evening much more so – Band with quite a procession of torches etc paraded streets, fireworks popped, glared & fizzled, dynamite anvil guns fired on plaza, flags waved, & everybody rejoicing – Last evening's east bound passenger train was held up by two men after the regulation style, about a mile east of Humboldt at 2 oclock this morning – express car & safe blown open and treasure & money taken – Passengers not molested, & nobody hurt . . . Tooth convalescent –

July 15 . . . Surrender of Santiago confirmed – details given – unconditional surrender of Santiago with neighboring country forts and towns comprising the east end of Cuba, with the troops, comprising the Fourth Corps of the Spanish army, over 20,000, US agreeing to ship these troops back to Spain under parole – cheapest and best way to get rid of them . . . Many members and hopeful friends arrived from various parts of the State today & this evening to attend meeting of Nevada State Central Committee of the Silver Party . . . My big troublesome left lower jaw molar . . . has become quiescent . . . For the last 2 yrs it has been very sensitive to cold or heat . . . now it has abruptly become insensible to cold, but not to heat – don't understand the philosophy of the phenomenon –

July 16 . . . Reno was full of political candidates & politicians today – making it lively – C C Wallace [political agent for the CP RR] of course – I mixed with them a little . . .

Sunday, July 17 . . . Had irrigating and *irritating* spat with Alf Jr 4 PM . . . The evening train from Cal, brought my wife and Bessie home . . .

July 20 – Clear & hot – Evening down town met —— Kennedy, old time 6 mile Canyon miner, etc, on his way to Butte, Montana, leaving Comstock for good – Con Va & all other mines have shut down – The last faro game at Va closed Tuesday night – Not one game running there – 1st time in history of the Comstock – Billy Cann the Va photographer was married here to Miss Watkins of Va this PM & left tonight for honeymoon in Cal – Sam gone on fishing trip up river with George James –

July 21 . . . My 69th birthday – had a last years apple kept till now and cut it for this occasion, giving Bessie half – Very much wilted and wrinkled but still sound & good – It would have kept longer – Dont think another one in State – From Cornelia as my birthday presents I received a nice book, "The White Company," a beautiful poetic birthday card, and a Pilgrim postal card – one of the new style of postals authorized by Govt – 6½ by 4¼ inches – requires a 2 ct stamp . . .

[Clip, *Reno Evening Gazette:*] The Comstock's sun has nearly set, and when it is entirely hidden by old Mount Davidson one of the most wonderful towns and mining camps this world has ever seen will go down with it.

Virginia City was a place of 20,000 inhabitants a few years ago, and no city in the land, big or little, enjoyed more of the luxuries of life than did Virginia. Twenty dollar pieces were more plentiful than nickles are to-day. . . . The whistles that blew to welcome General Grant in the seventies are now silent; many of the old hoisting works have been dismantled by the hand of man, and many more are being dismantled by the hand of nature. Only four whistles are now left to sound the departing glory of a once prosperous place. Con. Virginia sold for over $900.00 in 1875 and now it is selling for only 35 cents, and is not worth that. Everything about the place is fast going to decay, and the Comstock lode and Virginia will soon only be remembered in history.

July 23 . . . The Foley estate case has occupied the present week in the Dist Court here – Mrs Hartley was present . . . and among the interested auditors. [$25,000 to eastern heirs, the rest to Mrs Smith, Foley's widow.]

July 26 – Same – Hottest yet – 95° – Hon Frank G Newlands returns tomorrow morning from Washington, D.C. to Reno – It is rumored that he proposes to stand in for US Senator in place of Stewart this Fall – The port of Guanica . . . was taken early this morning by a US gunboat . . . Spain officially applied to US for peace today, for the first time, through the French Ambassador, Cambon – I commenced a *"Woods' Creek in '49"* story this PM . . . Mrs Alice M Hartley has commenced suit to recover Foley's dead sons share in his father's estate –

July 27 . . . 100° in the shade at 4 PM – at the Palace corner . . . PM I wrote on my new story – The mines of the Comstock being closed down, the miners and others are getting out of there fast as they can – Most miners go to Butte City, Montana . . . The fact is that the old Comstock nut is pretty well cracked and used up, the meat taken out and the shell remains – A strong agitation is now being made toward pumping out the lower levels, and resumption of deep mining – The reason of the suspension in 1868 was more the total lack of paying ore at those lower depths than anything else . . .

July 29 . . . Senator Stewart and wife returned from Washington this AM, & went on the PM local to "their home in Carson" –

July 30 . . . US ultimatum reply to Spains cry for peace completed today . . .

Sunday, July 31 . . . Still about 100° – At 5 PM I finished composition of my new story "Woods' Creek in Forty-Nine" – 16 pages legislative bill sheets . . . At 8 PM when I went down town, heard that Sam was drowned today in Independence Lake – Rushed back home – they had also heard of it – Down town again – tracked up story – no such telegram received at office – Finally concluded there was nothing in it – He has been out about a week with George James a class mate, fishing, hunting, etc – Was at Overton near Lake Tahoe last Tuesday & got separated from James, & lost in the mountains – 27 hours without food – Turned up all right at Independence, and wife got letter from him this morning, saying would be home tomorrow . . . At 10:30 was at telegraph office – no dispatch about Sam received – Came home feeling all right . . .

Aug 1 . . . Revised my new story . . . Postal card from Geo James to his father this morning – At Independence lake, & will be home tomorrow – all right –

[Clip, *San Francisco Examiner:*] The Heney divorce case came up in the District Court Saturday, and already seems about to assume an interesting position with relation to law. Alfred Chartz appeared for Mrs. Heney and ex-Secretary of State O. H. Grey, for the husband, an inmate of the penitentiary, convicted of robbing the Carson Mint. . . .

The attorneys say there is more in this case than appears on the surface. When Heney was convicted he was fined $5,000, but the Government, when it sought to levy, found that he had anticipated it, and all the property was in his wife's name, and after a long legal battle the Government got the worst of it. Mrs. Heney was intrusted by her husband with everything, and he was charged with having stolen about $30,000 from the Mint. All during his trial she was very devoted, but now seeks to obtain a divorce, but does not intend to give up any of the property.

Heney's attorneys will present an action to make her return the property, and the Government will watch the proceedings closely and will join in the proceedings as soon as it is apparent that Heney has any property or that the transfer was not a legitimate business transaction. His attorneys think they can get the best of the Government here again, and this is where the legal battle will be.

Aug 2 . . . Light thunder showers – About 4 PM Sam & his mate, George James, returned from their ten days outing . . . Both look rough & dirty but had good time –

Aug 5 . . . Sam went off down river today with Prof Hillman of the University, geologizing on various soils – About $\frac{9}{10}$ths of Shafter's army at Santiago down with malarial & yellow fever and all ordered back to America . . . Great trouble – At Puerto Rico our troops are carrying all before them without fighting . . .

Aug 6 . . . The Carson mint is being dismantled, machinery . . . being taken down & shipped away –

Sunday, Aug 7 . . . I completed my new story in every respect – 3 illustrations . . . Penciled pictures of camp of the *Pilgrim Mining Co* at Woods', *Dr H D Cogswells office & home* (Deerskin Cottage) near Curtis' Creek and a full length picture of *the Dr himself,* in hunting costume, buckskin suit, rifle etc – Inclosed private note, and mailed it to M H de Young of the SF Chronicle [See Appendix for text of story – The sketch of the Pilgrim Mining Company camp appears in the picture section of Volume 1 of these journals.] . . . Spain yields all to the US & peace will probably be concluded & hostilities cease next week . . .

Aug 8 . . . Adolph Sutro died at SF at 2:30 this morning – 78 yrs old . . . Worst upset of inkstand this PM I ever had – up my sleeve, in table drawers, on my pants, carpet, floor, etc – jet black –

Aug 9 . . . Spain's reply not received officially yet – is being translated . . . 4,000 feet of snowsheds burned today beyond Truckee . . .

Aug 10 . . . Lively work was done reconstructing the destroyed railroad, and by 3 PM the delayed trains were enabled to pass . . .

Aug 12 – AM clear & hot – PM cloudy with light thunder showers – War with Spain ended today by the official signing of the "protocol" at 4:23 PM, at Washington – Both Govts notified all their military & naval forces and ordered immediate cessation of hostilities –

Aug 13 . . . The blockade of Cuba and Porto Rico is raised – Sampson was bombarding Manzanillo, when protocol was signed yesterday – don't know how he came out . . . Sutro's will is long document, & likely to meet much litigation – Resumption of deep mining on the Comstock is taking shape in San F – leading Mining Cos holding meetings, etc – It is officially stated that the war has cost $150,000,000 –

Sunday, Aug 14 . . . Copied "Decayed Veneration" in good shape for preservation –

Aug 15 . . . Mrs Clarise Kluge of S.F. claims to be a contract wife of Sutro, & that her son Adolph, 7 yrs old, and daughter Adolphine 5 yrs old are by him – She goes in therefore for a share of Sutro's estate . . .

Aug 16 . . . Wife's Turk's Head cactus, which bloomed, one flower, April 14, in full bloom of 9 flowers today – She loaned it to Pinniger's drug store show window & it was taken there last evening in just full bloom . . . attracted crowds of people all day . . . Last Saturday Dewey and Merritt demanded the surrender of Manila in one hour – refused – then commenced shelling & directly the white flag up, and unconditional surrender – Took possession & raised Am flag – News of peace signed had not been received, & only to be by way of Hong Kong in 4 or 5 days – owing to cable being cut off – This puts a different face on the Philippine part of the peace settlement –

Aug 17 . . . I copied "Decayed Veneration," & have now three copies . . . In the brief battle at surrender of Manila we only lost 5 soldiers killed & 43 wounded – No sailors – Made Aguinaldo & his insurgents stay outside – wouldn't let them come into Manila at all – Made them very angry and they tried to fight us, but to no purpose . . .

Aug 20 . . . Silver party primaries for 13 delegates State Convention Sept 8 – 358 votes polled, said to be the largest ever cast at a primary election in Reno – The result favors Lem Allen for Governor. About all of Shafter's army have been shipped back to the US, and the Spanish soldiers back to Spain, from Santiago . . . The American flag was officially raised at Honolulu, Hawaii on the 12th instant, with all due national and military observances, it token of the Hawaii being annexed to the United States.

Sunday, Aug 21 . . . Bessie left for Cal on evening train . . . Her school resumes a week from tomorrow –

Aug 23 . . . Last evening I met Tom O'Hara a miner, boss, etc in Gold Hill at the time I was there – He came down this evening and took the east bound train on his way to Butte, Montana, leaving wife & family in Gold Hill – living in Harry Gorham's old house – Told me will give me $50 if I will sell his house, furniture & all for $500 – House cost originally $5,000, & furniture over $1,000 – Was Harry Gorham's furniture before he moved into the Jones mansion & sold to O'Hara – Tom says he must leave the old Comstock because its played out – Two crowded carloads of Indians – 20 or more – left here yesterday for Sacramento & vicinity to pick hops . . . The Silver primaries at Va & Gold Hill, Saturday 397 votes – GH polled the 97 votes –

Aug 24 . . . Meeting of Republican citizens held this evening at Judge Linn's office, and selected a lot of names to be voted for at the Rep primaries next Saturday for delegates to Rep State Convention – Sept 15 –

Aug 25 . . . Rec'd M.S.S. of my Woods' Creek story, returned from SF Chronicle –

Aug 26 . . . Gilbert McM Ross, a well known Comstock assayer 20 yrs ago or more, subsequently out in Humboldt county, has been appointed Supt of the Con Cal & Virginia, Mexican and Ophir mines – D B Lyman has resigned as Supt of them & going to leave on acc't of ill health, etc . . .

Aug 27 – Republican primaries for delegates . . . There being no opposition whatever, only the one ticket . . . a small vote polled – 140 in all . . . The Populists also held primaries, casting 19 votes . . .

Aug 28 through Sept 6 [AD suffering chills & fever morning & evening and treating them with quinine & cayenne pepper in gin – Of additional interest:]

Aug 29 . . . Schools & University all resumed today – Goodwin registered & started in Freshman on her 1st year in the University – Alfred went on his 3d year, and Sam started on Post Graduate course, teacher of pupils, etc, for which latter he gets $20 a month . . .

Sept 1 . . . The *Reveille* says that for the first time in nearly a third of a century not a steam whistle is heard in the town of Austin – Yesterday Gov Sadler rec'd a telegram from Genl Corbin, at Washington, DC, ordering the Nevada troops of the war to be mustered out . . . They have to return all arms, equipments, etc, and pass surgical examination same as when mustered in . . . This last is in case of future applications for pensions . . .

Sept 2 . . . Jason Libbey and Curtis Seagraves, who left here June 1 for work at the Keswick mine . . . returned this morning to resume their studies – They got in about 3 months work to very good advantage & look none the worse for it – good boys . . .

Sept 3 . . . Guy Walts . . . Sam's chum – has gone to Genoa to take charge of & open the public school there – good position & good, capable young teacher . . .

Sept 7 – Clear & pleasant – Democratic State Convention today, held in Clough & Crosby's hall – Effected temporary organization, appointed committees on Credentials, order of business, platform, etc, and at 3 PM adjourned till 10 AM tomorrow – Then the Silver Party State Convention starts in, and a fusion of the two parties is figured upon – The Silver delegates have already arrived, making over 200 in both conventions – The numerous candidates, friends, lookers on, etc make up biggest lot of the kind I ever saw . . . Reno is filled to overflowing with the most prominent men of the State – Very lively times are expected tomorrow – John W Mackay, and son Clarence & wife arrived in San F from the East, by northern route yesterday for a few weeks visit – Edgar E Sutro, son of Adolph has brought suit at SF to contest his father's will – grounds insanity, undue influence, etc – insane since 1882 . . . The Populist primary for delegates to county convention took place here today – Convention to be held on the 17th inst, same day as the Democratic and Silver Conventions –

Sept 8 . . . Silver Party Convention commenced at Wheelmen's Hall – organized and got as far as nominations . . . Democrats also in session . . . got as far as nomination & adjourned . . . The great question of fusion is now the stumbling block with both parties, each waiting for the other to be the first to propose . . .

Sept 9 . . . Both Conventions fought to a finish, unable to fuse – Both had Conference committees on the subject – The ultimatum of the Democrats was: We will give you all the offices, if you will merge or fuse the whole thing into a *Democratic* convention, accepting our platform, etc – The Silverites were reminded of the fusion offer of the devil to Jesus Christ: "All these things will I give unto thee if thou wilt fall down & worship me," so they indignantly refused to fuse on those terms – Both parties nominated full State tickets in the PM and adjourned sine die – Evening the Dems were out with the Wheelmen's Band whooping her up, serenading their candidate for Governor, George Russell, etc . . . *Nominations of Silver Convention:* For Congressman: Hon Francis G Newlands; Governor, Reinhold Sadler; (by 108 votes to 48 for A C Cleveland of White Pine) Lieut Governor, James R Judge of Ormsby; Supreme Judge, C H Belknap . . . *Democratic Nominees:* Congressman was passed (for Newlands) Governor, George Russell of Elko; Lieut Gov, W C Grimes of Churchill; Supreme Judge, C H Belknap of Storey . . .

Sept 10 . . . Populist State Convention today – Annexed nominations were made [for Congress, Thos Wren, Washoe; governor, J B McCullough, Washoe; lieutenant governor, W H Coffey, Storey; secretary of state, G T Leavitt, Lyon] – new Central Committee chosen & convention adjourned sine die . . . Owing to the belligerent and troublesome attitude of the insurgents at Manila, and even the possibility that terms of peace may not be satisfactorily concluded with Spain, President McKinley has ordered further mustering out of troops suspended for the present.

Sunday, Sept 11 – Same – The delegates, candidates etc having about all departed, Reno is herself again – I was talking with Lem Allen this evening on the sidewalk in front of the Arcade Hotel, with lots of people passing & repassing. We were talking about the recent Silver Convention, where he was beaten by Sadler in nomination for Governor – a rancher named Bowen stepped up to Lem, shaking him cordially by both hands exclaiming: "Hello! Lem Allen bless your old soul, I'm mighty glad to see you. Confound it all, but they did get away with you didn't they?" Just then a fine looking, neatly dressed, middle aged woman with handsome gray eyes and strong minded expression pressed in remarking in a firm clear voice: "So you're the Mr Allen, are you? And how did you come to allow yourself to be got away with by a dam'd leather-headed son of a bitch like that? I thought you was more of a man. I've got no use for *you.*" Then she turned away and walked up the sidewalk in the most dignified manner imaginable. Everybody burst out laughing of course, while Allen stood paralyzed. He gazed after her majestic form disappearing in the crowd and directly broke out into a roaring laugh that could have been heard a mile. "What devil of a woman was that?" said he – "I never saw *her* before. Well that settles it. Ive got nothing further to explain. I guess the beer's on me; come in boys." This woman was formerly a well known character in Eureka, when Reinhold Sadler lived there. He incurred her displeasure, and she used to pitch into, abuse and insult him publically whenever she was drinking or got on the warpath. He had her arrested a few times, but it only made it the worse for him when she got out. At one time especially in front of his residence, before his family and friends she cursed him for all she could think of, closing by turning her back, jerking up her dress, exposing her bare butt, and telling him: "Now you can kiss my arse you dam son of a bitch." She was a Welsh woman, very handsome and stylish and well educated. At one time she was married to a Mr McCullough who was killed in a fight, lastly she married a Mr Savory, from whom she got divorced. Some months ago she was convicted of selling whisky to Indians out at Winnemucca, and was recently discharged from prison – She is now ranching with the Mr Bowen she was with when she encountered Allen this evening –

Sept 12 . . . One year in Reno today – Went to Justice Linn's court room and got registered as a voter . . .

Sept 13 . . . PM I wrote a three page gossipy letter to the Wells *Herald,* George Vardy's paper, weekly, published Thursday's at Wells, Humboldt County, Nev – Mailed it on the east bound train at 9 PM – When I met him last Thursday he desired me to correspond for his paper saying he would pay me, etc – George I Lamy – editor & proprietor of the Gardnerville, Douglas County *Record* Carson valley – (weekly, started 3 mos ago) whom I met at same time also desired the same, and I may comply – This evening down town I met John Dobbie a 26 years resident Comstocker, leaving there finally for Costa Rica – He was a well known miner, shift boss, etc, and goes in employ of the Jones syndicate, with others, to a gold mine in Costa Rica, owned by the syndicate – Charley Colburn, W H Pratt, and Morgan Johns go with him from the Comstock, all good mining men – I had a long & interesting chat with John Dobbie over old times – we ate oysters, etc, and I saw him off . . .

Sept 15 . . . The Rep State Convention met at Wheelmen's Hall at noon . . . In the caucus it was agreed by a vote of 30 to 37 that the convention should pass any nomination it saw fit – Dr Patterson and S Summerfield were so strongly against the proposition that they withdrew from the Convention – It was also agreed that any nomination passed could be filled by the new Central Committee if deemed expedient at any time before election . . . The nominations having been all agreed upon in caucus, there was no contest but all went by acclamation or Secretary casting the ballot . . . Congressman, *Passed* – Governor, Wm McMillan, of Storey – Lieut Governor, J W Ferguson, Churchill – Secretary of State, *Passed* – Justice Supreme Court, *Passed* . . .

Sept 17 . . . Received a copy of the *Nevada State Herald* of Sept 16 . . . Had my first letter in it . . . The Democratic, Silver and Populist County Conventions were held today, each in separate hall . . . After much discussion and conferring the Dems and Silverites finally agreed to fuse on the following respective division of county offices: [Democratic: senator, one assemblyman, assessor, clerk, short term commissioner, treasurer. Silver: three assemblymen, sheriff, district attorney, long term commissioner, recorder and coroner.]

Sunday, Sept 18 . . . Race horses arriving from the conclusion of the California State Fair at Sacramento and elsewhere, and gamblers, hobos, Fair followers, etc got in lively . . . sat up most of the night writing a four page letter to the Gardnerville Record . . .

Sept 19 . . . First day of the Nevada State Fair . . . very fair attendance for the first day – Cattle getting in, and a very good start on exhibits at the Pavilion . . . PM I fixed up a nice picture, belonging to Mrs Lindsay which she has sent for – lithograph – 20 x 28, entitled *"Aban-doned,"* representing a horse harnessed to wagon, his mate lying dead, also his master, from an Indian raid, on the Plains . . . Evening down town . . . Numerous soldiers from Carson came down on a 30 days furlough this evening – Been paid off, so many of them got on their beer & had jolly good time . . . Committee of Comstock mining supts at Va made report, Sept 12, in favor of pumping out & resuming work on lower levels . . . Sam T Shaw & his dramatic Co open a weeks engagement at the Reno Opera House . . .

Sept 20 . . . Improved attendance at the Fair – PM & evening I wrote 3 page letter . . . to the Nevada State *Herald* . . .

Sept 21 . . . Rec'd copy of Gardnerville *Record* with my letter *not in it* – "Comstock Day" and big attendance at Fair – Splendid racing – Got free season ticket to the Fair for "Alf Doten and family" – Should have had it sooner but better late than not at all . . . Met G McM Ross, Supt, this morning at train returning to the Comstock from S.F. . . . Continu-ation arrangements of mining Cos completed, & pretty sure Comstock lower levels will be pumped out soon for exploration & deeper mining – Cost estimated at $100,000 –

Sept 22 . . . Fair at its best at grounds & in town – AM I visited the Pavilion for 1st time – last of the exhibits getting in, including that of the Agricultural Experiment Station – Quite a lot of choice fruits, vegetables, home preserves, dairy products, some pianos and sewing machines and a few pictures, and a most excellent and extensive exhibit of fancy needlework, embroideries, quilts, rugs, etc – But generally speaking this was the poorest Pavilion exhibit I have yet seen at any Nevada State Fair . . . Met Geo I Lamy . . . Said my letter to *Record* arrived too late . . . as he prints on Monday – Must get my copy in Friday . . . Reno is full of soldier boys, and many of them are rather inclined to be drunk & disorderly . . .

[Clip, *Journal:*] Old Gold Hill is about to lose its identity. A resolution has been passed by the Board of Commissioners of Storey county consoli-dating the townships of Gold Hill and Virginia, and the two townships will be known as Virginia Township No. 1 after December 31, 1898.

Sept 23 . . . Biggest crowd & best time yet at the grounds – Bicycle racing in addition to horse racing – This being "Reno Day" most of the

stores closed, & all attended the Fair – Evening a huge pyrotechnic pano-
ramic spectacular show entitled "Battle of Manila" given at the race
track – $1 admission – I didn't attend, but big crowds did. I went to
Pavilion & found it empty from everybody going to the big show – Shaw's
Dramatic Co draws full houses every night –

Sept 24 . . . Very good at the Pavilion – windup exercises and big
dance – Goodwin went with friends – took my pass ticket along . . .
Republican County Convention at Wheelmen's Hall . . . Col H B
Maxon made Chairman, Higgin's Secy and W Fogg asst secy – Alf Doten
Sergeant-at-arms – I was elected by strong acclamation – no rival . . .
Committee reports were read & adopted & Convention proceeded to select
a new County Central Comm of 13 – For State Senator P L Flanigan of
Reno was nominated by acclamation – For Assemblymen S J Hodgkin-
son, G W Robinson, L A Blakeslee, and Tom Pixley . . . The Secy &
Asst of Convention and I as Sgt-at-arms – each received $10 – I paid a
couple of small bills, $2, & went home to supper with $8 in my pocket . . .

Sunday, Sept 25 . . . Reno is rapidly settling down from her Conventions and Fair boom . . . Wild mountain quail are reported in the papers
as coming down into Virginia City . . . Tonight I wrote a three page
letter to send to the Carson *News* . . .

Sept 27 . . . Bought me a pair of pants at Jacob's for $3 – had to have
the legs shortened an inch or so, making them 29 inches inner seam – by
44 around the waist . . .

Sept 29 . . . Got my old shoes new heeled for 50 cts – Morning wrote
& sent a 3 page letter, No 3, to Wells *Herald*, and evening a 4 page letter
to Gardnerville *Record* . . .

Oct 1 . . . Evening attended formation of McMillan Republican Club,
at the Court House . . . Not very good attendance . . .

Oct 3 . . . At train met J P Jones . . . Only had a few minutes talk
with him – Will be here again shortly, he says . . .

Oct 4 . . . The Wallace grand combination of circus, menagerie, etc,
the best & most extensive of all traveling exhibits arrived early this morning from the East – 2 long trains – afternoon & evening shows – admission $1 – everybody went & got money's worth – best show of the kind
ever here, they all said – Only Goodie went, from our family . . . much
pleased – The street parade at noon finest . . . I ever saw . . . town

was full – C C Powning died early this morning, about time the circus was arriving – showed on his big reserved lot on Powning's Addition . . . & the rings were in center, on very spot where he planned to build his residence, to be best in county – and he lying dead within sound of the clown's jokes and general hilarity – It is estimated that over 3,000 were audience at each performance . . . PM I wrote No 4 for the Wells Herald . . .

Oct 6 – Clear, cool & pleasant – PM, big funeral of Powning from Masonic Hall – I counted it in passing – nearly 400 on foot including the various Orders to which he belonged, and 100 University cadets – band, pall bearers, etc – About 80 carriages – Masonic Cemetery – Jones and Newlands in the carriages – Quite a number from Va & Carson – Evening wrote 4 page letter to Gardnerville Record – No 3 – Took most of night – Bed at 5 – Tom Zeimetz murdered by Antonio Patagna at Dayton yesterday –

[Clip, *Virginia Daily Evening Report* – Patagna believed Zeimetz had cheated him out of some Como mining claims, and knifed him.]

Oct 11 . . . PM wrote 4 page letter to Wells Herald . . . Also sent private note concerning my recompense . . .

Oct 12 . . . The battleships Oregon and Iowa sailed from New York today under sealed orders, but supposed to be for Manila –

Oct 13 . . . PM and night I wrote 6 page letter to Gardnerville *Record* – took all night . . .

Oct 15 . . . The boys harvested the crop on our big old pear tree this PM, as the fruit is dropping off rapidly – Got fully two barrels of the pears – All hard & will not ripen till about December . . . Hon A C Cleveland, independent candidate for US Senator in opposition to Stewart, spoke at Opera House this evening – Two big bonfires in front, and band of music – Fair audience, not crowded – music – spoke an hour – Raked down Stewart & his "crime of '73" and strongly advocated "home rule" – Congressional representatives of Nevada in at Washington should live in Nevada . . .

Sunday, Oct 16 . . . Ed Seitz was fatally run over by a freight train at the Virginia street crossing about 12 oclock last night – long train was standing on track, & he on his way home tried to pass it by climbing over between two cars – train started & he fell – one leg cut off above knee &

other below . . . good sort of man, & good friend of mine – used to be sheriff of Elko county . . .

Oct 18 . . . This evening Gazette had a comm[unication] from me over my own signature – *Stultified* – column & a quarter – About Miners Union Republican indorsement and Secy J F McDonnell . . . PM & evening wrote over 4 page letter to Wells Herald . . .

Oct 19 . . . At the annual meeting of the Con Va M Co, San F, Monday, Patrick Kervin was elected Supt in place of G McM Ross, who will still continue as Supt of the Ophir and Mexican . . .

Oct 20 . . . PM & night wrote No 5 for Gardnerville Record . . . Evening I attended big Silver meeting at Opera House – 2 bonfires, anvils, band, etc . . .

Oct 21 . . . At registry just closed, Virginia registered 1011 votes and Gold Hill 206 . . .

Oct 22 . . . Evening I attended speaking of Hon B F Leete, independent candidate for US Senator – at Opera House – No bonfires, guns or music, but good fires in stoves – Rather slim audience – He spoke 2 hours on money question, Hawaii & the Phillipines, and trusts and corporations – Read it all – rather dry & prosy . . .

Oct 24 . . . Senator Jones and brother Sam returned from Cal by morning train and went on to Gold Hill – I met them at the train . . .

Oct 25 . . . PM wrote 5 page letter – No 7 – to *Herald* . . . letter from Geo I Lamy returning my last letter, No 5 – His letter says "can't use it as the election rush crowds out everything. When you write again, *after election,* make your letter *non political,*" etc . . .

Oct 26 . . . Evening, Senator Jones came down from Gold Hill & went on train at 10 for San F – I saw him at the Riverside Hotel short time – promising . . . Warlike trouble reported with the Shoshones in Nye County – Aid called for –

Oct 27 – PM wrote No 6 . . . for the *Gardnerville Record* – Also private letter to Lamy about compensation . . .

Oct 28 . . . The *causus belli* of the Shoshone Indian war in Nye county was: Last Friday – the 21st – a white man named McLeod, and a Shoshone Indian named Ballard, had taken a load of hay from Reese River to Midas, where the Indian got full of whisky and took a bottle along in the wagon. It got broken on the way home and the Indian accused McL of breaking it, and in anger he cut him about the face & head with a knife, threatening to kill him – When they got home the Indian got on the war path again and attacked McLeod, who in self-defense gave him a terrible thrashing, nearly beating and kicking his head off. His Indian friends took up on his part and made threats against the whites. The Governor was telegraphed to, and 75 rifles were sent there at once. Latest reports say the war has subsided and the settlers not afraid – "great cry and little wool."

Oct 29 . . . Evening attended speaking of J C Campbell, lawyer, orator, etc, San Francisco – at Opera House – under auspices of my McMillan Club – Gave one of the best Republican speeches I ever heard – Bonfires, brass band, anvils, etc – Crowded house . . .

Oct 31 . . . Reno & Comstock members of "Torrey's Rough Riders" mustered out in Florida – 13 of them got here at noon, all right . . .

Nov 1 . . . PM I wrote 4 page letter (No 8) to the Wells Herald . . . The "Halloween" boys didn't succeed in getting away with yard gates, because Sam and Alf took 'em in the house –

Nov 2 . . . Evening I was at speaking of Hon Tom Wren at Opera House, Populist nominee for Congress . . . bonfires and brass band – Slim house . . .

Nov 5 . . . Evening I attended last Silver party rally of the campaign, at Opera House – bonfires & anvils, but no music – plenty of chin music inside – crowded house – Speakers were Genl J C Hagerman, Chas D Lane, the rich owner in Utica mine, Angel's, Cal, chairman of the National Silver Party, Mr M F Taylor, a leading bimetallist of Colorado, & fine speaker, Senator Jones, Senator Stewart, Sam Davis and Gov Sadler – All did well . . .

Sunday, Nov 6 . . . Candidates stirring around lively, Reno seemingly being considered the chief battleground of the campaign . . . V&T passenger express did not leave till 11 AM. On it were Stewart and Jones, Gov Sadler and Sam Davis for Carson – Jones for Gold Hill – Had brief interview with him in the car . . .

Nov 7 . . . AM I met D B Lyman down town & he showed me a telegram from John W Mackay, San Francisco, telling that *Judge Rising fell dead at 1 oclock today* in San F – PM by request of Nate Roff of the

Journal, I wrote an obituary editorial . . . The burning out of tunnel No 13, west of Truckee with adjoining snow sheds has cut off all trains completely . . . Evening I attended last grand Republican rally at Opera House – Bonfires, anvils & brass band – Big house – speeches by State & county candidates . . .

> [Clippings from the *Journal* and *Gazette* – Judge Richard Rising was a prominent attorney in early Virginia City mining litigation and then served as judge of the First District Court for more than twenty-five years – Noted for his integrity and judgment – Many notable decisions and very few Supreme Court reversals.]

Nov 8 – Clear & pleasant – cold – General State Election day – Schools and saloons closed and everybody attending to election – At 9 AM I cast my first vote in Reno, in the 5th Ward, in which I reside, at the polls held in the old Congregational church, next block above my residence – Sam and Alf also voted there, casting the first vote of their life – Mine was Republican as always – Some passengers, and newspapers & express got around the destroyed tunnel 13, on foot, or otherwise and got cars through to Reno this morning and during the day – PM I wrote No 9 for Wells *Herald,* 5 pages, and got it off in east bound train at 8:40, the regular time – Election passed off very quietly – and when I went home to bed at 11, the vote counting indicated Republican victory –

Nov 9 . . . Everything has to be transferred around the destroyed tunnel & will for the next week or two . . . badly caved in places – 900 ft long – Washoe county returns complete – Republican principally, & McMillan, governor, but returns from the extreme eastward counties, not so favorable . . .

> [Clip, paper unspecified – Eva Greenwood, county charge, sixty years old, commits suicide by taking laudanum.]

Eva Greenwood was one of the old time boss demi monde at Virginia City.

Nov 10 – Same – At 8 AM train for Va I met Frank Osbiston, my old Comstock friend – Haven't seen him for over 20 yrs – Knew each other at a glance – He went to Va on business . . . The tunnel blockade still seriously interferes with travel . . . Election returns still coming in indicate Rep Governor & mixed otherwise . . .

Nov 11 – Same – Evening at Opera House with Nick Hummel of the Wadsworth *Dispatch* – Good house & good play – "Under the Dome" – melo drama founded on the great naval disaster in the harbor of Apia,

Samoa, a few years ago, when the US war ship Trenton sank, with the band playing the "Star Spangled Banner" – We got away up in the gallery for the 1st time for me – Very spectacular piece – good scenic effects, etc – Bed 11 – The V&T noon local train off for the blockade –

Nov 12 . . . Evening met old Jim Townsend, just in from Bodie . . . Same old Jim . . . On his way to S.F. to be treated for a chronic rupture . . .

Sunday, Nov 13 . . . AM was with old Jim Townsend, dined with him & Allen Bragg and saw him off for SF on westbound train arriving at 1:30 PM ($6) . . .

Nov 14 . . . Blockade raised early this morning . . .

Nov 15 . . . PM wrote no 10, 4 pages (cash called for) & sent it to the Wells Herald . . . Returns about all in indicate Sadler elected sure –

Nov 17 . . . Evening & night I wrote 5 page letter, No 7, to Gardnerville *Record* – inclosed note calling for coin . . .

Nov 22 – Clear & pleasant – PM wrote No 11, 4 pages – & sent it in evening train at 9 to the *Wells Herald* (pay called for) – Corbett-Sharkey fight in NY this evening – Henry Riter had the dispatches at his saloon, and big crowd heard the bulletins read aloud as fast as received. Quite an excitement in SF and all over the country regarding it. Dispatches said the Lenox Athletic Club rooms densely crowded to see the fight – 20 rounds contest – catch weights, for championship of world. Sharkey 178 lbs, Corbett 183 lbs – Sharkey knocked Corbett down in second round – All other rounds lively fighting & about even – no blood & little hurt – Ninth round close quick fighting and clinching. McVey, Corbett's second jumped into the ring to interfere, & was hustled out by Chief of Police – Referee stopped the fight, declared Corbett disqualified by this interference and decided Sharkey winner – also declared all bets on the contest off. Decision generally approved. Corbett made crestfallen.

Nov 23 . . . The steam whistle of the C & C shaft, Va, blew at noon today for 1st time in several months – renewed old time sound for the Comstock – The Gazette this evening figures Sadler's plurality in State at 22, from semi-official tabular statements from all quarters – & says a recount of entire State has to be made for Governor – 12 votes for McMillan, gained by re-count will elect him –

Nov 24 . . . Lively snowstorm at 8 AM whitened the ground – Chilly

Thanksgiving Day – We had roast pork and cranberry sauce for dinner – got no turkey today – Evening wrote 4 page letter to Gardnerville Record . . .

Nov 25 . . . Letter from Geo R Vardy . . . with $5 . . .

Nov 26 . . . The Nevada State *Journal* . . . announces "change in ownership" – E D Kelley retiring, owing to his new business, (elected State Surveyor General) and his partner, Judge Wm Webster becoming full sole proprietor by purchase of Kelley's interest . . .

Sunday, Nov 27 . . . Full official State returns show Sadler 22 plurality ahead –

Nov 28 . . . Evening completed a 5 page sketch about "the last of the Comstock camels" –

Nov 29 . . . PM & evening wrote No 12 for Wells *Herald* . . .

Nov 30 . . . Sent a letter tonight to G R Vardy, *Wells Herald*, calling for "*pay*" . . .

Dec 1 . . . PM wrote letter to Geo I Lamy, of the *Gardnerville Record*, inclosing my bill for $20, for services as Reno correspondent . . .

Dec 3 – Very frosty morning – Clear, fine day – Evening at theater – Ed Piper passed me in – "A Boy Wanted" – Very lively and amusing variety performance, singing, dancing, Two female acrobats, all sort of general cutting up & queer situations – no plot – just very lively fun – 10 ladies & 12 gents – good troupe, from the East . . . The Reno Evening *Gazette* contains . . . telegram from Winnemucca announcing candidacy of Newlands in place of Stewart –

Sunday, Dec 4 . . . *Journal* this morning has column telegram from Winnemucca announcing Newlands for Senator, and indorses it – Creates quite a stir –

Dec 6 . . . PM & evening wrote No 13 . . . to Wells *Herald* . . .

Dec 10 – Same – 2° below zero early this morning – PM & evening wrote 2 page letter to Hon M H de Young, SF, to learn about my story, "Wildcat Joe," sent to Chronicle last June 16th and not yet appearing or sent back – Also letter to Wells Drury S.F. inquiring about Jim Townsend – The treaty of peace between Spain and the United States was signed by the joint peace commissions at 8:45 this evening at Paris . . .

Dec 13 . . . PM & evening wrote No 14 . . . for Wells Herald . . .

Met Jim Townsend at morning train, returning to Bodie from S.F. – Looked 10 years better than when I put him aboard the train for S.F. . . . Surgeons at S.F. doctored up his ruption by hypodermic injections, but did not consider safe to make capital operation at his age . . .

Dec 14 . . . The bones or remains of Christopher Columbus were shipped from Havana, Cuba yesterday for Spain there to be re-interred forever –

Dec 16 . . . Between 9 & 10 AM two sections of the great 1st Regiment New York Volunteer Infantry arrived . . . They stopped about an hour, & the boys had quite a run about town . . . About 500 of them in this lot today – Others just arriving in S.F. Many are in the hospitals at Honolulu and at SF sick with typhoid fever – 50 of them dead from it & other sickness, mostly at Honolulu – They dont like that country . . .

Dec 17 . . . Letter from Geo I Lamy with $15 . . .

Sunday, Dec 18 – Clear, warm & pleasant – News from Va City says that Ben Higbee died there this morning – One of my oldest friends on the Comstock – Was rooming at Morton's when I came there from Como and also roomed there – Was on police most always and latterly about the railroad depot – last of all was janitor of the Court House – 71 yrs old, native of Boston – leaves wife at Va – Evening I wrote letter to Geo I Lamy, Gardnerville – acknowledging receipt of the $15, and wanting the $5 balance due –

Dec 19 – Cloudy and blustery – threatening storm – Very dusty – Wife rec'd letter from Sister Lizzie Doten – long nice one *to us both*. And it mentions a package also sent – I sent letter with 50 cts stamps to Cagwin & Noteware, ordering a book just like this for next years Journal . . . The Reno Gazette this evening reports telegram received this PM by the Rep State Central Comm at Carson from Eureka stating that Judge Fitzgerald has thrown out 171 votes in Eureka county as being illegal, on contest between Gregovich and Powell for Assessor of that county – This will give McMillan a plurality of about 30 votes over Sadler for Governor – *electing McMillan* Governor – Matt Brannan of Carson reported fatally shot there today – Bed 11 – Very cloudy & threatening – State election returns officially canvassed today at Carson by the State Board of Canvassers –

Dec 20 . . . PM & evening I wrote and sent No 15, 4 pages, to Wells Herald . . .

Dec 21 . . . Sent 2 page letter to Hon J P Jones, Palace Hotel, SF, inclosing some newspaper clippings, etc . . .

Dec 22 . . . Met Gov Sadler down town & had quite a talk with him – "Forefathers Day." We received a small bon-bon box of chocolate & other candies from Lizzie . . .

Dec 23 . . . About 11 AM Richmond P Hobson, the hero of Santiago came on west bound regular train on his way to SF and Manila – Big crowd at depot to see him – He addressed people from platform of car for about 10 minutes, while train stopped – made very neat rapid speech – no shake hands or kissing – Fine looking young fellow – looks just like his pictures in the papers . . .

Sunday, Dec 25 – AM cloudy – PM clear & pleasant – Christmas observed as usual – I received a beautiful Plymouth Pilgrim pictorial Calendar from A S Burbank – Evening I wrote a brief letter to M H de Young, Chronicle, SF, about Gubernatorial and Senatorial election in Nevada – He made a telegram in his paper of my last letter to him on the Senatorial contest here . . .

Dec 26 – Clear & pleasant – moderate – Evening wrote & mailed 2 page letter to Wm McMillan, Va City, about Governorship, and the Senatorial problem – Bed 12 . . . I received a big book from Bro Charlie entitled "The Bradford History" – Very interesting book, being a historical record or journal of the Pilgrims by Gov Bradford – The inside title of the book is Bradford's History "Of Plimoth Plantation," from the original manuscript – Printed by Wright & Potter, Boston 1898 – on the fly leaf Charlie wrote – "Brother Alfred, with love from Brother Charlie" – 9½ x 7 inches, 2 inches thick – cloth – 555 pages – 9 illustrations, the only Pilgrim portrait being Edward Winslow –

Dec 27 . . . We rec'd a Christmas package from Cornelia . . . PM & evening I wrote and sent No 16 to the Wells Herald . . .

Dec 29 . . . I was at home PM & evening overhauling my Austin file of the *Reese River Reveille* . . .

Dec 30 . . . Received today a letter from George R Vardy, Wells Herald – Been sick etc, & unable to attend to my importunities for pay – poor etc, but will have more money in a few days & will send me some –

Dec 31 . . . Received envelope from Geo I Lamy of the *Gardnerville Record* inclosing $5 draft on Wells, Fargo & Co . . .

Seeing the Bottom

Books 75–79
Jan 1, 1899 – Nov 11, 1903

Alf, nearly seventy, gets a legislative reporting assignment in Carson and, despite the obvious, is shocked and bathetic when Mary writes that he mustn't come home again. While often sounding more cheerful in this forced freedom, he now receives a monthly dole from Mary, scrounges from old friends and strangers alike, calling the handouts "loans," occupies the bar and lobby of the respectable Arlington Hotel as if it were his club, using its letter paper for his writing and its newspapers for his clippings, while rooming in much cheaper places and becoming something of a laughing stock, a "Husband on a Salary" who nonetheless announces himself a candidate for the legislature. Though a glimpse of his deterioration leads Mary, her own health uncertain, to lift the ban, Alf stays on in Carson with a stiff-necked remnant of pride, more and more alone, more and more in the past, more and more in quite literal dreams of reconciliation with his wife and children and justification in the eyes of his Plymouth family. Almost incredibly, he straightens himself out for weeks of hard work at the most exacting kind of reporting, and he still shows his never-failing enthusiasm for Republicanism, the big parade, the spectacular show, the lottery chance, and the gadgetry of a new age. But the pride, often indistinguishable from querulousness, leads him to antagonize the younger strangers now editing the newspapers, and is no match for the bottle and time.

Reno and Carson City
Jan 1, 1899 – Dec 31, 1899

Sunday, Jan 1, 1899 . . . PM a steady snowstorm started in from the southward and five or six inches covered the ground by dark . . . PM and evening I finished and copied in good shape my four page letter, closely written, to Miss Lizzie Doten . . .

Jan 2 . . . SF papers give full accounts, telegraphic, of the occupation of Cuba by Uncle Sam . . . Big drifts on the V&T RR in Washoe Valley – Evening train half an hour late, came in double header with big snow plow loaded 10 ft high with snow – I received letter from Cornelia . . . Spiro Vucovich died at Va Saturday aged 70 – after 8 years breaking down – One of my best old friends – and one of oldest Comstockers –

Jan 3 . . . Rec'd from Cornelia a fine album pamphlet: "Pilgrim Plymouth" . . . PM & evening I wrote No 17, 4 pages, and sent it to *Wells Herald* . . .

Jan 4 . . . Snow 6 or 7 ft deep at Truckee & on Summit . . . PM made out my bill to Wells Herald, 17 letters at $5 per letter – $85 –Rec'd $5, leaving $80 balance due . . . The Carson *Appeal* has absorbed the Carson *Weekly* . . .

Jan 5 . . . Rec'd letter from SF Chronicle asking me if I would go to Carson & report legislature & to wire reply – Did so at once: "Will fill legislative proposition satisfactorily. Will write tonight" – Evening I wrote to *Chronicle* on the reporting proposition, & also gave something to print on the Senatorial et al propositions, as its letter said: "We have been publishing your comments on the Senatorial situation, and would like to know whether you could make it convenient, when the game gets warm, to go to Carson and report the Legislature for us. We would not care for extended accounts, but simply enough to give us the drift each day – say 300 or 400 words – while the business is hot – Wire an answer." Also wrote to J P Jones, Palace Hotel SF for $100 – guess I won't get it . . .

[Clippings from San Francisco's *Examiner* and *Chronicle* say that Mrs Alice M Hartley, who shot and killed State Senator M D Foley in July, 1897, has married lawyer William S Bonnifield of Winnemucca – The groom's uncle, as a member of the Board of Pardons, had voted to release Mrs Hartley from prison in January, 1897.]

Jan 6 . . . Senator Stewart came on morning train from San F with Col Jack Chinn, an old political lobby warrior from Kentucky, Black Wallace, Billy Sharon, George Nixon, et al – Stewart & Chinn & Sharon went on up to Carson . . .

Jan 7 . . . Another carload of pipe for the Comstock deep drainage arrived last night from the east . . . This morning's SF Chronicle arrived . . . with my Thursday evening letter . . .

Sunday, Jan 8 . . . The requisite papers were filed yesterday in the Supreme Court at Carson for the McMillan vs Sadler gubernatorial contest – Hon Trenmor Coffin of Carson and Judge Cheney of Reno Atty's for McMillan, and Hon Thos Wren of Reno and Hon William Woodburn of Carson attorneys for Sadler . . .

Jan 10 . . . Received letter from George R Vardy of the Wells *Herald* inclosing $10 and objecting to my bill . . . Sent note to Tim Dempsey, Carson, to secure me a room in my old lodging house over his saloon . . . Sent no regular letter to Wells Herald tonight . . . I quit from poverty of sustenance . . .

Jan 11 . . . PM & evening light snowstorms here . . . heavy in the Sierra – delaying the trains – 10 ft reported at Summit . . . My old friend Major John H Dennis slipped & fell yesterday, so he has to go on crutches – was acting as editor of the *Journal* –

Jan 12 . . . Sent brief letter to Hon C C Goodwin of the Salt Lake Tribune, asking chance to report session, etc – Visited my old friend John H Dennis at his lodgings at Mrs Caldwell's near the depot . . . gets round room a little on crutches – in bad fix and very despondent – was sitting up, trying to write editorial . . .

Jan 13 – Variable – Colder – Occasional light snowstorms – At 8:30 AM left on train for Carson – The Dan Sully theatrical company on board from San Francisco, also more Nevada legislators . . . Arrived about 10 AM – Found that my room that I sent for . . . was taken & I couldn't get one there – Secured one at the Stone House lodgings – Bought me a new coat and vest at Abe Cohn's Emporium – $9 cash – five times as much snow here as in Reno – fine sleighing – very slippery everywhere – Met lots of the legislators – Arlington House full of them – It is always general headquarters – Newlands makes it his headquarters, Stewart at the Ormsby, Cleveland ditto – much buzzing, cutting and contriving – Evening at Opera House – Sully company in "Uncle Rob," a very pretty domestic drama, with music dancing and singing varieties, etc – good house – Bed at 12 – very hard bed & cheerless room but I was very tired and slept well, like a corpse on a marble slab or a cooling board at the morgue or in an undertakers shop – A fearful bed – made my hips sore – Unlucky day – *Friday 13th* –

Jan 14 – Same – Got me a room at the French Hotel – The Excelsior Hotel – next to the Opera House – Mrs Brault's, and moved my things to it from the Stone lodging House – paying 50 cts for my last nights lodging – At 4:30 PM I commenced and wrote my first regular telegraphic dispatch to the SF Chronicle – 3 pages – about 600 words – finished it & got it into the hands of the operator, Miss Hattie Humphrey's at 7 oclock – Evening about town – Bed 10:30 – Moderate & thawing –

Sunday, Jan 15 . . . Legislators all in and greatest political buzzing day of all – "Just before the battle" – Evening got off my second telegram to *Chronicle* . . . Caucuses of both houses held this evening, nominating all the officers & attaches – Strictly Silver party . . . Republicans held no caucus – no use – Bed 12 – good bed – slept bully . . . Got letter from Salt Lake Tribune . . .

Jan 16 . . . Both Houses called to order at 12 M – swore in members, officers & attaches and adjourned . . . telegraphed about 600 words to SF *Chronicle* . . .

Jan 17 . . . Evening attended speaking of Newlands at Opera House – Bonfires in streets, brass band, etc – Theater densely packed with ladies & gents – Newlands spoke over 2 hours, making the best effort of his life – Much applauded – His theme, of course was the hard talk and hard charges made against him by the opposition – Met Judge Webster from Reno, after the speaking and arranged to report for the *Journal* for $5 a week, both Houses – Bed at 12 –

Jan 18 through 21 [AD reports to *Chronicle* and *Journal* – No details.]

Sunday, Jan 22 . . . Hon T N Stone, Deputy Secy of State died very unexpectedly at 2 PM today from heart failure, at his residence . . . 65 yrs old – native of NY & leaves a wife & 3 children here – Was member of State Senate nine years ago – also Supt of Public Schools in Elko County, and was Principal of the State University when it was at Elko – Was Deputy State Controller last 4 yrs . . . evening at Arlington wrote & mailed 2 page letter to wife . . .

Jan 23 – Clear & very pleasant – Reported for Chronicle and Journal as usual – Wired also 478 words to Salt Lake Tribune on the Senatorial situation – Much stir about it – A test vote this PM showed that the Assembly stands equal Stewart and Anti-Stewart – 15 to 15 – Got letter from wife inclosing one from Bessie, Santa Clara – Had a hard days work – Bed 11 – Very tired & lame – Busiest day reporting I have had for many a day –

Jan 24 . . . Stewart won Senatorship in both houses today on 1st ballot – Quite a stir – I reported as yesterday – *didn't get chance to eat* . . .

Jan 25 . . . No joint ballot in joint convention, today, but Journals of the two Houses showing that he had a majority in each House he was declared elected . . .

Jan 26 – Clear & very pleasant – Assemblyman Gillespie of Gold Hill the renegade Republican absentee, who was bought by Stewart to dodge the roll call and thus give him one majority in Assembly appeared again today in his seat, answered to his name – All proceedings against him squelched, no questions asked, etc – Stewart rules – Leidy of Esmeralda, also bought by Stewart, whose case came up on committee report today was whitewashed & exhonorated – Wicked as usual – Bed 11 – tired – I bought ½ doz collars last evening at Abe Cohn's for 6 bits, but managed to leave and lose them somewhere before I got to bed – Had my name written on the package, but couldn't get run of it today – gone to —— Got very lame left shoulder from a bit of a tumble *up* the Capitol north steps last evening – outside – Wired 409 words to Tribune today . . . Andrew Robert who owns and keeps the Globe saloon has recently received a barrel, 51½ gallons, Old Continental Whiskey direct from Louisville Kentucky . . . He showed me the bills today . . . Costs him a little less than $3 per gallon delivered at the saloon –

Jan 27 . . . PM & evening I wrote letters to *Journal*, SF *Chronicle* and

Salt Lake *Tribune* . . . Evening about town – Bed at 2 oclock – Received this morning the following telegram from S.F. Chronicle: "We only desired you to cover Senatorial fight in Legislature. We dont care for anything further – M H de Young." So I only sent letter . . .

Jan 28 . . . At 8 PM went up to the grand Stewart reception, given by him & wife to the "members of the Legislature and friends" – Big crowd present – House crowded – Very tasty arrangement – Fine lunch of choice good things, salads, fruits candies etc, hot coffee & tea – And *magnificent punch* made by Mrs Stewart herself – Very pleasant and agreeable occasion . . .

Sunday, Jan 29 . . . PM was at State House & wrote letter to wife . . .

Jan 30 . . . Recd a printed "correspondents check" from Chronicle to fill out . . . left it at telegraph office for the operator to fill out for me . . .

Jan 31 . . . Reported as usual – Sent short note to SF Chronicle inclosing the "Correspondents check" filled out . . . My letter to Tribune came today in Sunday Tribune in good shape with my name attached – 585 words – Bed 11 – very blustering and light snowstormy –

                                    Salt Lake City, Jan 31, 1899
Alf Doten Esq, Carson, Nevada –
Dear Sir – Your letter was in the Tribune of Jan 29 and was just right – Send others from time to time as matters of general interest developes – Yours &c   William Nelson, Managing Editor   Tribune

Feb 1 – Variable – Stormy, wintry, very blustering, with light snowsqualls – Got telegram from SL Tribune relative to a new Nevada RR incorporation & to get information regarding it – Evening, Opera House – "Yon Yonson" Co – Big house & 1st rate little play – with a good plot to it – Very amusing as well as interesting – Best I have seen for long time – Bed 12:30 . . . Sent a very strong 2 page letter to Vardy of the *Wells Herald* tonight, calling him down on his neglect or refusal to pay me –

Feb 2 . . . Tim Dempsey sold out his saloon this PM to Dick Kirman – Evening I went with him on visit to his family – His daughters Nellie on piano and Pearlie on violin entertained me very pleasantly – and I played violin a little, sang "Rock a bye Baby on the tree top" etc . . .

Feb 3 . . . I got onto that new Nevada RR proposition for Lincoln County, Incorporation papers filed yesterday PM with Secy of State – I found it & sent synopsis of it to Tribune and also to SF Chronicle & the Reno Journal . . .

Sunday, Feb 5 . . . Telegram . . . here says big fight between Americans & Filipinos, at Manila – 2 Ams killed & 100 wounded – First fight with them . . .

Feb 6 . . . Jacob Klein, one of the oldest & best known & influential citizens of Carson died at SF last evening of stomach & heart troubles – Been there sick several weeks – quite wealthy – Firm of Wagner & Klein, Carson Brewery for years back, but owned whole business latterly – About 65 yrs old – Very benevolent, & many a poor family as well as business man will miss Jake Klein more than anybody – I received 2 checks from SF Chronicle, one for $50, and other for $20 . . . also received my 3d weeks salary of $5 from *Journal* – Total $75 – Big field day for me – Biggest lot of money at one time for last 2 yrs at least . . .

Feb 8 . . . Latest news from Manila is that the killed, wounded and prisoners, Filipinos, amounted to about 10,000 – & we didn't lose 100 killed – Slaughtered the poor devils – did as we pleased . . .

Feb 9 . . . Both houses of the Legislature held AM & PM sessions & adjourned till Monday in order to visit Reno & the State institutions tomorrow . . . Letter from wife says mother has a paralytic stroke of half her body – & may not live more than a day or two . . . I wrote her a reply this evening . . .

Feb 10 . . . PM I wrote & sent 3 page letter . . . to *Tribune* – Evening wrote similar one . . . to the *Chronicle* . . .

Feb 11 . . . Left Carson at 11 AM for Reno . . . Passing up street Met McFarland & was told of mother Stoddard's death – Found all the rest all right, at home – Mrs Andrews there as "help" – and good – Evening down town awhile – Slept over Riter's saloon . . .

Feb 13 . . . Funeral of mother Stoddard at 10 – Kissed her a last good bye – and followed her to her grave in cemetery north of town – Funeral private – six carriages, including hearse and the Riverside 'bus load – services at house and grave by Rev Mr Jones – Back home in ½ an hour – Dinner – Long talk with Sam & he went with me down to depot at 1:30 and I took local train for Carson . . . Found the package of six collars I lost . . . on my table . . . The chambermaid, Miss Thomas, found it in sweeping under the bed . . .

[Clips from the Reno *Journal* and *Gazette* – Mrs Sarah Abbott Stoddard, native of Middlebury, Connecticut, dies of a stroke at age 82 years and 4 months.]

Feb 16 – Very fine & springlike – Woman Suffrage resolution came up this PM in Senate – To amend article [blank] of Constitution by striking out word "male" wherever it occurs – Crowd of ladies present – Resolution lost by a tie vote, 7 to 7 – Lord absent – not a constitutional majority – I made longer report than usual – Evening was at Capitol & wrote 3 page letter to William Nelson, managing editor SL *Tribune* inclosing my statement of acc't, also the one from business dept of the *Tribune* – great discrepancy – want it explained – Bed 12 –

Feb 17 . . . Long report to Journal – and 2 three page letters to *Chronicle* and *Tribune* . . . Found in yesterday's SF *Examiner* notice of death of Dr Washington Ayer who attended me when I was so badly injured at Fort John . . . Native of Haverhill Mass aged about 76 . . .

Sunday, Feb 19 . . . PM copied 2 page letter to wife . . . In it I offer to send her $20 if she likes . . .

Feb 20 . . . Reported Legislature as usual . . . The new Comstock drainage pump in the C & C shaft started into practical operation today and worked even better than was anticipated – seems like a big substantial success right at the start . . .

Feb 21 . . . Evening I sent letter to my old friend John H Dennis, Reno, inclosing picture of Dr Washington Ayer whom he knew at time of my Fort John Calamity in 1854 – John attended me there like a more than brother and I owe him a debt of gratitude I can never repay – Recd letter from Wife asking me to not come home again, because our children dont like me – Is it separation? Great God! . . .

Feb 22 . . . Washington's birthday, holiday – no Legislature – AM I wrote and mailed letter . . . to Geo R Vardy, calling time on him – 2 PM, parade of the "Darktown Band," our local brass band, dressed as nigger wenches – Best thing in that line I ever saw – fine music etc – "Darktown Cadets," about 40 small boys, blacked face, & wooden muskets following – They marched principal streets and then to Capitol Park, where they gave open air concert for an hour or two, "Cake walk," etc – Big crowds of spectators, & genuine novel gala day – Evening they gave a ball at the Opera House – all "coons," constituting the principal young girls and lads of the town – Crowded, and extremely enjoyable, even to the jam of spectators – great success in all respects . . .

Feb 24 . . . Senate started in at 10 AM for 1st time – did good days work, and held first evening session at 7:30 – Many ladies present, expecting the Woman Suffrage bill to come up but it didnt have a chance – Another bill on public lands from US to Nevada taking till time to adjourn . . .

Sunday, Feb 26 . . . Worked hard on a letter to Sam . . .

Feb 27 – Variable, Cloudy – Finished copying my letter to Sam this evening after the Senate adjourned and sent it by evening mail – 12 closely written pages – longest letter I ever wrote in my life – all on family matters – Received letter from Eunice, also a letter from Bessie intended for mama, but got in wrong envelope – A bad streak in it – also letter from Salt Lake Tribune, inclosing check for $4.16 balance due for January work – Total from Tribune $8.54 – Bed 12 – Eunice says she is 75 yrs old – Recd my last weeks *Journal* salary today –

Feb 28 – Cloudy and ferociously dusty – Reported Legislature as usual – Got letter from Geo R Vardy, *Nevada State Herald*, Wells, Elko County offering me $25 in settlement, *as soon as he can get it*. Evening I was at Opera House. Hi Henry's Musical minstrel variety show – over 50 people – Biggest house ever in Carson and best performance – Henry best cornetist on earth – Affluence of fine singing, and royal band music – Best entertainment of its kind I ever saw, especially two acrobats best ever here or anywhere – Parade at noon – Over 20 pieces, right through blinding fierce cyclones of dust – Bed 1 –

March 1 – Variable with stronger ferocious wind than yesterday, from the S.W. Heavy snow clouds in the mountains, & occasional snow flurries were blown down here – Dust all blown away and only coarse gravel left – Got letter from wife and one from Sam both tabooing me worse and worse – Evening sent brief letter to wife, inclosing Eunice's and Bessie's – Busy day in Legislature as usual and evening session of Senate considered the woman suffrage amendment to State Constitution to amend article 2, by striking out, wherever it occurs, the word "male." After much argument it was lost by vote of 7 to 5 – 2 absent – no "constitutional majority" – Bed 11 – still very blustering & cold – but no snow or rain –

March 2 through 5 [AD writes a sharply demanding note to Vardy, reports the Legislature and a citizens' meeting about water, bums $3 from one legislator and $5 from another and works most of Sunday on a long letter to his wife.]

March 6 – Clear & very pleasant – warm – Legislature in big session – being the 50th and last day, but they had too much business for it & will take a day or two longer – *no pay* after the 50th day – must work for nothing – No Senate session this evening but the Assembly did – Had up the Woman Suffrage bill – crowded with ladies but bill was *lost* – 15 to —— Bed 12 – Finished my long letter to wife this evening in Senate chamber – 8 pages – to be sent tomorrow – Also inclosed "Decayed Veneration" the Alfred cursing and abusing episode – Received kind brotherly responsive letter from John H Dennis, Reno, today –

March 8 . . . Letter from wife, returning "Decayed Veneration" – and telling me I must not come home – must stay away from Reno, etc – Borrowed $10 from Senator Comins yesterday & today and $5 from Lem Allen – Evening session of both houses – lots of ladies . . .

March 9 . . . The busiest day of the legislature – Borrowed $5 from Kelley of Austin . . .

March 10 . . . The Senate started in at 9 AM – Assembly at 10 AM – 54th day – Passed a few bills & resolutions, made nice parting speeches – Lem Allen, Speaker of Assembly was presented with nice watch chain, and Speaker pro tem H H Coryell, a fine gold watch – Both houses adjourned sine die at the noon hour . . . I reported both houses & finished up my work and cleaned up at 4 PM . . . Have $66 in purse . . .

March 11 . . . PM was at Governor's office and took list of principal bills signed by him and made laws – 20 of them out [of] 67 – 127 in all passed by the Legislature, so many yet to be passed upon by the Gov . . .

March 12 through 26 [AD sends final legislative letters to the *Chronicle* and the *Tribune* and asks February settlement from them, receives an angry note and no money from Vardy, watches a new type of quartz mill in operation and sees a Merganthaler linotype machine (purchased from the *Enterprise*) at work in the *News* office – Exchanges letters with Mary, writes to his son Sam and his sister Eunice, and sends a long, reminiscent letter to his brother Sam on the fiftieth anniversary of his departure from Plymouth – Relates the details of a fatal hunting accident suffered by young Harry Diamond of Gold Hill, and notes the deaths of four more old Comstockers and the fact that flooding has finally extinguished a fire which has been burning for thirteen years at the 1750-foot level of the "big bonanza" – Pastes a clip into the journal which reports the predictions of Professor Rudolph Falb that submarine earthquakes will soon make islands of Florida and California, and that the earth will be partially, if not completely, destroyed by collision with a comet on November 13.]

March 27 . . . Court week – In US Dist Court, involving title to Silver Peak property & mines – 20 or 30 witnesses et al been here for a week – other cases also – McMillan vs Sadler for Governor of Nevada in Supreme Court – McMillan et al present . . .

March 28 . . . Last night I dreamed one of the most brilliantly pleasurable dreams of my life – Gold Hill was in bonanza again, better than ever, houses & everything being rebuilt with brick & stone on big scale – perfect beehive of industry, & I all right in it.

March 29 . . . Evening at Opera House – Traveling country show of sort of stereopticon, kinetoscope or "Edison's Projectoscope" exhibition – Wonderful pictures – city fire Alarm, bucking broncho rider, Bull fight, Spanish, 2 scenes, 3 rounds of a prize fight, naval & land battles connected with our Spanish war – some 30 pictures in all – 3 miserable tunes on a miserable graphophone – very slim houses, last night & tonight – leaves tomorrow – Really wonderful pictures, animated & moving, exactly like life – 10 cts, 25 & 35 cents admission – A scientific wonder its only recommendation – rather prosy & tedious – Bed 12

March 31 – Variable, blustering & cold – snowing all day in the Sierra – PM I attended libel suit in US Dist Court of Chiatovich vs Hanchett, in connection with Silver Peak – Chiatovich storekeeper there for last 25 or 30 yrs – one horse place. Hanchett working the mines, got much in debt to C – C levied attachment on a bar of bullion of Hanchett – H soon settled up on the square – Then he posted notices to all his employes not to trade or have anything to do with C – No good man to associate with, etc – boycotted him – hence this suit by C. for $10,000 damages. The Jury was charged at 6 PM & after being out for couple of hours, brought in verdict for Chiatovich of $4,700. Bed 12 – Today I received from wife a copy of *Old Colony Memorial* March 25 – In it brother Charlie gives good item of Pilgrim Mining Cos departure, with me from Plymouth, March 18, 1849 . . .

Sunday, April 2 – Clear & pleasant – Easter Sunday I walked around & took an outside look at all the churches with singing & services going on, just before noon, winding up at the brewery, then to the post office, then to dinner – felt better for it . . .

April 5 . . . The Silver Peak cases which have occupied exclusive attention of the US Dist court for last 2 wks came to end today – Jurymen venire of 75, witnesses, and lawyers (Campbell, and Metson from S.F.) from here & elsewhere all discharged for the term . . .

April 7 . . . Wrote & sent duplicate 5 page letters to SF Chronicle and SL Tribune giving summary or synopsis of the recent Silver Peak suits . . .

April 8 . . . Storey county hospital totally destroyed by fire at 1 oclock this morning – originating from kitchen – 37 patients – all escaped but Jos Richardson, an old timer 65 yrs old who got burned up trying to rescue some of his belongings . . . Rose at 6 AM and sent a 5 page letter to Reno *Journal* on Silver Peak . . . Rec'd very short, pointed letter from Bro Sam – Somewhat jammed himself, so can't lend a cent – In the SF *Examiner* of yesterday, Wells Drury gives a very neat & pleasant little old time Va Comstock sketch, entitled "The Prima Donna's Bow to the Comstock Boys" . . . I am mentioned in it – created much amused comment . . .

> [The clipping has Col K B Brown, the "former popular chief of Virginia City's Volunteer Fire Department," regaling some San Francisco friends with stories of the "good old days," when "the shows . . . were so poor that if there was any fun in them the fellows had to make it themselves." – Max Walter, owner of the largest music hall, had imported an "old maid vocalist" and billed her as "Mlle. Antoinette," and the boys decided to have some "sport" with her without wounding her sensibilities more than by suggesting that "she was old enough to be worthy of a pension":]
>
> "Mlle. Antoinette was dubbed 'Aunty' by the crowd as soon as she appeared on the stage, for she couldn't sing a lick on earth, though Max had no idea of her lack of ability.
>
> "Aunty's first effort was a ditty called 'Fair, fair, with golden hair, under the willow she's sleeping,' . . .
>
> "Well, you should have seen those young blades when Aunty finished her solo. They fairly went wild with pretended enthusiasm and applauded until it seemed that the roof would come down. There were no bouquets in those days and so the fellows pitched a half bushel of half dollars on the stage, and Aunty came back in response to the encore. She sang 'Under the Willow' again and once more the applause was deafening. Max rubbed his hands with glee. . . . She got through with the second rendition of the song with some difficulty, for the thin air of Virginia City, caused by the excessive altitude, severely taxed the lady's lung power. . . . [She]

tried to bow herself into the seclusion of her dressing room, but it was no use . . . [Max tried other acts, and a speech to excuse his prima donna, but the call rose ever louder for Aunty.] The old lady came to the front, showing signs of distress. She was panting heavily, and though she opened her lips, not a sound escaped. Another hatful of silver coin was hurled onto the stage and as Manager Max led off his overworked singer he made another attempt to stem the tide of popularity . . .

" 'Then we'll go home,' shouted Hank Blanchard, the spokesman, and they marched out, followed by the entire audience.

"Next night the fellows formed in line on B street in front of Colonel Bob Taylor's law office and marched to Manager Max's place of amusement. In response to their summons Max came out on the sidewalk and anxiously asked how he could serve them.

" 'We came to find out if you are willing to arrange your program to suit us,' said Alf Doten, who had superseded Blanchard as leader of the claque. When he said that all the boys asked was that Aunty should be the only performer of the evening and that she should agree to sing nothing but 'Under the Willow,' Max threw up his hands in despair, for though he had a genuine admiration for Aunty, he began to think that his patrons had gone crazy.

" 'Impossible!' he began, but the crowd would hear no more. They swore that they paid their money to hear Aunty and if that privilege were denied them they wouldn't go to the show, and away they marched to the 'Sawdust Corner,' everybody in town following, for it was no use paying to get into a concert hall when there was more fun to be had on the outside for nothing. Manager Max blew out the lights, more mystified than ever. . . . But Aunty saw the point, and the next day when the stage started for Reno over the Geiger grade Max's prima donna was aboard, accompanied by two salt sacks full of silver coin she had providently swept up from the stage after she recovered from the fatigue of singing in the light air of that mountain climate."

Sunday, April 9 . . . Our University basket ball team of 13 young ladies got beaten 7 to 3 yesterday at Berkeley, Cal . . . Tim Dempsey left for Lovelock this evening expecting to go into the saloon or hotel business there . . .

April 11 . . . Yesterday our University Basket Ball team beat the Stanford team at Palo Alto 3 to 2 – good! My great Silver Peak article did not appear in either the *Chronicle, Tribune* or *Journal* – Broke my last Chronicle $20 today –

April 12 . . . Letter from wife, offering . . .

Sunday, April 16 . . . Sent letter to wife . . . striking her for loan of $30 . . .

April 17 . . . My Silver Peak article came published in Sunday's SF *Chronicle* and Reno *Journal* – Makes about 1½ columns in each – Makes 218 lines in *Chronicle* – head not counted . . .

[Clip, *Nevada State Journal:*] The important lawsuits connected with the Silver Peak mines, which have occupied the attention of the United States District Court at Carson the last two or three weeks, employing some of the best legal talent of Nevada and San Francisco, besides a small army of jurymen, witnesses, etc., being concluded, the following resume of the matter will be read with interest: . . .

The entire group of Silver Peak mines is now virtually owned by John I. Blair, a citizen of New Jersey, ninety-seven years old, and reported to be worth as many millions as he is years of age. He loaned money liberally to some of the original locators long years ago, and subsequently through the formation of new working and speculative combinations, bonding of the mines, etc., the whole Silver Peak mining property became secured to him by mortgage to the extent of $573,978.71, which measurably indicates the estimated value of the property. . . .

Some six or eight years ago L. J. Hanchett, a well known Nevada mining man of ability and experience obtained a lease and bond of the mines, erected a thirty stamp mill and prosecuted the work of development with considerable success, notwithstanding natural disadvantages from lack of adequate water power, contested titles, etc. About three years ago, however, Hanchett became somewhat involved financially, and was sued by Blair for royalty on the ore he had taken from the mines, to the amount of $11,000, and an attachment by the United States Marshal was placed on the store of his son, L. E. Hanchett, at Silver Peak. This suspended all mining work and Hanchett the older brought a counter suit against Blair, claiming title through his lease and bond.

Last week on trial of the case of Hanchett vs. Blair in the District Court, Carson, Judge Hawley decided that Hanchett had no legal interest in the Silver Peak property entitling him to make any defense against foreclosure of Blair's mortgage. In other words, whatever interest or claim he may have in the property is subsequent to and subject to the lien of Blair's mortgage of $573,978.81. Judgment was accordingly ordered entered for Blair in the aforesaid goodly sum.

Then came a very pertinent and interesting libel suit—Chiatovich vs. Hanchett. John Chiatovich, the principal storekeeper of the town, to whom Hanchett was indebted, several months ago brought suit and levied an attachment on a bar of bullion in the express office belonging to Hanchett. This overt act precipitated hostilities. Hanchett promptly raised the money, raised the embargo on his gold brick, paid Chiatovich his demanded indemnity and then proceeded to make a formal declaration of war, typewritten copies of which he posted in prominent public places, reading as follows:

"Notice to Our Employes: As John Chiatovich entertains for us feelings of animosity, and as his actions have tended to interfere with our business, and his expressed intentions are to hinder and embarrass us still further, we deem it advisable, in our own interest, to abstain from all communication with him. We especially request our employes to refrain from association with him, either directly or indirectly, and to disclose to him nothing that might tend to indicate the present condition of our business . . . and suggest that no one of our agents, representatives or employes trade or deal with Chiatovich in any manner whatsoever. His interests are so antagonistic to ours, his purpose is so manifestly hostile, that those who favor him cannot complain if we consider them as equally unfriendly to us."

This warlike, boycotting manifesto was promptly responded to by Chiatovich with a libel suit for defamation of character and injury to his business, claiming $10,000 damages. This case was also tried last week before Judge Hawley, resulting in favor of Chiatovich to the amount of $4,700.

Lastly, occupying the first three days of the closing week, came the suit of Hanchett, the younger, against United States Marshal Humphrey and his bondsmen, for levying upon his goods and closing his store at Silver Peak. The marshal did that at the instigation of the Silver Peak Mining Company, he being protected by an indemnified bond in so doing, the proposition being that the goods and store belonged to L. J. Hanchett instead of his son, L. E. Hanchett, who now brought this suit, claiming $6,800 damages. It being satisfactorily shown that L. E. Hanchett was the real owner, the jury, after long figuring and deliberation, brought in a verdict in favor of young Hanchett for $5,760.

This ended the Silver Peak cases in the United States Court for the present term. The main case of Hanchett vs. Blair, involving title to the Silver Peak mining property itself, is to come up at the next term.

April 18 – Clear & pleasant – Rec'd letter from wife with PO order for $15 – can't spare any more at present – Bed 11 – cold – Tim Dempsey is keeping a hotel out at Lovelock, on the CP Railroad, Humboldt Co –

April 21 – Same – cooler – no frost this morning – Arbor Day – Legal holiday – Schools closed, also stores, etc – trees set out by various parties, etc – S H (Harry) Day, my good friend the Carson Postmaster presented me a copy [of] *The Bounding Billow,* published on board Admiral Dewey's flagship Olympia, at Manila "at intervals," by L S Young, editor, and H B Glover, printer, "In the interests of American Man-O-Warsmen" Manila P.I. Nov-Dec 1898 – Vol 1, No 7 – pamphlet form, 6½ by 9 inches – 14 pages, 2 columns each – "value per copy, 20 sen" – full of spicily written items and matter incidental to the war and that locality – naval notes, bits of incidental poetry, etc, and one page of 14 advertisements, principally tailors, barbers and hair cutters, all located on shipboard, on "Starboard st, Larboard st, Galley Square, No 1, Forecastle, Cor Starboard Spud Locker & Bell Alley, Sand Chest Avenue," etc. Describes some of the neighboring battles on land, and when the battleships took a hand at shelling, etc – Altogether a very unique & interesting little paper – Announces this as the "farewell issue," saying: "Our mission ended with the approaching close of our eventful cruise" – bidding everybody farewell, etc. One item says: "This issue is printed on captured paper, and even though the war is over, we still derive benefits from the downfall of the Dons."

April 25 . . . Norris Bros big trained animal show of small animals, ponies, dogs, monkeys, goats and the smallest elephant in the world came down from Va where performed yesterday & last evening – Fine parade at 11 AM, with its excellent brass band in fine band wagon throughout town – Children all let out of school – PM matinee crowded. Big tent lower part of town – Evening ditto . . .

April 28 . . . $4.90 from SF *Chronicle* for Silver Peak article – sent receipt, and item from the following:

> [Unidentified clip, repeating information from the *Walker Lake Bulletin* of April 26 – US Marshal Emmitt posts notices of sale of numerous Silver Peak mining properties to satisfy mortgages of $642,140.85 held by John I Blair.]

Jerry Piper, old barkeep, etc, cousin to John Piper died this morning in chair sitting in sheriff's office – worn out – heart failure – 50 yrs old – Germany . . .

April 29 . . . Thick ice formed all about town – considered a settler on fruit prospects – McMillan vs Sadler for Governorship of Nevada, on demurrer & answer showed points in favor of McM in Supreme Court today. Finality of the contest set for June 5th – I wrote & sent report of it to *Journal* . . . The Filipinos having been badly whipped every time in several battles, etc lately are suing for peace –

April 30 through May 8 [More snow and freezing weather – AD writes to his wife, revises his Silver Peak piece for the *Salt Lake Tribune* and sends a note with it congratulating proprietor C C Goodwin on his return from the Silver Party to the Republican, celebrates Dewey Day with "flags and drinks & general patriotic hilarity," gets his first haircut from a barber in two years, finds he weighs 207 lbs, and, with great difficulty, trims his toe nails.]

May 9 . . . I only spent 2 bits for anything this day – broke into my last dollar in doing so . . .

May 10 . . . Spent my last 2 nickels this evening – for a good drink of "Old Continental" Whisky – Bed at 11, *Broke* –

May 11 . . . Busted, had to borrow $2, & run behind for grub – But I had a good catfish dinner – Mrs Roberts presented the fish & I had them fried at my hotel . . .

May 13 . . . The Carson News this evening published my Silver Peak article, copied from the SL *Tribune* of the 10th, in full – I read proof – credited to me – Just 2 columns in *News* . . . The Comstock Brass Band at Virginia had a "Horrible" ball last evening – Been advertising it last month or two in the three papers there – Been giving free open air concerts every Saturday evening of the season – Had "Horrible" street parade yesterday PM – Horrible masquerade ball at Piper's Opera House last evening – Only 37 maskers on the floor. The Enterprise gave list of names – Band boys very indignant at such shabby patronage at the hands of the unappreciative public, and expressed themselves so in morning *Enterprise* – No more free open air concerts from them – Yet the tickets were only 50 cts – This evening our Carson band gave an open air concert in Capitol Park – Very fine, and greatly attended and enjoyed – The whole town there. Children playing tag, rolling in the green grass, etc – beautiful scene –

May 17 . . . PM at room writing a letter and statement . . . to Hon Webster Patterson, atty-at-law, Elko, placing my account against the *Wells Herald,* balance due $70, in his hands for collection . . .

May 19 . . . An old soldier named Theodore Mills, who lives with Bird out to the north of town got into town yesterday, & got patriotically drunk – He left for home in evening with his old double barrelled shotgun, a revolver & a jug of whisky – About 11 oclock he was down below my hotel apiece & around toward the railroad shooting his old gun off hilariously – The police got after him but kept out of range for an hour or two, till his ammunition and whisky all run dry, then they captured & took him to the station house where he is still cooling off – He said he was after the Filipinos – Fired 20 shots or more, terrorizing the women & children & men of the neighborhood – said to be an old woman in the case who wouldn't let the old rooster in – Anyhow he whooped things up and was a celebration all to himself – Big time . . .

May 20 . . . Thos N Buckner died at Va last evening from apoplectic stroke on Thursday – 73 yrs old – Tom was one of the old Comstock faro sports, like Joe Stuart, "Kentuck," et al – but square man and good citizen – Native of Kentucky, crossed the Plains in 1849 – leaves a wife at Va – no children – He prospered much in stocks a few years ago in bonanza days & was $300,000 ahead, but lost it again . . .

Sunday, May 21 . . . Letter from wife with $15 postal – Got a short bit left – not broke . . .

May 23 . . . Had a most beautiful & affecting dream last night . . . I had come home in Reno, and as I passed into the house I saw people hurrying out. Parties were exercising on bicycles just outside, Sam said, and had met with a severe accident. I hurried out also, thinking that perhaps my wife in attempting to ride had tumbled off her wheel and was hurt. They were bringing in some one on a bed. It was Alfred. He was just recovering from a long spell of typhoid fever and in trying to ride, fell off through weakness and was seriously injured. I hastened to his bedside and knelt. He looked pale and worn but sadly extended his hand, which I eagerly grasped as he said: "Oh, papa, I was wrong to you; will you forgive me?" What more he said I did not know, as his voice was choked with emotion. I could not speak one word, but bending low my head as I clung to his poor, thin, wasted hand and arm I wept as I had never wept before. I felt all unconscious of the presence of any but my boy, remembering him only as I knew and loved him in his childhood, before contact with companions of his manhood had demoralized his heart, and alienated him from his loving old father. A heavenly sunshine glowed within my soul, and the sorest grief of my life had passed away with my tears. The blessed time I had so longed for had come, and I was so happy. But 'twas a dream too sweet to last, and its very brightness awakened me to reluctant realization that it was only a dream. But all day it has been with me, glowing warmly around my heart, soothing all other sad troubles into calm peaceful quiescence.

May 26 . . . At the Appeal office I borrowed a copy of the *Artemisia*, a new annual just issued by the students of the State University . . . University matters 156 pages, and 36 pages advertisements, total 192 pages – classes, teams, associations, etc, history of University, etc – very fully illustrated with photos of faculty, classes, teams, etc – Sam's picture & Alfred's among them – Goodwin also has a neat story: "A Little Quaker Sinner" – Book got up in good style and shows considerable literary ability – Price $1 – The Silver Peak sale took place yesterday at Hawthorne, by US Marshal Emmitt – Whole property was bid in for John I Blair for $665,000, that being the full amount of his mortgages with accruing costs – One of the biggest mining sales of modern times – Emmitt told me of it when he returned on evening train for Reno – I telegraphed 50 words of it to *Tribune* and *Chronicle* . . .

May 27 . . . PM I wrote letters to SF Chronicle & SL Tribune . . .

May 30 – Fine & just right – It was *Memorial Day* . . . Sent a three page letter to wife . . . two pages of which were a personal kindly criticism of the new annual, the *"Artemisia"* . . . Very elaborate private criticism – A lively incendiary fire about one o'clock this morning . . . destroyed Vonderhyde's and James F Lind's harness stores and Lary's paint store between. The fire was set in a narrow alleyway north side of Vonderhyde's . . . The greater part of the stock in the stores was saved – Buildings owned by D Circe. Loss $2,500, no insurance. Lind had the only insurance, on his stock – $500. Very suspicious circumstances induced his immediate arrest as the incendiary and he was placed in jail. Excited crowd gathered around threatening lynching, and officers prudently took Lind to the State Prison for safe keeping. He was returned to jail this morning, and released on $2,000 bail this PM; John Vieira & M Downey sureties.

May 31 . . . My letter on Nevada Copper mining, etc, of Saturday last came back in the SF Chronicle of yesterday . . . I won $1.25 terminal prize in The Little Original Benificia Publica Co . . . Makes second prize I have drawn in *those* style of public lottery . . . This $1.25 has cost me at least $40 in my small monthly investments – [Notes that son Alfred has graduated from the University] . . .

> [Clip from an unidentified newspaper; AD attributes it to Jim Townsend:] It is said that Mark Twain is greatly distressed by the death of a favorite cat which he had owned for many years. He didn't exhibit symptoms of distress when, in '63, in Virginia City, he cruelly administered to Mrs. Burr's pet tabby an injection of pepper-sauce and mustard which drove her (the cat) to climb a church-tower and jump off, thus committing suicide. This catastrophe excited considerable comment at the time.

June 1 . . . The changes in the Insane Asylum administration at Reno resultant upon the late general election went into effect today, Dr Bergstein being ousted & Dr Patterson put in his place – other employes ditto –

June 2 – Variable & cool – The county Grand Jury today had J F Lind's incendiarism charge before them . . . and finding no positive evidence against him but a strong alibi in his favor, ignored the case & discharged him & his bondsmen – His wife & daughter testified that he was at home & abed at time of the fire & couldnt possibly have set it – Mrs Dolan, a neighbor, corroborated their testimony – She testified that she saw and spoke with Lind as he went from his residence to the fire – at alarm. I received a letter from C D Van Duzer, Winnemucca saying he is going to start publishing *The Nevada Magazine,* early in July and asking me to write a 2000 word article for its first issue on the *Early Journalism of Nevada* . . .

June 3 . . . Evening I sent off letters to Chronicle and Tribune with statement of acct, also to C D Van Duzer accepting his proposition . . .

Sunday, June 4 . . . Fixed up a "pome," "Uncle Zeb Sees a Hoss Race," that Harry Day . . . gave me . . . wrote letter to accompany it and will send it to J W E Townsend, Miner-Index, Bodie Cal tomorrow – The "pome" was given to Harry by Ex Gov Burke of North Dakota when he was here a few weeks ago as Government Land Office Inspector . . . Andy Roberts & wife & little 12 yrs old daughter Pearl went catfishing over to Washoe lake today – He caught 200, wife 150, & Pearlie 7 – Big catch – Bed 1 – Spent my last dime today – broke & running behind –

June 5 . . . Roberts gave me a dozen catfish for my dinner, got them cooked at my hotel & enjoyed them – The contested election for Governor of Nevada – McMillan vs Sadler – came up at 10 AM in Supreme Court. I attended. Returns from 8 counties from last election to be canvassed – Nye County occupied today – 263 ballots – 63 objected to & filed for decision by the Court – Sent brief report, 1 page, to *Journal* . . . At 11:20 oclock just as I was getting into bed, fire bells and whistles sounded a loud and persistent alarm of fire . . . I could see no light or other indications, and finally concluded I was not needed so went to bed and sleep.

June 6 . . . The fire last night was a small wood shed or outhouse at rear of the Episcopal church west part of town – Church badly scorched, but saved – incendiary fire – attempts were also made to burn the big schoolhouse near by, also the Catholic Church – Fire bugs evidently getting in their work again . . . The Governor contest went on . . . count of Nye and Lyon counties completed, and that of Lander nearly so – Sent 2 page letter to wife . . .

June 9 . . . Evening Livingston's saloon received special telegraphic report of the big fight between Jim Jeffries and Bob Fitzsimmons at Coney Island, New York this evening for $20,000 and the championship of the world – Fitz licked Jim Corbett here a year ago last March 17 but this time he got knocked out in the 11th round – point of the chin – Had to be packed out of the ring . . .

Sunday, June 11 . . . Met W E F Deal at morning train on way to Va – told me he & others of Bd of Regents had given Sam a position in the University with 4 or $500 a year –

June 12 . . . The Supreme Court got through with relator McMillan's part of the case, and after considerable argument of counsel on the technicalities involving the identifying marks etc on the ballots, & other irregularities, adjourned till next Monday at 10 AM – There are over 700 of the objected ballots for the Court to consider and decide upon and probably be a basis for future expectations in that line – Through Arthur Morris, Deputy Secy of State I succeeded this PM in getting Governor Sadler's signature for Wells Drury – wrote it with a quill pen, and was in ordinary condition – good medium signature . . .

June 13 . . . Evening attended band open air concert in Capitol Park – Fine – all the kids in town, parents, dogs etc were there – glorious time on green grass, & even I got down & rolled in clover – had tough time getting up again . . .

June 14 . . . PM I wrote & sent 2 page letter to Major John H Dennis of the Reno Journal, on the Governor contest . . . Andy Roberts & wife caught about 250 catfish yesterday at Washoe Lake, & they gave me 15 which I ate fried for my dinner.

June 16 – Clear, warm & pleasant – 90° – At evening train the locomotive suddenly and very [loudly] blowing off steam through safety valve, frightened Bray's dray team of 2 horses so they ran away, directly colliding with Dr Benton in his one horse light open buggy, with Sam Robinson on seat beside him in front of the Carson Exchange – One horse reared up and plunged over on top of Benton, smashing both him and the light vehicle to the ground and then ran the dray wagon over him – Kind hands gathered him up, took him into Circe's Carson Exchange, where he was washed off & fixed up with a doctor's care, & he was taken home on a bed in a wagon – No bones broken but he was badly strained & bruised all over – good for a week or two in bed – Had a leg broken, & otherwise severely hurt in being thrown off a runaway wagon over at Franktown a couple of years ago – More than his share of such luck – His head badly cut by horses hoofs this evening, But skull not cracked . . . Hon Richard Parke Bland, Congressman from Missouri, died at his residence, Lebanon, Missouri yesterday – He was the Dick Bland, lawyer, I knew on the Comstock in the earliest times – Made a great record in Congress since then – a national record, and especially so in the advocacy of silver –

June 19 – Clear, breezy & pleasant – Attended the Governor Contest in Supreme Court again today – The Judges were busy with the 708 objected ballots all the week, since adjourned, even working yesterday so as to be on hand at this morning's resumption – They rendered their decision, counting all but those which were written upon or showed erasures – thus sustaining objections to 49 ballots by relator McMillan and 13 by Sadler, respondent – This puts McMillan about 16 ahead of Sadler, but now comes Sadler's side of the count . . .

June 22 . . . Letter from wife with $15 . . .

June 24 . . . 2 page letters to *Chronicle* and *Tribune* about the Gov Contest . . .

June 26 . . . Through Charlie S Peters, one of a goodly party of Carsonites who went over to Marlette lake fishing etc, Saturday, I received a fine lot – about 1½ doz of trout – They met my boy Sam there. He and Guy Walts are out on a camping trip . . . I took the trout to Andy Robert. Mrs R cleaned them all & I gave her all but four for myself dinner tomorrow – Finest lot of trout I ever saw, I think – Evening I sent short letter about it to wife . . .

June 27 . . . Ormsby County was on deck in Court today . . . At 5 PM court adjourned for the term, or until July 6 . . . when Empire precinct, Ormsby County, and White Pine and some few other returns will come in for Supreme Judicial adjustment – both parties having concluded to go the whole pig . . . I took Harry Day . . . to dinner with me at noon . . . to help me enjoy my trout from Sam – And we did – had 2 apiece which was plenty – Best tasting trout I ever ate . . .

June 28 . . . PM engaged at room on elaborate letter to Hon J P Jones . . .

June 29 . . . At train met my boy Sam – Just arrived from Lake Tahoe, on way to Reno – In his rough camping trip costume, leggings, etc. Was awful glad to see him, but only for five minutes, as he left on the train . . .

June 30 . . . PM I commenced writing "The Early Journalism of Nevada" . . . Johnny Carroll, a colored friend of mine from Washoe lake dined with me at my hotel –

July 1 . . . PM was at State Printing office & got a supply of paper cut for my note-book. Also list of all the newspapers in the State. 31 of them, against about 100 twenty years ago . . .

July 4 . . . Fine day and very pleasant little celebration of our patriotic American holiday – Decorations on all public and business buildings very excellent & elaborate . . . About 250 in all procession – limited but very neat turnout – Usual exercises . . . Evening fine bicycle parade – Carson band, 16 pieces, on bicycles framed together & pushed along, 4 abreast – original & good . . . plenty of lantern & other decorations – Big govt post office building finely trimmed & illuminated – Chinese lanterns lighted in all directions, flags everywhere also eternal fusillade of crackers, bombs, fireworks, rockets, red fire, etc – big hay wagon loaded with men & boys with big supply of active fireworks, which took fire returning down town, vacating the wagon very lively – No damage – no runaway – Evening show best of all . . .

July 5 . . . Reno took the cake on fireworks yesterday – one at 1:30 AM in the Chinatown section destroyed 25 buildings and another at 10 AM destroyed about a dozen more . . . Cobb's building also burned – The celebration and parade otherwise didn't amount to much . . .

July 6 . . . Governor contest on again – recanvass of ballots of Empire precinct, and of White Pine county, took all day, but went to a finish – resulting in little or no advantage to either side – McMillan side rests . . .

July 8 . . . Gov's contest – Respondent had Sheriff, County Clerk, Justice of the Peace and Constable of Washoe county as evidence relative to voting boundaries of Reno Township south line – showing that ranchers outside voted in Reno for township officers . . .

July 11 . . . Wrote some on my Early Journalism job – Was at State library awhile looking at file of *Enterprise* . . . Rec'd Bodie Miner-Index of last Saturday, Jim Townsend's paper, and in it was my version of *"Uncle Zeb Sees a Hoss Race,"* which old Jim appropriates to himself . . .

July 13 . . . The lawyers with the judges inspecting the rejected ballots in Supreme Court today –

July 17 . . . Sent letter to Townsend this morning, about names, etc of old time printers & editors . . .

July 18 . . . 95° – Sam came up from Reno this morning on his wheel, in 4 hours, to see US weather observer Smith and State observer Friend in connection with his new position as Prof of Meteorology, etc – After he got through He found me in my room at work – I went with him a little about this part of town, Postoffice, Arlington etc, introducing and at the railroad corner bade him good bye & saw him off home – Bed 11 – A party out serenading made beautiful music with guitars, mandolins etc this nice cool pleasant moonlight evening –

July 19 . . . Jos R Ryan has been appointed Supt of the bonanza group of Comstock mines, Con Va, Ophir, Union et al . . . Heber Holman has been appointed Supt of the Gould & Curry, Best & Belcher and Utah . . .

July 20 . . . Work as usual . . . I find plenty of bedbugs in this old shack of a lodging house – Old timers – ravenous –

July 21 . . . My *70th* birthday – good health – good appetite – weigh about 205 lbs – lame as usual, but not more so than a year ago – In fact I feel a year younger than then – Recd $2.35 from SF *Chronicle*, pay for May – Also rec'd nice letter from sister Lizzie . . . congratulating me on my attainment of "three score and ten" birthday, and being "the *seventh* in our family who has attained that distinction" – She also sent me a nice book of 350 pages entitled *Bob, Son of Battle*, by Alfred Ollivant. It is analytical of dog nature and man nature, acting and reacting on each other . . .

July 22 . . . Letter from wife with $15 – 4th . . .

July 24 – Variable – AM hot & sultry – 89° – PM cloudy, with thunder and fresh, cooling SW breeze but no rain in Carson – some outside – Work as usual – Got my *Early Journalism of Nevada* job fully written up in pencil – makes about 10,500 words – double what is required – Have to boil it down, which is worst part of the job – Governor case on today in Supreme Court – arguments of counsel . . . Bedbugs so plenty that my landlord & lady took my bed all apart & out on front porch today for treatment. My board & lodging bill all square to date & today commences new acc't – Paid $11.75 in full with yesterday noon dinner – being four weeks to date, with 2 extra dinners, Harry Day and Johnny Carroll –

July 25 . . . Work revising my job – Arguments in Governor contest closed and case submitted to the Court – which is expected to decide in a month or two – Received a nice book from Cornelia today . . . *"David Harum"* by Edward Noyes Westcott.

July 27 . . . Got all pencilled complete – 40 full pages – 11,000 words by actual count – commence on the boiling down to 6,000 words . . . tomorrow – Letter from Webster Patterson . . . my atty to collect the $75 balance due from Vardy of the *Wells Herald* – says has written him, but no answer & will visit him shortly . . .

July 28 . . . PM I wrote duplicate 2 page letters to *Tribune* & *Chronicle* . . . about Schissler & Co's mine at Jumbo district . . .

July 29 . . . At State Printing office, Capitol, etc, getting information – Our new *Nevada Magazine* made its first issue today – from the *Journal* office Reno . . .

July 31 . . . Commenced copying off my Journalistic article – Big Job – Jim Turner a long time resident of Carson left . . . for Butte City Montana . . . been staying for long time at my little old French hotel . . . has worked in the box factory here for years . . . Final closing of the factory lets him out . . . General favorite among Carson friends –

Aug 1 . . . Jim Turner leaving . . . gave me a chance, so I moved from my room, No 9 into No 17 which he vacated – gave me quite a busy job arranging things to suit, but I get a much better room at the same price, and better than all I get away from the countless herd of bed bugs that have been tormenting me . . .

Aug 2 – Clear, breezy & pleasant & comfortable – about 80° – PM I worked at revising my job – 7 PM received from SF Chronicle "Townsend, wealthy candy man this city, recently divorced and Mrs King said gone Nevada to be married – If ceremony took place your town send three hundred words – Please warn if you get nothing – M H de Young" – I started on track at once & at 8 replied by telegraph, "Parties not arrived – no marriage license issued – Will look out" – Alf Doten –

Aug 3 . . . The Carson evening News had my last Friday's letter on Jumbo district copied from the *Salt Lake Tribune* . . .

Aug 4 . . . At the office of the *News* this noon I found a copy of the new *Nevada Magazine* & they gave it to me – Ordinary looking, yellow cover pamphlet – not stylish – 79 pages good reading matter, including history of Reno by F H Norcross – 12 articles in all, by as many authors . . .

Aug 5 . . . My rich San Francisco candy man . . . fooled us all by going to Lake Tahoe via Truckee with his Mrs King and to Tallac & down to Genoa, where they got married Tuesday and went back by way of the lake to SF. . . . Got a copy of the new Nevada Magazine at the *Appeal* office, left there for me by Haley, one of the proprietors –

Aug 7 . . . The Morgan mill on Carson river at Empire got up steam, blew whistle and started up machinery last Saturday preparing to work ore from Con Va mine – Been idle for last two or three years or more –

Aug 8 – Clear, breezy & pleasant – Got the first instalment – one third – of my Journalistic job off on evening train for Van Duzer, Winnemucca – Also sent letter to Van Duzer – Received letter from J F Haley, Reno, business manager Nevada Magazine calling for copy & also relative to history of Carson article – Ed Walsh is to write for the magazine – Replied by evening train – then went down & saw Walsh at his store in Ormsby House block – Bed 12 – Under orders from Washington the shipment of the treasure from the Carson Mint to San Francisco commenced today – $800,000 by this evening train – All coined silver dollars, in small strong canvass sacks $1,000 in each sack, each weighing 60 pounds – total today 22½ tons – five or six millions still in mint –

Aug 9 – Same – Met Ed Walsh in street this AM and agreed to take the job off his hands of writing "Carson, the Capital City of Nevada" for the Nevada Magazine – PM was at State House getting material for it from Secy of State – etc – Bed 11 – Met A C Pratt on street today and got him to give me the copy of the Thompson & West's History of Nevada, belonging to him that I borrowed from the *News* office about six weeks ago and have been using since – Pratt formerly Surveyor General of Nevada – Deputy Secy of State etc –

Aug 10 . . . AM busy picking up Carson information . . . Big picnic from Va & GH, Episcopal Sunday School children, Treadway's Park . . . Between 3 & 4 hundred in all – Only one this year – none last . . . A third shipment of $800,000 this evening from the Mint to the Sub Treasury San Francisco.

Sunday, Aug 13 . . . Very breezy – Cooler – Great day for Carson – Relay bicycle race 50 miles between Reno & Carson . . . Special trains – Probably over 1,000 people from outside . . . The Renos beat Carsons by ½ a mile . . . I rec'd photos of self and Wells Drury from wife & got Frank Hall's photo from him, but failed in mailing to Winnemucca . . . Just before daylight this morning I dreamed that a friend of mine and myself killed somebody – It was outside, somewhere. He had threatened to kill me for something I wasnt guilty of – we met him – I gave my friend a big club and he knocked him down – Then with a smaller club I struck him on his head two times, each time breaking his skull with a dull ringing sound – But I killed him all the same, and feel very uncomfortable about it ever since – looked like a Mexican some – I didn't attend the relay race, the strong SW wind was unfortunate for the race – I missed my mailing, and altogether it seemed like an unlucky "13" day for me – also killed that man in my morning sleep, realizing that it was the thirteenth of the month . . .

Aug 14 . . . Got after Frank Hall and got him to go with me to the spot in SW corner of Carson where he & his brother built their log house, Nov '51 – first in Carson, & took up ranch – called it Eagle ranch & named Eagle Valley from a big eagle Frank shot and stuffed with hay for a sign over the door – On the rising ground just back of Ex Gov Adams's present residence – Also got Frank signature, fixed up my own and sent mine, Wells Drury's and Frank Hall's this evening to C D Van Duzer, Winnemucca, to illustrate Part 1 of my Early Journalism article – Frank's for my Carson write up . . . Met J F Haley, Van D's partner this morning for 1st time – pleasant young fellow – says the type of the . . . second number of the magazine will be set at the Carson *News* office . . . Frank Hall is 76 yrs old . . .

Aug 15 – Same – Commenced writing up Carson today – did 3 pages – Met Sam Longabaugh of Empire, the old Carson river wood driver and got some items from him and promise to send me his photo for illustration – The last of the $800,000 daily shipments from the Carson Mint to the US Sub Treasury, San Francisco went by this evenings train, making $5,000,000 in all – Been no miscue or trouble of any kind in the handling or transfer – Great care, and plenty of "shotgun messengers" along . . . 15 tons in all . . .

Aug 16 through 24 [AD steadily gathering material for his Carson article, including photographs of Longabaugh and Farmer Treadway, and writing long hours on the piece – Also receives another lot of rainbow trout from his son Sam and notes that "Johnny Myers opened his handsome new store saloon at south end of town this evening in hilarious style – free lunch, town band played in front, etc."]

Aug 25 . . . Fought to a finish taking my last M.S.S. to *News* office at 2:10 PM just completed – Hard old siege – At 5 PM went to *News* office and read proof of Carson complete – Over 6000 words – through at 9 – Bed at 11, very, very tired –

Aug 26 . . . Rose at 7 AM after 8 hours good sleep and rest – much recuperated – *News* office at 10, added about 300 words more to Carson, read revised proof – hour at noon dinner – returned to office and read proof of Early Journalism – All through at 3 PM . . . The type of my matter, & all the rest . . . was boxed up and shipped to the *Journal* office, Reno by this evening train – I sent letter to Van Duzer, striking him for some money . . . Evening I called on Tim Dempsey at his residence – Tim came home from Lovelock last Tuesday sick with malarial fever . . . Bad water at Lovelock . . .

Sunday, Aug 27 . . . Slept till 8 AM – Good and needed rest – Did but little today –

Aug 29 . . . PM trimmed my toe nails and mended my sox – The US transport arrived Saturday last at San F with the California Regiment from Manila, discharged. Greatest parade reception on water & on land, ever seen in America – City and bay in a blaze of glory, music, feasting, marching, etc till nobody could rest – Papers loaded down with pictorial accounts of it . . . I received a copy of *Brotherhood of Locomotive Engineers Journal,* for June, 1899, from my good old Fort John friend Fred W Clough . . . It contains a well written article by himself, on *The Calaveras Grove of Big Trees,* illustrated by nine large & beautiful half tone pictures –

Aug 30 . . . The great silver-mouthed orator with a silver short bit in his peculiar mug, Wm J Bryan, the political chattering magpie, passed through Reno last evening at 10:10 with his wife, on a visit to the Pacific Coast – made a speech at every town or stopping place on the road – Talked & shook hands 15 minutes at Reno depot while the train stopped – Quite a big crowd – made nice talk . . .

Aug 31 . . . PM wrote & sent 4 page letter to SL *Tribune* . . .

Sept 1 . . . *The Indian Advance,* a new monthly paper, 2 bits a year, commenced its issue today & was scattered all about town – A decided novelty published by the students of the Stewart Institute, government Indian School at the mouth of Clear Creek, some 3½ miles south of Carson – 8½ by 12 inches . . . 4 pages – 3 columns per page . . . W L Taylor a first class white printer, etc, employed to run the printing dept & track the Indian boys & girls compositions – Exceedingly well made up & printed, interesting reading matter . . . Got letter from Webster Patterson, Atty, Elko, returning my papers in my Vardy case, giving up as a bad job . . .

Sept 2 . . . Rec'd letter from Van Duzer, with PO order for $5 – the first I have received from that resource – PM was down town as far as Geo H Meyers and Ed Walshs stores consulting on my pay for Carson write up –

Sunday, Sept 3 . . . PM remodeled a six bit black shirt I bought this AM . . .

Sept 4 . . . Put on my new shirt today and got my hair trimmed in good style . . . The various Comstock Companies have signed the Contract with Electric Power Co in Truckee river, Floriston, to supply that power by wire to the Comstock . . .

Sept 5 . . . In yesterday's San Francisco *Bulletin* I find account of death of D P Pierce whom I knew at and about Milpitas, Cal, when I was a rancher near there, long years ago – He also came to Como when I was there, and together with a Mr Wicker ran the quartz mill there for a short time, after I left – He also found me in Austin when I was running the *Reveille,* he being engaged in milling and mining at Lewis, a few miles north, toward Battle Mountain. He was Superintendent of the Betty O'Neil mine and mill at Lewis – About my age – Evening down town at the Magnolia – Lively conversation with Gov Sadler – on war and politics –

Sept 7 . . . PM down at State House & State Printing office – got photo of Maute, State Printer, also a half-tone portrait of Sam Davis – Rec'd letter from Van Duzer . . . Great preparations to receive W J Bryan tomorrow PM – Democratic-Silver Committees, gents and ladies went over to Lake Tahoe by carriages this evening to meet him and family . . . wife & 3 children . . . Anniversary of my terrible mining accident, at Fort John Amador Co, Cal, Sept 7, 1854.

Sept 8 – Clear & pleasant – PM wrote & sent letter to A Skillman, *Eureka Sentinel* desiring photos of himself, Geo W Cassidy, W W Hobart and

Fred Hart – Between 3 & 4 PM special trains from the Comstock & Reno brought over 1,000 people to see & hear Bryan – Over 100 also came in carriages from Va, Silver & Dayton – Carson looked like a fair or picnic day – Big cannon north of town fired salutes at intervals during the PM – Comstock Brass Band, 8 pieces, came down with the crowd, and the Carson Band and the Indian Band made up a pretty good welcoming assortment of music, playing on street & in the Capitol grounds – Bryan & party arrived from Glenbrook & got off stage at the Ormsby House about 5 PM – washed & fixed up, & at 5:30 Bryan commenced speaking from west porch of the State Capitol – Gov Sadler presided and introduced, and Congressman Newlands was among the dignitaries on the platform – Huge audience – 2,000 – in the park fornenst him – Made a splendid speech – champion orator – Spoke 50 minutes, closing at 6:20 – left on train for Reno ½ hour later to take train east – The Va train special – 8 coaches crowded also left directly afterward – Altogether rather interesting occasion – Met lots of my old Va friends today –

[Clippings on the speech – The *News* calls Bryan "a splendid specimen of the college senior wrangler, always ready to sacrifice facts as well as logic to . . . making an impression." – He said silver is a live issue, and that Democrats were more likely to destroy trusts because "they were better and wiser people. Under this head he rung the changes on his favorite expression, 'the struggling masses,' and every time he used the expression Sam Davis, who was the chosen leader of the claquers, set up a yell which met with a faint response in the audience." – Claimed, but did not, of course, prove that Republicans fostered trusts, and preached the "ancient fallacy" that the war was a rich man's war fought by the poor, and that the Philippines should be turned over to the natives – "The only attempt he made at arguments was to quote from the Bible to prove that it was wrong to acquire the Philippines," while failing to state that conditions were now different from those in Biblical times – Said "There was nothing bad, or that he considered bad, that was not laid at the door of the Republican party." The *San Francisco Chronicle* was equally against Bryan's position on the Philippines, saying that "no man . . . who holds such sentiments as these" is worthy or competent enough to be president – The *Appeal,* on the contrary, saw Bryan as talking honestly about how the Republicans had tried, in vain, to bury the silver issue and the trust problem, while the Administration "had placed the dollar above the value of mankind" – As for his position that the Philippine war was one of "conquest and not of liberty," "everyone voted it a masterpiece of eloquence and logic." – "People blocks away could hear the eloquent voice of this great speaker and at the conclusion of his convincing talk the people fairly yelled themselves hoarse" – The same issue of the *Appeal* recounts an anecdote about Bryan trying on half a dozen hats, looking for his own when leaving the Ormsby House after lunch, none of them fitting because "Mr. Bryan wears an eight and a quarter hat."]

Sept 9 . . . Letter from Van Duzer, inclosing PO order for $4 . . . I finished reading *David Harum* this evening, and like it very much – better in some respects than anything I ever read –

Sunday, Sept 10 . . . Evening sent *David Harum* to wife, with a 2 page letter accompanying –

Sept 11 . . . The second or September number of the *Nevada Magazine* arrived . . . Saw it on sale at bookstore – I am in it all right – both Carson and Journalism articles in full – with excellent pictorial illustrations . . . [See Appendix for text of "Early Journalism of Nevada."]

Sept 12 through 19 [AD revises part two of his article on journalism and mails it to Van Duzer, suffers severe stomach pains, which he relieves with whiskey laced with absinthe, & notes that the coining machinery of the Carson Mint is being shipped to New Orleans & Washington and that the State Fair has opened in Reno with a fifty-mile bicycle relay race in which Reno defeats Oakland by 2⅜ miles.]

Sept 20 – Clear & pleasant but very warm – 90° – Sent 2 page letter to wife, by evening train – The Supreme Court rendered its decision late this PM in the Governor contest – McMillan vs Sadler, declaring Sadler elected by 63 plurality over McMillan – It was 22 at general election – but the defects of the Australian ballot law or system have increased it to 51 more than the expressed will of the people – Several Chinese bombs were fired on street in honor of the event, and a big wood rack wagon loaded with schoolboys and girls, drawn by 4 horses went up and down street, they singing, shouting and horn blowing, etc – At the depot the telegraph boy found me & gave me a telegram from the SF *Chronicle:* "Send 250 decision in governorship contest – M H de Young" – I only had an hour, but just before 8 oclock closing time, I had my dispatch in hand in the telegraph office – About 400 words – sent it to both *Chronicle* and SL Tribune – About town awhile and bed at 11:30 – Dreyfus pardoned yesterday in France & released –

Sept 22 . . . The SF *Chronicle* . . . of yesterday had my telegram in good double-header style with double column cut of Gov Sadler . . .

Sept 23 . . . Gave copy magazine to Sam Longabaugh . . . Also sent a copy to Hon J P Jones, Hoffman House, New York City . . . At *News* office found copy of SL Tribune of 21st – Had my telegram on governorship decision, about 6 inches, with a *7 inch head* . . .

Sept 25 . . . Morning train . . . brought 40 or 50 folks from Reno, and the Elleford dramatic & variety Co, which plays during the week – It being fair week here . . . Evening met with Johnny Hepworth of Como when I was there, & we affiliated – as we have naturally ever since – Plenty of games and sports in the saloons . . . especially at the Criterion (Livingstons) and the Ozark – all the sports and camp followers from the Sacramento and Reno fairs being here – two Coons with banjo and guitar, playing & singing in the hall of the Criterion, and three more at the Ozark – Town lively – Bed 11 – Tired –

Sept 26 . . . Met Haley . . . Paid me $5 on acct . . .

Sept 27 . . . Met Sam Calvin this evening – recently from Cape Nome – Says its a big rich country, & he made big money there – Goes back there in the Spring . . . Came to a definite understanding today with Haley as to my terms for writing for the *Magazine* – I charge $20 for Carson write up, and $40, thus far, for "Early Journalism" . . .

[Clipping, *San Francisco Examiner,* Sept 27 – "Here is Hope for Men Who Drink" – A British Medical Association survey of 4,234 deaths shows that Total Abstainers live an average of 51.22 years, Habitual Drunkards 52.03, Free Drinkers 57.59, Careless Drinkers 59.67, and Habitually Temperate 62.13.]

Sept 28 . . . Recd letter from wife with $15 – (Sixth) – squared up my board & lodgings bill . . . Sent a copy of this number of *magazine* to Col Wm Nelson, Managing editor of *S.L. Tribune* with compliments of Alf Doten – When I mailed it on evening train I met James H Crockwell . . . Had pleasant talk on Comstock times, etc – It was his little daughter Ada, 12 yrs old, who got fatally burned that time, and when dying, surrounded by her family . . . and many friends, calmly recited the Lord's Prayer in confident, childish voice, same as was her taught invariable habit every night before going to sleep, closing with . . . "God bless papa, God bless mama, God bless Earlie, God bless Lulu, God bless Lawrie and God bless poor little Ada. Amen." – And while all present silently and soulfully wept, her gentle spirit passed into the eternal rest and sleep that have no trouble or waking forevermore . . . The unavoidable annual visitation of the hay fever has got onto or into me . . .

Sept 29 . . . PM I visited the Fair grounds & race track – trotting, pacing, running races, thats all . . .

[Clip, Virginia *Report* – Edward T Plank, Comstock printer, Nevada assemblyman, and president of the International Typographical Union, died in Boise, Idaho, on September 26.]

Ed Plank worked on *News* for some time before I got through – He was one of the best of printers and a *true friend* of mine. A good man among men –

Sept 30 . . . Rec'd proofs of my "Early Journalism" – 2nd part . . . The Ormsby Fair came to a conclusion today . . . Several accompanying darkies gave a "cake walk" in gay style, front of grand stand, as a feature attraction – very amusing . . . Haley returned to Reno tonight – He told me that 1st edition of *Magazine* was 3,000 copies and this second edition was 2,800 copies – He lied like blazes – Editions only about 500 or 600 – and about all sold . . . Newspapers all full . . . of Dewey's reception in New York – Grandest ever seen . . .

Sunday, Oct 1 . . . Exodus of all the Fair contingent, horses, horsemen, sports, darkies, hobos and camp followers . . . PM wrote on an article on the Australian ballot . . . A press telegram from Manila says the Nevada Cavalry left there for home on Friday on the transport Ohio . . .

Oct 2 . . . Fifty Years ago today I landed in San Francisco . . . Hadn't a cent in my pocket when I landed, and same today . . .

Oct 3 . . . PM I finished my Tribune Australian Ballot article, 6 Pages, & sent it – Also sent 4 pages on same subject to the SF Chronicle – Evening about town – very cold – saloons etc all had to have fires . . .

Oct 4 . . . The snowsheds near Cisco . . . were burned for about two miles last night . . . mailed Sept no of *Magazine* to Jim Townsend, Bodie . . . Great and glowing accounts of reception of Dewey in Washington Monday . . . was presented with his sword of honor, by President McKinley today . . . Richest & finest sword ever presented – Pres't said: "There was no flaw in your victory; there shall be no faltering in maintaining it."

Oct 5 . . . Milton Smith who was barkeep at the Arlington last Spring and went to Bodie to same position, returned today . . . Says Jim Townsend has sold his paper, the Bodie Miner-Index . . . Old Jim is too sick

& broken down to run it any longer – He will come in from there & probably go to his married daughter's home in Oakland –

Oct 6 . . . PM wrote & sent 2 page letter to Geo R Vardy, *Wells Herald*, dunning him for the $25 he promised to pay me . . .

Sunday, Oct 8 . . . At noon Mike Conlon, my best old Comstock miner friend found me – He just in from a prospecting trip, horseback, over in Alpine County . . . PM we were together . . . Took supper . . . cruised about town some – Bed at 10:30, he taking room & bed at my hotel – Mike gave me the cane I wear, three or four years ago, at Virginia.

Oct 9 . . . Mike Conlon remained visiting with me and not allowing me to pay for the entertainment – The SL Tribune of Saturday . . . contained my communication on Australian Ballot . . .

Oct 10 . . . My grand good old friend Mike Conlon got away for the Comstock about 1 PM – I went down to Raycrafts stable with him, and saw him off in his own good style – old white hoss, with blankets & comforter thrown across instead of saddle, bale rope bridle, etc . . .

Oct 11 . . . When I got out of bed at 7 AM there was full six inches of snow on the ground . . . At morning train met George Freyer with J J Hepworth, of Dayton – By invitation I dined with George – new aquaintance – great friend and admirer of Miss May-Ethelyn Bourne, a writer in the Nevada Magazine – seems very soft on her and loves to talk to me about her, and have me sympathetically help him win her – sad case – He is about 40 years old, and a miner principally – says she is about 26 – and lives out in Humboldt . . . He owns a gold mine nine miles from the Humboldt House on the railroad . . .

Oct 13 . . . Letter from Van Duzer proposing me to canvass Carson for subscriptions to *Magazine* . . . letter from *Tribune* with $6.50 cash to date . . . Nearly a bit an inch . . .

Oct 14 . . . 3 or 4 ft of snow reported on the summit . . . PM wrote on a long letter to J P Jones – NY – Harry Day, Postmaster gave me nice privilege to write in his private office . . . warm & comfortable . . .

Sunday, Oct 15 . . . The Boers & the British have got to fighting the last 2 or 3 days in South Africa – Both sides well prepared for an active bloody war and are starting in on it . . .

Oct 16 . . . At morning train I found old John W McKinney – He has been out at Shaw's Springs 2 miles north of town for a week trying to soak out his rheumatism, but he is still very badly crippled with it, so that I had to help him to board the 10 oclock local train for Reno, en route to his home at Lake Tahoe – Says he lives at mouth of the little creek just south of Blackwood, where I & Chubbuck & Harrison Gray ran a lot of big trout up the little shallow stream and clubbed & stoned them to death as they tried to escape over the ripples – in the old time – John looks same as ever, but older, and I had to carry his little valise for him to the car & help him up the steps – He is on his last legs and not good ones . . .

Oct 17 . . . AM I worked rewriting and revising Part 3 of *Journalism* . . . PM worked at revising or mending my oldest coat, put it on and in evening took my newest one . . . to Jacobs for repairs & rejuvenation . . .

Oct 18 . . . Patrick Crowley who murdered Wm Nicholls with an ax on the 1200 ft level station of the Savage mine Sunday night, July 20, 1890, slipped over the wall of the State Prison yard about 11 AM today & escaped but was subsequently re-captured near the Brunswick mill . . . Much excited discussion about town, politics, religion and Odd Fellowship being involved in his case and badly mixed – Sheriff Quirk, a son of Nicholls and others were in town this evening, much interested . . .

Oct 20 . . . Recd copy of DeLamar Lode, containing my Australian ballot article copied in full from SL Tribune & my name to it . . .

Sunday, Oct 22 . . . I completed Part III of my Early Journalism just in time to get it into the mail . . . Worked hard all the PM at Postoffice to finish it . . . Trouble with my heart last night . . . Waked up by it about 2 oclock with bad fluttering palpitation – and much dead oppressive & acute pains across breast & shoulders – lasted an hour or so, & I slept again –

Oct 23 . . . Recd $1.65 from SF Chronicle . . . The SL Tribune paid me $1.10 for the same special on Sadler decision . . . therefore I make it that Tribune pays 2 cts a line for special telegrams and the Chronicle 2½ cts per line –

Oct 24 . . . Received . . . ten copies Nevada Magazine for October, from Van Duzer . . . brief note from wife with seventh $15 – Evening sent her a letter – got my coat & vest from Jacobs . . . The Magazine is enlarged a little, also the price advanced from $1.25 to $2.50 per year –

Oct 26 . . . I wrote & sent 2 page letter to Van Duzer, and about 300 words of letter to SF Chronicle, about escape and recapture of Jimmy McCarty from State Prison – last evening about 6 – and captured by porter, Selden Richards, front of the Arlington on sidewalk about 4 AM. Took him to station house, & went back to prison this morning – 27 yrs old – from Storey County, for 27 yrs for shooting & killing an Italian, coming to town with a load of wood and McCarty wanted one of the horses & the Italian refused, so McCarty had to shoot & kill him, then ran away & was captured all right – Wont be a "trusty" and get out again very soon – On evening train I found old Jim Townsend, bound for SF & had short chat with him – Gave him copy of the Nevada Magazine for October – His address below will be East Oakland, Substation No 2 –

Oct 27 . . . PM I wrote a 3½ page letter to SL Tribune about the State Prison escapes . . . Ben Shaw, a clothing dealer at Va, and Andy Mahoney, a clothing drummer won $15,000 jointly in the Mexican Beneficencia Publica lottery, drawn yesterday –

Oct 28 through Nov 6 [AD sends a copy of the September *Nevada Magazine* to a Chas S Mann of Pennsylvania, who collects data on the first three newspapers of each state, copies of the October issue to Nelson, the *Tribune* editor, and J P Jones, and copies of one or the other or both to his wife, Fred Clough, Bessie, Eunice, Lizzie and Cornelia – Also writes to Van Duzer about canvassing, and to wife, Jim Townsend and others, reads proof on Part III of "Early Journalism," procures a letter from Pratt to prove his ownership of the Thompson & West *History of Nevada*, receives further installments of "The Clown's Protege," and hears telegraphic returns of the Jeffries-Sharkey fight in the Criterion Saloon. Writes, November 3, "Arrived at Woods' Creek and the golddiggings . . . 50 years ago this evening."]

Nov 7 . . . Rec'd Jim Townsend's photo, from him at Oakland – very good – cabinet size – no hat on – mailed it with brief note to Van Duzer. Capt Linscott's company Nevada Cavalry . . . arrived at San Francisco Sunday – well received by Gov Sadler, Lieut Gov Judge, & other Nevadans and friends – breakfasted by Newlands, and marched to Presidio where they are to be mustered out in ten days – Regiments of soldiers from the east and middle & western States pass through Reno almost daily, bound for Manila – The Boers still continue beating the English . . .

Nov 9 . . . Received brief note from Van Duzer with a receipt book and authorization to canvass for subscribers to the Nevada Magazine . . .

Nov 11 . . . PM I was at office rooms of Prof Ring the State Supt of Pub Instruction, overhauling the old register and record of the Pacific Coast Pioneers – Rec'd brief note from Hon J P Jones . . . saying: "My dear Doten – Your various letters have been received, for which I wish to express my thanks to you. I am going out to the coast very soon, and will see you when I get to Carson, and hope to have the opportunity of talking matters over with you fully. Very truly yours, Jno Jones." I mailed reply tonight . . . Also rec'd letter from Nelson . . . will rely on me for annual review of Nevada . . .

Sunday, Nov 12 . . . PM I wrote out for Jas D Roberts, guard of the State Prison a certificate that he was and still is a member in good standing in the Pacific Coast Pioneers . . . I found Roberts' name on the Registry book of the Society yesterday – It was in his own handwriting, under date of June 1, 1874 when he joined, stating that he was born in the Year 1826, and came from Cincinnati, Ohio across the Plains to California in 1849, arriving September 10 . . .

Nov 17 . . . PM I was at trial in Dist Court, before Judge Macks, of Mrs Emily Estes charged with cattle stealing, in connection with Maher and McKenzie – Maher has gone to State Prison for 5 years, McKenzie acquitted, and this evening jury brought in verdict of acquittal in her case – Handsome young woman of 26 . . .

Nov 18 – Variable – fine day – The 1st Nevada Cavalry, Capt Linscott, 48 in number . . . came to Reno by morning train at 8 & were gloriously received – 84 in number when they went to Manila – Excursion train from the Comstock & here went down leaving here at 10 – 5 coaches from Va and one hitched on here . . . about 300 persons in all – National and Emmett Guards from Va – Indian football team from here went down to contest with University team – about 20 Indian boys – Governor and State officers, et al went – Grand procession . . . this PM, with banquet & ball in evening – Great time – Two of the Cavalry boys came up on the PM local, to see their parents & friends & home at Gardnerville – Bed 12 . . .

Nov 21 . . . Met Gov Sadler & got him to subscribe one year for the *Magazine* – paid cash $1.50 – my first sub . . . I attended reception to members of 1st Nevada Cavalry Co at Odd Fellows Hall – given by ladies of the Red Cross – About a dozen of the soldiers, including Capt Linscott and Howard P Davis – Singing, music, recitations and dancing – About 200 or 300 people present, with Gov Sadler & State officers, etc – About

11:30 adjourned to front hall & had fine banquet – Gov was toast master or chairman – numerous *attempts* at speech making – closed with several pieces by the Carson Band and a little dancing, about 1 . . .

Nov 22 . . . Was about town canvassing . . . got 3 . . . Recd letter from wife today with 8th $15 . . .

Nov 24 . . . I wrote some on a sketch of Farmer Treadway and one of Sam Longabaugh, for the Magazine for Dec . . .

Nov 27 . . . Got five new subs – Had 10 before – Evening sent a list of 15 to Van Duzer . . .

Nov 28 . . . The Nevada Magazine was received by the News and Appeal today – for November – Has last of my "Early Journalism" – Part III . . . The Sacramento Bee of Monday has nearly two columns from Part II . . . including what I wrote about Fred Hart and Mark Twain . . .

Nov 30 . . . Everybody enjoyed Thanksgiving as usual . . . I had good turkey dinner at my hotel – Very nice, but not old home like . . .

Dec 2 . . . Letter from Van Duzer – asks me to canvass for ads – says Haley his partner has got out of concern – had to get rid of him – no good –

Sunday, Dec 3 . . . 2 big page letter from Van Duzer telling of Haley's out, and giving me full agency swing in this and Storey Cos, advertising & all . . .

Dec 8 . . . PM & evening wrote on an article "Pacific Coast Pioneers" for Magazine if wanted . . . Capt Fred Linscott of the 1st Nevada Cavalry, recently returned from Manila has been appointed military instructor at the State University –

Dec 14 . . . At State Library for information, & elsewhere – evening sent letter to Managing Editor of *SF Chronicle* – want my "Wildcat Joe" story I sent him June 16, 1898 returned – Stayed writing in my post office, till 10, and finished writing my Pacific Coast Pioneers article . . .

Dec 18 . . . I worked most of day in PO and completed copying my Pioneer article & mailed it to the SF Chronicle – 17 pages – 6,040 words – principally compiled from my Legislative pamphlet [of] April 1887 . . . [See Appendix for text of the article.]

Dec 19 . . . The Nevada State Band, 24 pieces left last evening for the grand Pioneer Golden Jubilee at San Jose, Cal – The Indian Band could not go, as intended by reason of small pox at the Institute . . . I worked Harry Day's type writer this evening short time, very successfully – never tried one before – wrote: "This world is all a fleeting show for man's illusion given" – My first lesson – It is a 35 "Blickensdorfer" machine.

Dec 20 . . . Skirmished for Magazine subs at lower and south end of town – got four – Rec'd letter from wife with $16, the $1 extra, she said, being for my Christmas dinner – Evening I took another lesson in type writing . . .

Dec 21 . . . PM was at the State Controller's office and got the quarterly reports of all the producing mines throughout the State for my Nevada review – Evening made a commencement of the job . . .

Dec 22 . . . *Forefathers' Day* – I am 279 Pilgrim years old today . . .

Dec 23 . . . Recd from Van D 4 new magazines, December, Very good – pictures of old Farmer Treadway and Sam Longabaugh in it, also the sketches I wrote of them – Wife also has a commencement of a story in it entitled: "The Singular Story of the Hortons and the Mortons" . . .

Sunday, Dec 24 . . . Rec'd Pilgrim Calendar for 1900 from Alfred S Burbank, my Plymouth nephew and namesake – Rec'd it remailed by wife . . . evening I remailed it to her with 1 page Christmas letter . . . Wrote on Nevada review most of day, and till 10:30 in evening – was at Arlington awhile, and Bed at 1, after wishing several friends a Merry Christmas –

Dec 25 . . . Christmas Day – Observed as usual – smooth and easy – I worked most of day at my job in Post office – Evening sent brief letter to Sears, Roebuck & Co Chicago Ill ordering a violin, by request of Tim Dempsey, for his little daughter Pearl – to cost $3.25 . . .

Dec 27 . . . Worked hard on my Nevada review all day . . . completed only in time to send it off by mail, at 6:15 . . . Rec'd by mail today a fine book from Sister Cornelia . . . entitled "Richard Carvel" . . . Winston Churchill author . . . Also rec'd from her son Alfred, my nephew, three photo Pilgrim pictures: "The Embarkation," the old county Court House, Plymouth, and Coat of Arms of the Bradford family . . .

Dec 29 . . . Rec'd from Alfred Burbank a nice photo of "Training Green" opposite our "Old House at Home" with soldier's monument on it – I recognized the old hip roofed Pilgrim house on north side of green, where I learned my ABC's from old lady Dyke . . .

Sunday, Dec 31 . . . Evening about town – At midnight big ringing of all the bells and horns and pistols . . . watch meetings at some of the churches . . . Good bye old year – I ended it dead broke – not a nickel in my pocket . . . Great wrangling among the newspapers and scientists and literary people generally as to when the 20th century begins – The Century Dictionary and Cyclopedia, Page 6550 says: "The twentieth century will begin not, as supposed in January 1900, but in January 1901" –

BOOK NO. *76*

Carson City
Jan 1, 1900 – Dec 31, 1900

Jan 1 through 8, 1900 [AD receives twelve copies of the New Year edition of the *Salt Lake Tribune* (64 pages for 5 cts) with his Nevada piece in it, sends notes & copies of the December *Nevada Magazine* to Senator Jones and Jim Townsend, gets his Pioneer article back from the *Chronicle,* revises it and sends it to Van Duzer, and notes that the Carson *News* is reprinting his whole Nevada write-up by installments.]

Jan 9 . . . Met old Matt Callahan in town this evening – from his ranch on Galena Creek . . . Comstock old timer, one of the most noted – His old brick yard down below Chinatown, at Virginia, was where all the boys used to go for a scrap, or "to fight it out" anyway they chose –

Jan 12 . . . Evening "Nance O'Neil Co" in play of "Magda" . . . but I was not there – Met Mr Barton Hill at Arlington, after show was over & had a long & interesting chat together . . . He is an old theatrical manager and agent on the Pacific Coast – Bed 1 –

Sunday, Jan 14 . . . At the depot yesterday morning . . . officer Ed Patterson picked up old pair of spectacles on platform – finding no owner, and as they suited the focus of my eyes exactly he gave them to me – quite convenient and desirable – steel bowed and cheap kind – worth about 4 bits – but good –

Jan 16 . . . Rec'd statement from SL Tribune with check for $10 in payment for Nevada write-up . . .

Jan 17 . . . A big blue-bottle eared fly, the first of the season was crawling on the window of my room this morning . . . an old stowaway of the winter – He's all right, but I will attend to his relatives later on. A brother of his was the first to thus appear to me last year, and I banged him out of existence first round. Over 1,000,000 of his relatives got more than even on me later on, even getting the bed-bugs to stand in with them. Bad luck as well as bad policy to thus kill the first fly of the season, especially the old *"bottle ear"* . . . Indian "Joe Pete," who killed Will Dangberg – 18 yrs old – last September 14 in Carson Valley, & has been hunted for ever since, was captured, or gave himself up & was brought to county jail, here, at 3 o'clock this morning . . .

Sunday, Jan 21 . . . My right heel which has been troubling me very sorely last few weeks disturbed my rest last night – Examining my shoe this morning I found a bad nail sticking up & eradicated it – thats whats the matter – heel very sore all day but improving – The violin I sent for to Sears, Roebuck & Co, Chicago, arrived today – evening I took it from express office to my quarters in the Postoffice – Tim Dempsey paid all costs . . .

Jan 22 . . . I opened the box and found the violin all right – went to work, regulated the bridge, strings, etc, tuned it up and it played splendidly – magnificent violin – much better than I anticipated – worth $20 – but cost just $3.90 . . . At 6 PM Tim Dempsey came . . . and we transported the violin over to Tim's residence – Dennis Canney was there on a visit, also Mrs D and the 2 girls, Nellie and Pearlie – They gave us some music, Nellie on piano, and Pearlie on the new violin, which she took kindly to – then I made a few brief remarks telling Pearlie the violin was a present to her from her papa, and that I had merely did the business part in procuring it for her – She was happiest of the happy, and we had lots of music, and she sang and danced & did the cake walk, and I played some, and never enjoyed a pleasanter little evening episode . . .

Jan 24 . . . PM wrote & sent letter to Van Duzer . . . with list of 16 new subscribers – Have not heard from him lately, and newspapers say he has been getting married . . . Hear unfavorable rumors as to failure of the Nevada Magazine – May not come out again – "Mebbyso" – Bed 1 –

Jan 25 . . . Received bundle of papers from Phila Inquirer including the last end of that story, "The Clown's Protege" that I have been after so long . . . I read last of it and bundled the whole to Bessie at Reno – with a nice letter to her . . .

Jan 26 . . . Evening wrote page letter to Sears Roebuck & Co, inclosing $1 worth of stamps, ordering a good violin case for Pearl Dempsey's fiddle, some sheet & other music, catalogues, etc – Bed 12 –

Sunday, Jan 28 . . . I wrote out a petition heading to be signed by best people, requesting re-appointment of Harry Day as Postmaster . . . First number of *"The Weekly,"* a new Carson weekly was published this morning . . . Pretty good for first attempt. Medes & Smith, two 14 yrs boys proprietors etc – $1.50 per year – The South African war seems approaching a culmination in the defeat of Buller's English army & surrender of Ladysmith –

Jan 29 . . . Letter from wife, with the regular $15 . . . Evening I sent wife a good responsive letter – Squared up my hotel bill for 5 weeks to date . . . $13.75 . . .

Jan 31 . . . Accomplished about nothing today, excepting receiving $15.50 through Nick Wylie as my half of a mutual winning in the Little Benificia Publica lottery . . .

Feb 1 . . . About town, canvassing, etc – rec'd 2 copies of January number of Magazine – Fallen off a little, & not up to the standard – Evening mail I sent a 2 page letter to Wm Nelson . . . remonstrating about the small sum of $10 allowed for my New Years Nevada write up – Was at Arlington late – Bed 1 –

Feb 5 . . . The pine trees on the tops of the Sierra, west of Carson were heavily coated with frozen snow this morning . . . looked like solid silver . . . Sent 3 page letter to J P Jones by evening mail, with January Magazine – Strong letter – he must stand in . . .

Feb 7 . . . The fiddle box for Pearl Dempsey's fiddle arrived . . . and I took it to the Dempsey residence – the music, box of resin etc inside – whole cost, expressage et al, $2.42 . . .

Feb 9 . . . Evening attended lecture of Hon F X Schoonmaker on "China, the Shadow on the World" – One of the best lectures and orators I ever heard – at Methodist Church – plum fully crowded . . . Uncle Fred Dangberg, Carson Valley rancher was my lecture companion –

Feb 10 . . . PM wrote & sent letter to Sears, Roebuck & Co ordering pair of pants, $3.20, pocket knife, 47c and "Consumers Guide," the big catalogue of the house . . . The measurement of pants I stated "Short and stout" . . . waist 46 inches, seat 52; . . . inseam 29 – Also sent page letter to wife – Evening I visited Tim Dempsey's family – the girls played piano & new violin for me, and I played violin and sang . . .

Sunday, Feb 11 – Clear & cold but pleasant – Rec'd brief note from Van

Duzer with 6 copies Dec & 6 January Magazine – I sent 6 Jan to Col E D Boyle, Gold Hill, his wife having a fine piece of poetry in that number – At morning train . . . I was introduced to Joaquin Miller, just arrived from Reno & Cal – walked with him down to State Capitol, looking for Sam Davis – couldn't find him – Then Doc Benton took Miller in his buggy out to State Prison to show him the prehistoric tracks, etc – Lost him after that – long gray hair & whiskers – quiet, pleasant gentleman – Bed 1 – Letter from Nelson of Tribune, Salt Lake, with clipping from Tribune on the Century Conundrum – Nelson is on opposite view from me on it – Genl Robt M Clarke died at 2:15 PM in San Francisco – Evening session of the telegraph office only being from 5 to 6 PM Sundays the news did not arrive till too late for me to telegraph story to SL Tribune in accordance with instruction of last June 13, so I went to RR depot and did it from there – press telegram saying that [Clarke] was 64 yrs old – native of Lancaster, Ohio – came here in 1865 – engaged in practice of law – was connected with most important mining and land cases and prominent in politics – prostrated and nearly died last June from stomach and heart troubles. Immediate cause of death paralysis and apoplectic stroke – Leaves wife and 2 grown children, and a brother, Major W G Clarke here – This is about what I telegraphed to the Tribune – Doc Benton took Miller out to Sam Davis' ranch & back after got back from State Prison & he went up to Va on evening local – To speak there tomorrow evening –

Feb 13 . . . Remains of Genl Clarke arrived by the morning train & taken to his residence . . . Ex Gov Blasdel came from San F with Clarke's remains – Had quite a talk with him, and saw him off on the evening train, returning to SF . . . Evening I attended lecture of Joaquin Miller, at Methodist Church – densely crowded – Little faulty in some respects but generally very poetically pleasing and good . . . Just a year today since Grandma's funeral and I last parted from wife & family in enforced exile –

[Two clips on Miller – The *Appeal* reports the lecture was entitled "Lessons not Learned in Books" – The poet looked just like his pictures, dwelt upon beauty and how many were blind to it, recited some of the wisdom of Buddha, some of his own poems, "enthusiastically received," then changed into his Klondike clothes, which "did not look stylish but they did look warm," and gave a description of that region and its people, while the audience "listened with wrapped attention" – The Virginia *Report* found that "a careful census of the tonsorial artists of Virginia taken yesterday brought forth a unanimous expression of opinion that the unbarbered poet was 'no good.'" – Also recounts how Miller, "something of a jester," went into the *Enterprise* office and asked for Mark Twain or Dan De Quille, and, when informed they weren't in, "departed with a sigh of regret."]

Feb 14 . . . Funeral of Genl Clarke this PM, from residence . . .

Feb 15 . . . Evening at the Opera House – Play of the "Sea Queen" by local talent – Lary the printer did up the scenery in the best and most popular style – lots of good singing, fair acting . . . is the old operetta of "Lurline," used to be played by Pauline Markham, with Lydia Thompson's Blonde troupe –

Feb 16 . . . Evening at theater again – "Sea Queen" – $335 house last night, 220 this evening – Finest *spectacular* piece I ever saw – Bed 1 –

Feb 17 . . . Evening F X Schoonmaker gave another lecture at the Methodist Church, his masterpiece, entitled "The Morality, Arts and Literature of China" – by special request – Good house – I attended by request – He spoke very interestingly for about 2¾ hours – Had quite an interview with him afterward, with others at the Arlington – Bed 1:30 –

Sunday, Feb 18 . . . Letter from SL Tribune, with check for $10 additional pay for my Nevada write up . . .

Feb 20 . . . Wrote a short letter to Senator J P Jones . . . asking his influence to get Harry Day reappointed Carson Postmaster . . . Got me a 2 bit bottle of liquid Boston blacking and blacked my shoes for the first time tonight since I left Reno . . .

Feb 21 . . . Evening at Opera House – Jules Grau's Opera Co in comic two act opera of "Wang" – 28 people including 10 or 12 women – good orchestra – Very lively and amusing opera – lots of good singing, strong choruses, etc – burlesque elephant about 6 ft high – very good – Had a good house, & everybody well pleased . . .

Feb 22 . . . Washington's birthday – Flags displayed – newspapers suspended, and business ditto to certain extent – I attended matinee in PM – The good old opera of "The Bohemian Girl" – rendered in first class legitimate style – Best I ever heard it – good house, and splendid satisfaction – Evening the comic opera of "Paul Jones" – I didn't attend – This closes the engagement & troupe goes to Reno tomorrow – And I most certainly did enjoy the opera this PM better than any before in my life – such glorious singing – "Then You'll Remember Me," etc. Bed 12 . . .

Feb 23 . . . PM wrote & sent letter with January Magazine to Jim

Townsend . . . and wrote & mailed letter with 12 copies December number to go to Sam Longabaugh . . . Dr Leslie E Keeley of Keeley cure for drunkenness fame died in Los Angeles Cal Wednesday, of heart failure – aged 68 . . .

Feb 24 . . . Letter from wife with $15 . . .

Feb 26 . . . My pants etc, arrived today . . . Plenty big enough – Found that I had made a mistake in ordering & so got side pockets instead of hip pockets as I wanted – Took them to Jacobs the tailor for him to make the desired alteration . . . Neither of the seven lottery tickets which I bought this month won a cent – drew blanks, all . . .

Feb 28 . . . Evening attended lecture at Methodist Church, by Mr Jay William Hudson – the last of the Star Course of 3 lectures at same place – Subject "Boer and Briton" – Young man about 27 or 8 yrs old – small and not very prepossessing, but a very able and finished speaker – causes of the South African war, the Boer country and the Boers – and the fighting English – Crowded house – very entertaining discourse – siding with the Boers, therefore well received & applauded – Bed 1 –

March 1 . . . PM I wrote 2 page letter to Geo E Roberts, Director of the Mint, Washington D.C. desiring a chance to bring my old report of the Comstock production . . . up to date . . .

March 3 – Stormy – Commenced snowing in the Sierra by 7 AM & kept at it all day . . . Sent letter to Jos R Ryan, Supt Con Va for a little piece of compressed wood –

Sunday, March 4 . . . Snowing steadily in the mountains all day . . . The California papers say grand rain storm throughout the State . . . Very much needed, owing to long continued drought –

March 6 . . . Evening train from Va brought me letter from Jos R Ryan . . . accompanied by piece of condensed or compressed wood, from the 1650 level of the Con Va mine – Been there 20 years or more . . . close grained & good for the purpose – composite gavel, for use at the National Republican Convention at Philadelphia in June – Joe Ryan is Chairman of the Democratic State Central Committee in this State . . .

March 7 . . . Got letter from Jim Townsend, Oakland, today, also brief note from Van Duzer – [The trial of] Indian Pete the murderer of Dangberg, at Gardnerville, took place last week at Genoa, and he was found guilty of murder in the first degree – Evening train sent letter to Jos R Ryan acknowledging receipt of compressed wood, & a letter to B F Smith, Stewart, Canton Co Ohio who wants the wood to make a gavel, telling him I will send it in 3 or 4 days – Evening wind blew furiously from Southward . . . Blew in a window of south side of US Dist court rooms . . . Snowed in the Sierra all day –

March 8 . . . The big wind of last night blew down chimneys on county building, Arlington House & elsewhere and did considerable damage . . . blew at rate of 65 and 70 miles per hour . . . Snowed in the mountains all day . . . Procured compressed wood from Ex Gov Colcord of the Mint, and Mountain Mahogany from George A Wilcox, Co E, 31st Mass regiment, civil war . . .

March 10 . . . Sent long 5 page letter to Cornelia . . . also a page letter to wife . . . Got letter from Van Duzer relative to how to get out the next Magazine –

Sunday, March 11 . . . Letter to B F Smith, Stewart, Athens Co Ohio, inclosing piece of compressed wood from 1650 level of Con Va mine, and a piece of mountain mahogany, to represent Nevada in the composition of a gavel made of wood of all the States & Territories, for use by the presiding officer at the Republican National Convention . . .

March 12 . . . Quite a hot summery day – 73° in the shade . . . I interviewed Dunn of the Carson News . . . relative to getting the Magazine printed here this time – 800 copies, 60 pages reading and ad & no half tones – gave me his figures $1.90 per page – Wrote it to Van Duzer . . .

March 14 . . . Sent letter to B F Smith, Athens County, Ohio, inclosing the 2 pieces of manzanita and sagebrush wood from Doctor S L Lee, given day before yesterday for the gavel – each piece I sent was about ½ by ⅜ inch thick, by 3 inches long . . .

March 15 . . . Finished, copied & sent my 3 page letter to Eunice . . . R K Colcord . . . sent for me about 2 PM – visited him at his office in the Mint – had received letter from Roberts, Director of the Mint . . . desiring to negociate with me on report of Comstock . . .

March 16 . . . Was at Controllers office, studying up the resources for my Govt mint job . . . Met Ed Harris today from his mine at Washoe, & took notes on 2 stories of his: *the log in Washoe Lake from Mars* and V&T RR toad story –

March 17 . . . St Patrick's Day . . . Big ball at the Armory Hall, by the Band – Charley Bray pinned a sprig of imitation shamrock on the lapel of my coat this morning, the Queen having proclaimed that the Irish may wear it hereafter – Didn't wear it long – "Nothing too good for the Irish" now, since the good fighting they have done in the British army in South Africa . . .

Sunday, March 18 . . . Evening train 2 page letter to wife – also a 1 page letter to Director Roberts . . .

March 19 . . . Was about town, & at State Capitol on information for Comstock report . . . Also commenced writing a story, "The Frog That was Run Over" for Black Cat competition . . .

March 21 . . . John Hill took charge of the Arlington House this morning, having bought out the lease of Bob Grimmon – Hill has been until recently commissary and clerk at the State Prison – First rate man – L C Hobart graduated from a 30 days term of the Keeley Institute last evening . . . says he feels as well as he ever did in his life – Joe Long, employed in the freight dept of the SP, at Reno drew the $7,500 prize in the Little Honduras lottery last week – I completed my Toad story this evening – 9 pages – about 2300 words . . .

[The manuscript is a mixture of the usual brief tall tales with an effort at connection and a surprise ending – After a totally irrelevant sojourn at Steamboat Springs, a Professor from Pennsylvania, socializing in Washoe City, uses his special X-ray machine to read on the mind of an old newspaper reporter, *"Look out for the Engine, When the Bell Rings!—Lyon"* – To excited demand, he explains it must have been imprinted there from the horrifying experience, back in the winter of '72, of being nearly decapitated by a train when he fell from his horse one icy night on the way to Carson to report a bulldog-wildcat fight – He noticed a sign nearby that said "Look out . . ." and a last-minute glance upward showed him the name of the locomotive, "Lyon" – His head held in place by a handkerchief from his best girl, he covered the fight anyway, which ended when the one-eyed cat got away, and made a "scoop on all the other Comstock reporters and didn't lose my head over it either." – Another man arrives, hears of the X-ray experiment and story, and is reminded of a time when he was engineer on the V&T Railroad and, one freezing night, ran over one of the big, warm-blooded toads peculiar to Nevada sagebrush country – While the former engineer digresses on cold and warm blood, his journal is brought to him which he uses to verify the incident and, seeing the date of the entry, the old newspaperman suddenly tears open his collar, showing his scars, and cries, *"I was the toad you ran over that night."*]

March 22 . . . I revised & polished up my new Toad story . . . Last Saturday night I dreamed that my boy Sam appeared from somewhere, saying that he had concluded to give me a thrashing – I tried to persuade him that I had done nothing to merit it, but he came at me rough – I did my best to stand him off, and last of all I was trying a right swing and upper cut and hit the head board of the bed so hard that it hurt my fist and woke me up –

March 24 . . . I finished my new story "The Warm Blooded Toad of Nevada," and sent it by evening mail . . . Dr Guinan, old resident and very prominent physician and surgeon died in Chicago this morning . . . from a surgical operation . . . It was his younger son, Julian, who shot and killed Chas A Jones, US Attorney Genl of Nevada couple of years ago on acct of his sister Jessie . . .

Sunday, March 25 – Variable, with fierce gales from the SW in the PM & evening – got letter from wife with $15 – also letter from Van Duzer – making up a joint stock Company & going to put in a $1,500 plant at Lovelock, to run a weekly newspaper and the Nevada Magazine – Replied to both . . . Jimmy Cummings, for several years mail clerk on the V&T passenger train, express – was arrested last evening at Va by the US Marshal for robbing the mail during last few months – registered letters – US Inspector and secret service detective got onto him – traced registered letters to him, etc, fixing guilt fully and indisputably upon him – placed under $2,000 bonds – Been leading rather a lewd, fast life in Reno, nights, opium, drink and gambling – spending double his salary – a man was put on in his place 2 wks ago, he being laid off temporarily, they said – but they were weaving the web around him – got a sure dead sinch on his guilt, and he saw that they had, and knew could only lead him to State Prison – About 8 oclock this evening he committed suicide in the International Hotel – Comstock raised boy – about 34 years old – Bed 11:30 – Clear but blowing like the devil –

March 26 . . . Jimmy Cummings committed suicide with a big dose of morphine instead of a pistol . . . Saves the costs of prosecution and imprisonment, and gives somebody else a chance to take his place . . .

March 27 . . . The two registered letters, causing the arrest of Cummings were from Dayton and Sutro . . . One contained $80, and the other $62 . . . Parties were taking inventory of furniture, etc in my lodgings house this PM, preparatory to my landlord, Savage, closing out –

March 29 . . . Otto Schultz the butcher having put an attachment on my landlord of $190 meat bill, he had a man busy getting ready to move all the bedding, furniture etc out, and I have to move on also tomorrow . . . Colcord of the Mint received telegram from Roberts . . . accepting my terms for Comstock report . . .

March 30 . . . Furniture all moved out of my lodging house today, so I got out myself, bag and baggage by noon, getting into room 7 in the Alta, or "Stone" lodging house. Mrs Kelly, a nice looking landlady . . .

Sunday, April 1 . . . Indian Pete, the condemned to be hung Indian murderer, escaped from the jail at Genoa last night, & not recaptured . . .

April 2 . . . About 4 PM a heavy snowstorm set in . . .

April 3 . . . Full ten inches of snow fell . . . Before night, with sunny PM, none remained . . . Glorious good storm for Carson & vicinity – At noon a couple of bicyclists gave open air exhibition of best trick riding anybody ever saw, on the broad concrete pavement in front of Postoffice . . .

April 4 . . . Met my old Comstock Va friend Tom McDonald in town this AM . . . to stop a few days at Shaw's hot springs . . . He made a winning of $500 in lottery, couple of weeks ago – and is enjoying it – Evening attended Republican meeting at Court House – first of the campaign – selected delegates to be voted for at the primaries next Saturday to the State Convention Apr 19th – Also started a Republican Club, with 55 signing the roll, Alf Doten included . . .

April 6 . . . Finished & sent my 5 page letter to Hon J P Jones . . . The general discussion of the day is now Dewey's big Presidential blunder –

[A clip from the *San Francisco Chronicle* of April 5 expresses outrage at Dewey's decision to run for president, partly because he had absolutely refused before, saying he was a professional sailor, but principally for his remark that he had changed his mind when he discovered that the job wouldn't be very difficult because all the president had to do was obey Congress – The article accuses Dewey, though reluctantly, of wanting the office merely to increase his social standing in Washington.]

April 7 . . . PM, Republican primaries at Curry engine house for 7 delegates to State Convention . . . Chas E Bray, Robt Grimmon, T R Hofer, Arthur G Meyers, George T Mills, Saml Platt, George A Tyrrell were elected – no opposition – 81 votes cast – Indian Joe Pete . . . still at large – Sheriff Brockliss offers $500 for him dead or alive –

Sunday, April 8 . . . Snowing in the Sierra most of the day . . . Harry Day got off his application to President for renewed Postmastership this evening mail, with all indorsements, etc –

April 10 . . . Studying up my Comstock report . . . Met C W Patterson, ed & prop of Yerington Rustler at the train & had quite a chat – just in from Lovelock – going to start a new weekly paper there called "The *Argus"* – Independent paper – Lovelock *Tribune* is already located & running there, and next is the *Standard* – all *weeklies* – small room for 3 in a bed –

April 13 . . . Lots of political buzzing from the Silver State Central Committee meeting of yesterday at Reno, and the proposed fusion, etc with the Democratic party, Populists or anything to beat McKinley – PM at Assessor's office . . . Joe Josephs received a letter today from Senator Jones on the Postmastership proposition for Harry Day – adverse . . .

April 14 . . . PM I finished getting statistics of tailings working and bullion production from quarterly statements of Supts . . . for 7 years past . . .

April 17 . . . All day on Comstock report . . . Evening at Opera House – Ward and Vokes' queer company in the "Floor Walkers" for only tonight – good house – and well amused audience – Mixed up lot of queer comicalities, dancing and singing specialties, etc, including a phenomenal female basso contralto voice in women quartette – sounded to me like a euphonium – 30 or 40 in the Co, about half women – beautiful dresses and undresses, high kicking etc . . .

April 18 . . . Was shown by Harry Day letter from Stewart and letter from Jones, both to Gov Sadler, et al in response to his application for Postmaster – Stewart says T R Hofer is agreed upon by he & Jones . . . That settles it . . .

April 19 – Clear, fine breezy day – Recd letter from Van Duzer . . . saying that he is unable to continue the Nevada Magazine, therefore must let it go dead and give up – Will return subscriptions to subscribers if they ask it – Also received letter from wife inclosing $1.50 for some unexplained reason, and stating that her pay-day will not be until the 27th – Republican State Convention here today brought delegates from all parts of the State – Held at Opera House, Wm McMillan chairman – after usual style – elected 6 delegates and 6 alternates to National Rep Convention at Philadelphia June 19 – Well attended – few proxies – adjourned 4 PM – Met lots of old acquaintances, from Austin, Va, Reno & elsewhere . . .

April 20 through 26 [Rain and snow – AD works on his Comstock report, writes his wife, attends Norris & Rowe's small animal circus, notes another suicide, also the death of his old Como friend Captain Charles Witherell, and the fact that Hofer's appointment as postmaster has been sent to the Senate by the president.]

April 27 – Variable – hard black frost this morning – much ice – good bye fruit – Busy on job – 1 PM grand street parade of the Carson Band – "paper" parade with "paper masquerade" in evening – Band all dressed in various costumes with bright colors, all paper – very fancy – & amusing – also had big white elephant on street, with two men inside to navigate him – big cloth and paper & frame affair – Had him at ball in evening – led the grand march – Event of the day . . .

April 28 . . . A week or two ago a couple of San Francisco young men appeared in Carson as organizers etc of the Liquor Dealers Protective Association and collected $10 each from all the saloons in Reno and Virginia and also did very well here, collecting $10 from each man whom they could get to join – giving him a fine looking certificate in return, of membership in good standing, etc – They were frauds of the 1st water, and got every saloon and liquor dealer to join, all except Andy Robert and Livingston – They were too practical and shy – I worked hard all day on my three tabular statements in mint report . . .

Sunday, April 29 – Rainy – Rained all last night, and very heavily for an hour or two this morning, as well as more or less all day – Glorious rain for the country – Rec'd letter from wife with $15 – She also sent me a Memorial, from Plymouth – Apr 21 – with an item in it about Bro Sam at a public gathering – old veteran, etc . . .

[The item says Samuel H Doten, at 88, was the oldest member of the 39th reunion of the "Minute Men of '61" and "stood the fatigue apparently as well as any of the boys in the parade."]

May 3 . . . Miss Amy G Solomon, one of the young lady clerks in the Postoffice, who will be let out soon, when the new postmaster, Hofer comes in, handed me her album yesterday to write something in . . . Whenever I call for a letter at the delivery window she takes a look, and generally replies, with a sorrowful look: "Nothing for you Mr Doten," or oftener, *"not a thing,"* just as though calling me a "naughty thing," for asking a civil question – made it a standing joke, so I wring it into the last line of the pokery – The scrap pleases her very much:

> Amiable art thou, Amy,
> Amy able, kind and true,
> And I'm happily included
> Among thy friends, who are not few.
> And should any ask me wherefore
> All should not thy praises sing,
> Ah! cordially would be my answer:
> "Naught prevents us, 'not a thing.' " . . .

May 4 . . . Letter from J P Jones, explaining how it was that Harry Day could not have been reappointed Postmaster . . .

May 5 through 9 [AD works long hours on his Comstock report, and notes that a Woods' Diggings and Como acquaintance of his, William McGrew, has an illustrated article, "Captain Truckee, A Reminiscence of '49," in the Sunday (May 6) issue of the *San Francisco Bulletin,* and that "Old Bill Gibson" has left for Cape Nome & "Many others talk of going also."]

May 10 – Variable – cooler, with strong blustering SW wind – Took morning train at 10 AM for Virginia City, Joe Ryan, Supt, and Charley Fish, Prest, Con Cal & Va Co on board bound from San F to the Comstock – arrived at Va 11:30 – The steep old Union st up side Mt Davidson seemed steeper than ever to me – Met quite a number of old friends and acquaintances to shake hands with – Visited old Joe Douglass et al – Virginia looks poorer and more dilapidated than ever, and so do the old timers – Only about 250 or 300 miners working on the whole Comstock – No ore yield at all during 1899 – none reported – 2 PM went up to County Auditors office, and commenced taking from the Assessors record book the quarterly reports of Supts of the ore yield of the Comstock for past 7 years, from '92 to date – Deputy Sheriff Kennay and a young lady clerk assisted me – quit at 4 – office hours – Met Miss May Dunlop in the hallway as I came out, & had pleasant little talk – Father and mother dead – She is a teacher in the public schools here, and acts a mother to her two little sisters – youngest only 5 yrs old – Took dinner at old Otto Eckelman's – Evening about town observing and affiliating – Visited Billy Brady, colored janitor at his room in the Douglass building – engaged room on the 3d floor, near Billy's room – The Dailey Dramatic stock Co playing at Pipers Opera House – Commenced raining and snowing about dark and kept at it busily all night – Bed at 11 – tired – slept good –

May 11 – Cloudy – About 6 inches sloppy snow on ground – AM I completed my job at Court House – noon dinner at Otto's – Visited Charley Brown, undertaker, at his old home over his shop on B st – badly bunged up with rheumatism and general dilapitude – visited him because he sent a man to ask me to – Didn't meet Jose Salinas, nor Mike Conlan this time – Was at Con Va office, and got mining proceeds, etc from Johnny Mahoney, clerk – Met Jim Kinkaid, supt of Curry, etc, & got more mining items . . . Snow passed off very rapidly during AM and streets & sidewalks got pretty good shortly, although slippery and dangerous for me in morning – Met N B Parsons my old newspaper carrier and friend – selling lottery tickets – bought one for 2 bits, Little Honduras . . . At 5:10 left on train for Carson . . . Was at Postoffice an hour – taking notes, etc – then at Livingstons awhile, hearing telegraphic returns of Jeffries and Corbett fight – Then at Arlington – Bed at 2 – very tired – Big snow fell on all the mountain ranges last night – Rained here and in Reno heavily –

May 12 through 22 [AD collects statistics and photographs and writes on his report, watches two performances of the "Quaker Doctors," a street medicine show, and notes that the hoisting works of the old Baltimore Mine on American Flat have burned.]

May 23 . . . Have been working *very* hard on my Comstock job this week commencing at 7 AM and working till 10 PM – only taking an hour at noon for eating, etc – same today & fought to a finish at 4:30 PM . . . 14 pages, or 4,500 words, and three tables, A, being gold & silver yield of the Comstock Lode by calender since commencement in 1859 to 1900 . . . B, Mill tailings, and C assessments and dividends . . . Tedious, hard job, since April 10 – Bed 11:30 – Collis P Huntington the great CP RR magnate arrived this evening – didn't see him – but everybody else were at the depot . . .

May 24 . . . Morning I carefully revised my Comstock report all through, and at 10:30 AM placed it in the hands of R K Colcord at the US Mint building . . . Collis P & party went in one of his cars to Mound House this morning early & took Supt Yerington's private car over the narrow gauge, C&C RR – went on speedy arranged time – 30 or 40 miles an hour, clear through to end of road –

May 25 . . . Added 500 words more to my Comstock narrative, getting in about the big timber felling of the big bonanza – the fire that smoldered in it 17 years, compressed wood, etc . . . Collis P & party returned about 6 PM and went on through to Reno with their special . . .

Sunday, May 27 . . . Busy most of day at the Postoffice fixing up & adding to details of my Comstock report . . . letter from wife with $15 . . .

May 28 . . . Theodore R Hofer Jr and his sister, Miss Hazel Hofer were at Postoffice most of the day taking lessons in mail work & business of the office & will till they take charge officially –

May 30 . . . Memorial Day . . . At 11 AM the Carson Band . . . escorted 20 GAR veterans and five carriage loads of citizens, flowers etc to the Cemetery north of town, where usual services were held . . . I got my Comstock report figuring completed at 3 PM and took the whole racket up to the Mint, to be forwarded with Mint report . . . this evening – I enclosed my bill for $150 . . .

May 31 . . . AM I straightened up my odds and ends of writings & figurings in the Postoffice, & at noon took away books, papers & all belonging to me to my room in the Stone lodging house . . . feel like an orphan thrown out in the cold world – Evening at 8 I was present at the genuine turning over of the Postoffice . . . from Harry Day to young Hofer . . . Met Mangus, my old Comstock printer friend today . . . over from California . . . says old Jim Townsend is nearly dead with rheumatism, general breaking down – old age, etc –

June 1 . . . Saw copy of *Black Cat* for June at Mrs Fox's store – gave list of prize story competition winners – I not in it . . .

June 2 through 7 [AD corresponds with wife, writes *Black Cat* to return his "Toad" story, turns down an invitation to run the *Gardnerville Record* while Lamy takes a vacation, and "skirmishes" for loans.]

June 8 – AM hot, sultry – About noon clouded up with heavy thunder clouds . . . some rattling good thunder all the PM . . . good, square rain all around, but not here . . . Bed at 12 – cool & very pleasant – The Yerington Rustler . . . has gone out of existence, and in its place appears the Lyon County Monitor, a similar weekly, published by the Monitor Publishing Co – C W Patterson formerly ed & prop of the *Rustler* has rustled out and now runs the *Argus*, a weekly at Lovelock . . . The

Crown Point mine, has changed out of the Jones-Hayward control to the
Sharon-Morrow, etc, control, with Billy Sharon Supt, who is also now
Supt of about all the Gold Hill mines – Met old Joe Douglass this AM at
the Arlington, down from Va en route for Walley's Springs, Genoa for a
week or so for his rheumatism – The Reno Ledger commenced Wednesday as a semi weekly, with R R Crawford editor and W L Brandon business manager – Independent Democratic – W J Bryan, for President and
Hon Frank G Newlands for reelection to Congress . . . Walter Crowninshield, better known as "Pony" when I lived and moved in Como, away
back in 1863–4, was found last Tuesday dead on the ground about 50
feet from his cabin, two or three miles below or east of Como – where it
had evidently been lying over a week, head badly mutilated and not known
how, as much decomposed from lying there in the hot sun. Coroners
inquest was held, and considering condition, etc, wood was procured and
remains were effectually cremated. I remember well that old "Pony," like
myself always kept a diary, writing up the days doings regularly every
night when he went to bed, as I am doing now – The last entry of his
diary was just two weeks ago, May 26 – It is therefore inferred that he
died next day, Sunday. Careful study of the situation shows that he had
gathered a sack full of pie plant from his garden, to take to Como or send
to Dayton – that he got his old saddle horse to ride, as usual – Whether
the saddle turned in mounting, or in his reaching for the sack, his foot
caught in the stirrup and he was fatally dragged on his head, similarly
inferred, is unknown – but his shoe being found – also the saddle – indicated his dragging till it got loose – But he was not found till seven days
later . . . He may have laid helpless a day or two in the hot sun before
death came to his relief – Owing to stage of decomposition, however, he
probably was summarily killed outright – hope so – Was the last of the
old Comoites staying in the district after I left – living always alone like
a hermit, yet always the same genial good old "Pony" of old Como days.
I used to print letters from him occasionally when I was running the *Gold
Hill News*. About 20 years ago . . . I recorded the death by cremation
in his cabin of George W Walton, speaking of him as the "last of the
Comoites," and now "Pony" goes out on the same cremating proposition.
The Virginia *Enterprise* of the 6th says:

[The clip says that Crowninshield was a native of Massachusetts, and
 reports the surmises on his death – Another, from the *Virginia Chronicle,*
 repeats the same information – A longer one from the *Lyon County
 Times* says that Crowninshield, who left a son in Mason Valley, was born
 in Rhode Island 76 years before, had come to Nevada in 1860 and had

been a pony express rider on the eighty-mile stretch from Van Sickle's ranch to Placerville – He went in with the first rush to Como, had great faith in the camp, and became "despondent" when it collapsed – Except for the legislative session of 1893, when he was elected assemblyman and lived in a cabin at Treadway's Park in Carson City, he had lived alone, with horse, dog, cat and chickens, in a cabin under some pines about a mile from Como, going down to Dayton once or twice a year.]

June 9 . . . Trenmor Coffin's little boy had about 70 Belgian hares on exhibition today in a place opposite the Postoffice, which he has cultivated & raised during last 6 months – Fine little animals – most of them from one doe which cost $25 in Los Angeles, served by a $500 buck for $20 – Very interesting exhibit –

Sunday, June 10 . . . Received through the Carson mint a check for $150 from the US Treasury department . . . This very prompt payment was decidedly unexpected and seemingly complimentary . . . The Carson brass Band gave its first open air evening concert last evening from their stand in Capitol Park – Big audience, of course – Reed returned from a fishing trip to Marlette Lake this evening – met my boy Sam, and Geo James there enjoying themselves – Sam sent about a dozen nice trout by him to me – I took them at once to Andy Robert for his wife to take care of, & give some to Harry Day & I.

June 11 through 18 [AD deposits $80 of his check, repays $10 borrowed from Colcord and $2.50 from Judge Hall, sends Comstock photos to go with his report, receives an article from B F Smith describing the Republican gavel, which is made of historic pieces of wood from every state, goes to another Band concert, meets Lily Schneider, now Mrs Greaves, once his assistant engrossing clerk, and is shocked by her appearance, the result of having nursed her husband through typhoid and come down with it herself – "completely broken down – 20 yrs older – great brown circles around her eyes – reduced to a skeleton."]

June 19 . . . The Republican National Convention commenced at noon today . . . Telegrams speak of the . . . *gavel* as the "big" gavel, and the "ungainly" gavel that was "brought down with a tremendous whack" . . .

June 20 . . . The gavel is mentioned in press telegrams received today as *"a heavy square oak piece, fitted with a handle and looked more like a maul than a gavel for the presiding officer"* . . .

June 21 . . . Rep Nat Convention at Phila nominated McKinley for

President and Rooseveldt for Vice Prest, and adjourned sine die – Drew out $30 – Bed 11 – This was the longest day of the year.

June 23 . . . Telegraphic news in all the papers says that recently accumulating troubles with China result in their now trying to drive out all foreigners, especially missionaries – and declaring war against all other nations of the world – strong fighting already started in with Russia and other powers at *"Tien-tsin"* in which 800 Americans had to participate – US Consulate destroyed, etc – Looks like the biggest war of the world just now starting in.

June 26 . . . Woodford's station Hotel, above Genoa on Carson river and the old emigrant road . . . was destroyed by fire Sunday night . . .

June 28 . . . *Hawaii* was formally admitted as a Territory of the United States on the 14th of this month – Great celebration there . . .

July 2 . . . Our boss battleship Oregon which went ashore last Thursday on the Chinese coast, reported in status quo – probably lost . . .

July 3 . . . The Indian School Band, Carson Base Ball club, et al – 2 coaches full, went to Wadsworth by evening train, to assist in celebration tomorrow there, being no celebration here . . .

July 4 . . . At 10:45 telegrams on the Arlington bulletin board said: Reno wins (50 mile) relay race, Sacramento vs Reno, by one mile – Keddie of Reno breaks coast record – 5 miles . . . Carson wins base ball game at Wadsworth – score 7 to 6 . . .

July 5 . . . The Dem Nat Convention at Kansas City nominated Bryan this PM by acclamation –

July 6 . . . Kansas nominations completed and convention adjourned sine die – Bryan President and Adlai E Stevenson of Illinois for Vice President – S was Vice President under Cleveland's 2nd and last term – A very weak ticket, which will be beaten about 16 to 1 in November . . .

Sunday, July 8 . . . AM made best neck tie of all – PM met John J Hepworth from Como, was there when I was, and is still trying to develop a paying mine there . . .

July 9 – Clear, fine & warm – PM met my old friend Louis ("Joe") Guggenheim just pardoned out of State Prison – Happy to see him out – Judge Hebbard of San Francisco decides Reno marriages all right – Bed

12 – Guggenheim went to SF tonight – Got letter from wife – Says Alfred chosen Ass't Principal of Wadsworth public school –

July 10 . . . PM I wrote 2 page pen letter to Van Duzer, Winnemucca, inclosing a full page statement of my financial account with the *Nevada Magazine* . . . Balance due me $12.30 . . . In SF Examiner of yesterday found account of death of Dr Henry D Cogswell, San Francisco, who was at Curtis' Creek gold diggings and Woods' when I was, in winter of '49 – Big dentist in San Francisco and capitalist since then – died very wealthy – 80 yrs old – Had to draw out my deposit of $50 today –

[The *Examiner* clip says Cogswell, the "Pioneer Philanthropist," was famous for his gifts of fountains to several cities, "to provide pure drinking water for man and beast in crowded city streets" – A firm prohibitionist, he also endowed Cogswell Polytechnic College in the Mission district of San Francisco – A loose clipping, from the *San Francisco Chronicle* of June 12, 1901, reports that Cogswell believed his spirit would return and inhabit his statue, on one of his fountains – This notion, and his twenty-year interest in spiritualism, occultism and theosophy, was being used by the children of his sister to try to break his will on the grounds of insanity.]

July 13 . . . My good old Comstock, 6-mile Canyon friend for about 36 yrs, Tom Hulley died about noon today . . . Aged 60 yrs, native of Yorkshire, England – Thrifty mill and mining man and latterly for 5 or 6 yrs been with Bob Logan trying to develop a paying mine at Palmyra . . .

July 16 . . . Sent a 2 page letter to B F Smith, Stewart Ohio commentarily criticizing his or our Republican national gavel . . . The Crown Point mining works, Gold Hill are being dismantled – The machinery sold and removed and mine to be worked hereafter through the Yellow Jacket mine – electric power –

July 18 . . . Yesterday the telegrams indicated assuredly that the Chinese or "Boxers" insurrectionists had killed all the foreign legations or ministries in Peking . . .

July 20 – Same – Hottest – 95° . . . About 5 PM Frank G Newlands, candidate for re-election to Congress and Hon C A Towne of Minnesota, arrived in a buggy from Virginia where they spoke last evening on behalf of the Democratic party – First gun of the campaign – Anvil salute of a dozen bangs or more saluted them – Evening the band turned out & played front of Opera House, and at 8 meeting called to order by Alf Chartz – House full of men & some women – Va Glee Club, quartette, Ernest Hall, Fred Trewillian, Alfred Borlini, and [blank] Tobin present, sang several Newlands campaign songs in pretty good style – & band played couple of orchestral pieces – Governor Sadler presided & stage full of state officials, etc – Newlands spoke first, then Towne spoke an hour & 20 minutes – Very good speaker & orator – Better than Bryan – more lyrical and argumentative, doing better than anybody speaking or arguing in a bad cause – hence considerably inconsistent and demagogue – Classes himself as a Silver Republican . . . Aspired for nomination for Vice President at Kansas City but beaten by Stevenson – He & Newlands just from the East, he engaged to campaign for Newlands – After the show, a festive time at barroom of the Arlington, at Newlands' expense, he there setting 'em up, glee club singing, and all the old bums in town getting in on the drinks – Great time – Bed 12 – And so ends the 71st year of my life.

July 21 . . . Letter from wife with $15 – says Bessie in Reno for her vacation – My 71st birthday – quiet and reasonable – The "Independents" Base Ball Club from San Francisco arrived, & gave a good battle with the Virginia Reports at race track this PM – SF beat Reports, 25 to 5 . . .

Sunday, July 22 . . . "Independents" played the Carson nine a very lively base ball game . . . beating them 20 to 4 – so the Independents are very triumphant, getting away with the whole bakery, and a cake walk home tomorrow . . .

July 25 . . . Finished the pencilling of a 3 page letter to Dr J L Cogswell, dentist, of San Francisco, relative to writing the biography of his brother Dr H D Cogswell . . .

July 26 . . . Copied my 3 page letter to J L Cogswell, and mailed it with the September number of the Nevada Magazine, containing my write up of Carson and the "Early Journalism of Nevada" . . . Received 4 page letter from B F Smith, my gavel friend . . . Also book, birthday present from Cornelia, entitled *"To Have and to Hold,"* by Mary Johnston . . . must be very popular work – 200th thousand . . .

July 28 . . . Recd another short letter from B F Smith . . . inclosing . . . clippings of acknowledgments from President Wm McKinley and Hon M A Hanna, each acknowledging receipt of a gavel (He made 2 of them) speaking highly and thankfully, etc of the souvenirs – The Rep State Central Committee met here this PM at the Briggs House Parlor and arranged for the Fall campaign . . . Finished reading my new book *"To Have and to Hold"* – Of most absorbing interest – Strongest written, boldest in incidental conception and working up of historic material and force of character I ever read – Founded on the settlement of Jamestown, Virginia . . .

July 30 . . . Sent my new book . . . to wife . . .

July 31 . . . About 2 PM I had come from lunch and was picking my teeth in front of the Arlington when my son Alfred suddenly walked to me smiling, extending his hand, saying "How de do Mr Doten?" – And I said "Oh Alfred, Im so glad to see you," and a big lump got in my throat and tears in my eyes, so I couldn't talk for awhile – I asked about all at home, & we had a pleasant little talk together, so strangely in contrast with our last parting in Reno that it made me ever so happy and forgiving – He came up from Reno yesterday, and has been busy with Smith, the US weather service man, and Prof Ring – will be here 2 or 3 days yet – We talked together for 15 or 20 minutes, then he went back to Prof Ring's office – I wrote and sent a 2 page letter to wife, mostly on the subject . . .

Aug 3 . . . About noon, I sitting in chair, front of Arlington Alfred passed a time or two and finally spoke to me, and I told him of a grip that had come on train from Reno & was at Express office – must be for him, although agent wanted to deliver to me – same name, but care of Prof Ring – so he went & got it all right –

Aug 4 . . . Got nice 4 page letter from Bessie . . .

Sunday, Aug 5 . . . PM wrote & sent 2 page letter to Bessie – didn't see Alfred all day – guess he must [have] attended base ball game . . .

Aug 7 . . . Letter – 3 page – today from Wife – most cold-blooded of all I ever received from her – Only one inference or conclusion for me to make from it – The greatest war of the world is now on in definite shape – China against all other nations – The allied forces marching upon Pekin from Tien-tsin had big battle yesterday, in which the allies lost 1200 killed, and the Chinese 3 or 4 times as many –

Aug 8 . . . Was at morning train, 10 AM – looked in at Circe's Carson Exchange and saw Alfred, and had a few minutes general talk with him . . .

Aug 9 . . . Saw Alfred pass down street today – Worked at room all day, fixing shirts, etc – Bed 12 –

Aug 11 . . . PM I was at Prof Ring's office getting some items from the old Pioneer register about Dr Harris, Sam Baker, etc . . . Met Alfred on my way to Ring's & we had pleasant talk together for five minutes . . . China wants to make peace – US Government sent ultimatum last Thursday, demanding free communication with our legation at Peking, immediate cessation of hostilities against legations, full protection for them and all foreigners, restoration of order, etc, etc – Gov't anxiously awaiting reply, as war may not be averted . . .

[Clip, Virginia City *Report* – Dr Elias B Harris, who died August 9, "was one of the most noted practitioners in Nevada, and a pioneer of the Comstock, having come here in 1859 and constructed the first mill ever erected in the State in Gold canyon near Silver City. . . . He was prominently identified with Republican politics in this State, and was one of our foremost citizens."]

Sunday, Aug 12 – Same – warmer – Took morning local train at 10 AM for Reno – Excursion rates . . . Arrived at 11:40 – went up home – found Bessie, wife, and Sam at home – Brief chat with them, hunted up some of my writings, especially "Woods Creek in Forty-Nine" – and left on my return to Carson at 1:35 – arriving at 3:30 – About town, etc – Bed 11 – tired and unhappy – Bessie leaves for Cal tomorrow morning –

Aug 13 – Same – Received a letter from wife, dated Sunday PM, after I had left for Carson, in which she apologized for any apparent inhospitable treatment, regretted my short visit, and removed the bar to my coming home to live whenever I saw fit. Very different from her cold blooded letter of last Tuesday – PM I was down to Prof Ring's office for an hour – Went to see Alfred but only met him for a few minutes, as he was going out somewhere – Ring took him and Frank Peterson, his office boy, over to Lake Tahoe, with his own team yesterday – Alfred enjoyed the trip very much –

Aug 14 . . . Andy Robert and wife went this morning on a camping or outing expedition over to Marlette Lake for the week – Got me to keep an eye on his business while he is gone – Julian Boubisse also –

[Clip, *News:*] A telegram was received in Carson today announcing the death of Collis P. Huntington in New York this morning.

When Collis P Huntington was here . . . he had his wife along in his private car, and being 81 yrs of age & infirm accordingly, he was being very vigilantly & carefully cared for – Personal advertising letter from

Sears Roebuck & Co – Want to send me a new big catalogue book & give my old one away, telling to whom I gave it . . .

Aug 15 . . . My landlady, Mrs Kelly is sick, so I have to "make up" my own room – Dr Lee says she is afflicted with "cerebro spinal menginitis," which should knock out most anybody – She is a hard working little frail woman which with the hot weather has caused a sort of breakdown –

Aug 18 . . . Republican primaries for delegates to State Convention . . . I was at polls and voted – "Professor Montague's Great Australian Bird Hippodrome and Cockatoo Circus" at Opera House last evening, this PM matinee and evening performance – Good entertainment, well patronized . . .

Aug 20 . . . Completed, copied and sent 5 page letter to wife . . .

Aug 22 – Clear & pleasant – Recd a letter from Mrs Ella Beach . . . daughter, I think of old Jim Townsend, informing me of his death, on the 10th instant in Illinois – Wrote it up and took it to the evening *News* – staid and read proof, etc – The allied troops have entered and taken Pekin with little or no opposition and it looks like the Chinese will not make much of a fight against the world –

> [AD's item pasted in – Reports Townsend's trip to Oakland and death in Illinois at age 77 – No biographical sketch – ". . . died at peace . . . leaving no money behind . . . Good-bye liberal-hearted, genial old boy, far better than the general average of millions that have preceded you into the mythical beyond."]

> [A second clip, from the *Appeal,* reports Senator Stewart's public endorsement of McKinley and repudiation of Bryan – The *Appeal* recalls, sarcastically, Stewart's scathing denunciations of McKinley four years before, thinks this the first time in history that the troops stood firm but the general deserted, and feels that Nevada Silverites, who helped Stewart through a close election, have been sold out cheaply for imperialistic doctrine.]

Aug 23 . . . Sent a page & a half letter to Mrs Ella Beach . . . inclosing clip of my last evening item . . .

Aug 24 . . . This mornings *Appeal* says: [Clip – Official denial that J P Jones has turned Republican] . . . Evening the big fight between Fitzsimmons and Sharkey . . . Telegrams taken at the Criterion saloon – Livingston's – crowded audience – Sharkey knocked out in 2nd round – My landlady, Mrs Kelly, is convalescent and able to get up and around, the last day or so – very severe sick spell – had doctor and a woman nurse . . . Bob Logan felt pretty good tonight – won $100 on Fitz – set 'em up for the boys . . .

Aug 25 . . . PM I wrote & sent a good page letter to Hon J P Jones . . . asking him to define his present political status, tell us if that Chicago telegram is true or not . . .

Aug 27 . . . PM wrote & sent a second letter . . . to Dr J L Cogswell, asking reply to my proposition . . . My landlady now all right and on deck as before . . .

Aug 28 . . . Letter from wife with $5 – Met old Dick Sides this PM at the Arlington – In from Winters' ranch, Washoe Valley, which is his home for several years past – One of the first Comstock locators – The Dick Sides mine was his location – next north of Gould & Curry – Hasn't been in Carson for nearly 20 years till now – 75 years old – Theodore Winters 77 yrs now . . . My son Alfred came up from Reno yesterday to consult with Smith, chief of the US Weather Bureau, relative to new instruments for the Weather Service at Reno. Wife says in her letter that in the destruction of the U.S. Agricultural Experiment Station at the State University Sunday PM: "All Sam's work, botanical and entomological, of the past seven years went up in smoke, at which he naturally feels very badly. When he will go to Washington, if at all, remains to be seen." . . .

Aug 29 . . . Alfred still in town, & I not seen him – He called on the Robert girls at their home this AM – I went down to Prof Ring's office at 4 PM, found it all locked up . . . & concluded that the Prof took Alfred home to Reno with his own team – Sent a page letter to wife, embodying the above . . .

Aug 30 – Cloudy, but pleasant – Republican State Convention at Virginia City today – Well attended by delegates from all parts of the State – Nominated E S Farrington of Elko for Congress, Trenmor Coffin of Ormsby for Justice of the Supreme Court, for Presidential Electors, Enoch Strother of Virginia, D B Lyman, Reno, Simon Bray, Austin. For Regents, State University, long term G W Turrittin, Reno, short term Mark Averill, Virginia – Selected new State Central Committee and at 9:30 PM adjourned sine die. Big prize fight this evening at Madison Square Gardens, New York, between Corbett and McCoy, under auspices of the 20th Century Club. Audience about 10,000 – McCoy got knocked out in the 6th round – Dispatches taken at Livingston's Criterion saloon – with big crowd to hear them read as fast as brought in – Bed 12 – Milo C

McMillan was Chairman of the Republican State Convention at Virginia today, and M R Averill, Secretary.

Sept 1 . . . Got 2 page letter from Dr J L Cogswell, San Fran – today – Didn't think I had any show for writing up his brothers biographical obituary – said no money provision for it in his *last* will –

Sunday, Sept 2 . . . Commenced a letter to Dr Cogswell's widow on same subject as to his brother . . .

Sept 4 . . . Commenced taking a 2 grain capsule morning and night, of quinine this morning, and will follow it up throughout my hay fever season . . . Letter to Hall Chemical Co for sample of advertised anti-fat treatment, inclosing 4 cts postage for return – and letter to . . . Maine for advertised lightning calculating pencil, & year subscription to *Sunshine* – monthly paper . . .

Sept 6 . . . Silver Party and Democratic State Convention at Va today did not get beyond temporary organization, selection of some Committees etc . . .

Sept 7 – Cloudy & cooler – breezy – The two conventions at Va yesterday closed today sine die – They *fused,* the Silver party being gobbled in & swallowed out of all further right or record by the good old Democratic party – Only nominations allowed the Silver Party were Richard Kirman for Presidential Elector, and J N Evans of Washoe County for long term Regent State University – The full ticket nominated stands as follows: Presidential Electors: John H Dennis of Washoe; John Weber, White Pine; Richard Kirman, Ormsby; & Congressman, Francis G Newlands, Washoe; Justice of Supreme Court, A L Fitzgerald, Eureka; University Regents, long term, J N Evans, Washoe; short term, W W Booker, of Elko – A Democratic State Central Committee was selected, with C H Stoddard of Reno as Chairman, and John H Dennis of Reno, Secretary. Judge Fitzgerald and Congressman Newlands addressed the convention, and there was other speechifying. No more Silver Party – all fused into Democratic bullion and cooled down to regular party shape and work. Delegates, et al left for home by evening train, many stopping off here – Met many of them at the Arlington this evening – The *Wells Herald* office was destroyed by fire night before last – loss $2,000 – no insurance – Some of the material was saved.

Sunday, Sept 9 . . . I wrote and sent 3 page communication to SF Chronicle on the political situation in Nevada . . .

Sept 10 . . . 3½ page letter to Salt Lake *Tribune* . . .

Sept 11 . . . Got transcript from my old Pacific Coast Pioneers register of Sam Baker's record as Pioneer 49'er, etc, for a certificate I am making for him . . . The San Francisco journals are filled with elaborate pro-fusely illustrated accounts and glowing descriptions of the semi-centennial Jubilee Celebration of Admission Day – when California was admitted into the great American Union, Sept 9, 1850 . . . 100,000 visitors to San Francisco from all sections – Native Sons of the Golden West, with the few old Pioneers, take the leading part of course, and run things for all they are worth and in up to date style . . . Quite a num-ber of people have gone from here, the Comstock, Reno and other parts of Nevada . . . Fearful hurricane blowing 100 to 120 miles an hour with cloudbursts of rain devastated Texas Saturday, destroying Galveston and other towns . . .

Sept 13 . . . Relief in food, clothing, money etc pouring promptly into Galveston from all parts of the US . . . The wife of Walter Scott *Cone* ("Scotty") died at Reno yesterday morning . . . immediate cause of her death was dropsy – She was about 65 years old and a former resident of Virginia City, known as "Dutch Kate," keeping a house in the "tender-loin" quarter – "Scotty" was a well known gambler and sport. He married her and they went to Reno, where they built a fine house on the Powning Addition which they afterward sold –

Sunday, Sept 16 . . . PM wrote and sent a full page letter to Hon George R Vardy . . . sympathizing in his loss by fire of his "good little journalistic establishment" . . . I donated to him the full amount of my bill against him . . . Also brief letter to Van Duzer . . . drumming him up on returning my *Pioneer* article . . .

Sept 20 – Clear & pleasant – as usual – PM I copied and sent 4 page carefully written letter to my dear sister Cornelia, Plymouth . . . Eve-ning down town – attended meeting of my Republican Club . . . at Dist Court room – elected 25 delegates to County convention . . . Met Johnny Kent at evening train, from Virginia on his way to State Fair, Reno, for a day or so – Has got the miners consumption – used to be stout and portly, but now wasted away – lost 40 pounds in last year or so – About 50 years old – Cornish miner – and good friend of mine for very many years on the Comstock . . . Newlands with his Comstock Glee Club also passed down to Reno, where he addresses the Bryan Club this evening – They were at Dayton Tuesday, and at Yerington . . .

last evening . . . At the Club meeting this evening, during a brief recess, E E Roberts, a young lawyer now teaching school at Empire and candidate for District Attorney, and Ed Dupuis, a young Carson lawyer and also candidate for the same office, had a bit of a scrap, but were separated after a few blows and a mix up – No harm done, but the meeting was rather inharmonious anyhow – Dupuis had called Roberts a "carpet bagger," etc, which made R angry and strike D. Bad for a *Republican* meeting –

Sept 22 . . . Republican primaries . . . for delegates to County Convention – No opposition . . . Polled 84 votes . . . beating the Democrats or Silver party, held Thursday, by 31 votes . . .

Sept 24 . . . The Elleford Dramatic Co and Jessie Norton came from Reno on morning train for the week – Fair started at 1 PM with Carson Band playing at Depot and along down street to the race track – Good attendance there for opening day – No agricultural or cattle exhibits – only racing for this Fair . . . Evening attended theater – Fully crowded house – Play, "The American Girl" – Excellent . . .

Sept 25 . . . AM I finished & copied a 3 page letter to sister Eunice, & mailed it – PM I reported the Silver Party County Convention . . . for the News for $1 – also Democratic fusion with them on one Assemblyman, and the constable – only . . .

Sept 26 . . . Reported the Republican County Convention . . . for the News, and got $3 for it – good to get . . .

Sept 27 . . . Best day of the Fair thus far . . . Plenty of gambling games in the various saloons with plenty of cappers, suckers etc . . .

Sept 28 – Fine clear day – PM I visited the Fair . . . No agricultural or cattle show, just simply horse racing, only this and nothing more – Met lots of Comstock and Reno friends . . . Best day of the Fair – Prof A H Hoff, aeronautist, made a very fine balloon ascension about 5 PM, after the breeze went down – parachute jump of 100 ft or more – Passed over south end of town, landing safely – I was lucky to see it from the Arlington sidewalk – with others who were notified – Ed Bettencourt living down near the race track shot Jack O'Brien this morning about 4 o'clock – O'B was a horse "rubber," at race track – was drunk and got into Ed's yard prowling about – Ed fired 3 pistol shots – only one hit, passing through right thigh – Bed 12 –

Sunday, Sept 30 . . . Cool frosty nights . . . have nipped the tomato and squash vines considerably – The tree leaves are also yellowing and falling fast – Letter from wife with $15 and promise of more . . .

Oct 1 . . . Squared up room rent . . . Got letter from Geo R Vardy, Wells *Herald* in humbly appreciative response to mine . . . donating him my bill of $25 against him – quite refreshingly amusing –

Oct 2 . . . My '49 arrival in California anniversary – 51 years – *Poorer* than when I arrived, but richer in *humanity* and appreciativeness between man and man than ever – Expended about a dollar celebrating the event with other old '49ers . . .

Oct 3 . . . Lily Leale Schneider . . . returns to her husband in New York – name *Greaves*, a newspaper man – I think she is in the last stages of Consumption and will hear of her death shortly – hope not, but —— . . .

Oct 4 . . . The whole Sierra range abreast of Carson white with snow, down into the foothills . . . letter to Mint Director Geo E Roberts . . . about starting up of the new electric power of the Comstock on the 15th instant . . .

Oct 6 – Variable & very pleasant – very heavy white frost this morning – Wrote and sent over a page, carefully pen written, copied letter to wife, inclosing a page from the SF Bulletin on styles of penmanship – Bed 12 – Had a delightful dream, toward morning – was in Gold Hill – met "Abby," brother Sam's first wife, young and sweet as when I first knew her – she kissed me lovingly and we wandered about town together, coming to a boarding house at lower end of town, kept by sisters Cornelia and Eunice, both looking young and fresh as when I left them at home in old Plymouth – We all went happily cruising about together, incidentally finding, at my nice Gold Hill home, our new sister, my wife, Mary, who with me showed and introduced them around, visiting the various mining works and points of interest, up and down the steep lines of steps and stairs of the hillside streets and habitations – and all so cheerful, prosperous and happy – But 'twas a dream too sweet to last, yet making me feel happy all day afterward –

Oct 9 . . . A new daily evening paper started at Virginia yesterday by Wm Sutherland, publisher, called *Campaign Notes* . . . Politix, straight Republican. Van Duzer is around organizing Bryan Clubs & making speeches, etc . . .

Oct 10 . . . Senator Stewart arrived . . . Met him on sidewalk opposite Postoffice at noon & had brief talk, together with Harry Day – He will be here till after election he said . . .

Oct 12 . . . Evening attended first meeting of the Ormsby County Bryan Club at their room little south of the Postoffice – Well filled – Van Duzer spoke an hour & said little – The Comstock Quartette, present, & sang half dozen pieces . . .

Oct 13 . . . Rec'd letter . . . from Committee on Comstock Electric Power celebration inviting me to participate next Saturday, the 20th . . .

Oct 16 – Clear and divine – "Indian Summer" – golden foliage & falling leaves – Hon James W Haines died at his home in Genoa at 5 PM on Friday last. "Old Jim Haines" was one of Nevada's most active and enterprising citizens, holding important positions in public and private life and highly respected by all. He was an able representative of Douglas County in the State Senate and always vigorously prominent in politics and a straight old black Republican – He leaves a wife and daughter, well provided for with valuable property. His funeral took place at Genoa this afternoon & was well attended by friends from here, including Hon W M Stewart, also Steve Gage who came up from Sacramento for the purpose.

Oct 17 . . . PM commenced writing up the Comstock . . . relative to the Electric future . . .

Oct 19 . . . Sent off 5 page letter to SF Chronicle about the Comstock – Writing another for SL *Tribune* . . . Bed 12 – with clothes on . . .

Oct 20 . . . I rose at 3 AM . . . and went to work on my SL Tribune letter . . . Big celebration at Virginia today, of advent of the electric cheap power in mining and milling, superseding steam altogether – quite a number of stock and mining men from San Francisco went up on morning train, also some few from Reno and here – Brass band met them on arriving at depot & escorted them up town – Va gay with flags, dynamite, etc – After lunch they visited the new Gould & Curry mill, and saw it start crushing ore when the electric power was turned on – old G & C tunnel near by lighted with electric lights, etc – Evening a big banquet at the International, etc – I had made all preparations to attend, but at last moment, when train was coming I had severe attack of the *shits* which lasted me over an hour, just squarely and disgustingly knocking me out – So I didn't go and lost all the fun . . .

Oct 22 . . . I put the annexed epigram into the News this **PM** – They got the first word wrong, making it Ambitio*n*'s instead of Ambitio*us* –

ON CASTING OUT DEVILS.

Ambition's greed, two years ago,
  Put treacherous devils into Newlands,
The people now should, at the polls,
  Cast out those devils—also Newlands.
              — Boxer.

Oct 23 . . . Evening at theater – Boston Lyric Opera Co – comic opera of "The Idol's Eye" – Pretty good – musical, pleasant & amusing . . .

Oct 24 . . . Rec'd copy of SL Tribune with my big Comstock letter in it . . . Evening at Opera House – Big Republican rally – Bonfire in street and Farrington, Coffin and Sam Platt addressed the meeting, especially F. – who made a most excellent, substantial Rep talk – Carson Band officiated all through – About half a house – not very enthusiastic, but all right anyhow . . .

Oct 25 . . . Hon A C Cleveland of White Pine arrived on morning train – A small weekly illustrated campaign paper called *Pandora* is being issued at Reno, by Copeland, Lary et al – Democratic and for Newlands . . .

Oct 26 . . . PM Republican speaking at Opera House by Hon Victor B Dolliver, of Iowa, US Senator, etc – Splendid orator – best I have heard for years – good fair audience, which he owned & was with him for the time – He took evening local train for Va where he speaks tonight – Employed by National Rep Committee – Band played – Evening J H Roberts from San Francisco, another employe, spoke at Opera House – Good square Republican talk, but mostly dry statistics, historical etc – fair audience – Band played, and big bonfire in street . . .

Sunday, Oct 28 . . . The Sierra well whitened and looks wintry – A quiet, pleasant Sabbath, but the various candidates for office made a day of it, getting around lively among their friends, on the streets and in saloons . . .

Oct 29 . . . Letter from wife with $10 . . .

Oct 30 . . . Evening big bonfires on street – Band played, and big audience of all politix gathered into Opera House – Newlands for Congress and Judge Fitzgerald for Supreme Judge spoke – Had Comstock quartette – Newlands spoke 3 hours – They ran town late – Bed 3 –

Nov 1 . . . This evening grand Republican rally at Opera House – crowded audience – Addressed by George B Chandler of Illinois – good straight American talk – best talk and orator I have ever heard in this State – better than Dolliver . . .

Nov 3 . . . Wrote an editorial on *Bryans Jawbone* for the *News,* and one on Newlands for the *Weekly* – That for *News* didn't appear . . .

Sunday, Nov 4 . . . Letter from wife with $30 . . .

Nov 5 . . . About town most of day among the electioneering element . . . The Weekly had my editorial, King Cole Newlands, in this morning. The Capitol saloon, opposite the State Capitol, on Main st was opened tonight in great style, band of music and bonfire in street – great free lunch, etc . . .

> [Clipping of AD's editorial – Opens with a quote from "Old King Cole" and a tortuous analogy between the nursery rhyme and Newlands's congressional campaign, to the effect that he uses loud music to cover up defects in his arguments – Asserts that Newlands has done nothing for Nevada, not for silver, not even for irrigation: the "only practical thing in that line he ever effected was the irrigation of the voters' throats." – Had tried to knife Stewart two years before and rob him of "his hardly earned Senatorship." – Notes wryly that Newlands has a lot of money, but Nevada needs "a more practical and efficient Congressman." – Concludes, "as a local epigrammist puts it," with his poem from October 22, only this time the last line is misprinted, and corrected on the clipping in pencil.]

Nov 6 . . . Election passed off quietly – Carson style – saloons rigidly closed, etc – Read telegraphic returns at Arlington & other places till 2 oclock, when I went to bed – Showed McKinley elected without doubt by big majorities throughout the East, as well as Pacific Coast –

Nov 8 . . . The election returns coming in from all parts of the nation make people, especially Republicans, feel good – Looks like clean sweep – McKinley reelected by bigger majority than ever . . .

Nov 9 . . . At evening train I found Senator Jones on his way to San Francisco – Had short confab with him on the grievance between us – said he was "coming back in a week or so," etc – Guess he lied . . .

Nov 10 . . . Thick fog or "pogonip" in morning . . . According to completest returns, McKinley has nearly or quite 300 electoral votes out of the 447 . . .

Sunday, Nov 11 . . . Senator Stewart has gone back to Washington, and Van Duzer has retired to Winnemucca from his campaigning – He has been elected to the Assembly from Humboldt County –

Nov 13 . . . 3 page letter from wife. Says Sam has gone to New Haven with Dr & Mrs Stubbs as delegates to a convention which is to open sessions at Yale College . . . Alfred comes home from Wadsworth nearly every Friday night . . . Latest news from Bessie she was well & happy . . .

Nov 15 . . . Took all measurements and filled order to Sears, Roebuck & Co for coat, vest and pants . . . Bought me another new shirt, dark, fine striped sateen . . . which with my other new shirts and undershirts and sox fixes me for the winter. Evening about town – bed 12 –

Nov 19 . . . Snowing in the Sierra more or less all yesterday and followed it up this morning – PM it got down into town . . . The Carson Weekly this morning had my little editorial, "The Passing of the Jawbone."

[Clip, signed at the bottom, in pencil, "Alf Doten":] William Chinnings Bryan has been a devout believer in the efficacy of chin music and jawbone, especially in conducting a political campaign. He won his sword and his commission as colonel by judicious use of his trusty jawbone, but the combination was too binding on him and he was only too glad when his brief and bloodless military campaign was over and he could return to the free and unlimited use of his jawbone—sixteen to one.

Whatever of patriotism he may have possessed he laid aside with his sword and uniform and he should also have doffed his title as colonel as not being honestly earned or belonging to him. In fact, considering his treasonable utterances and attitude in opposition to the government, it was both inappropriate and dishonored—too much jawbone. In his recent desperate political campaign it was his chief weapon, and like Samson in the Bible, he smote his adversaries hip and thigh with it, or thought he did. He talked himself and party to death and now he is buried beneath the great Democratic landslide, to be resurrected nevermore. Bryan's jawbone rests in peace and the country is safe.

Nov 20 . . . Fierce & blustering snowstorm . . .

Nov 21 . . . Rained quite steadily from before daylight till nearly noon – snowed in the mountains . . . water dripping down into my room very copiously – Had to get my landlady's wash tub to catch it . . .

Nov 22 – Clear, cool & pleasant – The late storm covered the whole Pacific coast as well as this State, and did a vast amount of good – Nobody objects – More snow piled up on the Sierra than for many years, at this time . . . .

Nov 24 . . . At train met James Langan & wife, nee Kate Shanahan, of Gold Hill, en route for Santa Monica, to live, deserting the old Comstock forever – Had very pleasant chat with them – Jas Langan has been prominent miner, underground foreman, shift boss, etc, for 31 years that I know of – Married Kate only a year or so ago – she was old restaurant neighbor of ours, next to *News* office in Gold Hill . . .

Sunday, Nov 25 . . . Letter from wife with $15 – says Sam visited her relatives in Conn & mine in Plymouth . . . The widow of John Piper died at the State Insane Asylum yesterday –

Nov 26 . . . Met Steve T Gage – been up to Genoa visiting family of his recently deceased friend Jim Haines – Had good pleasant talk with him about old times on the Comstock when we were there together from 1864 down, or till he left to join in employ of the Central Pacific Railroad where he has been ever since – home in Oakland . . . I saw him off . . .

Nov 28 . . . PM wrote page letter to Hon P L Flanigan, State Senator, Reno on $100 business scheme . . .

Nov 29 . . . Thanksgiving . . . I dined by special invitation with Harry Day and his landlady, *May Williams* . . . we had nice turkey – pie – oranges – coffee and a very pleasant time – Miss Jessie Burke, a pretty little lady of about 14 also formed one of the party . . . After dinner Harry ran his gramophone on a lot of various music for an hour or so, and at 9 I took leave – was at Arlington for awhile, reading the papers, etc – Bed at 12 . . .

Nov 30 . . . Oscar Wilde died this PM at a small, obscure hotel in the Latin quarter of Paris from the effects of an abscess in his ear and head. A few friends attended his deathbed. His great *sodomy* scandal & trial of five years ago caused his terrible downfall, with 2 yrs imprisonment from which he emerged a mere wreck of the talented man that he was. He died in poverty and crushing disgrace – too aesthetic for this world . . .

Dec 1 . . . Got a real nice 5 note page letter from wife, all about Sam's return and his visit to our relatives . . . he found old Bro Sam, Charlie, Cornelia, et al, but his time was limited so that he was there only about 24 hours or less & had to get on to Chicago . . . where he overtook Dr Stubbs and wife . . .

Dec 4 . . . Sent letter to E G Siggers, Patent Soliciting Dep't Washington, D.C. for his book on patents – Also to Dr Austin Albro, Box 229,

Augusta, Maine – Also to **Dr F G Kinsman Box 952, Augusta, Me,** both . . . for "Heart Tablets" for heart disease, which they advertise to send sample box free . . .

Dec 5 – Clear & pleasant – Evening at Opera House – *free show* – "The Great South African Salesman" – House crowded – Sold lots of *jewelry,* snide & otherwise – had piano music, and a young assistant with guitar and some songs – also some fun with some of the small kids of Carson – But the boss was the slickest salesman, and the cleanest, most truthful bunco game man on earth – He roped in lots of money – $365 dollars from the people of Carson, including numerous representative ladies – good Carson society crowd – Slickest bunco game I ever saw – Sold watches, rings, jewelry, cutlery and his audience . . . Bed 1 –

Dec 6 . . . The grand Fakir who ran the Opera House and the people of Carson last night registered at the Arlington as I Cramwell ("Ike") . . . He said to his audience last night that he would be more talked about today than anybody in Carson, and he has been all this day, everybody admiring him for his ability to play suckers, and ridiculing themselves or friends for suckers . . .

Sunday, Dec 9 . . . 4 PM by special invitation I went down to Harry Day's & dined with he & Mary – Fine roast chicken. Plymouth Rock rooster, she raised in back yard – hatched last Spring – weighed 8 lbs dressed – cranberry sauce, baked sweet potatoes, orange pie, apples, oranges & bananas – Passed pleasant evening with gramophone music, stories, etc . . .

Dec 10 . . . Got letter from wife with $5 – Borrowed some more and got my package of clothes from Sears, Roebuck & Co which arrived at Express office Saturday . . . Total $12.50 . . .

Dec 11 . . . PM wrote & sent another letter to Hon P L Flanigan, Reno for $100 . . . Judge Troutt of the Superior Court, San Francisco decided yesterday that Reno-California divorce marriages are invalid –

[Clip from the Sacramento *Evening Bee* of the 10th – The ruling, in an estate case, established a precedent for invalidating marriages performed in Nevada if they took place before the expiration of the one-year waiting period which California law required following a divorce.]

Dec 14 . . . Recd letter from P L Flanigan declining the $100, so I sent him one asking for $40 . . .

Sunday, Dec 16 . . . At 4:30 with my new coat and vest on I went down to Harry Day's . . . to dinner – "pot luck" . . .

Dec 17 . . . Got reply letters from Dr F G Kinsman, and Dr Austin Albro, Augusta, Maine . . . got no tablets but their reply letters discovered to me that they are one and the same person, same printed literature, circulars, blank order, etc – identically – guess *they* [being] a *he* is an advertising fraud . . .

Dec 18 . . . PM was at State Controller's office, getting items on taxable property in Nevada for present year – Total valuation, $24,184,-559.77 – Total State tax, $241,845.59 . . .

Dec 19 . . . Was at Mint getting mining returns . . .

Dec 21 . . . The Haverly's Mastodon Minstrels . . . here by morning local train – have their own big car, with eating & sleeping arrangements, etc – Street parade at noon – 16 members on foot, plug hats, etc – and 16 [in] fine brass band – finished parade in front of the Postoffice, where they played some very fine pieces – Evening I was at Opera House – good audience and exceedingly good entertainment – minstrel and variety . . .

Dec 22 . . . Started in writing up Nevada for the Salt Lake Tribune New Years edition . . . "Forefather's Day," and I the only one in Carson to note the fact . . .

Sunday, Dec 23 . . . Wore my new coat & vest – wrote considerably on my Nevada review in my room and at the Arlington – Recd letter from wife inclosing $20 . . . Recd those packages of heart tablets from the Augusta Me, twin doctor – little wooden boxes exactly alike . . .

Dec 25 . . . Busy at room writing most of day – Rec'd nice 5 page letter from sister Eunice inclosing silk pocket handkerchief – At 5 PM I went to Harry Day's to Christmas dinner . . . at 9 oclock was at my room & went to work . . . Made a night session of it . . .

Dec 26 . . . Sent 7 pages . . . to Tribune . . .

Dec 27 . . . Got balance of my Nevada review off to Salt Lake Tribune by evening mail . . . about 4000 words I think – The Indian pupils of the Indian school . . . were in town with their fine brass band this PM . . . and this evening gave regular performance – admission 2 bits – good house – A couple of Indian boy orators did pretty well but the rest of the crowd didn't amount to much . . . Got book from Cornelia . . . *"Eben Holden"* . . . Irving Bacheller the author . . . Special town election today on the question of "Shall Carson City be bonded for the purpose of purchasing the water works and the water rights of the Carson Water Company?" . . . 143 no to 23 yes . . .

Dec 28 . . . Recd letter from wife, inclosing present from Cornelia of a nice linen handkerchief . . . Also rec'd from Bessie, a fine photograph of herself, with card saying "Merry Christmas, with love from Bessie" . . .

Dec 31 . . . Was about town during the evening considerably as usual on the occasion – Very cold but occasion observed as usual at churches or anywhere else – bell ringing, fire crackers etc in plenty at 12 – Bed at 3 – Clear and nearly down to Zero . . . I had but 15 cents left today, so I spent it before midnight so as to close out the year flat broke . . . It is generally claimed in the newspapers etc that this is the passing of the 19th century – this night at 12 . . . I still don't see it in that light, no more than I did a year ago . . .

BOOK NO. *77*

Carson City
Jan 1, 1901 – Dec 31, 1901

Jan 1, 1901 – Clear and cold – Early morning thermometer . . . stood at 2° above Zero . . . New Years Day . . . observed . . . with mutual calls, good wishes, egg nog and good cheer after the old style . . . I received 10 extra copies of the Salt Lake Tribune, New Years number this morning – 76 pages! – My Nevada review in it in good style – 3 columns . . . Wm Crisler re-elected constable of Carson in Republican ticket . . . has been getting crazy for some time past and this evening got violent and fighting at the Arlington House – Had to be taken to jail for safe keeping. In the last drawing of the Beneficencia Publica (Mexican) lottery, Nick Wylie & myself . . . drew a terminal prize of $1.25 . . .

Jan 2 – Cloudy and cold, with furious west wind . . . snowing in the Sierra – Morning mail sent copies of the Tribune to James H Kinkead, and J W O'Donohue, Virginia City and to wife, also gave copy to Dunn of the Carson *News* and to J H Smith, weather observer, and to Harry Day . . . Evening at Arlington out of the big wind & dust – in good company – comfortable and cozy – Bed at 2 . . . 3 Drs examined and pronounced Crisler insane this morning, & he was taken to the Insane Asylum at Reno . . .

Jan 4 – Rainy more or less all day . . . plenty of snow falling in the mountains . . . Got letter from wife . . . inclosing . . . Bulletin No 49 Agricultural Experiment Station . . . all about the Carpenter Worm . . . by Samuel B Doten . . . B.A. Entomology – on the Station Staff – So there he is regularly installed as one of the Professors of the University . . .

Sunday, Jan 6 – Moderate and very rainy . . . snow in the mountains . . . more snow on the Sierra now than for last 3 Winters all put together . . . The water privilege through the roof and ceiling of my room is flowing finely, requiring the washtub's constant use as a calamity catcher. In fact my room resembles a shower bath to a certain extent – Old Uncle Billy Cradlebaugh died this PM at his home, Cradlebaugh's bridge, on Carson river, 6 miles south . . . 83 years old in April next – Native of Circleville, Ohio & came here in about 1850 – unmarried – Mexican war veteran . . .

Jan 9 . . . Some heavy snowsqualls . . . Finished reading "Eben Holden" this evening – Like it very much indeed – Was about town in PM – got ½ doz calendars from as many sources and will send one or more of best to wife tomorrow with "Eben Holden" – Evening mostly at Arlington as usual . . . This cold snap has given the ice harvest a better chance and all the ice men are hard at work . . .

Jan 11 . . . Evening at Opera House – Carson Band Concert, closing with a very light and farcical farce entitled "Spasms," by local talent, the principal feature being J R Pavilla a very excellent contortionist and acrobat . . .

Jan 18 . . . The majority of the outside legislators got in today . . . The new Sunset telephone posts are all up and the wires being strung . . .

Jan 19 . . . Carson was a buzzing beehive of political and office seeking industry, mostly about the Arlington – the headquarters . . .

Sunday, Jan 20 . . . About 8 oclock in the evening both houses caucussed in their respective chambers in the State House and chose all their officers and attaches – taking till nearly or quite midnight – Republicans had to take a back seat there only being five in each house – so the Dem Silver Bryanites had it all their own way . . . short note to Sacramento *Bee,* asking job of reporting of Legislature –

Jan 21 . . . The 20th session of the Nevada Legislature commenced at 12 M today, both Houses being called to order at that time . . . Both proceeded to organize by choice of full list of officers & attaches . . . I reported Senate for myself, not having secured definite arrangements with any paper as yet – rather discouraging outlook for me – The army of expectants who got left . . . evacuated the premises . . . and Carson subsided to proper Legislative basis – with plenty of gambling games, etc, especially at Livingston's Criterion building, where a very excellent trio of musicians . . . attracted crowds – violin, flute and a big Irish harp – up stairs . . .

Jan 22 . . . Bought me a new pair of 50 ct eye glasses to compensate for my failing vision . . .

Jan 23 . . . Reported as usual, but altogether uncertain as to who for – finally wrote out my report to send to the Reno Journal . . . Evening about town – Visited Opera House turned into a skating rink – roller skates, bicycle style – little wheels with solid rubber tires – Wm Hy Doane manager – Big crowd and grand time – Carson band did up the music in fine style – All the big SF, Salt Lake and other papers filled with pictorial accounts of the Queen's death – Bed 12 –

Jan 24 . . . Rec'd reply from the Sac Bee – my correspondence not required – Associated press does it.

Jan 25 . . . Edward VII was sworn in and proclaimed King of the United Kingdom of Great Britain and Ireland and Emperor of India, today in London with all the time honored observances, pomp and public enthusiasm – The Queen's body is embalmed and the funeral is to take place Feb 2 –

Jan 26 . . . E E Copeland, an attorney, at Reno, about 40 yrs old, was found drowned this morning in a big water ditch on the south side of the river, below the Riverside hotel – He had been dissipating during the night and started for his home about 2 oclock, pretty drunk – He wandered around through the snow, crossing the Truckee river on the railroad bridge and turned up toward the Riverside Hotel, finally tumbling into the ditch face downward, too drunk and chilled to crawl out or save himself, although the water just merely covered his body – only about 18 inches deep – leaves a wife and two children –

Jan 28 . . . Ran my legislative report as usual, and was told by Hon W W Webster of the Assembly, son of Judge Webster, proprietor of the Reno *Journal* to keep right on with the report . . . for awhile at least – all of which is very encouraging and hopeful . . . Received a four page letter from wife – first in two weeks – longest interval ever occurring in our mutual communication, personal or written, since we married – Pleaded extra busy . . .

Jan 29 . . . The inquest over Copeland at Reno yesterday showed that he was very drunk that night, pawned his watch for $2.50, had a quarrel, broke his cane, was refused drinks on account of his condition – was in the "tenderloin" quarter as late as 2 o'clock . . . Jury brought in a verdict of accidental death – Met Gottwaldt at noon . . . said my engagement was all right to report for *Journal* . . . for $5 per week . . .

Jan 30 . . . First dividend of our Carson Lottery Syndicate, Nick Wylie, Harry Day and myself, for the present year – won a $1.25 prize, 41⅔ cts apiece, each buying 2 two bit tickets – or 50 cts each as "assessments," so we came out a few cents behind – It was one of Harry Day's tickets that won . . .

Jan 31 – Stormy & cold – One of the most wintry days of the season – Commenced snowing heavily about 6 AM . . . 6 or 8 inches falling . . . After PM adjournment I wrote 3 page legal cap letter to the *Reno Ledger*, weekly, and delivered it . . . to Bert Crawford, the editor, who is Sgt-at-arms of the Assembly . . . Telegraph says that C C Wallace the great political boss of Nevada for several years past, died suddenly of heart failure yesterday in Mariposa county California – Past 72 yrs of age – was "Black" Wallace . . .

[Clips from the *News* and the *Appeal* say that Wallace, as political agent for the Southern Pacific, probably put more men in office in Nevada (or kept them out) than any other influence, and both agree that he was famous for keeping his word to friend and foe alike – The *Journal,* which AD does not clip, says: "While Wallace, the politician, will ever remain in condemnation . . . we will revere the memory of Wallace, the man."]

Feb 2 . . . Rose at 6 and wrote a correspondence, 6 pages, & sent it to Gardnerville Record . . . PM fixed up similar dose & sent it to the Salt Lake *Tribune* . . . Got letter from wife with $15 – Evening about town . . .

Sunday, Feb 3 . . . PM wrote 4 page correspondence & mailed it to SF Chronicle . . .

Feb 4 – Variable, and snowstorming . . . Big sleighing . . . Legislature held AM & PM sessions . . . I reporting as usual – Getting down to their work . . . wrote a 4 page letter to wife . . . The Vanderbilts & Co have bought out the Huntington & other old originators & owners of the SP or main continental railroad and own it & all connections – Grandest railroad transaction on record –

Feb 6 . . . Recd SL *Tribune* . . . containing my correspondence . . . Recd through the Mint here today a copy of the "Treasury Annual

Reports . . ." – It is better executed than any of its predecessors – Has my Comstock portion of it better than was got up before – 12 pages and 4 cuts – really big cap for me as well as the Dept . . .

Feb 7 . . . Gardnerville Record had my letter in today . . .

Feb 8 through April 3 [The *San Francisco Chronicle* turns AD down in favor of Associated Press reports, but he reports daily for the *Journal*, and weekly, with occasional special dispatches, for the *Tribune, Record* and *Ledger*, and writes as always to his wife, who continues to send him money – Of interest:]

Feb 9 . . . The first fly of the year (or century) crawled out of a crack and put in his appearance on my window sill in the morning sunlight – He acted very slow and rheumatic and I didn't kill him . . .

Feb 11 . . . Papers and press telegrams from the East tell much about a Mrs Carrie Nation, an anti whiskey enthusiast engaged in wrecking drinking saloons in Topeka & other Kansas towns, where the prohibition laws are not enforced – She goes in with a hatchet and slashes, smashes and wrecks things, assisted by other kindred spirited women – Creates much excitement, but nobody killed as yet – Says strong drink killed her first husband and now she is on a killing crusade to kill it and get even as far as possible – She is a woman of about 54 yrs old, of respectable appearance but says the Lord has put her onto this crusade and she must obey – Has been on the warpath the last three or four weeks – Been arrested a time or two but released – Holy terror to all saloon keepers, who seem to be defenseless, and seem to think her real name should be Helen Dam Nation . . . Senator Flanigan's bill No 9 to repeal our Nevada prize fight law was lost this PM in the Senate by a vote of 10 to 3 –

Feb 14 . . . The lottery bill came up at 2 PM in the Senate – Senate Concurrent Resolution No 11 – providing for organization and regulation of a lottery in this State – passed at last session 2 yrs ago and laid over under the Constitution for ratification by this Legislature . . . But this Senate by a vote of 10 to 3, 2 absent, declared against such ratification, and therefore the lottery scheme falls dead and defeated in the Senate, with no chance for redemption in the Assembly . . .

Feb 15 . . . In AM Senate roasted the devil out of the Reno Journal for sundry capitalized squibs scattered through its columns yesterday reflecting upon the Senatorial actions and possibilities regarding voting on the lottery question – Sent a page letter to Judge Webster this evening regarding it, inclosing the News legislative report of today . . .

[The "squibs," placed between short articles, offered such observations as: "Any Senator who supports the lottery amendment after voting for the anti-lottery resolution is a liar and a traitor." "Nevada is on the brink of ruin and dishonor." "If you got your price, leave the state with it. Nevada may bear her disgrace, but not the author of it."]

Feb 19 . . . Met Assemblyman Ed Holmes of Gold Hill this evening at the Arlington and he lent me, to read, a copy of the Gold Hill Daily News of August 4, 1866 – Philip Lynch Editor and Proprietor – 7 Columns to page – Bigger & better paper than exists in Nevada today – Very interesting to me, who was working on it a year or two later, soon becoming its proprietor and enlarging it to 8 columns per page . . .

Feb 25 . . . Senate PM session only 10 minutes – then went into "executive" session – closed doors, reporters & all excluded, on the Insurance bill, vetoed by the Governor and passed over his head – Most of 48 Insurance Cos doing business in this State withdrawn their business – will take no new insurance in this State – "Bid for incendiarism" – Insure your house for 3 times its value, and set fire to it to get insurance and they have to pay full amount named in policy. Hal Mighels goes on a business trip tonight to San F – leaves me to do the Legislative reporting for him for 3 or 4 days – Bed 1 –

Feb 26 . . . Did up my double reporting job very promptly & successfully today –

Feb 28 . . . Met George R Vardy of the Wells Herald in town this PM – we shook hands and passed along – first time I have met him since our falling out – He is a dam stinker all the same –

March 2 . . . My busiest day – Rose at 5:30 – wrote 5 page letter to Gardnerville Record . . . reported Senate . . . for the News and Appeal as well . . . PM I wrote 5 long page letter to Salt Lake Tribune . . .

March 4 – Clear and springlike – The grass grows greener on the Capitol lawns . . . Busiest day of my legislative reporting . . . both Houses, for both Carson papers as well as the Reno Journal, and an extra amount at that, both Houses being unusually industrious – I was all right in Saturdays Reno Ledger, on "Legislative Gossip," little over a column – I find in the Ledger the following 2 items: [Retirement of Mrs Nora Webber, Virginia City postmistress, and death of A R Gandolfo.] Mrs Webber is widow of old Dr Webber whom everybody on the Comstock used to know so well – And "Tony" Gandolfo was my old Austin friend, of Crescenzo & Gandolfo, International Hotel proprietors, Austin – Bed 12 – Clear & fine –

March 5 . . . Hard days work at my double reporting – Hal Mighels has returned from San Francisco, but leaves me to do his reporting as yet . . . Carson Lottery Syndicate wins $5 approximation prize . . .

March 6 . . . Found that the Syndicate won $2.50 instead of $5.00 – so I collected it and paid each member his one third – 83⅓ cents – or 80 cts each, retaining the 10 cts extra . . . for my Secretary salary . . . Evening by special invitation I attended banquet at the Arlington given by citizens of Carson to the members of the Legislature . . . 2 big tables occupying the whole big dining room – Fresh shell oysters, turkey, salad, white wine and claret – coffee, beef tea, fruit, cake & all that sort of thing – Nevada State Band did fine music, Plenty of good talkers, etc – Bed 1 . . .

March 8 . . . Evening I attended Opera House – Minstrel show and concert of the Nevada State Band – Crowded house – Very good performance . . . First part was regular up to date minstrel show – all black face – Rest, variety, vaudeville – songs – instrumental solos, overtures etc, trapeze – "Cynthia" a young girl dancing contortionist, peculiarly slim and good . . .

March 9 . . . My right testicle is terribly swollen to ten times normal size from some cause or other . . . I dont know – Very sore and has to be slung up –

Sunday, March 10 . . . Sick day for me – Morning I worked making a sling for my testicle, which troubles me badly – got chilled from a cold already started, with a restless night last night – Was at Arlington and got warmed up, also got a big hot dose of brandy, ginger, peppermint and other ingredients that Tim Dempsey the barkeeper knows how to fix up – Then went and got some soup, hot coffee etc at Johnny Anderson's restaurant and went to my room, turned into bed and slept couple of hours – good refreshing sleep – got up feeling much better . . . Evening at Arlington . . .

March 11 . . . Legislature stood in well on work, accomplishing little of importance as usual, excepting demonstrating that although this was the last day of the session, the fiftieth, they failed to get through with the business before them and would have to run some days longer . . .

March 13 . . . The Senate concurred in Assembly amendments to the big "General Appropriation Bill," and passed it, and sent it to enrollment and the Governor – So settles that bill which no Legislature can adjourn sine die without passing – It foots up to nearly $350,000, for the years 1901-2 . . .

March 15 . . . In the Assembly was the fun of the session – The Third House, with Governor Sadler presiding – Very funny and hilarious episode – But the big revenue bill, passed by the Assembly, lies stranded "on the table" of the Senate . . .

March 16 . . . Both Houses came to adjournment, sine die, at 3:30 PM today, all requisite bills being passed and business completed . . .

Sunday, March 17 . . . St Patrick's Day – Many observers of it in "wearin' of the green," neckties, shamrocks, etc – I visited my old friend Ed Sweeney on King street, above the brewery – had his big Irish flag and American flag strung across the street after his usual annual style, entertaining visiting friends in home open house way, with a drop of the "craythur" etc . . . Marchie Kelly left for Tonopah, the new mining district in Esmeralda or Nye County this evening –

March 18 . . . Hardesty's Senate Bill No 10, was the now famous insurance bill vetoed by the Governor 2 yrs ago and passed over his head this session and is now the law . . .

March 19 . . . Jim Yerington left last evening for Buffalo, NY to take charge, as Commissioner, of the exhibit of Nevada at the Pan-American Exposition . . .

March 20 . . . Marchie Kelly returned this evening from Tonopah – Didn't like the country or chances for work, or the mining prospects, so turned round & came back . . .

March 21 . . . Harry Day presented me with a beautiful picture the first part of this month entitled *"My First Violin"* – told me 'twas special present from May Williams – printed in colors, and represents a little girl playing the violin – Came with "Happy Hours" a monthly paper, Augusta, Me . . .

March 23 . . . My swollen right testicle has abated so that don't have to be slung up – 3 times ordinary size yet . . .

March 29 . . . PM down at State Capitol getting list of laws passed at this Legislature – Was discovered in Secy of States office about 3 PM that the Hardesty insurance bill . . . was of no effect, lacking signatures of Van Duzer and Judge, Speaker and Prest of the two Houses . . . So the whole vexatious Insurance problem is very satisfactorily & summarily solved – the bill being a self vetoed nullity – All Insurance Cos withdrawing business from this State can soon get in as before . . . no extra session needed to be called as was feared would have to be – The big joke on this Legislature telegraphed all over the coast by Associated Press . . .

Sunday, March 31 . . . PM and evening busy writing up synopsis of the bills passed . . . over 40 of them – giving Governor's action thereon – Vetoed seven . . .

April 1 . . . Completed 4 page letter to Gardnerville Record, including my legislative synopsis or summary . . . All the County Assessors from all the 14 various Counties of the State came in this morning attending a ten days convention . . . to work some concerted plan whereby taxation shall be made more equalized . . . H R Mighels paid me $5 today and I paid it to Mrs Kelly for my room rent to Friday last – This is *"Holy Week"* but I had a bit of a spat with Mighels because he wanted to jew me out of $3 . . .

April 3 . . . PM wrote & sent letter to Judge Webster of Reno Journal inclosing my summary of bills . . . Latest telegrams from Manila say Aguinaldo took the oath of allegiance yesterday to the United States – The Reno Gazette comes enlarged Apr 1, and improved, and set with Merganthaler linotype machine – 7 columns per page as before, but columns two inches longer, and widened about $\frac{3}{16}$ of an inch . . .

April 4 . . . PM I attended Assessors Convention – It got through and adjourned sine die at 3:30 – Then I visited Supreme Court – The Insurance bill invalidation argued, and submitted at 4 PM, when court adjourned till Monday next . . .

April 5 – Variable, blustering – cool – About town, observing – At 7:50, just 10 minutes before closing time of the telegraph office, the messenger met me on the street, giving me following, just rec'd here at 7:30 PM – "Salt Lake 5 – Alf Doten Carson Nev Rush three hundred words railway decision. Tribune" – I soon studied out what was wanted – clipped it from the evening News and sent it in 15 minutes after receiving the dispatch – Mr Franklin Leonard, Supt of the Sutro Tunnel Co met me at the Arlington, and I incidentally took him over to my room and showed him a copy of my gov't book – The Production of Gold & Silver in the US for 1899 – $20 for the Tunnel Co – Bed 12 –

Sunday, April 7 – Clear, cold & pleasant – Easter Sunday – all churches well attended and everybody feeling religiously happy – The Knights Templar from Virginia and Reno, came on morning trains and at about 11 AM marched down street from Armory Hall, north of the depot and went to the Episcopal Church, attending service as is their established custom once a year. 45 or 50 of them in all, Bearing three flags – richest regalia of any Order – richest of black silk velvet cloaks, military chapeaus with white ostrich plumage – cloaks loaded with silver ornaments and silver lace, etc – and all carried swords. Those regalias cost from $100.00 to $700 each – those from the Comstock being, of course the richest – being bought in bonanza times – when silver was plenty and nobody cared a dam for expenses – They had a fine lunch and refreshments at the hall on return from Church, and all went back home on the PM and evening trains – Bed 12 . . . About 4:30 PM recd at my room following telegram from the SL Tribune: "Keep close watch on land office and Court officials for developments in fight for railroad grade in Lincoln County and keep us advised – Tribune." My telegram I sent Friday evening came in all right in Saturday's Tribune . . . just 300 words –

April 8 . . . State Teacher's Institute commenced today for a week in the Senate Chamber – Nearly 100 teachers from all parts of the State, mostly young ladies – Alfred came, from Wadsworth, but wife did not – Met him on the street and he gave me a letter from her, inclosing $5 – she said she had very sore inflamed eye . . . didn't know for sure whether would come at all – The Supreme Court decided against the Hardesty insurance bill becoming a law this AM – PM I got hold of the type written decision, condensed it into about ⅓ of a column in the evening News & after it went to press I clipped and telegraphed it to SL Tribune – Sent also a ten word dispatch of it to the Gardnerville *Record* . . . Evening at theater – play was *"The Evil Eye"* a very lively vaudeville show by a travelling company from the East – Very good indeed . . . good singing, music and some extra good dancing, including the Electric Ballet, in which the clothing or dresses of the dancers in a sort of May pole dance sparkled with small electric lights about a dozen or more apiece, from head to foot – beautiful effect . . .

April 10 . . . The Teacher's Institute progresses finely – crowded attendance – great interest taken – About 120 teachers present . . . First Institute held here in 23 years, and best ever held in the State . . .

April 11 . . . Wife and Sam came on morning train and attended the Institute – So did I with them, more or less – Wife & I took lunch at noon at Ormsby House together – She gave in a poem, "Tainted," in the AM, and Sam a brief ½ hour discourse on "Insects," etc in the PM – Saw them off on evening train to Reno, not to come back . . .

April 13 . . . Recd page letter from Will W Booth, Tonopah – son of old John Booth, Austin – going to start a weekly paper in that famous new mining camp & wants to know about procuring a half medium Gordon press he knows of now at the Carson News office – Went and found out he couldn't – not for sale – would take $450.00 or more to replace it – made item of his intentions . . . Sent page letter, explanatory, etc, directed to Sodaville, Nevada – on the C&C RR, nearest RR point to Tonopah . . .

April 15 . . . Met George James, of Reno, Sam's college mate . . . is here in connection with a job in the Treasurers office . . . putting in electric alarms and other safety arrangements . . . He lent me a book to read and criticize, entitled "Miss Devereux of the Mariquita," by Richard Henry Savage . . . early Comstock scenes and incidents – One of the most mendacious yarns I ever tackled, I think – He evidently never saw or experienced what he wrote about – merely a heterogeneous lot of familiar names of localities and characters picked up from old timers or writings woven into a sensational bonanza of strong romance – Too infernal tough for close reading or serious criticism by any honest Comstocker . . .

> [Unidentified clipping:] Here is a way to tell how fast you are traveling in a railway car. Every time a car passes over a rail joint there is a distinct click. Count the number of these clicks in twenty seconds and you have the number of miles the train is going per hour. This is a simple matter of arithmetic, as the length of the rails is uniform.

April 16 . . . Met Alex Fleming at Arlington – Used to be with me at Como in old best times – His old daddy I knew as locator & a chief pillar of the town – Alex is now prosperously located 12 miles this side of Placerville, Cal, ranching, etc – Over here on a festive visit to his many old friends – 55 yrs old . . . gave me $2 out of natural exuberant festive generosity, for old times and old Como sake – Wouldn't have it any other way . . .

April 19 . . . I finished reading "Miss Devereux of the Mariquita" . . . It is a well constructed, vigorously written romance – with unusual strength of profanity, affluent wickedness and bold rascality . . . with easy mendacity and reckless sacrifice of truth to sensational effect . . . Brings in plenty of genuine names, characters and incidents, historical, etc, but leaves the impression with me that he picked it up second hand and never was on the Comstock at all – probably a stock broker or dealer in San Francisco – His mining terms and expressions show that he never was a practical Comstock miner – He speaks of the famous Vigilance Committee as "101" when it was 601, and has most of his mining in "Grizzly Gulch" at Va or Gold Hill – No such gulch in that section – Many other gross discrepancies, etc, but as before remarked he spins a very bold, dashing, lively and absorbingly interesting yarn, especially so to an old Comstocker like me . . .

April 20 . . . Letter from Will Booth, Tonopah – Wrote page letter in reply, about type purchasing possibilities here – also mailed a type sample book . . .

April 23 . . . This PM Harry Day loaned me "Robert Greathouse," a 573 page Comstock novel like "Miss Devereux of the Mariquita," which I loaned him in return – Robt G is by John Franklin Swift, 1870 – Formerly US Minister to Japan . . . Supt Colcord of the Mint yesterday received a bagfull of books from Hon Geo E Roberts . . . his annual report of Gold and Silver Production . . . C tells me to come and take what I wish of them – He has sent copies to the newspapers, and they are giving complimentary notices, etc . . .

April 24 . . . Was at *Appeal* office this PM inquiring for some old type, long primer, bourgeoise and nonpareil, that Will Booth wants – didn't have any to spare . . .

April 25 . . . Rec'd 3 page letter from Mrs Cora N Stoddard, wife of Charley Stoddard, Reno, and daughter of Mrs S J Cross of Como when I was there – asking me to write something on the death of her mother – Think I will do so . . .

April 26 . . . Sent a full 3 page letter to Bessie this evening, together with that picture of "My First Violin" . . .

April 27 – Clear, cool & very pleasant – At my room – just before morning train time, 10:10 AM I recd following telegram from Salt Lake: Watch for C S Varian, and see if he files any maps or documents in land office – Tribune – I watched – He arrived on PM local about 4 – went direct to the US Dist Court chamber – I waited around and finally made out to get off the result, as follows at 8 oclock telegraph closing time: "C S Varian in US Dist Court this PM filed complaint as vs Utah & California RR Co asking for restraining order. Defendants given till June 7 in which to show cause why the injunction should not be dissolved" – Evening had a lively chat with Varian, my old time legal friend and politician – Hadn't seen him for 20 yrs or more . . .

Sunday, April 28 . . . Pencilled off a memorial tribute to Mrs Cross . . . Rec'd letter from Crawford of Reno Ledger . . . will pay the $13.50 as soon as able – Bed 11 –

April 29 – Rainy . . . snow fell in the mountains – I completed my Cross *"Memorial Tribute"* . . . copied off in good shape for printer & inclosed it with page private letter to Mrs Cora N Stoddard . . . I advise her to publish it in Reno Journal . . . Latest Comstock sensation is defalcation of John F McDonnell, Secy of Va Miners Union – $1,100 – Said to have skipped out for California . . .

April 30 . . . Recd letter from wife with $15 . . . President McKinley started yesterday on his great western tour to Pacific Coast, launching of big US war ship Ohio, etc – Mrs Nation the Kansas saloon wrecker of a few weeks ago was crazy then, or has proved so since, for telegraph says she is now confined in a padded cell in jail at Wichita, Kansas, crazier than a bed-bug . . .

May 3 . . . Met Geo I Lamy of the Gardnerville Record . . . He paid me $25 on account, so he only owes me $5 balance . . . Recd nice little 4 page note letter from Mrs C N Stoddard . . . Wrote . . . short letter to Sheriff Jas Quirk, Va City . . . for placard & photo J F McDonnell . . .

May 4 – Clear & very Springlike – The shade trees all over town are opening their leaves . . . and apples, pears & all other fruits are in full blossom & promise . . . Got through reading *"Robert Greathouse"* . . . Dont like it – Not well written or constructed – Semblance of truth & historical in some instances, but too prosy in love story incidentals, legal dialogue, etc . . . Good material poorly worked up – Attained considerable degree of notoriety as an early Comstock story or novel, founded upon some facts in noted legal contests . . . unprincipled proceedings, mining rascalities, etc – bringing in the semblance of sundry leading mine manipulators, legal lights, etc . . .

Sunday, May 5 . . . Rec'd another letter from Mrs Cora N Stoddard . . . stating that in view of too much delay on part of Journal in publishing my *memorial tribute* she had concluded to drop it . . . She apologizes for the trouble she gave me . . .

May 7 . . . Evan Williams reported dying in San Francisco this evening – His wife & daughter left here on special train about 9 oclock . . .

May 8 . . . Flags on the bank & also on State House ½ mast in token of the death of Evan Williams, about 9 last evening . . .

[Two clippings – The *Appeal* says Williams, a pioneer resident on the Comstock in the early 1860s, was superintendent of the Mexican Mill at Empire, president of the Bullion Bank in Carson, and Ormsby County senator from 1885 to 1891 – The San Francisco *Bulletin* notes that he was superintendent of the Nevada mill when that company was defendant in the Fox vs Hale & Norcross litigation, and copies from a Reno paper the further information that Williams once ran a butcher shop in Gold Hill, then became an accountant for the Crown Point in the 1870 bonanza, and had recently sued "his former friend, Senator Jones" for an accounting of various business transactions, but had died before the case came to trial.]

May 9 . . . Met Charlie H Fish at late morning train going up to Va – Prest Con Va Co – Declared 10 ct dividend, 1st for some years . . . Evening was at *Appeal* office & read proof of Memorial Tribute to Mrs S J Cross . . .

[The "tribute" is more about the importance of the Cross family and their "young gals from Sonoma" (Cross having come from Sonoma County, California) in the sociable days of Como than it is about Mrs Cross, who is called "a noble-hearted wife, mother and friend."]

May 11 . . . Letter to Mrs Cora N Stoddard with 8 copies Carson Appeal, containing my *Memorial Tribute* on her mother's death . . .

Sunday, May 12 . . . Recd from wife yesterday copy of *Seattle Daily Times,* big paper like SL *Tribune* – containing big column editorial notice, complimentary . . . of my Comstock report . . . Best editorial notice I ever had –

["The Famous Comstock Lode," from the *Seattle Daily Times* of May 4:] A most interesting and entertaining story is told in the annual report of the treasury department treating of the production of gold and silver of the

United States and touching the famous Comstock Lode as it is properly called—the same having been written for the government by Mr. Alfred Doten, of Virginia City, Nevada, which is located at the very entrance of this famous lode, consisting of nearly forty independent mines.

The story is interesting not only because of the number of years which have elapsed since gold was discovered at this point, for that took place nearly forty-two years ago, but by reason of the enormous amount of wealth which has been taken therefrom—the yield up to the close of the year 1899 having reached the enormous sum of four hundred million dollars. . . .

In spite of the enormous yield, however, of the Comstock Lode, this same writer declares that nearly "eighty million dollars" has been expended in the development of the Comstock Lode, including its forty independent mines, while the total dividends paid to stockholders are slightly below $134,000,000—to which the famous Consolidated California and Virginia mines contributed $84,000,000 alone against an assessment of less than three and a half millions in the beginning. . . .

May 15 . . . Got a nice little letter from Mrs Cora N Stoddard . . . deep gratitude for all I have done in the matter –

May 16 . . . Sent page letter to Wm Nelson of SL Tribune, regarding Lincoln railroad . . . PM funeral of Wm Crisler who died at 6 PM yesterday – took place from hall of K of P, of which he was a member – well attended by members on foot and in carriages – I rode with Doc Benton . . .

May 17 . . . Mrs McKinley nearly died in San F yesterday or day before from heart troubles, nervous exhaustion, etc . . . reported better and improving, but Presidents visit is curtailed . . .

Sunday, May 19 . . . President McKinley witnessed launching of the big battleship Ohio at San F. yesterday 2:30 PM – Mrs McK too ill to attend – Over 50,000 people saw it . . .

May 20 through 31 [AD notes the progress and safe return home of the McKinleys and party, corresponds with Mary and brother Sam, follows the short-line suit for the *Tribune* and writes other pieces, notes further compliments upon his Comstock article in the Virginia *Report* and Wells *Herald,* gives copies of the Mint report to friends and family, applies to Roberts of the Mint, with clippings enclosed, for chance to report again and begins to gather material – His landlady, Mrs Kelly, quits, worn out and unable to make any money with only five roomers – He attends sessions of a Catholic Mission being held by two Paulist fathers, and a public lecture, "From Plymouth Rock to the Rock of

Peter," given by one of them, Father Wyman – "One of the cleanest voiced preachers I ever heard."]

June 1 . . . Rec'd 8 copies of the Seattle Daily Times of May 4 which I sent for . . . Old Comstock Pioneer Dick Sides died at Theodore Winters' ranch, Washoe Valley yesterday PM – aged 75 years . . . The famous Wedekind silver mine, near Reno sold yesterday for $175,000 to John Sparks the great cattle rancher . . .

Sunday, June 2 . . . $2500 already collected for Carnival expenses & plenty more coming in or available –

June 3 . . . PM I attended hearing before Judge Hawley, US Circuit Court, of argument for continuance of temporary injunction in the Oregon Short Line railroad case against the Utah & California, or Clark line – The injunction expired today, and P L Williams, chief Attorney of the Short Line Co . . . gave the argument – Judge Hawley's decision will be given at 10 AM tomorrow – I sent 210 words dispatch to SL Tribune . . .

June 4 . . . Attended Court – Judge postponed his railroad decision till 2 PM, when he decided no new injunction to issue, but that plaintiff should notify deft to appear June 24 & show cause why further injunction should not be abandoned . . . in other words the case has to come up in court then for trial and final adjudication . . . I got off a 250 word telegram to the *Tribune* . . .

June 6 . . . Made two new reportorial note books, 70 leaves each, to fill my own old covers that Major Dallum gave me nearly 40 yrs ago, when I first started in reporting for the *Va Daily Union* – That pair of old covers has been my daily pocket companion ever since . . .

June 7 . . . Sent Seattle Times to Sisters Eunice and Lizzie . . . Also . . . to Fred W Clough, Angel's Camp Cal –

June 8 . . . Wrote page letter & mailed it to the Gardnerville *Record* . . . The Con Cal & Va M Co declared another 10 ct dividend yesterday – Tom Tennant gave me a copy of the Elko Independent of June 7, in which was published a column letter from son Sam, relative to the cut worm infesting and destroying the alfalfa fields of Starr Valley & other parts of Humboldt County . . .

June 11 . . . Busy most of day at room, evolving and constructing a new and original style of catheter case . . .

June 12 . . . Miss Hettie Humphreys died here this morning, aged 34 years – She was born in Dayton, Nevada, where her father died when she was but 10 yrs old – She taught school there as soon as able, for two years, was 2 years telegrapher at the V&T RR station Franktown, and since then has been telegrapher here for the Western Union Tel Co – She was a weakly, hard working little woman, suffering much from illness and bodily pain, incapacitating her from work for several months past, ending with her death – everybody who knew her was her friend . . .

June 20 – Partially cloudy, but very warm – 86° . . . Finished making a new pocket document case 8½ x 3½ x 1 inch – Also finished up a catheter case, 9 x 4 and ⅜ inch – Recd from Will Booth No 1, Vol 1 of his new weekly paper, the Tonopah Bonanza, dated June 15, 1901 – 4 five column pages – size of page sheet 13 x 19 inch – By Tonopah Pub Co, W W Booth Manager & Editor – 9½ columns ads & rest reading matter . . . Tim Dempsey closes out as barkeep at Arlington tonight and goes as barkeep at the Ozark – Dick Bright takes Tim's place at the Arlington – Bed 12 –

June 21 . . . The Midway Plaisance location is the block surrounding the Government building . . . Carpenters commenced the erection of the requisite buildings for the 12 shows of the Midway this morning . . .

June 24 . . . Five booths are in course of construction . . . letter to Gardnerville Record . . . then went up to US Circuit room – Court in full session, Judge Hawley presiding – The great Lincoln County Short Line–Clark Co railroad suit – All the big lawyers in it arrived on a 3 coach morning special from Ogden, Varian with them, of course – I reported case to SL Tribune before 8 PM – about 350 words . . . Rec'd letter from wife with $15 . . .

June 25 . . . Reported Court as yesterday – Testimony all in – and all documentary – at 2:30 PM, when Judge J R Kelley, general solicitor for the UP RR opened the argument for plaintiff . . . Balloting for Queen of the Carnival this evening . . . Miss Nellie Epstein won by about 3,000 majority – 17,000 votes in all –

June 26 . . . Judge Kelley finished argument at 3 PM . . . Varian gave 15 minutes – then came T E Gibbon, leading atty and Vice Prest of Clark line, for defense . . .

June 27 . . . Very hot day – 91° – At Court cool and nice – Gibbon occupied whole day & didnt finish . . . Got off telegram . . . My telegrams return in due time regularly published in the Tribune –

June 28 . . . 94° – Defense got in all their argument – Gibbon closing at 11 . . . followed by Whittemore for an hour . . . PM, P L Williams, Genl Atty Short Line, went in for wind up on the part of pltff . . . Took me till 9 oclock, 3 hours to write out and send my telegram . . .

June 29 . . . 92° . . . Nevada grade railroad injunction case closed argument and was submitted for decision at noon today . . . wrote up & sent telegram to Tribune . . . Most of the principal buildings in town are decorated & all others decorating with Carnival and national colors . . .

Sunday, June 30 . . . Letter from Geo E Roberts Director of the Mint . . . "I have concluded to authorize you to prepare such an article and will allow the sum named ($150) therefor. I am not prepared to offer any suggestions, save that you give quite fully an account of the attempt made in the last year to reopen the mine . . ." . . . John M Daniel, "Kentuck," old Comstock sport died at Circe's Carson Exchange Hotel this morning at 2 oclock from stones in the bladder . . . E E Bingham, formerly of the Tuscarora Times-Review and Chief Clerk of the late Assembly is now lessee of the Reno Journal, commencing tomorrow – John H Dennis is in with him as editor –

July 1 – Clear, breezy & Cooler – Whole City decorated grandly – nobody ever saw the like – Lots of strangers getting in and all the Midway show people will arrive tomorrow . . . Evening took a walk down to the Ozark saloon, where Tim Dempsey is running the bar – Had lots of nice violin and piano & bass viol music & songs – Bed 12 – Somehow this morning in making my toilet . . . my wedding ring, gold, was lost from my left little finger . . . Discovered loss about 4 PM – downtown – Went straight home . . . Swept room completely and *found it* – Never happier in my life . . . The gentle breezes from the west today shook up the decorations considerably . . . blowing down most of the Chinese paper lanterns strung across the street at frequent intervals with other decorations, flags, etc.

July 2 . . . High west wind blew down a couple of the Midway show booths this PM . . . Town full of strangers . . .

July 3 . . . Carnival commenced at 8 oclock AM, engine house bell 20 strokes – tennis game, base ball – Band played up & down street –

Midway shows all opened – I attended two: the "coon" show, 15 cts, and "Baby Krause," 10 cts . . . Fakir tables & booths everywhere . . . Wrote a page nice letter to Will W Booth acknowledging receipt and admiration of his paper the *Tonopah Bonanza* . . .

July 4 – Clear, pleasant and *just right* – Special trains from Reno, brought about 2,500 people – also 4 or 5 hundred from the Comstock, notwithstanding they held a little local celebration up there – Flags and decorations all right – Big parade just before noon – Marshal Flanigan & aids, horseback – 14 young ladies, horseback – Carson Band, Woodmen afoot – over a dozen *floats* – Fire Dept – Indian Band and school floats, etc – Over a thousand people in it – Exercises east side of State House . . . I was about town considerably – met *Sam Pidge* et al from the Comstock, Sam especially – The great relay race, wheels, PM, Reno won – Evening I took ride on smallest railroad in the world, 10 cts, and paid 25 cts to see theater, *"Little Egypt"* – Bed 12 – Four of the floats carried pupils of the Indian School – Escorted by their band, about 40 pieces – They also had a small Gordon press printing 8 x 6 dodgers & distributing as they passed along – This is what it said:

> Fifty years ago the government controlled us with powder, now a better weapon is used. Then life was taken and primitive happiness destroyed; now hope is instilled and our future brighter. Reason and justice prevails.
>
> The Indian.

July 5 . . . Town still crowded . . . PM fine parade of the Queen along the main street, with band, floats, etc – Great fun, racing, broncho busting, lassoing, etc at race track – Evening exercises and dancing before the Throne at State House, east side – Big floor for the purpose – Evening I attended shows of Midway: "Poses Plastique," "Art Exhibition," Juvenile Show and "Little Egypt" – Bed 12 – Fun still going on . . .

July 6 – Same – Warmer – 94° – *Mardi Gras* and closing day of the Carnival – Everybody supposed to be en masque – I made one out of a bit of bunting, green, with a red nose – Lots of racing & other fun down at the race track . . . Evening, King Rex arrived with his retinue and was given the key of the City – At 7:30 PM special train brought about 200 from Reno, and one from the Comstock about 50 – Grand procession right then, southward from the Depot – Several floats, Queen, Maids of Honor to the Queen, etc – Everybody masked & joined in the queerest and most hilarious fantastic procession I ever saw – clowns and acolytes & all that sort of thing – Evening big dancing on the floor constructed on the lawn, east side of Capitol Park – I was there awhile – electric lights, bully band etc – Plenty of fun, more than ever – all over town – Plenty of fireworks – Capitol Park beautifully illuminated – Chinese lanterns, etc – Bed at 2 – very tired, yet glad. The Midway shows ran late tonight for their closing – Fire about 10 in evening . . . destroyed couple of buildings in Chinatown –

Sunday, July 7 . . . Show people all getting out, also their booths, and the general supernumeraries – Wonderful difference . . .

July 10 . . . My old landlady, Mrs Kelly returns to take charge . . . "The Cat Comes back" . . .

July 11 . . . Rec'd No 4 of Tonopah Bonanza – Had portion of my letter to Will Booth July 3d, about Carnival . . .

July 12 . . . Met George I Lamy – paid me $5 balance . . . Rec'd $12.86 check from SL Tribune – Bed 12 –

Sunday, July 14 . . . Carson quieter than usual – 3 or 4 hundred went down to the great relay bike race at Reno, between the Garden City, San Jose, Cal, Wheelmen and the Reno team – 50 miles – Reno beat San J by 1 mile & 12 ft, Championship Pacific Coast . . .

July 16 . . . A telegram received by the Schneider family, this AM from New York City says that their daughter (Lily Leale Schneider that was, but now wife of Mr Greaves, a newspaper man of that city) died there this morning at 4 oclock – consumption probably . . . Morning passenger & mail was over 3 hours late, owing to immense travel over the CP RR – 80 trains last 2 days Epworth Leaguers to big convention at San Francisco – freight trains abandoned to accommodate the wonderful rush . . .

Sunday, July 21 – Clear & hot – 93° – My 72nd birthday – Was about town more or less but on good behavior – Bed at 12, broke – not a cent in my purse – But I received a check for $22.14 from the SL Tribune today bringing my pay for June up to $35 in the railroad case . . . Met Jas M Leonard, Ass't Supt Comstock (Sutro) Tunnel Co, in company with L C Hobart his father in law, up from Sutro – Was about town with them some – Got items about tunnel etc –

July 22 . . . Was on hand at US Dist Court – good full audience, including Herron, Ryan, Garber & other big railroad lawyers from S.F. & elsewhere & local attorneys to hear Judge Hawley's decision in the Lincoln railroad case – Took him 1½ hours to read it – so I telegraphed about 350 or 400 words of it to Tribune – He simply sustained the injunction etc . . .

July 23 . . . Rec'd letter from Jas M Leonard, Sutro . . . giving items and asking about photographer –

July 25 . . . Sent a page letter to Jas M Leonard, about photographer – not able to send one, but recommending other sources – Billy Cann of Va for instance . . .

July 26 . . . Letter from wife with $20 – Been back home to Reno a week – Bessie came a week before . . . Sam still out in the Sierra – Met Alfred on street today & evening – He is let out at Wadsworth, & trying for posish at Austin . . . Board of Pardons this PM decided against pardon for Crowley the Savage mine Nichols murderer, 3 to 2 – Governor and Woodburn for him, but the 3 justices of the Supreme Court against him . . . *Correct.* Sent telegram about 350 words about it to Salt Lake Tribune –

July 27 . . . Bought a black alpaca thin coat $2.00 & pr shoes $2 . . . Dined at Anderson's restaurant on mess of nice catfish from Carson river presented by Andy Robert who caught them day before yesterday – Very fine eating – At train yesterday morning I met Col P J Keyes on his return to Va from San Francisco with W S Chapman a big capitalist interested with him in his mines in 6-Mile Canyon – Chapman was here in the early times, and his name appears on the county map, covering the bottom lands along Carson river below Empire & near Brunswick . . .

Sunday, July 28 . . . PM I finished a three page letter to Tribune . . .

July 29 . . . PM I finished elaborate 3 page letter to wife & sent it . . . Evening down town – at Ozark Saloon – Met & conversed lively with Jim Butler the discoverer of Tonopah, sold a week or two ago for $360,000 – Jim got lots of cash, and is very naturally liberal with it . . . At the Ozark saloon this evening I listened to the latest and best of Edison's phonographic instruments I ever saw or heard – wonderful instrument –

July 30 . . . Hottest yet – 97° ! ! ! – 3 men campers from Cal, pitched their tent near the old box factory, south end of town day before yester-day – One of their number being sick a doctor was sent for and found a well developed case of smallpox – All 3 were taken to county pest house and placed under rigid quarantine . . .

Aug 1 – Somewhat cloudy, but very warm – about 94° – Went on morning train to Virginia, arriving at noon – Met many of my old friends and acquaintances, including Jose Salinas and was kept busy shaking hands and chatting as I passed along C street – The old hill up from the depot seemed longer and steeper than ever – sidewalks more dilapidated – general air of dilapidation in passing through Gold Hill & Virginia – Visited the three newspaper offices, *Enterprise, Chronicle* and *Report,* all of whom made note of my arrival – Met Miss May Dunlop on sidewalk front of her home on C st & we had pleasant old time talk – I wore my new shoes, and the left one hurt my toes so badly that I had to change it for old one I had taken the precaution to bring along in my valise, which I took to Con Ahern's Crystal saloon – Found Leon M Hall at his rooms in the International and we had talk about Comstock changes to electrical works, and machinery, etc, information I require – he being Consulting Engineer, etc – Dined with Jose Salinas at Otto's old restaurant – Evening about town – Bed at 12, in Douglass building – 3d story, my old colored friend, Billy Brady janitor, took charge of me – Old Joe Douglass not at home – met him in Carson yesterday morning on his way to Walley's Springs, Genoa, for a weeks mud bath to soak rheumatism, whisky and other cussedness out of him – Bed at 12 – sultry, so I laid on top of bed, uncovered, and slept excellently –

Aug 2 – Same – Met Leon M Hall at his rooms, and he gave me a written statement he prepared relative to Comstock electric changes etc – 5 pages – PM about town gathering information & visiting old friends, McGurn, et al – Met Dr P Manson on C st, and by invitation dined with him at the City Bakery, kept by E Bonafous & Son – Bed at 11 – sultry –

Aug 3 – Same – hotter – must have been 96° – more consultation with Leon M Hall – PM at Con Va office awhile, consulting with O'Donahue, Ross, et al – Pay day – Only about 250 miners working Comstock, mostly at Con Va – Took a walk down below the RR depot to old Chinatown – Very few houses left there & very few Chinese – gone – dilapidated relics – At 4:20 PM left on train to Carson – Evening about town some – Bed 12 – very tired – Leon M Hall also came down on same train, bound for San Francisco –

Aug 4 through 8 [AD gathers more mining information, corresponds with family, notes that the Selby reduction works near San Francisco has been tunnelled into and robbed of $280,000 in gold bullion, that the other two campers in the pest house have come down with smallpox, and that, after fumigation against bedbugs, "my landlady's infernal, diabolical, sulphuric and odoriferous lubricators and disinfectants make my room smell worse than 40 drugstores."]

Aug 9 – Same – Rec'd letter from SL Tribune, with check for June services, of *$7.86* – Should have been $10, but —— At noon I met J M Leonard, Asst Supt Sutro or Comstock Tunnel Co – He drove up with his wife from Sutro in buggy – Brought several newly taken views of the new mill and surroundings at mouth of Tunnel for me to select from for illustrations of my Comstock govt report – Got lot more desired information from him, and he returned to Sutro this evening – Then I went to the US Circuit Court room, and from Clerk T D Edwards got hold of document of injunction applied for and granted, this AM – Clark line vs Short Line for all the road or right of way from Clover Valley Junction to the California and Nevada State line, about 170 miles – I wrote out telegram about 300 words, & sent to SL Tribune at 4 PM – Then strayed down street and in front of the Magnolia saloon was overhauled by Doc Benton in his buggy – made me get aboard and drove down street to Johnny Meyers' corner where we overtook a two horse old time California prospectors rig – two men, father and son – arrived by Placerville route – The elder was *Tom Frakes,* one of the three Frakes brothers who rescued me when I was caved on and buried in the gold diggings at Fort John Amador Co, Cal Sept 7, 1854 – 47 yrs ago – Haven't seen him since till now – Half a century almost . . . Fred W Clough had told him I was here, so he inquired and Doc Benton brought about this very interesting and happy meeting – I would not have known Tom – nearly 70 yrs old now, wrinkled, gray, dusty and dirty, but the dear old friendly, brotherly light beamed warm as ever from his blessed blue eyes and came home to my heart and soul as in those olden golden days. I got aboard with Doc again and we escorted the rig down to the open fields below or south of town where was a fine camping ground, and left them there for the night – God and everybody else bless old Tom as I do and will while life lasts. Bed at 11, tired but serenely happy.

Aug 10 . . . AM met Tom Frakes with Doc Benton at Arlington – jolly talk, etc – At 2:30 PM met Frakes with his son in their rig driving up street on their way out . . . Tom bade me a last goodbye and passed on – They are to camp out near Franktown . . . fill up on catfish breakfast then journey on to Reno for next nights rest, & would meet Major John H Dennis . . . Sent a page letter on evening train to Dennis . . . Tom looked happy and content, ready for any emergency . . . Tom was native of Pennsylvania – His brothers Jesse and John have both died since I saw them last – Tom married since then and got wife and 4 children, one having died – This son with him is named Thomas Edward Frakes, 38 yrs old . . . Home . . . Sutter Creek . . .

Aug 12 . . . Attended US Circuit Court & heard Judge Hawley read his decision, granting writ of injunction in favor of Central Pacific RR Co vs the various County Assessors, restraining them from assessing and collecting the big taxation raise of $20,000 a mile – Sent telegram of it to Tribune, also made a column synopsis of the long decision & sent that by mail . . . Jack Winters who stole the bullion from Selby's smelting works . . . was detected & arrested day before yesterday . . . Says he did it alone – gives up all the bullion and claims the $25,000 reward offered – also must go free & unprosecuted for his generosity.

Aug 17 . . . At 9 AM left on excursion train for Reno – the great Ringling Bros circus . . . there today . . . 8 coaches & 3 flats took 700 people from Va and here . . . The street parade at 11 AM biggest and grandest I ever saw . . . nearly 100 cages, numerous gents and ladies horseback, in Chariots etc – 7 bands of music, including a chime of huge bells and a steam Calliope – 8 camels, 21 elephants and many other wheeled representations – Passed through all the principal streets – people from wide surrounding country present crowding the sidewalks and afterwards the largest tent ever seen on this coast – Capable of seating 15,000 people – Had about 10,000 today – or more – Claimed that daily cost of concern comes up to $7,000 – Took lunch or dinner with my family at 1 PM and passed next few hours in pleasant home converse principally with Bessie & wife – left on return excursion train at 6:05 . . .

Sunday, Aug 18 . . . Rec'd 11 photos of Eureka Cyanide Works, and vicinity, Carson River . . .

Aug 19 . . . PM commenced on my write up of Comstock report for Gov't – Pencilled off 3 legal pages, Sutro Tunnel portion . . . Sunday's Salt Lake Tribune contained ¾ page sketch with illustration cut of Judge Charles Carroll Goodwin, chief editor of that paper – Headed: "The Record of a Great Editor," "Written Fitz-Mac for the Colorado Springs Gazette" . . .

Aug 22 . . . Morning train 3 hours late on account of big fire destroying 3,000 feet of snowsheds other side of Truckee . . . Evening met old

George Wedekind of Reno, discoverer of now famous Wedekind mine, also John Sparks the rich fine cattle stock breeder . . . Case before Judge Hawley about injunction on mine . . . The $280,000 worth of bullion stolen from the Selby Works . . . has all been recovered from the mud and water of the Bay near the Selby wharf . . . Jack Winters . . . was sentenced yesterday to 15 yrs at State Prison at Folsom – He asked to go to San Quentin, but wasn't given his choice . . .

Aug 23 . . . Wrote considerably on my job, getting in the Cyanide part of it . . . Wedekind case argued and submitted . . .

Aug 24 . . . The trial of Kelly vs Kelly before Dist Judge Mack yesterday & today creates great sensation – Hugh Kelly sues his brother Joe for half interest in grocery store which Joe has fired him out of – testifies that Joe alone committed the famous V&T RR robbery $3,700 dollars on train west of Carson 7 yrs ago in charge of paymaster George Mills to pay off the hands all along the road – Joe gave him part of the money and they started business with it later on – Judge put case out of court at noon today, saying Court couldnt divide stolen property between thieves . . .

Sunday, Sept 1 . . . Wrote much on the electric part of my Govt job . . .

Sept 5 . . . John L Considine, editor & proprietor of the Virginia *Evening Report* has leased the Va *Evening Chronicle,* from the McCarthy estate, taking possession today as editor, etc – putting George Warren of the Chronicle, (reporter, etc) in his place on the *Report* – quite a sensational change –

Sept 6 . . . About 2 PM came telegraphic news of the attempted assassination of President McKinley – Shot at Pan American Exposition, Buffalo, N.Y. by Fred Neilson a confessed Polish anarchist from Detroit. One shot in breast & other in stomach – Assassin immediately arrested, giving reason that he was simply doing his duty. At 6 PM bullet had been extracted from breast and he was resting easily, but considered fatally wounded. Great excitement, and prisoner threatened with lynching but held safely for investigation . . .

Sept 7 . . . News from President McKinley occupying all public attention – Still living at last accts . . . Sam's regular salary in the University is fixed at $1,000 a year.

Sept 9 . . . Worked figuring on my job – PM visited Supt Colcord at Mint & got items from him – President improving . . .

Sept 10 . . . President seems to be getting all right, but my landlady must be on a drunk – Had to take care of my own room, since Friday last –

Sept 11 . . . President able to take beef tea nutriment, & getting better fast – Emma Goldman and other Anarchists arrested . . .

Sept 14 . . . Telegrams & papers say President McKinley died at 2:15 AM . . . got letter from Leon M Hall accompanying three views of the Floriston Electric Power works, on Truckee river . . . Telegraph reports great excitement against the prisoners and all anarchists, in Buffalo, Chicago, etc – Flags at ½ mast all over Carson . . . Vice President Roosevelt took the oath of office as President this PM . . .

Sept 16 . . . Rec'd photo of Gold Hill from Reno this AM – Bird's eye view taken from Divide, looking down Gold Canyon – Very good picture – cost 2 bits – Billy Cann – State Fair at Reno commenced today . . .

Sept 17 . . . Special train each day for the Fair . . .

Sept 19 . . . Presidents funeral at his home, Canton Ohio, took place about noon today – Exercises held throughout the US about same time – I was in attendance at Opera House – Tastefully draped in mourning, flags, flowers – densely crowded – lasted over 2 hours – Many buildings draped – flags ½ mast, and all business houses, saloons etc closed . . .

Sunday, Sept 22 . . . The State Fair crowd . . . came on the PM local . . . The Elleford dramatic Co. came this morning for a weeks run . . . Got my big mining table completed . . .

Sept 23 . . . A 'bus came down from the Comstock this morning & got on regular run to & from the Fair grounds – It was marked Virginia and Gold Hill – one of the old time line, of Jake White's – Took off my hat in due reverence as it passed . . . Trial of Szolgosz, McKinleys assassin commenced today at Buffalo, N.Y. – Emma Goldman and other anarchists arrested are discharged . . .

Sept 25 . . . Szolgoscz trial ended yesterday – Murder 1st degree – I wrote till 3 oclock tonight . . .

Sept 27 . . . 3 PM I walked down to the race track & took in the Fair – Big attendance – many from Reno & the Comstock, & all town were there – streets deserted – Plenty of hoss racing, but I went to see the 50 mile bicycle race between a good team from Sacramento, and Carson team – Carson won by about 12 feet – Evening I was down town & visited Ozark Saloon awhile – Fine band of music, big fiddle, little fiddle, piano and cornet – Also a sort of hula hula, Little Egypt, one young woman dancer on stage – N.G. . . .

Sept 30 . . . Col Jack Haverly the famous minstrel & theatrical manager, died at Salt Lake yesterday PM, of heart trouble – about 70 yrs old, native of Pa – latterly been engaged in mining matters about that section –

Oct 1 . . . I did make out to fight my job to a finish – getting it safely packed and into the mail at 4:30 PM . . . together with photos of Gold Hill, Gould & Curry mill, Eureka Cyanide plant, Electrical Power House . . . etc . . . My Carson Lottery Syndicate won $1.25 . . .

Oct 2 through Dec 31 [AD much "about town" – Spot reporting, letters to Tonopah *Times-Bonanza,* correspondence with family, and regular check from Mary – Many personal meetings – Little detail – Of interest:]

Oct 4 . . . Wife forwarded me copy of Plymouth O. C. [Old Colony] Memorial of Sept 28, from which I clipped [clipping about cutting big Chestnut tree beside former Doten home] – Remembering and thinking of that old tree, as only *I can,* this feels to me like vandalism – "children continuously pelting it in the autumn to get the chestnuts" is such a damned old *Chestnut* that it should have become forgivingly endurable by this time – Oh! I would like to have been present, with potent ability to sing:

> "Woodman, spare that tree, touch not a single bough,
> In youth it sheltered me, and I'll protect it now."

Oct 7 . . . By evening train sent crisp letter to R R Crawford of Reno Ledger for the $13.50 he owes me . . .

Oct 8 . . . Joe Pete . . . who killed Will Dangberg near Gardnerville about a year ago, and last week killed his own father in law, was shot and assassinated by his own brother last night near Markleeville – so that ends the Joe Pete episode –

Oct 15 . . . Recd by todays mail letter from Hon Geo E Roberts, Director of the Mint . . . a US Treasury note . . . for $150.00 . . . Also rec'd letter from wife, with $5 greenback . . .

Oct 17 . . . Took AM train to Va – Most of passengers got off at

Mound House for Tonopah – Went to California Bank – got Check cashed for 150 – leaving $100 with Bank at present – Met lots of old friends . . .

Oct 21 . . . Negociated satisfactorily with old Joe Douglass, & was placed in full possession of my old time effects, also my last old time room, No 5 – Slept there tonight in my old bed, happier than for years . . .

Sunday, Oct 27 . . . Got all packed up – Mike Conlon helped me, but too late to get hauled to the depot . . .

Oct 28 – Big snow storm most of day . . . PM got Tom Dick to ship my goods to depot – $1.50 – got shipping receipt – $2.50 more, and also old pioneer picture I had at Andy Youngs saloon $5.00 and left for Carson by evening train . . .

Oct 29 . . . Szolgosz electrocuted at 7:20 AM today –

Oct 30 . . . My things, 1,150 pounds – 16 pieces arrived yesterday PM, and I got them all hauled this PM by Charley Bray to Harry Day's house . . . *All paid up in Carson* – Bed 11 – I weigh just 200 lbs today –

Nov 1 . . . PM wrote & sent page letter to Will W Booth, Tonopah Bonanza . . . on Nevada Political Senatorial Status, Jones and Newlands – in response to his of Oct 12th –

Nov 4 . . . PM was at my new place, Harry Day's – straightening up desk and things . . .

Nov 6 . . . Evening at Opera House – "A Female Drummer" played – Big Co & good house, at $1 admission – Grand conglomeration of nothing – Worst I ever saw – no plot, nothing but general fun and cutting up – Bed 12 –

Nov 11 . . . The Eureka Tailings Works on Carson River have been shut down for a month . . . Being removed to the Morgan Mill, 6 miles above – Have worked out all below . . .

Nov 14 . . . Daggett died in San Francisco day before yesterday of tumor of the liver – Great notices of his death in all the papers . . .

[A clip from the *San Francisco Chronicle* reports the large funeral, which included many old newspapermen – Sam Davis of the *Appeal* and Joseph Goodman, once associated with Daggett on the *Enterprise,* served as pallbearers – The *Journal* says Daggett left Ohio at age 16 to cross the plains alone, the Sioux thinking him a lunatic, until he joined up with a wagon train – In California he made a stake in the mines, went to San

Francisco and started a "literary journal" called *The Golden Era* and a newspaper, the *Mirror* – After the paper failed he came to the Comstock as associate editor of the *Enterprise* under Goodman and stayed on as manager until he went to Congress for the special session of 1879.]

Nov 15 . . . Evening at Livingstons hearing telegraphic report of big prize fight between Jeffries and Ruhlin at Mechanic's Pavilion, San Francisco – Ruhlin beaten in five rounds – fairly outclassed . . . Got letter from Wm Nelson of SL Tribune for me to write up Nevada for New Years issue – Bought me a new walking stick or cane today at Mrs Fox's store – counterpart of my old Mike Conlon cane, which is worn too short . . .

Sunday, Nov 17 . . . Met Albert Lackey at evening train leaving Gold Hill with his family to make their future home at Oakland California – Been Supt of the Overman mine 23 years . . .

Nov 20 . . . Fixed up and sent to the Overland Monthly my story of "Woods' Creek in Forty-Nine" . . .

Nov 23 . . . Recd letter from Will W Booth, Tonopah – Down on W L Butler – says he's no good . . .

Nov 28 . . . At 4 PM went to Thanksgiving dinner at Harry Day's – Only himself, May Williams & myself – Good turkey & all the fixings – Spent evening very pleasantly till 9 – Went to Arlington awhile – read papers and Bed at 11 . . .

Nov 30 . . . University second 11 came up from Reno by morning train for a bout with the Indian School football team at their ground . . . They were met and welcomed by the Indian Brass Band, 16 pieces, all dressed in Indian rig, yellow fringes down their pants, sort of plug hats with turkey feathers stuck in them, shawls or blankets, and all were painted Indian style – Comical and strange for the producers of such good music – Good part of Carson went out to see the game – And it was closely contested, coming out 0 to 0 . . . I won a terminal prize of $2.50 in the Beneficencia Publica Lottery . . .

Dec 2 . . . I attended arguments of attys in US Circuit Court before Judge Hawley in the Wedekind mine case . . . My good old friend and Pioneer Gotth Haist of Virginia, died there at 7:30 last evening, after a long illness – Nearly 80 yrs old . . .

Dec 3 – Stormy . . . The Wedekind case came to submission on points and arguments to the Judge, who will hold it under consideration for awhile . . . Would have attended the funeral of Gotth Haist today, but simply couldn't . . .

Dec 4 . . . Old Jim Orndorff, a Comstock old timer, and latterly of San Francisco saloon business, etc, came on morning train, & will go on to Tonopah tomorrow – Had not met him for about 15 or 20 years . . .

Dec 7 . . . James Heney took the pauper's oath today and was released from State Prison after being in there six years for robbing the US Mint, Carson City –

Dec 12 . . . About town – Met James Heney . . . at train this morning, bound for Virginia – Shook hands with him, etc . . .

Dec 13 . . . Got letter from Will W Booth, Tonopah, about mining Patent advertising –

Sunday, Dec 15 . . . Judge Wm Webster of Reno died in San Francisco yesterday PM . . .

Dec 16 – Clear & very pleasant – Fixed up neckties, and wore my Mexican Pearl scarf pin – Bed 10 –

Dec 17 . . . Commenced writing up State of Nevada . . .

Dec 20 . . . Worked extra hard today and completed my write up of Nevada for the SL Tribune and sent if off by evening mail – 10 pages . . . Evening I was up stairs [with] Andy Robert's family, and the girls sang and played me much fine music – and I sang them "Shoo-la-gra" and "Little Boy Blue," and played some on the mouth organ – Had real nice time . . .

Dec 24 – Put my Mexican Pearl on exhibition at Davis & Kirman's this PM – Evening wrote it up in the Appeal . . . calling attention to the exhibit . . .

> [Two clips, very much the same; one from the *News,* and this from the *Appeal:*] In Davis & Kirman's show window is exhibited a genuine Mexican pearl which was taken from the stomach of a shark, off the coast of Peru in September, 1849, by Alf Doten, on his way to California. The hungry monster was following the ship and was caught with a shark hook . . . Alf got possession of his stomach, expecting to find it loaded with human bones and things. But it did contain a lot of fish bones and abalone or pearl oyster shells, among which was the pearl. It is of extra size and rare beauty. He had it mounted in pure gold as a scarf pin at Virginia City twenty-five years ago and preserves it as a precious relic of the days of '49.

Dec 25 . . . Christmas Day . . . Got package from Bessie . . . inclosing four silk handkerchiefs, a box of candy, and $5 in coin – Bed at 10 –

Dec 26 . . . Wrote an item in the evening News regarding my Mexican Pearl – corroboratory, etc – My "Woods Creek in 49" story, returned to me from the Overland Monthly, declined – I gave it to Johnny D O'Brien, reporter for the SF Call who has been at home here in Carson on Christmas visit and left on return to SF this evening – with instructions to get it into the Call if he can . . .

Dec 27 . . . Met George Paynter this PM at the Arlington, son of old George R Paynter who used to edit the Enterprise . . . Old George is mining over in Tuolumne County, near Jamestown – Married again – 87 years old . . .

Sunday, Dec 29 . . . By mail today I received from Plymouth "The Crisis," a fine book by Winston Churchill . . . relating to Commencement of our Civil war and Abraham Lincoln's time – 7 fine illustrations – Guess its pretty good – Postage 18 cts – Nothing came with it to tell who its from – Bed at 10 –

Dec 31 – Clear and very pleasant – Evening "Devil's Auction" Troupe played at Opera House to a big audience – I paid a dollar to get in, and got the full worth of my money – Best show I have seen for many a day – Variety show, etc – After the show, met Fox of the trained dogs part of the show, with others – Was in on the New Years bell ringing and general blow out, and went home at 1:30, with a mince pie, a present from old Schneider, the baker.

BOOK NO.  78

Carson City
Jan 1, 1902 – Dec 31, 1902

Jan 1, 1902, through March 1 [AD joins friends on New Year's day, continues "Capitol Notes" & special reports to the *Journal,* writes to Kinzle & others about the Centennial, to Keyes & Shay about their several-times postponed suit, to Bessie, Mary, sister Cornelia and Senator Jones, gets his half-fare V&T pass renewed for a year, notes that Governor Jones of Nevada is seriously ill in San Francisco and that Carson has had another day of earthquakes, suffers a couple of brief illnesses himself and sees Gracie Plaisted & Dramatic Company in *Tina* and Palmer's Dramatic Company in *Trilby* – Of additional interest:]

Jan 1 . . . Was about town considerably, participating in the general observance of the New Year . . .

Jan 2 – Showers in early morning laid the dust admirably – Think street sprinkler no more needed – Cloudy all day – threatening – Received 6 extra copies of Salt Lake Tribune, New Years edition – 64 pages – My write up of Nevada occupies 2 full columns – Bed 10:30 – Col E D Boyle was thrown out of his buggy by 2 horse runaway team this AM on his way from Como or Palmyra to Dayton with W H McQuarrie – collar bone broken and severe concussion of the brain, blood gushing from ears and nostrils, & he in semi unconscious condition ever since – McQuarrie's neck was broken and he died immediately – Boyle has charge of tunnel operations at North Rapidan mine, Palmyra – actively working –

[These Nevada "write ups" consist of very general and statistical information about agriculture, railroads, tax revenues and cattle raising, often repeated from the previous year's account, but are mostly taken up by the same mining information he puts in the Mint reports, with the emphasis on the Comstock, though booming Tonopah gets some space.]

Sunday, Jan 5 . . . Col E D Boyle has recovered his senses and is coming out all right – The Carson Appeal copied nearly one of the columns from my Nevada write up . . .

Jan 10 . . . Evening met 2 Calkins Bros of the Pacific Coast Miner – R C Leeper constable at Reno was shot & badly wounded at 6 oclock last evening while attempting to arrest a negro named Bill Scott – They emptied their guns at each other – Leeper received 2 shots, one in the hand and the other in the abdomen – Scott got 2 balls, one in pit of the stomach, and the other near the navel – He didn't die, as expected and Leeper is reported as having a fighting chance to live . . .

Sunday, Jan 12 . . . Leeper & Scott . . . both improving . . . Calkins Bros went up to Gardnerville yesterday on business for their paper, the Pacific Coast Miner – They wish me to act as correspondent for it at $10 per month – 2 letters per month –

Jan 13 . . . Bill Scott was brought up from Reno last night on a special train & taken to the State Prison to keep the people from hanging him in case Leeper dies – Half a dozen officers and a doctor came with him – Brought on a cot – [Scott died in prison the next day.]

Jan 15 . . . Sam A Crescenzo, late Dist Atty of Lander Co died of pneumonia at Tonopah . . .

Jan 17 . . . Rec'd $18.12 from SL Tribune in payment of account to Jan 10 . . .

Jan 18 . . . At 1 PM meeting of State Central Committee held at Hofers office, next to the News – About 30 present from most parts of the State – Very lively meeting, best in last 6 years – George H Mills, Chairman & E D Vanderlieth Secretary – Filled vacancies in Committee – Increased Nye County three members, Oddie, Brougher and Warburton, and Washoe two, Cottrell & Smith – Adopted an address to Republicans in this State – 5,000 copies ordered printed & distributed . . .

Sunday, Jan 19 . . . Two pneumonia Tonopah patients at the Arlington, McKay and Beacham . . . Rose early and wrote a 3 page letter for Tonopah Bonanza . . . PM wrote & sent 5 page letter to SL Tribune . . .

Jan 20 . . . Wrote 7 page article for Calkins of the Pacific Coast Miner, about Nevada Reduction Works, Davis & Gignoux proprietors . . .

Jan 21 . . . My new landlady, Mrs Carter took possession yesterday, & took hold today – made up my room for first time –

Jan 25 . . . PM I got my old "Mary had a little lamb" lamp in trim . . . and lighted and burned it this evening again . . .

Jan 27 . . . Judge Healy about town drunk – Some naughty boys blacked his face and hair, making him look ridiculous – Tim Dempsey fell in a fit of vertigo at his home about 4 PM while standing looking out of a window . . .

Jan 29 . . . Tim Dempsey was up & around town this PM, crazy & out of his head . . . McKinley Day today – 1st commemoration of his birthday as a national holiday – Observed in public schools – flags displayed etc –

Jan 30 . . . Met "Doc" John O'Toole this evening at Arlington – Old time friend on Comstock – Figured strongly at Tonopah – had father & mother there with him – He nearly died of pneumonia – All 3 went to Virginia a few days ago, where both died of pneumonia contracted at Tonopah – He feels naturally very blue, but will go back [to] Tonopah in a day or two –

Jan 31 . . . Tim Dempsey is slowly recovering from his attack of delirium tremens but has to keep his bed as yet, with watchers –

Feb 4 . . . About town as usual – Tim Dempsey was able to appear on the street a short time . . . Electric light introduced into hallway of my lodging house & on sidewalk for first time tonight –

Feb 7 . . . Evening I sent a telegram, 150 words to Tribune on new Tonopah excitement – Met Matt Callahan & affiliated . . .

[The "Tonopah excitement" may actually refer to nearby Sodaville. As the *News* of the 10th put it, with prospectors fanning out in all directions the "rich strikes and new discoveries out Tonopah way are being announced so fast these days that they are difficult to keep track of," with each new site immediately claiming it would soon rival Tonopah itself.]

Sunday, Feb 9 – Variable but pleasant – no rain – Judge T W *Healy*, committed suicide probably early this morning at Harry Day's brick house, where he has roomed for the last two years, by shooting his head from temple to temple with a 38 caliber bulldog revolver – Did it lying on the bed with his clothes and boots all on – Will found on table near by – Been dissipating drunk the last 3 or 4 weeks – lived alone & like a hog – apart from his fellow men – Inquest said he was 64 years old – but he was 74 sure – and native of Ireland – Was a Pacific Coast Pioneer, of 1849 – Been in this State about 40 years, and in early days became prominent politician, literary man etc, but latterly gone to the dogs with drink, etc – Col E D Boyle reported dead from pneumonia at Dayton this PM about 4 oclock – Think about 60 yrs old & native of Ireland – Send 300 words telegram on Healy to Tribune & also to SF Chronicle . . .

Feb 11 – AM furious wind and dust brought out the street sprinkler – At 2 PM funeral of Judge Healy, from Kitzmeyer's undertaking shop – About a dozen women and 3 dozen men present – Rev Mr Dodge officiated and had choir of 2 women & 1 man and John Meder organist – Commenced raining but ½ doz carriages got out to funeral, which was paid for by private subscription, public – very good – Healy was a Catholic, but they wouldnt bury him or have anything to do with him because he suicided – By evening train passed Col E D Boyles remains bound for San Francisco, from Dayton, accompanied by his son Emmett – Boyle was a Mason and a Knight Templar, but his wife being a strong Catholic, persuaded him in his dying moments to be baptized into the Catholic Church, so the Masons had to repudiate *him* . . . Mrs E D Boyle could not go with her husbands remains to San Francisco, because she is very ill with pleurisy at Dayton – Riverside flouring mill burned last night – $40,000 loss – Smallpox has closed the schools of Reno – ½ doz cases or more since Saturday – University quarantined, etc –

Sunday, Feb 16 . . . My old sporting friend on the Comstock, Scotty Cone, who married Dutch Kate long ago and she died, and who has been living in Reno for several years past, was found lying on a bench in the Riverside park early yesterday morning, unconscious – He was taken to the Hospital and died there at 3:40 this morning – He was about 68 years old and considerably run down at the heel as a sport – ready & willing to die – His real full name was Winfield Scott Cone –

Feb 21 . . . Wildey Lodge No 1, I.O.O.F., Gold Hill, the oldest lodge in Storey county is to be consolidated with Virginia Lodge No 3, making only one lodge in Storey County – There used to be four . . . Virginia Lodge now carries the number, *one,* and all the ancient glory connected therewith –

Feb 24 . . . The Reno public schools reopened this morning – All the pupils were compelled to show that [they] had been successfully vaccinated within the past five years –

Feb 25 – Heaviest storm of the entire winter, commenced raining about 9 AM and kept at it steadily & good all day & into evening . . . news from Cal are big rains . . . Snowing heavily when I went to bed at 11 –

Feb 26 – Big snowstorm all day . . . fully 8 inches of snow on the streets . . .

Feb 27 – Snowstorming all day – The local train from Virginia got blockaded about American Flat . . . Deluging rains & snows in California, and the old Sacramento overflowing its banks and whole Country, like as in old times, 50 years ago . . .

Feb 28 . . . Storm appears to be broken – Mails on time . . .

March 1 . . . Started in snowing about noon and kept at it steadily all the PM and evening . . .

Sunday, March 2 . . . Clouded up again toward evening, with more snow – The morning local train from Va didnt get through at all – Regular mail train from Reno was over an hour behind time . . . No western connection . . . week ago today, the 4 inch Davis Calyx drill being put down in the east wall of the Comstock, Brunswick Lode, got "fitchered" in the hole at 470 feet depth & hasnt been able to run since – Davis the inventor was sent for at San Francisco & came, but couldn't do anything with it as yet . . .

March 3 . . . Took my Will Booth letter to train this morning, forgot about it and brought it back in my pocket, same as I have done before – dammit – PM worked at my Day room some . . . Paid my rent today for last month $4 –

March 4 . . . PM fixed key to Day room, & gave up old one to Dr Huffaker – Harry Days ticket . . . in our lottery syndicate won $12.50 . . .

March 8 . . . The Democratic and Silver Party Central Committees held meetings at Reno today which were very fully attended . . . business of merely routine character was transacted in Joint assembly of Committees . . .

March 11 . . . Old Joe Budd, veteran of the Civil war, aged 73, died in a barbers chair this PM, while having his hair and shaggy old beard slicked & trimmed up – He used to be a prominent stage driver over the Placerville route in the early days & was an old resident of Carson, but leaving no relatives here – He had received his pension money $12 per month yesterday. The barber noticed that Uncle Joe [was] becoming very quiet and supposed he had dropped off to sleep as usual under his soothing manipulations, but when he tried to wake him up for his pay he found he had passed out into the mythical beyond. What a pleasant, agreeable death – comfortable, easy and serene, in a barbers chair . . .

> [Clip, Virginia *Report*, March 12:] Alf Doten, in his weekly letter to the Tonopah Bonanza, pronounces the Brunswick lode drilling project a "dead failure." Alf's knowledge of drills is extremely limited, but as a bore, he is at the head of his class.

March 18 . . . Tim Dempsey went down to Reno Sunday to be a barkeeper in a new saloon – Met old George Wedekind of Reno today. He is up with his sons, and Sparks and an army of lawyers on the suit of Wedekind vs Bell, et al before the Supreme Court . . . Worked at Day room on desk – The Odd Fellows had a grand time last night at Virginia consolidating Va & Gold Hill Lodges into one . . .

March 20 . . . Rec'd letter from Wm Nelson of the Tribune, asking me to furnish him with list of names of prominent individuals & their wives in this State – The good and devoted wife of Col E D Boyle died at Virginia at residence of Col F C Lord about 11 AM yesterday – She never recovered from the shock of his recent accidental death . . .

March 21 . . . Morning wrote & sent 2 page communication to Va Chronicle based upon my Thos J Linton, RI, correspondence on Irrigation – solve the Comstock drainage problem, etc – Also put similar one in this evenings News . . .

> [The piece in the *News* reports on some correspondence between AD and Linton, of Providence, who makes grandiose claims for an "irrigating machine" with which he "can lift water 3000 feet as easily as I can lift it one foot." – AD comments that, though Linton fails to name his source of power, whether compressed air, electricity, "or just the familiar 'hot air,' which propels so many other great schemes for Nevada," the thing might be feasible, and could easily supply Tonopah with all the water it needs, make the arid desert bloom, and drain the troublesome deep levels of the Comstock – "He settles the irrigation and all other water questions without a doubt—also perpetual motion and the attraction of gravity."]

March 22 . . . Attended the Supreme Court on the Wedekind and Bell mine case argument short time this PM. Been arguing since last Tuesday, & finished today, & taken under advisement – Great array of legal talent on both sides – All went home tonight . . .

[The *News* indicates the suit came about because Wedekind felt he could follow the lead of the ore vein west under the property of the Conroy ranch, and preferred to go to court rather than buy the property for $4,000 – One Bell then bought the property for $6,000, sank his own shaft to tap the vein, and everyone went to court – Bell won the first case and Wedekind the appeal, and thus to the supreme court.]

Sunday, March 23 . . . Wrote a 2 page Comm & sent to SF Chronicle, on the Wedekind Case . . . Evening met Jim Orndorff just back from Tonopah, at the Arlington – Had long & very pleasant chat together about old times on the old Comstock . . .

March 24 . . . Was with my old friend Jim Orndorff considerably . . .

March 25 . . . Was with Jim Orndorff somewhat and saw him off on the evening train for San Francisco . . .

March 28 . . . Worked at my Day room – Mrs Guy Thorpe & daughter arrived today – Mrs T & husband own ⅚ of the Day house, which has been sold to Dr Huffaker . . . So I am getting my things ready to move out, and the Dr started in today trimming trees and getting ready to occupy the premises . . .

April 3 . . . Rose early & wrote & sent 3 page letter to Tonopah Bonanza – No 10 – Rest of day wrote & sent 5 page letter to SL Tribune – Johnny T Jones was let out of State Prison this AM having completed his term of sentence . . . He took the paupers oath this morning which knocked out the fine . . . Got friendly letter today from Tim Dempsey, Reno, where he is barkeep in a big fine saloon & doing well – George Senf – "Graphy" – the old boss Comstock telegraph operator when I got married, & for years the Manager of the Western Union Telegraph office at Virginia, died in San Francisco Tuesday last . . .

April 5 . . . A big traction motor for Fred Dangberg of Carson valley arrived, last evening from San Francisco on local train – was unloaded and straightened out today, and at 5 PM left for its Gardnerville destination, by its own volition – It weighs 33,800 pounds – Will run 20 fourteen inch plows in gang, and plow 40 acres per day – It created quite a sensation passing through the streets . . .

April 10 . . . A locomobile from Reno, the first, belonging to O J Smith, or in his charge came to Carson this PM, via Virginia – Created quite a sensation, being first ever seen here, at Va, or in Reno. Punctured a tire and had to lay up in front of Raycroft's stable for repairs – Horseless carriage puts up at a horse stable . . . sent sharp little note to R R Crawford asking for the $13.50 he owes me for journalistic services at last Legislature – over a year ago – Think I will drop him hereafter as no good . . .

April 14 – Clear & pleasant – Andy Robert commenced his new concrete sidewalk – About noon, met Franklin Leonard, Prest Sutro Tunnel Co & daughter on street, also his Attorney, Chas C Boynton, San Francisco – Had case in Circuit Court, against Alf Chartz, on attorney's fees, between them & Occidental M & M Co – got me to make report of it in evening News and paid me $10 for it – I also sent it to the SF Chronicle – comes up again next Monday – Evening Kickapoo vaudeville and medicine show at Opera House – free – full – Bed 11 –

April 15 . . . Accomplished my removal from the Day residence, sold to Dr Huffaker at noon today – Got the whole lot, 1150 pounds, big desk, secretary and all hauled and delivered at my room in the Stone lodging house – Worked hard all the PM till 6 – putting up shelving, and fixing up . . . Dismantling the Mexican mill, and cleanup of the millsite commenced yesterday at Empire – Only 2 more of the old regular Comstock ore mills remain – the Brunswick and the Morgan – Mexican mill owned by J P Jones, et al . . .

April 17 . . . Recd brief note from wife with $5 inclosed – Recd from George E Roberts . . . copy of his annual report of Production of Gold and Silver in the United States for 1900. In it is my Comstock report . . . 14 pages and 7 cuts: Gold Hill – Sutro Tunnel Mill – Gould & Curry Mill – Eureka Cyanide Plant – Cyanide, Zinc & Precipitating Dept – Electric Power House, Truckee River – Interior View of Power House – I have the only cuts in the book . . .

April 19 . . . Andy Robert finished his new concrete sidewalk today – I wrote & sent friendly letter to Tim Dempsey, Reno – one to C D Van Duzer, Golconda, to send me copy of his 1st issue of his Nevada Miner, February . . . Evening attended entertainment of the Kickapoo Medicine Co at Opera House with Andy Robert – 2 bits admission – Big house – Gave best showing of moving pictures, etc I ever saw by far – Whole show fully 3 hours . . .

April 21 . . . Met with Franklin Leonard, and his atty, Boynton – on same court business as last Monday – Also Atty Huffaker, Frank M – Worked lots in various directions today but accomplished nothing satisfactory – Got letter from Will Booth, saying would send me some money . . .

April 22 through May 5 [AD reports heavy frosts, works at arranging his crowded room, writes letters to *Bonanza, Tribune, San Francisco Chronicle* and wife, receives $15 from wife & $13.90 for monthly "string" from *Tribune.*]

May 6 . . . The new, or reorganized band, with Prof Hendricks as leader was out on the street for the first time this evening in open air concert – Besides the old regular musicians there were over half new and many very young men in short pants and stockings – 38 pieces in all – But they played several good pieces well in front of the Federal building, Postoffice, giving a good harmonious volume of sound –

May 7 . . . The Reno Journal tells of the death of Col Frank F Osbiston by a Denver Col telegram – died recently in Australia – no particulars –

[The *Journal* carries a short note – Osbiston, a "pioneer of Reno," came there as "confidential agent" for the Bank of California after being superintendent of the Savage mine on the Comstock – A clip from the *San Francisco Chronicle* says Osbiston was born in 1834, was secretary and assistant superintendent of the Yellow Jacket, then agent for the bank under Ralston and Sharp, and finally superintendent of the Savage under Mackay and Fair.]

Sunday, May 11 . . . Two young girls aged 15 and 19, daughters of Vonderhyde the harness maker were drowned in Carson river about noon today 4 or 5 miles from town – boating on river with their brother & another young man – boat got caught in current and went over a dam – the boys escaped but the girls did not – Bodies not recovered at dark tonight . . .

May 12 . . . Havent recovered the bodies of the Vonderhyde sisters yet – Their mother was confined with a baby last night . . .

May 13 . . . Jim Butler of Tonopah notoriety arrived from Reno on the PM local & was here tonight at Arlington – met him – Wrote 2 page letter to Tribune about the Vonderhyde drowning . . . Also wrote & sent page letter to T J Osborne, Pioche, about prominent men of Nevada –

May 14 . . . The body of Miss Lola Vonderhyde, aged 20 . . . was recovered today from Carson river, about a mile from where the accident happened – Many people with boats and grappling hooks dragging the river above the Mexican dam – Jim Butler with his wife left for Tonopah this morning . . .

May 15 . . . I wrote & sent page letters to George Watt, Sheriff of Lander County, E A Skillman, Editor Eureka Sentinel, J J Hill, Recorder Humboldt Co, W W Booker editor Elko Independent, and J M Lynch editor White Pine News, all to secure list of most prominent men of Nevada . . .

May 16 . . . Received $10 greenback through Trenmor Coffin from Will W Booth of the Tonopah Bonanza this morning, Coffin coming direct from there on morning train . . .

May 19 . . . Jewett Adams gave me an item this morning which he clipped from a Virginia City paper many years ago reading thus: "Bully for Alf Doten. His better 'alf has given him another little "Alf" and he is happy. He is continually "Doten" on the little rascal, and has already had a case set up to put him at work at the trade in a few weeks. Long may old Alf and young Alf live to grace the Comstock." I put the item in a letter to wife . . .

May 20 . . . Heavy frost last night . . . killed lots of garden truck, and probably much of the fruit blossoms . . . Play of "A Husband on a Salary" at Opera House tonight was not pretty well attended . . .

May 21 . . . Recd letter from J M Lynch, editor White Pine News, inclosing poll lists marked as I desired . . . Done 1st rate, promptly and good – Good man – W S Beard, Deputy Assessor of Washoe sent me a printed tax list, totally unmarked, and of no use . . . Cuba raised her flag as a free republic among the nations yesterday . . .

May 24 . . . The body of Ada Vonderhyde recovered this forenoon near the Mexican dam – 2 miles below where the accident occurred – Evening I sent telegram of it 90 words to SL Tribune . . .

May 26 . . . Recd Copy of No 1 of Goodwins Weekly . . . I attended Episcopal church ceremonies at funeral of the Vonderhyde sisters, Lola and Ada at 2 PM – church perfectly crowded – Ceremonies after the usual business style of the church, with no extra remarks by preacher Darnielle – 60 carriages in procession including hearse, etc –

[A clip from the *Appeal* of May 20 gives a short notice of the new twelve-page publication, "filled with the sound writings" of "Judge" Charles C Goodwin, who had retired from the *Salt Lake Tribune*.]

May 29 . . . Wrote & sent 6 page letter to Tribune – none to Bonanza, as my last one was not published . . .

May 31 . . . Chas L Calkins editor of *Pacific Coast Miner* for whom I wrote article on Nevada Reduction works Jan 20th died at Lovelock last Tuesday . . .

June 2 . . . Met Bob Gordon from Tonopah yesterday & today & saw him off on the evening train for his old home Cincinnati Ohio which hasnt seen since he left there in 1865 – Has made $50,000 in Tonopah – Only going on a visit to his father, whom he hasnt seen for 27 years – short visit he says – He got me to take dinner with him, and gave me $20 gold piece – Recd letter from wife with $15 . . .

June 3 . . . Peace declared in London between the British and the Boers day before yesterday . . . Boers got about all they asked except their independence . . .

June 4 . . . By evening mail sent letters to T J Osborne, Pioche, Nev to hurry up his returns or quit – Also to George Watt, Sheriff of Lander to same effect – Also sent letter to same effect to Sheriff Wm McCormick of Douglas this AM . . .

June 7 . . . I concentrated all my energies today on a letter to George E Roberts, Supt of the Mint at Washington – 2 page letter – Commenting on his recent visit to this coast on acct of $30,000 shortage in San Francisco mint, also commenting on his recently published "Production of the Precious Metals . . ." in which I occupy prominent place with my Comstock report, and asking a chance to do it again for $150 . . .

Sunday, June 8 . . . Alfred employed as Clerk at Flanigan warehouse, bookkeeping etc – doing well . . .

June 10 . . . Wrote letter to Sheriff Quirk of Va to send me lists of registered voters of last election, and I would mark them & not depend on him any longer . . .

June 11 . . . PM I got *Lennie Lichtenberg* of Gold Hill to help me mark Storey County returns all right – He is down here on the Masonic Grand Lodge business . . .

June 12 . . . Recd brief note from Will W Booth Tonopah Bonanza saying: "Friend Alf I will make a remittance to you tomorrow or next day. Dont send any more letters for a while. I havent got room. I will get out twice a week before long." . . . US Weather Observer Smith showed me a letter from Alfred today. He has taken charge of the weather Station at the University, and asks Smith's assistance in some things –

Sunday, June 15 . . . Got letter from wife with $5 inclosed – She also sent me a copy of the Old Colony Memorial of June 7th which had the following extremely interesting items:

[Clips report the quiet marriage of Elizabeth "Lizzie" Doten and her friend Mr Z Adams Willard, "a wealthy and highly respected citizen of Brookline," and the ninetieth birthday of Major Samuel Holmes Doten, to whom the townsfolk sent many tokens of their esteem, and for which his brother, Captain C C Doten, "hoisted his flag."]

Sent letter to wife this evening expressing my ideal feelings in this very important matter in our family history –

June 18 . . . Met Tom Tucker, manager at Incline, Lake Tahoe & he told me Sam & party from University . . . had been at Incline for about a week, boating, fishing and having big time . . . Report of the Precious Metal Product of the U.S. came yesterday, so today I got my quota and sent them . . . to wife, Charlie, Leon Hall, Alex McCone, Franklin Leonard . . .

June 19 . . . Recd from Tribune statement of account for May, with check in payment, $12.94 –

June 23 . . . Evening at Opera House – Russell's Players, a traveling Comedy Co, about a dozen strong . . . Play was "Michael Stroghoff," a Russian blood & thunder – They did it up brown . . .

June 25 . . . Finally and fully completed my long and perplexing job . . . of making a list of the *Most Prominent Leading Representative* Citizens of Nevada, taking in every one of the 14 counties & their various precincts – Makes 57 pages, 1,670 names – Wrote a five page letter, explanatory etc, to Col Wm Nelson managing editor of the Tribune, making 62 pages in all and shipped the whole off by evening mail . . . I feel relieved . . .

June 26 . . . Today was to have been Coronation of King Edward of England, but he has just had operation performed for Appendicitis and is most probably dead – Anyhow the coronation is indefinitely postponed – Bed 11 –

June 28 . . . Nice little banquet this evening at Arlington to Jas Yerington by his eastern capitalist friends – Brass & string band and everything high toned . . .

Sunday, June 29 . . . Completed & sent 2 full page letter to Brother Sam . . . The Yellow Jacket tunnel of the V&T railroad burned out today from one end to the other – 450 feet long – cutting off the passage of all trains – Have to transfer now from Va to Gold Hill, where the Express and all other trains have to stop – Shallow tunnel and is said to have caved – 2nd tunnel from Gold Hill toward Virginia.

June 30 . . . Completed & sent 3 page letter to Sister Lizzie – Mrs Z Adams Willard, 25 Regent Circle, Brookline, Massachusetts . . .

July 1 . . . Wrote and sent 2 page letter to Sister Eunice . . .

July 2 . . . 100 or more went from Carson to the Reno Carnival opening today . . .

July 3 . . . Took evening train for Reno – 7 cars, crowded – Arr at 6:15 – streets crowded, and Carnival in full progress – Blaze of electric lights, fine decorations – music and hell a poppin everywhere – Reported myself at home and found only Sam there – rest out on the streets – I witnessed the grand procession with the Queen *Carmelita Avanzeno* proceeding through principal streets to the Coronation, which took place across the river, next to the public park, opposite the Riverside Hotel – I didn't attend but 5 or 10 thousand did – Was about town, mingling with old acquaintances, etc – Home at 10:30 & to bed in wifes room & bed, but still saw only Sam – Rest all abed . . .

July 4 . . . Big Reno 4th of July parade at 11:30 – 40 floats representing social & business interests etc, including Queen Carmelita and staff, 5 bands of music – Finest parade ever in Nevada . . . The usual ceremonies took place at the Park . . . oration by Sam Platt . . . Joe Ryan, Supt of Con Va mine was Chief Marshal . . . Was well treated all day and deliberately *didnt spend one cent* – First Fourth I ever passed on the Pacific coast that I did not spend liberally – did this today for a novelty although I had $23.50 in my pocket – Met old Jim Orndorff and pretty much all the old sports I ever knew and Tim Dempsey and everybody else . . . Big rain storm about 6 PM spoiled the bicycle parade . . . also the big ball at the park grounds, where Gov Sadler was to open the dance with the Queen – But he was too *drunk* for that . . .

July 5 . . . AM down town . . . PM I visited the Carnival grounds . . . Evening at 8 grand bicycle parade – 70 bikers, in costume, masks, etc, wheels got up in fine style – 6 big bike floats – 2 brass bands – Queen in grand carriage – Two automobiles, first I ever saw – They went to Carnival grounds to big postponed ball – A rather light Mardi Gras procession with King Rex and a brass band, 4 floats & few followers . . .

as a wind up – Many merry maskers . . . This AM while chatting with a friend in front of the Palace Hotel, by the boot black stand, some sly rogue pinned a programme to his coat tail, and to mine a big placard which said in big letters "A Husband on a Salary." We detected and got rid of them directly –

Sunday, July 6 . . . Breakfast at 10 – wife, Alfred, Goodwin, Sam & I – Sam was fishing up the river yesterday and caught about a dozen small rainbow trout so we had them for breakfast, I being accorded the majority of the fish – delicious – At 11:30 I took leave of my family, to go back to Carson . . . James Senseney, a friend of Sam's, about his age has rented my old room since early last November at $7 per month – Cruised about town till regular time to leave on local train 1:20 PM . . . Evening about town . . . Found Tim Dempsey, barkeeping at the Oberon saloon, owned by Charles Dreyer – One of finest saloons in town –

July 7 through 13 [AD rests himself "considerably," writes letters, including a brief one to his wife, and a communication to the *Tribune,* notes that trains are running through the Yellow Jacket Tunnel again, and receives a gift of trout from Sam.]

July 14 . . . The little carnival parade this evening in Carson, was the finest kind of a burlesque on the Reno Carnival – The little tot of a queen only 4 yrs old kissed her hand right & left to the passing applause, & her car was followed by about a dozen more stalwart young maids of honor – 8 or 10 bicycle floats, etc – Created much general amusement –

July 16 . . . Replied to a letter from Dr D A Sykes, Salt Lake City, asking information about Tonopah – Told him the population is 2,500 – Miners employed, 400 – number of physicians, 10 – Water to get in from Twin river, 65 miles south, in three or four months – Present water supply from outside springs & wells – $3 per barrel . . . Evening I got my old banjo strung up all right and played some old time tunes on it – Haven't used the old banjo . . . since I left it in Joe Douglass clutches at Va . . .

July 21 . . . My 73d birthday – Passed as usual – John W Mackay died in London Saturday PM . . . 71 yrs old – 2 years younger than I – Bed at 11 –

July 22 . . . All the daily papers from Cal & Salt Lake full of pictorials on death of John W Mackay – Recd letter from wife with $15 . . .

July 23 . . . Recd letter from Geo E Roberts, Director of the Mint, telling me to report Comstock . . . also the Tonopah mines – Compensation $150 as before – shall do it –

July 24 . . . Wrote 5 page letter to Tribune all about *The Deceased Millionaire* John W Mackay . . .

July 25 . . . Evening was at Livingston's Criterion saloon with rest of town getting returns from the great championship fight between Jeffries & Fitzsimmons – Fitz got knocked out in the eighth round . . . retires from the ring forever . . .

July 26 . . . Primary election of Silver Party for delegates to State Convention held today – 199 votes cast . . .

July 28 . . . Rec'd good long nice letter from sister Lizzie, explanatory of her new position in life, marriage, etc . . .

July 29 . . . PM I attended funeral ceremonies of Frank Hall, my oldest Carson friend, and who so prominently figured in my write up history of Carson City in the Nevada Magazine couple of years ago – He died peaceably & happily at home, well cared for by his married daughter, Mrs Bowman . . . Died principally of old age, having no disease, but just tired and quit, past 80 yrs of age . . . but I think from what I know of his habits that if he had been allowed 2 or 3 good drinks of whisky per day he would have lived longer – wouldn't have been so *tired* . . .

July 30 . . . PM I wrote on a John Mackay letter for the SL Tribune – Bed at 11 –

July 31 . . . Completed my John Mackay letter of stories – 8 pages and sent it this evening – One of the best letters I ever wrote . . .

Aug 4 . . . Had to break that $20 that Bob Gordon gave me to square up lodging, grub & other bills – Used most of it doing so – Held it long time, straining the point . . .

Aug 7 . . . The Supreme Court of California has decided all Reno marriages of divorced parties from California legal – In other words an absolute divorce in Cal is all right, and parties at liberty to marry again . . . without waiting a year . . .

Aug 9 . . . Voted at the Rep primaries for 11 delegates to State Convention – Only one ticket . . .

Sunday, Aug 10 . . . Wrote letters to J R Ryan, Supt Con Va, and G

McM Ross Supt Ophir, to send me a report of Con Va & Ophir 1901 – Also to J W O'Donahue, Secy Con Va, to same effect – Also wrote letter to Leon Goldstein . . . SF for copy of mining Stock Record of Jan 1 . . . Met Will W Booth at the Arlington and he paid me $20 . . .

Aug 16 . . . Worked on information as usual . . . This evening I recd copy of Tonopah Miner of Aug 15 . . .

Aug 17 . . . Morning wrote & sent . . . letters to J E Gignoux . . . of the Nevada Reduction Works (old Rock Point Mill) Dayton and to Franklin Leonard, Supt Sutro Tunnel Co . . .

Aug 20 . . . PM worked in State Library wrestling with file of the Virginia Evening Report for Comstock product items . . .

Sunday, Aug 24 . . . Took the 10 AM local train for Reno . . . Went directly home – Bessie had left Saturday morning . . . so I was much disappointed . . . wife gave me a postal order for $15, she was about to send me – Alfred off on an excursion to Lake Tahoe – Sam and Goodwin at home – I dined with them, and left at 1:20 PM on return to Carson – May Williams, Harry Day's woman on board, returning from a 10 days visit to friends in Reno – Chatted with her all the way . . .

Aug 26 . . . State Controllers office etc, on information – The State Conventions of the Silver Party & Democrats commenced today in Reno for nomination of Gov & other State officers, Congressman, etc . . . great interest taken – fusion or no fusion or confusion . . . tomorrow comes the circus – two ringed circus, you bet . . .

Aug 27 . . . Rec'd from Leon M Hall copy of magazine entitled The Journal of *Electric Power* and *Gas* . . . Handsomely illustrated article on Comstock electrical works by himself – Just what I wanted . . .

Aug 28 . . . The big joint convention of the Democracy & Silver Party at Reno today resulted Governor Sparks, Lem Allen Lieut Gov . . . Fused and nominated full ticket –

Sunday, Aug 31 . . . Evening sent page letter to Wm McClure Gotwaldt, of the Reno Journal objecting to his criticism of my recent Comstock report . . .

[The offending clipping, from the *Journal* of Aug 28, credits the statistical part of the Mint report to R K Colcord, and notes an apparent error in the figures – The piece concludes:] The report contains a rehash of the history of the Comstock lode, which includes a fine picture of the interior and exterior of the Best & Belcher mill and other illustrations prepared by Alf Doten.

Sept 3 . . . Met Johnny O'Brien, reporter on the SF Call and raked him down on my "Woods Creek in Forty-Nine" story I gave him to get into the Call – but he never did and never replied to three letters . . . got letter response from the Sutro Tunnel – also from T L Oddie, Genl Manager Tonopah M Co – 2 pages – very unsatisfactory . . .

[Clip, Reno *Journal:*] Some days ago The Journal wrote, with a pair of scissors, a six line squib about Mr. Alf Doten's review of the history of the Comstock lode. The item in question was really an unkind and undeserved criticism of Mr. Doten's work, as the writer was later convinced upon perusing it.

This is the fifth time that the government has employed Mr. Doten to write up the great lode. The first time was in 1887. This latest work brings the history of the Comstock right up to date, including tabular statements.

The new features of the latest report are principally the change from steam to electricity, the cyanide plants and the proposed extension of the Sutro tunnel. The work is a literary gem as well as an accurate historical resume and The Journal regrets having treated it so lightly in the previous criticism.

Sept 5 . . . Sent another letter to Oddie . . .

Sunday, Sept 7 . . . All day today I worked strongly, completing two letters to be sent to the Tribune next week . . . "Nevada State Doings," and . . . "Some of the Old Comstock Millionaires" . . .

Sept 11 . . . Recd long type written letter from T L Oddie, with a photo of the Town & mines of Tonopah . . . John Sparks big Barbecue today near Reno –

Sept 13 . . . The Rep Convention got through at Reno today . . .

Sunday, Sept 14 . . . Got a fine photo of James L Butler the discoverer of Tonopah from T L Oddie . . .

Sept 16 . . . Took morning train to Virginia City – Met several of the old boys etc – Went after information, etc, from Kinkead et al & accomplished all I went for and came back on evening train . . . Letter . . . from Oddie . . . inclosing *corrected* bullion returns – Total output to July 1, 1902, $1,470,405.44 . . .

Sept 19 . . . Announced myself for the Assembly in evening News – First time in my life I ever ran for office – Evening mass meeting, Republican, at Court House . . .

[Clip from the *Appeal,* Sept 20:] Alf Doten has his political card in another column, which states that he is a candidate for Assemblyman, subject to the decision of the Republican convention.

Alf Doten has probably attended as many sessions of the Legislature of Nevada as any man in the State. He has always occupied the reporter's seat, and as a consequence knows as much parliamentary law as any man that could be sent. If the Republicans are looking for men that know the legislative business from A to Z, he is the man to select.

Sept 22 . . . Demo-Silver Ormbsy County Convention held today – Couldnt fuse – Democracy pulled out and the Silver party went on to nominate a ticket . . .

Sept 23 . . . Republican County convention today – I attended – got left on nomination for the Assembly – didn't get it – Harry Day tells me that his woman, May Williams was married in Reno last Saturday to George Kellar, section boss on the V&T RR . . .

Sept 24 . . . I completed my Comstock report, fully this AM – PM commenced on Tonopah . . .

Sept 25 . . . Rose at 4 and put in a long hard steady days work on Tonopah – Finished it by 4 PM and shipped both it and the Comstock report by evening mail . . . 20 pages Comstock with 7 photos – 10 pages Tonopah & 2 photos, one of the town, & other of J L Butler . . .

Sept 26 through Oct 2 [Frosty mornings – AD sends additional Tono-pah material to Roberts of the Mint, gets after O'Brien of the *San Francisco Call* again about his "Woods' Creek" article, writes his wife & his daughter Bessie, gets $15 from his wife and makes a start on his annual hay fever.]

Oct 3 . . . Wrote 2 page for the Evening News, correcting Van Duzer in the last number of his Nevada Miner, issued on the 15th – my article headed *Erratic Statements – Tonopah as Compared With the Comstock* . . . made over half a column . . .

Oct 8 . . . Evening grand rally of Fusionists . . . Gov, Sparks; Lieut Gov, Lem Allen, etc – Town band – Big bonfires on street . . . H F Bartine principal speaker . . . Afterward at Arlington . . .

Oct 9 . . . Evening Beaty Bros moving picture show at Opera House – big double horn phonograph or gramophone, played several good pieces – pictures [illegible] assassination of McKinley, electrocution of his assassin – McKinley's funeral – Galveston Cyclone, Mt Pelee in erup-

tion, and a host of other pictures, humorous, pathetic & otherwise . . .
Crowded house . . .

Oct 11 . . . Sent short letter to Tribune Distribution Company, Salt
Lake about their plan to distribute $27,000 on guessing the vote of Utah,
Idaho & Wyoming at coming election – Big thing . . .

Sunday, Oct 12 . . . Met John Sparks this evening – just back from an
electioneering trip up the valley – We had pleasant chat together . . .

Oct 14 . . . Sam Baker, my old Pacific Coast Pioneer friend died at
the Ormsby Co Hospital – the Poor Farm – this morning at 5 o'clock . . .
Have had him written up at his own request for last 8 years – Arranged
for it to appear in the Carson Appeal . . . Old Sam was born in Belfast
Ireland Dec 1, 1829 – came to America at age of 15 – Participated in the
Mexican war – came to California, landing in San Francisco March 14,
1849 – came to Nevada in July 1860 –

Oct 16 . . . 2 PM funeral of Sam Baker – I attended, riding out to the
grave in one of the carriages with relatives and friends . . .

Oct 17 . . . Recd from SL Tribune $13.10 for my Sept correspond-
ence . . . Also rec'd big package, 20 pounds or more . . . of blanks
& circulars for Tribune's big $27,000 guessing contest – Guess they want
to make me agent . . . US Senator J P Jones . . . passed up to Gold
Hill today, registered as a voter and passed down this evening, bound for
Santa Monica –

Oct 18 through 21 [AD writes letter to *Tribune* and notes deaths of
three more acquaintances, Ben Moore, Hank Metz & Jim Hurley.]

Oct 22 . . . Uncle Billy Musgrove, pioneer of Carson, found dead in
his house – Heart disease – 75 yrs old – Alone – He attended Sam Baker's
funeral the other day and wanted me to ride with him in his buggy, but I
was otherwise engaged – But nobody not even himself expected he was
going to die next – Ah well we must go whether our time comes or not –
But its getting uncomfortably near onto *me* – Don't like it . . .

Oct 24 – Variable – cloudy – & cold – Morning train from Reno arrived
an hour late, accompanied 15 minutes later by special car, with Wm
Jennings Bryan on board, direct from the East – He spoke at Salt Lake &
other points along the route – and comes employed by Newlands to help
him out in his fight for the Senate – He was accompanied from Reno by
Newlands, Van Duzer et al – Only stopped about 15 minutes to wood up

the locomotive, shaking hands and conversing with people on the platform & then passed on up to Virginia where he spoke this PM – accompanied by Newlands, Van Duzer, Governor Sadler, et al – Got back from
Va nearly 4 PM – Opera House densely packed with men of all parties,
women & children – Town band escorted him from depot, and played in
the Opera House – Commenced speaking at 4:10 closing at 5:25 – One
of the best orators in the U.S. Spoke strongly for silver, Newlands & Van
Duzer, deprecated the return of Republicans to the old party, picked the
Government to pieces, and wound up in a grand howl against imperial-
ism – He made a very interesting & entertaining speech and was much
applauded – Then he left on his special for Reno where he speaks tonight
and goes back to his home in Nebraska, speaking at Winnemucca and
Elko on his way – I was about town in the evening – Bed at 11:30 –

Sunday, Oct 26 . . . Recd from the SF Call . . . my story "Woods
Creek in Forty-Nine" . . . Worked with Harry Day some this PM getting up Club in the Salt Lake Tribune guessing contest . . .

Oct 28 . . . Harry Day got off our SL Tribune guessing match club
. . . 10 members, 2 guesses each . . . Evening, Grand Dem Silver
rally . . . Bonfires, town band, and Va Quartette Club . . . Not enthusiastic . . .

Oct 30 . . . Evening Republican speaking at the Opera House . . .
Densely crowded house – Cleveland for Governor spoke first and did 1st
rate . . . E S Farrington for Congress followed with the best address of
the season, beating Bryan badly – Greatly applauded throughout – Long
ways the best and most satisfactory meeting yet – I affiliated with the
orators & everybody else in crowds at Arlington et al afterward . . .

Oct 31 . . . Sent 10 estimates, 50 cts each to Tribune guessing contest,
all on my own account & risk . . .

Nov 1 . . . Sent off 2 more guesses each from Alfred Doten and Dan
De Quille – Both in name of Doten – Alf Doten 184,900 – Dan De Quille
216,200 (1849 & 1620) Received letter from Hon George E Roberts,
Washington, DC . . . "Sir I enclose herewith check . . . in your favor
for the sum of one hundred and fifty dollars . . ." . . . Evening attended
speaking at Opera House, Jimmy Sweeney for Atty Genl and Sam Davis
State Controller . . .

Sunday, Nov 2 . . . News telegraphically came at noon from Reno of
the death of Tim Dempsey, this AM after a 2 or 3 days sickness . . .

Great rushing around of political aspirants, treating, etc – At 4:30 PM Camminetti, the Chairman of the California Democratic State Central Committee, arrived . . . escorted by the town band direct to Opera House – Bonfires – One Johnson from Tuscarora made a hell roaring speech, followed by Camminetti . . . Good Newlands talk for couple of hours & shot out for Reno . . . to talk there this evening . . .

Nov 3 . . . Electioneering red hot . . . saloons getting rich . . . Tim Dempsey's remains arrived by AM train . . . taken to Odd Fellows Hall, awaiting relatives from the East – will be finally buried at Virginia, beside relatives – Evening grand Republican rally at Opera House . . .

Nov 4 . . . Grand General Election Day . . .

Nov 5 . . . Election returns actively looked for and received from everywhere . . .

Nov 6 – Cloudy, with very light rain in the AM – Tim Dempsey's funeral took place about 3 PM from Odd Fellows Hall – He belonged to 3 societies, Odd Fellows, K of P, and Workmen – The IOOF buried him and the other two stood in $3,000 and $2,000 each in insurance – $3,000 K of P – good attendance of the Orders and friends – Procession 55 on foot, and 27 carriages – Buried in the catholic Carson Cemetery, aside from all religious propositions, Catholic or otherwise . . . Was to have been buried at Virginia, in Catholic cemetery, by the side of relatives, but the catholics refused to allow him to be buried in their consecrated ground, or to perform funeral services by reason of his being a member of the Orders – Therefore the Orders performed all the rites and ceremonies according to their ritual – Very good singing by a choir of ladies and gentlemen – He owned a lot in the catholic Carson Cemetery, otherwise he could not have been buried there –

Nov 8 . . . Dominic Circe, landlord of the Carson Exchange Hotel for many years, and prominent in Carson Community died about 5:30 this evening from chronic affliction, cancerous condition of the stomach . . .

Nov 11 . . . The event of the day was Circes funeral – I visited the hotel at noon & viewed the remains – At 2 PM I went to Catholic church & attended funeral ceremonies, conducted by Father Gartland – church full – The AOUW order escorted – 38 on foot and 53 carriages . . . several old time friends of mine attended from Silver City – Buried in Catholic cemetery here . . .

Nov 14 . . . Billy Pennison died at his home in Va at 1 oclock this morning – Born in London in April 1836 . . . One of the oldest Comstockers and Chief of the Fire Dept both Volunteer and Paid for many years – Big friend of mine . . . The remains of the late John W Mackay arrived in New York from London on Wednesday last accompanied by his wife and daughter Princess Colonna – funeral strictly private & body buried in the family mausoleum at Greenwood cemetery by the side of his son, John W Mackay Jr . . .

Nov 22 . . . Important Comstock case before Judge Hawley in the US Circuit Court yesterday & today – Fred Ritter, Vs the Lynch estate for possession of the slum pond pile of tailings – below the old Chollar workings in the ravine – from the old Hoosier State Mill – 30 to 60 thousand tons – Ritter claiming it under a placer mining location made ten years ago . . . got through at 3 PM with all evidence – has now to be printed, and arguments of counsel a week or so from now . . .

Nov 27 . . . Thanksgiving Day . . . I found some turkey at principal saloons and did not suffer for good cheer . . . Schneider, the baker made me present of a big mince pie, a nice little pan of baked beans, and a small loaf of nice rye bread – Big drop in price of silver in the East & Europe . . . down to 47¼ per ounce . . .

Nov 28 . . . Wrote brief note to William Nelson . . . accepting his desire for me to do the Nevada write up, as before, for the New Years edition of the Tribune – 2 columns, with cuts – Evening about town . . .

Dec 1 . . . "Stetson's Double Spectacular Production of Uncle Tom's Cabin" arrived . . . Gave great street parade at noon, 2 bands of music, Uncle Tom's cabin on wheels, little Eva and something else, drawn by Shetland ponies – Gave performance to good house at the Opera House in evening – Good Uncle Tom & little Eva – best clog, jig and cake walk dancing seen here for years – excellent orchestra . . . 30 or 40 people, bloodhounds & other dogs – A really good show . . .

Dec 5 . . . PM I wrote a 2 page letter to Hon J P Jones, Mills Building, or Palace Hotel, San Francisco, deliberately complimentary and dunning him for $5,000 or $10,000 on old scores – Don't think he will admire it . . .

Dec 10 . . . By evening train sent order to Sears, Roebuck & Co, Chicago, for new coat, vest & pants – Sent postal order for $10 accompanying . . .

Dec 11 . . . Today I received SL Tribune of the 9th . . . giving full list of winners in the great guessing contest on the aggregate vote of Utah, Idaho and Wyoming at recent general election – Raymond Sullivan a 10 yrs old boy living at Eureka, Utah, guessed the exact vote 169,181 and won 1st & 2nd prizes of $5,000 each . . . 2nd prize was for nearest to exact number – All of our club guesses were about 7,000 too high . . . All my private guesses were a dead failure from same cause . . .

Dec 12 through 21 [AD records the deaths of Billy Brummett, David Norrie, "divining rod" prospector, and Jake Webber, "20 years the younger of the Pacific Coast Pioneers many" – Receives a passing visit from his son Sam, "like a bright ray of sunshine to my soul," who gives him $10 – Writes a regular letter to the *Tribune* and works at his New Year's letter.]

Dec 22 . . . Worked hard, early & all the time on my Tribune New Years writeup – And I completed it just in time for mail . . . 11 pages and cuts of Virginia City and Tonopah . . . Rec'd letter from wife with $15 today . . .

Dec 24 . . . Rec'd 6 page letter from Sister Eunice, with very rich white silk pocket handkerchief, also a copy of a monthly magazine, entitled "Out West" . . . Also from Bessie a little bundle of five silk white pocket handkerchiefs . . .

Dec 25 – Same – a little cloudy & dusty – streets not being sprinkled as last year at this time – Christmas Day – Observed as usual with church services but more outside happy meetings & greetings & the chief saloons showed up fine turkey & pig lunches, etc – I dined with old Doc Benton at Johnny Myers saloon, south end of town, with many others – Splendid layout at tables – Turkey, roast pig, sourcrout, salad, doughnuts, etc – Best dinner I have had for many a day – And Schneider the baker gave me a small mince pie and cake to take home with me – Received $6.25 from the SL Tribune – Bed 11:30 – Started in using my new handkerchief from Eunice today, as the *best one* I ever had in my life – Intend using it as such –

Sunday, Dec 28 . . . Governor elect Sparks arrived on morning train & left on evening . . .

Dec 30 . . . Found that I had drawn $10 in the December drawing of the Little Benefencia lottery, San Francisco . . . Our Carson Syndicate . . . won nothing . . . during this year we have only won $15 at a cost of $18 . . . Package from sister Cornelia . . . containing a nice white silk pocket handkerchief and a book entitled "The Conqueror," by Gertrude Franklin Atherton, being the true and romantic story of Alexander Hamilton as great American Statesman of Washington's time . . . He died 47 yrs old – Too great to live any longer . . .

Dec 31 . . . Lem Allen, Lieut Gov Elect was in town today . . . Evening about town some till 12 oclock and the ringing of fire bells & popping of pistols & guns announced the incoming of the New Year 1903 . . .

BOOK NO. *79*

Carson City
Jan 1, 1903 – Nov 11, 1903

Jan 1, 1903 – Clear and very pleasant – The finest New Years day I think I ever saw . . . sent letter to R R Crawford of Reno Ledger dunning him for that $13.50 which he owes me for reporting the Legislature 2 yrs ago nearly – About town considerably . . .

Jan 2 . . . Recd ½ doz extra copies of the big 64 column, extra edition of Salt Lake Tribune containing my 3 column New Years article with 2 Tonopah cuts . . .

Jan 3 . . . The Cal papers are full of Clarence Mackay's success in getting telegraphic cable through to the Sandwich Islands from San Francisco – messages interchanged commencing New Years evening . . . Evening at Opera House – Recital of Miss Adelina Raffetto, a Carson born girl about 20 yrs of age – Has received good stage and elocutionary education in the East . . . recitations: "Pauline Pavlovna," "Lady Gay Spanker," "Portia" scene from "Merchant of Venice," balcony scene from "Romeo and Juliet," "Magda," and "Leah the Forsaken." Fine stage figure, fine voice, fine action & elocution and took immensely – much applauded encored & called before the curtain . . .

Sunday, Jan 4 . . . Rec'd letter from Sister Lizzie – 6 pages, note paper – cool and "at home" like . . .

Jan 5 . . . Big crowd came from Reno to see inaugural swear in of Governor Sparks . . . US Dist Court in session drew big crowd from Tonopah on a case . . .

Jan 6 . . . AM wrote a page article on Nevada Lottery for Jimmy Wiggins, of Empire – Among the Tonopah folks in town on lawsuit, etc, is old Jim Butler discoverer of Tonopah – met & affiliated with him . . .

Sunday, Jan 11 – Clear, cold . . . Miss Rafetto had good house at Pipers Opera House Va last evening – about $400, same as here . . .

Jan 14 . . . PM wrote & sent page letter to Major John H Dennis, editor of Reno Journal, & page letter to Hon Nate W Roff, Reno for them to secure me position as reporter of the Senate . . .

Jan 15 . . . Bought $4 ticket, biggest of all in Mexican lottery today . . . The highest prize is $60,000 and I am after it . . .

Jan 17 – Same – Morning 8° . . . Big crowd of legislators and would-be attaches, etc, in town – Barkeeps all busy, especially at the Arlington, which is headquarters for everybody – Bert Crawford in town – wants to be sergeant-at-arms again – Paid me $4 on account – still owes me $9.50 . . .

Sunday, Jan 18 . . . At 7 PM caucuses held by both parties at State Capitol – chose attaches . . . Harry Day's gal, May Williams, came home to him from her run in Reno yesterday morning – Glad to get back . . .

Jan 19 . . . Legislature convened today – both Houses, at 12 M – New members, officers, and all attaches sworn in . . . Chaplain prayed – Senate Bill No 1, *To Create a Legislative Fund*, $40,000 to pay per diem, mileage, salaries & other expenses of the session passed with the greatest unanimity, and at 1:30 adjourned . . . most of the disappointed ones . . . went home tonight – Bert Crawford included, not paying me another blessed cent . . .

Jan 21 . . . Reported as usual – made arrangements with Ernest Bingham, lessee etc of the Reno Journal, to report the Senate for the session, at $10 per week . . .

Jan 24 . . . PM wrote some "State Capitol Notes" . . . and sent to the Reno Journal . . .

Jan 26 – Very rainy from early morning . . . At 2 PM great conference meeting of both houses on the Irrigation question – in Assembly Chamber – Frank Newlands leading spirit of course, as his election comes off tomorrow – [blank] Taylor of the US Hydrographic and geological survey was present with Newlands and both talked . . .

Jan 27 – AM rain, PM snow and very steadily all day . . . At 12 both Houses elected Frank G Newlands US Senator from Nevada – Senate 4 for Hawley, 13 for Newlands – The Assembly 5 for Hawley and 30 for Newlands . . .

Jan 28 . . . Commenced on new 5 gallon can of Elaine coal oil today, burning in the stove in my room – Reported as usual – Newlands declared elected US Senator . . . in joint session . . . Newlands gave a sort of off hand informal reception at 9 in the evening at the Arlington House – Plenty of drinkables & dry cakes & cheese – cheap – But plenty of speaking besides Van Duzer and Sam Davis – Bed at 2 – Sent 4 page report to Tribune of the Legislative conference on irrigation . . . Snow 8 inches deep this morning . . . Bed at 2, clear & very low down – Will hit Zero this time – 57° in my room . . .

Jan 30 – Snowstormy and warmer . . . Farmer Treadway died last evening –

> [Clips from *Goodwin's Weekly,* the *Appeal* and the *News* – Aaron D Treadway was born in Connecticut in 1815, operated brick businesses in several states, served as a lieutenant in the Mexican War, and went west to Sutter's Mill in 1849 – He moved to Washoe City in 1859 and was among the first settlers in Carson City where, in 1866, he bought the land that became one of the popular resort areas in the "palmy days" of the Comstock.]

Feb 2 . . . My friend W W Booth, editor & propr of the Tonopah Bonanza has been appointed postmaster there and is such now – Supt H M Yerington of the V&T RR slipped & fell on the sidewalk front of the Mint Saturday, bumping his head pretty hard and straining his hip badly – Has Dr Packard of Va to attend him – Badly hurt – may die . . . Wrote out my annual report as Secretary of the Carson Lottery Syndicate for the year 1902, before I went to bed – We have come out just $4.25 ahead on the three years, or $1.41⅔ apiece – 3 of us . . .

Feb 7 . . . Ordered Coat and Vest – dark blue serge through Sammy Cohn today . . . $12.50 . . .

Feb 9 . . . The Freeman & Lynn Commercial Men's Mastodon Minstrels . . . Paraded street at noon – magnificent band – Played in evening at Opera House – Very crowded audience – largest for years – Regular minstrel performance . . . About 50 in the crowd – fine orchestra – Closed with solos, bag punching act and very dextrous club and balls juggling, very good indeed . . .

Feb 12 . . . I got, at the mint this PM, a sample copy, sent to Colcord, of the annual report of Mint Director Roberts . . . My Comstock and Tonopah report was in it all right but with none of the cuts I sent with the report . . . Arlington House thermom registered 6° above zero . . . Room temperature 49° . . .

Feb 14 . . . Senate held good session AM & PM – AM session got away with the big irrigation bill that Newlands has been waiting for to make him big in the US Congress & Senate – He can go home now . . .

> [Newspapers clarify that this is Assembly Bill 16, the detailed implementation of the Truckee canal project in the Fallon, Nevada, area – Federal money had been provided under the Newlands Reclamation Act passed by the US Congress in 1902, and the Department of the Interior was to be in charge of the project.]

Feb 15 . . . Met my son Alfred about noon today – up from Reno with a couple of his boy friends – Saw him but a moment – & he was off with them again – Didn't meet him afterward because I was so busy writing, and guess he went back home this evening.

> [Unidentified clip, copied from the Chicago *Record Herald*:] Mr. Jones, whom Mr. Newlands succeeds, is called the father of the Senate, having served in that body continuously since 1873. When his term expires on the 3d of March, he will have completed his thirtieth year and fifth term, a record that has been surpassed by three men only and equalled by only two others.

Feb 20 . . . Wrote & sent page letter to Nelson of Tribune – complaining of treatment of my letters –

Feb 23 . . . Evening Gov Sparks grand inauguration ball at Opera House – Crowded – $5 a ticket – Big supper on the stage – spectators in gallery – I got in & got fine standing place next wall on lower floor – Hall finely decorated – hundred or more electric lights . . . No public observance of the day beyond display of few flags and advent of a big lot of people . . .

Feb 25 . . . During any spare time, even to my 2 hours nooning, I was busy writing up a burlesque on Miss Annie Martin's account of the ladies' dresses at the big inauguration ball – I wrote [up] the gents, a dozen of them, choice ones – gave it to the Appeal . . .

> [A clip from the *Eureka Sentinel* describes the ladies and their formal wear – AD's version, in the *Appeal*, signed "Criticus," gives the descriptions of, amongst others, former governor Sadler, J D Torreyson, and Will U Mackey, the "floor director" of the ball:]

Mr. S—dl—r, hair scrambled, with tobasco sauce dressing. Coat and pants, swallow's tail of dark Manila; boots delicately shined; general style, festival; waltzing style, away up.

Mr. T—son, hair a la Piute chief; magnificent double-breasted sweater, rubber moccasins; general style, Republican; waltzing style, con-fusion.

Mr. M—c—k—y, hair auburn crest; necktie, wire silver; complete suit of bird's eye porphyry with side drift ruchings; general style, superintendent; waltzing style, unfitchered.

Feb 26 . . . Recd brief letter from Wm Nelson of the Tribune saying: "The matter of which you wrote has been entrusted entirely by the present management to the news editor. I do not see, therefore, that there is any chance for different handling of your correspondence . . ." – Also received the following: "You are invited to attend a dinner given by Hon William Randolph Hearst, at the Brigg's House, Thursday, March 5th, 1903. To the members of the Nevada Legislature, Twenty-first session" . . .

Feb 27 . . . Very busy day in legislature – Between times I got off a 4 or 5 page letter to the Tribune – got in the PM report on Journal all right – Bed at 12 – Very very tired – The poles and wires are being set and strung through Carson for the new electric power . . . Power comes from Floriston on the Truckee River . . . via Virginia . . .

March 2 . . . In what little spare time I had today, I was looking up the old lottery bill of 4 and 2 yrs ago . . .

March 3 . . . Wrote up a lottery bill, for Jimmy Wiggins of Empire, who is going in on the racket & trying to get this bill, amending the State Constitution so as to allow lotteries . . .

March 5 . . . About 9:30 went to the Hearst banquet . . . at the Briggs House, given by W R Hearst the great newspaper proprietor to the Nevada Legislature for its big memorial of gratitude to him, Feb 16 – for getting the tariff put off from Coal – He sent $350 to Sam Davis to get up this banquet, and he did it. Over 100 at the well spread tables – oysters, chickens, 3 kinds of wine, including Champagne – tongue, cake & all sorts of good grub – Sam Davis was toast master, and we had lots of speaking, etc – Ran till past 2 . . .

March 6 . . . Evening the Senate met at 7:30 – ran short time & went into executive session on a State University proposition, with Closed doors – To give it a new Metallurgical laboratory, $6,000 appropriation . . . Bed at 11:30 –

March 7 . . . Rec'd from Sammy Cohn my new coat and vest . . .

March 9 . . . Last day of the regular 50 days session – But they didnt finish, & have to go on to a finish without pay . . . Held AM, PM and evening sessions . . .

March 11 . . . Hardest days work I ever had reporting Legislature . . . Reported for both News and Appeal . . . The big General Appropriation Bill, providing for expenses of governing Nevada for next two years . . . foots up to $377,390 . . .

March 12 . . . The big General Appropriation bill passed the Assembly last evening with some few amendments which were concurred in by the Senate this AM which settles it . . .

March 14 – Clear & pleasant – Held AM & PM sessions and adjourned over till 10 AM Monday next – Tonopah got beaten in the Senate this PM on removal of Nye County seat from Belmont to Tonopah – I telegraphed it in 17 words to the Tribune this evening – And at 8 oclock this evening reception of Gov Sparks, tendered to Legislature & personal friends, at Armory Hall – Big crowd of the elite of Carson, including all the best looking women present – Not overcrowded, just right, and best function of the kind ever occurring in Carson – Reception room had whisky, champagne punch, and very choice claret punch, also numerous tables with little parties of 4 to 8 persons, with hot coffee, cake, ice cream etc – Plenty of nob ladies as waiters – Hall very tastefully decorated, and splendid band, cornet, clarinet, 2 fiddles, piano and bass viol played by Ernst Hall, caller – all from Gold Hill, except John Meder pianist – Crowd held the fort till 12, when it being Sunday, had to quit & go home – Bed 1:30 – This evening must have cost Sparks about $500 –

March 16 . . . Legislature fighting to a finish . . . Evening the members, especially including the outsiders under name of "The Coyotes," gave a very splendid dance at Armory Hall, free, and all the same as the Governor's ball . . . Hall full and everybody happy – They danced till along toward morning, outdoing the Govs ball . . .

March 17 . . . St Patrick's Day – Legislature adjourned Sine Die, at 12:30 noon – 58th day – Three great anniversary events occurring, *Legislature adjourned, St Patrick's Day,* anniversary of *Fitz Corbett prize fight,* and all indulging therein – Got off my Reno Journal letter in good style – About town considerably – Bed at 11 very, very tired – Sent page letter to wife . . .

March 19 . . . Great events taking place in the world – Prest Roosevelt is to be in Carson May 19 on trip to Pacific Coast – The purchase of the Panama canal has been decided in Congress – Henry Riter of Reno has bought the old Bowers Mansion in Washoe Valley . . .

March 20 . . . AM filled out my "string" of account against SL Tribune for February and sent it to Mr Rivers the Business Manager, direct, for 1st time . . . Otto Eckelman who kept the Capitol Restaurant Virginia so many years & was prominent member of our Society of Pacific Coast Pioneers, died in San Francisco this morning – about 80 years of age –

> [Clip, *Journal:*] Alf Doten Jr., bookkeeper for the Flanigan Warehouse Company, is spending a short vacation at San Jose.

March 21 . . . PM busy in Governors office . . . getting list & description of bills passed upon by the Governor . . . 112 passed or approved by Gov . . . Picked out 62 of the best & most important and sent to the Reno Journal . . .

March 26 . . . PM was at Circuit Court awhile – Occidental M Co vs Sutro Tunnel Co, commenced this morning . . . My last Sunday's letter to Tribune came today in Wednesdays Trib, badly mangled & cut up into specials, one dating from *Tonopah* – and some of it left out, as well as my name – no good.

March 28 . . . PM sent page letter to business manager of Tribune giving him a new "string" of acct for February, based on "specials" instead of regular correspondence . . . Also sent page letter to Ernest L Bingham Propr of Reno Journal, rendering my bill of $60 for reporting Legislature, for the whole term, etc – Evening about town . . .

March 31 . . . Met E S Mangus one of the old Va & Gold Hill typos yesterday & today – Over from California, & on the lookout for a job, but stands poor show nowadays, where type setting machines are all the go . . . worked for me on the Gold Hill News 3 or 4 years . . . Says he is going to Tonopah . . .

April 1 – April Fool Day – Snowstormy . . . Wrote & sent 4 page letter to Tribune – *all "specials"* – Bed 12 – 3 years in Alta Lodging House today –

Sunday, April 5 . . . PM wrote a 5 page special & sent it to Tribune on the Sutro-Comstock trial . . .

April 7 . . . My Comstock-Sutro [trial] came to an end & was submitted to the jury at 4 PM – One hour and a half afterward they gave verdict for Occidental, Potosi & Chollar Mining Companies with $50,000 damages for breach of contract, etc – Sent 70 words telegram on subject to SL Tribune . . .

April 8 . . . PM attended Court – New Jury in case of Frank A Wells, killed by a live electric wire, March 1, 1902 at Reno . . . $40,000 damages claimed . . .

April 9 . . . Wrote out itemized bill of my February "string," amounting to $26, & sent it with page letter to Rivers . . . Also sent a carbonized copy of the string, with page letter to Col Wm Nelson . . .

April 11 . . . Borrowed $30 from Harry Day this noon . . . Met Dr Peter Manson from Virginia at the evening train – leaving the old Comstock for good, bound for Fresno, Cal where he bought a ranch and established a home for his wife and four red headed sons 19 years ago. He told her then that he had to go back to the Comstock to make money to give the ranch a good start, but promised that he would only stay away four years . . . only able now to redeem his promise . . .

April 14 . . . Letter from daughter "Goodie," Reno telling me wife in S.F. in care of an occulist, & she running school instead – also intending to inclose me $5 today, but she forgot to inclose it. Sent her a letter, the first in my life to her, this evening – showing her mistake . . . My special, 3 pages, to the Salt Lake Tribune, last Friday has got left out . . .

April 15 . . . Blank letter from Goodie, inclosing the $5 . . . Rec'd from SL Tribune . . . $14.35 in payment of my February "string" . . . Which is incorrect and not enough. Also recd letter from A L Philips, News Editor Tribune . . .

April 16 . . . The Jury in case of Wells electrically killed at Reno a year ago was out all night from yesterday noon and brought in verdict for plaintiff, Wells as against the Nevada Electrical Light & Power Co, Reno for $500 damages out of $40,000 claimed – generally considered to be a very unsatisfactory & inefficient verdict – Should have been at least $5,000 or nothing . . .

April 18 . . . Got letter from wife today, dated from "The Oaks," San Francisco, telling me she has been there last 2 weeks having her eyes treated by an occulist – Almost lost her sight through overwork in her school business – Will be there another week at least . . .

April 22 . . . PM I completed writing a scorching 3 page letter to the News Editor of the SL Tribune . . . calling for quits on bad treatment of my writings – Closing out on my Tribune correspondence . . .

[Clip, *Eureka Sentinel:*] Mrs. M. S. Doten, assistant principal of the Reno high school, has resigned. Mrs. Doten has been teaching continuously for the past twelve or thirteen years. Lately she went to California to have her eyes treated and the doctors have ordered her to give up her teaching.

April 24 . . . The grand feature of today was Norris & Rowes great animal show – Big parade on street at noon – and big 2,500 or 3,000 people house this PM, on grounds south of town, near the box factory . . . 3 elephants, 2 llamas, 1 genuine camel, monkeys, dogs et al – Japanese acrobats, contortionists, etc – Best show of the kind I ever saw . . .

Sunday, April 26 . . . Got letter from Mr Perry S Heath, Publisher and General Manager of the Salt Lake Tribune – also one from A F Philips, news editor . . . I am let out from the Tribune I guess – by Philips . . .

April 29 . . . SL Tribune has missed coming yesterday & today – Guess they have cut me off the list . . .

May 1 . . . Sent page letter to E L Bingham Reno Journal, wanting my $60 – Also letter to daughter "Goodie," otherwise Miss Goodwin S Doten, acknowledging receipt of $15 received this AM . . .

May 2 . . . PM wrote & sent 4 page communication to the SF Chronicle on Van Duzer . . .

[A clip from the *San Francisco Bulletin* of April 30 reports the death of William McGrew in a hospital, from kidney disease – 75 years old – McGrew had been employed by the *Call* and other papers as reporter and editor until the last few years, when he was "too feeble to do much work."]

The clipping about Wm McGrew, hits me hard and sad. He was the boy who walked with me from Woods diggings in March 1850 to Stockton, perfect strangers, but took kindly to each other – slept together in the tules the one night, shot at ducks – played the fiddle & flute together at houses on the road & parted in Stockton – Met him a time or two since, the last in Como in '63 . . . Vale – God bless him . . .

May 5 . . . Rec'd 6 page closely written letter from wife – still at "The Oaks" . . . eyes slowly improving . . . Also recd letter, 5 pages from E L Bingham of Reno Journal, repudiating my bill of $60 for legislative reporting . . .

May 6 . . . Rec'd nice letter from Chas W Coe, San Jose, Cal, engaged with his brother Harry running the Rancho San Felipe in the Mount Hamilton hills, 14000 acres – lots of live stock cattle etc – He has bought the late Gen Nagle's beautiful home in San Jose and invites me to call & see him – Often heard his father and mother speak of me and always most kindly and has my old chest I brought round Cape Horn – His father was my old friend H W Coe who used to have the hop ranch near San Jose where I used to frequent – the same Coe that I knew in the mines of Rich Gulch Mokelumne over 50 yrs ago – Says his father died prematurely from tongue cancer several years ago, and mother died a helpless invalid Jan 17, 1901 . . .

May 7 . . . Was at State Library couple of hours today overhauling newspaper files on my disputed Reno Journal report . . .

May 14 . . . I finally completed my 7 page Bingham letter and sent it to him by this evening's train . . . Big preparations started in to welcome Roosevelt – Big arch across Main st today, from my lodging house across to the Arlington Hotel . . .

May 15 . . . Wrote 2 page letter to Major Dennis, editor of the Reno Journal, about Bingham, inclosing with it a full rewritten copy of my letter to Bingham . . .

May 16 . . . Snow in the air nearly all day . . . Borrowed $20 more dollars from Harry Day . . .

Sunday, May 17 . . . Hired gang hard at work all day decorating main st with numerous criss-cross lines of flags . . .

May 18 . . . Everybody decorating big . . . Made presentation today of my old Pioneer flag that I have carefully kept so long, to the State, as described in the annexed item which I wrote and published in this evenings *News* . . .

> On behalf of the few remaining members of the Society of Pacific Coast Pioneers, President Alf Doten this day presented to the State of Nevada, through Governor Sparks, at his office in the Capitol building, the old flag of the Society. This flag will adorn the broad table or desk of President Roosevelt at his speaking tomorrow, with the inscription "Flag of the Pacific Coast Pioneers" lettered across it. [A brief summary of the flourishing days of the society, and of the presentation of their cabinet, worth $10,000;] and now the Old Boys last of all surrender their old flag. It is of the true blue American style, twelve by eighteen feet in size, and was presented to the Society by Hon. Thos. B. Rickey many years ago. . . .

May 19 – Clear – A little frosty this morning – very pleasant day – Grand Presidents Day – Special trains from all directions at half rates – The whole Comstock, Silver City, Dayton etc – rushed in any way to get in. The whole of Carson Valley, Washoe valley, Como, and even from Tonopah contributed, many coming from Reno – Eight crowded coaches came from the Comstock early – Carson street was a forest of flags and the decorations a thousand times finer & more profuse than ever before seen. The Indian Band played and the Capitol Park was densely crowded. The main avenues had to be roped to keep the crowd back – all the public school children were there each with a flag, and they sang the "Red White & Blue" etc – Miss Nellie Milligan sat at reporter's table with me, & took speeches of Governor and Roosevelt shorthand for the Evening *News* – At 8:45 the big Presidential train pulled in from Reno, President and party got aboard the carriages in waiting and came down street – About 20 carriages, escorted by GAR veterans – came into park at NW gate, discharged cargo at State Capitol and passed out SW gate – Platform built over front steps and occupied whole west front porch – about 200 people, State, city & county officers on platform – Fully 15,000 people in the Park – Governor Sparks introduced Roosevelt in brief speech at 9:05 – spoke nearly half an hour – very plain distinct & forcible speaker – good sensible speech, much applauded – Carriages came in as before, loaded up and passed out – plenty of body guards – Whole vast multitude followed to the RR depot & saw Prest & train off on return to Reno having spent only an hour in Carson – Is booked for an hour in Reno, then goes over the mountains – next to Oregon and back East – Carson crowded all rest of the day or till outsiders thought it time to go home – President told Jas A Yerington that Carson had given him a better, handsomer and more thoroughly enjoyable reception than at any point on his whole route from the East & in California so far – At 3:30 PM I footed it to John Q A Moores house north of the RR to attend wedding of his daughter Chrissie to John Casey McDannel of Tonopah . . . After nice chicken dinner, with cake, wine, etc bride and groom left on evening train . . . Saw them off & dispersed – Knocked about town, and the Arlington & home at 10 – Bed at 11 – exceedingly tired – Got 7 page letter from Major J H Dennis . . . He is at the "Nevada Sanitarium" or Advent Hospital – Been there last 2 weeks being treated for nervous prostration and throat trouble – Was before that at the Nevada General Hospital from first of the year except about a month –

[Several clips on the president's visit – Both the Reno and Carson papers commented on the superiority of Carson's decorations, despite its relative poverty – From the *News,* Carson's weather was its miserable self the day before, but rose to the grand occasion with a sparkling day; also, an item about the "Lugger magazine revolver" with leather case which was presented to the president by the governor: "Mr. Roosevelt was as pleased over it as a child, and it is safe to say that he will not travel far before trying it." – Also notes how many children the president shook hands with – From the *Appeal,* an anecdote about Governor Sparks' chair, made from intertwined elks' horns, "delicate as a barbed wire fence," used by the president on the platform – A great expense, not in purchase price, but in medical bills for children's injuries and clothing bills for ladies' ruined dresses – The governor developed a great affection for the chair from all the times he had to bring it back in from the woodshed where his wife always put it when she had a chance – From the *News* again, the introduction by Governor Sparks ("We have the second Andrew Jackson with us here today"), and the full text of Roosevelt's speech – He opened with praise for the pioneering work and the development of the state, and moved on to the central theme of working for the children and the future, this theme used somewhat indirectly to justify the reclamation-irrigation project already under way, and the fact that Nevada's watershed is located in California was used as the reason that federal control was felt necessary – The same subject served as a basis for advocating other conservation projects, to guard against overgrazing or "destructive lumbering" that might ruin the watershed – "The State of Nevada has led the way, not only through the peril of national legislation for irrigation, but also in the willingness to test the work . . ." – The speech closes with confidence that Nevada will prosper, and that, of all her crops, the crop of children most pleases him: "I am sure they are alright in quality and quantity . . . I believe in your stock and am mighty glad that it does not show any sign of dying out." – "The President took his seat amid tremendous applause. The school children waved their flags, women threw their handkerchiefs in the air and men hurled their hats at the tree tops."]

May 20 . . . Wrote and published in the evening *News* the [Moore-McDannel] marriage item . . . and Eno Moore went to office and got a dozen copies . . .

Sunday, May 24 . . . Completed and sent four page letter to Perry S Heath, Publisher & General Manager Salt Lake Tribune, about my ruined correspondence . . .

May 26 . . . Rec'd 3 page letter from wife today – Still at "The Oaks" . . . Waiting for Goodwin to get through her University graduation and come down and join her . . .

May 30 . . . Recd note from M H de Young of the SF *Chronicle* returning my communication on Van Duzer regretting that it was "unavailable" – Also 2 page letter from Bingham, of the Reno *Journal* objecting to my charge of $60 for reporting Senate –

June 1 . . . Sent page letter to R R Crawford, Reno Ledger, dunning him for the 9.50 he still owes me – and page to George R Vardy, Wells, Nev, dunning him for the $25 he owes me and written promise to pay from 3 or 4 yrs ago . . .

June 4 . . . Ross Lewers, my old Washoe valley friend has lost a son and a daughter within the last week – the son Ed last Saturday May 30 about 12 M, by a placer mining accident near home, being caved on, and the daughter Ellen at Stanford University Cal, from pneumonia on Tuesday last – Hard on Lewers & surviving family – daughter buried at Reno yesterday, and son the day before.

June 5 . . . Recd letter from Goodwin, Reno, with $15, to my surprise, not expecting any – She leaves tonight to join her mother at San F and go to Pacific Grove, near Monterey for 5 or 6 weeks benefit to her eyes, and recuperation – Also received from Goodwin a copy of the second great Nevada University annual for 1903, the "Artemisia" . . . Very fully illustrated – Goodwin Stoddard Doten the literary editor . . .

June 10 . . . Wrote page letter . . . to Geo E Roberts . . . applying for my job of writing up annual report of the Comstock and Tonopah . . . The old Bowers Mansion, Washoe valley, bought by Henry Riter of Reno was thrown open yesterday as a public Summer resort – Been closed as such for many years . . .

June 12 . . . Recd letter from Wm Nelson, editor of the Salt Lake Tribune: "Have gone carefully over the subject matter of your claim, and this evening handed the papers and letter to Mr Heath, with my recommendation. Yours as ever, William Nelson, Editor Tribune" . . .

June 17 . . . Finished reading The Conqueror . . . Pretty good for history of Alexander Hamilton and the incidents leading to the Revolutionary war – Bunker Hill anniversary day today (1775) but the Conqueror don't say a word about it anywhere – speaks of the first pitched bloody battle of the revolution at *Brooklyn Heights* . . . ignores Lexington and Concord also, and forgets to mention Massachusetts and Connecticut as chief promoters and originators of the Revolution . . .

June 18 . . . Rec'd 2 page note paper from wife – At Pacific Grove –

popular summer resort near old Monterey . . . "Goody" with her – Says dont like it much, but I can write to her there, for a week or more yet . . .

Sunday, June 21 . . . Arlington House lighted throughout with electricity for 1st time tonight . . .

June 23 . . . Met Prof Ring on street, & he told me it was Bessie who is the "Miss Doten" who is to take charge of the intermediate school, Gardnerville – She gets the position through Guy Walts . . .

June 24 . . . PM I completed and sent 3 page letter to Major John H Dennis, of the Reno *Journal,* relative to effecting a settlement, between the paper and myself . . . About 6:15 o'clock this evening, old Charley Blue – nigger – at the Arlington got into a quarrel with the chief cook . . . in the kitchen, stabbed him just below the right ear with an old sheath knife, & he laid down and died in ten minutes. Blue walked down to the Sheriffs office immediately and gave himself up & was jailed – Chinese Chief Cooks name was Lu How – about 40 or 45 years old . . .

June 25 . . . Prehistoric footprints are discovered day before yesterday near Gardner's, south of town and being developed by J A Yerington – look like the tracks of rhinocerosses – Major Laughlin, Inspector of Indian Reservations, paid the Walker Lake Reservation a visit last week to arrange matters with the Indians for throwing open the reservation. Giving the Indians all the valley and pasture lands, and opening the mountain and mineral sections to the whites.

June 27 . . . The Reno *Journal* says wife arrived there last night, so I wrote her a 3 page letter this evening mail, from the Arlington . . . But best of all, I recd brief letter from Bingham of the Reno Journal inclosing check for $60.00, with attached [typewritten] letter:

Dear sir:--
   I enclose you a check for sixty ($60) dollars, being the amount of your claim against the Nevada State Journal for services rendered. I take the same stand that I always have that it is an unjust bill, that we don't owe it. But I have learned a lesson in this case which will probably make it cheap in the long run and that is, to be a little less particular of the feelings of others and say "no" and enforce with an insult if the recipient is too dense. I do not want any thanks or any receipt for this amount it is a present---a gift, and wish to be spared any further annoyance and persecution.   Yours respectfully,
                                        [signed] EL. Bingham

Used some of the money immediately to pay up delayed bills – all right – Will reply tomorrow – Bed at 12 – Happy over my Journal triumph – *He* tried to swindle me and didn't make it –

June 29 . . . Letter from wife . . . Eyes still sick but general health good – Sam out at Elko, on the grasshopper problem . . .

June 30 . . . Charley Blue's case came up before Justice Stone this PM – argued, and Judge held him in $500 to appear before the Grand Jury next week. Gov Sadler and Edmund James went his bail, & he was released from Custody –

July 4 – Clear & pleasant – Independence Day – Big Carnival at Virginia – Rose at 6 – Was on hand at depot for special train from Reno at 8:30 – Came – 5 coaches & 10 flats . . . crowded – All could not get aboard from Carson – Waited an hour for 2nd special section – Came about a dozen cars – 5 coaches – I got on coach, arriving at Va about noon – C street densely crowded and decorated – About 6,000 people present – women & children predominating – sidewalks patched up & benches arranged along street for people to sit on – Big procession started down C st from Taylor – lots of horsemen, footmen and floats – about 1,000 people in it . . . 4 bands of music . . . Grandest display for last 15 or 20 years – Wound up at Piper's Opera House – Big audience – I was one – Music, singing, poem, reading Declaration – H F Bartine made one of best orations of his life – well and heartily applauded throughout – After that I was about town, meeting and affilliating with quite a number of old acquaintances – took 4:20 PM train for home – being afraid to stay later & go with big crowd on 11 oclock special . . . Evening about town some – Bed at 2 Very tired – The last special arrived from Virginia shortly after 2 oclock, when I was going to bed –

July 10 . . . Mr W S Guffey of Pittsburg, Pa, a coal oil multi millionaire who represents a Pa syndicate in the purchase and running of the North Rapidan mine, at Palmyra, near Como and the Boyle tunnel connected therewith during the past year or two, returned from a visit to the tunnel yesterday. 28 men employed at $3.50 per day struck for $4, so he has shut the mine or tunnel down entirely discharging all hands. Tunnel in 3,500 feet, requiring 800 ft more to reach the ledge . . .

July 14 . . . Evening attended the McKanlass hot coon show – full house – wound up with an afterpiece, 25 cts extra, for men only – I staid to it – "Miss Perry" in her "Filipino" dance – *Little Egypt* only more so –

Better muscled – wiggled her arse more vigorously and suggestively – A German Jewess, I think, and lustful bitch – Bed at 12 –

July 15 . . . With Johnny Moore on a coal oil striking proposition, in connection with W S Guffey . . . Guffey has been at Walley's Springs the last few days, but returned this PM – Johnny furnished him some samples of the oil shale, to get analyzed . . .

July 16 . . . About 3 oclock this morning I was awakened by a persistent dream that my bed and everything else in my room, books, papers, etc, and for aught I knew all out of doors was covered ultimately by newspaper sheets and all sorts of white paper with two letters c/z thus printed closely in large primer type all over. Somehow the impression forced itself upon me that it spelled *u/p sep*. Anyhow it also became impressed upon my mind that this was a new era in my existence and it took several minutes walking the floor to get thoroughly awake, and drive the peculiar vision out of my mind . . . PM was with Johnny Moore watching around on the oil proposition . . .

July 17 . . . Recd short note from Sam with $6, saying that he wrote me in place of his mother because her eyes were very tired . . .

July 18 . . . Received letter from Geo E Roberts, accepting my Comstock & Tonopah reporting proposal, for $150.00 – Mr W S Guffey . . . left this evening . . . May return here next year at this time – Saw him off on train . . .

Sunday, July 19 – Clear, warm & pleasant – About town, etc – got 5 page note letter from Sister Lizzie, with $5 greenback inclosed . . . as a birthday present – Bed at 11:30 – My son Sam's recent strong raid out in Elko, and Paradise valley trying to solve the grasshopper pest problem which was threatening to destroy all the crops came to a sudden and unexpected termination. Frosty nights on the 7th and 8th . . . laid the grasshoppers out cold, and summarily solved the problem.

July 20 . . . Wrote & published in the News of this evening . . . item on the recent Como mining strike and final shut down . . .

[The clip adds little information to the journal entry of July 10 – The jocular tone and sardonic closing comment that the rights of labor had been vindicated seem to support Colonel Guffey – The miners had been working under an agreement to stay at $3.50 per day until paying ore was found, but a "walking delegate" from the Silver City Miners' Union talked them into the strike.]

July 21 . . . My 74th Birthday – Celebrated it with becoming modesty – Wrote & sent page letter to Col W S Guffey, Palace Hotel, S.F. inclosing clip from the News that I published yesterday . . .

July 22 . . . Wrote & published in the evening *News* an article signed "Diogenes" relating to the three Carnivals, in Carson, Reno and Virginia the last 3 years, and Renos delinquency therein . . .

July 24 . . . Busy figuring on Comstock product for 1902, also of Tonopah, at Controllers office . . .

July 25 . . . Got after the bed bugs in my bed today with insect powder and a blogun – Breathed so much of it into my lungs that almost killed me – severe congestion . . . At 6:30 PM a special went to Reno with the Carson Wheelmen and band . . . to meet and bring up the Capital City Wheelmen, Sacramento, Champions of the Coast for a grand relay race for the Championship – Returned at 11, music, torches, bonfires, procession down street to hotel . . .

Sunday, July 26 . . . The great event of the day was the 50 mile relay race . . . Band on the street to commence – and everybody down to the track – Sacramento won by a few feet, some said "two wheels" . . .

July 29 . . . Big Episcopal & other Sunday school picnic to Bowers Mansion – 4 crowded coaches – 300 persons . . .

July 31 . . . Went out to Johnny Q A Moore's house, north of the RR round house to dinner at 5 PM – Occasion his 74th birthday . . . Had fine chicken dinner, with ice cream, etc for finish . . .

[A clip from the *Nevada Appeal* reports a July 27 prison break at Folsom, California – The thirteen escapees took several prison officials, including the warden, as hostages.]

Aug 3 . . . The escaped convicts from Folsom, Cal, had battle with 8 militiamen pursuers in wooded ravine, near Grand Victory mine – 6 miles south of Placerville . . . Three militiamen killed . . .

Aug 4 . . . Letter to J P Woodbury, Empire, for summary of all the tailings of Lyon and Storey counties for 1902 . . . A Placerville, Cal, dispatch says that Roberts, one of the escaped convicts has made his way to around Carson . . . work has been resumed at the North Rapidan mine, Como . . . Miners Union Terms $4, acceded to . . . Virginia City got too poor to support electric street lights, and had to discontinue them on the 1st instant – Poor Virginia . . .

[Clip, *Virginia Chronicle:*] Officer Ferrel, accompanied by his thorough-bred bloodhounds, Jumbo and Bess, which he recently sold to Warden Considine of the [Nevada] State Prison, left last night on the local for Sacramento whence he will immediately go to Folsom and thence take the field after the escaped convicts. . . .

Aug 5 . . . Wife reports her eyes still bad but comparatively comfortable – Says Bessie will probably marry in October . . .

Aug 7 . . . James P Roberts one of the Folsom escapes, was captured near Davisville, Cal at 2 PM yesterday . . . Seavis the negro convict . . . also captured . . .

Sunday, Aug 9 . . . Bed bugs outraged me so badly last night, in spite of all the dopes and powders of my landlady, that today she had to take out my bed, bedstead and all for heroic treatment – I have the only buggy corner in the house . . . She put me to sleep in room 10 tonight . . .

Aug 10 . . . Charge of manslaughter against Charley Blue, for killing Lu How . . . ignored today by Grand Jury, so Blue remains at liberty – I completed & sent . . . letter to T L Oddie, Gen'l Sup't Tonopah Mining Co . . . Instructions as to what he may be kind enough to report to me . . .

Aug 11 . . . Big picnic of K of Pythias at Bowers Mansion today – largely attended from Comstock, here and Reno – Mrs Carter completed the . . . unbugging . . . Slept *at home* again . . .

Aug 12 . . . According to the SF papers the pursuit of the Convicts is about abandoned by their pursuers, who seem to be afraid of them – Reported that 5 of them have made their way over the Sierra by the old Carson river route & into Nevada by Woodfords – Those bloodhounds from Nevada State Prison – not heard from . . .

Aug 14 . . . Officer C P Ferrell of Reno who took the two bloodhounds from this State Prison over to California and tried to trail the escaped convicts got back here with them yesterday . . . says he got on track all right, but the posses wouldnt stand in and help . . . all left the hunt and he followed them a couple of days, five of them over toward head waters of Carson river and was glad to get back here with the dogs after his 10 days hard tramp and travail – Evening Jeffries and Corbett big fight for champion heavy weight of the world at San Francisco . . . Big crowd at Criterion saloon . . . to hear dispatches . . . Corbett got knocked out in 10th round, by a solar plexus blow, same as Fitzsimmons gave in their memorable fight here . . .

Aug 17 . . . The escaped convicts . . . are heard of near south end of Lake Tahoe robbing for grub, but otherwise peaceable and unpursued – Bed at 11 –

Aug 18 . . . Richard J, otherwise Dickey Jose with his star company of minstrels – 30 or 40 – arrived on morning train from Virginia where they played last evening to crowded house . . . I got letters from Supt Ryan and Secy J W O'Donohue of the Con Va and Ophir mines . . . Evening at theater – 20 in first part – 12 or 14 in band – Splendid setting of 1st part, usual minstrelsy – 4 end men, black face, all others white – Singing & dancing very fine – Good afterpieces, tumblers, burlesque band, etc . . . House crowded – 1st class prices – $1 & 50 cts . . . Raymond Bone a Comstock raised boy is leader, with 1st violin in Dickey Jose's orchestra – Dicky Jose told me today that he weighs 247 pounds – About 35 yrs old –

Aug 20 . . . Great international England and America yacht race for the championship cup, between Sir Thomas Lipton's yacht Shamrock No III and American Reliance commenced at Sandy Hook, N.Y. today . . .

Aug 24 . . . Two more of the convicts, Murphy and Woods were captured in Reno yesterday – Been working in the hay fields of Carson valley, and were in Carson yesterday, eating, drinking & making themselves at home, then footed it to Reno – Third one of them who escaped capture at Reno, reported caught at Wadsworth but not confirmed . . . Hon A C Cleveland died yesterday at his ranch . . .

[Four clips on the unexpected death – Cleveland was born in Maine about 1840, arrived in California in 1858, and came to Nevada in 1863 – Served as state senator and assemblyman, but lost out in two gubernatorial races and one try at the US Senate – Engaged in ranching, lumber and mining, and "gained a fortune by work and sacrifices that would have discouraged the average man" – Heart disease was the cause of death.]

Aug 25 . . . From 10 till 4 PM going through the Va Report file of '92 in State Library on Comstock mining yield . . .

Aug 26 . . . Recd today letter of information from Jas M Leonard relative to the Sutro Tunnel . . .

Sunday, Aug 30 . . . Met Johnny Moore on street about 2 PM & had long chat about our oil shale project – He went to the place and back on Wednesday last – about 50 mile trip . . .

Sept 1 . . . Recd letter from wife with $15 inclosed . . . said Bessie was home last four or five days – sent for by Goodwin on account of wife having a strong attack of nasal hemorrhage – weakening her considerably – Bessie will remain for several weeks . . . Also rec'd letter from James M Leonard with desired Tunnel information, & copy of *Mining Stock Record* of Jan 1, 1903 which I desired . . .

Sept 2 . . . Sent page letter to Col Wm Nelson, SL Tribune – on settlement – Wrote couple of letters for Tom Muckle, to Ed Swift, Gold Hill and Tom Dick Jr, Virginia, relative to hauling 2nd hand brick to Carson – Evening paid my landlady $5, closing room rent, for October – She is packing up to leave . . .

Sept 3 . . . The Yacht race today came off all right, and Reliance won by about a mile & a half. This being the 3d out of 5 settles the champion cup in favor of America, as usual, and perhaps forever as Sir Thos Lipton, the most persistent, says he is going to give up the 50 years contention and let us keep the cup for all of him –

Sept 4 – Same, breezy & cooler – 88° – Mrs Carter and little boy Loverne got away for their new Reno home by morning train – I saw them off – She left my lodging house in perfect order, clean and good – Only occupants now are myself, Jack Wing, Guy Spencer, and the new baker from San Francisco, Henry Hanks. $5 pr month, each, we paid her – she paid Otto Schultz, proprietor, $15 per month for the concern – small profits – Wrote a brick furnishing contract for use in rebuilding the State Orphans' Home – to furnish good 2nd hand brick from Va to the Orphans Home grounds at $9.81 cts per thousand – Wrote this for Tom Muckle, contractor & builder – Afterward wrote for him order for his wages working on Broughers new mansion $29.50 – Mixed up affair – 4 concerned – Bed at 11:30 feeling lonely & sad at loss of my real good landlady & little son – gave him a 2 bit package of candy at parting – She told me of a little memorandum book she had left in a cupboard inadvertently, and I just mailed it to her.

Sept 5 . . . Took morning train . . . to Va . . . Had a tough climb of the steep hill from the depot, with my wobbly tired old legs – Went after Comstock information – Jim Kinkead, Leon Hall, et al – got considerable – Met Fillebrown and many other old acquaintances & had rather of a pleasant time – spent 6 bits – left on return at 4:20 & got home all right, tired but mentally refreshed – Found Leon Hall on train, going to San F. Interviewed him – The Va *Chronicle* changed hands today, from J L Considine, lessee, to J M Davis, lessee . . .

Sept 9 . . . Mrs Downey, wife of M A Downey the furniture merchant, took charge of my lodging house today . . .

Sept 11 . . . Have my job well started – couple of pages written and Assessment & Dividend table completed in good style –

Sept 12 . . . Got tailings report from Woodbury all right – $401,200 all – Bed 12 –

Sept 14 . . . Sometime along the first of last week, Dr Price, a horse doctor performed the operation for appendicitis on Harry Day's dog "Bob." It was a perfect success, the dog dying on Friday – dead.

Sept 15 – Clear & cool with white frost . . . Sent hurry up page letters to J H Kinkead and Leon M Hall – last – Wrote as usual – Bed 12 – 42 degrees – Bob Logan loaned me a book to read, entitled "The Argonauts of California," by C W Haskins – Pub 1889 – good sized book of 500 pages – two thirds full of lively California stories, and the other third a complete register of the ships and argonauts who arrived, also Pioneer Associations, etc, etc – Bark Yeomans arrival among them, with my name and all hands – My name spelled *Alf*. Doten – Never spelled or pronounced that way till I came to Nevada and adopted it as my *"nom de plume"* –

Sept 18 . . . The outrageous driving out of the Chinese from Tonopah last Tuesday night is a theme of much indignant discussion . . . Johnson Sides the best known old Piute in Nevada died on Tuesday in a hop field, near Pleasanton, California, where he and his people from this State were employed picking hops – He was very old, probably 80, and went with his people to Cal hoping to benefit his health, and died as he wished right among them in the hop field – Was buried in the Odd Fellows burial ground near Pleasanton . . .

[Clippings from the *Appeal* and the Virginia *Chronicle* discuss the trouble in Tonopah – Early reports were confused, but a mob ranging anywhere from twenty to a hundred men, apparently mostly white cooks and waiters belonging to Tonopah Labor Union Number 224, had ransacked the small Chinese section, dragging several Chinese down the canyon and leaving them out on the desert, about midnight – One man apparently was beaten to death – Tonopah citizens, including members of the Miners' Union, quickly called a meeting, and several arrests were made, including the president of Number 224 – Trouble started when a Joe Quong took charge of the North Star restaurant – Both papers, outraged at the violent incident, predict that China will demand indemnity and that Nye County will have to foot the bill.]

Sunday, Sept 27 . . . Met son Alfred this PM at Arlington, with some young men friends – Came up for a run and returned on evening train – He only gave me time for a few minutes chat with him. Has to wear eyeglasses all the time now, he says.

Oct 1 . . . Snowstormed some up in the hills – Fall day – Breezy – Ray Richard came home this AM from S.F. Brought along a young female Jaguar, cat, about 3 months old he bought of a man from Central America . . . pet and tame but kept on chain – 1st I ever laid hand on – Completed the Comstock this evening, ready for the printer – 18 big pages . . .

Oct 3 . . . Got the financial part of my Tonopah report, relating to bullion product of Tonopah figured up properly in the Mint, by Will David, Clerk – Total yield of Tonopah in bullion since commencement in 1901 to 1st of last July amounted to:

Tons	Silver	Gold	Total
16,988	$2,028,198.97	$922,392.76	$2,950,591.73

lacking $49,408.27 of being $3,000,000 – Pretty good for Tonopah – Telegraphed George Roberts . . . this evening "Will send both reports complete by Oct tenth" – Feel sure I can do it now . . .

Oct 5 . . . Wrote considerable on Tonopah today . . . James Holbrook an old resident died here yesterday afternoon from diabetes, dropsy, etc aged 64, native of Maine – Was at one time Deputy State Controller, and was Deputy US Marshall awhile before he died – Tom W Raycraft died at Genoa home of Raycraft family yesterday – 1 of the 9 Raycraft brothers . . . Met Matt Riehm at train today & he told me Maggie Moore often inquires about me in her letters . . .

Oct 7 . . . Running evening sessions on my Tonopah report . . .

Oct 10 . . . Bed at 5:30 AM – rose at 10 – Got in the finishing touches of my report, etc – Tried to register & mail it on time – couldnt well do so – will tomorrow . . .

Oct 12 . . . Got my job registry so it positively goes on to Washington tonights mail – feel relieved [See Appendix for the report, "Bullion Production From the Comstock Lode and Tonopah, 1902."] . . . Johnson Sides was buried at Reno last Friday – big funeral, many white citizens besides all the Indians in it . . .

Oct 13 . . . Got letter from Bessie, Reno, going to return to Cal tomorrow morning & be married next Monday, a little sooner than she expected – didnt give me his name but guess its all right – I wrote her a nice page letter . . . She says he is a good man – has a prune ranch – sold his short crop sooner than expected so sent for her to come and marry him right away – Will be married in Episcopal Church Santa Clara, and Eunice will give her away . . .

Oct 14 – Clear, cool & pleasant – Bed at 12 – The Reno Gazette is changed from a 6 to 8 column paper, same size & style as the Journal – improved – Allen C Bragg retires as editor and Manager and Chas A Norcross takes his place and interest in the concern, Gazette Publishing Co – Old Bob Jones whom I knew as milk rancher at American Flat in the early times died in Reno last Sunday, aged 73 years – tough old case – hard parent – caused his daughter to commit suicide at home from cruel treatment and the death of his two sons by freezing to death on the Ophir grade one cold Christmas eve – horseback, trying to get home from Truckee meadows, with a young calf in obedience to father's command, who would beat them half to death if they did not obey orders – He always treated me well – didn't dare do otherwise, the cowardly old brute, and child murderer – His boys were found frozen to the ground and their horses standing by them –

Oct 17 . . . Harry Day's woman, May Williams has recently got married again, this time to a man named Gomez, over at Truckee . . . At the recent drawing of the Little Louisiana lottery, Henry Fothergill won $400, the highest prize on ten cent tickets – poor hard working man – comes good to him . . .

Oct 19 . . . Bessie gets married in the Episcopal church, Santa Clara, today . . . "God bless you my children" – I should have given away the bride, were I present, but Eunice does so in my absence . . .

Oct 20 . . . Got . . . wedding notice reading as follows:

Grant Barton/Bessie T. Doten/Married/Monday, October nineteenth/nineteen hundred and three/Santa Clara, California/At home/after Nov. 5th/Cupertino.

Only this and nothing more – My old legs that have been getting wobbly and shiftless last year or so are almost giving out now – very heavy & *tired* all the time, very hard getting up stairs. Breath getting very short also – Heart bothers me also . . .

Oct 21 . . . Letter from Sam with $9 – from Col Nelson of SL Tribune growling at my writing to him on settlement, says its out of his hands . . .

Oct 22 . . . At 2 PM I walked . . . up to Parson Davis residence to a wedding – 6 blocks – long walk for my present dilapitude – Hadnt seen old parson for last 2 or 3 yrs, as too old to get out & around any more – Sam Davis' father – Episcopal minister – Marriage of James Lamb to Mrs E E May, the widow of my old Hank May of Empire, deceased 6 or 8 yrs ago – Jim got me for best man and for best woman, Mrs Belle Gavin, of Empire – widow – We 4, with parson & wife constituted the whole crowd present – a festive lot of good old timers – the youngest, Mrs Gavin being surely 50 – Old Jim over 60 and his bride not much younger – and Parson Davis wife & himself oldest of the lot – I being 74 – This is Mrs Lamb's third, first one, Mike Donovan, killed by a fluming accident – Old parson just did make out to go through the marriage ceremony with strongest assistance of his wife – But he made it – Then we had a nice little wedding cake lunch, with angelica wine – jolly talk, and all hands left about 4 PM, having occupied nearly 2 hours with our fun – plenty of *kissing* – Dont know where the wedding party passed the night – but they were loaded for bear – Home very leg weary – Evening attended Nevada State Band Minstrels . . .

Oct 26 . . . Evening at Arlington was interviewed by A H Ten Broeck, mining operator etc north of Reno – Wanted to know all about the Comstock – Told him – Bed at 12 after bathing my legs in alcohol . . .

Oct 27 . . . Our Carson Lottery Syndicate won $5 . . .

Oct 28 . . . It was my lively & good old friend, George Schissler who got killed in the Mexican mill Adams plaster works this morning – Body brought to town but so badly mutilated that I didn't care to look at it . . . Good bye old George – few if any best friends have gone before that were more appreciative than you –

Oct 29 . . . Geo Schissler was of Knights of Pythias . . . brief funeral by K of P at train time, evening, when remains shipped east to his old home in Michigan – A younger brother accompanied him . . . PM met

Billy Kent his mining partner, from Virginia & we had lots of old time talk . . .

Oct 30 . . . Walk with much difficulty with frequent rests – shortness of breath, etc – both legs swelling . . .

Sunday, Nov 1 . . . About home most of day, not feeling well – PM wrote & sent 2 page letter to wife – Evening at Arlington awhile . . .

Nov 2 . . . Wrote & sent page letter to George E Roberts (personally) about not sending acknowledgment of receipt of my reports, or cashing my $150 bill for same – Bed at 11 very lame and *tired* – I never get rested any more – Old Clabe or Claiborne Gunter, one of the oldest faro dealers and gamblers on the Comstock died at his post last Saturday evening at Virginia . . . only 2 or 3 more of his kin remain –

Nov 3 . . . Recd letter from wife with $15 – Legs still lamer – can't get up the long 28 flight of stairs to my lodgings without taking a rest or two – Paid my landlady my room rent . . .

Nov 5 – Principally clear & pleasant – At home most of the day . . . Have Dr Huffaker working on my care – Bed 12:30 – And as I slept the first 2 hours, I got into one of the queerest dreams of my life – dreamed that I was traveling horseback among some of the central mining towns of the old California gold diggings in company with half a dozen brothers & uncles of our Doten family, being the first time we had ever all met together. Just at dark we arrived at the cabin or abode of one of the relatives, for the night – His wife called him out one side shortly & showed him a letter she had written to more relatives a few towns away, calling his attention particularly to the tail end of the letter which was stuffed into a long envelope, like a sausage about 14 inches long. He commenced reading out to us all the chopped and stuffed chunks of wit, wisdom & humor, until all enthusiastically called a quit on the reading, heartily indorsing every word and sentiment, and then every man of us signed it as his own, passing it along to its destination feeling that we had done something grand, that we could think happily over the rest of our lives. And the more I thought it over, the more I couldn't sleep from studying & reflecting over the contents of that stuffed tale, and finally I had to get up and write this regarding it.

Nov 6 . . . Had to get some one else to get my mail from the PO since last Monday – Afraid to chance those big stone steps – Sitting in the Arlington this PM, chatting with Uncle David Hull, I inadvertently got my left shin too near the stove allowing it to draw a big blister 2 or 3 inches in diameter . . .

Nov 7 . . . PM I called on Dr Huffaker and arranged to shut down my personal works for next wk or 10 days – deciding the thing 3 or 4 days, keeping my room & bed – Bed at 12 – Freezing –

Sunday, Nov 8 . . . Johnny Moore only one that called, till after 4 PM – Harry Day came, like good angel, with sundry little supplies – I wrote & mailed by him letter to wife – page – giving her first knowledge of present sad condition – Evening to myself and newspapers brought to me . . . This is one day in my life, that living up stairs, I failed to strike the main street . . .

Nov 9 . . . PM had to get out & to the Arlington privy – Home again at once – Mrs Downey my landlady made up my bed this PM . . . Harry called on me this evening – nobody else today – The Dr called about 11 oclock PM, 1st time . . .

Nov 10 . . . Very quiet at home – Johnny Moore and Harry Day called by turns and each kindly procured needables, medicine, etc for me – P H Mulcahy also called with Harry – The Dr didnt come at all . . .

Nov 11 – Cloudy, cold with fearful wind and dust storm all day – Blew down fences and all moveable things – Everybody staid at home and I had nobody to visit me – Had to get along as best I could – not even the Dr calling to see me – Bed 11:30 – still continues bad as ever – can't let up –

[*Carson City News*, Nov 12, 1903:] Alfred Doten, one of the old pioneers of California and Nevada was found dead in bed this afternoon at about 2 o'clock by Mrs. Downey proprietor of the Alta House, where he roomed. His body was still warm showing that he had been dead only a few hours. He was last seen alive by Mr. Downey who visited his room at 11 o'clock last evening, leaving him feeling as well as usual. He passed away peacefully and quietly as there was no sign of a struggle. . . .

Mary continued to live on in Reno until her death in 1914 at age 69. The married daughter, Bessie, died of typhoid fever at age 31, in 1905, while on a visit to Reno; and the youngest daughter, Goodwin, committed suicide with chloroform in 1911 at age 30, after the death of her fiancé. The two sons, although both lived in Reno, had little to do with one another. The older, Samuel, a moderate man, was director of the university's Agricultural Experiment Station and a well-known professor; he died in 1955 at age 79. Alfred Jr., whose temperament was much like his father's, was part owner of a Reno warehouse until his death at age 48 in 1926. His obituary mentions that Millie, his stepsister, was then living in Illinois. Although both sons were married, neither had children, and Bessie's daughter was the only grandchild.

Appendix

Charter of the Pilgrim Mining Company

[Transcribed here from the manuscript copy in the Doten Collection; mentioned in the journal entry for May 1, 1849.]

Articles of agreement in two parts, by and between Bradford Barnes, and the other owners of the Barque Yeoman of Plymouth of the first part, and James M. Clark and thirty nine others, members of the Pilgrim Mining Company of the second part, made and concluded at Plymouth in the county of Plymouth, State of Massachusetts, this [blank] in the year Eighteen hundred and forty nine, for the purpose of engaging in mining operations in California and prosecuting such other business as may be further agreed upon by the parties interested. Witnesseth –

That the said party of the first part, for, and in consideration of the covenants and agreements hereafter to be kept and performed by the parties of the second part do covenant and agree as follows –

First – To let the above named Barque Yeoman for a two years voyage to California to be used for freighting or any other lawful business, while there and return to Plymouth – to put and keep her in suitable order for such voyage with suitable accommodations for forty men at our own expense, and also to allow the sum of thirty five and two thirds dollars to the officers of the said Barque per month, during the passage out, payment to be made at the conclusion of said voyage by the said owners –

Secondly – The parties of the first part also agree, to furnish and supply, on account of the voyage, good and sufficient provisions for forty men for two years, together with such implements for mining, and such other articles as the parties may judge nescessary to effect the objects of the undertaking, the cost and expense of which with interest shall be refunded to the parties of the first part, from the proceeds of the expedition as hereinafter specified, and they are also to select the Master for the said vessel –

The parties of the second part, in consideration of the covenants and agreements herein mentioned, to be kept and performed by the said parties of the first part do severally and individually agree –

First – To associate themselves together to be called the "Pilgrim Mining Company," to embark in said vessel on the voyage or expedition faithfully and constantly, to pursue the contemplated business of mining and such other business as may be deemed expedient for the interest of all concerned for the space of two years, including the time spent on passages, that they will endeavour to promote according to the best of their respective abilities, the interest of all parties to these covenants and agreements, and to obey and support such rules and regulations as shall be adopted for the government of the said expedition –

Secondly – That they each one for himself will give seperate bonds, to the said owners, with sufficient sureties each in the sum of two hundred dollars, severally binding themselves to perform the covenants and agreements set forth in this instrument to be performed, with said party of the first part, it being expressly understood that the said company are not to be held liable to said owners for the debts default or liabilities of any one of its members.

Thirdly – It is further provided that if either of the parties of the second part shall obstinately refuse or neglect to fulfill said covenants and agreements herein mentioned, that the individual so refusing or neglecting shall forfeit his share in all right, title, and interest in the proceeds of the voyage or expedition and also all that he may now or hereafter produce or posess, so far as shall be sufficient to indemnify them for any and [all] damages for such neglect or refusal, which shall go to joint-stock fund –

The parties of the first part, and the parties of the second part also agree –

First – That there shall be paid to the Master of the vessel, from the joint stock, a commission of five per cent, untill such sum may amount to five hundred dollars, which sum shall be the extent of his perquisite for the service as Master, after which payment, the said parties agree, that two thirds of the proceeds shall belong to the owners of said Barque untill such amount shall be sufficient to repay them, with interest. The other third part shall be the property of said Mining Company to be divided as the rules and by-laws of said Company provide –

Secondly – It is to be distinctly understood that all purchases of fresh provisions and produce, not provided by the owners shall be paid for, one third by the owners, and two thirds by the Mining Company –

Thirdly – That after the above named deductions for the payment of the Master, Owners &c, the proceeds arising from the further prosecution of the objects of the expedition, whether from Mining or earnings of the vessel shall be joint stock property, of which one third shall belong to the owners of the vessel, and the other two thirds to said Mining Company, subject to the foregoing considerations –

Fourthly – That if any member of the Company die before the voyage is completed, his share of the proceeds shall be in proportion to the time elapsed from the departure from Plymouth to the time of his decease compared with the whole time employed in the enterprise and no member shall be deprived of any portion of his share, for sickness unless caused by his own misconduct.

When the time arrives to take passage for home, should the said Mining Company and the Master of the vessel think proper and choose some other conveyance to return, and the vessel can be suitably disposed of, such an arrangement may be made by an agreement of the representatives of the parties and the vessel sold for the benefit of the owners –

And for the faithfull performance of all the covenants and agreements herein mentioned, the said parties hereunto individually set their names and seals and hereby firmly bind themselves, their heirs, executors, and administrators, at Plymouth this thirteenth day of March in the year One thousand eight hundred and forty nine –

Names of the owners of the Yeoman

Benjamin Barnes	James M. Clark
Bradford Barnes	Corban Barnes
John Gooding	Southworth Barnes
Ellis Barnes	Samuel Doten
James Collins	George Simmons, Jr.

Names of the Pilgrim Mining Company members

Ellis B. Barnes	Henry Chase
Winslow B. Barnes	John E. Churchill [Ship's steward]
Nathaniel S. Barrows, Jr.	Silas M. Churchill
Ozen Bates	James M. Clark
Seth Blankenship [Second mate]	[Master of the *Yeoman*]
Caleb C. Bradford	John B. Clark
[Ship's carpenter]	George Collingwood [First mate]
George A. Bradford	William Collingwood
Thomas Brown	James T. Collins

Names of the Pilgrim Mining Company members (continued)

Nathaniel C. Covington [President of the Pilgrim Mining Company]
Nathan G. Cushing
Alfred Doten
Chandler Dunham
Richard B. Dunham
William J. Dunham
Sylvanus Everson
George P. Fowler
William A. Gifford
Franklin B. Holmes
Henry B. Holmes
Henry M. Hubbard
Elisha J. Kingman
Edward Morton
Henry M. Morton
Alexander O. Nelson
Augustus Robbins
Francis H. Robbins [Secretary of the Pilgrim Mining Company]
Ellis Rogers
Thomas Rogers
William Saunders
Robert Swinburn
James T. Wadsworth
John Ward

Woods' Creek in "Forty-Nine"

[Unpublished manuscript by Doten, written in July and August of 1898. See journal entries for January 3, 1850, March 26, 1871, and August 7, 1898.]

Among the earliest noted and most productive placer diggings in the southern part of the California gold mining region were those of Woods' creek, in Tuolumne county, about seventy miles from Stockton, amid the pine-clad hills of the old Sierra Nevada. The principal rush of the fortune hunters, during the Fall of 1849 was to Woods', although many struck out for still more newly discovered diggings away farther south along the range.

The youthful argonauts, including representatives of all nations, rather enjoyed the tramp across the broad level plains of the San Joaquin valley, packing their blankets and things, frequently resting beneath shady oaks, and chewing the big sweet acorns that dropped from the branches over-head. The road was also lined with freight trams and pack trains to and from various localities. Occasional parties were met coming back from the mines, sick or disappointed, one gang of thirty Chinese who had been driven out, saying: "Mines no good; Melican man he no likee Chinaman."

Knight's Ferry, on the Stanislaus river, was the best camping place, where the cool flashing water was knee deep, in crossing, and plenty of luscious salmon to be had for the catching. Many were shot with rifles, and Indians standing mid-stream, speared and sold them for a dollar apiece – ten or a dozen pounders at that. From here the road was over rolling ground with numerous dry gulches amid the low trees and aromatic shrubbery of the foot-hills skirting the southern flanks of the famous long, level-topped Table Mountain for numerous miles, until reaching the main objective point, Woods' crossing of Woods' creek. And right here a dozen of us made our first camp in the gold diggings, on the left hand side of the road, where it descended to cross the creek to Curtis', Sullivan's and other new creeks and diggings beyond. Our cabin or camp, when completed, was sixteen by twenty feet square, with rough log walls four feet high, a canvas roof, and, at one end was a small kitchen addition, thatched with pine boughs, a stone fireplace and chimney finishing up the outfit in comfortable style. Then somebody with a bit of charcoal wrote *Pilgrim Mining Co.* in big letters along the side of the canvas roof and we were ready for business. [Doten's sketch of the camp appears in the picture section in Volume 1 of these Journals.]

Charley Heffernan's store, with wooden stockade walls, was a few yards directly below us, on the bank of the creek, and fronting it, on the opposite side of the road was Swope's store. Both naturally dealt in goods suitable for miners' use, selling at a profitable advance on Stockton rates, with freight added. And a decidedly important addition was "freight," when in the middle of Winter it got up to a dollar a pound, owing to the almost impassable state of the road from Stockton. Thus molasses was $10 a bottle, vinegar $16, and whisky jumped from four bits to a dollar a drink; in fact it jumped clean out of sight entirely on one extra bad occasion when the copious rains and floods destroyed what little bottom there was left to the road. This was reckoned among the hardships.

Woods' Crossing, with its two stores, was looked upon as the initial point of trade, distribution and divergence for the surrounding mines and down the creek. Some hundreds of miners worked along the banks, flats and bed of the creek, or in the connecting gulches and ravines, but phenomenally rich strikes were not frequent, and a man with ounce – $16 – diggings was considered in big bonanza luck. Half an ounce a day was pretty good, and perhaps five dollars a day may be stated as a fair general average – many made less, and the sick or disabled ones nothing. Those newly fledged "miners" had the disadvantages of inexperience, impaired health from long travel by land or sea, lack of proper food and shelter, unsuitable mining implements, and many other adverse conditions to contend with, therefore it was that the miners of that famous "Winter of '49" were not as financially successful as those of the heavy Winter of '52.

Jamestown, about a mile above Woods' on a flat at the left hand side of the creek, was a mere suggestion in name of the present flourishing metropolis. It was made up of a few miners' cabins and tents scattered around near Butterfield's store, which was the most pretentious wooden house in the camp and naturally a central rallying point. Moreover, Butterfield's wife was the only woman citizen of that locality, like as Mrs Heffernan was the only one down at Woods' Crossing. Indeed the inspiring sight of a white woman in those new regions was a notable rarity, and many a gray-shirted miner traveling the hillside trail past Jamestown on a Monday, paused to gaze upon the array of white sheets, pillow cases, table cloths and other linen goods, and real woman's dresses fluttering from Mrs Butterfield's clothes lines. It made him think of home and mother and wipe away a tear.

And those festive miners about Jamestown were inclined to feel a little aristocratic over the idea of having the only white lady, and regarded Mrs Butterfield as a sort of mascot, inducing good luck to any of them working or prospecting within range or compass of the glance of her eye. The diggings around Jamestown paid well, and the community prospered better than the average, consequently the Butterfields also prospered, and the boys were only too happy to pay Mrs B. three dollars apiece for the eggs derived from the half dozen hens she so thriftily nurtured and encouraged, engaging them for weeks ahead, about Christmas time. She lost thousands of dollars by not having more hens. Whether it was originally named Jamestown or Jimtown doesn't matter, both names were familiar to it then and have been ever since. Just above Jamestown, off to the left, was a glimpse of the end of Table Mountain, showing a very prominent vein or body of snow-white quartz, but it merely attracted passing attention as a peculiarity. Nobody cared for quartz, or looked upon it as liable to some day develope into a richer gold mine than any of the surrounding placer diggings.

Coarse gold predominated at Jamestown and throughout Woods' creek and its tributary gulches, and especially up at Sonora and Shaw's Flat, half a dozen miles or so above. Coarse nuggets were quite frequently picked up on the surface, about Jamestown, and the abundance of coarse gold glitteringly revealed among the grass-roots on Shaw's Flat after a heavy rain was what caused its immediate recognition and occupation as one of the richest and most promising gold discoveries.

The coarsest piece of gold found in '49 was unearthed by a drunken, lazy old Mexican in crevicing around among some abandoned prospect holes within the town of Sonora. It weighed twenty-two pounds and nine ounces, and contained about five pounds of quartz. As soon as he could wash off the dirt he took it to his favorite monte bank and lost $500 of its value inside of an hour, by which time he had become too drunk to play any longer. With such a good hold on it for a starter, it did not take the bank long to win the rest, and become sole proprietor. It was not a very handsome nugget, but it was valued at $5,000, and went to San Francisco, doubtless finally closing its destiny in the melting pot.

Sonora, Shaw's Flat, Columbia, Bald Mountain, Jamestown and adjacent localities yielded numerous good fortunes. Taking a section of ten miles square, including the various mining localities mentioned, for honest, substantial golden merit and liberally demonstrated production it was unsurpassed, if not unequaled by any other golden section of its size in California. It was also a fine, salubrious section, well wooded and watered, and even in that hard old Winter of '49 it was very little troubled with severe cold or wintry snows, although plenty of deep eternal snow shrouded the higher mountains of the Sierra, not far away.

The principal sickness of the Forty-niners was scurvy, and dysentery or diarrhea. Scurvy came from eating too much salt pork and flapjacks and the lack of vegetable food and fresh meat – good hunters were few and hardly anybody knew how to cook. Nearly half of them were more or less afflicted with scurvy, for which the most effective or available medicine was potatoes, from New Zealand, bought at Swope's store for $3 a pound, scraped raw into vinegar – $16 a bottle – and fed to the patient with a spoon.

Doctor Carnduff, an eastern patent medicine man down at Hawkin's Bar, on the Tuolumne river, was noted as having a sure cure for diarrhea. A miner nearly dead from it – and dissipation – went to him one day and after paying the stipulated fee, an ounce of gold, was given a plainly written prescription with strict directions to go right straight home with it, which he did. Then he read this: "Quit whisky and eat acorns." The miner was so profoundly impressed with such a condensed chunk of wisdom that he proceeded to get well forthwith and permanently.

But, speaking about doctors, a prominent figure appears among the interesting memories of those days; a kindly personage still well remembered by many of the old boys. His home and office was a neat little cabin some three or four miles from Woods' Crossing, on the left hand side of the mail road where it approachingly declines toward Curtis' creek, another new and lively mining community. It was built of sawed lumber, was about ten by fourteen feet square and the roof was elaborately shingled with deer skins, indicating its occupant to be a mighty hunter, yet his professional shingle, tacked to the corner near the front door bore the peaceful legend: *"Dr H D Cogswell, Dentist."* Written placards, posted at outside conspicuous points among the diggings also advertised: "Dr Cogswell, dentist, deerskin cottage, main road, near Curtis' creek." [Pencil sketch of cabin.]

The doctor was nice looking, in the full vigor of early manhood, fine light figure, pleasant bright black eyes, and full beard carefully trimmed to a regulation inch all around. He wore a genial smile and a fine fringed buckskin hunting suit, carried a trusty rifle that he handled like a true American sharpshooter, and pictured upon the background of distant memory he appeared something after this style: [Pencil sketch of doctor.]

He could pick, shovel or pan when he took a notion, interested himself considerably in mining and mercantile pursuits, possessed lots of good practical sense and judgment on all popular subjects and was naturally popular with all who knew him – a right good man among men. And when you come to dentistry, that's where he was chief, and a comfort to know and find, in case of painful or defective mastication. He came from Rhode Island, and was proud of his country and his people. Nobody knew any more how the gold got into the diggings, or had better philosophical ideas generally than the doctor. Said he at one of his frequent visits to our camp:

"Gold is where we find it, and the safest rule for finding it is to go where it is and follow it up. Whether it rained down or was thrown up matters but little. Gold is good to fill teeth with but not as a filling for the stomach. Gold is also good to make money of and corrupt politicians with. It is also exceedingly handy to have in one's pocket when needed, and is highly useful in many ways but we can't eat or drink it.

"Water is infinitely more valuable than gold. Next to woman water is God's greatest blessing to man. Without water California's gold would never have been found, or if found it would never have been washed out. Gold has caused the great rush of emigration hither from all quarters of the globe, yet let all this gold be worked out in the next fifty years California will then be greater in her population and prosperity than ever, all from her great wealth of pure water in rivers, lakes and the noble mountain streams of her grand old Sierra Nevada.

"Give a man dying of thirst a purse of gold and he will sadly reject it in despair, but place a cup of water to his parched lips he will eagerly imbibe it with soulfelt thanks for true salvation and renewed life. Ah! if we could only furnish food to our fellow man as freely as we can water, the world would be well fixed and ripe for the millenium.

"Every cup of water we give to the thirsty increases our hopes of heaven, and with many it is their only hope of ever getting there. And now for this free lecture on hydraulic philosophy please give me a cup of water and I'll go home. Good bye."

A year or two later I found the good doctor following his dental practice in San Francisco, as full of life and successful business energy as ever, and got half a dozen teeth filled in order to meanwhile enjoy another good lecture from him on gold and hydraulic philosophy.

His fellow pioneers sympathetically rejoiced with him on his progressive accession to deserved munificent wealth, noting that his liberal heart expanded with his success, and now, since his death, whenever I read or hear of the beautiful free water street fountain he presented to the general public of San Francisco, I softly and complacently remark "that's him" and imagine each sparkling drop of water to be one of the jewels of his consistency, and a tear to his memory.

The hardships and sufferings endured by the Forty-niners have often been imagined and described, yet there is not one of them living at the present time but will agree that our hardships and sufferings were not to be even mentioned in comparison with those of the Klondike gold seekers of the present day. We came to a land already famed for its general beauty, fine climate and undeveloped resources, a land which even without its rich gold revelation was fairer and more promising than many of us left behind. None of us froze to death on the way nor after arriving, neither were the rivers or the gold diggings themselves ever frozen. Food was scarce at first, but nobody starved to death and the seemingly wild stories we read and heard, of the richness and extent of the mines, we found to be all true – they were even better and more extensive than represented. There were no frozen humbugs or frozen flies in California.

One Saturday evening one of my partners and myself were returning from Shaw's Flat to our camp at Woods' Crossing. We had seven or eight miles to travel, on a late start, and a storm was commencing, but we knew our trail. A couple of miles out, the shades of evening thickened with cold showers, and soon broad snowflakes like ghostly flapjacks were floating down upon and around us. We were in for it and doing some very active sprinting, for the trail was fast disappearing.

"The big old hollow tree!" shouted George, breaking into a lively run, "let's make that, quick!" We struck out with hearty good will, plunging along the obscure hillsides and across the dark, muddy ravines till directly with hilarious whoops we rushed into the wide open hospitable shelter of that great, hollow-hearted old sugar pine tree.

This being our half-way house of refuge, after a brief rest we concluded to make ourselves at home for the night. Taking advantage of a temporary lull in the storm we dragged together a lot of dry limbs and logs and soon had a roaring good fire. Then we dressed a jack rabbit I had shot that morning, split him in halves, broiled him nicely on the clean hot coals, and with the aid of some sea biscuit we had a supper fit for the Mikado, washed down with a social draught of Adam's ale from a babbling brook near by.

Indian hunters through numerous generations had builded their camp fires against the north base, or lee side of that big old sugar pine, which was ten or a dozen feet in diameter, until it had become well burned and hollowed out, making a very eligible sheltering place for man or beast, neatly carpeted with dry leaves scattered in by the winds. It was not large enough to lie down in, so after supper we sat side by side on the floor with the charred black walls to lean against swapping odd stories, and George smoking his pipe. A coyote, hungry hoodlum of the wild animal race, attracted by the scent of our jack rabbit cookery, serenaded us from the hillside with his sharp, varied barks and yelps, venturing within range of our bright firelight. There was only one of him, but he barked in the various keyed voices of a dozen, all at one time. "Ah!" exclaimed George, smiling regretfully toward him, "what wonderful game a fellow sees sometimes when he hain't got no gun."

Complacently we congratulated ourselves on our luxurious quarters, and when the wind roared through the trees, and occasional whirls of snow lightly sprinkled our faces, our hearts were filled with sorrow for the hundreds of poor homeless fellows who were doubtless lying about, exposed to the fury of this pitiless storm. We needed no blankets, but sat leaning snugly against each other and slept gloriously, notwithstanding that envious coyote on the hillside, only a few rods away, ambushed beside a big rock, who glared and barked viciously at us all night.

> We were nice and warm amid the storm,
>   And "as happy as a clam,"
> For our fire was bright, our hearts were light,
>   And we didn't care a yam.

It was daylight when I was rudely awakened by George's elbow punching me in the ribs. "What's the matter here?" said he nervously. "I can't get up." I tried to help him, but still he couldn't make it. Then I discovered that I was in a similar fix. We had deliberately seated ourselves in a solid bed of pitch that had been dripping down from the interior of that tree for centuries. It was of unknown depth but undoubted tenacity, and the heat of our bodies had done the rest. There was no other way for it but to cut each other loose, which we did with a pocket knife, leaving the seats of our pants by way of sign and warning to all future lodgers. Talk about the hardships and sufferings of Forty-niners, here now was some of it. We didn't mind being jeered and joked at by our fellow miners on the way home to Woods', but we modestly detoured around through the chapparal in passing Jimtown.

Charley Heffernan, whose store, as previously stated, was a few yards directly below our camp at Woods' was a very pleasant sociable gentleman and we were not long in becoming acquainted. He was a stout built, ordinary sized man about thirty years of age with brown hair and eyes, and a heavy mustache, the indescribable peculiarity of which, combined with the expression of his mouth became impressed into my mind, and was tragically brought out in memory many years afterward. He came from New York around the Horn in 1846 on the ship Thomas H Perkins, commanded by Captain Arthur, with a portion of Colonel Stevenson's famous regiment of California volunteers, he being corporal in Company F, Captain F J Lippit. His wife, accompanying him, was an Irish woman, and sister to Jack Powers, a private in the same regiment, and subsequently a very noted bandit and highwayman in the early days of southern California.

On the voyage between New York and Rio Janeiro a child was born to the Heffernans, upon whom they bestowed the name of Arthur Perkins Heffernan, in honor of Captain Arthur, his ship and themselves, and by that name the youngster received holy church baptism when the ship put in at Rio. In their store at Woods' little Arthur was the chief joy of his parents, and a prime favorite with all the miner lads and others who traded there. He played around in the dirt as he pleased, and was a bright, happy little baby boy – the only one in the whole camp.

One Sunday in November, shortly after our arrival, happening into the store, Mrs Heffernan said to me: "'Come here mister, please, I want to show you something." Passing through a cloth partition to the rear part of the store, used as parlor, kitchen and sleeping room she pointed to a corner of the earthen floor. "There sir," said she, "this mornin' I left my little Arthur asleep in his bed on the ground while I was talkin' to Charley, out in front. I wasn't gone so very long, and whin I come back, what do you think? I saw a big rattlesnake! crawlin' around Arthur, and he still fast asleep. Oh! you should have seen me. I sprung like a tiger, and I catched up my little boy quick. There's nothin' in the world I'm so afraid of as a snake, but I was too brave to let him kill my boy – wasn't I, Artie, darlin'? I screamed Charley, Charley! come here quick, for God's sake! And Charley did come; he jumped all over the snake, and killed it dead, and then he t'rowed it out on the hillside.

"But stop now while I tell ye the strangest part of it. 'Twasn't half an hour afterward, what should I see but that same dirty divil of a snake, as I thought, come crawlin' in the back door there, wid blood in his eye, still lookin' afther me little boy. I didn't scream for Charley this time, but grabbed this pick handle and wint for the snakin' baste, I bate him to rags this time, I did, and whin I t'rowed him out, there laid the one that Charley killed. Then I thought I'd killed his ghost, sure, but Charley and others that come in whin the battle was over, explained that rattlesnakes runs in pairs, and this one was jist huntin' after his mate. An' *this* is what he found!" shouted she giving the pickhandle a triumphant whirl like a shillaly.

A little later on, came Christmas Day, which was welcomed and observed with much popping of guns and pistols, shouting and general jollification much after the present style in some respects, Christmas being about the only holiday much celebrated in those early times outside of the Fourth of July. That evening the inspiring sound of joyous revelry down in Heffernan's store attracted my presence for a brief observation. A lively gathering of festive miners were having a jolly good time, regardless of expense, singing, dancing and cutting up as they pleased, but all companionably happy, for those Forty-niners were not like the tough elements arriving later on.

"Black Sam," a very "likely" young Virginia darkey, mounted on a pork barrel, with a cracked old fiddle, sawed out some of the most inspiring tunes, from "Ole Zip Coon" to the "Arkansaw Traveler," and the boys came down on the "double shuffle," "Virginny Reel" and various styles of jigs with full-booted emphasis, jarring the rocks on the hillside. And they had a quadrille where the ladies were represented by some of Mrs Heffernan's old skirts, and the style they did put on was excruciating. Little Arthur, too, wouldn't be left out, but trotted around gleefully, with his childish laugh and prattle, reaching up for manly hands to help him dance a little bit, but most of the time he was in the arms of one or the other of the miners, and the scanty supply of candy or sweetmeats in the store was all his. He laughed, sang and shouted, the merriest, happiest little pioneer of them all, and cried bitterly when his loving mother took him away to his little bed. Ah! how well for him it were that he had gone to sleep then, in the arms of the Angel of Death.

Twenty years later, at Virginia City, Nevada, I knew a young man named Arthur Perkins. There were several other Perkinses on the Comstock, and it never occurred to me that I had ever seen or known him before, yet his heavy, dark mustache had a peculiarly familiar look that made me think backward, sometimes. He was rather of a good looking young fellow, inclined to tough and evil associations, and was for several months employed as piano player in Scott's dance house, on South C street, a big public saloon where, every evening, demi-monde ladies balanced partners, and all promenaded to the bar with much harmonious regularity.

On the evening of March [5], 1871, Arthur Perkins was enjoying a little run about town, with a mate, who, like himself was hilariously tight. At the International saloon they amused themselves playing rough tricks and "joshing" their acquaintances. Bill Smith, a quiet, good natured Welsh miner, well known generally, happened to come in, and soon they turned their attention to him. He joked back as good as they sent, and directly Perkins, angry or pretending to be, jerked out the revolver he always carried and poked it into Smith's face, saying: "How'll you have it?" or "where'll you have it?" when the pistol went off, and Smith fell dead on the floor with a bullet through his brain.

"Great God!" exclaimed Perkins stepping back, "I didn't mean that; I didn't go to do that." He was immediately arrested and taken to jail. Great was the public excitement, for this wanton killing had followed closely upon the heels of frequent deeds of murderous violence, incendiarism, robberies and lawlessness, occurring of late, already causing the formation of a secret vigilance committee composed of several hundred of the most popular and responsible citizens, organized for the summary punishment or banishment of the evil-doers who were causing this state of terror and excitement throughout the community. Meetings were held, and a night or two after the Smith murder, the Committee captured the jail on B street and told Perkins he was wanted.

Arthur took the matter coolly and like a philosopher, for he understood the situation fully, and knew just what to expect. They marched him up by the old Ophir works above A street, to the trestle of a mining car track, stood him up on a short piece of plank placed across the track, his arms and legs tied, and a stout rope leading from his neck to a beam overhead. Then they kindly advised him to give a good jump straight up, when they would quickly remove or turn away the plank, thus allowing him a clear, effective drop down through between the rails. He approved the grim utility of the idea, and the last words of Arthur Perkins, as he gave a vigorous, resolute spring upward, were:

"Turn her loose, boys!"

The coroner being informed of this midnight tragedy went up there early next morning and found Arthur still hanging, and upon his back was pinned a placard bearing the figures "601." This was the first official public record or announcement, as it were, designating the name of the Committee, as it was always called afterward. It is known that the members were all successively numbered on joining the organization, therefore presumably, 601 was the number of the Secretary. Moreover all the notifications or warnings, banishing evil-doers after that, emanating from the Committee, bore the fateful signature "601," same as were all the similar warnings of the famous San Francisco Vigilance Committee signed "No 33, Secretary."

When I stood beside Arthur's coffin, at the undertaker's and gazed earnestly upon the countenance now calm and still in the repose of death, the peculiar feature or expression of his mustache and mouth struck vividly home to my recollection, and I involuntarily exclaimed: Charley Heffernan! And my impressions proved to be correct, for a woman with whom he had been living now stated that his full, real name was Arthur Perkins Heffernan and that he was originally from Woods' creek, Tuolumne county, California, where his father, Charles Heffernan, kept a store. This was corroborated by a younger brother who came over from California on learning of the tragic event, through the newspapers. He told me he had often heard his mother tell the rattlesnake story, and, said he: "What a God's blessing it would have been to him and the rest of us if the snakes had killed Artie and made a good little boy of him forever."

Thus sadly ended the reckless career of the pioneer white baby boy of the Woods' Crossing mining camp. Old gray-haired men were seldom met with among the hardy miners of Forty nine, but little children, almost never – being naturally scarcer than women. Not so now, however, for the advancing march of civilization and improvement has brought newspapers and railroads to the Woods Creek and Jamestown section, and as for women and children, a friend from there says: "The chapparal is full of 'em."

The Three Marthas; A Love Story

[A semiautobiographical tale by Doten, printed in the Virginia Daily Union *of July 30, 1865.]*

CHAPTER FIRST.—MY FIRST MARTHA.

I never could understand why or how it was that I fell in love with little Mattie B——.

I was a house carpenter apprentice, eighteen years of age, full of warm blood, happy ideas and lofty aspirations, and considerably addicted to playing the flute.

I was very fond of the society of young ladies, and of course had my favorite among them, and occasionally had experienced a temporary feeling of something more than brotherly regard for some one or the other of them, but I had never been downright in love before.

Mattie was just "sweet sixteen." I call her little, because she was in comparison with the other girls around, and it may have been that the idea of "the choicest sweetmeats are generally done up in the smallest packages," had something to do with it. Be that as it may, she, like myself was very fond of music.

Before I was much acquainted with her I used to be attracted by hearing her play the piano, and stand under the parlor window listening for an hour at a time. The piano has been a favorite instrument with me ever since.

I was always rather backward and retiring in the society of young ladies, although of a very impressible, ardent temperament; but by degrees I sought her society, and shortly became well enough acquainted to sit by her at the piano, and soon the notes of my flute were to be heard commingling its strains with the lively notes of the piano.

An odd feeling of loneliness came over me occasionally while I was at work at my daily avocation, and amid the busy noise of saw, hammer and turning lathe in the carpenter shop, and sweet thoughts—a pair of rosy cheeks and hazel eyes—would enter, like rays of sunshine beaming upon my heart, causing me to shove the jackplane or the handsaw, sometimes with a strange vehemence as I thought of the approach of evening and its anticipated pleasures.

Why was it that after playing merry tunes and gay music for awhile, that we somehow would naturally select some sweet, simple love song? Why was it, that when we played and sang "Thou, thou reignest in this bosom" that our eyes would occasionally meet in a sly, sidelong glance, given, by a strange coincidence, at the same moment, causing the red blood to mount to the brows of either? Why was it that twelve o'clock always came so soon, and even one o'clock, without our noticing the intervening lapse of time at all?

Yes—and why was it that late one evening, we stood by the front door, as I was taking my departure, she holding a lamp, and I with my hand on the door knob? It wasn't the first time we had stood that way; but, somehow on this occasion there was something on my mind more than usual—an ungratified wish—and my courage had never before been equal to the emergency. In fact it was hardly so now, but as I gazed into the depths of those beautiful eyes, and wishingly upon those pouting, rosy lips, I felt suddenly inspired, and with a low murmur of her name I suddenly bent forward and, with one arm about her waist, I imprinted a burning kiss upon those pouting rosy lips aforesaid. A heavenly kiss! for it met with a full response; and for an instant two souls mingled together in a state of ecstatic bliss.

A blank in my existence occurs about that time. I remember nothing of the intervening space between that front door and my father's house. The long down hill and the long up hill pass at once into oblivion, and I seem, with feet together and hands outstretched to lean forward with closed eyes and fly, even as we see pictures of angels in the act of doing.

Honey, sugarhouse syrup—nothing can convey any adequate idea of the sweetness of my dreams that night; but my mother wakes me up in the morning and is surprised and happy to notice the thoroughly blissful expression that beams o'er the countenance of her boy.

I see my little Martha again and again, and I am never so happy as when in her company. Each evening seems shorter than the other. That hateful old clock with eternal click, seems always to run about three times as fast as usual when we are together, and I never leave her, even after the sweetest of kisses, without a strange, indefinite feeling of ungratified wish, and blissful anticipations of the next evening.

All is flowers, moonlight and sunshine with me now, and the world rolls on wheels.

I astonish my "boss" with the extraordinary vim with which I shove the plane or swing the shingling hatchet, and quite often, as I lay down my hammer after driving a nail, I draw a long breath and gently exclaim, "O! Martha, Martha."

I build lofty castles in the air, and my future pathway seems strewn with flowers and glowing with the beams of hope and promise. I see a little white cottage, with green blinds, roses climbing the porch, hollyhocks and sunflowers in front, and fragrant flower beds all around it.

It is *our* cottage, built with my own hands and my little duck of a Martha sits at the window singing, or stands in the door waiting to give me the welcome kiss, as I return from my daily toil, "happy and content," like the fattest of Swimley's boarders.

I am filled with the brightest hopes, noblest ideas and loftiest aspirations—eternally longing to be doing something good and grave that shall win a smile of approval from Mattie.

I see her ride along the street with her father, and think of how if those horses should become frightened and unmanageable, and come frantically tearing down street, scattering all living things in their way right and left, I would bravely rush out to the rescue and seizing them both by the foaming bits, bring them to a stand still, while Mattie and her father alighted in safety, her smile being amply sufficient reward for the danger I had encountered for her sake.

Then again I picture to myself a band of burglars forcing an entrance into her house in the still depths of the night. I happen along. I hear a shriek—I dash madly into the back door, which they have forced from its hinges. At the head of the stairs I meet a huge burglar. We grapple. His comrades come to his assistance, and in one wild, desperate struggle we all roll down the stairs together. I spring to my feet—I knock them down as fast as they can pick themselves up. There are seven of them, and they are a match for me, as I have no weapons but my fists. Why does not assistance come? Suddenly the report of a pistol, and all is chaos—I am shot.

When I come to my senses I find myself in a bed, amid a strong smell of camphor and with a bad taste in my mouth.

I gaze wildly around, for I see many faces and think they are all burglars, and I clench my swollen fists preparatory to knocking them all down, but my eye rests on Mattie, with a big bottle of camphor, bathing my head with her own plump little hand, and I know that everything is all right. I hear the voice of the doctor, in reply to anxious inquiries from my mother, who has just arrived, telling her that the ball only glanced on my skull and that I will be all right in a day or two. I feel all right *now,* and astonish them all by sitting upright in bed.

Her father calls me a "brave fellow"—Martha says nothing, but her eyes talk.

My mother is proud of her brave boy, and from the others around me I learn that I came just in the nick of time, for the burglars had just succeeded in forcing the door of Martha's chamber, thinking it the door of the pantry where silver plate was kept, but my sudden appearance had frustrated their attempts, so they had only got off with a bottle of hair oil and a pewter washbowl.

I imagine myself a man. Like to have people call me "Mr. Doten" instead of "Alf.," and often my sisters detect me examining my chin and upper lip before the looking glass for some faint trace of an incipient beard.

The form of a brawny young shoemaker rises in my memory. That shoemaker has the audacity to make love to Martha, and I have to look upon him as a rival. His name is Jenkinson, but the boys all call him "Jinks," for short. He has a large nose, and he is bigger and older than I am, and has a moustache.

He calls me "boy," and annoys me all he can. Yes, he even insults me sometimes when Martha is with me. She tells me to take no notice of the fellow, and that she "hates him and his big nose."

He becomes inflamed at the idea of Martha never bestowing more than a friendly smile upon him, and one evening, coming home from singing school with Martha, he meets up and wipes me across the face with a stocking full of wet sand. My blood boils and I cannot speak a word, but my mind is made up.

I see Martha home, wash my face from the foul insult, and bidding her "good evening," I go after "Jinks."

I meet him on the sidewalk, and stepping in front of him I spit full in his face. Blows follow—I put in the best I know how. A ring is formed around us of his friends and mine, who will see fair play. I receive a staggerer which closes my left eye, and I fall amid a shower of stars.

I rise for the second round, and come at him again. He taps me on the forehead, and I counter on that big proboscis of his making the claret fly copiously, amid cheers from my friends. He staggers back, but soon comes up again for the third round. I am getting weak, but I give him the best I have got.

Suddenly another shower of stars, and with a wild whirl I fell again.

When I rose again. I saw Jinks walking away down street with his friends, and naturally conclude that I have got the worst of it.

Sam Pogue, the constable, makes his appearance from "round the corner," and whispering in my ear as he quietly pats me on the back, says: "Well done my little rooster—you'll lick him yet."

My mother puts beefsteak on my obscured eye, reads the Bible to me, and tells me how wicked 'tis to fight, but I think—"Just wait till my eye gets well."

My father (an old sea captain and a regular old war horse) pats me on the head and tells me: "Never mind bub, we'll fetch the scoundrel yet."

I say nothing, but think numerous things.

My sisters are apparently neutral, but still say they "would like to see me whip Jinks. He ought to be whipped." I concur.

Martha comes to see me, for I feel ashamed to go to her. She is sorry that I fought, but doesn't blame me. She says "that big nose of Jinks' is swollen as big as her bonnet, and thinks he ought to have been put in jail for fighting. She wishes she was a man."

My big brother Sam takes me down into the barn and talks to me. He illustrates thus:

"When he struck at you that time you oughter stuck your elbow up like thus, and then you oughter returned on his conk—his bugle you know—like that. Go for the smeller all the time; that's his weak point."

Sam and myself privately meet in the barn every day and "illustrate."

Two weeks later, with Sam for my second, Jinks and myself meet by appointment, accompanied by a few friends of each, in a huckleberry pasture, and in four rounds he gets most gloriously whipped.

I escape with scarce a scratch, while he is led home stone blind, that huge nose of his having swelled up into his eyes and looking like a parboiled beef's heart.

After this I have no more trouble with Jinks. He treats me with respect, and I talk to him just the same as though I had never whipped him and couldn't do it again.

Alas for human happiness, "the course of true love never does run smooth."

Martha's father had gone to Charleston, South Carolina, on business, where he was taken very sick. His family was sent for, as it was thought he would not live long, and hastily they packed up and left.

Oh! how shall I describe that sad parting? My heart starts wildly beating even now as I think of it. But oh! we did not once think that would be a final separation. No. We would soon meet again, never more to part, and be happier than ever.

> "Wi' many a vow and locked embrace,
> Our parting was fu' tender,
> And, pledging oft to meet again,
> We tore oursel's asunder."

Two months passed by, and every week we exchanged the most loving of letters, full of sweetness and protestations of eternal love and fidelity.

"There's a divinity that shapes our ends, rough hew them as we will." That's so.

Wild stories were afloat, and golden tales were told of a far off country called California, where the yellow precious metal lay scattered about in profusion, even abounding in the sands, in the beds of the rivers and mountain streams. Yes, fortunes were lying about loose there, waiting for the hand of the enterprising adventurer to come and gather them up.

Ships were being fitted out and leaving every port, loaded with fortune hunters, and at length I too became imbued with the exciting "gold fever," and a ship being up for California, raising a company in my own native town, I joined them.

Martha tried in her letters to dissuade me from it, saying her father was nearly recovered and they would start for home soon; but no use, I was bound for California, but I would be back in two years at the outside, with a fortune, and then all our fondest hopes would be realized. It was all for *her*.

I will not speak of the long seven months' trip around Cape Horn, of the perils we encountered, or of the romantic pleasures of "sailing o'er the broad blue sea," but amid all, the happiest moments to me were when I was dreaming of my old home and Martha.

For over a year after I arrived in California I got letters regularly every mail from her, filled with assurances of love and constancy, which I returned with interest, and anticipated the happy time when we should meet again.

By and bye her letters became less frequent, and I could not understand why they became so short and the tone of them gradually cooler and less loving.

Was it possible? No! I would not believe it.

But, alas! letters came from friends who told me the sad, cold truth. Martha's love had become estranged, and another had supplanted me in her affections.

I immediately wrote to her, asking her in plain terms if this was all true.

She replied that there might be some grounds for my believing it, and said "it was true we had enjoyed many happy hours in each other's society, and had imagined ourselves in love with each other, but we were both very young and had really mistaken our feelings. She felt that we would always remain the warmest of friends and should consider me as such."

I at once replied, reminding her of the many sweet moments we had passed side by side, and absolving her from all vows and promises. Yes, we would always remain friends, but we need not continue our correspondence."

Oh! the wild heart achings—the soul weariness of that unhappy time. The saddest feeling of blighted hopes that had come o'er the spirit of my happy dream. Martha was lost to me forever. Not many months later I read the notice of her marriage in one of the home papers.

Heigho! I read it with a sigh and a pang of regret as I again thought over the bright dream of the past—a foretaste of Heaven, too sweet, too bright to last.

> "Twas a light that ne'er can shine again
>   On life's dull stream.
> No: there's nothing half so sweet in life
>   As love's young dream."

CHAPTER SECOND.—MY SECOND MARTHA.

Four years passed by with their variations of winter, summer, clouds and sunshine, and I was a miner living on the banks of the Mokelumne, and the proprietor of a rich claim in the bed of the river.

A short distance below was Tom Langford's ranch, where he dwelt with his pretty wife Martha, and, as everybody thought, happily—but I knew better. He was kind enough to her, and did by her as well as any husband could, but there seemed to be a lack of sympathy between them.

He was a steady going, business like man of the world, too much absorbed with plans and speculations as to present and future operations, to pay a great amount of attention to his wife. She was handsome, smart and intelligent, possessed of the form of a Venus or Psyche, and with a pair of eyes of deep melting blue, full of soul and ever seeking for an answering glance of sympathy.

She was very fond of music, and I used to visit the house often, on which occasion we used to sing together, she accompanying on the fine piano which Tom had presented her. It might have been the piano or her name which caused that chord to thrill within my heart—that chord which had been silent so long—or it might have been the melting eyes that carried my thoughts back to other scenes and reviewed the happy memories of other days.

However that may have been, it is certain that her society had great attraction for me, and my visits became more and more frequent, she sometimes gently chiding me for not coming oftener.

Tom noticed our intimacy, but did not seem to care much, in fact rather liked it, and seemed to think it took quite a burden off his shoulders. She was pleased and happy when I was with her, and that was just what he liked, for he was always willing to contribute to her happiness by all the means in his power when he could do so without interfering with his other pursuits.

Pleasant evenings, especially moonlight ones, when my daily toils were over, I would go to the ranch, and Martha and I would wander forth among the wild roses and hazel bowers that skirted the river side, arm in arm, and pleasantly chatting or gaily singing together some sweet ditty. Sunday's, too, we would go out for a horseback ride among the hills, mounting to the tallest hights from whence we could enjoy the grand scenery of the Sacramento and San Joaquin plains, with old Mount Diablo in the distance.

At other times seated side by side on the sofa, with my arm around her waist, she would lay her head on my shoulder, and with her great blue eyes fixed tenderly on mine, she would listen to some wonderful tale I was telling of incidents on land or sea.

It wouldn't do for this state of affairs to last much longer.

I was now fully persuaded that she, as well as myself, was head over ears in love. My conscience accused me most violently, and I began to absent myself from the house, not going there for several evenings at a time, but in such cases she would either send or come for me, and then I had to apologize and make all possible atonement in the way of singing and amusing her for my long absence.

As I said before, it would not do for such a state of things to exist much longer. Tom was a good friend of mine, and I would do naught to injure him. Martha and I myself were too loving altogether, and, by degrees I came to the conclusion to leave.

My claim was paying poorly, and one day a stranger came along and I "took him in;" that is to say, I sold him my claim for all it was worth.

The next day I packed my horse with all my worldly goods, and left camp, passing by way of the ranch in order to bid Martha and Tom "good bye."

Of course both were struck with surprise at my sudden departure, and Martha at once burst into a flood of tears.

Tom tried to dissuade me from going. We had lived neighbors for over a year, and been on the most intimate terms. Why did I leave? What had he done? What had Martha done? Hadn't I always been used right in his house? A cloud passed across his brow. There was something wrong between him and me and I must explain. He demanded an explanation. "He wished no trouble, but before I could throw off on him that way I must satisfy him with some sort of an explanation."

Well, I took him one side and I *did* explain, shielding Martha, and criminating myself all possible.

He heard me patiently through, with a broad smile on his countenance, and then laughing exclaimed:

"Well Alf, is that all? Why, Lord bless your soul, take her by all means. If she's happier with you than with me, take her, but don't leave. Wait till I go in and talk to the poor gal."

I saw him enter the house and sit beside her, with his arm fondly around her waist, kissing her in the most fatherly manner.

I could bear no more, I would trust myself no longer. I turned up the first ravine to the right, and at once lost sight of the house. In less than ten minutes I heard the clatter of Tom's horse as he dashed off down the main road, hunting me.

I watched him a moment or so from the brow of the hill and then passed along, leading my horse on my journey southward.

I never saw them more, but the last I heard of them was a year afterwards, at which time Tom and Martha were still living pleasantly together on the same old ranch.

CHAPTER THIRD.—MY THIRD MARTHA.

It is not over five years ago, since I fell in love with a pretty little school teachess in Santa Clara Valley. One of the sweetest and most loveable little schoolmarm's you ever saw, and her name was Martha.

I say I fell in love with her. 'Twas something of the sort, at any rate.

I have no doubt the name had something to do with it, but somehow I was always partial to "schoolmarms," and one named Martha, why, that was the very thing—couldn't be better. Pretty, smart, intellectual and spicy, and name Martha, surely I was born under a lucky star.

The name of Mary was also a favorite name with me, but that of my first Martha was printed on my right arm in India ink on the passage round Cape Horn, and there it remains to this day.

It won't take long to tell all about this Martha. I don't like to dwell on the subject much, for I feel a little sore over it.

She taught school at the little town of M——, and I became acquainted with her at a picnic.

She was very fascinating and easy in her manners, and had numerous admirers who were constantly vieing with each other in the assiduity of their attentions but from her treatment of them after I made her acquaintance, I flattered myself that I had got the inside track; in fact Martha was mine, mine alone.

I became sentimental. I talked poetry to her, and descanted glowingly upon the beauties of nature, and the pleasure of meeting with souls attuned in harmony with one's own as we walked arm in arm about the picnic grounds.

I left her when the picnic was over, at the door of her boarding house, after a stipulated promise to call and see her next Sabbath.

Now I lived across the Valley at a distance of seventeen long miles, and it was no small ride to see her every Sunday, and back home again, but do it I did, rain or shine, or the mud ever so deep. Horseflesh had to suffer.

I was farming there, and couldn't help thinking how nice it would be to have this Martha to take charge of my home. In fact I fixed it all up in apple pie order in anticipation, and ran my face at an Israelite clothing store for a gorgeous bob-tailed coat and white vest.

I made Martha lots of presents of books, little fancy articles, and all that sort of thing, and it was a pleasure to see her rogueish black eyes light up on such occasions, although at times there was a queer mischievous look mingled with the happy expression of her pretty countenance, that I could not at all understand—then.

Those sparkling black eyes of hers never had the depth-of-soul look about them that characterized those of my other two Marthas, and I never could be by her side, conversing ever so lovingly, without the sudden rogueish flashing of those eyes giving me a queer sensation of apprehensiveness of some approaching disaster to my suit.

It was night. The disaster *did* come, and if I was a profane man, I could curse more or less in very bitterness of spirit, even now as I think of it.

The last Sunday that I rode over to see her, I was dressed within an inch of my life, with beard trimmed nicely, and oil on my hair, for the important time had arrived, and I intended to "pop the question" that day.

They said Martha was at Church, so I went there also.

I looked about a while, and soon espied her; but who was that fine looking gent sitting beside her? What business had he holding one side of the singing book with her as they sung?

I asked myself the popular question of: "Why is it?" several times, but could divine no satisfactory solution to the problem.

After the meeting was over I saw them march off, arm in arm together, smiling, and looking particularly agreeable—to themselves no doubt— that fellow and my schoolmarm.

I rode down the road two miles and back in very desperation of soul; drank a glass of lager; ordered dinner for two at the hostel and ate it all myself, in the most wrathful manner.

I felt better, but not reconciled.

In the evening I called on Martha at her boarding house.

I was ushered into the parlor, and there they sat, side by side on the sofa, he with his arm around her waist, and she leaning up against him, "like a sick kitten to a hot brick."

They at once arose, and in the coolest, most self-possessed, (I won't say devilish) manner, she said, "Mr. Doten, allow me to make you acquainted with Mr. Jones, a very dear friend of mine, from San Francisco."

I bowed to Jones, giving a ghastly smile as I did so. I took Jones by the hand, and jerked his arm up and down like a pump handle a few times and sat down.

I saw through it all at once. This accounted for the ring which she wore with J. Jones engraved on the inside. This accounted for the letters she received from San Francisco, and the newspapers with J. J. marked on the margin.

I was dumbfounded. I could hardly speak a word, but muttering something about a "violent headache" I hastily got out of the house, mounted my horse, and made the quickest trip home on record.

People must have thought I was riding express or after the doctor.

The Living Hinge; Or, The Seventeen Pots of Amalgam

[Written by Doten, and printed in the Territorial Enterprise *of July 21, 1867.]*

CHAPTER I.—PROSPECTIVE.

Some four or five miles east of the town of Como, Palmyra District, is a small lake which looks very pretty at a distance, but does not amount to much on close inspection. It is a couple of hundred yards or so in diameter, is very shallow, and contains no fish or anything of the sort, except a few sullen, disconsolate frogs, who merely stay there out of pure reckless desperation, because they can go nowhere else, there not being another drop of water for miles around.

What that pond was put there for, unless it might be for the accommodation of the few mountain sheep which sometimes stray over in its vicinity, no one could ever say. It is away from any mines, and the low, rolling hills on either side are completely barren of all vegetation except a very inferior article of sage brush, interspersed with here and there a solitary tuft of bunch grass. Even if there was a large population dwelling around the rocky margin, the water would be of little use as a beverage, as in the winter it freezes solid, and in the summer it is too warm and disagreeable for anything but an emetic.

Captain Henry C. Smith, one of the first projectors of Como, for some reason or other took a notion to dub this ridiculous scrub of a lake "Como" also. He must have been in a very imaginative mood, to thus transfer the pretty little name of that lovely lake in Italy, so often sung of by enamored poets, to this horribly unromantic locality. The name, however, recoiled back in judgment upon him, and he was ever afterwards known as "Como" Smith.

A little over three years ago I was a resident citizen of Como, a very remarkable town in many respects, when one takes into consideration the remarkable character of its population. There was more real fun enjoyed and real hard work done up there than could be realized by any one unacquainted with the place; others may have their own opinion, but I will say for Palmyra District, abandoned as it is, that it can show more deep shafts, tunnels and extensive thorough prospecting work than any other district of like character in the State of Nevada.

One day I resolved myself into a grand exploring expedition, and, with a shot-gun on my shoulder and a small hammer stuck in my belt, took a tour of observation and prospective inspection throughout the land away to the northward and eastward.

I found no rich ledges, although I cracked open every suspicious looking quartz stone I came across, neither did I see any game, except a little cotton-tailed rabbit which sprang up some two hundred yards ahead of me.

Now any old sportsman will agree with me that two hundred yards was a pretty long range for a shot-gun, and when I fired I had no expectations of hitting that rabbit. Sure enough I didn't.

Along in the afternoon I came around to Lake Como, and just as I came in sight of it my attention was attracted by the strange actions of a man standing on the shore of the lake.

He was standing sideways towards me, bowing vigorously at the lake, sometimes bringing his head nearly to the ground in the vehemence of his adulation. Occasionally he would pause, and after reaching behind him with something I could not at first distinguish, he would go on working himself up and down as before.

He ceased as soon as he noticed my near approach, and when I came up to him he bade me "good evening" in response to my salutation, remarking, smilingly, "Well, I presume you must have thought a little strange of my actions just now, but I assure you it was unavoidable on my part. I have a peculiar requirement, consequent upon my condition in life, and although I rather dislike being detected in this as a general thing, yet on the present occasion I am heartily glad to see you, for I am in a small bit of a difficulty. Will you please do me the favor to oil me?"

As he made this odd request, he handed me, with all imaginable gravity, an oil feeder, such as is used in oiling machinery, and bent over with his back towards me.

"Squirt it right here," said he motioning towards the small of his back. "That's the only place what needs it."

As might well be supposed, I was more or less wonderstruck by this very queer little episode, and hardly knew at first what to make of it, but quickly arriving at the conclusion that the man was a little luny, I resolved to humor the poor devil. So I took the feeder and attempted to squirt with it, but it failed. It was empty.

"Why, look here, my dear fellow," said I, "you haven't got any oil in this thing. What do you mean? how do you expect me to oil you without oil?"

"Oh, you're very much mistaken," laughed he, "for its over half full; try it now; let me hear the bottom snap in and out."

I did so, and although no oil came forth, he exclaimed:

"That's it! good! that feels all right."

Then he swayed his body up and down at a great rate for about a minute, and straightened up, saying with a long drawn breath of relief:

"There now. I'm all right once more, thanks to your kindness. I tried it mighty hard before you came, but somehow couldn't reach the right spot."

CHAPTER II.—A DEMENTED CHRISTIAN.

"I ain't nobody's fool, as you already perceive. I'm an educated man and used to be a Universalist minister once. I found myself too much naturally inclined to be a regular built sinner, so I just turned preacher in self defense and as a matter of precaution, for I didn't want to land in Tophet after shuffling off this mortal coil.

"And then, too, Universalist ministers are much better than those of other denominations, because believing as they do in sure and inevitable present punishment here on earth for all sins committed, either morally, physically, or any other way, they act in accordance with such belief, striving to avoid the consequent punishment, while others who preach up the doctrine that all punishment for sin committed is reserved for the great hereafter—punishment of the hell fire and brimstone order—are disposed to take chances on its remoteness, intangibility, and possible non-existence—also on repenting in time to get around it.

"Come, now—you know yourself that it's much easier and pleasanter to travel in the path of sin and iniquity than in the straight-laced, unsociable ways of those who feel that they have got a sure thing on being punished for any sin they may commit, and punished, too, just in proportion to the enormity of the sin or crime committed."

He was a small, lightly built man of about fifty-five, with dark hair, whiskers, and mustache, considerably mixed with gray. He had high cheekbones, narrow forehead, and a pair of the queerest little brown eyes anybody ever saw, set closely on each side of a thin, wedge-like nose, which projected out from his face like the figure-head of a down-east fishing schooner. He was dressed in a well worn suit of grey, with a little old brown felt hat on his head; his boots conformed with his general appearance, in being rather dilapidated; and from the old leather haversack which lay on the ground with a hammer beside it, I judged that he also was a quartz prospector.

And such a little rattle-head to talk as the old fellow was! He hardly allowed me to get in a word edgeways, but kept right on chatting freely like an old acquaintance.

"Now I think of it," continued he, "you must think me rather a strange chap—eccentric, maybe. Everyone else thinks me so; why shouldn't you? But then I ain't strange; I ain't eccentric at all. Everything has its own proper peculiarities; why shouldn't I? Now this little peculiarity of mine is simply this: I've got to be oiled or I can't work; and right where you squirted that oil is the grand working joint of my organism. Great God! if I should ever allow that to get disabled with rust so it couldn't work, I'd be stiff as a wagon tongue forever afterwards, and fit for nothing except old iron.

"I may say I wasn't successful as a preacher. I drew mighty poor houses. Even when I tried street preaching I couldn't make the thing win. No crowd would stay by me any length of time, unless some fools or other would get to hooting at me and mocking me, when I'd get more or less wrathy, and the excitement would draw a good big audience for a short time.

"You oughter seen the huge audience I raised one Sunday evening in San Francisco. It was my last. I felt mightily pregnant with the spirit of truth, and I let myself out. I don't remember now just all what I said. I only know I was full of burning, fervid eloquence; but the boorish rabble before me only laughed and jeered at my excited, earnest words, which, alas! fell as pearls before swine.

"Then I told them in the sad bitterness of my soul that they were no better than the Jewish rabble who made themselves so disagreeable at the crucifixtion of Christ. I said I was poor, and anyone stealing my purse would steal trash, but I was a proud-hearted man. Pride and poverty was the downfall of old Cole's dog, but I was willing that such, too, should be my downfall. Then I became fiercely angry and sprang down from the steps on which I was standing, in order to drive the whole crowd off into the bay, even as the devil did the herd of swine into the sea of Galilee, when a couple of stout men with stars on their breasts laid violent hands on me and hurried me along the street so fast that the houses and all passing objects reeled into chaos, and I into a thick black night.

"It was a long, long, strange night, and when I was conscious it was daylight once more. I found myself—don't laugh at me, please—I found myself transformed into a hinge, a real living iron hinge, on the front door of the Insane Asylum at Stockton.

"I was none of your common, insignificant hinges, but a large, handsome, portly, well oiled hinge, bending my jointed back gracefully whenever the door was swung back for the admission of talent and respectability. The humbler degrees of society always have to pass in and out at side doors.

"Should you ever become a hinge, be a first class upper one, like I was; don't ever be a common butt, but a genuine high-toned wrought-iron strap hinge. There's honor in it.

"The honor in my case, however, was not sufficient to induce me to stay long, and although envied by all the other hinges in the house, I had a realizing sense that I was something besides a hinge, so one night I contrived to unscrew myself from the door and took quiet leave of the Asylum.

"Whatever happens to you in life, don't you ever allow yourself to be taken to Stockton. No one can be put to baser uses than they put folks to at that Asylum. I am told that the big soup-kettle in the kitchen was formerly a City Alderman, and the cook-stove itself used to be a member of Congress; all the hinges on the doors once swung round in the most respectable circles, and God knows what the shovels, mops and brooms used to be.

"The devil take Stockton! the devil take the Asylum! the devil fly away with everybody who's fool enough to be there! Whoop! Damnation!" and away the little fellow flew off the handle, as crazy as a Dayton bed-bug in May.

He was red in the face with passion, and wrung his hands about with great energy of gesticulation as he trotted vehemently back and forward; but his little crazy fit only lasted a minute or so, for directly the anger-flushed expression of his countenance gave way to one of pain, and he backed up to me saying, earnestly:

"Do, please, oil me again, sir; that's what's the matter with me; I was getting a little too dry and squeaky. Ah! there we are again all right, thank you, sir. You hit exactly the right spot."

He worked himself up and down with great satisfaction a few times, and then continued:

"You must think I'm a little wandering in my upper story; crazy, maybe, but I ain't; not a bit of it. I'm as sound as a saw-log, all except the small of my back, where the great joint of me is. If 'twasn't for that joint, I shouldn't know I was a hinge at all. I keep that a secret from everybody, and only oil up when I do so unobserved. But what are we doing here? It's getting late, and we'd better be traveling."

I agreed to this proposition, and being much amused with my novel companion, invited him home with me.

On our way we examined several quartz ledges which we came across, and I found the old man really quite a good judge of rock, as well as intelligent in mining matters generally.

He told me of vast amounts of copper ore which he had found existing only a few miles distant, and in the neighborhood of Walker River, which he said would some day be very valuable, when railroads should make transportation to San Francisco cheaper; also of gold and silver mines on the forks of Walker River, and about that section of the country, showing that he had been prospecting around pretty extensively for some time past.

We slept together that night at my cabin, and next day started out on a prospecting trip over to Walker River. The old man showed me all the copper, gold and silver discoveries he had made; but the richest gold quartz we saw was between the east and west forks of the river. We did not think it worth while at that time to locate any claims, leaving that for some future time, when perhaps we might go there to work and develop whatever riches there might be.

We were absent from Como about three weeks, and on my part I must say I enjoyed the companionship of that queer little rattle-brained old man very highly. He was often rather flighty in his ideas, but I knew how to manage and appreciate him, and keep him oiled up properly; so we got along finely, and he became more and more attached to me.

Sitting at our camp-fire during evenings, the old man was the best hand I ever saw at telling stories—and right interesting ones, too—generally of his traveling experiences and observations among mankind, and in me he never failed to find an attentive as well as instructed audience.

CHAPTER III.—WONDERFUL IDEAS.

One evening, after being apparently in a brown study for an hour, the old man said to me:

"Alf., my son, come sit down on this rock side of me, and I'll tell you something."

I complied, and, after gazing thoughtfully for about ten minutes at the kettle of beans cooking over the fire, he turned towards me with an unusually serious countenance, saying, as he passed me the oil feeder:

"Oil me up once more, and I'll tell you a story nobody ever heard."

I went through the imaginary process of squirting oil on the small of his back, as usual, and he proceeded:

"I never told you about what a great thief I was, but really I have stolen more gold and silver, and have been more successful in concealing it and avoiding all manner of suspicion than any one single man in the State of Nevada. Yes, that's so; I concealed it so effectually that I have never been able to get at it since; neither do I much think I ever will. I'm going to tell you all about it, and without fear—for now I have perfect confidence in you; and the secret I am about to impart to you may make you a rich man; yes, a rich man; richer than you dreamed of. You never laughed at me, but always oiled me right and good when I needed it; you are my friend, and you shall find that hinges are not all ungrateful. I am a machinist by trade; that is to say, I learned the business when I was a boy, but I have never followed it regularly since. I wish I had. Nobody ever had a more inventive head than mine, and being, as I said, a machinist, there's no telling what valuable and important inventions I might have developed, had it not been for my extreme poverty. I was always studying out something new and wonderful. Among scores of other schemes which would have startled the world as with an electric shock, had they been properly brought out, was this, my best one, the vast intrinsic merits and feasibility of which will strike you at once. It is simply a plan by which the broad deserts of Arabia, or the vast plains of the continent can be traveled with a common steamboat, with perfect comfort and safety, and in any chosen direction, even ascending and descending slight elevations, the steamer sailing along smoothly at the rate of fifteen or twenty miles an hour, with the same facility as she would on the Mississippi.

"This is the way I propose to accomplish this important project: I would take a light draught, flat-bottomed steamer, and under her and over her I will build an endless track with low sides to it. This track will be of a flexible nature, passing up under the stern and over across a series of wheels, carrying it length wise of the boat and down under the bow again.

"The track being filled with water, so that the boat floats, the wheels are set in motion by the machinery of the boat, same as the paddle-wheels are worked, and operating by means of cogs above and below, the track is set in motion and the steamboat driven ahead at the same time.

"Thus you will perceive, the passengers can travel with luxuriant comfort even in the most sweltering clime, the track passing continually overhead creating a strong current of air, as well as shading them completely from the fierce rays of the sun, while they recline at ease on the sofas of the hurricane deck, smoking their cigars, drinking sherry coblers, and all that sort of thing. Ah! it is one of the grandest projects of the nineteenth century, and had I only been properly supported and encouraged, thousands of my style of land steamboats would have been now traversing the vast prairies and broad alkali deserts of the American continent, as well as all other parts of the world. I should have made my mark, and been the richest and most prominent man in existence.

"With such a steamer, rivers, snow, ice, in fact all similar obstacles would prove no obstruction, and with sufficient provision and fuel I might traverse away into the far regions of the north, across the illimitable fields of ice, and embark upon that great open polar sea discovered and described by the more recent Arctic explorers.

"The water floating my steamer within my endless track being constantly in motion could not freeze, which circumstance, combined with the heat from the boilers, would have the effect to preserve the temperature immediately surrounding at a comfortable summer-like warmth, even in the highest latitudes.

"And then again my mind expands with the idea of what great and sensationally startling discoveries would be made in sailing still farther north on that open polar sea—for let me tell you there's *something beyond.* The explorers who stood on the margin of that great unknown sea had passed the broad frozen zone, and had arrived at where a warmer belt of climate was just commencing, and with ships at their command they might have sailed north until they had again passed through temperate and tropical zones similar to this part of the world, and to another frozen polar region beyond.

"This world is not, as is generally supposed, round like a ball, but like an immense, eternal cylinder, which has neither beginning nor end, the tropical and frozen zones succeeding each other at regular intervals and in endless series, each being similarly inhabited, and possessing the same general conformation. But then, dear me, how I am rattling along and digressing entirely from what I started in to tell you.

"As I said before, notwithstanding all my efforts and representations, I never could interest any people in my behalf who were possessed of the requisite wealth to assist me in the development of either this or any of my other schemes; in fact, many ridiculed me as a demented dealer in wild impracticabilities.

"My father was a poor Universalist preacher in Illinois, and, following in his footsteps, I, too, occasionally took to preaching by way of variety, for 'variety is the spice of life,' you know.

"When I did preach, it was with all sincerity, but I never could make it pay; after all, I was cut out more for a mechanic than a preacher. The most I ever received as a reward for my labors in the Lord's vineyard was a bare subsistence. At length after years of wandering service in that line throughout the Western States, I strayed down into Texas, Mexico, and finally found myself in California.

"After I got away from the Asylum at Stockton, I came across the Sierra Nevada to this State, and sought employment, carefully always concealing my real character, and oiling myself only when no one could see me. The first job I got was tending battery in a quartz mill, not over a thousand miles from Gold Hill, and it was not long before being promoted, step by step I became head amalgamator. This was just about two years ago.

"Now here we come to the points of interest—the secrets—in what I am going to impart to you. Oil me up once more, please. There, that's it; good!

CHAPTER IV.—THE HIDDEN TREASURE.

"I had the handling of all the amalgam—and it was rich amalgam, too—rich in gold. I used to steal that amalgam. There, now, don't look that way at me, I'm only telling you the truth. Yes, I used to steal it, just a little at a time.

"The owner of the mill was a fine man, an excellent good man in pretty much all respects, except one. He was a little too avaricious, and in an evil hour was induced to enter into an arrangement with a certain mining superintendent, by which first class ore was supplied to the mill from the mine, and rated as second or third class ore, the returns being made to correspond as such, thus defaulting the mining company, while the wicked superintendent and my employer pocketed a very desirable amount of extra cash by the operation. Ha! ha! they didn't pocket quite so much after I became cognizant of their iniquity.

" 'The wages of sin is death'—so the good book tells us—and as a true Christian I believed it to be my plain duty, pointed out by the Lord, to allow them as little of those sinful wages to atone for as possible, so every day I quietly abstracted of this amalgam all I could conveniently carry off, taking it to my little cabin and dropping it through a knot hole in the floor.

"Another object, too, which I had in view, was the accumulation of wealth sufficient to allow me to carry out some of my great schemes, especially the wonderful land steamboat arrangement I have described to you. I considered the Lord in this matter was now assisting me in supplying the means required, as well as making me an adjuster of sin in this amalgam arrangement.

"For months I followed up this practice. The ore paid far richer than any one dreamed of except myself, and although our naughty superintendent and mill-man evidently seemed disappointed somewhat in the yield of the amalgam, yet, strange to say, I remained unsuspected.

"At length this arrangement between them ceased from some cause or other, which I never cared to inquire into. Perhaps first-class ore was found less plenty in the mine, or fear of detection, or the stings of guilty conscience may have interfered in the matter: I can't say; be that as it may, however, we soon came down to working nothing but regular third-class ore, so I threw up my position and quit the concern. It was astonishing how fast that amalgam had accumulated. Along latterly, whenever I deposited a fresh lot, I had to take a stick and poke it away from the knothole. All underneath the floor seemed full of the precious stuff.

"Next thing was, how to dispose of it. I went to work and built me a small furnace, and retorting a few pounds at a time, I soon had quite a nice little lot of crude bullion, sufficient to furnish me with all the money I might want for present purposes, as it contained so much gold combined with the silver, that it was worth from four to eight dollars an ounce when refined.

"Becoming fearful lest my amalgam deposit might be discovered, by some unforeseen accident or other, I resolved to remove it to a more secure place, and after some little time spent in search of a safe locality, I decided on an old, abandoned tunnel, which I examined and thought would answer my purpose.

"This tunnel had been run at an early date by persevering prospectors, after some anticipated rich ledge supposed to exist at that particular point; in which, however, they were doomed to disappointment. The tunnel was about three hundred feet in length, and had several little drifts or branches to it, running in various directions. Into one of these branches I carried all my amalgam one dark, stormy night, in iron pots which I had procured for the purpose—such as are used on a cook stove—and placing them at the extreme end, with flat stones laid over them as covers, I carefully caved down all the loose rock and earth I could over them with a pick, and came away as soon as possible, for now a singular and unforeseen danger developed itself.

"The tunnel was not timbered at all, and although firm enough originally, the action of the atmosphere, and natural dampness, had caused that peculiar swelling and slacking of the stiff clayey earth and rock, so well understood by miners, and in many places the sides and roof of the tunnel were already beginning to fall in large scales.

"It was well that I got out of that drift as soon as I did, for my picking had started a cave, and for some moments heavy masses continued falling in from both roof and sides, completely filling it up nearly to the main tunnel in which I stood. I left, for the indications were, now that it had got started, no one could tell where the cave would stop. One thing was pretty morally certain; my treasure was secure, and if I never got at it again, probably no one else would.

"A day or so afterwards I put my crude bullion in sacks, and with an old wagon and two horses which I had purchased for the purpose I drove to Sacramento, taking the bullion with me in that way to avoid the possible suspicion consequent on shipping it by coach.

"In San Francisco I found no difficulty in converting it into cash, representing myself as running an arastra in Washoe, and returned here with over $15,000 in greenbacks in my possession.

"I have been wearing out fast lately, and something seems to tell me that in a few short months my great joint will give out entirely, in spite of oiling and attention, and I shall be tossed aside among the worthless things of the past. For of what use is a hinge when its gudgeon-pin and bearings are worn out? Oil me again, please. Ah! capital! Thank you; your complaisant kindness I ne'er shall forget.

"I am going home now to Illinois, and have got money enough to carry me through all right the rest of my life. I will tell you all about the precise locality of my old cabin (or rather where it stood, for it has since been destroyed by fire), and also exactly where to find that amalgam deposit. That is the grand secret I wish to impart to you; but not here, not here," said the little old man, looking apprehensively around. "Not here, for bushes have ears, and even the tattling winds whisper what is uttered in their presence. I'll write out full directions in a very few words, so that you cannot fail to understand, and find that hidden store of rich amalgam. There are seventeen pots of it, and the whole is worth over $50,000. The last time I was there—three or four months ago—the tunnel was caved and filled in nearly to its mouth, but you can get at the treasure by running a new tunnel for it, and you will be a rich man. But wait till to-morrow, when we arrive at Como."

I was considerably excited over what he had been telling me, for surely such a prospect of sudden wealth is agreeable for any poor miner or carpenter to contemplate, and I would have questioned him more particularly regarding it, but he totally repudiated anything further on that point, simply saying, "wait till we get to Como; just wait. I'll write it out for you. I'll write it in cypher, so nobody but you and I can read or understand it, and we'll be safe."

CHAPTER V.—THE MYSTERIOUS CIPHER.

"I have," said he, "an arrangement of letters studied out and perfected by myself the like of which no man ever saw or dreamed of before. It is a cipher arranged on a very simple but perfectly undiscoverable principle, yet in less than five minutes I can learn you the key to it so that you can read it with almost the same facility as common print, and we can communicate together in any part of the world by telegraph or letter, on the most private or important subjects, freely and openly, without the least fear of being detected or understood by outsiders. I will write out full directions for finding the treasure deposit, by means of this cipher, and learn you the key. Oil me once more and we'll go to sleep. Good; again; that's it; God bless you! I'll write it out for you in cipher. Wait till we get to Como.

We arrived at Como about sunset the next day, and after a hearty supper the old man left me, saying, "I'm going up-stairs a while. I'll meet you in an hour, at McCumber's saloon."

At the time appointed I was at the saloon, which was well-filled with men engaged in drinking, playing cards, billiards, etc., amusing themselves after the style usual at such places, when the old man entered hastily, with an expression of trouble on his countenance, which I had well learned to comprehend, and placing a slip of paper within my hand, said, "come out quick and oil me; I need it mighty bad; then I'll learn you the key to the cipher I just gave you. Quick! Oh, my God! There, I knew it!—listen how I squeak!"

The poor, demented old fellow stood in the middle of the floor, with his hands on his hips, painfully swaying backward and forward without bending his back, while the bystanders, attracted by his queer exclamations and appearance, gathered around. I felt in his pocket for the oil feeder, but it was not there.

"No," said he sadly, "I left it in my room, curse the luck, but what the devil are you all gaping at, you d—d baboons you; git!" This forcible remark with its accompanying gestures, brought forth peals of laughter from those around, and one tipsy fellow stepped up to him saying:

"Take a drink old toppy, suck down a little beverage; never mind the ile. Don't jerk around that way, its bad."

The old man's face was blazing with passion, and foreseeing trouble, I left him and ran for the oil feeder. I was gone only a moment, but when I returned, there he stood in the middle of the floor with his shirt off looking crazy as could be desired, swinging his fists wildly about and apparently oblivious of either friend or foe, while in a high old key and strain he was thus addressing the crowd:

"Yes, gentlemen, by h—l! you've jumped up a peaceable man. Don't talk to *me! Be calm?* Ain't I calm? What d—d man presumes to tell me I'm excited? Yes, d—n you all, you've jumped up the peaceablest man in the world. A peaceabler man never existed; but you've jumped me up, and d—n the first son of a gun of you that dares to speak or look cross at me! You're a set of miserable cur dogs, and for two bits I'd just waltz through you like a dose of strychnine through a lot of hound pups! *You'll* jump up a peaceable man, will you? Whoop! take that! you blasted scrub," and with a wild attempt to strike the nearest man to him, the poor little old fellow gave a whirl half round and fell flat on his back upon the floor, stiff and motionless.

From that time forward he never moved or spoke a word. He had received a paralytic stroke from which he could not recover. The poor old hinge was worn out at last; broken past all mending.

I removed him to Dayton the next day, and in the course of a couple of weeks to San Francisco, where he had the benefit of the best medical attendance which could be procured, but all was of no avail. He lingered along, still speechless and motionless, for two months, when he died without a struggle.

His secret died with him, for although evidently conscious at times of what was going on around him, yet he could never divulge the key to that remarkable cipher, although he gazed into my eyes with peculiar earnestness on various occasions, as though he longed to tell me something.

Sewed into various parts of his clothing were found over twelve thousand dollars in greenbacks, and after all the expenses of the funeral, medical attendance, etc., were paid, the balance was forwarded to his relatives in Illinois.

As for myself, three months after my return to Como, I removed to Virginia, where I have been ever since. I have studied over the mysterious cipher for hours and hours at a time, and can read it just as well now as I could when I first received it. The majority of the old man's other stories, aside from his peculiar theories and idiosyncracies, proved so correct, that I have often been inclined to believe there might be something in his amalgam treasure story, and the more so from the fact that in my perambulations I have found the ruins of a burnt cabin, with the remnants of what was evidently a small furnace and retort, but where is the old tunnel containing those seventeen pots of rich amalgam? I have searched for it all I am going to. I give it up. It is a riddle I cannot solve, but perhaps some one else can.

It must be within a mile of Virginia or Gold Hill, otherwise he could not well have carried those heavy pots of amalgam to it from his cabin all in the course of one night.

The American people are fonder of being humbugged than any other on the face of the globe, and I partake of the general characteristics of my countrymen; but how much humbug there may be in this matter, I leave the reader to judge.

Here is the mysterious cipher precisely as I received it from the old man. It is well worthy the study of the curious, and those skilled in deciphering puzzles. As to myself, I feel so much interested in it that I will gladly pay a good round sum, or even share whatever profits may be developed, with any person who will furnish me a manifestly correct solution or translation and full explanation of this lettered mystery, together with the key which unlocks it:

S	R	X	H	L	L	S	R	S	J	D	L	N	R	N
Z	H	D	W	S	S	H	Q	Z	H	B	S	T	X	J
J	I	Z	S	B	Z	D	D	C	D	Z	T	J	I	H
H	P	X	R	B	J	D	L	R	Z	D	Y	N	V	J
Z	Y	Z	D	Z	C	D	S	M	Z	Z	Z	L	L	G
R	X	Z	I	H	X	G	S	X	Z	F	R	I	I	V
L	G	D	H	L	S	T	N	J	Y	B	J	I	V	I
H	S	D	Z	S	Z	L	S	L	V	N	C	G	J	J
Y	N	H	Z	R	L	F	I	G	D	G	Z	E	N	D
Z	H	L	Z	W	O	I	L	J	J	N	J	F	E	L
T	H	J	S	Z	Z	X	I	N	J	Z	C	I	Z	I
X	Z	S	S	D	I	L	U	L	G	V	S	H	T	R
D	Z	T	L	Z	N	S	I	K	D	X	Z	X	D	J
X	H	H	V	I	D	Z	T	H	X	S	I	H	P	C
I	Z	Z	R	J	J	X	I	J	D	S	S	I	D	J

Four Devils. A New Year's Tale

[This story by Doten appeared in the Gold Hill Daily News *on December 31, 1877.]*

One New Year's eve several years ago four travelers were seated before a comfortable fire in the bar-room at Hunter's Station on Truckee river.

It was in the days of staging, long before the iron horse came snorting through that way with his long trains of cars from California, and from the East. People traveled more on their own hook and resources then than they do now.

Everybody, except these four travelers, had retired for the night. The beds were all full, consequently, these four, having no blankets, found the chairs better than nothing, before the comfortable log fire.

One was a Chinaman, who had been working all the season cooking at a lumber camp in the mountains, and was now on his way to the Comstock; the second was a Piute Indian, traveling nowhere in particular; the third was a jolly old Jack tar, bound for California, and the fourth was a little old man.

He was a queer-looking, blear-eyed, mild-mannered old fellow, with a very sedate, yet shrewd countenance, dressed in dark clothes, closely buttoned up, and a tight-fitting seal-skin cap on his head. Nobody observed where he came from, or when he came. They only noticed that he was at supper and had a fine appetite.

This little old man was inclined to be sociable. He wished his companions a "happy new year" and after some few preliminary remarks pulled a bottle of brandy out of his coat pocket.

"My good friends and companions," remarked he, "will you not join me in a little spiritual consolation, a cordial salutation to the new year, as it were; in other words, will you have a drink?"

The sailor and the Chinaman were willing, but the Piute was a little shy of strong drink.

The old man stepped to the table and got cups, sugar [illegible] a kettle of hot water in the corner of the fireplace, each soon had a cup of some-thing hot and good. Even the Indian liked it, weak and well sweetened.

"My friends," said the little man, "there's comfort in this, yet many people say there's the devil in it, but after all, that's merely a matter of superstition. I've been a preacher in my day, and many's the sermon I've preached on the devil, without knowing much about my subject. The devil, however, is a good pulpit assistant, yet none of us ever really saw him. Did you ever see the devil, John?" said the old fellow, smiling toward the Chinaman.

A CHINESE DEVIL.

"Yes, me see debble jessee one time. My fader see him plenty time. Debble makee plenty tlubble in China. He tly come China New Year allee time, but he no can do. Chinaman plenty fight 'im; shootee plenty fi'clacker; makee dlum music; burnee plenty joss paper."

"But what does the devil look like, John?" asked the old man.

"Oh, some time he big, allee same tseung, what you call 'im elepant; nudder time he little, allee same labbity.

"One time he come my fader housee. He allee same loi, what you call 'im mule. He speakee my old glanmudder: 'Samoon-chai (sweetheart) me likee you come along.' "

"Glanmudder belly ole woman; heap flaid; tly clawl under bed. Debble turn lound, kick 'im out tloo window; nebber see 'im no more."

"But that time when you saw him, John, how about that?"

"Yessee, me tell. Me see him Oloville. Me come down mines; gottee plenty gold; come China New Year. Dlink too muchee planty two day; gettee dlunk allee time. Me tly go home sleep. Debble jump down off housee; smellee stlong allee same powder. Me heap flaid; lun quick; shootee pistol, tlow joss paper, clawl under housee; stay moller mornin'."

"Yes, but you haven't told us how he looked, John."

"Oh, he gottee big head, allee same cow; plenty fire all over; lookee allee same hell; me no likee see 'im no more."

"A fine, graphic description of His Satanic Majesty, John," said the little old man. "Now let's all have a pull at the spirits, and then our aboriginal friend here will tell us what *he* knows about the devil."

A PIUTE DEVIL.

The Indian had been apparently as much amused as the rest at the Christmas story, and after another drink, needed no urging. He could talk pretty good English, too.

"You see, plenty Piutee man's 'fraid of the devil, but *I* ain't. He's pooty good feller sometimes, and sometimes he ain't. We call him in Injun, *Avee-ah-day-gah-Pah:* that's bad spirit. He goes all over the country and makes all the troubles and sickness. When he gits after you bad, it's no use, you got to go, so it's best to be good friends with him, you bet."

"Well, but what does he look like and where does he keep himself generally?"

"He don't look like nobody. Sometimes he's big smoke, and sometimes big water, and sometimes he's big wind, but he can git ye when he wants ye, *you* bet.

"I've seen him stand up like a big tree of water and smoke, and walk all over Pyramid Lake and Carson Sink.

"Once he went swimmin' through the big lake, what you call 'im Tahoe, and it doesn't never catch'em ice any more. Other lakes gits ice in Winter, but this one never doesn't. Injuns never has no boats on that lake and they never gets in the water, and they won't catch the fish. It's dam bad place.

"We all better let the devil alone, and treat him good. He'll git ye when he wants ye, *you* bet."   A SAILOR'S DEVIL.

It now came Jack's turn, and with another hot splice of the main brace all around, he gave his old waistband a hitch, shifted his chaw of tobacco over into his starboard cheek and started in:

"I agree with our friend, the Piute Dago, here, in sayin' that Old Jimmy Squarefoot isn't always the worst feller in the world, but I never saw him only once. That was off Cape Hatteras in the worst storm that ever was. Yes, and it was New Year's Day, too. The old ship was layin' to under foretopm'st stays'l and close-reefed maintops'l, and 'twas comin' on dark.

"All of a sudden one of the watch sung out, 'Breakers ho!'

"The old skipper was on deck in a jiffy. 'Where away!' says he.

" 'Right dead to leeward, sir.'

"Just then I happened to cock my eye aloft; and there sot the devil in the main-to'gallant crosstrees, with his tail wound round the mast like a ring-tail monkey, and smokin' his pipe as complacent as a Tonga Island pig. He was lookin' to the leeward and calculatin' how soon it would be before he'd take us in tow.

"I pointed him out, and the minute the old skipper clapped his eyes on him he whispered easy like a steam-engine: 'Yes, there's that d——d old cuss still tryin' it on. He thinks he's got me this time, but I'll have to raise him again.' Then he swelled up and grew red in the face with rage.

" 'Aloft there!' roared he, and his eyes fired up like stage lanterns.

"Old Jimmy looked down sort o' disappointed.

" 'Git out o' that! you d—d infernal old — — — ! — ! † + + † — ! ! !
— ! ! ! ! ! * ‡ ‡ ‡ ‡ * — — — ! ! ! ! ! ! ! .'

"The oaths he uttered would have made a Washoe bullwhacker die of envy. They went up in a perfect blue streak, and the old skipper himself grabbed a belayin' pin and sprang for the shrouds, goin' up there.

"Old Jimmy smiled on him in pure admiration, bowed by way of apology, and threw three or four flip-flaps in the air and disappeared.

"The wind shifted square round and moderated, and inside of two hours we was startin' along on our course with all drawin' sail set.

"But this sort o' reminds me of the old story of the boat's crew that was out after a whale. They got the iron into him, but when he jumped ahead he gave a flip of his tail that knocked 'em, boat and all, into eternity.

"Well, they brought up, of course, where all sailors go. They never expected anything else, and was satisfied with the place.

"But they would have their fun, and day after day they cut up more queer antics than ever was known of in hell before.

"They upset the wheelbarrows of brimstone, pulled the imps round by the tail, and played the devil generally with the whole institution.

"They never had so much fun in their lives, and was sorry they hadn't died sooner.

"The old bos'n was leader, and the worst in the lot. He beat old Jimmy at poker, euchre, or any game he wanted, and won all his loose coin, and if he had been there long enough he would have played him out of his whole institution.

"Old Jimmy tried every way to get rid of 'em, but they wouldn't go. He couldn't either coax, hire or drive 'em, and he was in deep trouble.

"One day a splendid idea struck him. He set the big gate wide open, and put a barrel of rum outside, with the head knocked in, and a tin cup hung on the side.

"After awhile the old bos'n happened that way and smelt it. 'Avast there, boys,' says he, 'wait where you are a minute 'till I see about this.' He took a dip at it, and then he stuck his fingers in his mouth, so, and whistled, this way, pipin' all hands to grog. 'Grog ho!' he sung out, and forth they rushed to the rum barrel.

"Slam! went the big gate, and old Jimmy felt so jolly over getting rid of them that he stuck his tail out of the key-hole and shook it at them.

"Quicker'n wink the old bos'n jumped for'ard, and caught hold of the tail and sang out, 'Avast, there, boys! lay hold here; haul aft main sheet— yo, heave, ho!' And they bowsed him chock up to the key-hole and took an overhand knot in his tail and there they left him.

"He begged hard, and [illegible] no use, they all hands got roarin' drunk and went on to Fiddler's Green, half a mile beyond, and it was a week before he could get his tail untied. He shut down on all sailors after that: wont have 'em there at all.

A SLY DEVIL.

The little old man was delighted as well as the Chinaman and Piute, and he declared that now he must set up the drinks himself in good style, and then he would tell his experience.

He took the cups aside and fixed up the hot beverages with extra care. It was getting along toward morning, and he laughed right jolly as he handed each his drink. When they had drained their cups he commenced:

"My convivial friends, as I have before remarked I have been a preacher, and I ought to know something about the devil. You have all seen him in one shape or another, and I am free to say that I too have beheld him frequently. He appears among us in all shapes, and we never know precisely when or where we are meeting him."

Just here he noticed with a peculiar twinkle of his eye that the Chinaman and Piute were both falling off asleep, and he turned his attention more particularly to Jack.

"The World, the Flesh and the Devil," continued he, "these, my maratime brother, constitute the great earthly Trinity. The World we know all about, also the Flesh, but the Devil is the great puzzler. Yes, my dear salt-water friend—"

Here he observed that the sailor also was fast asleep, and in a few minutes all three were snoring at a glorious rate.

The little old man gazed around at them gleefully, took another pull at the bottle, and then put it in his pocket, quietly remarking, "I wish you a Happy New Year."

*　　*　　*　　*　　*　　*

Morning came. The sleepers awoke.

The little old man was gone.

So also was the Chinaman's purse with $360 in it. So also were Jack's few half dollars and his plug of tobacco and his jackknife. So also was the Piute's horse and some other horses.

They never saw nor heard of that nice little old man any more.

The Chinaman remembered seeing him going up the chimney feet foremost, last of all, taking a drink of blue fire as he went, and Jack found big circles burned in the chair seat, where his tail had been coiled beneath him.

Then they knew that the real old sly devil of all had been their New Year's entertainer.

Early Journalism of Nevada

[Reprinted from Doten's articles in The Nevada Magazine *for September, October, and November of 1899.]*

PART I.

Considering age, and sparcity of population as compared with extent of territory, Nevada, since her admission to the American Union as the "Battle Born State," in 1864, has produced or utilized more newspapers and journalists, good, bad or indifferent, than any other of her sister States. The most notable and prosperous period in her early history was that signalized by the discovery of the world-renowned Comstock lode and subsequently other rich silver and gold mines in Eureka, White Pine, Lander, Lincoln, Esmeralda and other famed localities within her borders.

The Comstock silver discovery in 1859 started a rush of immigration to Nevada like as was that of "Forty-nine" to the newly discovered gold mines of California. Vigorous enterprising men in the prime of life, by hundreds and thousands came over the snow-clad Sierra Nevada and across the plains from the East, all eagerly seeking eligible fields for their varied abilities at mining or anything else in the new land of promise, and with them came the journalists with their presses.

During that early period of Nevada's wonderful prosperity mining camps and towns sprang magically into existence all over the broad State, for it would seem that about all the best and most productive mines were discovered during the first dozen years. Among the first public institutions of each newly organized community was its newspaper to herald forth its glowing prospects and share the fortunes of the camp. And those migrating printing presses, most of which had seen service in the mining towns and elsewhere in California, were about as varied in their styles and capacities as the editors, reporters or printers, who accompanied them.

The chief rallying and distributive point being naturally the Comstock—Virginia City and Gold Hill—which received the first general raid of immigration, there naturally gathered numerous searchlights of journalism; men with full heads of sound sense, comprehensive ideas and brilliant genius; embryo editors and reporters; fellows of infinite wit and affluent cheek; and better still, came with them, as a judicious saving clause, a splendid lot of first-class printers. All of these good journalists and printers not required on the Comstock soon branched out into other eligible fields looming up on all sides throughout the State.

One hundred and twenty-seven different newspapers, over half being dailies, have been started in Nevada at various times and places, and twenty-nine comprises the roll of the living at the present writing. The sagebrush was full of them, but with the disastrous decline of the great mining excitement and prosperity, and the consequent decrease of population in their respective localities, one by one they had to die. Some were resurrected under other names, other owners or in other places, but many of them still sleep beneath the sagebrush, with only memories on their headboards to mark their graves. And it will be observed that the three leading pioneer daily newspapers of the Comstock and the State, the Territorial Enterprise, the Virginia Daily Union, and the Gold Hill Daily News, all three died. The Enterprise was galvanically resurrected after nearly a year, but the Union and the News have remained dead.

The first "Directory of Nevada Territory," by J. Wells Kelly, in 1862, was a sort of preliminary skirmisher or organizer as it were, in the pioneer journalistic and business field. It was a well arranged, neatly bound book of 270 pages, containing the Organic Act, a historical sketch of Nevada, business advertisements, and names of residents in the principal towns, mineral discoveries, mining and milling descriptions, tables of distances and much other useful information relative to the wonderful new land of sagebrush and silver ore.

The first newspaper printed in Nevada was by Alfred James and W. L. Jernegan, at Genoa, Douglas county, fourteen miles south of Carson City. It was published as a weekly, commencing December 18, 1858—five years before Nevada became a State, and was therefore appropriately named the Territorial Enterprise. Eleven months later—November 5, 1859—it was removed to Carson where it was continued as a weekly. Meanwhile Jonathan Williams, having become sole proprietor by purchase, in October 1860, removed the Enterprise to Virginia City, making it the first paper published on the Comstock Lode. Joseph T. Goodman and Denis E. McCarthy, printers, became partners with Williams in March, 1861, and D. Driscoll soon after bought out Williams, who several years later committed suicide at Pioche. The Enterprise was changed from a weekly to a daily newspaper September 14, 1861. Goodman and Mc-Carthy bought out Driscoll October 28, 1863 and Joseph T. Goodman became sole proprietor September 15, 1865, remaining as such until February, 1874, when he sold out to the Enterprise Publishing Company, a corporation composed of William Sharon and the Virginia & Truckee Railroad Company. John W. Mackay subsequently at one time owned a half interest, but D. O. Mills with the Virginia & Truckee Railroad Company, is now considered to constitute the proprietorship.

When Goodman sold out he removed to San Francisco, where he engaged in stock brokerage and passed out of regular journalism. R. M. Daggett succeeded him as chief editor of the Enterprise, Dan de Quille retaining his position as local reporter. Judge C. C. Goodwin became associated with Daggett in the editorial conduct of the paper, and after the big fire of October 26, 1875, Daggett left him chief editor for a couple of years, when he resumed for a year. In 1878, however, Daggett was elected to Congress and Goodwin was again chief, finally severing his connection with the Enterprise in 1880, when Fred Hart succeeded him for a few weeks and Colonel Henry G. Shaw was called to the chief command. Col. Shaw resigned in 1885, Dan de Quille permanently preceding him a few months, after which there was a successive variety of editorial and reportorial efforts to sustain the paper, which together with the dropsical old Comstock had fallen into a bad state of decline. Notwithstanding all possible reduction of expenses, and with J. M. Campbell as the last lessee and J. W. Plant foreman, the business of the concern would not sustain it and therefore on January 16, 1893, the old Enterprise deliberately suspended publication.

It remained dead for nearly a year, or until December 3, when it was resurrected by J. W. McKinnon, who gave it a new lease of life which has been continued by successive lessees, Frank Blake and John Craise having it efficiently in hand during the past year with hopeful prospects.

Joseph T. Goodman was a brilliant and logical as well as a critical editor, and as a true poet he had few superiors, as attested by many a poetic gem from his facile pen, published in the columns of the old Enterprise. Rollin M. Daggett, his chief of staff, wrote the heavier editorials, political and otherwise in his own peculiar, vigorous style, and blatant demagogues, venal office holders or disloyal politicians winced beneath the keen strokes of his pen, the ink from which flowed green with sarcasm when occasion required. Yet he also was the author of meritorious poems that found favor in the eyes of numerous appreciative admirers. C. A. V. Putnam—"Old Put"—telegraph, paragraph and scissoring editor, was

also a good writer, as well as a practical printer, like Goodman and Daggett. Later on he was editor of the Daily Inland Empire, at Hamilton,
during the White Pine mining excitement, and served a four years term
as State Printer. He now dwells comfortably at the Printer's Home, Colorado Springs, and Goodman dwells in a fine country home near Stockton,
California, taking it easy, while Daggett, too aggressive to die, is in his
element writing editorials for the San Francisco Chronicle. He tried ranching near Napa for awhile after leaving the Comstock, raised hens and laid
stone walls, but the occupation was too tame, so he had to drop back on
himself, as it were.

The early newspaper publishers took more interest in poetic and literary
productions than those of the present day, probably from being more
tunefully inspired by general prosperity, and not impelled to the disagreeable study of ways and means. And they all took professional pride in a
handsome paper, good printing, good make-up and good presswork—
different from the slip-shod, slouchy, clam-boat styles observable in some
of our present journals.

The only Nevada editor who ever got rich, retired rich and stays rich,
was Joe Goodman of the old Enterprise. He was the early bird that got
the fat worm.

Charles C. Goodwin came to Nevada from California in 1861. He was
a highly educated gentleman, but having a few shrewd mechanical ideas
in his head requiring to be eliminated, he tried quartz milling for awhile,
and then ranching, meeting with an affluence of bad luck which impelled
him to be elected District Judge of Washoe county. Subsequently viscissi-
tudes of fortune in other parts of the State finally gravitated him into his
natural groove, journalism, and the editorial rooms of the Enterprise. He
was a very industrious editor, and his writings were always of a high order
of literary merit, full of noble sentiment and poetic rhythm as well as
sound common sense and aggressive power, exercising a potent influence
in politics and social government. He left the Enterprise in 1880 to take
chief editorial charge of the Salt Lake Daily Tribune, and the present high
standard of that popular journal is ample evidence of his eminent ability
and well deserved success. P. H. Lannan, one of the best and most popularly known former Comstockers, is ably and appropriately connected as
business manager and proprietor. He was not a thorough journalist in
Virginia City, but has developed all right on Salt Lake water.

"Dan de Quille" was chief among the early local reporters. At home in
his native State, Ohio, his Quaker parents named him William Wright,
which held all right until the young man came to Nevada. His early pros-

pecting companions among the placer diggings and rich mineral veins of Silver City near the Carson River knew him familiarly as Bill Wright, but in writing up the mining, social and festive resources of that lively camp for the Enterprise, with which paper he occasionally took pleasure in corresponding, he adopted the fanciful pen name of "Dan de Quille." His letters, written in a very genial, humorous style, pleased everybody and his adopted name was cordially endorsed as the only natural and appropriate one for him. In the Spring of 1862, Dan was called to Virginia and was not long in making himself famous as local editor or reporter of the Enterprise, which position he held with few interruptions until the fall of 1884—nearly twenty-three years.

Dan was a versatile, easy, off-hand writer, full of quaint, original humor and as an industrious wide-awake reporter he could pick up columns of lively and interesting items where few others could see anything at all. Moreover he wrote scientific articles or humorous sketches that were copied far and near. He published many very popular stories and eventually was inspired to write a book, but like other meritorious writers, made a financial failure of it, yet his "Big Bonanza" is a historical, very interesting and entertaining work which can be found in many libraries, public and private. He also published a condensed "History of the Comstock Lode," which, although correct and interesting for reading or reference, was of small profit to him.

With the decline of the Comstock Lode and the old Enterprise, Dan passed out of reportorial journalism into magazine and outside literary work, corresponding regularly for the Salt Lake Tribune, but by degrees he became a sad victim to rheumatism which finally rendered him almost helpless. With his wife and unmarried daughter he finally left Virginia, July 14, 1897, to make his home in West Liberty, Iowa, where his eldest daughter, married, resides. The change operated somewhat favorably, but finally a severe attack of la grippe seized him and he died March 16, 1898, nearly 69 years of age, his birthday being May 9, 1829. The good old boy wrote the obituary of many an old time friend, as his in turn is written now.

"Mark Twain"—Samuel L. Clemens—worked with Dan de Quille on the local department of the Enterprise in 1862–3, having previously been a correspondent from Aurora, Esmeralda county, and his career as an established popular writer dates from that time. His peculiarly, original style as a genuine humorist soon brought him into notoriety, but as between the two, Dan was the best and most reliable reporter, doing most of the regular routine work, while Mark filled in with humorous sketches and special reports.

Alf Doten was among the early developers of Como, or Palmyra mining district, in the nut pine range, about twenty miles south-east from Virginia, beyond the Carson river, which locality was attracting much attention by reason of the many fine looking quartz ledges discovered there. Como was a flourishing town of about six hundred inhabitants, with telegraph, express and postoffice, brewery, and of course, a newspaper, named the Como Sentinel. Alf was a prospecting miner, like most everybody else, but found time to amuse himself writing for the Sentinel, and corresponding for the Virginia Daily Union. One day he met Mark Twain, just arrived, having been sent to report upon the mining prospects and conditions of the new district, for the Enterprise, and they naturally affiliated. Mark was there about two weeks, making himself a popular favorite, writing humorous letters about scenes and incidents connected with the town, district and people, without making particular reference to the mines.

One pleasant Sunday Alf said to him: "Mark, you don't seem to get out among the mines and write 'em up. If you'll come along with me to the top of the hill, I'll point you out all the quartz ledges in the district, give you the names of the mines, and the aggravating particulars, just as good as if you tramped all around among them yourself. Splendid view, Mark; come along up and I'll give you the whole thing."

Mark's eyes twinkled genially as he quizzically responded in his peculiar drawling voice: "Say, Alf, do you know who you remind me of?"

"Well, no, Mark, I don't know as I do," replied Alf, with an inquiring smile.

"Well, you remind me of that fellow we read of in the Bible, called the devil, who took the Savior up on top of a high mountain, where he could see all over the world and offered to give him the whole thing if he would fall down and worship him. Only you aint the devil and I aint the Savior, by a blamed sight. How far do you say it is up there? Only half a mile? Well, no, thank you all the same, but I'm too derned lazy. Let's go down to the brewery."

So he made no special mention of the mines he was sent to report upon except in his last Como letter, written after he got back to Virginia— where he said:

"This new mining town, with its romantic name is one of the best populated and most promising camps, but as to the mines, I have started out several times to inspect them, but never could get past the brewery."

Mark soon went to San Francisco, where he worked some for the Call and other papers, meeting with little advancement until he returned from the Sandwich Islands and wrote up his famous lecture thereon, delivering the same to great audiences in both California and Nevada. His grand literary and financial success dates from that time.

Alf Doten was called from Como shortly after the foregoing incident, to be local editor or reporter of the Virginia Daily Union, a morning paper which at one time outranked the Enterprise, but by mismanagement the Enterprise was allowed to overshadow it and the Union's flag went down in financial distress and rank political change. Alf had been with it about a year and a half and was then called to the Enterprise where he localized for a similar period, finally leaving it for a long engagement on the Gold Hill Daily News with which stalwart journal he remained fourteen years.

The Virginia Daily Union was established November 4, 1862, by Church, Glesner & Laird, three good San Francisco printers. The plant was brought from California and had been used for about six months previously at Carson by John C. Lewis in publishing the Silver Age, the first daily newspaper printed in Nevada, Lewis selling it to Church and partners. They conducted the Daily Union as a first-class morning newspaper in every respect, contemporaneous with the Enterprise. Monroe Thompson was a regular editorial writer, also Tom Fitch, the "silver-tongued" orator, and others occasionally. George Marshall, Major F. P. Dallum and Alf Doten were local editors and reporters and Clem Rice was special legislative reporter. In May, 1865, through adverse circumstances, the Union passed into the hands of an association of printers, and in October following it astounded the Comstock political world by an abrupt radical change within twenty-four hours, from chief organ of square Union Republicanism to rank copperhead Democracy, with Orlando E. Jones as editor and Robert E. Lowery, local reporter. About a year later the old Daily Union died and W. J. Forbes, the humorous editor of the Humboldt Register bought and resurrected it under the euphonious name of the "Trespass." It did not trespass long, but passed through other experimenting hands and under other names until it became the Inland Empire, at Hamilton, White Pine county, thus finally dying in 1870 with no hope of further resurrection, its demoralized remains being removed to Stockton, California.

The Gold Hill Daily News was established by Philip Lynch, October 12, 1863. Hiram W. Hawkins and Charles A. Sumner were successively editors and Edward W. Townsend, author of "Chimmie Fadden," and "Major Max" was also one of the early writers on the News. Alf Doten became associate editor and reporter November 14, 1867, remaining there until Lynch died, February 13, 1872, when a few days later he became sole proprietor and editor. During the subsequent bonanza years of Gold Hill and Virginia, the News flourished immensely—ahead of all competitors. Captain George G. Lyon and W. W. Austin were successively employed in the editorial rooms and W. H. Virden, now Superior Judge of Mono county, California, was advertising manager and also reportorially in the mining department, which was a specialty with the News. Wells Drury and Arthur McEwen were also on the News for several months, also H. B. Loomis, George Phelps and others in reportorial and editorial capacities. Will U. Mackey, now foreman of the State Printing Office, graduated from the Gold Hill News.

When the great fire of October 26, 1875, destroyed the principal part of Virginia, including the Enterprise office, by special invitation, the entire Enterprise force, printers, editors and all came to the Gold Hill News office, were furnished all facilities, and the Enterprise was published next morning, as usual—never lost an issue. The Virginia Evening Chronicle also took advantage of the same hospitalities offered for a few issues, and thus all three papers were printed on the News press. The Chronicle, however, soon found another office at Virginia, and resumed printing there on a hand press furnished from the News office, most of its type and material having been saved, but the Enterprise utilized the News office for two months, or until its own building and plant was reconstructed at Virginia.

In its palmiest days the Gold Hill Daily News was considered the chief political and mining journal of the State, as shown by its bound files now in the State Library, and that of the State University, but with the exhaustion of the rich ore bonanzas and consequent decline of Comstock prosperity the News had also to take the down grade. February 21, 1879, its proprietorship merged into the News Publishing Company, Alf Doten remaining as managing editor until December 10, 1881, when he dissolved his fourteen years connection with the News and a month later left with his family for Austin, to edit the Reveille. Three months afterward the News died, and its costly plant was sold and removed to Wood River, where it was used during the short life of the Bellevue Times. Subsequently it went farther east and at last accounts it was warehoused in charge of a Montana sheriff.

Wells Drury officiated by turns as foreman, compositor and local editor of the Gold Hill News, being not only a prolific and versatile writer but a very handy all-around newspaper man in any capacity, from editor to "devil," as shown by his varied and extensive Nevada record. He even officiated at one time as Deputy Secretary of State under John W. Dormer, an experienced Nevada editor—now digging up great wealth in Klondike—and in 1887 he was Speaker pro tem of the Assembly, ending up his Nevada career as Secretary of the State Insane Asylum at Reno. From there he graduated to San Francisco, where he has since held several responsible journalistic positions, including managing editor of the Call, and is now special writer for the Examiner.

It cost piles of money to establish and maintain a first-class daily newspaper in those early and most flourishing days. The journalistic managers were comprehensive, broad-minded men, recognizing and employing the best literary talent and typographical ability and liberally and honestly paying for the same. Thus chief editors received $300 to $500 a month and reporters $40 to $60 per week—short hand reporters were a fancy priced novelty. Printers' union rates were $1 per thousand "ems," therefore it was a lazy typo who did not make $10 a day. Freight on presses, type and other heavy material was at high figures, building or rent high, salaries of employees high and regular daily press telegrams almost out of reach. The Enterprise, Union and News, when first established and flourishing paid from $500 to $1000 per month for full daily telegrams. No wonder that amid the dizzy whirl of bullion wealth, fluctuating millions and fortune's speedy changes, that even the most enterprising journals became stricken with paralysis and went down with the general mix-up.

PART II.

Fred H. Hart was a peculiarly brilliant and lively feature in his way. In the early seventies he began to attract attention as correspondent of the "Reese River Reveille," writing from White Pine, Belmont and contiguous localities under the nom de plume of "Van Jacquelin." His letters were spicy and interesting, and led to regular employment on that paper in 1874, and finally into partnership with John Booth, Hart editorially and Booth doing all the rest. During this period it was that Fred got up his famous little book, the "Sazerac Lying Club." He subsequently sold out his interest in the "Reveille" to Booth, and at one time made quite a popular mark as legislative reporter and outside correspondent for the "Gold Hill Daily News."

After that he was about Eureka for some time, not doing much, and finally through strong friendly influence he succeeded in getting into high position as editor of the "Territorial Enterprise" at Virginia City. There his career was remarkably brilliant as well as brief—about three months.

Inspiration of some kind got into him one evening to distinguish himself editorially, and he did most effectually succeed. James G. Fair was running for United States Senator from Nevada, so Fred devoted to him one long, two-column, pungent, paragraphic editorial, headed, "Slippery Jim," ridiculing his ability or capacity as a would-be statesman, and relating sundry current anecdotes of his alleged surreptitious mining methods and sly trickeries among his miners and mankind generally, both above and below ground.

Next morning when John W. Mackay read the "Enterprise" he wrathfully arose and struck a bee-line for the printing office. "Look here!" roared he, shaking the paper fiercely in the face of Cohen, the bookkeeper; "What damsonofagun wrote all this infernal trash about my partner? I own half of this paper myself, and won't have Fair abused and belied in it by anybody. I've a d—— good mind to take a sledge and smash h—— out of the bloody press."

By the most strenuous persuasion on the part of influential friends, John Mackay's wrath was partially appeased, and under the most stringent promises never to thus slop over again, Fred Hart's bald little scalp was allowed to remain in place. But alas, only a month later an east wind from the brewery struck him again, and under the resistless impulse he steered directly into and afoul of the Alta Mining Company—among the best patrons of the "Enterprise." Under heading of "The Alta Steal," he devoted a long-winded, viciously crotchetty editorial, like that on Fair, to showing what an atrocious band of mining rascals they were—stealing the best portion of the Justice mine adjoining—worst gang of thieves ever allowed to be pirooting around outside of State Prison walls, etc. There was a cloudburst, earthquake and war-dance, all in one, next morning when the Alta folks and their friends, waving aloft their gleaming machetes and tomahawks, came charging down upon the "Enterprise" office with blood in their eyes.

Poor little Fred Hart got wind of the coming cyclone, and struck out through the sagebrush across the north end of the Mount Davidson range with great alacrity, never stopping till safe on San Francisco's beautiful shore. His journalistic ship was wrecked forever, and he drifted about, picking up little jobs of reporting by way of precarious subsistence for a few months, finally dying August 30, 1897, in the Sacramento county hospital.

Denis E. McCarthy, after disposing of his interest in the "Enterprise" in 1865, went back to San Francisco, where he was variously engaged in journalistic work until Mark Twain returned from the Sandwich Islands and commenced his famous lectures thereon. McCarthy then became his business manager, and they traveled and worked well together, Mark doing all the talking, and Denis handling all the cash proceeds.

And this is how it happened that when they were walking to Virginia one night after lecturing at Gold Hill, and the footpads held them up on the Divide, Denis obediently passed over the bag of lecture money— about $750—to the robbers, while Mark stood obediently holding his hands up in the air till they had gone through all his pockets, taking his elegant gold watch and chain, pocketknife, corkscrew and all, leaving him not even so much as a toothpick.

It had always been a time-honored custom with those road agents between the two towns, whenever they found no money in a victim's pocket, to give him a rough shake-up and a lecture, like "Left all yer money in faro bank, like a d—— fool, did ye?" or "So You're a sucker from that d—— church fair and can't give an honest footpad a chance." Then they would slew him around and kick him unmercifully, by way of parting admonition, as long as he was within reach. But on this special occasion financial circumstances were different; moreover, the masked agents were Confederate generals, addressing each other as "Beauregard," "Stonewall Jackson," "Jeff Davis," etc.; therefore, all "kicking" was courteously dispensed with on their part, or considerately left to their two victims.

Mark and Denis steered direct for the "Enterprise" office as soon as they could, where they graphically told their tale of woe, Mark grieving more over the loss of his watch and chain than anything else, being a present from his friend, Judge Sandy Baldwin, worth about $500. This reporter tried to get him to sit down and write up the full account of the aggravating episode for the morning's paper, but he declared that his nerves were "too badly stove up," so he and McCarthy hastened to put the police on the track as soon as possible.

A week later, about 9 o'clock in the evening, Mark and Denis were seated in the California stage coach in front of Wells, Fargo & Co.'s, ready to depart, when half a dozen "Enterprise" printers, with the Chief of Police, stepped forward to bid Mark good bye. Chief Birdsall politely handed him an open package containing his stolen money, watch, pocketknife, corkscrew and toothpick, saying with a genial smile and shake of the hand: "Mr. Mark Twain, my name is Jeff Davis, and in behalf of our mutual friends, Beauregard, Stonewall Jackson, and—"

"Stop right there!" drawled Mark in an indignant tone, comprehending the whole matter at once. "I don't want to hear any more. I've always regarded you fellows—I can't call you gentlemen—as good friends of mine, but I look on this thing as a derned mean, unmerited outrage. You've deliberately made me suffer more privation and inconvenience than you think or care for, and I don't like it. You may think it a great joke, but I can't, and I don't thank you for it; go on, driver!" and he left, refusing to shake hands or bid them good bye.

McCarthy told afterward that for the first ten miles Mark was too deeply occupied with bitter reflections to speak a word, but finally he said: "Denis McCarthy, was you a party to this thing; did you know anything about it?" Denis mildly acknowledged that the boys had hinted to him a few points in the matter, but he had no idea that they would carry the joke so far. It took a whole lot of soothing talk, explanation and reasoning, but Mark never seemed to be entirely reconciled. The truth was, as far as McCarthy was concerned, they were obliged to have him in with them as an accomplice, or they could not have perpetrated the robbery without a genuine, desperate fight, for they well knew Denis McCarthy.

Some time before that, when Mark Twain was working on the "Enterprise" with Dan De Quille, in the local department, those wicked printers played a similar joke on their friend, the humorous joker. They bought a clay imitation meerschaum pipe, big as a man's fist, for four bits, got a tinsmith to mount it with tin in silver regulation style, finishing up with a long, cherrry-wood stem and mouthpiece, the whole rig costing about two dollars, yet looking to be worth about sixty. Then they got Dan to quietly post Mark, who as quietly proceeded to smuggle a few bottles of champagne and some cigars into the office, ready for the surprise party.

Along in the evening, when it was about time for Mark to be going home, the printers came into the local room where Dan and Mark were sitting at the table, busily writing. Both tried to look surprised when the foreman, with that magnificent pipe poised between thumb and finger, made the presentation speech. Mark had prepared a humorous little response, which he got off in good style, thanking his admiring friends for their rich, emblematic appreciation of his humble efforts, assuring them that this noble journalistic pipe of peace should be fondly smoked through all future generations of the Twain family, in cherished memory of this auspicious event.

"Say Dan," said he, "isn't there a bottle or two of that wedding notice wine left kickin' around under the table somewhere?" Dan found it, and there was much typographical and reportorial hilarity for a short time, while the wine and cigars lasted. Then Dan carefully wrapped and tied up the pipe and Mark proudly took it home.

Next evening Mark was late in getting around to work, and when he did come he was silent and morose. Finally, however, he squared himself back in his chair, with a face on him like a salivated grave-digger, saying, "See here, Dan. I've always considered you like a friend and brother, but after that infernal snide pipe affair last night I don't know. I took it home happy, and was happy all night till this morning, when I unwrapped the blamed thing and was loading it for a royal smoke; then I saw what a meersham it was. The wine and cigars cost me sixty times more than the cussed smokestack is worth, to say nothing of my chuckle-headed speech. I met Denis McCarthy down street, and he started in to read me your glorifying account of the derned scrape, but I just turned away and left him. I fully believe he was in with the rest of 'em, and you, too. Jokes are jokes, but I don't recognize this as one. I'll be cussed if I do."

What he did with that remarkable pipe, nobody ever knew, but it was never seen or heard of afterward, and any allusion to it brought an ominous scowl to his countenance, as a sufficient warning to desist. But it was well understood by all who knew him best that although he liked practical jokes on others, he did not seem to enjoy one upon himself.

These incidents, as well as the Como episode related in last month's "Magazine," are simply illustrative of Mark Twain's peculiar journalistic style and disposition. As a regular daily newspaper reporter he was neither great nor intended, his true literary sphere being that of a humorous descriptive sketch or historical story writer and book maker, as since shown to the world by his exceedingly popular works. And he certainly seems far more at home taking notes and observation in Rome or Jerusalem, or among the throned halls of European royalty than he was or ever could be, writing up local items for a Nevada newspaper.

The "Virginia Evening Chronicle" was started by E. F. Bean, and John I. Ginn, October 8, 1872, and soon became a lively and prosperous daily. Like its contemporaries, however, it passed through various changes of ownership until 1873, when it came into the hands of C. C. Stevenson, from whom it was purchased May 24, 1875, by Denis E. McCarthy, who well and popularly conducted it for ten years, or until his death, December 23, 1885. The Chronicle belongs to the McCarthy estate, and is leased to an association of good printers, under the able and long experienced management of John H. Coleman.

H. C. Street, Professor Frank Stewart, Arthur McEwen, John H. Dennis, R. D. Bogart and Sands W. Forman were each at times editors of the "Chronicle," and John I. Ginn, Bob Lowery, Sam Davis and Winfield Scott were successively reporters. Allen Kelly was also for some time reporter, afterward city editor of the S. F. "Examiner," and is now chief editor of the "Los Angeles Times."

Arthur B. McEwen was one of the most brilliant and forcible journalistic writers. D. E. McCarthy, proprietor of the "Virginia Chronicle," knew him in San Francisco, and in 1876 induced him to come to Virginia and take a position on his paper. As a thoroughly live reporter he soon made his mark; in fact, he made things a little hot for himself sometimes. He left the "Chronicle" and went on the "Gold Hill News," with Wells Drury, in the local department, popularly enlivening the columns of that paper with his brilliant wit and pungent paragraphs for about six months, when by reason of a belligerent lodging-house difficulty one night at Virginia he abruptly emigrated to Eureka. There—in March, 1878—he engaged with Alfred Chartz and Tom Watts, two good printers and journalists, in the publication of the "Daily Republican."

The paper sprang into popularity and flourished famously for a brief period, but finally over indulgence in trivial personalities with Edward Ricker, a railroad conductor, resulted, June 16th, in the death of Ricker, which tragical disaster summarily ended the promising career of the "Republican" a few days later.

McEwen finally returned to the Comstock and made a lively success for a couple of years as political editor of the "Chronicle," after which he went back to San Francisco, where his editorial career was prominent on the "Examiner" and other papers, and afterward on the New York Journal. Recently he was called to the responsible position as chief editor of the "North American" at Philadelphia. Chartz gradually passed out of public journalism into stenography and typewriting, and is now an able and successful lawyer, residing in Carson City.

Sam P. Davis was introduced from San Francisco by McCarthy, of the "Virginia Chronicle," shortly after the great fire of 1875, and materially assisted in getting that paper into good running order again after its fiery ordeal. Sam was already known to some extent in the journalistic fields of California and elsewhere, and for four years he did popular and efficient reportorial service on the "Chronicle." Then he went to Carson, and in November, 1879, became editor of the "Morning Appeal," the former editor of which, Harry Mighels, had died on the 27th of May previously. Sam, being a good writer, humorous, political and otherwise, figured well with the "Appeal," not only as a successful journalist, but it also helped him into good ranching near Carson City, and finally into public office, being elected State Controller at the last general election.

The "Daily Appeal" was started at Carson City May 16, 1865. It was a twenty-column weekly, owned by Marshall Robinson, E. F. McElwain and J. Barrett, with Henry R. Mighels as editor, one of the most brilliant and capable on the Pacific Coast. Six months later Robinson and Mighels were sole proprietors, so remaining till the close of 1870, after which sundry changes in ownership, style and name supervened. C. L. Perkins, H. C. Street and John Booth becoming successively proprietors and editors, and at one time D. R. Sessions was local editor. Finally, January 1, 1878, Mr. Mighels came in again, this time permanently as sole proprietor and editor of the daily "Morning Appeal"—making that its fixed designation.

Harry Mighels died May 27, 1879, and his widow conducted the "Appeal" until August following, when S. H. Fulton of the Elko "Post" was placed in charge, subsequently superseded by Sam P. Davis, who married Mrs. Mighels. The paper has prospered well under his management, and its prosperity is ably continued and promoted by Henry R. Mighels, lessee and editor, who is a worthy son of the original.

The "News," a newsy and active daily evening paper, is now the only one left to divide with the "Appeal" the journalistic patronage of Carson, H. C. Dunn, formerly foreman of the State Printing Office, and H. A. Lemmon proprietors, editors and good workers.

The Carson "Tribune" was started in July, 1872, and was owned and operated by the Parkinson family, R. R. Parkinson, the father, being editor, Ed J. Parkinson, the elder son, reporter and business manager, and Percy, the younger son, and three of his sisters doing all the rest. The genial old "Deacon" was a good editorial writer, Ed a good reporter, and all worked harmoniously together, but there was not business enough, so they sold out four or five years ago and moved up to Seattle. The Tribune plant also passed away to Reno a year or so later.

The Carson "Daily Independent" was started by W. W. Ross in July, 1863, Israel Crawford subsequently becoming editor and proprietor, and so continuing until it closed out, October 11, 1864. Col. A. C. Ellis ran the "State Democrat" as a campaign paper two or three months that same fall, falling out after the election.

The daily "Carson Post," morning and evening, posted in and posted out in 1864–5, under the auspices of J. C. Lewis, editor. Al Mills and Al Jones, printers, hummed the spicy little Carson "Daily Bee" a year on a job press, and Billy Cowan and Si Adams, two little twelve-year-old kids, ran a little seven by nine monthly called the "Carson Post" for four months. Some other young lads, the Olcovich brothers, ran a neat little "Carson Weekly" not long ago for several months.

The Carson "Daily Index," with Judge C. N. Harris, editor, had a lively but not lengthy run in 1880, and Ed Niles had a similar experience with his Carson "Daily Times" in 1880–81.

Wells Drury also pleads guilty to starting a paper or two in Carson, but plaintively remarks that there were extenuating circumstances, and such indiscretions should not be held out against him.

The "Carson Valley News," weekly, started by A. C. Pratt, editor and proprietor, in 1875, at Genoa, well represented the interests of Douglas county for about a year, the "Genoa Courier," by Boynton Carlisle, succeeding it. Others lived briefly and died permanently, but the "Courier" still lives and flourishes, with Smith & Williams, editors and proprietors. For the past year or so it has had a very promising, well-conducted rival in the "Gardnerville Record," George I. Lamy, editor and proprietor.

The "Como Sentinel," the first newspaper published in Lyon County, was started April 16, 1864, as a weekly, in the town of Como, Palmyra mining district, about eight miles southeast of Dayton, by H. L. Weston and T. W. Abraham, who brought the press and material with them from Petaluma, California. Como was a new and very promising camp of about six hundred people, situated in the heart of a wide mountain district, seamed with a large number of fine looking gold and silver bearing quartz veins or ledges, but the expected bullion product failing to materialize, people got out of there as lively as they had rushed in. Consequently the "Sentinel" judiciously weakened four months after its commencement, and removed to Dayton, where it immediately resumed under the name of the Lyon County Sentinel, Weston retiring, B. F. Cooper and Charles F. Paine came in as partners with Abraham. The great fire of July, 1866, which consumed most of the town, destroyed the "Sentinel." During its brief season of prosperity in Como the "Sentinel" was a very lively and enjoyable institution—and so was Como.

The "Lyon County Times" was started at Silver City July 4, 1874, by Frank Kenyon, as a tri-weekly, changing to a daily in March, '75, with Harry J. Norton editor. T. E. Picotte became editor and publisher in July, '78, John M. Campbell joining with him in December, '79. In November, 1880, it was reduced to a weekly, and, December, removed to Dayton, where Campbell continued its publication as sole proprietor. Fred W. Fairbanks bought a half interest in '83, and the other half in '85, since which time, under his able management, the Lyon County Times has prospered exceedingly.

The "Daily Mining Reporter," started at Silver City March 10, 1876, by Harry J. Norton and H. Scrimgeour, reporter, lasted just two months.

The "Sutro Independent," weekly, was started in July, '75, in the town of Sutro, at the mouth of the famous Sutro Tunnel, Adolph Sutro, proprietor, T. E. Picotte, editor. Frank B. Mercer succeeded Picotte as editor and publisher, November 1, 1876, staying with it under sundry trying vicissitudes, latterly doing every department, editor, typo, pressman, devil and carrier, by himself alone, with great facility and increasing poverty until, November 29, 1880, the "Independent" surrendered forever.

The "Esmeralda Star," weekly, was started at Aurora, May 10, 1862, by Edwin A. Sherman & Co., the press and material being that of the old "San Diego Herald," famed in the early history of California journalism, when Judge Ames was its editor, notably assisted by Lieutenant Derby, otherwise journalistically known as "John Phoenix," alias "Squibob." The "Star" rose to a semi-weekly, but dimmed and went down in March '64, yet rose again three weeks later as the "Esmeralda Daily Union," J. W. Avard, editor and proprietor. With the declining fortunes of that noted and lively mining camp it was subsequently reduced to a tri-weekly, then to a weekly, and finally died in October, '68. In the spring of 1870, Chalfant & Parker bought the historical concern and removed it to Independence, Inyo county, California, where it is still running as the "Inyo Independent."

The "Aurora Times," weekly, started by R. E. Draper and Bob Glenn in April, '63, became a daily in May, '64, but suspended in November following. It was revived a month later by Robert Ferral, who ran it through the winter and it died in the next spring.

The "Esmeralda Herald," Aurora, weekly, started by Frank Kenyon, October 13, 1877, with John M. Dormer, editor, was sold to M. M. Glenn, March 1, 1880, and died a year or so later.

The "Borax Miner," Columbus, weekly, by W. W. Barnes, in August, '73, based on the borax excitement and hopeful Democracy, lingered about four years before it finally died out.

The "Belleville Times," weekly, started in October, '77, by Mark W. Musgrove, lived about six months.

The "True Fissure," Candelaria, weekly, by John M. Dormer, editor and proprietor, started June 5, 1880, flourished well for a time but passed in its checks six years later, leaving Esmeralda county without a newspaper. Dormer was an excellent journalist and popular citizen, subsequently becoming Secretary of State for four years.

The "Washoe Times," weekly, was started at Washoe City, October 18, 1862, by G. W. Dickerson, with General James Allen as editor, and was the pioneer journal of Washoe county. Judge Charles C. Goodwin soon became its editor, and so remained until December 12, 1863, when J. K.

Lovejoy bought the paper and changed its name to the "Old Pah-Utah." He did not succeed to suit himself, therefore a year later he sold out and started a daily paper at Virginia City named "The Old Piute," which was short-lived, and successful principally in fastening its peculiar title as a nickname upon its proprietor, Lovejoy being known ever afterward as the "Old Piute."

The parties to whom he sold his Washoe City paper changed its name to the "Washoe Weekly Star," which dropped out of the journalistic firmament a few months later—in January, 1865. It was picked up by other successive owners, including J. C. Lewis—nom de plume "Snarleyow"—and lastly the Sheriff clapped his claw upon it, forcing a final suspension on the 20th of November following. Three weeks later "Snarleyow," meanwhile having got his back up, came in with the material of the defunct "Carson Post" and started the "Eastern Slope," which he vigorously and popularly conducted for over two years, or until owing to the decline of Washoe City he removed the concern to the new and lively town of Reno, where on the Fourth of July, 1868, he issued the first edition of the "Reno Crescent," the pioneer newspaper of Reno.

W. C. Lewis, his son, became associated with him as editor, and they ran a very good paper, sometimes as a daily, until June 30, 1875, when Col. J. C. Dow securing command, hoodooed it by changing its name to the "Daily Nevada Democrat," and it promptly ran into the ground. H. A. Waldo & Co. purchased the material after it had been stored away about a year, and used it in the publication of the "Reno Daily Record," commencing August 5, 1878. Two months later other parties owned it, and finally, November 1, 1878, S. F. Hoole becoming sole proprietor, he shut down the works and soon moved the erratic concern over to Bodie, California, where it was subsequently devoted to the publication of the "Bodie News."

C. C. Powning was a young man of prominent mark, not only in the early journalism, but also in the political and social history of Nevada. He was a native of Wisconsin, born February 23, 1852, and by the death of both his parents became an orphan when but three years of age. In 1863 he came with his grandmother to California, locating in Sacramento. Being a self-reliant, enterprising little fellow, when the Central Pacific Railroad was completed across the Sierra Nevada, he managed to secure position as newsboy on the passenger train.

The Sacramento "Daily Union" was the chief popular newspaper, and its proprietor befriending him, he naturally felt a degree of pride in being its representative, therefore soon commenced writing up his youthful observations in a series of letters which were published in the "Union" over the peculiar nom de plume of "Ning Pow"—the syllables of his own name reversed, or transposed. These letters took well and constituted his first effort in journalism. Meanwhile making his home in the new and promising town of Reno in 1870, he followed the real bent of his genius by getting in as office "devil" on the "Nevada State Journal," which was just being started.

"Ning Pow" made himself exceedingly handy at inking rollers, typesticking and whatever else he could do, and two years later he owned half the establishment. Two years still later—in 1874—he became sole proprietor. He ably edited and managed his paper with editorial assistance at times when required, took an active part in politics, and was elected State Senator from Washoe county in 1878, which high position he filled during his term of four years with marked ability and credit.

Powning always took a leading part in all public movement or organized enterprises, especially for the benefit of Reno and the general interests of Washoe county, and when declining health compelled his retirement from business and active public life, terminating in his death, October 4—a year ago—his fellow citizens realized the loss of a most energetic, public-spirited and influential friend.

The "Nevada State Journal," the daily morning paper of Reno, commenced publication November 30, 1870, as a weekly, with J. G. Laws, W. H. H. Fellows and E. A. Littlefield proprietors, under the firm name of J. G. Laws & Co. It was changed to a semi-weekly, February 5, 1873, and to a daily and weekly April 1, 1874, which arrangement still continues. Littlefield sold to his partner August 26, 1871, C. C. Powning bought Laws' half interest June 15, 1872, and the firm was Fellows & Powning until September 5, 1874, when Powning bought out his partner and became sole proprietor. In 1890 he sold to E. D. Kelley and C. H. Stoddard. Later on Stoddard sold to Judge William Webster, who bought out Editor Kelley's interest about a year ago, thus becoming sole proprietor. The Journal has since been ably conducted by William Webster & Son, with Major John H. Dennis as chief editor, and Thomas Smith local editor and reporter.

The "Journal" has always been pronounced in its nationally political character, either as formerly Republican and now Democratic, but under its liberal, comprehensive name, ignoring petty jealousies with neighboring localities, it has never failed to be a straightforward, honest exponent and promoter of the best interests of Reno, Washoe county and the State of Nevada.

Major John H. Dennis has been an active and efficient element in Nevada journalism and politics since 1863. He came "around the Horn" to California in '52, and in '54 this writer worked with him in the gold placer diggings at Fort John, Amador county, where neither of us got opulently wealthy, but we had lots of old-time funny experience as honest miners. He afterward prospected some of the journalistic and political croppings of that section, and served one term as Assemblyman from El Dorado county.

Then he came to the Sagebrush State, and in 1871 he became half owner in the "Reese River Reveille," a flourishing daily at Austin, Lander county. He sold out to John Booth in 1874, and bought a half interest in the Eureka "Sentinel," which he editorially conducted for three years, then sold to A. Skillman, the present sole proprietor, and with O. L. Fairchild for partner, bought the Tuscarora "Times-Review," subsequently selling out and leaving Fairchild sole proprietor.

During the Gosh-Ute Indian warlike uprising in Spring Valley, Dennis took an active part in organizing a small army at Eureka which promptly went forth to the rescue of the settlers. The "war" was a bloodless one, the rampant savages judiciously and unconditionally surrendering, and Dennis received his proud title of Major, as a tribute to his valor. Following the vicissitudes of journalism and politics, he has since wielded his trenchant pen—mightier than his sword—as editor of the "Nevada State Journal," Reno.

The Reno "Evening Gazette" was established by John F. Alexander, a graduate of the University of California, twenty-three years of age, with Thomas E. Hayden as partner, and its publication commenced March 8, 1876, as a live daily newspaper. The eight-page weekly addition was made a year later. Alexander purchased the interest of his partner September 2, 1878, thus becoming sole proprietor. He sold to R. L. Fulton and W. F. Edwards on the 19th of November following, and was subsequently elected Attorney General of Nevada, dying from consumption at the conclusion of his term of office. Fulton soon bought out his partner, Edwards, and became sole owner, editor and publisher. A year or two later Fulton sold to Preble & Young, who in turn later on sold to Porter & Bragg, Major Dennis meanwhile being editor for a couple of years. Finally it passed into the hands of the Gazette Publishing Company, under which firm name it is flourishingly conducted, with Allan C. Bragg as editor and manager. The Gazette is a newsy, wide-awake paper, well up to date, and giving latest daily telegrams from everywhere.

PART III.

The "Reese River Reveille" was established in the flourishing town of Austin, Lander county, situated in Pony canyon, east side of Reese River Valley, by W. D. Phillips, an able journalist, as well as printer, May 16, 1863, at first as a weekly and a month later semi-weekly. The paper flourished well, but declining health impelled its enterprising proprietor to sell out in the following October to O. L. C. and J. D. Fairchild, Phillips retiring to his old home in Illinois, where he died some months later. Adair Wilson and Myron Angel succeeded each other as editor, and May 24, 1864, the "Reveille" became a daily. Subsequently, it changed proprietors and editors, John H. Dennis and Andrew Casamayou being at one time thus connected.

John Booth & Co., including Fred Hart later on for a few months, became proprietors in 1875, with Hart as editor and Andrew Maute business manager, Booth finally becoming sole proprietor and editor November 26, 1878. Maute meanwhile became connected with the "Belmont Courier," sixty miles south of Austin, in Nye county, as proprietor and editor. Under John Booth's proprietorship, Alf Doten became editor of the "Reveille," and after Booth's death, March 13, 1884, J. W. Maddrill was editor and manager, succeeded by others.

The "Reveille" was a remarkable paper in several respects, passing through sundry marked vicissitudes during its checkered career. A heavy cloudburst on the summit of the Toiyabe range in the summer of 1876 caused a great flood to sweep down the canyon through Austin, doing much damage and carrying away the "Reveille" plant entirely—press, type, paper, ink, building and all—down into the flat at the mouth of the canyon, a mile below town. New material was immediately ordered by telegraph from San Francisco, a new building purchased, and less than two weeks later the "Reveille" resumed its daily publication, livelier than ever. It is now a well conducted semi-weekly, under the proprietorship of Attorney-General W. D. Jones.

The "Nye County News," weekly, was started at Ione, Nye county, by Henry De Groot and Joseph E. Eckley, June 25, 1864. It was the pioneer, but short lived, dying four months later. Eckley afterward became State Printer. The "Advertiser," "Silver Bend Reporter," "Mountain Champion," Grantsville "Sun" and other newspapers were started in other parts of the county at various times by Tom Fitch, Fairchild, Myers, Ragsdale and other promoters, but the "Belmont Courier" only remains in illustration of the "survival of the fittest." The "Courier," a thrifty, well managed weekly, was started February 11, 1874, by A. Casamayou and John Booth, both since dead, Andrew Maute becoming proprietor December, 1876, and so remaining at the present time.

Andrew Maute, like Eckley, was one of the early Nevada printers. He came from Nevada county, California, where he had been working as compositor on the "Transcript," and in the spring of 1863 he was similarly engaged on the "Washoe Times." He subsequently changed to the Carson "Independent," becoming one of its proprietors in 1864. Later on, when Charles L. Perkins was State Printer, Mr. Maute was foreman of the establishment. He was subsequently connected with the Carson "Appeal," and, as before stated, was foreman and business manager of the "Reese River Reveille" before becoming editor and proprietor of the "Belmont Courier." At the last general election Andrew Maute was chosen State Printer by a handsome majority, all of which is satisfactorily correct, although the principle has not always held good that the best and most meritorious has been chosen to the responsible position of State Printer of Nevada.

The "White Pine News" was originated at Treasure City as a weekly, in December, 1868, by W. H. Pitchford and R. W. Simpson—afterward of the Ward "Reflex," and flourished exceedingly as a daily during the famous Treasure Hill-Eberhardt mining excitement. Myron Angel was at one time editor, with John I. Ginn, reporter. George W. Cassidy made his first Nevada journalistic mark as reporter on the "News." W. J. Forbes leased it in May, 1869, and eight months later removed it down to Hamilton, which had been made the county seat. The "News" was a great paper in its time, but had to share in the decline of the mining excitement and general prosperity. A. Skillman and Fred Elliott bought it in 1873, and in 1875, Elliott retiring, Skillman ran it as a tri-weekly, then as a weekly, and finally, in November, 1878, suspended its publication altogether. In 1880 W. R. Forrest and W. L. Lewis bought the material, and the "White Pine News" is now published at Ely, E. H. Decker editor and manager.

The "Daily Inland Empire" commenced at Hamilton, March 13, 1869, with first-class press and material, and was one of the largest, handsomest and best conducted papers in the State, J. J. Ayers and C. A. V. Putnam—afterward State Printer—being proprietors, managers and editors. Its career was brief and brilliant, lasting only eleven months, or until April 13, 1870. It was revived for the political campaign four months later, under charge of George W. Cassidy, to assist in the election of L. R. Bradley for Governor. Soon after its object was accomplished, the material was sold to H. C. Patrick, who removed it to Stockton, California.

Shermantown, Schell Creek, Ward and Cherry Creek each also had its paper, with plenty of ambitious writers willing to help represent the best interests of White Pine county, even Cleveland, the leading agriculturalist and home rule politician, finally developing a literary proclivity for the development of campaign poetry.

The Pioche "Record," the leading pioneer journal of Lincoln county, was started as a weekly at Pioche, Lincoln county, September 17, 1870, by W. H. Pitchford & Co. Pat Holland soon bought them out, and taking R. W. Simpson in with him as assistant, they ran it for two years, meanwhile Frank Kenyon coming in as editor, when it became a flourishing daily, with its stated name, it having been at first inappropriately called the "Ely Record." It experienced various changes of ownership and fortune with the declining prosperity of the country, becoming a weekly again in 1877. It is run and edited by T. J. Osborne, secretary of the last Nevada Senate.

The Eureka "Sentinel," one of the most prominent newspapers in eastern Nevada, was born of the great Eureka mining excitement, making its first appearance July 16, 1870, as a weekly, A. Skillman & Co., proprietors, and Dr. L. C. McKinney, editor. In October following it became a tri-weekly, with A. B. Elliott and George W. Cassidy proprietors and editors. John H. Dennis bought out Elliott in December, 1874, and the paper became a full-fledged daily, with Dennis as chief editor. Two years later, Skillman returned and bought out Dennis, and after the death of Cassidy, in 1892, he became sole proprietor and editor, eventually reducing the "Sentinel" to a weekly and so continuing to the present time.

Abraham Skillman is a pioneer of the Pacific Coast and one of the oldest printers and journalists of California as well as of Nevada. In 1851 he was half owner of the "Pacific News," one of the very first newspapers published in San Francisco. The concern was twice totally destroyed by fire and was at last compelled to suspend from lack of printing material. In 1852 he started the Shasta "Courier," then the only paper in the State north of Marysville, which still flourishes, and is recorded as the second oldest newspaper published in California.

Coming to Nevada he officiated for a year or two as foreman of the "Territorial Enterprise" at Virginia, and at the time of the famous White Pine mining excitement in 1869 he joined in the grand rush for that silver-plated locality. In the spring of 1870, with G. A. Brier, formerly local reporter of the Gold Hill "Daily News," he started the "Reporter," a

weekly paper, at Shermantown, White Pine. Brier suddenly died the evening before the first issue of the paper, and, Shermantown being short-
lived, the "Reporter" soon passed away, Skillman removing the plant to
Eureka, using it in the creation of the Eureka "Sentinel," of which he is
now editor and proprietor. The "Sentinel," too, passed through episodes
of destruction by flood and fire, coming out all right, and still substan-
tially flourishes, with a truly skilled man at the helm. His long journalistic
career gives grounds for Skillman's claim of being the oldest newspaper
man on the Coast who is still in the business.

Hon. George W. Cassidy, one of the proprietors and editors of the
Eureka "Sentinel," for several years partner with Skillman therein, com-
menced his journalistic career as local reporter of the "Meadow Lake
Sun" in 1866, subsequently being connected with the "White Pine News"
and "Inland Empire." He served two terms in the Nevada Legislature as
State Senator from Eureka, and one term as Congressman from Nevada.
He was a vigorous writer, an able legislator and a very active politician.
His death at Reno in September, 1892, was from a bad cold and pneumonia contracted in public speaking during the vigorous political campaign. Cassidy was a forcible speaker, good at ready repartee, and his
reply to a person who interrupted his speech at a political meeting, accus-
ing him of not sticking to his Democratic party platform, will always be
remembered: "Platforms! my dear friend," replied Cassidy; "party platforms are only traps made to catch voters."

William W. Hobart also figured prominently among the early journalists of the "Great East," as the broad eastern county sections of the State
were termed, and was one of the owners and the brilliant and popular editor of the "Eureka Daily Leader" in 1879. He was twice elected State
Senator from Eureka to the Nevada Legislature, and served two terms as
State Controller. Mr. Hobart was not only an excellent journalist, but one
of Nevada's best and most efficient public officers. In 1891, having sold
out his interest in the Eureka "Leader," he removed to San Francisco,
where he has since resided.

The Elko "Independent," started by E. D. Kelley and Judge George B.
Berry, in October, 1869, was the pioneer paper of Elko county. Charles
L. Perkins, elected State Printer in 1870, was subsequently connected with
its ownership, also H. C. Street, W. B. Taylor and others. In the middle
seventies it was run as a daily, and it is still being run as a live Nevada
daily, with W. W. Booher editor and proprietor.

William J. Forbes was the pioneer journalist of Humboldt county, his
record as such being on the old "Humboldt Register," the press and mate-

rial for which he hauled across the Sierra Nevadas from Downieville, California, with an ox team. In connection with Charles L. Perkins, afterward State Printer, he established the "Register" at Unionville in May, 1863. The paper changed hands several times, and latterly had a somewhat erratic and precarious existence, finally dying at Winnemucca in December, 1876. The press and material fell into the hands of J. C. Ragsdale & Co., and C. C. Wallace was instrumental in getting it removed to Eureka, where it was afterward used in publishing the "Republican" and subsequently the "Leader."

Forbes, with his ubiquitous nom de plume of "Semblins," was famous throughout the State for his witty, terse paragraphs and quaint aphorisms, the most noted of which, referring to a suspicious executive transaction in the Territorial days, was: "Semblins knows that Governor Nye had a dam by a mill-site, but he had no mill by a dam-site." He ran the "Trespass," at Virginia City, for a short time, then the "White Pine News," and at Salt Lake he started "The New Endowment," which speedily proved an utter failure. Then he came back to Battle Mountain and published "Measure for Measure." There he was found on the morning of October 30, 1875, lying across his bed, dead and alone, his ending being characteristic of his eccentric life.

The "Silver State" was first published at Unionville, Humboldt county, in March, 1870, with John C. Fall as proprietor and H. A. Waldo managing editor. Five months later John I. Ginn was publisher, succeeded by John Booth, January 7, 1871. In August, 1872, R. L. Tilden & Co. assumed control, followed later on by John J. Hill and Peter Myers, who in 1873 became sole proprietors and moved the establishment to Winnemucca, its since permanent home. They continued it as a weekly until October 7, 1874, when they changed it to a daily, which it still is. Myers retiring, E. D. Kelley became partner with Hill, and achieved much well-deserved fame as the able editor of a well conducted journal. Mr. Kelley was a good editorial writer, forcible as well as logical and entertaining, and by its contemporaries the "Silver State" was considered a first-rate paper to clip items and extracts from.

George S. Nixon bought out Kelley & Hill in 1890, since which time the "Silver State" has maintained its full standard of excellence as a well-established journal, with latest, up-to-date improvements in its typographical and other departments, publishing full daily press telegrams from everywhere. It was enlarged considerably a few months ago, but, the experiment proving injudicious, it was relegated to its previous dimensions.

E. D. Kelley, its former editor, now occupies the responsible position of State Surveyor-General, and J. J. Hill has an unlimited franchise upon the office of Recorder of Humboldt county at the hands of his appreciative fellow-citizens. Thus virtue hath its reward even in journalism.

J. W. E. Townsend, more affectionately known in Nevada journalism as "Old Jim Townsend," or "Truthful Jeems," by the sarcastically envious, was a prominent figure among the pioneer printers and editorial fraternity, as he always has been ever since and will be until he dies. Jim is an original genius, always loaded to the muzzle with exuberant, mirthful witticisms, ready to be turned loose on any occasion. It's simply his genial, festive nature, and he can't help it. No more kindly dispositioned, generous-hearted man lives, sympathizing liberally with weaker and more suffering humanity, and always willing to divide his last dollar, if he has one, with a friend in need.

He worked professionally on the leading daily journals of Nevada, and about fifteen years ago he strayed over the southern border into Mono county, California, where he started a little weekly paper at Lundy, and finally gravitated into Bodie, becoming proprietor of the Bodie "Miner-Index," which he soon invigorated into the lively representative journal that it is today. His editorial columns sparkled with witty paragraphs and quaint aphorisms, which have been eagerly copied as "Jim Townsend-isms" by his journalistic contemporaries far and near. A few days ago he concluded that he was too old and tired of the daily journalistic grind, sold out his paper, and says he will come back and enjoy life among his old friends awhile.

And he also threatens to write and publish a book of his diversified worldly experiences, to be appropriately entitled "Truth, with Variations." The "truth" element will be his own philosophical deductions from personal observation and study of the heads of mankind and their natural storage capacity for good or bad ideas, all incidental events or occurrences in human life emanating from or being supervised by the human brain or fountain head. Heads that are never open for the reception of any new ideas or impressions are simply blockheads. Some heads close early and others close late, while the brainiest of all are always open. Then there are men whom over-wealth or over-education has given the big-head, or the swell-head, but the meanest of all is the swelled pin-head with no soul except on his feet, and dwarfed so low in the scale of humanity that he would have to stand on a brick to spit over a duck's tail. The "variations" are the readers who may dissent from Jim's peculiar ideas of truth, or consider it a case of "Jim-jams."

Mr. Townsend was born 76 years ago, is imbued with "spirit of '76," and don't care a continental dram for any other kind. He used to be a sailor man once, and sailed the briny ocean for years before he landed on the Pacific Coast and became a printer. In fact, he came around Cape Horn as mate of a ship to California, yet he never was a pirate or a buccaneer, nor a buckaroo. His old sea legs get rebellious sometimes and he thinks it rheumatisms, yet the trouble disappears whenever he goes down to San Francisco, sails across the bay, and smells the salt sea breezes and the tarred rigging of the ships. But the good old boy has quit sailorizing forever, and cannot end as the jack tars disposed of the dead "land lubber" at sea, when—

> They wrapped him in a "futtock shroud,"
> And buried him in the "lubber hole."

Among the first good printers in Nevada, arriving at Virginia City early in 1862, were Joseph T. Goodman and Denis E. McCarthy, who, becoming proprietors of the "Territorial Enterprise," sent back to San Francisco for their best typo friends. When the Washoe Typographical Union was formed, in May '63, and a dollar a thousand was the rate fixed for typesetting, the "Enterprise" had as good a force of printers as the world ever saw in a bunch. Each one was good for twelve hundred an hour as long as he could stand up to the case, making his ten dollars a day without half trying.

They were H. P. Taylor, now living in New York; Frank Mahon, wealthy rancher in San Mateo county, California; Wm. M. Taylor, in San Francisco; Steve Gillis, "picking pockets" in the gold diggings on Jackson Hill, California; C. M. S. Millard, in Illinois; George Thurston, Captain U. S. Army; Dick James, in San Francisco; O. G. ("Dick") Hicks, in New York; Sam Pope, foreman, "Record-Union," Sacramento; Peter Daley, in Portland, Oregon, and J. W. E. Townsend. Also Sam Martin, first President of the Union; Edward T. Plank, for thirteen years President of the International Typographical Union, and member of the 10th Nevada Legislature from Storey county (died at Boise, Idaho, in September last); A. J. Graham, Mike McCarthy, George T. Russell and Frank Huntley, all now dead. The pressmen were Jack McCarthy— brother of Denis—and George Eames, both dead. Between them they worked about 1,500 papers every day on a hand press.

On the Virginia "Daily Union" there were George W. Crowell, now in San Francisco; Orlando E. ("Dan") Jones, in Sacramento; John I. Ginn, El Paso; Timothy Leander Ham, S. F. Call; Harry Trayser, doctor in Chicago; George W. Blair, Sam Richardson and Pitney Taylor, dead; Jim

Conley, J. H. Bain, Pete Meyers, Mike Lynch, J. H. Huling, A. P. Church and Oliver and Charles Glessner—all now lost run of. Samuel A. Glessner, foreman of composition room; James L. Land, foreman of job printing department, and John Church, managing editor, were the proprietors. Tony Kramer was "fly boy" at the press, printer's devil, etc. Tony lost his sight a few years ago working in the State printing office and now meanders the streets of Carson stone blind, guided by his little son, selling photos for a living.

One day in the fall of '64 Mike Riley, the pressman of the "Union" office, was walking astride of the "outside" form or first page of the paper, dragging it along the floor by its upper edge toward the press, when it suddenly bulged in the middle, flew out, and the whole mass of type was disastrously "pied" all over the floor. It was the new Constitution of Nevada, eight columns, all solid agate type, and every "em" of it went out. The accident was as disastrous as it was unusual, and the only immediate remedy was to fill in the form with standing matter, old mining sales, doubled ads, etc. Tony was the greatest sufferer, for he had to shovel all that "pied" type into a box and put in all his spare time for the next two months sorting it out piece by piece—"a devil's own job," he called it.

Later on came Joe Harlow, State Printer twelve years ago, now in Oakland, Cal.; Wells Drury, on the "Examiner"; Jack W. Plant and Jack Matthewson, on the Stockton "Mail"; Bob Glenn, Portland, Oregon; Tom Watts, at the Printers' Home; Mike G. Foster, member from Eureka to the 16th and 18th sessions of the Nevada Legislature, now in Carson; also Sam Leonard, Dave Bond, Sam Spear and the two Barnses—"Bibleback" and "Shorty"—who were among the "early birds," all now dead. Andy Graham, Joe Harlow, Wells Drury, Dick Hicks, Jack McCarthy, Sam Leonard, George Russell, Sandy Warren, Ed Plank, Jim Huling, Tom Watts, W. W. Barnes, Charley Copp, J. D. Hoes and others of those model printers whose names cannot now be called to mind, worked also on the Gold Hill "Daily News" at various times, all good old boys in their line—all broke, as usual, if alive and out of a job, and if dead, we are sure they have gone where all good printers go.

And they were printers in those olden days, not blacksmiths, brokers nor cobblers—typos who could set a whole "galley" or column of type without an error, regardless of the blunders always made by even the best of writers.

One Sunday evening in Gold Hill, some of the "News" printers who were enjoying their holy day of rest in Dumars' saloon, across the street from the office, got into an animated discussion on correctness in type-setting, resulting in old Sam Leonard offering to bet the drinks for the crowd that he could set up the Lord's prayer in the dark without making a blunder. The bet was promptly taken, and Sam, in charge of a commit-tee of three, went across to the printing office. Every ray of light was excluded, and when Sam said he was through, the lights were turned on and the job inspected by committee of the whole. Sam had not made an error, and his friends were prouder of him than ever. Yet it was not because of the excellence of the feat accomplished, but the wonder was that a printer should know the Lord's prayer by heart.

Then there was old Doc Hoitt, on the "Enterprise," whose knowledge and convictions on the "art preservative" were logical, standard conclu-sions. Nothing could aggravate him worse than to be ordered to "follow copy" in his printing. Everybody who knew him was sure that he would arbitrarily and implicitly obey, even if a high wind should blow the afore-said copy out through on open third-story window.

But the most extensively noted of all typographical peculiarities was Hazlett, the wandering tramp printer. Where or how he originated does not matter, but, like the historic "Wandering Jew," he was seemingly condemned by some ruling power—perhaps the vengeful spirit of some dead printer who owed him a grudge—to be a sprinter forevermore. Any-how, he always kept traveling, mostly on foot, from one town to another wherever there was a printing office, throughout the United States. About once a year he would get around to the Comstock for three or four days, accept little jobs from his kindly brother printers in Virginia or Gold Hill, always at "distribing" type, to earn only money enough to keep him in food and drink—for he was too proud to accept charity—not more than a day or so at each office, when he would resume his endless journey, to be heard from next in Carson, Reno, or out along the railroad east or west.

The best single day's pay was made by Dan Jones on the old "Daily Union," Virginia, $45. But he had the "ad" case, and some fat "pick-ups" in mining sales helped him out famously that day.

Orlando E. ("Dan") Jones literally was "a fellow of infinite wit" and versatility. John Wilson, with his famous circus came to Virginia, and, his clown being sick and disabled, Dan volunteered to supply his place. He readily showed Wilson that he had been in the ring before, so Wilson at once starred him on the bills as "Dan Conover," the famous Shakesperian clown. That afternoon the big tent wasn't big enough for the audience. Dan was a brilliant success—covered with a spangled cloud of glory, and the crowd of admiring printers who witnessed his great triumph went and got enthusiastically drunk over it. But the most wonderful surprise, however, was next day, when they came wearily to work and found Dan there at his case busily throwing in type as usual, and perfectly sober.

One day in the Gold Hill "News" office the printers were discussing the suicide of Elkus, a clothing merchant, at Virginia that morning. He had been gambling recklessly the evening before and went to his room financially ruined. He methodically put on his best clothes, laid himself on his back in bed, tied a large sponge saturated with chloroform over his mouth by means of a towel, and quietly, serenely passed into eternal sleep. Carl Severs, the foreman of the office, philosophically remarked that it was the most sensible and soothing way of getting out he had heard of, and he believed he would follow suit himself that way shortly. Just two weeks later, faro, the printer's besetting sin, wrecked poor Severs worse than ever, and he was found in the morning precisely as Elkus was found.

The worst broken up printer anybody ever saw was old Sandy Warren when he won that $4,500 in the Havana Lottery. He was working right straight along, paying his whisky, grub and other current bills every Monday (the regular payday) when the calamity struck him. He had to quit work immediately and devote his entire attention to getting rid of this demoralizing wealth. He drank all he could stand and sat for hours industriously trying to buck it off at faro, but luck opposed him and he would win in spite of himself. The boys all kindly tried to help by striking him for a "twenty" or so, and he gave away what he could conveniently.

A friend met him one evening out on the "Barbary Coast" of South C street sitting despondent and alone on an old rum barrel. "Oh, Lord!" exclaimed he, "I'm mighty glad to have you come along. Been waitin' here more'n an hour with both pockets full of money, and the d—n footpads won't go through me. Take me somewhere and put me away. Oh, dear, Jim; I wish you could pick me up in the air fast asleep and dump me down alongside of my good old sister in Charleston, Massachusetts. She'd take care of me."

Next day poor Sandy struck it good. He put all he had left into Ophir mining stock on a liberal margin. Three days later he was restored to his normal condition—broke—and sticking type at his case again, happy and content.

Of the numerous other papers in every county throughout the State, which briefly lived and died, no extended mention is needed. Their ambitious editors tilted their free lances in limited journalistic engagements and quit, with honors easy. As to that matter, even among the best and foremost, notwithstanding the vigorous editorial contentions, political and otherwise, of these early exciting times, few hostile personal collisions resulted. The field of honor was sought sometimes, and pistols were used with fatal effect in two or three instances. There was a lively street duel or so and several pugilistic scraps between contentious reporters, all of which incidents furnished more or less stirring items for their papers, but they were the result of heated contentions in public journalistic service.

Blood atonement was followed by regret and forgiveness, and none more sincerely sorrowed over his fallen adversary than the victor himself. But all these unpleasant incidents, long past, need not now be recalled and were better consigned to oblivion. "Let the dead past bury its dead." As for the typos, their bloodless duels were generally with tongues, barkeeps or faro dealers.

The majority of those early times editors, reporters and printers mentioned in this veracious narrative are scattered broad or now lie peacefully in their graves beyond the troublings of the wicked, and of those old-time editors or reporters who still survive only the narrator himself remains— the last of the early Comstock journalistic Mohicans.

This elaborate review of the early journalism of Nevada is intended to illustratively set forth the historical works and doings of those ideal pioneer journalists, what they achieved and what they left for others to accomplish. They were simply wide-awake, capable men of the times, such as come to the front in all worldly emergencies. And there are others following in their footsteps, just as ready and willing to develop with times and circumstances and be the live journalists of any distinctive future period.

Some thirty years ago, about the time the Central Pacific Railroad got through from California, Brown & Mahanny, job printers at Virginia City, began publishing a little eight by twelve daily sheet called the "Footlight," because it merely contained the local theatre or show programmes and a few items relative thereto. When there was no show to advertise they would turn down the "Footlight," and with the advent of some new attraction turn it up again. By and by, as time intermittently progressed, John A. Mahanny removed to San Francisco, and David L. Brown, inheriting the "Footlight," got to picking up a few business advertisements and local items to fill up with, but whenever he saw any non-paying symptoms he would shut her down again—sometimes for months or a year or so. Everybody knew "Footlight" Brown. But he never suspended his job printing business and is running it yet.

One or two printers got in with him fifteen or twenty years ago and turned up the "Footlight," enlarging and making a smart little daily newspaper of it, which they called the "Evening Report." It flourished and slept by turns, some good editorial ability getting in occasionally, until within the last four or five years it has developed into a permanent live daily newspaper. John L. Considine, a Comstock raised boy, is editor, and Frank S. Cox, a young Comstock printer, is business manager. As a successive and successfully rejuvenated relic of old newspaperdom, it is interesting, and as a lively, well-conducted, newsy Comstock paper it is making a good "Report" of itself.

Among the latest live Nevada journals, besides those already made mention of, is the "Evening News," published at Carson by Dunn & Lemmon in lively, enterprising style, with gasoline engine power, typesetting machinery, etc. The Wadsworth "Dispatch" is a flourishing semi-weekly, the popular editor of which imbibed his journalistic ideas when a bright-eyed little lad carrying the Gold Hill "Daily News." Then there is the "Walker Lake Bulletin," weekly, published at Hawthorne, ably edited and conducted by Alf McCarthy, brother to Denis; the "Nevada State Herald," a newsy and admirable weekly published at Wells, Elko county; also, the "Free Press," "Tidings" and "Argonaut," published at Elko, same county; the wide-awake "Record," Gardnerville, Douglas county; the Yerington "Rustler," Mason Valley; the enterprising DeLamar "Lode," and the "Messenger," Pioche; the "Advocate" at Winnemucca; Lovelock "Tribune," Golconda "News" and the Reno "Plaindealer" complete the list.

Nine dailies, one tri-weekly, two semi-weeklies and seventeen weeklies, twenty-nine in all, comprise the number of regular newspapers now being published in this State, and all are doing their best to well represent the interests of their respective localities and the country at large, keeping pace with the times as were their illustrious predecessors in the early journalism of Nevada.

Last, but surely not least, comes the "Nevada Magazine." It is published once a month for the special information, delectation and home interest of our intelligent fellow citizens dwelling within the borders of this extensive and inherently prosperous State. Its contents carry its own recommendation, as the tree is best known by its fruits. Read and judge of its merits, and of its real desirability to every good citizen of Nevada.

The Pacific Coast Pioneers; History and Passing of Nevada's Most Noted Society

[Unpublished manuscript by Doten, written December, 1899.]

Among the most popular and interesting of Nevada's social public institutions in its time has been the Society of Pacific Coast Pioneers. It was organized at Virginia City in 1872, and during the bonanza days of the famous Comstock Lode it flourished splendidly, its roll of membership exceeding five hundred, including many of the prominent pioneers of the Pacific Coast, California and Nevada. Senators William Sharon, John P Jones, Wm M Stewart, and Hon Charles E DeLong were regular members, and included in the brief list of honorary members were Ulysses S Grant and John C Fremont.

It is the only society of its name, and as its name comprehensively indicates, it pertains to no particular State or Territory, but embraces the Pacific Coast of the great American Republic – principally California and Nevada – many of its members being also members, or eligible to become members of the Society of California Pioneers in San Francisco.

The grand rush of immigration to the Pacific Coast, consequent upon the world-stirring California gold discovery was in 1849 and '50, therefore this Society based the eligibility of its membership to include citizens of the United States residing or arriving on the Pacific Coast by land or sea, previous to January 1, 1851. The Society was organized as "a moral, benevolent, literary and scientific association, its objects being the cultivation of more fraternal union and pioneer fellowship among its members, and

"To create a library and cabinet, collect and preserve such literary and scientific objects as the Society shall at any time determine, and in all appropriate matters to advance the interests and perpetuate the memory of those whose sagacity, energy and enterprise induced them to settle in the wilderness and become founders of a new empire upon the Pacific Coast."

Subsequent to the great fire of October 26, 1875, which nearly destroyed Virginia City, the Society built a fine two-story brick building on B street, costing over $25,000 for headquarters, the hall for meetings, ante-room, library and cabinet being on the upper floor. The Society was then in its most flourishing condition, holding regular weekly meetings, and contributions to the cabinet and library came in from all sides.

The richest silver and gold ores from all parts of the Comstock lode, also valuable specimens of ores, minerals and curiosities from the eastern and southern sections of the State, also from other States and countries of the world came in liberal profusion, and the great cabinet of the Society soon became a valuable and famous exhibit, very attractive to mineralogical and scientific visitors, the intrinsic value of the ores being at least $10,000.

And in those prosperous days, when grand public picnic excursions by various societies, over the railroad, during the summer season were frequent, the old Pioneers outdid them all, one memorable excursion to the "Bowers Mansion," Washoe Valley, consisting of sixty cars, carrying over 3,000 people.

But bonanza days passed, one rich ore body after another became exhausted and the immense silver and gold bullion yield of the Comstock fell away more rapidly than was agreeable to anybody. And so also correspondingly declined the prosperity of the Pioneers Society, and as the population pulled out and scattered to California, Montana and other more prosperous or promising localities, so also the "Old Boys," whose ranks were already becoming thinned out by death and desertion, one by one "folded their tents" and went prospecting elsewhere. The few members of the Society remaining, kept up the organization, but their meetings subsided from weekly to monthly, and finally to semi-occasionally or "at the call of the President."

Meanwhile the Society became in "bad standing" financially, being heavily in debt, with no adequate income from dues or anything else. Indeed so many of the old boys had failed altogether to pay their regular monthly dues, that at a special meeting it was unanimously resolved and officially recorded that all dues should be abolished permanently and forevermore.

It was also resolved that all members who had been suspended in the past for non-payment of dues, should be reinstated to full membership. Once a pioneer, always a pioneer, and a pioneer society without pioneers, was like the play of Hamlet with Hamlet left out. Therefore every pioneer who ever legitimately joined and belonged to this Society is still a member in good standing, unless he is dead or gone somewhere.

Then the wise heads took into earnest consideration the present condition and future disposition of the Society and its belongings. Not many years more would pass away before the last of the Pioneers would pass out forever, therefore definite action was taken with the following results:

The Pioneer Hall building was disposed of and ownership transferred in liquidation of indebtedness to the Knights of Pythias lodge, then occupying it, on condition that the Pioneers should also occupy it whenever desired for meetings or society purposes, the Knights furnishing lights or fire as required.

The cemetery of the Society, wherein Dr S A McMeans, and Hon Charles E DeLong, the first and second Presidents, and several other members of the Society were already taking their final repose was similarly disposed of to the Masonic lodge whose burial ground adjoined, the Pioneers reserving their rights of burial there and the Masons agreeing to keep up the fences and grounds all right forever, the whole to be known as the Masonic Cemetery.

What few books remained in the library were divided up or left, and only the great and valuable cabinet remained to be finally disposed of to the best advantage.

The Hall and the Cemetery being thus safely given into good hands – "better than owning them ourselves," they sagebrushly remarked – next came the Cabinet. "We could get the intrinsic value out of it by having the ores milled or otherwise reduced," said they, "or we could sell the concern as it stands for a good price, but would that be right? It was kindly and appreciatively donated to us by our fellow citizens of Nevada and other interested friends in all parts of the country, not to sell or speculate with, but to constitute a cabinet which we would be proud in the possession and exhibition of. Other organizations and institutions want it, but we must place it where it will best answer its purpose and be more appropriately and naturally inherited, in our State Capitol, at Carson."

The result was that at a regular meeting of the Society of Pacific Coast Pioneers, held January 23, 1887, at their hall in Virginia City, a resolution was unanimously adopted, tendering to the State of Nevada, through its Legislature then in session, the aforesaid "Cabinet of ores, minerals, rare coins, museum of curiosities, pictures and other similar property now belonging to this Society, as a free donation to the State of Nevada, the same to be suitably placed in the State Capitol at Carson City, there to be properly arranged, kept marked and designated as the cabinet property thus donated by the Society of Pacific Coast Pioneers, provided that an appropriation shall be made by the present Legislature to cover the expense of removing the said property from its present position to the State Capitol."

Robert Patterson and James Delavan were appointed as special committee to represent and carry out the objects of the Society.

Responsive to the foregoing resolution, Senate Bill No 55 was introduced January 26, by Senator Boyle. It authorized the acceptance of the Cabinet property as offered by the Pioneers, with all details of arrangement, appropriation of $500 for its removal, etc.

The legislative proceedings on the occasion were very interesting and appropriate in both Houses, able and pleasing speeches being made by various members in eloquent tribute to the old Pioneers. The bill passed both Houses unanimously, and committees were appointed to make arrangements for the formal reception of the cabinet and other property donated.

On the evening of March 1, a grand reception and banquet was given by the members of the Legislature to the Pioneers, the occasion being the formal ratification of the presentation and acceptance of the cabinet property.

Quite a crowd of the "old boys" and their friends came down from Virginia on the evening express train, free transportation being generously given them by the Virginia & Truckee Railroad Co through Superintendent Yerington. They were met in good style at the depot by the members of the Legislature with the Carson Brass Band and escorted to the State Capitol together with a goodly number of Pioneers residing in Carson, Reno and other localities. The exercises at the Capitol were brief but pertinent, Hon Robt Briggs being master of ceremonies, and all were dismissed to meet at the banquet in the Opera House later on.

The spacious theatrical floor was very fully occupied with the banquet tables, chairs and guests, and the collation spread of choice eatables was glorious, although beans and flapjacks were not as prominent in evidence as should have been expected, but there was plenty of hot coffee, champagne and claret, and the excellent Carson orchestral band under the popular leadership of Charley Laughton with his violin played appropriate music, adding much to the enjoyment of the occasion.

George I Lammon, Secretary of the Senate, stepped upon the stage and called the Pioneer Society's roll of membership as it was ten years before, when it numbered over five hundred, but now not over one hundred responded to their names, each personal response being greeted with hearty rounds of applause.

Then everybody proceeded to appreciatively enjoy the feast of good things, and good fellowship, wit and good humor held their own.

Attorney General John L Alexander made the reception address, which was inspiredly eloquent, and one of the happiest efforts of his life. Letters pertinent to the occasion were read from absent Pioneers in San Francisco followed by the programme of toasts and sentiments which were well and felicitously responded to by Judge Leonard, Hon Thos H Wells, Rev James L Woods, Hugh J Mohan, Sam Davis, Hon Wells Drury (Speaker pro-tem of the Assembly), Hon W H A Pike and others.

Sundry old time pioneer songs and poetic recitations were interspersed, including "Beans," by Wells Drury, R M Daggett's beautiful poem entitled "My New Years Guests" – tastefully read by Hon George A Tyrrell – and Charley Laughton's singing of "The Days of Forty-nine" were all heartily applauded. Hon C E Laughton also read a beautiful poetic song written by C C Goodwin now editor of the Salt Lake Tribune, dedicated to and entitled "The Pacific Coast Pioneers," which was enthusiastically received.

Altogether it was one of the most pleasing and satisfactory occasions of the kind ever transpiring in the State of Nevada, and it was away past two o'clock in the morning before the festivities concluded and the guests parted company for bed.

The cabinet, museum and other property donated by the Pioneers was duly and successfully transferred to the State Capitol and is now elegantly placed in an apartment by itself, adjoining the official rooms of the State Superintendent of Public Instruction, where it can be freely seen by all interested.

It collectively constitutes not only a very interesting relic of the past but is a valuable and interesting exhibit of the mineral resources of the State of Nevada and of the Pacific Coast, as well as of specimens and curiosities from all parts of the world.

Choice and liberal samples of rich gold and silver ores of every variety and combination from the various mining districts of Nevada and the Pacific Coast are tastefully displayed on its substantial shelves. Also rich gold ores from California and elsewhere, and copper, tin, galena, cinnibar, carbonates, sulphurets and every description of ores from all parts of the American continent and the world, including native metals and their richest mineral combinations. The graphite, sulphur, soda, borax, salt and similar naturally abundant products of Nevada are well represented.

There are also agates from Colorado, garnets from Alaska and other precious stones from all quarters of the globe.

The numismatic exhibit includes coins, peculiar, ancient and rare from all nations and ages of the world, copper, silver, gold, brass, and bronze. Also Confederate notes of different denominations and other interesting paper money, both ancient and modern.

Among the curiosities are various specimens of petrified woods, shells, fossiliferous formations, ancient pottery from South America, fabrics and curiosities from Japan, together with a lot of queer old firearms, Indian war-club, bow and arrow and other weapons and articles of interest from the Hawaiian and other islands and shores of the Pacific. Also a case of samples of submarine telegraph cable, presented by Cyrus W Field.

The menagerie exhibit includes a large full-antlered deer, shot in the Sierra Nevada, and very artistically stuffed and mounted by Dr E B Harris, the sixth President of the Society, a huge California lion measuring about nine feet from end of nose to tip of tail, Alf Doten's famous little old Comstock war-dog "Kyzer," buffalo and white wolf heads from Colorado, also a magnificent full-antlered elk head from Montana, "velvet" deer horns, etc.

Among the pictures are two fine life-size, oil-painted portraits of Dr S A McMeans and Hon Charles E DeLong, the first and second Presidents of the Society, also painted portraits and photographs and engravings of Captain Storey, John James and other well known Pioneers, the "Landing of the Pilgrims" at Plymouth in 1620, the pioneer stage crossing the Sierra Nevada, and numerous small pictures.

A letter written by Daniel Webster in 1848, and a document signed by President John Quincy Adams and Secretary of State Henry Clay are among the literary relics, the whole forming a very valuable and interesting cabinet collection such as is possessed by few States even much older than Nevada.

The Society of Pacific Coast Pioneers still exists, although but few members remain near the old Comstock scenes of its former prosperity. They hold no regular meetings, and not unless required, when a quorum could be raised in Virginia, Carson or Reno, Alf Doten being President the last twelve years, and S D Baker Secretary.

But the former properties of the Society are advantageously disposed in trust as stated. It owes nothing and owns nothing except its historically interesting record books and its good old flag – the Stars and Stripes – has no expenses and needs no income, therefore is the most financially and independently solid of any Society in the State.

The Society of California Pioneers, with headquarters in San Francisco was liberally endowed with wealthy belongings which are legitimately and naturally passing into the hands of their heirs and successors. And Nevada's Society also in putting their worldly affairs into good ship-shape condition, and trimming their sails to the breeze that wafts onward into the glorious American futurity, but bequeath their old belongings in the grand Pacific Coast heritage created by the Pioneers to those who are following in their footsteps – the Native Sons and Daughters of "God's Country," the Golden and Silvery West.

Well and nobly do those sons and daughters respond to the sentiment and the trust. The resounding echoes of California's grand Golden Jubilee at San Jose ring with undying reverence and honors rendered by those children worthy of their noble parentage.

The last old Century passes, and the new one can find but few of the Pioneers and Argonauts of '49 and '50 to welcome its coming and adventurously prospect its possibilities.

They have had their day and their Century, yet will stay and see the new proposition properly inaugurated before the last old Pioneer "passes in his checks" and quits the game of life, fearing nothing in the mythical beyond worse than he has met and conquered here.

The shores and heights of the receding Century are studded and scored with monumental markings of the Pacific Coast Pioneers. Fremont the Pathfinder blazed the trail across the Sierra Nevada, followed later on by Stanford, Crocker, Huntington and other Pioneers with the iron horse and great transcontinental railroad.

Pioneers found the famous Comstock Lode, and Sharon, Fair, Mackay, Jones, Sutro and other Pioneers developed its vast riches as the contribution of the "Battle Born" State of Nevada to the financial benefit of the American nation and the world.

Sharon brought in his abnormally crooked railroad to the Comstock, Sutro bored his famous tunnel, four miles in length, to promote the exploring of its lowest levels and present day mining men are striving heroically to reclaim those bottom levels and drain and follow the long submerged footsteps of their illustrious predecessors.

San Francisco, Queen City of the Pacific, whose Golden Gate expansively opens out upon the trackless seaways toward the farther West, the Occident and the Orient, Alaska's golden strand and Klondike's frozen heart, is a grand monumental exhibit of the judicious foresight and indomitable enterprise of the old Pioneers.

Comparatively few died millionaires, and very many ended their days in poverty, yet all imbued with the standard energy and steadfastness of purpose characteristic of the true pioneer have played well their part in life's varied drama while health and strength lasted, true to themselves and those they loved best – "faithful unto the end."

> Then kindly remember the good deeds they wrought,
>   What they were evermore striving to do,
> And their many short-comings will vanish as naught
>   In memories honoring, genial and true.

Bullion Production From the Comstock Lode and Tonopah, 1902

[Written by Doten from July through October, 1903, and reprinted here from Report of the Director of the Mint Upon Precious Metals in the United States During the Calendar Year 1902 *(Washington, D.C.: Government Printing Office, 1903).]*

THE COMSTOCK LODE.

The anticipated financial advancement and prosperity of the old Comstock Lode during the past year has not appeared largely in evidence, yet there has been an advance and a strong tendency toward improvement over adverse circumstances. This has been promoted through the gradual introduction of electric power, during the last year or two, taking the place of the obsolete and expensive old steam machinery, all of which had to be accomplished by slow degrees.

There was an increased amount of ore produced and worked during the year, including low grade and mill tailings, bringing the bullion yield up to above that of the previous year, considerably above the million mark, and more extensive arrangements are being inaugurated for greater progress in that respect for the present and coming years.

The Consolidated California and Virginia mine has been in the lead for the last two or three years in both bullion production and advancing development, and its persistent, well-earned success has inspired other companies also to renewed effort. All the mines having at last discarded their old steam machinery for electric works, they are better prepared than ever to resume active operations for the renewed production of ore from deep mine workings and explorations again.

A great deal of dead work was performed in this way, by the efficient aid of the new electric machinery, especially in the Union and other big mines in the north end, Cedar Hill section, with good prospective results, and more men are employed in, on, or about the Comstock than for years past. But the great tendency underlying mining operations generally during the last year has shaped itself toward the resumption of operations at the lower levels of the mines, following the confident and lucrative example of the Consolidated California and Virginia.

One thing is certain, that the old Comstock is not yet played out, and whenever she undertakes to carry a mining boom on a large scale, she has both the means and the energy left to carry it through all right.

INTERESTING FINANCIAL EXHIBIT.

The following carefully revised and prepared tabular statement of the regular assessments levied and dividends disbursed in the rich financial history of the Comstock, from commencement until the first of the present year, recommends itself to the careful consideration of all practical students of mines and mining manipulation. It comprehensively includes the representative mines of the great lode, commencing at the north end and following in succession southward through Virginia and Gold Hill to Silver City, a distance of about 4 miles, or the length of the Sutro Tunnel:

Name of mine.	Number of feet.	Number of shares.	Total amount of assessment.	Total amount of dividends.
Utah Consolidated	1,500	100,000	$ 540,000	
Sierra Nevada	4,400	100,000	6,880,910	$ 102,500
Union Consolidated	1,000	100,000	2,745,000	
Ophir	675	100,800	4,865,408	1,592,800
Mexican	600	100,800	2,395,250	
Consolidated California and Virginia	1,310	216,000	3,497,100	84,324,900
Best and Belcher	540	100,000	2,792,273	
Gould and Curry	612	108,000	4,812,650	3,837,600
Savage	771	112,000	7,410,600	4,460,000
Hale and Norcross	400	112,000	5,817,980	1,850,000
Chollar	700	112,000	2,159,600	750,000
Potosi	700	112,000	2,275,920	
Bullion	943	100,000	3,145,000	
Alpha	306	105,000	331,800	
Exchequer	400	100,000	1,023,000	
Imperial Consolidated	468	500,000	2,221,000	500,000
Challenge Consolidated (including the Bowers and other small Gold Hill mines adjoining)	150	50,000	460,000	4,800,000
Confidence	130	24,960	568,588	204,490
Yellow Jacket	1,200	120,000	5,890,000	2,196,000
Kentuck	90	105,000	128,450	1,350,000
Crown Point	641	100,000	3,045,000	11,903,000
Belcher	1,040	104,000	3,684,600	15,397,200
Segregated Belcher	1,324	100,000	391,000	
Overman	1,200	115,200	80,640	
Caledonia	2,188	100,000	3,285,000	
Justice	2,100	105,000	3,720,750	
Alta	600	108,000	3,713,310	
Silver Hill	1,200	108,000	2,220,200	5,400
Total			80,101,029	133,273,890

Excess of dividends over assessments, $53,172,861.

SUPPLEMENTAL PROPOSITIONS.

This table is of especial interest to those who have paid, and are still paying, those inevitable regular assessments, as well as gratifying to the recipients of the munificent dividends, especially when they so liberally exceed the sum of the assessments. And it indicates the several dividend-paying mines, as well as the many which never gave up a cent; as, for instance, the misnamed Bullion mine, situated right in the heart of the Comstock, assessed in all over $3,000,000, which never yielded a pound of bullion nor a ton of pay ore. Yet that very mine, simply from the value of its location, is going to be utilized before long as a means of reopening valuable ore deposits in mines adjoining, which will yield plenty of gold and silver bullion.

Dividends cut but a small figure during last year as compared with the assessments; in fact, assessments were far in excess for the year, owing to the heavy expense of changing the ponderous and expensive old steam machinery from steam to electric power, which is universally done, about the last to adopt the change being the Consolidated California and Virginia, the great chief producing mine of the Comstock. Considerably over a million dollars was expended in new electric machinery along the lode during the year, inducing somewhat of a falling off of the ore product for the time, between 500 and 600 men, miners, mechanics, and electricians being employed. It will also be noticed that many of the mines, although continuously worked, utilized all their own product, as well as sundry assessments to pay running expenses. The best as well as the poorest portions of the extensive lode are clearly indicated in the table.

MINING CAPITALIZATION.

The number of feet and shares in each mining incorporation is also given in this tabular statement as a study in modern capitalization.

In the old Comstock incorporation days a share to the foot was common—1,000 feet, 1,000 shares—and even to-day it will be seen that the capitalization remains at the same reasonable figures that have ruled the stock market through all its wildest or its tamest vicissitudes down to the present time. The Utah Consolidated, the first mine on the list, and the only one having the present statutory number of feet—1,500—has only 100,000 shares, and next comes the Sierra Nevada with 4,400 feet and but 100,000 shares, upon which she paid dividends amounting to $102,-500; and so with a large majority of the rest regardless of their respective number of feet. But Comstock capitalization did not seem to be ruled much by the number of feet in the mine. At any rate, none of those mines split up their stock into wildcat hairs.

Silver Hill, now the only dividend-paying mine on the Comstock, pays regularly 5 cents per share on her 108,000 shares, with a comfortable amount left in the treasury. Five cents a share dividends on some million-share mines would bankrupt them forever.

Nowadays any new outside 1,500-foot mining claim is located and incorporated with its capital stock fixed and advertised at not less than a million or two million dollars. This, of course, is intended to facilitate the sale of the stock at low rates among the people, especially the few thousand shares considerably set aside for sale to raise "working capital—unassessable." The result is that those stocks do not find a ready market. Too much of a good thing. Comstock mining stocks continue to be regularly bought or sold at the regular daily stock-board quotations, based upon practical reasonable capitalization.

BULLION RESCUED FROM MILL TAILINGS.

The saving of gold and silver left in the ore tailings after passing through the mills did not amount to much in the earliest years of Comstock ore reduction. There was plenty of rich free-milling ore to be worked, and if the proceeds came up to 40 or 50 per cent of the assay value it was considered pretty good returns, the rest being allowed to run off down the canyons toward Carson River, or through the several large river mills directly into the river itself. About $60,000 is computed to have been thus lost before blanket sluices and other saving appliances were adopted at the mills to catch the heavy sulphurets, and huge dams and reservoirs placed for the purpose caught up many very extensive tailings deposits for future reference.

Gold being much the easiest amalgamated and saved in the mills, the greater part of the precious metals escaping was silver. Important improvements in ore reduction have gradually been adopted in milling, some claiming to work the ore to within less than 90 per cent of the assay value, consequently the mill tailings of to-day are not to be compared with those of the early times as a source of lucrative salvage. Various devices and concentrating appliances have been brought into use in times past to work these immense deposits of old tailings, but the cyanide process proves to be the best and most effective of all, giving largely increased results the last few years.

The various cyaniding ore-tailings plants of Carson River, Silver City, and Virginia, materially assisted by the great new Butters plant in Sixmile Canyon, give a much-increased aggregate bullion yield for 1902, as follows: Tons, 125,400; gold, $205,000; silver, $196,200; total, $401,200, being nearly four times that of the previous year. This, added to the annual production from the commencement, gives the following bullion summary:

Period.	Tons.	Gross yield or value.
To and including 1901	3,186,500	$18,048,633.16
For the year 1902	125,400	401,200.00
Total	3,311,900	18,449,863.16

THE CHAMPION CYANIDING PLANT.

The new and extensive cyaniding plant of the Charles Butters Company, constructed at great expense in Sixmile Canyon, 3 or 4 miles northeast, or below Virginia, did not achieve what it was popularly expected to do—more and better work than all the other cyanide plants of the Comstock put together—but although it much outdid any other single plant during the year, it is not yet completed and in full working order. More leaching or dissolving vats are to be added and improved appliances brought to bear in the matter, greatly increasing its capacity and effectiveness. It has cost about $400,000 thus far, and will cost as much more to perfect and carry out all its plans and details.

The Butters company has secured possession of a vast amount of old mill tailings, including some of the oldest and heaviest deposits, also several low-grade surface-ore propositions in the mines, as well as some mighty mining-shaft dumps of what was considered waste ore, or too poor to work in bonanza days, including those of the Hale & Norcross, Chollar, and other middle mines, enough to keep the plant in steady work for ten years at least. The Butters plant, being eligibly situated down in the steep canyon, a thousand feet lower than the surface of the mining shafts and dumps of Virginia, the tailings are very readily and cheaply conducted through wooden flumes by means of water directly to the plant for treatment, thus making the whole Virginia basin tributary to the plant without horses, wagons, or railroads.

A recent achievement has been the purchase of the great dump of the old Imperial mine, the largest on the Gold Hill slope of the Divide, estimated at 100,000 tons. This will all have to be hauled in wagons, about a mile, to the Best & Belcher, formerly the Gould & Curry mill, where, by means of the Kinkead gyratory grinders employed, the ore will be reduced to a coarse cyaniding pulp and sent smoothly and noiselessly down through the water flumes to the plant in the canyon. Other small mills are to be similarly employed on the low-grade mining ores, water flumes reaching out and doing all the transportation from any point, and eventually—in a year or two, perhaps—the already famous Butters plant, with its own cheap, improved application of the cyanide process, will become literally the octopus of the great tailings and low-grade ore proposition, adding numerous thousands to the annual production of the Comstock.

TOTAL GOLD AND SILVER PRODUCTION OF THE COMSTOCK LODE FROM DISCOVERY AND COMMENCEMENT, BY CALENDAR YEARS, TO DATE.

Years.	Ore (tons).	Gold.	Silver.	Total.
1859		$ 30,000.00		$ 30,000.00
1860	10,000	550,000.00	$ 200,000.00	750,000.00
1861	140,000	2,500,000.00	1,000,000.00	3,500,000.00
1862	250,000	4,650,000.00	2,350,000.00	7,000,000.00
1863	450,000	4,940,000.00	7,460,000.00	12,400,000.00
1864	680,450	6,400,000.00	9,600,000.00	16,000,000.00
1865	430,745	6,133,488.00	9,700,232.00	15,833,720.00
1866	640,282	5,963,158.00	8,944,737.00	14,907,895.00
1867	462,176	5,495,443.20	8,243,164.80	13,738,608.00
1868	300,560	3,391,907.60	5,087,861.40	8,479,769.00
1869	279,584	2,962,231.20	4,443,346.80	7,405,578.00
1870	238,967	3,481,730.16	5,222,595.24	8,704,325.40
1871	409,718	4,099,811.46	6,149,717.19	10,249,528.65
1872	384,668	4,894,559.86	7,341,839.79	12,236,399.65
1873	448,301	8,668,793.40	13,003,187.13	21,671,980.53
1874	526,743	8,990,714.06	13,486,071.09	22,476,785.15
1875	546,425	10,330,208.62	15,495,312.92	25,825,521.54
1876	598,818	12,647,464.08	18,971,196.12	31,618,660.20
1877	562,519	14,520,614.68	21,780,922.02	36,301,536.70
1878	272,909	7,864,557.64	11,796,836.47	19,661,394.11
1879	178,276	2,801,394.33	4,202,091.49	7,003,485.82
1880	172,399	2,051,606.00	3,077,409.00	5,129,015.00
1881	76,049	430,248.00	645,372.00	1,075,620.00
1882	90,181	697,385.60	1,046,078.40	1,743,464.00
1883	125,914	802,539.54	1,203,809.29	2,006,348.83
1884	188,369	1,261,313.60	1,577,438.40	2,838,752.00
1885	226,147	1,729,531.25	1,415,071.04	3,144,602.29
1886	238,780	2,054,920.15	1,681,298.31	3,736,218.46
1887	223,682	2,481,176.85	2,030,053.78	4,511,230.63
1888	271,152	3,169,209.07	4,458,058.66	7,627,267.73
1889	286,144	2,590,973.32	3,358,949.95	5,949,923.27
1890	286,075	1,992,349.03	2,988,523.56	4,980,872.59
1891	188,647	1,380,857.02	2,071,285.53	3,452,142.55
1892	133,678	1,043,158.86	1,130,088.77	2,173,247.63
1893	109,780	1,123,262.54	748,841.70	1,872,104.24
1894	97,049	768,880.63	512,587.09	1,281,467.72
1895	63,558	548,873.68	365,915.79	914,789.47
1896	39,240	340,253.36	226,835.57	567,088.93
1897	17,850	223,808.63	149,205.76	373,014.39
1898	10,766	123,023.89	82,015.92	205,039.81
1899	6,780	103,006.74	68,671.16	171,677.90
1900	35,300	381,123.56	319,441.70	700,865.26
1901	56,577	746,477.00	521,032.00	1,267,509.00
1902	96,490	785,030.59	495,944.96	1,280,975.55
Total	10,851,748	148,145,385.20	204,653,039.80	352,798,425.00
Total mill tailings added				18,449,863.16
Grand total				371,248,288.16

SUMMARIZED COMSTOCK BULLION YIELD.

No more expressive illustration of the grand bullion wealth, the munificent gold and silver production, and the varying fortunes of the old Comstock Lode can be given than the subjoined tabulated exhibit of its annual yield from the beginning, through the years of its world-renowned existence to the present time. It was originally compiled and published in its present form nearly twenty years ago, under Government auspices and direction, at considerable expense, from the most authentic and reliable authorities, and has since been revised and added to regularly, year after year, its authentic correctness always remaining uncontroverted and unimpeached.

Commencing with the few weeks of prospective work with pans and rockers, before winter interfered, although black silver sulphurets were found secondarily commingled with the rich free-gold discovery, no one fully understood its real value or importance, or how to utilize it; therefore only gold to the extent of about $30,000 was washed out of the surface diggings. The result of virtually the first year's real mining operations, in 1860—three regular stamp mills being brought over the mountains from California—was $750,000, considerably over one-half of which was gold. The next year, $3,500,000 was the product, and the next $7,000,000, and it was not until the fourth year that silver predominated in the first silver mine of the United States discovered as a gold mine, the yield for that year (1863) aggregating $12,400,000, or nearly $24,000,000 for the first four years.

THE LONGEST, RICHEST DRIFTS IN THE WORLD.

In 1864 the rich yield was $16,000,000, and in 1877 culminated the grand height and glory of the big bonanza days, the product for that calendar year being $36,000,000, the best year's record of the old Comstock. And it was during that year that the thousands of visitors were shown the famous "long drift" on the 1,550-foot level of the Consolidated Virginia and California mine.

The great bonanza was a regular shaped oblong body of high-grade ore carrying high values in silver and gold, three-fifths being silver. It was about 1,300 feet in length, and the aforesaid long drift was a crosscut through its widest part, the "heart" of the big bonanza, the drift being over 100 feet long, with top, bottom, and sides all in very high-grade ore, $1,000 per ton, without a pound of waste anywhere throughout its entire length. John Mackay, one of its principal owners, claimed it to be "the longest, richest drift anybody in the whole world ever saw, or would ever see again." No wonder, at the magnificent bullion yield and the liberal regular bonanza dividends, $108,000 per month.

A long, gradual decline followed, with the exhaustion of the rich ore body, the production of the Comstock falling below the million mark in [1895]. In 1901 it got up above it again, with a further increase for last year, 1902, to over a millon and a quarter, as shown in the table.

The total yield of the Comstock Lode to date, as given in this table, foots up to over $371,000,000, yet all who were familiar with the old-time mining and milling methods know that millions were handled with perfect looseness, with surreptitious leakages, especially in the flush and rapid early times, and that the square actual yield of the Comstock should amount to nearer $500,000,000. Some, in fact, guess it up to $800,000,-000 or more, and one of our sanguine-minded Congressmen recently published it at $600,000,000. The table, however, is not responsible for illegitimate estimates any more than for the $60,000,000 tailings' loss in Carson River. It is simply an honest record of what bullion was "in sight" and none other.

THE SUTRO COMSTOCK TUNNEL.

The old Sutro tunnel, commenced in 1869 and completed ten years later, in 1879, nearly 4 miles in length, has always been considered one of the most important factors in the Comstock mining situation. Intersecting the great lode at a central point in the Savage mine, nearly 1,700 feet in depth, or about midway between the surface of the principal shafts and the deepest mine workings, 3,300 feet, its chief practical service has been and still continues to be as a drain tunnel, all the water from the upper levels flowing out through it by gravitation, and 1,700 feet of pumping being thus saved in raising the water from the lower levels. The principal revenue of the tunnel for the general drainage of the lode has been derived from royalties per ton on ores extracted from the various mines, amounting in the most flourishing bonanza times to a munificent sum. Comparatively little ore now coming to the surface through the various mining shafts, the revenue of the tunnel is absorbed in keeping the vast amount of timbering throughout the tunnel and its branches in repair.

The drainage capacity of the tunnel and its branches, 7 miles in extent, is simply sufficient to handle all the water that is ever likely to be elevated from below its level by any present or future operation throughout the entire extent of the lode, including all water that may be added at any time from drainage of the Silver City or the American Flat districts or from any westward extension beyond the Comstock.

The only mine raising water from deeper working below the tunnel is the Consolidated California and Virginia, which with its electric pumps discharges into the tunnel the enormous quantity of 400 miners' inches of water per minute or 6,624,000 gallons every twenty-four hours, which it would be totally impracticable to dispose of in any other way. Indeed, were it not for this tunnel preserving the drainage, the 7,000,000 gallons flowing through it would have to be raised 1,700 feet to the surface or deep mining totally abandoned on the Comstock Lode.

ADVANTAGEOUS MILLING.

The practical facilities offered by the Sutro tunnel for the transportation of waste low-grade ores, etc., found in the various mining explorations of the lode, are far superior to any other method of utilization, as illustrated by the fine 10-stamp mill belonging to the company, constructed a couple of years ago, near the mouth of the tunnel. It does excellent work, reducing 60 tons per day of what was considered low-grade waste ore taken out of the tunnel workings in the Comstock. It only yields about $3 per ton, but costs little for handling and nothing for the water power furnished by the liberal stream flowing from the Comstock through the tunnel; therefore a good profit is realized. This water power is amply sufficient, and with increase from extensive Comstock pumping, the mill can and will be increased to double the capacity with perfect facility.

DISASTROUS BREAKDOWN.

A great breakdown of the powerful hoisting machinery at the C. & C. shaft of the Consolidated California and Virginia Mining Company occurred March 28 last, seriously affecting the revenue of the Comstock, that being the principal productive mine on the lode, and throwing over a hundred men out of employment for about three months. The long anticipated and prepared for changes from steam to electric power were being made, a 500-horsepower variable speed motor on balanced electric hoist, being introduced. The change included the starting of the new Reidler electric pumps, the first on the Comstock, and a large number of people, including some from San Francisco, were present, waiting to be lowered into the mine to witness the working of the pumps. Suddenly, with a dull crack, the huge 16-inch shaft of the hoisting engine broke, and everything came to a standstill. Many of the guests, however, went down into the mine through the shaft of the Union mine near by. The new electric pumps installed on the 2,150 foot level worked to absolute perfection, but no hoisting, or necessary lower water drainage could be performed until the engine shaft could be sent to San Francisco for repairs and returned to work. Electric hoists have also been installed in the Utah and Andes mines near by, air compressors and fans placed in other mines, and the means for more effective and remunerative work are better than ever, giving good promise for the future.

REVIVAL IN MINING OPERATIONS.

Since repairing the great machinery break, more men have been put to work in the Consolidated California and Virginia mine than before, and ore extraction with further mining development is resumed with renewed vigor and effectiveness. The submerging water of the lower levels has been reduced with perfect ease as fast as required, pumps lowered to within 200 feet of the bottom of the shaft, which is 2,500 feet deep, and considerable work done repairing and straightening up those reclaimed lower levels. Some good pockets and veins of ore have already been reached and more is anticipated, increasing the regular output of the mine.

Active mining is also to be resumed in a lucrative portion of the Best and Belcher mine adjoining the C. & C. shaft on the 2,050 foot level. The Ophir on the north is getting at increased ore resources, and the Sierra Nevada and Union are bringing their new electric machinery into effective prospecting work. The Yellow Jacket and Belcher mines in the Gold Hill section, being fully provided with electric machinery, are perfecting and developing plenty of low-grade ore. The old Brunswick mill on Carson River, after several years' rest, is being made ready to start up again on Yellow Jacket ore.

Away down at the south end, near Silver City, the old Silver Hill mine continues its regular output of ore that occasionally pays small dividends, being the only mine on the lode that does so. The Justice, Caledonia, and Overman are also producing some ore, and all are completing the introduction of electric machinery in place of their old steam works.

The increase in the bullion output in 1902 over the year before was not as much as was anticipated, but it will show a good further increase for the present year. The immense new Butters cyanide plant, and the smaller ones as well, will double their product, and, in fact, everything points to a general revival of mining operations all along the lode.

THE UNWATERING OF THE COMSTOCK.

And now, most important of all, comes the practical unwatering of the lower levels, which have remained fully submerged since October, 1886. The time had then arrived when it was found impossible, with the big hydraulic pump in the Chollar–Norcross–Savage Combination shaft—

3,260 feet vertical depth—to keep the immense flow of water reduced or controlled any longer; the utmost limit of power was reached, and the mines had to be allowed to fill up, the water subsequently rising over 1,500 feet, or nearly up to the Sutro tunnel level.

The mines of the Gold Hill section had already been submerged five or six years before by a great flood of water tapped by a joint drift being run into the 2,400 foot level of the Alpha and Exchequer mines.

During the last two or three years the successful working and continued deeper drainage of the Consolidated California and Virginia mine, by means of its improved hydraulic pump, and latterly by the much more powerful and effective Reidler electric pumps, has had the effect to drain or lower the submerging water in the adjoining mines along the lode for some hundreds of feet in depth throughout the Virginia section.

A combination of the companies controlling the Gould & Curry, Savage, Potosi, Bullion, Exchequer, Alpha, and Julia mines has now been formed, to be known as the Ward Shaft Association, under the efficient superintendency of Leon M. Hall, the well-known general Comstock electrical engineer. The object of this association is to put the Ward shaft in first-class condition for the active resumption of prospecting work and further exploration in all the mines mentioned, and also to reopen and work the good and extensive ore bodies known to exist in the Alpha and Exchequer mines before the submerging flood.

EXCELLENT BASE OF OPERATIONS.

The Ward shaft belongs to the Julia Mining Company, and is the most eligibly situated of any, being located at the "Divide," between Virginia and Gold Hill. It has been idle for several years past, but well housed, and its powerful machinery in good condition; this will, however, be superseded by adequate electric machinery. The shaft is 1,800 feet deep, extending below the Sutro tunnel, with which it connects by a short drift. The Ward is the best located and most eligible of any shaft in that section for the objects to be accomplished, and will render very efficient aid in the unwatering of the Comstock and deeper mining explorations. And in this connection it is proposed to put the old Sutro tunnel in a thorough state of repair and best possible condition throughout, for extended ventilation and drainage purposes.

ANOTHER STRONG POINT.

The old Forman shaft of the Overman and Caledonia mines, farther down the range, opposite Gold Hill, was also considered an important point in Comstock deep development, being sunk to the depth of 2,400 feet, with its powerful surface hoisting and pumping plant, costing over a million dollars. But after being idle for some years the works were destroyed by fire a few months ago. It was also made an initial point in the southern extension of the Sutro tunnel, with which it was connected, to the American Flat, Gold Hill, and Silver City mines.

This shaft is now being retimbered and put in the best condition for installing an air-lift elevator and auxiliary electric plants, to unwater the flooded lower levels of the Gold Hill mines. These levels are submerged to the depth of 1,500 feet or more, but when the bottom, or 2,700-foot level, of the Belcher mine is reached, better stringers of high-grade ore and better indications for an old-time bonanza will be met with near the south line than can be shown anywhere else along the bottom levels of the Comstock Lode.

THE BIG COMSTOCK DRILL NOT A SUCCESS.

The new and very promising proposition to cheaply prospect the eastern, or Brunswick section, of the Comstock Lode by means of a big drill, boring holes down from the surface, enterprisingly introduced by some of the middle mining companies nearly two years ago, has met with little or no tangible success thus far. It is known as the Davis calyx drill, and is simply operated at the lower end of a series of long poles, as in artesian well boring, except that the drill itself is like a hollow augur, cutting in a circle and bringing out a core. And it is of different sizes—from four to ten inches in diameter—as found requisite, its proprietor or managers using steam, electric, or any other power, as they see fit.

Commencing with a 4-inch drill they made rapid progress, but at 460 feet it struck loose material, and not having any shell or casing to protect it, got stuck or "fitchered," to use a common Cornish drilling term. They sent East for proper casing, and the drill was finally rescued after a month's rest. A smaller drill had next to be used, with smaller casing to correspond, driven down inside of the other. This had to be successively done until at the depth of 850 feet the drill used was too small for satisfactory demonstration. Other and larger holes were driven down at sundry points in the vicinity, reaching about the same depth and ending principally in very low-grade quartz or loose porphyritic vein matter.

The fifth and largest hole is, or was, being bored recently, but at last accounts it had not reached the depth of either of its predecessors, and the drill was badly stuck with no hope of release. The trouble is that, although the drill works well, even without casing, in the firm, smooth-surface porphyry, which it brings out in long, solid cores, it can not well help getting stuck, or "fitchered," in brittle loose quartz and vein matter. Mining men generally, who have interestedly watched the progress of this great drilling experiment, do not approve it as a cheap and effective method of prospecting for veins or deposits of ore at any great depths. It is too indefinite and uncertain. Even without waiting to examine or assay the drillings, the first sign of striking a quartz deposit is when the drill becomes "fitchered."

Tonopah, Nevada's Richest New Silver Discovery.

Tonopah prospered exceedingly during the last year—in fact, prospered to the extent of its present facilities. The town has grown to a population of about 4,000 people, including many families, fine residences and business buildings, a well-attended public school, 3 churches, 2 weekly newspapers, and a double stage line from the railroad, still 60 miles away.

During the last two or three months, however, the boss camp has come to a stand still, owing to delay in the projected establishment of extensive ore reduction works, the building of the railroad extension into Tonopah, water works, and necessarily limited ore shipments to Salt Lake and elsewhere for reduction. The Tonopah Mining Company, owning the original group of mines, have been shipping only their highest grade ores, extracted in the course of mining development, keeping only about 200 men steadily employed and about as many more are engaged in prospecting and developing other mining claims in the district. Thus it is that many people come and go, but the population does not increase, and the great Tonopah rush has subsided for the present.

The eight original claims of the group, located by Jim Butler and sold by him to the Philadelphia syndicate for $366,000, included all the eligible ledge croppings in sight, and each claim, consisting of 1,500 feet in length by 600 in width, adjoining each other, the whole group does not cover a great extent of ground. But their phenomenal silver richness, especially the Mizpah ledge, creating an immense excitement, enterprising miners came rushing in from all directions, and the whole surrounding vicinity was staked off into 1,500-foot claims very shortly, regardless of any ledge croppings or surface indications.

PRELIMINARY PROPOSITIONS AND CAPITALIZATION.

The main trend or strike of the outcropping ledges is nearly east and west, and a few of the claims outside in either direction from the main Tonopah group have developed good ore by sinking shafts down through the heavy porphyry or andesite capping which covers the general surface of the country. Scores of claims also run lengthwise in all directions, north and south as well as east and west, at cross-purposes, as though the locators were uncertain as to what direction the leads really do run in. Some in reality advocate the north and south theory as depth shall be attained, but the direction of the surface croppings may be relied upon to settle that point. The great multitude of outside claims are barren of results, the majority of them being owned by men who can not afford to sink deep shafts on any desperate uncertainty. They therefore philosophically prefer to visit and watch the success of their neighbors.

But meanwhile many have incorporated under the State laws and with all sorts of pretentious names, frequently getting the cabalistic word Tonopah in combination for interested effect. The favorite style is 1,000,000 shares, par value $1,000,000, advertising the placing of 200,000 shares or thereabouts on the market for sale as working capital to run the mine with. The result was a flood of wild-cat stocks drowning out the market, to the detriment of the really meritorious, legitimate stocks which, however, find private market with sufficient facility, the greatest objections even to them being their over-capitalization.

THE LEASERS AND REDUCTION WORKS.

During the few months that the leasers under Butler & Co. were so busily engaged in rushing out the rich ore of the surface croppings on 25 per cent royalty before their leases would expire, they shipped the richest selections to the Selby Reduction Works, San Francisco, and elsewhere, to get needed "working capital," at a cost of $50 or $60 per ton for transportation alone; and so diligently did they improve their time that when their leases expired they had accumulated 20,000 tons of ore on their various dumps. Considerably over one-half of that still remains on the dump awaiting cheaper reduction, which they will soon have right at home.

A comparatively small amount of all the ore that has been developed and uncovered in the mines of Tonopah has found its way to distant reduction works, but that has given good returns, as only the richest ore could pay the grievous expense of transportation. The true solution of the great Tonopah problem as to the real value of her average ores and mining lies in practical reduction works established right at the mines. This was strongly talked of being done on a large scale in the first year of bullion production, but somehow failed to materialize. The rich ore was shipped to smelters and mills all over the coast with various results, some lots hardly paying expenses. It is said that the best and most satisfactory returns were made by the Kinkead mill at Virginia, and two or three small mills of that pattern are contracted for to be placed at or near Tonopah. And it must be borne in mind that over three-fourths of Tonopah's bullion product is silver, not gold, making the ore more difficult to work, but being so very rich in silver it pays equal to a gold mine. Moreover, by modern improved processes and appliances, silver is worked very much cheaper than it was years ago, or before it was demonetized. Tonopah's wealth lies in her great abundance of silver; her mines pay richly for working, and any advance in the price of silver will make them pay still better.

THE FIRST MILLS FOR TONOPAH.

The first ore-reduction mill introduced at or near Tonopah a few weeks ago was a small Kinkead gyratory, or grinding mill, which operated very successfully, working that difficult ore up to above 90 cents of the assay value per ton. But it subsequently got involved in litigation and suspended. Other mills of the same kind were ordered for neighboring localities.

But the most practical immediate solution of the chronic problem is that of the fine mill now being erected by the Tonopah Mining, Mill and Development Company, right in the heart of the mines, to be completed and in crushing order before the next snow flies. It will consist of 10 stamps weighing 1,350 pounds each, in double battery, assisted by two powerful Huntington grinders, with pans, settlers, cyaniding tanks, and everything complete, capable of reducing 60 tons of ore per day.

It is being erected on the ground of the Midway Mining Company, its first object being to work the ore still remaining on the dumps of the leasers near by, followed by general custom work. When finished it will be one of the most thoroughly substantial and complete mills in the State and a credit to the company, which is composed of some of the chief mining men and leasers. It is officially announced that the main Tonopah mining company propose erecting at or near that place the largest and best milling and reduction works ever constructed in the West, some time next year. They have had it under consideration long enough to decide fully and do something pretty good in that line, but this other new mill is fast becoming an accomplished fact.

ENTIRE BULLION PRODUCTION OF TONOPAH.

The following tabulated statement gives the total silver and gold production of Tonopah during the two and a half years she has been producing bullion. The figures are strictly and officially correct. The apparent discrepancy or falling off during 1903 is accounted for by the returns of

1902, including proceeds from leasers' ore, and that of 1903 represents only the ore taken out in the course of development work and the bullion returns from the smelters or reduction works during the six months to July 1. The number of tons shipped are comparatively nothing as compared with the thousands of tons on the surface or in the mines awaiting the advent of home reduction.

Year.	Tons.	Silver.	Gold.	Total.
1901	2,534	$ 374,109.62	$202,035.82	$ 576,145.44
1902	11,258	1,234,270.99	558,858.30	1,793,129.29
1903 (Jan. 1 to July 1)	3,196	419,818.36	161,498.64	581,317.00
Grand total	16,988	2,028,198.97	922,392.76	2,950,591.73

The silver in this table, which amounts to 3,090,394.98 ounces, is figured into commercial value at regular market rates. The gold, amounting to $34,930.09, of course, has its own fixed standard value and is figured accordingly, but the price of silver bullion fluctuates somewhat under financial manipulations. Nearly three millions in two years and a half certainly is a splendid showing for so young a camp, especially in view of the policy adopted of not marketing any more of the ore than necessary to pay running expenses and holding it in reserve for cheaper reduction at home, avoiding costly transportation abroad. And it will be observed, in the table, that the ore selected for shipping realized about $174 per ton, one-fourth of which amount had to be paid for its transportation alone. No wonder they wanted to avoid that bit of expense and adopt home reduction. The Comstock only produced $3,500,000 in bullion during the same commencement period—two years and a half.

TONOPAH ORE "IN SIGHT."

If what is, or has been enthusiastically alleged to be, "in sight" in the way of fabulously rich ore at Tonopah were half true it would be the richest mining camp in the world. Pretended experts from all parts of the country have given the most glowingly exaggerated accounts of what they have seen in these mines, some putting at over $200,000,000 in sight, already blocked out in the mining depths by drifts, cross-cuts, and winzes, making Tonopah richer than a dozen Comstocks. Yet all they saw were naked walls to blindly guess at the value of, even measuring with a tape line on the same principle. All such sanguine estimates published, of vast blocks and extents of ore in sight are detrimental and misleading, and only fit to be put into prospectuses of wildcat mining companies interested in gulling the unwary.

The true criterion of mining valuation is the honest product, the bullion, not ore in sight. And gauged by the bullion product, the number of tons from which her silver and gold has been produced thus far, Tonopah makes a magnificent showing, needing no exaggeration.

Practical assays and milling tests have squarely proved the value of the vast resources of ore exported, and home reduction works will solve the whole rich problem in due time. Tonopah's best days are yet to come.

PRACTICAL MINING OPERATIONS.

Over 3 miles of underground work has been done by the main Tonopah mining company, a large part of this being in ore, working through three main shafts, the Siebert Valley View and the Desert Queen, the latter being used principally for the Tonopah Development Company, and all being connected underground. Every 100 feet drifts are being run on the ore veins and cross-cuts from the working shafts.

Winzes are also being sunk on the ledges to connect the various levels, and in this way the ore is being blocked out in good shape and the mine kept well ventilated.

It is simply impossible to estimate the amount of ore in sight, the drifts not by any means representing the real width of the ledges, as they vary from 1 or 2 to over 50 feet in width. The shafts and stations are all timbered in first-class style with Oregon pine timbers.

FIRST-CLASS MINING WORKS.

The large steel-hoisting works building contains a substantial 65-foot gallows frame over the main shaft, which most certainly is the best in the State, also a first-class hoisting engine driven by ample gasoline power; a 150-horsepower air compressor, and a large blower for supplying air down into the mining depths. Well-ordered machine shops are being added and, when fully completed, it will be a thoroughly first class hoisting establishment in every respect.

All the mining operations of the company are being conducted throughout in the most careful, systematic, and substantial manner, and the great amount of work done, besides the extensive surface equipments provided, have all been paid for out of the proceeds of ore shipped to reduction works, together with the great cost of said shipments. And best and most satisfactory of all this, a handsome amount of money has accumulated in the treasury of the company. Indeed, this famous property is unique in having more than paid its way from the very start.

THE BELMONT TONOPAH.

Active development work is being done on the property of the Tonopah-Belmont Development Company, which lies directly west of the Tonopah Mining Company's ground. The Mizpah and Valley View ledges both run into it on the 614-foot level. The main ledge is as large and of as high grade in this property as anywhere in the Mizpah claim, and from the fact that the ore shoots all dip to the east and that the main ledges are converging toward the Belmont, the belief is prevalent that it will eventually prove to be the greatest property in the camp.

Another working shaft is being sunk 2,000 feet east of the present workings, with which it will connect in due time.

THE MONTANA TONOPAH.

Another very important property, immediately adjoining the main group of mines in the north is that of the Montana Tonopah Mining Company. A series of half a dozen strong, high-grade ledges have been opened in its workings recently, which are nearly parallel to the Mizpah, and high-grade shipping ore is being extracted for reduction. This also bids fair to become one of the most valuable mines.

Immediately adjoining on the west is the Tonopah Midway Company's ground, in which has been opened up the same series of ledges discovered in the Montana, and high-grade milling ore is being extracted from them for reduction.

SOME MORE TONOPAH.

There are several other claims near camp which have recently developed high-grade ore, among them the Tonopah North Star, east of the Montana Tonopah Mining Company's ground. Good ore shipments are being made from it and it is expected that they will continue. It certainly is a very promising and valuable claim.

A very important ore discovery has also been made on the Grand Trunk ground, west of the famous buckboard claim of the Tonopah Mining Company.

On the south of the main Tonopah group the claims owned by the Gold Hill Mining Company, the Tonopah Fraction Mining Company, the Tonopah City Mining Company, and a number of other outside claims are about to be consolidated into a new company, to be called the Jim Butler Tonopah Mining Company, and active development will commence shortly.

STYLE OF REDUCTION WORKS DECIDED UPON.

No very extensive mine workings have been conducted below the 500, 600, or 800 foot levels of the mines, although shafts have been extended below 1,000 feet, also a diamond drill in the Mizpah mine, there being a vast abundance of rich ore already blocked out in the upper levels ready for lively extraction when required. Deep explorations are never necessary at present, there being ore enough opened out in the mines to run reduction works at full blast, close at home, for the next few years at least.

Tonopah ore being of a somewhat refractory nature, not giving up its values readily, the company has had it worked by various reduction localities and processes in California, Washington, and lastly at Salt Lake. The object has been to find out and decide upon the best and most advantageous process of working the ore before constructing the extensive milling or smelting works required. This point is now said to be settled, and early in next year the machinery and equipments for the largest milling and reduction works ever erected on the Pacific coast is to be landed in Tonopah. Meanwhile, the Midway mill, now nearly completed, and perhaps two or three Kinkead mills, will be giving pointers on practical home-ore manipulation.

INCREASED WATER SUPPLY NEEDED.

Meanwhile a better water supply and more of it has to be considered and provided for. The present resources, springs and wells, within a few miles of town are ample for careful present use, but measures are being taken to largely increase the supply by sinking for deeper wells and well connections. The strong vein of water recently struck in the shaft of the Rescue Mining Company is engaged to supply the new Midway mill.

Tonopah has a good, lively fire department, with good machines, but when the town has its first baptism of fire—same as all other new towns—about next July, sweeping both sides of Main street and the other streets, it may be shown how difficult it is to check a big conflagration without plenty of water. The great project mentioned last year, of a powerful company formed to pipe in an abundant supply of water from Twin Rivers—70 miles distant—totally failed to materialize, leaving Tonopah to find her much-needed water nearer home.

TONOPAH RAILROAD CONSTRUCTION.

And now, last of all, comes the railroad. Its necessity commenced and stayed with the prosperity of Tonopah, and the route being only 60 miles long from the Carson and Colorado Railroad over a rolling desert country, it was thought that somebody would build it at once. A franchise for the road passed the last State legislature, and at one time the aforesaid railroad company threatened to construct it. Now, however, comes the solid business, the Tonopah Mining Company, with a straightforward proposition to ignore all others in that line and build the road on its own responsibility, breaking ground for it at an early date and completing the road in full running order early next season. This is as it should be, for the Tonopah Company best knows whether their mines will justify the construction of the railroad or not, independent of the Carson and Colorado Railroad or any outside assistance, thus speaking highly and well for the real merits and solid future prosperity of the mines and the district.

The true, substantial future prosperity of Tonopah will come in some time next year with the big reduction works and railroad.

Index

Although every effort has been made to spell the names in this index correctly, the vagaries of Doten's handwriting and spelling are such that readers should check for possible variants of the names they wish to locate. The main headings are alphabetized letter by letter to the first mark of punctuation (disregarding apostrophes and titles such as Dr. or Mrs.), and the subentries are arranged chronologically. Where several main entries start with the same word, surnames come first, followed by place names and names of groups or businesses. Names of newspapers, plays, ships, and books are set in italic type. Maps and photographs are listed as being on the last page of text preceding a pictorial section.

Bishop, Dr. ....: superintendent, Insane
Asylum, charged with mismanagement,
1668; exonerated of charges of
mismanagement, 1669; removes one of
Alf Jr.'s teeth, 1726
Bishop, ..., acquaintance of AD, 1833
Bishop, A. W., 1745
Bishop, Madam Anna, 868, 1210
Bishop, W. W., 1424
Bistolfi, ..., musician, 1871
Black, ..., suspicious stranger with
lice, 173
Black, Mrs. ...., housekeeper, 377–394
passim
Black, ..., magician, 482
Black, ..., teacher at writing school,
574, 579
Black, ..., AD's rival, 635
Black, Judge ...., 1933
Black, John L.: killed his brother, 1702;
accused of murder, 1703; tried for
murder, 1709; death, 1722
Black, Sam J., killed by brother, 1702
Black & Bros. store, 864
Blackburn, Leslie F., 931, 992, 1326
Black Connor, 922
Black Crook, 1086, 1087, 1235, 1315
Black Crook Melodeon, Virginia City, 931,
970
Black Diamonds, 1564, 1811
Black-Eyed Susan, 979, 1125
Black Flag, or Brother Against Brother,
1796
Blackford, ..., Democratic candidate
for assembly, 729
Black Hawks, 1776
Blackstone, N., 522
Blackwater Jack. *See* Craze, Jack
Blaine, James G., 1519
Blair, Chris, 1708
Blair, George W., 2251
Blair, John L.: Sliver Peak lawsuit, 2027;
property sale, 2032
Blaisdell & Constable's Circus, 1006
Blaisdell Troupe of Swiss Bell Ringers, 868
Blake, ..., friend of AD, 508, 515,
519
Blake, E. D., 1917
Blake, Frank: chief printer, *Territorial
Enterprise,* 1926; journalist, 2227
Blake, Thomas: officer of California
Settlers and Miners Secret Fraternity,
488; Alviso land-grant dispute, rent
charged, 500
Blakely, ..., miner, 86
Blakely, S. H., 1698
Blakeslee, L. A., 2003

Blanchard, Hank, 1028, 1261
Blanchard, Kitty, 1118
Bland, Richard Parke, 2035
Bland Silver Coinage Bill, 1863
Blanding, ..., acquaintance of AD,
83, 91
Blane, Mary, 874
Blankenship, Seth: shipmate on *Yeoman,*
8; member, Pilgrim Mining Company,
68, 2179
Blasdel, H. G., 889, 894, 933, 980, 1082,
1111, 1213, 2058; candidate for
governor, 808, 897
Blaser, W. T., 1588
Blauvelt, H., 1061
Bleakley, Joe, 1804
Blessington, Audy, 919
Blewett, Harry, 1453
Blight, Andrew, 1533
Blind Tom, pianist, 1196, 1197
Blind Troupe, 1137
Bliss, D. L., 1851; general supply agent,
Virginia & Truckee Railroad, trustee,
Enterprise Publishing Company, 1218
Blizzard, ..., friend of Fred Lucas,
428, 431
Blood, Col. ...., 1225
Blow for Blow, 1034
Blue, Charley: preliminary hearing for
murder, 2161; charge of manslaughter
dropped, 2164
Blue laws, discussion, 422, 1761
Blundering Pat, 1086
Blythe, Helen, 1753
B'nai B'rith, 1211
Boardman, Charley, 681
Boardman, W. M., 1367
Bob, hired hand in Mountain View, 332,
333
Bob, 1749
Bob Ticket, 1121
Bodfish, ..., owner of lumber yard,
510, 513
Bodge, ..., owner of race horse, 181
Bodie, California, 1349, 1352
Bodie Miner-Index, 2250
Bodie News, 2242
Bodley, Tom, attorney, 659, 684
Boegle, Fred, 1795
Boer War: begins, 2047, 2049; defeat of
Buller's English army, 2057; lecture,
2060; peace declared, 2133
Bogart, R. D., 1250
Bohemian Girl, The, 2059
Bohman, Barney: hired hand, 339, 349,
359, 367, 371, 380, 387, 390–394, 400,
401, 412, 415, 416, 441, 450, 493–511,

546–549, 558–581; 614–639; initiated into California Settlers and Miners Secret Fraternity, 500

Boileau, ..., secretary, Pacific Company, 95, 129

Boland, Mrs. ...., applies for insurance, 1759, 1760

Bonafous, E., 2112

Bond, Dave, 2252

Bone, Raymond, 2165

Bonfanti, ..., performer, 1226

Bonfanti Ballet Troupe, 1084, 1085

Bonnell, Marion, 248

Bonnemort, ..., of the Utah Mine, 1303

Bonner, Bill, 370

Bonnie Fish Wife, 1049

Bonnifield, ..., lawyer for Henry Nofsinger, 1581

Bonnifield, M. S., 1935

Bonnifield, William S., 2016

Bonynge & Hawxhurst, stockbrokers, 1056, 1059, 1073, 1080

Booker, W. W.: Democratic nominee for University regent, 2079; editor, Elko *Independent,* 2132; journalist, 2248

Boone, ..., from Mountain View, 355

Bootblacks, The, 975

Booth, George, son of John Booth, 1495

Booth, J. E. ("Ed"), son of John Booth, 1505, 1554, 1555, 1557

Booth, John, 1450–1499 passim; *Silver State,* Unionville, 1114, 1147; vacations at Lake Tahoe, 1202; part owner, *Reese River Reveille,* 1214, 1361, 1396; offers AD a job, 1395; employs AD on *Reese River Reveille,* 1407–1429 passim; death, 1503; president, Society of Reese River Pioneers, 1505; obituary, 1505; funeral, 1506; will, 1508; career as journalist, 2233, 2239, 2244, 2245, 2246, 2249

Booth, Mrs. John, 1407, 1428, 1495, 1557

Booth, Merrick P., son of John Booth, 1414; Tuscarora, 1505; insanity, 1524; Spanish American War, 1984

Booth, Newton, governor of California, 1025, 1179

Booth, T. W., telegrapher, 1679

Booth, Will W., 1527, 1532, 2138; son of John Booth, quits job as compositor, *Reese River Reveille,* 1416; birth of son, 1416; discharged from *Reese River Reveille,* 1417; publishes the *Democrat,* Austin, 1425; loaned paper for *Democrat,* 1428; loses newspaper, 1439; Belleville, 1505; attempts to organize newspaper in Tonopah, 2101; begins

publication of *Tonopah Bonanza,* 2107; appointed postmaster, Tonopah, 2149

Booton, Brig. Gen. ...., 1742

Borax Miner (Columbus), 2241

Borlini, Alfred, 2073

Born to Good Luck, 1022, 1125

Borst, Virgil, 1351

Bosco, Carl, 1091, 1623

Bostich, ..., miner, 682, 695

Boston Lyric Opera Company, 2084

Boston Melodeon, music book, 7, 79, 152

Boubisse, Julian, 2076

Boucicault, Dion, 1219

Bouheben, August, 1815

Bourne, Miss May-Ethelyn, 2047

Bourne, Russell, 536

Bowden, Bill, 1689

Bowen, Ben, 243, 246, 264, 265

Bowen, Doc, 244

Bower, ..., acquaintance of AD, 853, 854

Bowers, Mrs. D. P., 1011, 1013, 1199, 1200, 1250, 1707

Bowers, Eilley Orrum (Mrs. Sandy): description, 1477; prediction of fires, 1514

Bowers, Lemuel S. ("Sandy"), 934; history written by AD, 1696

Bowers, Seth, 816

Bowers Mansion, becomes public summer resort, 2159

Bowie, H., 293

Bowie, Kate, 907

Bowler, ..., acrobat, 1695

Bowles, Sam, 839, 1055

Bowline, ..., sheriff, Mariposa County, 242

Bowman, Mrs. ...., daughter of Frank Hall, 2137

Bowman, Abby, 840

Bowman, Charley C.: defeated for president, Virginia Exempt Firemen's Association, 1614; initiated into Odd Fellows, 1728; argues with AD, 1807

Bowser, John ("John the Barber"), 742, 746

Bow Windows, bordello, 838, 862, 874–878 passim, 883, 906, 823, 976. *See also* Tyler, Jenny

Bowyer, ..., preacher at camp meeting, 558

Box and Cox, 255, 1132

Boxer Rebellion, 2072–2077 passim

Boyce, Fred, 1912

Boyd, Nellie, 1695

Boyden, ..., member, school district board of examiners, Austin, 1427

attorney, 1906–1918 passim; house burns, 1955; death, 2058
Clarke, R. M., Jr., 1584
Clarke, S. A., 1163
Clarke, Major W. G., 2058
Clarke, Willie, 1948
Clarke-Ward & Burch Co., 1940
Clark's Specialty Entertainment, 1784
Clarkson, E. W., 837
Clarkson, Louisa, 880
Clawson, Harry A., 1587
Clay, Henry, 121
Clayton's Ambrotype Studio, 643
Cleary, ..., famous athlete, 1590
Cleburne, Dr. ....: doctor of allopathic medicine, 949, 950, 1012, 1014, 1018; death, 1863
Clemens, Orion, 1972
Clemens, Samuel L. *See* Twain, Mark
Clemmo, Robert, 1680
Clendening, John, 614, 681, 684, 685; killed during secessionists' robbery of stage coach, 804
Cleveland, ..., prisoner, Nevada State Prison, 1078
Cleveland, Abner Coburn, 922, 2084; nominee for governor, 1873, 1875; elected delegate to Republican National Convention, 1919; refused nomination by Silver party for governor, 1999; independent candidate for U.S. Senate, political speech, 2004, 2017; Republican candidate for governor, 2142; death, obituary, 2165
Cleveland, E. R., 1394
Cleveland, Grover: nomination for presidency by Democratic National Convention, 1526, 1822, 1823; election, 1551; vetoes Bland Silver Coinage Bill, 1863
Cleveland brothers, travel to the mines with AD, 75
Cleveland's Minstrels, 1789
Clifford, ..., escaped convict, 1139
Clifton, Blanche, 1191
Clifton (Austin Junction), Nevada: description, 1405; depot, Nevada Central Railroad, 1491
Cline, Robert, 900, 902
Clockmaker's Hat, The, 523
Clooney, Martin, 1046
Clouds and Sunshine, 1332
Clough, Mrs. ...., of Fort John, 250
Clough, Fred W., 1788, 1799, 1801, 1812, 1844, 2041; engineer, Alta Mine, 1783
Clough, Orson, 1783
Coad, Miss ...., performer, 129

Coal mines: Berryessa Creek, 647, 649; Nevada, 815, 834
Cobb, George F., 1634
Coburn, Joe, 1035
Cochran, Edward Everett, 1709, 1717, 1719, 1901; marriage to Millie Stoddard, 1705; visits Illinois, 1840; leaves for Chicago, 1907; moves family to Illinois, 1920
Cochran, Esther Armorel, 1881, 1920
Cochran, Millie Stoddard, 1717, 1719, 1749, 1901; birth of daughters, 1742, 1881; visits Illinois, 1840; returns from Illinois, 1841; leaves for Illinois, 1920; birth of son, 1976; married life, 2173. *See also* Stoddard, Millie
Cochran, Sara, 1840, 1841, 1920
Cochrane, Robert, 1249
Cock fights, 907
Cocks, William, 1867, 1868
Code: how to decipher, xvii; entries, 926–1009 passim, 1930; used in short story, 2218
Cody, William, 1531
Coe, Charles W., 1083; son of H. W. Coe, 2156
Coe, Harry, 1083
Coe, Henry W., 427, 445, 571, 632, 675, 676, 679, 680, 708; neighbor of AD, 415; birth of child, 697; AD visits, 1083; death, 1922; reminiscence about, 2156
Coe, Mrs. Henry W., 707, 1083
Coe, Isabel, 1715
Coe, J. M., 1890
Coes, George, 523, 624
Coffey, W. H., 1999
Coffin, Gus, 669, 683, 699, 701, 705
Coffin, Trenmor: mint embezzlement case, 1905, 1911, 1915; receives secret payment from client Heney, 1921, 1952; assignments by client determined not to be fraudulent, 1965; attorney for McMillan in gubernatorial election contest, 2016; son, 2071; Republican nominee for justice of the supreme court, 2078; political speech, 2084
Cofran, ..., friend of AD, 310, 362–391 passim, 415, 426, 427, 442, 478, 480, 497, 499, 502, 522, 525, 544, 579, 657, 657, 674, 704, 834, 1082
Cofran, Mrs. ...., friend of AD, 362, 376, 416, 417, 487, 542, 544, 707, 783, 802
Cofran, Georgiana, 362–392 passim, 415, 417, 427, 484, 489, 501, 505, 522, 536, 537, 538, 539, 543, 577, 579, 1082, 1144; photo, 394

Dent, Col. Bob, 219–250 passim
Dent, Mrs. Bob, 244, 245, 249, 250
Denton, ..., women's suffrage debate, 1940
Denton, Ben, 1072
Denver, Frank, 1140, 1223; lieutenant governor, wounded in prison break, 1137, 1193
Denver, Mrs. Frank, 1141, 1204
Denver, Jennie, 1140
De Quille, Dan (William Wright), 812–898 passim, 913, 921, 924, 932, 940, 944, 948–993 passim, 1008, 1015, 1016, 1027, 1036, 1038, 1040, 1053, 1054, 1061, 1072, 1085, 1132, 1160, 1165, 1166, 1170, 1186, 1229, 1249, 1261, 1263, 1291, 1397, 1401, 1575, 1657, 1658, 1665, 1672, 1673, 1681, 1706, 1714, 1718, 1958; joins Crystal Lodge of Good Templars, 991; delirium tremens, 1071, 1087; discharged from *Territorial Enterprise,* 1119; leaves for Iowa with wife and daughter, 1959; newspaper comment on departure for Iowa, 1959, 1960; death, obituary, 1977; career as journalist, 2227, 2228, 2229, 2236; photos, 1152
Derby, Mrs. ...., Mountain View seamstress, 403, 404, 408, 515
Derby, ..., of the Alta Mine, 1303
Derby, Lieut. George Horatio, 241
Derby, Laura, 489
De Reamer, De Witt, 488, 504
De Rosa, Josephine, 1315
Derry, Pat, 871
De Shields, Capt. ...., Gould & Curry Mill, 893
Dettenreider, Mrs. ...., spiritualist lecturer, 883
Devany, George, 1173, 1176
Devil's Auction Troupe, 2121
Devlin, ..., Virginia City fight, 920
Dewey, George: victory at Manila, 1982; made admiral, 1983; reception in Washington, 2046; comment on decision to run for president, 2064
De Witt, John, 919
De Wolf, Mrs. E. T., 1187
Dey, Dick, 1644, 1657
de Young, Charles: of the *San Francisco Chronicle,* 1129; shoots Rev. I. S. Kalloch, 1350–1351; shot by Rev. I. M. Kalloch, 1362
Diamond, Harry, 2023
Dick, Capt. ...., Emerald Bay, 1208
Dick, Tom, 1825, 2118
Dickerson, G. W., 2241
Dickey, James W., 850

Dickinson, Anna, 1052
Dickinson, Elisha, 172
Dickinson, John, 169, 174, 192
Dickinson, Will, 174
Dickman, Conrad, 1106
Dickson, ... *See* Dixon
Dickson, George W., 1725
Dickson Comedy Co., 1802
Dick Turpin, 1091
Diehl, Rev. Israel H.: lecture on Solomon's Temple exhibit, 490; lecture on the Holy Land, 1061
Digger Indians. *See* Indians
Dill, Mrs. ...., restaurant owner, 817, 872
Dilley, J. S., 871
Dillon, John, 1816
Diman, ..., at Stockton, 75
Dimon, Mrs. ...., victim of murder and robbery, 236
Dinsmore, George, 1457
Dinsmore, Lizzie, 1457
Dinsmore, Mrs. Mary E., marriage to W. A. Hall, 1457
Diphtheria, 1294
Directory of Nevada Territory, J. Wells Kelly, 2226
Divine, Judge ...., miner, 682
Divine, Belle, 808
Divorce, 1169
Dixon, ..., present at murder of Alexander McDonald, 98–100
Dixon (or Dickson), ..., rents mare to AD, 373, 379, 632
Dixon, ..., fiddler, 666
Doane, Christina, 1294
Doane, Mike, 666
Doane, William Hy: secretary, Nevada Sportsman's Club, 1084; proprietor, skating rink, 1116, 1117, 2093; child dies of diphtheria, 1294; shoots Chinese cook, 1311; acquitted of murder, 1312
Doane, Mrs. William Hy, 1356
Dobbie, John, 2001
Dockstader's Minstrels, 1707
Dodge, Mr. and Mrs. ...., work for S. B. Emerson, 186
Dodge, Rev. ...., officiates at funeral of Judge Healy, 2126
Dodge, Ossian E., 808, 811, 814, 963
Dods, Henry, 1630
Dods, Mrs. Henry, 1630
Dogfights, 778, 785, 786
Dog Valley, 835
Doherty, Charles. *See* Dougherty, Charles
Dohrety, James, 780
Dolan, ..., Knights of Pythias, 1821
Dolan, Mrs. ...., of Carson City, 2033

1703; picture taken for Thompson & West's *History of Nevada*, 1383; writes autobiography for Thompson & West's *History of Nevada*, 1385; initiated into Harmony Lodge No. 13, Knights of Pythias, 1391; writes history of *Gold Hill Daily News* for Thompson & West's *History of Nevada*, 1393; leaves *Gold Hill Daily News*, 1395; begins work on *Reese River Reveille* (Austin), 1396, 1405; history of Austin for Cyclopedia Britannica, 1415; loses job on *Reese River Reveille*, 1429; begins correspondence from Austin to *Territorial Enterprise*, 1435; deputy U.S. marshal for special court case, 1455; moves from Austin to Carson City, 1558–1559; engrossing clerk, Senate, 1559; reporter for *Territorial Enterprise*, 1573; correspondent and agent for Associated Press, 1595, 1883; agent for Bankers & Merchants Mutual Life Association, 1689; compiles Comstock mining statistics for U.S. Mint, 1700; agent, Mutual Endowment and Life Association, 1745; secretary, Republican County Convention, 1827; vice president, Centennial Gravel Gold Mining Co., 1866; secretary, Storey County Republican Convention, 1873; resolution of commendation by Nevada Legislature, 1945–1946; "Woods' Creek in 'Forty Nine' " (reminiscence), 1996, 2181; correspondence with *Nevada State Herald* (Wells), 2001; correspondence with *Gardnerville Record*, 2001; sergeant-at-arms, Washoe County Republican Convention, 2003; reports Nevada Legislature for *San Francisco Chronicle*, 2015; asked not to return home, 2021; "Early Journalism of Nevada" (article), 2044, 2225; "The Pacific Coast Pioneers" (article), 2051, 2257; "Bullion Production From the Comstock Lode and Tonopah, 1902" (mining report), 2137, 2265; death, 2172; member, Pilgrim Mining Company, 2180; career as journalist, 2230–2231, 2245; photos, frontispiece, 394, 1152, 1856

Doten, Bessie Tahoe, daughter of AD, 1246, 1250, 1264, 1279; birth, 1230; starts going to school at San Jose, 1826; teaches at intermediate school, Gardnerville, 2160; marriage to Grant Barton, 2169; death, 2173; photo, 1856. (Bessie bore a daughter July 1904.)

Doten, Charles C., brother of AD, xix; visits AD in Reno, 1819; photos, 394, 1152, 1856

Doten, Cornelia, sister of AD. *See* Burbank, Cornelia Doten

Doten, Eunice, sister of AD. *See* Morton, Eunice Doten

Doten, Euphelia, sister of AD, xix, 83; photo, 394

Doten, Frank B., cousin of AD, 1697, 1723, 1767, 1786, 1836; teamster from Bodie, 1559, 1684, 1690, 1703, 1746; member, Pacific Coast Pioneers, 1745, 1839; injured in accident, 1766; death, 1872

Doten, James, cousin of AD, 70, 128, 187, 383

Doten, Laura, sister of AD, xix, 1841; photo, 394

Doten, Lizzie, sister of AD, xix, 953; spiritualist lecturer, 486; sermons, 681; "The Inner Mystery," 1054; *Poems of Progress*, 1141; visits Reno, 1730; marriage to Z. Adams Willard, 2134; photos, 394, 1152

Doten, Mary (Mrs. Charles C. Doten), visits the Dotens in Reno, 1819; photo, 1856

Doten, Mary Goodwin, daughter of AD, 1401, 1424; birth, 1374; changes name to Goodwin Stoddard Doten, 1989; graduates from high school, 1989; participates in Fourth of July exercises, Reno, 1991; begins at University of Nevada, 1998; story appears in University Annual, 2031; literary editor, *Artemisia*, 2159; death, 2173; photos, 1856

Doten, Mary Stoddard, wife of AD: wedding, 1205; birth of daughter Bessie, 1230; vacations at Lake Tahoe, 1232, 1254, 1279, 1298; mother and daughter Millie arrive in Gold Hill, 1255; birth of son Samuel, 1264; Mary's thirty-second birthday, 1270; birth of son Alfred, 1301; birth of daughter Mary Goodwin, 1374; teaches in Austin, 1423; takes examination for teaching certificate, 1427, 1428; miscarriage, 1473; offered job teaching school in Reno, 1487; accepts position in Reno, 1488–1489; work published in newspaper, 1724, 1763, 1767, 1771, 1776, 1815, 2052; initiated into Rebekah Degree No. 7, 1726; assistant principal, Reno High School, 1741, 1922, 1956; visits San Francisco, 1825; writes for *Nevada Magazine*, 2052; trouble with

Dumarsh, Margaret Ann. *See* Schuyler,
Fannie
Dumb Belle, The, 243
Dunbar, ..., laborer, 422
Dunbar, Samuel, 1503, 1513, 1529
Duncan, J. C., 378
Dung beetles, 1479
Dunham, Alexander, 82
Dunham, Chandler, 68, 2180
Dunham, Richard B., 63, 69, 2180
Dunham, William J., 2180
Dunlap, Wilson: broker, 1171, 1172;
absconds owing money, 1194; returns
from San Francisco, 1217; meeting of
creditors, 1219
Dunlop, May, 2067, 2112
Dunn, ..., of the Chollar Mine, 888
Dunn, ..., foreman, Justice Mining
Company, 1237
Dunn, Uncle Bill, 1863
Dunn, F. W., 1421, 1509
Dunn, Horace A., 2061, 2091, 2256; of
the *Nevada Tribune,* fined for contempt,
1899; part owner of the *Carson
Morning News,* 1904
Dunphy, Gen. William: cattleman, 1509,
1521; Democratic candidate for U.S.
senator, 1535
Dunwreath, Florence, 893, 936
Dupaix, Henry, 636, 696, 708, 716
Duprey, Willie, 1360
Duprez & Benedict's Minstrels, 1104
Dupuis, Ed, 2081
Durand, Dick, 723
Durand, Rosalie, 502
Durant, Jimmy, 1620
Durning, Charley: foreman, Manhattan
Mill, 1418; superintendent, Manhattan
Mine, 1465, 1467, 1469, 1471
Dutch Louis. *See* Sennewald, Louis
Dutch Pete, at Rich Gulch, 81
Dutton, ..., San Francisco, 674
Duval, Charles, 840
Dwight, Mrs. ...., mother of Governor
Jewett W. Adams, 1583
Dwyer, Billy, 1167
Dyer, ..., photographer, San
Francisco, 704
Dyer Brothers, grocers, Austin, 1514

Eagan, John, 741, 790, 799
Eagar, Mrs. ...., acquaintance of AD,
997, 1005, 1006
Eagle Eye, 1091
Eagle Valley, Nevada, 2040

Eames, George, 2251
Earle, Rev. A. B., 925–929 passim
"Early Journalism of Nevada," article by
AD, 2044, 2225–2256
Earthquakes, 260, 329, 455, 456, 1004,
1026, 1071, 1072, 1077, 1159, 1302,
1670, 1816, 1877, 1883, 1911, 1953
Easly, ..., schoolmaster, 514
Eastern Slope (Washoe City), 892, 2242
Eastern Star, Mrs. M initiated into, 1115
East Lynne, 703, 1034, 1115, 1121, 1199,
1604, 1630, 1797
Eastman, Rev. R. S., 1344, 1356, 1420;
pastor, St. John's Episcopal Church,
Gold Hill, 1361; member, school district
board of examiners, Austin, 1427;
leaves Austin, 1446; moves to La Porte,
Indiana, 1493
Easton, Mrs. ...., Mountain View, 436
Eaton, Jim, 748
Eaton, John, 837
Eaves, ..., former mayor of Virginia
City, 1885
Eaves, Gus, 1885
Eaves, Harry, 1885
Eckert, ..., of the Washoe Brewery,
908
Eckfeldt, J. R., 1922
Ecklemann, Otto, 1669, 1678, 1681, 1764,
1767, 1811, 2067, 2153
Eckley, J. W., 1362, 1740, 2245
E Clampus Vitus, Austin, 1421
Eclipse Mine, 880
Eclipses: of the moon, 217, 1385, 1709;
of the sun, 1270, 1323, 1359, 1721
Eddington, Jimmy, 931
Eddy, H. M., 963; elected Common
Council, Virginia City, 833
Eddy, Mrs. H. M., 875
Eddy, Joe, 1855
Eddy, Kate, 1681
Eddy, Peter, 1676, 1677
Eddy, William Henry, 1690
Edgerton, Henry, 1023
Edgington, Abe, 1260
Edgington, Lillie, 1217
Edison, Thomas A., 1323
Edward VII, 2093, 2134
Edwards, ..., miner, 95
Edwards, ..., wants to organize
newspaper in Como, 757
Edwards, ..., actor, 1249
Edwards, ..., prizefighter, 1566, 1568
Edwards, A. L., 1263
Edwards, George, suicide, 115–116
Edwards, George, son of W. S. Edwards,
986
Edwards, Harry, 1039, 1040, 1068, 1312

Fanchon or the Little Cricket, 922, 926, 994, 1041, 1089, 1115, 1215
Farini, Professor ...., music teacher, 1088, 1106, 1114
Farley, Jim, 239
Farmer, ..., landlord, St. Charles Hotel, 254
Farmer, Miss ...., school teacher, 1642
Farmer Stebbins, 1919
Farm machinery: threshing machines, 186, 559, 610; Strong's harvester, 429, 442; Burral reaper, 432; Willard's patent seed sower and harrow, 442, 454; fruit picker, 501; reaping machines, 555; Leland's harvester, 616
Farnum, Harrold, 1625
Farrand, ..., of Virginia City, 863
Farrand's Amalgamator, 816
Farrell, Capt. ...., from Virginia City, 823
Farrell, Ed, foreman, Manhattan Mine, 1446, 1510
Farrell, Mike J., 1421, 1543, 1566; bookkeeper, Manhattan Mine & Milling Co., 1413, 1415; state senator, 1418; chief clerk, Manhattan Mill, 1468; member, Reese River Pioneers, 1475; visits Gold Hill, 1584
Farrell, Mrs. Mike J., 1568, 1584
Farrington, E. S.: political speech, 2084; Republican nominee for Congress, 2078, 2142
Farrington, Frank: local editor, *Gold Hill Daily News*, 812, 834, 864, 905, 994, 1004; becomes night foreman, Yellow Jacket Mine, 872; local editor, *Trespass*, 917; visits Japan, 1146
Farron's Comedy Company, 1711
Fatherland, 1742, 1870
Faulds, P. K., 1719, 1748
Faust, 1136, 1654, 1712
Fay, Harley S., 728, 742, 743, 746, 762, 773, 781
Fazio or the Italian Wife's Revenge, 1013
Fear, Jim, 518, 519, 520, 528
Feeny, Mark, 1805
Fegan, John B., 1605
Felix, ..., of Lemoine Froment & Co., 664
Fell, James, 1765, 1789
Fellows, W. H. H., 2243; foreman, *Reese River Reveille*, 1422; fired from *Reese River Reveille*, 1423
Felser, Noah, 1260–1263 passim
Female Detective, The, 922
Female Drummer, A, 2118
Female Gambler, The, 922

Fenner, ..., Gold Hill, 1221
Fenton, ..., Rich Gulch, 86
Fenton, Bill, 102
Fenton, K., 104
Ferguson, ..., shot accidentally, 479
Ferguson, Cora, 1705
Ferguson, J. W., 2001
Ferguson, R. D., 834, 838
Ferguson, Honorable W. T., 442
Fernande, 1116
Fernandez, John, 165, 176, 177, 182
Ferral, Robert, 2241
Ferrell, Officer C. P., 2164
Ferrend, Major George E., 1101; marriage to Miss Mary Margaret Burke, 1148; suicide, 1241
Fessenden, Col. ...., from Boston, 895
Feusier, ..., Virginia City treasurer, 876
Feusier, Frank, 830
Feusier & Co., 864
Fidelia or the Fire Waif, 1247
Field, Mattie, 838, 1140
Field of Honor, The, 1655
Field of the Cloth of Gold, 1085, 1118
Fielding, Frank, 1592, 1637, 1764, 1858, 1859
Fieley, ..., Storey County school trustee, 1867
Figot, William. *See* Tigot, William
Fillebrown, T. H., 905, 1606, 1607, 1620, 2166
Fillmore, Lizzie, 821
Fillmore, Millard, 306, 307, 308
Fillmore, Minnie, 821
Filopoena, 652, 657
Finch, Tom, 1071; marriage to Ellen Shaw, 1061; saloon robbed, 1096; owner, Capital Billiard Saloon, 1256
Fine, ..., musician, 471–473 passim
Finigan, Mike, 1574
Finkham, Capt. ...., of the hay scow *Express*, 657
Finlayson, Miss ...., kindergarten teacher, 1647
Finlayson, Flora, 1678
Finlen, Miles: fatally injures opponent in fight, 1703; indicted for murder, 1704; trial, 1708
Finley, Mrs. ...., 875
Finley, ..., Virginia City, 878
Finn, ..., Virginia City, 880
Finn, John, 1104
Finney, Rev. ...., 546, 600
Fire departments: elections, 823, 917, 981, 1037, 1191; salary cut, 835; races, 1053; Washoe Engine Company No. 4,

1294; Exempt Firemen's Association, 1566; Reno, 1734–1735
Fire engines: Sacramento, 255; San Francisco, 261; Virginia City, 1167, 1217; photo, 1152
Fires (arranged in alphabetical order): American Flat, 1346, 1386, 2068; arson, 929, 956, 1029, 1034, 1098, 1107–1108; 1132, 1135, 1138, 1142, 1169, 1585, 1734, 1841, 1930, 1931, 1932, 2032, 2033; Austin, 1413; Baltic Switch, 1384, 1385; Bay State Mill, 1118; Belcher Mine, 1239, 1315; Bowers Mill, 1050; Campo Seco, 188; Carson City, 1304, 1590, 1803, 1841, 1915, 1930, 1931, 1932, 1940, 1955, 1962, 2032, 2033, 2110; Chicago, 1209; Chinatown (Virginia City), 1058, 1085, 1208, 1696; Chollar-Potosi Mine, 1054; Cliff House, 1880; Dayton, 890, 1099; the Divide, 1385, 1395, 1580, 1637; Empire, 1111; Fort Homestead, 1377; French's Hotel, Milpitas, 586; forest fires, 311, 446; Geiger Grade, 1057; Gold Hill, 1097–1098, 1111, 1290, 1294, 1315, 1346, 1352, 1353, 1359, 1361, 1366, 1368, 1369, 1380, 1397, 1595; Gold Hill mines, 880, 1041–1042, 1043, 1054, 1087; Gold Hill schoolhouse, 1827; Gould & Curry Mine, 1672; Hale & Norcross Mine, 1377; Imperial Mine, 1256, 1348, 1373; Lady Bryan Mine, 1331; Mokelumne Hill, 188; newspaper account, 1734; Original Keystone Mining Co., 1585; Palmyra range, 936; Phoenix Mill, 900; Piper's Opera House, 1098; in railroad tunnels and snowsheds, 1177, 1218, 1347, 2134; Reno, 1343, 1632, 1730, 1733, 2036, 2126; Sacramento, 132; San Francisco, 380, 1853; Seattle, 1731; Silver City, 1039, 1343; Spanish Gulch, 155; Succor Hoisting Works, 1226; University of Nevada, 1904; Utica Mine, Angel's Camp, California, 1963; Virginia City, 812, 825, 832, 851, 874–897 passim, 902, 910, 923, 931, 956, 983, 1025–1038 passim, 1057, 1059, 1069, 1104–1117 passim, 1127–1143 passim, 1172, 1176, 1191, 1212, 1252, 1258–1262 passim, 1277, 1377, 1595, 1598, 1608, 1709, 1739, 1771, 1850, 1861, 1880, 2025; Wadsworth, 1514; Wells, Nevada, 2079; Winnemucca, 1801; Woodford's Station, 2072; Yellow Jacket Mine, 1209
Firmin, Annie, 983
First Night or The Debutante, The, 985

Fischer, Henry, 745–788 passim, 792, 818, 934, 1302, 1955
Fish, ..., agent, Stedman Clothes Washer, 1117
Fish, ..., Washoe County commissioner, 1727
Fish, Charles H., 1184; president, Consolidated Virginia Mine, 1902, 1918, 2067, 2104
Fish, H. L., senator from Reno, 1552, 1561
Fisher, ..., leaves the mines, 82
Fisher, ..., preacher, 510
Fisher, ..., barley clipper, 611, 613, 614
Fisher, Mrs. ...., dressmaker, 1210
Fisk, ..., from Russian River, 526
Fisk, Lizzie Basye, 1343
Fitch, J. B., 1145
Fitch, Thomas, 575, 576, 758, 871, 891, 1015, 1016, 1732; *Eastern Slope,* Washoe City, 892; lecture on expansion of United States, 961; political speech, 1102, 1107, 1283, 1768; lecture on Sutro Tunnel, 1238; journalist, 2231, 2245
Fitzgerald, ..., dies of smallpox, 1382
Fitzgerald, A. L.: Democratic nominee for supreme court justice, 2079; political speech, 2084
Fitzgerald, John, 1553
Fitzgerald, Thomas, 951
Fitzsimmons, Judge Hugh, 1172, 1261, 1280, 1339, 1363
Fitzsimmons, Julia, 1219
Fitzsimmons, Robert Prometheus, 1934, 1942, 1947, 2034, 2077, 2137
Flack, ..., Summit City, 854
Flagg, H. H.: broker, 987; proprietor, Knickerbocker Mine, 1140; banking and brokerage suspension, 1148–1149
Flanagan, Willie, 1377
Flanigan, P. L., 2003
Flannagan, Michael, 1651–1652
Flannery, ..., sergeant-at-arms of Assembly, 1885
Flanningham, J. P.: justice of the peace, 1379; secretary, Centennial Gravel Gold Mining Co., 1616, 1625, 1632; funeral, 1741
Flattery, ..., saloon shooting, 816
Fleming, Alex, 2101
Fleming, Miss Ida, 1420
Flenders, ..., from San Jose, 654
Fleur de The, 1171
Fleury, Mademoiselle ...., performed, San Francisco, 702
Flick, Mrs. ...., Virginia City, 984
Flint, ..., public speaker, 239
Flint, ..., prospector, 688

in execution on *Gold Hill Daily News,* 1342

George, Henry ("Harry"), lecturer, 1389

George, J., 832

Georgia Minstrels, 1330, 1723, 1815

German, George, 244, 249

Germania Singing Society or Glee Club, 813, 833

German Lover, 1086

German Sanitary Fund, 1104

German Soldier, A, 1878

Gerrans, Mrs. ...., Virginia City, 1899

Getchell, Lysander W., 1406, 1410, 1433, 1482, 1489, 1504, 1508, 1510, 1522, 1543, 1556; Republican nominee for sheriff of Battle Mountain, 1425; delegate to Republican National Convention, 1511; parents visit from Maine, 1512, 1513; London Mine on Lavage Ledge, 1513; regent, University of Nevada, 1562, 1586, 1587; returns from visit to Maine, 1614; returns to Silver City, Idaho, 1902

Getchell, Mrs. L. W., 1406, 1410, 1482, 1505, 1522

Getchell, Noble H., son of L. W. Getchell, 1433, 1522, 1902

Gettis, ..., Milpitas, 689

Getzler, Charles H., 1247

Getzler, Sue Robinson, 911, 912, 914, 916, 918, 919, 982, 1001, 1007, 1009. *See also* Robinson, Sue

GH. *See* Gold Hill

Gibbon, T. E., 2017, 2018

Gibson, Mrs. ...., of Austin, 1517

Gibson, Nellie, 1245, 1247

Gibson, W. D. C. ("Bill"), of Virginia City, 1235, 1277, 1279, 1281, 1297, 1306, 1318, 1353, 1355, 1404, 1786, 1891, 2067; Indian agent from Pyramid, 1567, 1632; superintendent, Stewart Indian School, 1811

Gibson, William, postmaster, Austin, 1408, 1433, 1436, 1487, 1503, 1512, 1554, 1574

Giddens, ..., actor, 1249

Gifford, Fred, 1934

Gifford, William A., 73, 2180

Gignoux, Lieut. ...., 1988

Gignoux, J. E., 2124, 2138

Gilbert, ..., store owner, near Fort John, 213, 217, 219, 225, 227, 232, 235, 243, 246, 249, 250, 253

Gilbert, ..., Austin rancher, 1524

Gilbert, Col. F. P., 1380

Gilbert, Joe, 1542

Gilbert, Donnelly & Girard Farce Comedy Company, 1688

Gilbert's Melodeon, Milpitas, 580, 624, 657, 702

Gilder, Frank, 1210

Giles, Miss Freethy, 1797

Gilkey, Mr. ...., at Milpitas, 669

Gill, ..., from Austin, 1684

Gillespie, Adam, 1227, 1246, 1268, 1280, 1291, 1300, 1307, 1308, 1320, 1648, 1757; newspaper carrier for Gold Hill & Silver City, 1158, 1236; puts attachment on *Gold Hill Daily News* for debt, 1337; judgment against *Gold Hill Daily News,* 1340; levies execution on *Gold Hill Daily News,* 1342

Gillespie, Matt, 1258, 1261, 1263, 1266, 1588; Gold Hill carrier for *Gold Hill Daily News,* 1303

Gillespie, W. A., 2018

Gillespie, William M., 838, 839, 861, 863, 868, 870, 872, 874, 878, 880, 881, 882, 887, 895, 910, 930, 931, 932, 933, 1041, 1115, 1516, 1606; photo, 1152

Gillet, ..., lives at Russell's Diggings, 217

Gillett, ..., Savage Mine, 1303

Gillig, Mrs. ...., Virginia City, 1275

Gillis, Billy, 967, 1031, 1036; publisher of local directory, 1009, 1010

Gillis, Steve, 969, 972, 1595, 1740, 1772, 2251

Ginn, John I., 1012, 1141, 1166, 1199, 2237, 2246, 2249, 2251; editor, *The Daily Safeguard,* 1024; marriage to Kate Mosser, 1142; birth of child, 1169

Girofle-Girofla, 1252

Gladding, J. F., 1175

Glanningham, ..., justice of the peace, 1397

Glassman, William, 1738

Gleason, ..., Spanish Gulch, 180

Gleason (or Gleeson), Mrs. ...., 1036, 1039, 1045; death, 1060

Glenmore, ship out of Richmond, Virginia, 16

Glenn, Bob, 2241, 2252

Glenn, Dick, 149, 168, 171, 174

Glenn, M. M., 2241

Glessner, Charles, 2252

Glessner, Oliver, 2252

Glessner, Samuel A., 867, 915, 977, 2231, 2252

Glover, E. F., 887

Glynn, Maggie. *See* Hayes, Liz

Goetz, Henry, 1690

Goff, ..., of Warm Springs, 651

Golconda News, 2256

Goldbarm's store, saloon, in Como, 745, 756, 762

Kennedy, John M.: killed in mine fire, 1676; funeral, 1677
Kennedy and Mellon's Store, 815
Kenney, Mrs. ...., spiritualist lecturer, 985
Kent, Capt. ...., traveling agent, Bankers & Merchants Mutual Life Association, 1745, 1748, 1750
Kent, Billy, 2171
Kent, Johnny, 2080
Kent, Jule, 1097
Kent, Lucy, 912
Kentuck. *See* Daniel, John M.
Kentuck Mine: fire, 1041, 1043; map, 1152
Kentucky Derby, Ten Broeck beats Molly McCarty, 1321
Kentz, Charley, 815
Keough, William, 1765
Kermeen, J. J., 1935
Kermeen, Walter: arrested for arson, 1935; tried, 1969
Kerrin, Hugh, 934; elected chief, fire department, 917; firemen's election, 981, 982
Kerry, 1219
Kervin, Patrick: backs expedition to Klondike, 1961; elected superintendent, Consolidated Virginia Mining Co., 2005
Ketchum, ..., at Como, 785
Key, ..., ranch overseer, 559
Key, Bob, 773
Keyes, E. W., 1023
Keyes, Col. Pat J., 1710, 1711, 1712, 1828, 1849, 1875, 1930, 1932, 1951, 2111; suit for wages as superintendent, Keyes Mining Company, 1802, 1806
Keyser, D., 1724, 1725
Keyser, George, son of D. Keyser, 1724
Kickapoo Vaudeville and Medicine Show, 2130
Kidd's Dam, 853
Kilfoyle, W. W., 854, 858
Killeen, Mrs. ...., of Virginia City, 1134
Killeen, Jim, of Virginia City, 1717
Kill or Cure, 977
Kilrain, ..., prizefighter, 1733
Kimball, ..., fireman, killed, Petaluma Mill explosion, 1170
Kimball, William: secretary, Mt. Davidson Lodge No. 3, I.O.O.F., 1447, 1509; funeral, 1794
Kimball Opera Comique and Burlesque Company, 1785
King, Mrs. ...., nurse, 1301, 1302
King, Angela Starr, 862

King, George, 1329
King, James, of William: murdered at San Francisco, 268–286 passim; funeral, 282
King, Mrs. James, 271
King, Jim, killed at Mason Valley, 1949
King, Joe, 1532, 1696
King, Sammy, 1461, 1495, 1554
King, Thomas S.: brother of James King of William, 271; shoots A. A. Cohen, 335; newspaper editor, 378
King, Rev. Thomas Starr, 541; description of service at Unitarian Church, San Francisco, 703; death, 766; AD summons to seance, 1073, 1099
King, W. R., 1370
King Alfred Mine, accident, 1411
Kingman, Elisha J., 68, 2180
Kingsbury, Alice, 926, 927, 928, 929
King's Fool, The, 1724
King's Gardener, The, 933
King's Ranch, Reese River, 1420
Kinkaid, Jim, 2068
Kinkead, John H.: political speech, 1332; governor, 1341; visits Austin, 1421; former governor of Nevada and Alaska, 1602
Kinney, Sheriff ...., 1897
Kinney, Mr. ...., raises carrier pigeons, 1990
Kinzle, M., 1625, 1789, 1814, 1817, 1843, 1853
Kiota Hollow, 59
Kiralfy, Arnold, 1315
Kiralfy Combination, 1315
Kirby, Joe, 1319
Kirby, Dr. P. T., 1050, 1147, 1148, 1150, 1158, 1172, 1201, 1208, 1221, 1232, 1233, 1272, 1583, 1595, 1608, 1863; marriage to Miss Lucy Harris, 1194; resident physician, county hospital, 1291; fifth wedding anniversary, 1316; funeral, 1718
Kirby, Mrs. P. T., 1243, 1254
Kirchner, Harmon, 1935, 1936; death, 1937
Kirk, ..., shot by Indians, 83
Kirk, George: served notice by Vigilance Committee, Virginia City, 1125; hung by Vigilance Committee, 1133
Kirk, Leopold, 881
Kirk & Co. Drugstore, 871
Kirkbride, Rev. ...., 1535
Kirman, Dick, 1323
Kirman, Richard, 2019; Democratic nominee for presidential elector, 2079
Kiss in the Dark, 1046, 1085
Kit, the Arkansas Traveler, 1143
Kittrell, ..., political speech, 1330

Le Favre, Aline, 1159, 1160, 1161
Legal Document, A, 1811
Legate, Charley, 1607, 1668, 1677, 1719
Leidy, ..., assemblyman, Esmeralda County, 2018
Leland, Mrs. ...., Austin friend of AD, 1518, 1523, 1574
Leman, Walter, 1111
Lemmon, H. A., 1899, 1900, 1904, 2256
Lemmon, J. G., 905, 1207
Lemoine Froment and Co. of San Jose, 664, 665
Leni Leoti, 175
Leon, W. F., 1418
Leonard, Franklin, 2099, 2130, 2138
Leonard, James M., 2110, 2113
Leonard, O. R., 1424, 2261
Leonard, Sam, 2252
Lepava, John, 1624
Lernhart, A., 1882
Les Cloches de Corneville, 1327
Leslie, ..., comedian, 1004
Lester, ..., workman, at Austin, 1414
Lester, Jessie, 817, 820
Lester, Lisle, 960, 691, 971, 973, 974
Le Tour De Knell or the Chamber of Death, 1117
Levy, ..., owner, Hotel Alturas, 862
Levy, J., 1096
Levy, S., 620, 621, 641, 671, 673
Lewers, Ed, 2159
Lewers, Ellen, 2159
Lewers, Ross, 2159
Lewis, ..., watchmaker in San Jose, 496, 519, 522, 619
Lewis, Abe, 787, 791
Lewis, Bill, 289, 291, 292
Lewis, Horace, 1693
Lewis, Miss Jeffreys, 1604
Lewis, John C. ("Snarleyow"), 1790, 2231, 2239, 2242
Lewis, W. C., 2242
Lewis, W. L., 2246
Lewis, shipwreck, 665
Lewis brothers, Austin, 1533, 1534
Lew Johnson's Refined Minstrels, 1750
Lew Morrison Comedy Company, 1620
Libbey, Jason, 1970, 1987, 1998
Lichtenberg, Lennie, 2133
Lieb, Beatrice, 1890
Liebman, ..., Virginia City, 909
Light, Ham, 934, 1100
Lightner, ..., secretary, Ophir Mining Company, 745
Lights & Shadows, 1787
Lights O' London, 1823
Lightston, Frank, 533

Lilly, Chris, 298, 299
Lilly Clay's Collossal Gaiety Company, 1735
Limantour, ..., forger, 321
Lime kiln, operated by AD and partners, 148–172 passim; map, 394
Limerick Boy, 1126
Lincoln, ..., sheriff, 798
Lincoln, Abraham, 566, 567, 576, 578, 766, 823, 836; nomination for president, 545, 785, 794; elected president, 580; support in Nevada, 802; assassination, 831, 843
Lincoln and Johnson Club, 806
Lincoln Hose Co. No. 1, 944
Lind, James F., 2032, 2033
Lind, Jenny, 79
Lindsay, ..., fiddler, 715–755 passim
Lindsay, Miss ...., of Reno, 1705
Lindsay, ..., stone cutter, 1922
Lindsay, Annie Batterman (Mrs. R. H. Lindsay), 1360, 1389, 1394, 1404, 1705
Lindsay, John S., 1093, 1780
Lindsay, Luella, 1780
Lindsay, R. H. ("Bob"), 1174, 1204, 1345, 1356, 1360, 1388, 1389, 1404, 1429, 1434, 1561, 1562, 1610, 1674, 1703, 1707, 1711, 1715, 1744, 1748
Lindsay Company, 1781
Linehan, Patrick, 1608, 1609
Lingard, ..., actor, 1250
Lingard & Company, 1134, 1135
Linn, ..., of Milpitas, 639
Linn, ..., justice of the peace, 1967, 1991, 1997
Linn, James, 797–799
Linscott, Fred M., 1986, 1988, 2050, 2051
Linton, ..., deputy sheriff, 664
Lion Brewery, 385
Lippincott, Mrs. ...., lecturer, 1141
Lipton, Sir Thomas, 2165
Liquor, influence on miners, 350–354
Liquor Dealers Protective Association, 2066
Lisle, Jake, 1484
Litchfield, William M., 1367
Little Barefoot, 922, 1089, 1115
"Little Dog Kyzer," poem by AD, 776
Little Don Giovanni, 1094, 1197 ,
Little Egypt, 2109
Little Emily, 1785
Littlefield, E. A., 2243
Little Lord Fauntleroy, 1749, 1828
Little Mother, 1118
Little Nell, the California Diamond. *See* Gibson, Nellie
Little Puck, 1747

Randall, Dr. Andrew, 302
Randall, Gracie, 1345
Randall, Mary, 1345
Randall, Capt. William, 50, 72, 269
Randall, Willie, 1243, 1254, 1320
Randolph, Edmund, 501
Rankin, McKee, 1118, 1637
Rann, Roger, 1167
Rany, Bill, 145
Rape, 123, 979, 1148–1149, 1363
Rapidan Claim, Palmyra District, 733
Rapp, John, 1102
Rapp, Matthew, 1102
Rappahannock Claim, Palmyra District, 733, 739
Rapson, Matt, 1846
Rassett, Joseph, 766
Rathbone, Gus, 144–167 passim, 234, 496, 627
Rathbone's Saloon, 651
Rathbone's Store, 451, 457–472 passim, 481, 492–497 passim, 503, 530, 621
Rattlesnake Dick, prisoner at Nevada State Prison, 1078
Rawley, ..., grain buyer, 424
Rawley & Adams, 390
Rawson, Charles, 1070, 1411, 1424, 1447, 1509, 1624, 1669, 1686, 1719
Raycraft, Jim, 1887, 1895
Raycraft, Mrs. Joe, 1930
Raycraft, Tom W., 2168
Raymond, Charles F., 1715
Raymond, J. P., 390, 415, 522, 544, 624
Raymond, J. T., 1068, 1126, 1127
Raymond Holmes Troupe, 1501, 1502
Rayner, C. W., 1096
Raynor, Harry, 940, 943
Rea, C. H., 1004
Reardon, ..., Milpitas, 675, 677
Rebekah, Daughters of, 1696, 1726, 1761, 1868
Rebel Chief, 1086
Reckenzaun, Frederick, 1736
Red Cross, 1986–1990 passim, 2050
Redfern, John, 783
Red Gnome, 968
Red Jack. *See* Woods, Red Jack
Red Jacket Mining Company, 754
Redpath, ..., land-grant dispute, 526, 545
Reed, ..., Milpitas thresher, 486
Reed, E. P., 645, 677
Reed, Frank, 1162
Reed & Collins Comedy Variety Troupe, 1823
Reed's Minstrels, 1632
Reek, George J., 1426

Reel, Cyrus, 1016, 1018
Reese, Mart, 1076, 1078
Reese River goldrush, 751
Reese River mines, 1442–1443
Reese River Pioneers, 1475, 1505, 1506
Reese River Reveille: office destroyed by flood, 1324; AD begins working for, 1405; female apprentice, 1419, 1422; history of publication, 2232, 2233, 2244, 2245, 2246
Reformed Cattle Doctor, The, 409
Regan, Charles, 1962
Regular Fix, 849, 1118
Reichel, Prof. Frank, 1810, 1812, 1813
Reick, Louis, 1864
Reid, Whitelaw, 1820
Reihm, Mott, 1882
Reilly, James A., 1878
Reinhart, F. W., 1095
Remington, Moses, 1119
Remmerfield, Joe, 224
Renfrew, P. C., 725, 773
Renfrew, Mrs. P. C., 718, 725, 759, 760, 774
Reno, Nevada: auction sale of lots, 999, 1701; description of townsite, 998, 1047; railroad, 1008; destroyed by fire, 1343; need for fire department, 1734–1735; water supply, 1735; carnival opens, 2135; map, 1152, 1856; photos, 1856
Reno Crescent, 2242
Reno Daily Record, 2242
Reno Elite Minstrels, 1817
Reno Evening Gazette: Mergenthaler linotype machine used, 2099; change in management, 2169; history of publication, 2244
Reno Ledger, 2070
Reno marriages, 2072, 2088, 2137
Reno Reduction Works, 1646, 1649
Rentz-Stanley Novelty & Burlesque Company, 1710
Reporter, State Capital, 1018
Republican National Convention: of 1876, at Cincinnati, 1277; of 1880, at Chicago, 1364; of 1884, 1518; of 1892, at Minneapolis, 1820; of 1896, at St. Louis, 1922; of 1900, at Philadelphia, 2071
Republican State Convention: of 1868, at Carson City, 1020; of 1872, at Reno, 1175; of 1874, at Winnemucca, 1235; of 1876, at Carson City, 1281; of 1878, at Eureka, 1328; of 1880, at Carson City, 1367; of 1882, at Reno, 1422; of 1886, at Carson City, 1639; of 1888, at Winnemucca, 1704; of 1892, at Virginia City, 1817; of 1896, at Carson City,

Stevenson, Charles C. *(continued)*
proxy at Republican State Convention,
Eureka, 1328; receives bill of sale for
Gold Hill Daily News, 1342; votes proxy
at Republican Convention, Austin for
AD, 1363; divorce, 1363; delegate to
Chicago Convention, 1363; elected to
Republican Central Committee, 1368;
elected president, Garfield & Arthur
Club, 1368; elected treasurer, Republican
Central Committee, 1370; appointed to
confer on consolidation within Storey
County, 1375; marriage to Mrs. Frame,
1386; chairman, Silver Convention,
1564; elected president, Nevada Silver
Society, 1566; 60th birthday, 1618;
nominated for governor, 1639; political
speech, 1641; elected governor, 1647;
reception, 1654; accused of underhanded
methods in controlling mines, 1697;
death, 1775
Stevenson, Mrs. C. C., first wife, 1363, 1364
Stevenson, Mrs. C. C., second wife, 1389,
1711, 1825
Stevenson, Charley, grandson of governor,
1655, 1751
Stevenson, Col. Jonathan D., 1860
Stevenson, J. L. ("Lew"), 1230, 1586,
1618, 1730, 1735, 1736
Stevenson, Mrs. J. L., 1647
Stevers, ..., Virginia City, 1805
Steve's Blacksmith Shop, 249, 253
Steve's Store, 140, 141
Stewart, Mrs. ...., performer, 849,
1007, 1111
Stewart, ..., comedian, 1875
Stewart, Charles, 1920
Stewart, Frank, 807, 1348, 2237
Stewart, George M., 1534, 1565
Stewart, Joe, 1386
Stewart, W. H., 62, 365
Stewart, William M., 864, 896, 901, 1015,
1638, 1647, 1733, 1932, 1994, 2016,
2017, 2083; political speeches, 1108,
1644, 1714, 1715, 1777, 1827, 1829–
1831, 1931, 1969, 2006; suit filed
against, concerning Sutro Tunnel, 1227;
addresses Nevada Silver Association,
1602; elected U.S. senator, 1654, 1837,
2018; chairman, senatorial Irrigation
Committee, 1740; reception on election
as senator, 2019; endorsement of
McKinley, repudiation of Bryan, 2077;
Pacific Coast Pioneers, 2257
Stewart Indian School, 1894, 2041;
smallpox epidemic, 1900, 1901; football
games, 2119
Stickney's Great Circus, 1012

Still Waters Run Deep, 1098, 1114, 1127,
1142
Stirling, ..., 167, 170, 174; Fort John,
167, 170, 174
Stith, Isaac F. ("Ike"), 800, 805, 904,
1657, 1695, 1696
Stivers, Mrs. ...., housekeeper, 338,
349–390 passim
Stivers, S. E., 1847, 1848
Stockton, California, 646; picture, 394
Stoddard, ..., coroner, 1609
Stoddard, Capt. Asa A., 1264, 1286, 1386
Stoddard, C. H., 1640, 1802, 2079, 2243
Stoddard, Mrs. Cora N., 2102, 2104
Stoddard, Mrs. Mary Elizabeth Calista:
sends trout to AD, 1171; courted by AD,
1185, 1194–1204; married to AD on
yacht in middle of Lake Tahoe, 1205.
See also Doten, Mary Stoddard
Stoddard, Millie (née Millie Abbot Sperry;
Mary S. Doten's daughter by an earlier
marriage): arrives in Gold Hill, 1255;
vacations at Lake Tahoe, 1279, 1323;
bridesmaid for Mrs. Richardson, 1356;
seventeenth birthday, 1431; works for
Lindsays, 1625; marriage to Edward
Everett Cochran, 1705. *See also*
Cochran, Millie Stoddard
Stoddard, Samuel G., brother to Mary
Stoddard Doten, 1498
Stoddard, Mrs. Sarah A., 1255, 1729;
mother-in-law of AD, 1214; vacations
at Lake Tahoe, 1279, 1298, 1323;
mining deeds made over to, 1339, 1340;
birthdays, 1392, 1483, 1969; death,
2020, 2021; photo, 1856
Stokes, Sheriff ...., 632
Stone, Rev. ...., San Jose minister,
530, 640
Stone, ..., performer, 929
Stone, ..., justice of the peace, 1970
Stone, Amy, 922, 927, 929, 969, 1041,
1042, 1275
Stone, H. F., 927
Stone, M. N.: attorney, moves to Salt
Lake City, 1763; Democratic nominee
for justice, Supreme Court, 1424
Stone, T. N., 2018
Stonehill, E. B., 1339, 1340
Stoner, ..., undersheriff, 1122
Stoneyer, ..., preacher at camp
meeting, 558
Storer, T. B., 1355, 1589, 1594, 1660, 1624,
1680, 1704, 1773
Storey, Prof. R. C., 1885, 1912
Storey County, 1875. *See also* Consoli-
dation of Virginia City, Gold Hill, and
Storey County

U.S. Mint, Carson City branch *(continued)*
shipped to San Francisco, 2040; coinage
machinery shipped to New Orleans and
Washington, 2044; photo, 1856
U.S. Post Office, 1598, 1993
University of Nevada: new site selected,
Reno, removal from Elko, 1587; corner-
stone laid, 1596; admission policies,
1742, 1743; field day, 1819; fire, 1904;
smallpox, 1905; *Student Record,*
monthly magazine, 1950; football games,
1971, 2119; girls' basketball team, 2026;
Artemisia, yearbook, 2031, 2159; legis-
lature asked to approve metallurgical
laboratory, 2151; photo, 1856
Unknown, The, 1643, 1695
Unmasked, 1190
Upchurch, Father ...., founder of
Ancient Order of United Workmen,
1592
Upside Down, 1718
Upton, ..., Carson City, 818
Urridias, Don Jose, 521, 549, 559, 560,
564, 586, 595, 597, 615, 619, 620, 631,
635, 662
Urso, Camilla, 1083, 1089, 1219, 1724,
1870, 1949
Utah Mine, map, 1152
Utica Mine, Angel's, California, 1963

Va. *See* Virginia City
Vacation or Harvard vs Yale, 1568, 1650
Vail, Hugh, 1701
Vail, John Randolph, 1695
Valencia, Antonio, 986
Valentine, John J., 1519
Vallejo, Gen. Mariano Guadalupe, 617
Valpey, Cal, 642, 646, 647, 659
Valpey, Charley, 666
Valpey, Horatio, 635, 647
Valpey, Lizzie, 638, 639, 652
Van Bokkelen, Gen. J. L., 798, 828, 933,
1201
Vance, John A., 225, 237, 246, 247, 249,
259
Vance's Store, 225–229 passim, 239. *See
also* Last Chance House
Van Cott, Mrs. ...., revival service,
conducted by, 1213
Vanderlieth, E. D., 2124
Vandervoort, Gen. Paul, 1829
Van Doren, Miss ...., from Carson
City, 753
Van Doren, Henry, 724, 759, 775, 778,
780, 830

V&T. *See* Virginia & Truckee Railroad
Van Duzer, C. D., 2082, 2141, 2142;
begins publication of *The Nevada
Magazine,* 2033; political speeches, 2083,
2149; elected assemblyman, Humboldt
County, 2086; publishes *Nevada Miner,*
Golconda, 2130
Van Dyke, Miss ...., Salvation Army,
1948
Vane, Alice, 1214
Van Emon, George B., 1784
Van Etten (or Van Netten), David, 355,
369–371, 420, 435
"Van Jacquelin," 2233. *See also* Hart,
Fred H.
Van Nostrand, ..., from Fort
Churchill, 799
Van Reiper, ..., at Stockton, 83
Van Sickle's Station, 713
Vantine, ..., San Francisco, 702, 706
Vanwinkle, A. J., 730
Vanwinkle, Harvey, 253
Van Zandt, Dr. J. W., 1233, 1348
Vardy, George R., 2001, 2096
Varian, Charley, 1330, 2102, 2103, 2107
Varney, ..., musician, 1277, 1278
Vattu, Hypolite, 1024
Vaughn, Dr. ...., patent medicine
man, 53
Vaughn, ..., teamster, 253–255
Vaughn, Alpheus, 1916
VDU. *See Virginia Daily Union*
Vennum (also Venom), O. H. P., 517, 520,
526, 546, 547, 632, 659
Verdi, Nevada, map, 1152
Vernon, Ida, 821, 976
Vesey, Ed, 717
Vesey, H. M., 717, 1204, 1232
Vesey's Hotel, Gold Hill, 757
Vesser, Charley, 526
Vesser, Francis, 469, 518
Vesser, Henry, 456–472 passim, 480, 488,
500, 502, 521, 528, 548, 553, 577, 631
Vesser, Sarah, 469, 471, 518
Vestal brothers, 471
Veteran, The, 1601
Victaver, Dr. ...., veterinarian, 414
Victim of Circumstances, 1166
Victoria, Queen, death, 2093
Victorine, 1034
Vigilance Committees: San Francisco, 258,
269, 275, 281; Aurora, 765; Virginia
City, 1119–1123, 1125, 1133, 1137, 2191
Vim, 1694
Vincent, Charles ("Scrub"), reporter, 891
Vincent, Charley, minstrel, 1157
Vineyard, J., 775, 776, 779, 784, 789, 792

Vining, Nelly, 940

Virden, William H. (Billy), 722, 725, 739, 756, 759, 775, 781, 783, 785, 824, 838, 845, 848, 878, 891, 902, 927, 1176, 1198, 1200, 1201, 1205, 1209, 1211, 1213, 1233, 1241, 1246, 1252, 1256, 1258, 1265, 1268, 1270, 1274, 1276, 1282, 1286, 1298, 1305, 1313, 1329, 1330, 1333, 1340, 2232; candidate for Constitutional Convention, 727; elected delegate to Republican County Convention, 755, 773; elected delegate to Convention to elect delegates to 1864 Constitutional Convention, 782; becomes bookkeeper for AD, at *Gold Hill Daily News,* 1161; stabbed by jealous husband, 1195; accidentally shoots himself, 1207; expelled from Masons, 1212; marriage, 1242; attends Odd Fellows Convention, Winnemucca, 1252; moves into lower level of Doten house, 1259; ill, 1272; vacations at Lake Tahoe, 1282; elected Grand Representative, Odd Fellows, 1297; father arrives, 1300; Grand Representative from Nevada to Grand Lodge, Odd Fellows in Baltimore, 1301; returns from Baltimore and goes to San Francisco, 1303; returns from San Francisco, 1304; candidate for county assessor, 1329; levies attachment on *Gold Hill Daily News,* 1342; owner, provisions store, 1344; moves out of AD's house, 1345; sues AD for wages, 1346; decision on suit for wages, 1347; superior judge, Mono County, California, visits Virginia City, 1858; photo, 394

Virden, Mrs. William H., 1248, 1249, 1257

Virginia, circus performer, 220

Virginia Amateur Dramatic Club, 1699

Virginia & Truckee Railroad, 1075, 1191, 2134, 2227; tunnels between Virginia City and Gold Hill, 1055; completed to Crown Point Ravine 1066; completion 1067; Reno to Steamboat Springs section finished, 1141; first regular through passenger train from Reno to Virginia City, 1175; train wreck, 1599–1601; maps and photos, 1152, 1856

Virginia Choral Society, 1076

Virginia Chronicle, 1239; editorship changes, 1250; change in ownership, 1252; printed in offices of *Gold Hill Daily News* after fire of 1875, 1262; description of press room, 1726; trouble in management, 1845; change in management, 1917, 2167. *See also Virginia Evening Chronicle*

Virginia City: description, 716; county hospital, 816; Common Council, 833; greenback currency used, 882; freight wagons, 895; masquerade ball, 924; elections, 925; price war among clothing stores, 1001, 1002; baseball club, 1063; earthquakes, 1071, 1072, 1077; Vigilance Committee, 1119–1125, 1133, 1137; water supply, 1206; busline to Gold Hill discontinued, 1385; consolidation with Gold Hill, 2002; registered voters, 2005; carnival for Independence Day, 2161; discontinuation of electric lighting, 2163; maps and photos, 394, 1152, 1856

Virginia Daily Union, 905; AD begins correspondence with, 726; AD becomes local editor, 806, 811, 828; sold to O. E. Jones & Co., 835; sold to Democrats, 867; history of publication, 2226, 2231; printers, 2251, 2252

Virginia Dramatic Company, 1607

Virginia Evening Chronicle, 1160, 2232, 2237, 2238. *See also Virginia Chronicle*

Virginia Exempt Firemen's Assoc., 1611, 1614, 1687, 1689, 1694, 1807, 1809, 1821, 1833, 1836, 1844, 1858, 1864

Virginia Glee Club, 813, 833, 862

Virginia Mastodon Minstrels, 1845

Virginia Melodeon, 727

Virginia Zouaves, 822

Virginius, 1717

Vista, brig out of Edgartown, 71

Vivandiere, 702

Vivian, Charles, 1131

Vivian DeMonto's Superb Company, 1901

Vogrich, Max, 1361

Voight, Dr. ...., Virginia City, 868

Vokes, ..., performer, 2065

Volcano Hall, 239, 243

Vollmer, Mrs. ...., Austin, 1517

Vollmer, A. D., 1706

Volunteer, The, 1929

Vonderhyde, ..., harness maker, 2131

Vonderhyde, Ada, 2132

Vonderhyde, Lola, 2131

Von Gulpen, Madame ...., singer, 337

Von Hartman, Newton & Co. Magic Lantern Show, 1135

Voorhees, Miss ...., performer, 243

Vucovich, Spiro, 999, 1617, 2015

W, Mrs. *See* Whittingham, Nettie

Wade, ..., veterinarian, 355, 356, 391, 428, 429, 443, 447, 448, 495, 552

Wade, Tom, 197

DATE DUE
